Copyright ©IBID Press, Victoria. First published in 2001 by IBID Press, Victoria,
 Published by IBID Press, Victoria.

Library Catalogue: Green J. & Damji S.
　　　　1. Chemistry, 2. International Baccalaureate. Series Title: International
　　　　Baccalaureate in Detail

ISBN: 1 876659 41 6

Cover design by Adcore.
Published by IBID Press, 36 Quail Crescent, Melton 3337, Victoria, Australia
Printed by Shannon Books, Victoria, Australia.

FOREWORD TO THE SECOND EDITION

So why the second edition? Well a multitude of reasons, but there is no doubt that the catalyst was the publication of the revised Chemistry syllabus earlier this year. There were however many other reasons, such as the opportunity to go from monochrome to the new trendy duochrome format. Then of course there were the mistakes! Some of these we spotted ourselves (unfortunately after the book had gone to the printers!), others were spotted by our readers. A sincere thankyou to all of you who made the effort to e-mail us about them and hopefully we have eliminated the ones you spotted in the new edition. Finally there was the more general feed back about things you would have liked to have had included, that were missing – again our thanks for this. You will find quite a lot of new material in the second edition, including "Extension" material – things that are not in the IB syllabus, but that many of you teach because of other demands.

Is the Preface the place for thanks? Well we have already done it twice, so better continue. John and Sadru would like to sincerely thank Chris Talbot from Singapore. Not only did he give us extensive feedback on the first edition, he also solicited most helpful comments from those in tertiary education on various sections. We found this so useful that we have asked him to read through the whole of the second edition, before publication this time. We can assure you that it would have been less accurate and less "user friendly" if it had not been for Chris' eagle-eye and thoughtful suggestions. Finally both authors would like to thank their editors from IBID, who have been most patient with their flexible interpretation of the word "deadline" and their innumerable requests for them to do the virtually impossible in terms of layout and presentation.

We think that the second the second edition is an order of magnitude better than the first – we hope you agree. No doubt there are still things that are not quite right and so please continue to e-mail us about ways the third edition can be better still.

John Green & Sadru Damji, July 2001.

FOREWORD TO THE FIRST EDITION

This text has been produced independently as a resource to support the teaching of the Chemistry course of the International Baccalaureate. The examples and questions do not necessarily reflect the views of the official senior examining team appointed by the International Baccalaureate Organisation. The statements from the IB syllabus are reproduced with the permission of the IBO.

In writing this book the authors hope to share material that they have found useful over the years, with other Chemistry teachers in the context of the new International Baccalaureate Chemistry syllabus. Those familiar with this will find a close correlation between the order in which the book deals with topics and the order in which they appear in the syllabus. The text is accompanied by a series of exercises, most of which have accompanying answers, making this a useful resource for self-study to reinforce normal classroom teaching.

The work has been divided up into several categories:
* Core work that is fundamental to all studying the subject
* Advanced work for those aspiring to knowledge of a higher level
* Option work for those wanting a greater depth of knowledge of particular topics
* Extra material to support the contents of the other sections

The category to which the contents of a particular page belongs can be ascertained by looking at the key in the outer margin of the book and/or the syllabus statement (in the shaded box) from the guide for Chemistry published by the IBO in 1996. In some cases, as for example material relevant to Option A and Option B in the I.B. syllabus, then the work may belong to more than one category. Coming from different continents the authors have tried to bring some uniformity to the nomenclature - for example all of the "sulphur"s should now appear as "sulfur"s. Nevertheless there will almost certainly be some inconsistencies and we hope that these will be taken as a positive reflection of the international nature of publication!

Again, in spite of a great deal of time and trouble having been invested in its production, the authors are certain that they will (indeed they already have!) discovered some things that they would, on reflection, have done differently. Minor errors, places where a section could be re-worded to give greater clarity, things that have been omitted that in retrospect it would have been better to include etc. Also as time goes on, the way in which the syllabus is being interpreted will become clearer. If this edition is good, the next should be even better. To this end, the authors would like to invite both teachers and students using this book to comment critically upon its contents. Feedback has never been easier than in these days of e-mail.

We would like to receive your views: John at <lpcuwc@hkbu.edu.hk,
Sadru at< DAMJI@fs2.ucc.on.ca>

Speaking of the electronic age, it may be of interest for readers to know that during the production of this book, written by one author in Toronto, the second in Hong Kong and a publisher in Melbourne, the parties made extensive use of electronic communications. Manuscript and proofs were exchanged electronically with consequent savings in time, energy and paper.

We hope that you, the reader, will find some of the same satisfaction in using this book that we have experienced in its production.

John Green & Sadru Damji, January 1998.

ACKNOWLEDGMENTS

In writing this book I would like to acknowledge all the help and assistance, sometimes given unwittingly, from colleagues and students at both Kristin School and at Li Po Chun. I am also most grateful to my co-author, the publisher and editor for many helpful suggestions and for being forgiving on deadlines. Most of all my thanks to my wife Ann and to my two daughters Kirsty Alison and Katy for their patience and support throughout the lengthy process of writing this book.
John Green

This book is dedicated to the three very special loves of my life, Hussain, Aly and Nish, and to a personal friend Diamond Ismail. Special thanks to all my students, past and present, from Lester Pearson United World College, Li Po Chun United World College, and Upper Canada College whose thirst for knowledge makes teaching such a wonderful and satisfying profession. I am deeply grateful to John Eix, a mentor and a colleague for inspiring me to be a better teacher, and to Ron Ragsdale and Arden Zipp from whom I have learnt a great deal through doing IB workshops together. Special thanks to my co-author, the publisher and the editor for all their useful suggestions and support in completing this text.
Sadru Damji

CONTENTS

STOICHIOMETRY

1

Chapter contents

SOME FUNDAMENTAL CONCEPTS

Chemistry is a science that deals with the composition, structure and reactions of matter. It is involved with looking at the properties of materials and interpreting these in terms of models on a sub-microscopic scale. Investigations form an important part of any study of chemistry. This involves making observations, and using these in the solution of problems. A typical investigation requires choosing a problem, working out a way of attempting to solve it, and then describing both the method, the results and the manner in which these are interpreted. Namely, "a scientist chooses, imagines, does and describes". Along with many other syllabuses practical work is a requirement of IB Chemistry.

Matter occupies space and has mass. It can be subdivided into **mixtures** and **pure substances**. Mixtures consist of a number of different substances, not chemically combined together. Thus the ratio of these components is not constant from one sample of mixture to another. The different components of a mixture often have different **physical properties** (such as melting point and density) and **chemical properties** (such as flammability and acidity). The properties of the mixture are similar to those of the components (e.g. a match burns in both air and pure oxygen), though they will vary with its exact composition. The fact that the different components of the mixture have different physical properties means that the mixture can be separated by physical means, for example by dissolving one component whilst the other remains as a solid. A pure substance cannot be separated in this way because its physical properties are constant throughout all samples of that substance. Similarly all samples of a pure substance have identical chemical properties.

Pure substances may be further subdivided into **elements** and **compounds**. The difference between these is that an element cannot be split up into simpler substances by chemical means, whilst a compound can be changed into these more basic components.

The interpretation on a sub-microscopic scale is that all substances are made up of very tiny particles called **atoms**. Atoms are the smallest particles present in an element which can take part in a chemical change and they cannot be split by ordinary chemical means.

An **element** is a substance that only contains one type of atom (see Section 2.1 page 60), so it cannot be converted into anything simpler by chemical means. (n.b. 'type' does not imply that all atoms of an element are identical. Some elements are composed of a mixture of closely related atoms called isotopes - again, see Section 2.1 page 60). All elements have distinct names and symbols. Atoms can join together by chemical bonds to form **compounds**. Compounds are therefore made up of particles (of the same type), but these particles are made up of different types of atoms chemically bonded together. This means that in a compound, the constituent elements will be present in fixed proportions such as H_2O (water), H_2SO_4 (sulfuric acid), CO_2 (carbon dioxide) and NH_3 (ammonia). The only way to separate a compound into its component elements is by a chemical change that breaks some bonds and forms new ones, resulting in new substances. The physical and chemical properties of a compound are usually totally unrelated to those of its component elements. For example a match will not burn in water even though it is a compound of oxygen.

If a substance contains different types of particles, then it is a **mixture**. These concepts in terms of particles are illustrated in Figure 1.1.

Figure 1.1 - The particles in an element, a compound and a mixture

Element	Compound	Mixture

Copper, water and air provide good examples of an element, a compound and a mixture respectively. Table 1.1 summarises the characteristic differences between these substances.

Table 1.1 - The properties of a typical element, compound and mixture

	Proportions	Properties	Separation
Element Copper - a pure element	Contains only one type of atom.	These will depend on the forces between the atoms of the element.	Cannot be converted to a simpler substance by chemical means.
Compound Water - a compound of oxygen and hydrogen	Always contains two hydrogen atoms for every oxygen atom.	Totally different from its elements, e.g. Water is a liquid, but hydrogen and oxygen are gases.	Requires a chemical change, e.g. reacting with sodium will produce hydrogen gas.
Mixture Air - a mixture of nitrogen, oxygen, argon, carbon dioxide etc.	The proportions of the gases in air, especially carbon dioxide and water vapour, can vary.	Similar to its constituents, e.g. supports combustion like oxygen.	Can be carried out by physical means, e.g. by the fractional distillation of liquid air.

The term **molecule** refers to a small group of atoms joined together by covalent bonds (see Section 4.2, page 121). If the atoms are of the same kind, then it is a molecule of an element, if different it is a molecule of a compound. Most elements that are gases are **diatomic** (composed of molecules containing two atoms). Examples are hydrogen gas (H_2), nitrogen gas (N_2) and oxygen gas (O_2). The halogens (F_2, Cl_2, Br_2 and I_2) are also diatomic in all states. The noble gases (He, Ne, Ar, Kr, Xe and Rn are **monatomic** (i.e. exist as single atoms).

THE TYPES OF ATOMS

There are 92 kinds of atoms, and hence 92 chemical elements, that occur naturally and about another seventeen that have been produced artificially. Only about thirty of these elements, given in Table 1.2, are usually encountered in chemistry and most of chemistry would deal with about half of these, shown in **bold** type. Each element is given a symbol that is used to write the formulae of the compounds that it forms. The significance of the atomic number and relative atomic mass of the elements will be explained in Sections 2.1 1.2 and 2.1).

Table 1.2 - The most common chemical elements

Element	Symbol	Atomic Number	Relative Atomic Mass
Hydrogen	**H**	**1**	**1.01**
Helium	He	2	4.00
Lithium	Li	3	6.94
Beryllium	Be	4	9.01
Boron	B	5	10.81
Carbon	**C**	**6**	**12.01**
Nitrogen	**N**	**7**	**14.01**
Oxygen	**O**	**8**	**16.00**
Fluorine	F	9	19.00
Neon	Ne	10	20.18
Sodium	**Na**	**11**	**22.99**
Magnesium	**Mg**	**12**	**24.31**
Aluminium	**Al**	**13**	**26.98**
Silicon	Si	14	28.09
Phosphorus	**P**	**15**	**30.97**
Sulfur	**S**	**16**	**32.06**
Chlorine	**Cl**	**17**	**35.45**
Argon	Ar	18	39.95
Potassium	**K**	**19**	**39.10**
Calcium	**Ca**	**20**	**40.08**
Chromium	Cr	24	52.00
Manganese	Mn	25	54.94
Iron	**Fe**	**26**	**55.85**
Cobalt	Co	27	58.93
Nickel	Ni	28	58.71
Copper	**Cu**	**29**	**63.55**
Zinc	**Zn**	**30**	**65.37**
Bromine	Br	35	79.90
Silver	Ag	47	107.87
Iodine	I	53	126.90
Barium	Ba	56	137.34
Lead	**Pb**	**82**	**207.19**

A complete periodic table can be found inside the back cover

- Parts of the names where there are common spelling difficulties have been underlined.

- You should know the symbols for the elements, especially those in **bold** type. Most of them are closely related to the name of the element (e.g. chlorine is Cl). Elements that were known in early times have symbols that relate to their Latin names (e.g. Ag, silver, comes from *Argentium*).

- Note that the first letter is always an upper case letter and the second one a lower case, so that, for example Co (Cobalt) and CO (carbon monoxide) mean very different things.

EXERCISE 1.1

1.   A grey solid when heated vapourised to form pure white crystals on the cooler parts of the test tube leaving a black solid as the residue. It is likely that the original solid was

A   an element.
B   a metal.
C   a pure compound.
D   a mixture.

2.   Which one of the following is a chemical property rather than a physical property?

A   Boiling point
B   Density
C   Flammability
D   Hardness

3.   Which one of the following is a physical change rather than a chemical change?

A   Combustion
B   Distillation
C   Decomposition
D   Neutralisation

4.   Decide whether the sketches below represent elements, compounds or mixtures.

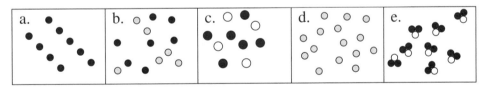

5.   State whether the following refer to an element, a compound or a mixture:

a)   Easily separated into two substances by distillation.
b)   Its components are always present in the same proportions.
c)   Its properties are similar to those of its components.
d)   Cannot be broken down by chemical means.
e)   Very different properties to its components.

1.1 THE MOLE CONCEPT AND AVOGADRO'S CONSTANT

1.1.1   Describe the basis of the mole concept, and apply it to substances.

The mole concept applies to all kinds of particles: atoms, molecules, ions, formula units etc. The amount of substance is measured in units of moles. The approximate value of Avogadro's constant (L), 6.02×10^{23} mol^{-1}, should be known.

1.1.2   Calculate the number of particles and the amount of substance (in moles).

Convert between the amount of substance (in moles) and the number of atoms, molecules or formula units.   © *IBO 2001*

Atoms and molecules are inconceivably minute, with equally small masses. The masses of all atoms are not however the same and it is often convenient to be able to weigh out amounts of substances that contain the same number of atoms or molecules. The same amount of any substance will therefore contain the same number of particles and we measure the amount of substance in moles. It is for this reason that the mole concept is important.

It is found, as shown in Figure 1.2, that exactly 12 g of a particular type of carbon atom (^{12}C) contains 6.02×10^{23} atoms of carbon. (Note - this very large number is expressed in scientific notation. For a further explanation of scientific notation refer to page 43).

Figure 1.2 - Illustrating Avogadro's constant

6.02×10^{23} mol^{-1} is called **Avogadro's constant** (L or N_A). This number of any particle, i.e. atom, molecule or ion, is known as one **mole** (symbol: mol) of that substance. A mole is therefore simply a number, just like a 'dozen' but much larger. The number of

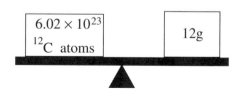

moles present is known as 'the amount of substance' and is given the symbol n. Thus $n(\text{Fe})$ means the amount of iron atoms in moles.

The amount of a substance (n) can be calculated from the number of particles (N) by applying the formula:

$$\text{Number of moles} = \frac{\text{Number of particles}}{6.02 \times 10^{23}}$$

This can be written as $n = \dfrac{N}{6.02 \times 10^{23}}$ or $N = 6.02 \times 10^{23} n$.

A sample of water that contains 3.01×10^{25} water molecules therefore contains

$$\frac{3.01 \times 10^{25}}{6.02 \times 10^{23}} = 50 \text{ moles of water molecules.}$$

This is very similar to saying that 36 oranges is $\dfrac{36}{12} = 3$ dozen oranges.

The formula may be rearranged to calculate the number of particles.

For example 0.020 moles of carbon dioxide will contain
$0.020 \times 6.02 \times 10^{23} = 1.2 \times 10^{22}$ molecules of CO_2.

This number of molecules of carbon dioxide will contain 1.2×10^{22} atoms of carbon but 2.4×10^{22} (i.e. $2 \times 1.2 \times 10^{22}$) atoms of oxygen, because each molecule contains one atom of carbon, but two atoms of oxygen and the total number of atoms is 3.6×10^{22} (i.e. $3 \times 1.2 \times 10^{22}$). Note, therefore, how important it is to state what particles are being referred to.

EXERCISE 1.2

Take the value of Avogadro's constant as 6.02×10^{23} mol^{-1}.

1. How many atoms are there in 5 moles of sulfur atoms?

    A 1.20×10^{23}
    B 6.02×10^{23}
    C 6.02×10^{115}
    D 3.01×10^{24}

2. Which one of the following is not the same number as the rest?

    A   The number of molecules in 4 moles of CO_2.
    B   The number of hydrogen atoms in 2 moles of H_2O.
    C   The number of chloride ions in 4 moles of $CaCl_2$.
    D   The number of hydrogen atoms in $\frac{1}{2}$ mole of C_3H_8.

3. The number of atoms present in 0.10 mol of ethene (C_2H_4) is:

A 3.61×10^{22}
B 6.02×10^{22}
C 3.61×10^{23}
D 6.02×10^{23}

4. One mole of water contains

A 6.02×10^{23} atoms of hydrogen.
B 2.01×10^{23} atoms of oxygen.
C 6.02×10^{23} atoms in total.
D 6.02×10^{23} molecules of water.

5. The number of atoms present in 36 molecules of glucose ($C_6H_{12}O_6$) is

A   24
B   36
C 24×36
D $24 \times 36 \times 6.02 \times 10^{23}$

6. The mass of one atom of carbon -12 is

A   1 g.
B   12 g.
C $12 \times 6.02 \times 10^{23}$ g.
D $12 \div 6.02 \times 10^{23}$ g.

7. A sample of phosphoric(V) acid H_3PO_4 contains 1.2×10^{23} molecules.

a)   How many moles of phosphoric(V) acid is this?
b)   How many atoms of phosphorus will there be?
c)   How many atoms of hydrogen will it contain?

8. a)   How many molecules are there in 6 moles of hydrogen sulfide (H_2S)?

b)   The formula of gold(III) chloride is $AuCl_3$. How many chloride ions are there in 0.30 moles of gold(III) chloride?

1.2 FORMULAE

1.2.1 Define the term molar mass *(M)* and calculate the mass of one mole of a species.

1.2.2 Distinguish between atomic mass, molecular mass and formula mass.

The term molar mass (in g mol^{-1}) can be used for all of these.

1.2.3 Define the terms relative molecular mass (M_r) and relative atomic mass (A_r).

The terms have no units.

1.2.4 State the relationship between the amount of substance (in moles) and mass, and carry out calculations involving amount of substance, mass and molar mass.

1.2.5 Define the terms empirical formula and molecular formula.

The molecular formula is a multiple of the empirical formula.

1.2.6 Determine the empirical formula and/or the molecular formula of a given compound.

Determine the: empirical formula from the percentage composition or from other suitable experimental data; percentage composition from the formula of a compound; molecular formula when given both the empirical formula and the molar mass.

© IBO 2001

CHEMICAL FORMULAE

Chemical formulae are a shorthand notation for elements, ions and compounds. They show the ratio of the number of atoms of each element present and, in the case of molecular covalent substances, it gives the actual number of atoms of each element present in the molecule or ion. For example, the formula for magnesium chloride, which is ionically bonded, is $MgCl_2$. This tells us that in magnesium chloride there are twice as many chloride ions as there are magnesium ions. The formulae of ionic compounds can be deduced from the electrical charges of the ions involved (see Section 4.1, page 116).The formula for glucose, which is a molecular covalent compound, is $C_6H_{12}O_6$. This tells us that a molecule of glucose contains six carbon atoms, twelve hydrogen atoms and six oxygen atoms. The formulae of covalent compounds have to be memorised or deduced from their names. The carbonate ion, which is a covalently bonded ion, has the formula CO_3^{2-}. This tells us that the carbonate ion consists of a carbon atom bonded to three oxygen atoms, and thus has gained two electrons (hence the charge). Brackets are used to show that the subscript affects a group of atoms, for example the formula of magnesium nitrate is $Mg(NO_3)_2$, showing that there are two nitrate ions (NO_3^-) for every magnesium ion (Mg^{2+}). Sometimes brackets are also used to indicate the structure of the compound, for example urea is usually written as $(NH_2)_2CO$ rather than CN_2H_4O, to show that it consists of a carbon joined to two NH_2 groups and an oxygen.

Sometimes compounds are hydrated, that is they contain water molecules chemically bonded into the structure of the crystals. This is known as **water of crystallisation** or hydration and it is indicated by the formula for water following the formula of the substance and separated from it by a dot. For example in hydrated sodium sulfate crystals seven molecules of water of crystallisation are present for every sulfate ion and every two sodium ions, so its formula is written as $Na_2SO_4 \cdot 7H_2O$. When the crystals are heated this water is frequently given off to leave the anhydrous salt (Na_2SO_4). Similarly blue hydrated copper(II) sulfate crystals ($CuSO_4 \cdot 5H_2O$) form white anhydrous copper(II) sulfate ($CuSO_4$) when heated.

EXERCISE 1.3

1. The formula of the cadmium ion is Cd^{2+} and that of the benzoate ion is $C_6H_5COO^-$ What is the formula of cadmium benzoate?

    A $Cd(C_6H_5COO)_2$
    B CdC_6H_5COO
    C $Cd_2(C_6H_5COO)_2$
    D $Cd_2C_6H_5COO$

2. An ore contains calcium hydroxide, $Ca(OH)_2$ in association with calcium phosphate, $Ca_3(PO_4)_2$. Analysis shows that calcium and phosphorus are present in a mole ratio of 5:3. Which of the following best represents the composition of the ore?

    A $Ca(OH_2) \cdot Ca_3(PO_4)_2$
    B $Ca(OH)_2 \cdot 2\ Ca_3(PO_4)_2$
    C $Ca(OH)_2 \cdot 3\ Ca_3(PO_4)_2$
    D $Ca(OH)_2 \cdot 4\ Ca_3(PO_4)_2$

3. If the formula of praseodymium oxide is PrO_2, what is the formula of praseodymium sulfate?

    A Pr_2SO_4
    B $PrSO_4$
    C $Pr_2(SO_4)_3$
    D $Pr(SO_4)_2$

4. Write the formulae of the following common compounds:

    a)   Sulfuric acid   b)   Sodium hydroxide
    c)   Nitric acid   d)   Ammonia
    e)   Hydrochloric acid   f)   Ethanoic acid
    g)   Copper sulfate   h)   Carbon monoxide
    i)   Sulfur dioxide   j)   Sodium hydrogencarbonate

5. Write the formulae of the following:

    a)   Sodium chloride   b)   Copper sulfide
    c)   Zinc sulfate   d)   Aluminium oxide
    e)   Magnesium nitrate   f)   Calcium phosphate
    g)   Hydroiodic acid   h)   Ammonium carbonate
    i)   Methane   j)   Phosphorus pentachloride

MOLAR MASS

Because atoms are so minute, a scale is used to indicate the average mass of atoms and molecules relative to each other. The mass of average atom of the element, relative to an atom of (carbon -12 isotope) having a mass of exactly 12, is known as its **relative atomic mass** (A_r). Similarly the mass of a molecule on this scale is referred to as its **relative molecular mass** (M_r, previously sometimes referred to as RMM). This scale is approximately equal to one on which a hydrogen atom has a relative atomic mass of 1.

Note that because they are ratios, relative atomic/molecular masses do not have units. Fluorine atoms are about 19 times as heavy as hydrogen atoms and so have a relative atomic mass of about 19. Relative atomic masses are shown on the periodic table and those of the common elements are given in Table 1.2. Most are approximately whole numbers, but some are not because these elements exist as mixtures of isotopes (see Section 2.1, page 60). With elements it is very important to differentiate between the relative atomic mass and the relative molecular mass. Thus nitrogen, for example, has a relative atomic mass of 14.01, but a relative molecular mass of 28.02 because it exists as diatomic molecules (N_2).

The **atomic mass** of a substance is the mass of one mole of that substance and hence has units of g mol^{-1}. Similarly the **molecular mass** of a substance is the mass of one mole of the molecules and is therefore the sum of the atomic masses of the elements that it is composed of. For example the molecular mass of sulfuric acid (H_2SO_4) is:

$(2 \times 1.01) + 32.06 + (4 \times 16.00) = 98.08$ g mol^{-1}.

The **formula mass** of an ionic substance is similarly the sum of the atomic masses of the atoms in the formula. If a substance contains water of crystallisation, then this must be included in the formula mass, for example the formula mass of sodium sulfate heptahydrate crystals ($Na_2SO_4.7H_2O$) is:

$(2 \times 22.99) + 32.06 + (4 \times 16.00) + (7 \times 18.02) = 268.18$ g mol^{-1}.

The atomic mass, the molecular mass and the formula mass are often collectively referred to as the **molar mass** (M). The term molar mass is a particularly useful term because it can be applied to ANY of the above (atoms, molecules, ions etc.).

EXERCISE 1.4

1. The relative molecular mass of iron(III) sulfate $Fe_2(SO_4)_3$ will be

    A   191.76
    B   207.76
    C   344.03
    D   399.88

2. A certain substance has a molar mass (to 2 significant figures) of 28. Which of the following is not a possible formula?

A CH_2O
B   Si
C C_2H_4
D   CO

3. Calculate the relative molar mass of the following (correct to 1 decimal place).

a)   HI   b) $NaClO_3$ c) $(NH_4)_2HPO_4$
d) $(CO_2H)_2.2H_2O$ e)   chromium(III) oxide   f)   iodine trichloride

MOLES AND MASS

As one mole of hydrogen atoms (i.e. 6.02×10^{23}) has a mass of 1.01 g, then the same number (6.02×10^{23} = one mole) of fluorine atoms ($A = 19.00$ g mol^{-1}) will have a mass of 19.00 g. Similarly the mass of one mole of any substance will be equal to its molar mass in grams. If one mole of fluorine atoms is 19 g, then 76 g will be four moles, hence the amount of substance may be calculated from its molar mass using the formula

$$\text{Amount of substance, } n = \frac{\text{Mass } (g)}{\text{Molar Mass (g mol}^{-1})} \qquad n = \frac{m}{M}.$$

4.904 g of sulfuric acid will therefore contain:

$$\frac{m}{M} = \frac{4.904 \text{ g}}{98.08 \text{ g mol}^{-1}} = 0.05000 \text{ moles of sulfuric acid}$$

[**Note** - It is important to pay attention to significant figures in calculations. A short description of the scientific notation and significant figures is given later in the chapter.]

The equation may be rearranged to calculate the molar mass from the mass and the amount of substance, or to find the mass from the number of moles and the molar mass. For example the mass of 3.00 moles of carbon dioxide is

$$n \times M = 3.00 \text{ mol} \times 44.01 \text{ g mol}^{-1} = 132 \text{ g of carbon dioxide.}$$

Similarly if 0.200 moles of a substance has a mass of 27.8 g, then its molar mass (M) will be

$$M = \frac{m}{n} = \frac{27.8 \text{ g}}{0.200 \text{ mol}} = 139 \text{ g mol}^{-1}$$

Knowing the mass of a given number of atoms or molecules means that the mass of one atom or molecule can be calculated. For example as the molar mass of the hydrogen atom is 1.01 gmol^{-1}, 6.02 x 10^{23} atoms of hydrogen have a mass of 1.01 g, hence the mass of a single atom is:

$$\frac{1.01 \text{ g mol}^{-1}}{6.02 \times 10^{23} \text{ atoms mol}^{-1}} = 1.68 \times 10^{-24}\text{g atom}^{-1}$$

Similarly the mass of one molecule of glucose ($C_6H_{12}O_6$, $M_r = 180.18$ g mol^{-1}) is:

$$\frac{180.18 \text{ g mol}^{-1}}{6.02 \times 10^{23} \text{ molecules mol}^{-1}} = 2.99 \times 10^{-22} \text{ g molecule}^{-1}$$

EXERCISE 1.5

1. What is the mass of 0.700 moles of Li_2SO_4 taking its molar mass as exactly 110 g mol^{-1}?

   A   15.4 g
   B   77 g
   C   110 g
   D   157 g

2. 0.200 moles of a substance has a mass of 27.0 g. What is the molar mass of the substance?

   A   13.5 g mol^{-1}
   B   27 g mol^{-1}
   C   54 g mol^{-1}
   D   135 g mol^{-1}

3. One drop of water weighs 0.040 g. How many molecules are there in one drop, taking the molar mass of water as exactly 18 g mol^{-1}?

   A 1.3×10^{21}
   B 2.4×10^{22}
   C 3.3×10^{22}
   D 3.9×10^{22}

4. What is the mass (in g) of one molecule of sulfuric acid (H_2SO_4)?

   A   98.08
   B $98.08 \div (6.02 \times 10^{23})$
   C $98.08 \div 7$
   D $98.08 \div (7 \times 6.02 \times 10^{23})$

5. A polymer molecule has a mass of 2.5×10^{-20} g. What is the molar mass of the polymer?

    A 1.5×10^4 g mol^{-1}

    B 2.4×10^{43} g mol^{-1}

    C 6.7×10^{-5} g mol^{-1}

    D 4.2×10^{-44} g mol^{-1}

6. Calculate (correct to 3 significant figures) the mass of

    a)   3.00 moles of ammonia.

    b) $\frac{1}{4}$ mole of Li_2O.

    c)   0.0500 moles of aluminium nitrate.

    d) 3.01×10^{23} molecules of PCl_3.

    e) 2.60×10^{22} molecules of dinitrogen monoxide.

7. How many moles are there in

    a)   28.1 g of silicon   b)   303 g of KNO_3.

    c)   4000 g of nickel sulfate   d)   87.3 g of methane?

8. a)   0.30 moles of a substance has a mass of 45 g. What is its molar mass?

    b) 3.01×10^{25} molecules of a gas has a mass of 6.40 kg. What is its molar mass?

9. Some types of freon are used as the propellant in spray cans of paint, hair spray, and other consumer products. However, the use of freons is being curtailed, because there is some suspicion that they may cause environmental damage. If there are 25.00 g of the freon CCl_2F_2 in a spray can, how many molecules are you releasing to the air when you empty the can?

10. Vitamin C, ascorbic acid, has the formula $C_6H_8O_6$.

    a)   The recommended daily dose of vitamin C is 60.0 milligrams. How many moles are you consuming if you ingest 60 milligrams of the vitamin?

    b)   A typical tablet contains 1.00 g of vitamin C. How many moles of vitamin C does this represent?

    c)   When you consume 1.00 g of vitamin C, how many oxygen atoms are you eating?

PERCENTAGE COMPOSITION AND EMPIRICAL FORMULA

Knowing the formula of a substance and the atomic masses of the elements, then the **percentage composition** may be found by calculating the proportion by mass of each element and converting it to a percentage. For example the relative molar mass of carbon dioxide is

$$12.01 + (2 \times 16.00) = 44.01$$

Oxygen constitutes 32.00 of this (2×16.00), so that the percentage of oxygen by mass in carbon dioxide is:

$$\frac{32.00}{44.01} \times 100 = 72.71\% \text{ oxygen by mass.}$$

The **empirical formula** is the simplest whole number ratio of the atoms of each element in the compound. This is also called the simplest formula. For example the molecular formula of glucose is $C_6H_{12}O_6$, but its empirical formula is CH_2O.

If the mass of the elements in a compound is found by experiment (*empirical* means "by experiment"), then the amount of each element may be found using its relative atomic mass and the formula:

$$n = \frac{m}{M}$$

EXAMPLE
2.476 g of an oxide of copper is found to contain 2.199 g of copper. What is its empirical formula?

SOLUTION
The oxide therefore contains 0.277g (2.476 – 2.199) of oxygen. The amount of each element can therefore be calculated using the relative atomic masses (O = 16.00; Cu = 63.55).

$$\text{Amount of oxygen} = \frac{0.277\text{g}}{16.00 \text{ g mol}^{-1}} = 0.01731 \text{ mol}$$

$$\text{Amount of copper} = \frac{2.199 \text{ g}}{63.55 \text{ g mol}^{-1}} = 0.03460 \text{ mol}$$

The whole number ratio of oxygen to copper may be found by dividing through by the smaller number

Ratio of O : Cu = 0.01731: 0.3460 = 1: 1.999 (dividing by 0.01731)

The simplest whole number ratio of oxygen to copper is therefore 1: 2, so that the empirical formula is Cu_2O.

In some cases this does not give whole numbers and then multiplying by a small integer will be necessary. For example a ratio of Fe:O of $1:1\frac{1}{3}$ gives a whole number ratio of 3:4 when multiplied by 3. Percentage composition data can be used in a similar way.

CORE

EXAMPLE

What is the empirical formula of a compound of phosphorus and oxygen that contains 43.64% phosphorus by mass.

SOLUTION

In 100 g, there are 43.64 g of phosphorus and 56.36 g (i.e. 100 − 43.64 g) of oxygen.

$$\text{Amount of phosphorus} = \frac{43.64 \text{ g}}{30.97 \text{ g mol}^{-1}} = 1.409 \text{ mol}$$

$$\text{Amount of oxygen} = \frac{56.36 \text{ g}}{16.00 \text{ g mol}^{-1}} = 3.523 \text{ mol}$$

The whole number ratio of phosphorus to oxygen may be found by dividing through by the smaller number:

Ratio of P : O = 1.409 : 3.523 = 1 : 2.5 (dividing by 1.409) = 2 : 5 (multiplying by 2)

In this case it is necessary to multiply by a small integer, in this case 2, in order to produce a whole number ratio. The empirical formula is, therefore, P_2O_5.

Similar techniques may also be applied to calculate the amount of water of crystallisation in hydrated salts, by calculating the ratio of the amount of water to the amount of anhydrous salt.

SUMMARY

- Calculate the amount (in moles) of each element (or component).
- Find the simplest whole number ratio between these amounts.

EXPERIMENTAL METHODS

Empirical formulae can often be found by direct determination, for example converting a weighed sample of one element to the compound and then weighing the compound to find the mass of the second element that combined with the first (see exercise 1.6, Q 13). Another method is to decompose a weighed sample of the compound and determine the amount of one of the elements that results. This second method is the one that is usually used to determine the formula of a hydrated salt (see exercise 1.6, Q 14). There are also many other methods for determining percentage composition data, too numerous to mention.

The percentage composition of organic compounds is usually found by burning a known mass of the compound in excess oxygen, then finding the masses of both carbon dioxide (all the carbon turns to carbon dioxide) and water (all the hydrogen turns to water) formed. The mass of oxygen can be found by subtracting the mass of these two elements from the initial mass, assuming that this is the only other element present.

EXAMPLE

6.00 g of an organic compound forms 8.80 g of carbon dioxide and 3.60 g of water when it undergoes complete combustion. What is its empirical formula?

SOLUTION

Amount of CO_2 = amount of $C = \dfrac{m}{M} = \dfrac{8.80 \text{ g}}{44.0 \text{ g mol}^{-1}} = 0.200 \text{ mol}$

Amount of H_2O = amount of $H = \dfrac{m}{M} = \dfrac{3.60 \text{ g}}{18.0 \text{ g mol}^{-1}} = 0.200 \text{ mol}$

Therefore amount of $H = 2 \times 0.200 = 0.400 \text{ mol}$

Mass of $C = n \times M = 0.200 \text{ mol} \times 12.0 \text{ g mol}^{-1} = 2.40 \text{ g}$

Mass of $H = n \times M = 0.400 \text{ mol} \times 1.01 \text{ g mol}^{-1} = 0.404 \text{ g}$

Mass of $O = 6.00 - 2.40 - 0.40 = 3.20 \text{ g}$

Amount of $O = \dfrac{m}{M} = \dfrac{3.20 \text{ g}}{16.0 \text{ g mol}^{-1}} = 0.200 \text{ mol}$

Ratio $C : H : O = 0.200 : 0.400 : 0.200 = 1 : 2 : 1$;
therefore the empirical formula is CH_2O.

MOLECULAR FORMULA

An empirical formula only gives the ratio of the elements. In the case of a molecular substance, the actual number of atoms of each element in the molecule could be any multiple of this. In order to decide which, it is necessary to know the approximate molar mass.

Ethyne and benzene, for example, both have the same empirical formula (CH), but the relative molar mass of ethyne is ~26, whereas that of benzene is ~78, so the molecular formula of ethyne must be C_2H_2 (2×CH) whereas that of benzene is C_6H_6 ($6 \times$ CH because $\dfrac{78}{13} = 6$). In the case of the empirical formula P_2O_5, the molecular formula could actually be P_2O_5 or it could be P_4O_{10}, P_6O_{15}, P_8O_{20} etc. The relative molecular mass of P_2O_5 would be 141.94 ($2 \times 30.97 + 5 \times 16.00$). In order to know which molecular formula is correct, it is necessary to have information about the approximate molar mass of the substance. The molar mass of this oxide of phosphorus is found to be ~280 g mol^{-1}. It must therefore contain two P_2O_5 units, hence the molecular formula is P_4O_{10}.

EXERCISE 1.6

1. What is the percentage by mass of silver in silver sulfide (Ag_2S)?

    A   33.3%

    B   66.7%

    C   77.1%

    D   87.1%

CORE

2. Of the following, the only empirical formula is

A N_2F_2
B N_2F_4
C HNF_2
D H_2N_2

3. A compound of nitrogen and fluorine contains 42% by mass of nitrogen. If the molar mass of the compound is about 66 gmol⁻¹, what is its molecular formula?

A NF
B N_2F_2
C NF_2
D N_2F

4. An organic compound which has the empirical formula CHO has a relative molecular mass of 232. Its molecular formula is:

A CHO
B $C_2H_2O_2$
C $C_4H_4O_4$
D $C_8H_8O_8$

5. 3.40 g of $CaSO_4$ (M = 136 g mol⁻¹) is formed when 4.30 g of hydrated calcium sulfate is heated to constant mass. How many moles of water of crystallisation are combined with each mole of calcium sulfate?

A 1
B 2
C 3
D 4

6. 2.40 g of element Z combines exactly with 1.6 g of oxygen to form a compound with the formula ZO_2. What is the relative atomic mass of Z?

A 24.0
B 32.0
C 48.0
D 64.0

7. Of the following, the only empirical formula is

A $C_{12}H_{22}O_{11}$
B $C_6H_{12}O_6$
C C_6H_6
D C_2H_4

8. A certain compound has a molar mass of about 56 g mol^{-1}. All the following are empirical formulae for this compound except

A CH_2
B CH_2O
C C_3H_4O
D CH_2N

9. The empirical formula of a compound with the molecular formula $C_6H_{12}O_3$ is

A $C_6H_{12}O_3$
B $C_3H_6O_2$
C C_2H_3O
D C_2H_4O

10. What percentage of 'chrome alum' [$KCr(SO_4)_2 \cdot 12\ H_2O$; $M_r = 499.4$] is water?

A $\dfrac{18.01}{499.4} \times 100$

B $\dfrac{12 \times 18.01}{499.4} \times 100$

C $\dfrac{18.01}{499.4 - 18.01} \times 100$

D $\dfrac{12 \times 18.01}{499.4 - (12 \times 18.01)} \times 100$

11. What percentage by mass of sodium thiosulfate pentahydrate ($Na_2S_2O_3 \cdot 5H_2O$) is water?

12. a) 2.0 g of an oxide of iron contains approximately 0.60 g oxygen and 1.4 g iron. What is the empirical formula of the oxide?

b) A compound of silicon and fluorine contains about 73% fluorine by mass. What is its empirical formula?

c) A compound of carbon, hydrogen and oxygen only, with a molar mass of ~90 g mol^{-1} contains 26.6% carbon and 2.2% hydrogen by mass. What is its molecular formula?

13. 1.000 g of tin metal burns in air to give 1.270 g of tin oxide. What is the empirical formula of the oxide?

14. A 1.39 g sample of hydrated copper(II) sulfate ($CuSO_4 \cdot xH_2O$) is heated until all the water of hydration is driven off. The anhydrous salt has a mass of 0.89 g. Determine the formula of the hydrate.

CORE

15. The red colour of blood is due to haemoglobin. It contains 0.335% by mass of Fe (iron). Four atoms of Fe are present in each molecule of haemoglobin. If the atomic mass of Fe=55.84 g mol^{-1}, estimate the molar mass of haemoglobin.

16. A 200.0 mg sample of a compound containing K, Cr, and O was analyzed and found to contain 70.8 mg Cr and 53.2 mg K. Calculate the empirical formula of the sample.

17. The formula molecular formula of the insecticide DDT is $C_{14}H_9Cl_5$. Calculate the molar mass of the compound and the mass percent of each element.

18. The percentages of carbon, hydrogen, and oxygen in vitamin C are determined by burning a sample of vitamin C weighing 1.00 g. The masses of $CO_{2(g)}$ and $H_2O_{(l)}$ formed are 1.50 g and 0.408 g, respectively.

    a)   Calculate the masses and amounts of C and H in the sample.
    b)   Determine the amount of oxygen in the sample.
    c)   From the above data, determine the empirical formula of vitamin C.

19. The percentages by mass of C, H, and N in an unknown compound are found to be 23.30%, 4.85%, and 40.78%, respectively (N.B. these do not add up to 100%. Why?). Determine the empirical formula of the compound. If the molar mass of the compound is 206 g mol^{-1}, what is its molecular formula?

20. Efflorescence is the process by which some hydrated salts lose water of crystallisation when exposed to the air. 'Washing soda' ($Na_2CO_3 \cdot 10H_2O$) is converted to the monohydrate ($Na_2CO_3 \cdot H_2O$) when exposed to the air. What is the percentage loss in mass of the crystals?

1.3 CHEMICAL EQUATIONS

1.3.1   Balance chemical equations when all reactants and products are given.

Distinguish between coefficients and subscripts.

1.3.2   Identify the mole ratios of any two species in a balanced chemical equation.

Use balanced chemical equations to obtain information about the amounts of reactants and products.

1.3.3   Apply the state symbols (s), (1), (g) and (aq).

Encourage the use of state symbols in chemical equations.   © IBO 2001

The chemical equation is a record of what happens in a chemical reaction. It shows the formulae (molecular formulae or formula units) of all the reactants (on the left hand side) and all the products (on the right hand side). It also gives the

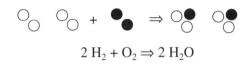

$$2\,H_2 + O_2 \Rightarrow 2\,H_2O$$

number of each species that are required for complete reaction. The example shows the reaction of hydrogen and oxygen to produce water.

The first stage is to write a word equation for the reaction. The reaction of calcium carbonate with hydrochloric acid, for example, which produces calcium chloride, carbon dioxide and water can be represented as

Calcium carbonate + Hydrochloric acid $\Rightarrow$ Calcium chloride + Carbon dioxide + Water

The next stage is to replace the names of the compounds with their formulae, so that this equation becomes:

$$CaCO_3 + HCl \Rightarrow CaCl_2 + CO_2 + H_2O$$

Finally the equation must be **balanced** by placing coefficients, also called **stoichiometric coefficients**, in front of some of the formulae. These multiply the number of atoms of the elements in the formula by that factor and represent the number of moles of the species required. Because matter cannot be created or destroyed, at least in chemical reactions, there must be the same number of atoms of each element on both sides of the equation. In the example above, there are two chlorines on the right hand side, but only one on the left hand side. Similarly the hydrogen atoms do not balance. This can be corrected by putting a '2' in front of the hydrochloric acid, so the final balanced equation is

$$CaCO_3 + 2\,HCl \Rightarrow CaCl_2 + CO_2 + H_2O$$

This means that one formula unit of calcium carbonate will just react completely with two formula units of hydrochloric acid to produce one formula unit of calcium chloride, one molecule of carbon dioxide and one molecule of water. Scaling this up means that one mole of calcium carbonate reacts with two moles of hydrochloric acid to produce one mole of calcium chloride, one mole of carbon dioxide and one mole of water. The amounts of substances in a balanced equation are known as the **stoichiometry** of the reaction, hence these equations are sometimes referred to as **stoichiometric equations**. Note that the formulae of compounds can never be changed, so balancing the equation by altering the subscripts, for example changing calcium chloride to $CaCl_3$ or water to H_3O, is incorrect.

It is sometimes helpful to show the physical state of the substances involved and this can be done by a suffix, known as a **state symbol** placed after the formula. The state symbols used are (s) - solid, (l) - liquid, (g) - gas and (aq) - aqueous solution. Adding these, the equation for the reaction between calcium carbonate and hydrochloric acid becomes

$$CaCO_{3\ (s)} + 2\ HCl_{(aq)} \Rightarrow CaCl_{2\ (aq)} + CO_{2\ (g)} + H_2O_{(l)}$$

It is often better to write the equation for a reaction occurring in aqueous solution as an **ionic equation**. This is particularly true for precipitation reactions, acid-base reactions and redox reactions. An example would be the reaction between aqueous lead nitrate and aqueous sodium chloride to precipitate lead chloride and leave a solution of sodium nitrate.

$$Pb(NO_3)_{2\ (aq)} + 2\ NaCl_{(aq)} \Rightarrow PbCl_{2\ (s)} + 2\ NaNO_{3\ (aq)}$$

The reaction actually involves just the lead ions and chloride ions, so it is better written as

$$Pb^{2+}_{(aq)} + 2\ Cl^-_{(aq)} \Rightarrow PbCl_{2\ (s)}$$

The hydrated nitrate ions and sodium ions are present in both the reactants and products and so do not take part in the reaction. They are known as **spectator ions**. Ionic equations are far more general than normal equations. This ionic equation, for example, states that any soluble lead compound will react with any soluble chloride to form a precipitate of lead chloride.

EXERCISE 1.7

1. Which one of the following equations best represents the reaction between iron and hydrochloric acid?

    A $Fe + HCl \Rightarrow FeCl + H$

    B $Fe + HCl \Rightarrow FeCl + \frac{1}{2} H_2$

    C $Fe + 2\ HCl \Rightarrow FeCl_2 + H_2$

    D $Fe + 2\ HCl \Rightarrow FeCl_2 + 2\ H$

2. What numerical value of **Q** is required to balance the equation below?

    $$2\ H_2S + Q\ O_2 \Rightarrow 2\ SO_2 + 2\ H_2O$$

    A   2

    B   3

    C   4

    D   6

3. The equation for the reaction of sodium sulfate with barium nitrate to form a precipitate of barium sulfate is

$$Ba(NO_3)_2 + Na_2SO_4 \Rightarrow BaSO_4 + 2\,NaNO_3$$

Which one of the following is the correct ionic equation for this reaction?

A $Ba^{2+} + SO_4^{2-} \Rightarrow BaSO_4$

B $Na^+ + NO_3^- \Rightarrow NaNO_3$

C $Ba^{2+} + Na_2SO_4 \Rightarrow BaSO_4 + 2\,Na^+$

D $Ba(NO_3)_2 + SO_4^{2-} \Rightarrow BaSO_4 + 2\,NO_3^-$

4. Write in numbers, in front of the formulae, to balance the following equations.

a) $CaO + HNO_3 \Rightarrow Ca(NO_3)_2 + H_2O$

b) $NH_3 + H_2SO_4 \Rightarrow (NH_4)_2SO_4$

c) $HCl + ZnCO_3 \Rightarrow ZnCl_2 + H_2O + CO_2$

d) $SO_2 + Mg \Rightarrow S + MgO$

e) $Fe_3O_4 + H_2 \Rightarrow Fe + H_2O$

f) $K + C_2H_5OH \Rightarrow KC_2H_5O + H_2$

g) $Fe(OH)_3 \Rightarrow Fe_2O_3 + H_2O$

h) $CH_3CO_2H + O_2 \Rightarrow CO_2 + H_2O$

i) $Pb(NO_3)_2 \Rightarrow PbO + NO_2 + O_2$

j) $NaMnO_4 + HCl \Rightarrow NaCl + MnCl_2 + Cl_2 + H_2O$

5. Write balanced equations for the following reactions.

a) Copper carbonate forming copper oxide and carbon dioxide.

b) Nickel oxide reacting with sulfuric acid to form nickel sulfate and water.

c) Iron and bromine reacting to give iron(III) bromide.

d) Lead(IV) oxide and carbon monoxide forming lead metal and carbon dioxide.

e) Iron(II) chloride reacting with chlorine to form iron(III) chloride.

f) Ethanol burning in air to form carbon dioxide and water.

g) Silver reacting with nitric acid to form silver nitrate, nitrogen dioxide and water.

h) Manganese(IV) oxide reacting with hydrochloric acid to form manganese(II) chloride, chlorine and water.

i) Sulfur dioxide reacting with hydrogen sulfide to form sulfur and water.

j) Ammonia reacting with oxygen to form nitrogen monoxide and water.

1.4 MASS RELATIONSHIPS IN CHEMICAL REACTIONS

1.4.1 Calculate stoichiometric quantities and use these to determine experimental and theoretical yields.

Mass is conserved in all chemical reactions. Given a chemical equation and the mass or amount (in moles) of one species, calculate the mass or amount of another species.

1.4.2 Determine the limiting reactant and the reactant in excess when quantities of reacting substances are given.

Given a chemical equation and the initial amounts of two or more reactants: identify the limiting reactant; calculate the theoretical yield of a product; calculate the amount(s) of the reactant(s) in excess remaining after the reaction is complete.

1.4.3 Apply Avogadro's law to calculate reacting volumes of gases.   © IBO 2001

REACTING MASSES

In chemical reactions matter cannot be created or destroyed, so that the total mass of the products is equal to the total mass of the reactants. If a gas is given off or absorbed, then the mass of the solids and liquids will appear to change, but if the gas is taken into account, mass is conserved.

Chemical equations give the amounts of substances related by a chemical reaction. Consider the reaction of methane with oxygen:

$$CH_{4\,(g)} + 2\,O_{2\,(g)} \Rightarrow CO_{2\,(g)} + 2\,H_2O_{(l)}$$

One mole of methane (i.e. 16 g) will react with two moles of oxygen molecules (i.e. $2 \times 32 = 64\,g$) to form one mole of carbon dioxide (i.e. 44 g) and two moles of water (i.e. $2 \times 18 = 36\,g$). The total mass is 80 g on both sides of the equation, in accordance with the principle of conservation of mass, but the equation allows us to predict that burning 16 g of methane will consume 64 g (= 2×32) of oxygen. What if only 4 g of methane is burnt? This is $\frac{1}{4}$ of the amount of methane, so it will consume $\frac{1}{4}$ of the amount of oxygen, i.e. 16 g.

If the molar masses are known, the masses of substances related in a chemical equation may be calculated by applying the formula $n = \frac{m}{M}$. These calculations are best thought of as being carried out in three stages as illustrated in the examples below:

EXAMPLE

Consider that you had 10.00 g of sodium hydroxide. What mass of hydrated sodium sulfate crystals ($Na_2SO_4 \cdot 7H_2O$) could be produced by reaction with excess sulfuric acid?

SOLUTION

Stage One - Calculate the amount of the substance whose mass is given.

$$\text{Amount of NaOH} = \frac{m}{M} = \frac{10.00 \text{ g}}{40.00 \text{ g mol}^{-1}} = 0.2500 \text{ mol}$$

Stage Two - Use the balanced equation to calculate the amount of the required substance.

$$2 \text{ NaOH} \quad + \quad H_2SO_4 \quad \Rightarrow \quad Na_2SO_4 \quad + \quad H_2O$$

2 mol   1 mol

$$\therefore \text{ mol } Na_2SO_4 = \tfrac{1}{2} \text{ mol NaOH}$$

0.2500 mol $\tfrac{1}{2} \times 0.2500 = 0.1250$ mol

Stage Three - Calculate the mass of the required substance from the amount of it.

Mass of hydrated sodium sulfate $= n \times M = 0.1250 \text{ mol} \times 268.18 \text{ g mol}^{-1} = 33.52 \text{ g}$

(N.B. the molar mass of the hydrated salt must be used)

The procedure is exactly the same irrespective of whether the calculation starts with the mass of reactant and calculates the mass of product, or calculates the mass of reactant required to give a certain mass of product, as illustrated by a second example.

EXAMPLE

What mass of sodium hydrogencarbonate must be heated to give 8.80 g of carbon dioxide?

SOLUTION

Stage One

$$\text{Amount of CO}_2 = \frac{8.80 \text{ g}}{44.01 \text{ g mol}^{-1}} = 0.200 \text{ mol}$$

Stage Two
$$2 \text{ NaHCO}_3 \Rightarrow \quad Na_2CO_3 + \quad CO_2 \quad + \quad H_2O$$

2 mol   1 mol

$2 \times 0.200 = 0.400$ mol   0.200 mol

Stage Three
Mass of $NaHCO_3 = 0.400 \text{ mol} \times 84.01 \text{ g mol}^{-1} = 33.6 \text{ g}$

SUMMARY

- Calculate the amount of the substance whose mass is given.
- Use the balanced equation to calculate the amount of the required substance.
- Calculate the mass of the required substance from the amount of it.

EXERCISE 1.8

1. When butane is burnt in excess air, the following reaction takes place

$$2\ C_4H_{10\ (g)} + 13\ O_{2\ (g)} \Rightarrow 8\ CO_{2\ (g)} + 10\ H_2O_{(l)}$$

How many moles of oxygen are required to react with five moles of butane?

A   6.5
B   13
C   32.5
D   65

2. When magnesium is added to aqueous silver nitrate, the following reaction takes place

$$Mg_{(s)} + 2\ AgNO_{3\ (aq)} \Rightarrow 2\ Ag_{(s)} + Mg(NO_3)_{2\ (aq)}$$

What mass of silver is formed when 2.43 g of magnesium is added to an excess of aqueous silver nitrate?

A   107.9 g
B   21.6 g
C   10.8 g
D   5.4 g

3. When heated potassium chlorate(V) decomposes to form potassium chloride and oxygen. The unbalanced equation is:

$$KClO_{3\ (s)} \Rightarrow KCl_{\ (s)} + O_{2\ (g)}$$

a)   Balance the equation.
b)   How many moles of $KClO_3$ are needed to produce 0.60 moles of oxygen?
c)   What mass of $KClO_3$ is needed to produce 0.0200 moles of KCl?

4. What mass of copper(II) sulfate pentahydrate ($CuSO_4 \cdot 5H_2O$) can be produced by reacting 12.00 g of copper(II) oxide with an excess of sulfuric acid?

5. Pure compound A contains 63.3% manganese and 36.7% oxygen by mass. Upon heating compound A, oxygen is evolved and pure compound B is formed which contains 72.0% Mn and 28.0% oxygen by mass.

   a) Determine the empirical formula for compounds A and B.

   b) Write a balanced equation which represents the reaction that took place.

   c) How many grams of oxygen would be evolved when 2.876 g of A is heated to form pure B?

LIMITING REAGENTS

The quantities of reactants related in the section above are the precise amounts, or stoichiometric amounts, required to just react with each other. More commonly there will be an excess of all of the reagents except one, so that all of this last reagent will be consumed. This reagent is known as the **limiting reagent** because it is the amount of this that limits the quantity of product formed. It may be identified by calculating the amount of each reagent present and then dividing by the relevant coefficient from the equation. The reagent corresponding to the smallest number is the limiting reagent.

EXAMPLE

Consider the reaction: $H_2O_{2 (aq)} + 2KI_{(aq)} + H_2SO_{4 (aq)} \Rightarrow I_{2 (s)} + K_2SO_{4 (aq)} + 2H_2O_{(l)}$

What mass of iodine is produced when 100.00 g of KI is added to a solution containing 12.00 g of H_2O_2 and 50.00 g H_2SO_4?

SOLUTION

The mole ratio from the equation is

	H_2O_2	:	KI	:	H_2SO_4
	1	:	2	:	1

The actual mole ratio of reagents present is

	$\frac{12.00}{34.02}$	:	$\frac{100.00}{166.00}$	:	$\frac{50.00}{98.08}$
=	0.3527	:	0.6024	:	0.5098
=	1	:	1.708	:	1.445
Ratio divided by coefficient =	1	:	0.854	:	1.445

It can be seen that even though there is the greatest mass of KI, it is still the limiting reagent, owing to its large molar mass and the 2:1 mole ratio. The maximum yield of iodine will therefore be $\frac{1}{2} \times 0.6024 = 0.3012$ moles. This is the **theoretical yield**, which can, if required, be converted into a mass:

Theoretical yield $= n \times M = 0.3012$ mol $\times 253.8$ g mol$^{-1} = 76.44$ g

There is an excess of both H_2O_2 and H_2SO_4. The amounts in excess can be calculated: 0.6024 moles of KI will react with:

$\frac{1}{2} \times 0.6024 = 0.3012$ moles of both H_2O_2 and H_2SO_4 (both a 1:2 mole ratio).

Mass of H_2O_2 reacting $= 0.3012 \times 34.02 = 10.24$ g,
therefore mass in excess $= 12 - 10.24 = 1.76$ g

Mass of H_2SO_4 reacting $= 0.3012 \times 98.08 = 29.54$ g,
therefore mass in excess $= 50.00 - 29.54 = 20.46$ g

In practice the theoretical yield is never achieved owing to impurities in reagents, side reactions and other sources of experimental error. Supposing 62.37 g of iodine was eventually produced, the **experimental yield** can be calculated as a percentage of the theoretical yield:

$$\text{Experimental yield} = \frac{62.37}{76.44} \times 100 = 81.59\,\%.$$

EXERCISE 1.9

1. Consider the reaction:

$$2\,Al_{(s)} + 3\,I_{2\,(s)} \Rightarrow 2\,AlI_{3\,(s)}$$

Determine the limiting reagent and the theoretical yield of the product from:

a) 1.20 mol Al and 2.40 mol iodine.
b) 1.20 g Al and 2.40 g iodine.
c) How many grams of Al are left over in part b?

2. Freon-12 (used as coolant in refrigerators), is formed as follows:

$$3\,CCl_{4\,(l)} + 2\,SbF_{3\,(s)} \Rightarrow 3\,CCl_2F_{2\,(g)} + 2\,SbCl_{3\,(s)}$$

150 g CCl_4 is combined with 100 g SbF_3 to give Freon-12 (CCl_2F_2).

a) Identify the limiting and excess reagents.
b) How many grams of Freon-12 can be formed?
c) How much of the excess reagent is left over?

3. Aspirin is made by adding acetic anhydride to an aqueous solution of salicylic acid. The equation for the reaction is:

$$2\,C_7H_6O_{3\,(aq)} + C_4H_6O_{3(l)} \Rightarrow 2\,C_9H_8O_{4\,(aq)} + H_2O_{(l)}$$
$$\text{salicylic} \qquad\quad \text{acetic} \qquad\qquad \text{aspirin} \qquad\quad \text{water}$$
$$\text{acid} \qquad\qquad \text{anhydride}$$

If 1.00 kg of salicylic acid is used with 2.00 kg of acetic anhydride, determine:

a) the limiting reagent.
b) the theoretical yield.
c) If 1.12 kg aspirin is produced experimentally, what is the percentage yield?

GASES AND AMOUNTS OF SUBSTANCE

At constant temperature and pressure:

It is found that a given volume of any gas always contains the same number of particles (i.e. molecules except in the case of the noble gases, see Section 5.2, page 170). This is known as Avogadro's Law. It means that in reactions involving gases the volumes of reactants and products, when measured at the same temperature and pressure, are in the same ratio as their coefficients in a balanced equation. For example when carbon monoxide reacts with oxygen to form carbon dioxide, the volume of oxygen required is only half the volume of carbon monoxide consumed and carbon dioxide formed:

$$2\,CO_{(g)} \quad + \quad O_{2\,(g)} \quad \Rightarrow \quad 2\,CO_{2\,(g)}$$
$$\text{2 vol} \qquad\qquad \text{1 vol} \qquad\qquad \text{2 vol}$$

This may be used to carry out calculations about the volume of gaseous product and the volume of any excess reagent:

EXAMPLE

$10\ cm^3$ of ethyne is reacted with $50\ cm^3$ of hydrogen to produce ethane according to the equation:

$$C_2H_{2\,(g)} + 2\,H_{2\,(g)} \Rightarrow C_2H_{6\,(g)}$$

Calculate the total volume and composition of the remaining gas mixture, assuming that temperature and pressure remain constant.

SOLUTION

Ratio of volume of reactants to products is in the ratio of the coefficients:

$$C_2H_{2\,(g)} \quad + \quad 2\,H_{2\,(g)} \quad \Rightarrow \quad C_2H_{6\,(g)}$$
$$\text{1 vol} \qquad\qquad \text{2 vol} \qquad\qquad \text{1 vol}$$
$$10\ cm^3 \qquad\quad 20\ cm^3 \qquad\quad 10\ cm^3$$

Hence it can be seen that the hydrogen is in excess:

$$\text{Volume of remaining hydrogen} = 50 - 20 = 30\ cm^3$$

The total volume of the gas mixture that remains is $40\ cm^3$, comprising of $10\ cm^3$ ethane and $30\ cm^3$ hydrogen.

Under specific conditions:

If the temperature and pressure are specified, then the volume of any gas that contains one mole may be calculated (see the ideal gas equation, Section 5.2, page 170). This is known as the molar volume. There are two sets of specific conditions that are frequently used in calculations involving this concept:

Standard temperature and pressure (s.t.p.) | Room temperature and pressure (r.t.p.)

Temperature = 0°C (273 K)   Temperature = 19.6°C (292.6 K)

Pressure = 1 atm (101.3 kPa)   Pressure = 1 atm (101.3 kPa)

Molar volume = 22.4 dm^3 Molar volume = 24.0 dm^3

Using these the amount of gas can be calculated from the volume of the gas under these conditions using the formula:

$$\text{Amount of gas} = \frac{\text{Volume of gas}}{\text{Molar volume}}$$

This may be abbreviated to:

$$n = \frac{V_{stp}}{22.4} \qquad \text{or} \qquad n = \frac{V_{rtp}}{24.0}$$

as appropriate, where V is the volume of gas in dm^3.

EXAMPLE

How many moles of oxygen molecules are there in 5.00 dm^3 of oxygen at s.t.p.?

SOLUTION

$$n = \frac{V_{stp}}{22.4} = \frac{5.00}{22.4} = 0.223 \text{ mol}$$

This equation may also be rearranged to calculate the volume of gas under these conditions, knowing the amount of gas. The relationship between the amount of gas and its volume can then be used in calculations in the same way as the relationship between mass and molar mass.

EXAMPLE

What mass of sodium hydrogencarbonate must be heated to generate 10.0 dm^3 of carbon dioxide, measured at room temperature and pressure?

SOLUTION

Stage One - Calculate the number of moles of the substance for which data is given.

$$n = \frac{V_{rtp}}{24.0} = \frac{10.0}{24.0} = 0.417 \text{ mol}$$

Stage Two - Use the balanced equation to calculate the moles of the required substance.

$$2\,NaHCO_3 \quad + \quad \Rightarrow \quad Na_2CO_3 \quad + \quad H_2O \quad + \quad CO_2$$

2 moles   1 mole

$2 \times 0.417 = 0.834$ moles   0.417 moles

Stage Three - Calculate the result for the required substance from the number of moles.

Mass of sodium hydrogencarbonate = $n \times M = 0.834 \times 84.0 = 70.1$ g.

EXAMPLE

What volume of air (assumed to contain 20% oxygen), measured at s.t.p., is required for the complete combustion of 1.000 kg of gasoline, assuming that this is totally composed of octane (C_8H_{18})?

SOLUTION

Stage One - Calculate the number of moles of the substance for which data is given.

$$n = \frac{m}{M_r} = \frac{1000}{114.2} = 8.76 \, mol$$

Stage Two - Use the balanced equation to calculate the moles of the required substance.

$$2C_8H_{18} \quad + \quad 25\,O_2 \quad \Rightarrow \quad 16\,CO_2 \quad + \quad 18\,H_2O$$

2 moles   25 mole

8.76 $\frac{1}{2} \times 25 \times 8.76 = 109.5$ moles

Stage Three - Calculate the result for the required substance from the number of moles.

Volume of oxygen = $n \times 22.4 = 109.5 \times 22.4 = 2543$ dm^3

Volume of air = $2543 \times 5 = 12260$ dm^3

EXERCISE 1.10

1. According to the equation below, what volume of nitrogen dioxide would you expect to be formed from 20 cm^3 of nitrogen monoxide, assuming that the volumes are measured at the same temperature and pressure?

$$2\,NO_{(g)} + O_{2\,(g)} \Rightarrow 2\,NO_{2\,(g)}$$

A   10 cm^3

B   15 cm^3

C   20 cm^3

D   30 cm^3

2. Four identical flasks are filled with hydrogen, oxygen, carbon dioxide and chlorine at the same temperature and pressure. The flask with the greatest mass will be the one containing

A   hydrogen.

B   oxygen.

C   carbon dioxide.

D   chlorine.

3. How many moles of hydrogen molecules are there in 560 cm^3 of hydrogen gas measured at s.t.p.?

    A   0.0250

    B   0.050

    C   25.0

    D   50.0

4. What volume would 3.20 g of sulfur dioxide ocupy at r.t.p.?

    A   1.12 dm^3

    B   1.20 dm^3

    C   4.48 dm^3

    D   4.80 dm^3

5. Potassium nitrate ($M_r = 101$) decomposes on heating as shown by the equation below. What mass of the solid must be heated to produce 10.0 dm^3 of oxygen gas, measured at r.t.p.?

$$2\ KNO_{3\ (s)} \Rightarrow 2\ KNO_{2\ (s)} + O_{2\ (g)}$$

    A $101 \times \dfrac{24.0}{10.0}\ g$

    B $101 \times \dfrac{10.0}{24.0}\ g$

    C $\dfrac{1}{2} \times 101 \times \dfrac{10.0}{24.0}\ g$

    D $2 \times 101 \times \dfrac{10.0}{24.0}\ g$

6. A mixture of 20 cm^3 hydrogen and 40 cm^3 oxygen is exploded in a strong container. After cooling to the original temperature and pressure (at which water is a liquid) what gas, if any, will remain in the container?

7. To three significant figures, how many methane molecules are there in 4.48 dm^3 of the gas at standard temperature and pressure?

8. If 3.00 dm^3 of an unknown gas at room temperature and pressure has a mass of 5.85 g, what is the molar mass of the gas?

9. What is the density of ammonia, in g dm^{-3}, at s.t.p.?

10. sulfur dioxide, present in flue gases from the combustion of coal, is often absorbed by injecting powdered limestone into the flame, when the following reactions occur:

$$CaCO_{3\ (s)} \Rightarrow CaO_{(s)} + CO_{2\ (g)}$$
$$CaO_{(s)} + SO_{2\ (g)} \Rightarrow CaSO_{3\ (s)}$$

What volume of sulfur dioxide, measured at r.t.p., can be absorbed by using 1 tonne (1.00×10^6 g) of limestone in this way?

1.5 SOLUTIONS

1.5.1 Define the terms solute, solvent, solution and concentration (g dm^3 and mol dm^3).

Concentration in mol dm^{-3} is often represented by square brackets around the substance under consideration, eg [CH$_3$COOH].

1.5.2 Carry out calculations involving concentration, amount of solute and volume of solution.

1.5.3 Solve solution stoichiometry problems.

Given the quantity of one species in a chemical reaction in solution (in grams, moles or in terms of concentration), determine the quantity of another species.

© IBO 2001

Sometimes when a substance is mixed with a liquid, it disintegrates into sub-microscopic particles (i.e. atoms, molecules or ions) to produce a homogenous mixture of two or more substances - this is known as a **solution**. The liquid, present in excess, in which the dispersion occurs is known as the **solvent** and the substance dissolved in it, which can be a solid, a liquid or a gas, is known as the **solute**. A solution is different from a **suspension** (fine particles of solid in a liquid) because it is transparent, does not settle out and cannot be separated by filtration.

The **solubility** of a substance is the quantity of that substance that will dissolve to form a certain volume of solution in that solvent (water is assumed unless another solvent is stated). The units vary from source to source (the quantity may be in moles or grams, and the amount may be in 100 cm^3 or in 1 dm^3), so this is always worth checking. It is important to also note that solubility varies with temperature. With solids it usually (though not always) increases with temperature, for gases it decreases with temperature. If a certain volume of solution contains a small amount of dissolved solid it is said to be **dilute** and if it contains a large amount of solute it is said to be **concentrated**. Care must be taken not to replace these with the terms **weak** and **strong**, as these have a very different meaning in chemistry (see Section 9.2, page 290). A **saturated solution** is one in which no more solute will dissolve at that temperature, and excess solute is present. Sometimes, temporarily, the concentration of a solute (or its component ions) can exceed its solubility and in this case the solution is referred to as **supersaturated**. This can occur if the temperature of a solution is changed, or more commonly, if the substance is produced in a chemical reaction. In this case the excess solid will eventually separate from the solution as a **precipitate**.

CONCENTRATION

The concentration (c) is the amount of substance (n) contained within a given volume (V) of solution. In chemistry this is given as the number of moles of the substance in one cubic decimetre (dm^3; note that this volume is equivalent to 1 litre). Concentration can therefore be calculated using the formula:

$$\text{Concentration of solution} = \frac{\text{Amount of solute}}{\text{Solution volume in dm}^3}$$

This can be written as: $c = \dfrac{n}{V}$.

For example we can calculate the concentration of the solution formed when 4.00 moles of glucose are dissolved in 5.00 dm³ of water?

$$c = \frac{4.00 \text{ mol}}{5.00 \text{ dm}^3} = 0.800 \text{ mol dm}^{-3}$$

Although the preferred unit for concentration is mol dm⁻³, because 1 dm³ is equal to 1 litre (L), concentration may also be quoted as mol/L, mol/dm³, mol L⁻¹, or even just 'M'. 2 M sulfuric acid is therefore sulfuric acid with a concentration of 2 moles per litre. International convention recommends that this use of 'M', and the use of the term '**molarity**' instead of concentration, be discontinued.

Because we frequently refer to the concentrations of species in chemistry, the convention has arisen that square brackets around a symbol means 'the concentration of', so that [NaCl] = 0.5 M means the concentration of sodium chloride is 0.5 mol dm⁻³.

The concentration of the solution formed by dissolving a given mass of a substance may be found by substituting in the concentration formula above, having first calculated the amount of the substance using the formula $n = \dfrac{m}{M}$.

EXAMPLE

If 2.00 g of sodium hydroxide is dissolved in 200 cm³ of water, what is the concentration of the resulting solution?

$$\text{Amount of NaOH} = \frac{2.00 \text{ g}}{40.0 \text{ g mol}^{-1}} = 0.0500 \text{ mol}$$

$$[\text{NaOH}] = \frac{0.0500 \text{ mol}}{0.200 \text{ dm}^3} = 0.250 \text{ mol dm}^{-3}$$

Note that the 200 cm³ of water has to be converted to 0.200 dm³ before it can be substituted in the equation. Similarly this process can be modified to calculate the amount (and hence the mass) of solute present, or the volume of the solution required.

EXAMPLE

What mass of hydrated copper sulfate crystals ($CuSO_4 \cdot 5H_2O$) is present in 17.3 cm³ of a 0.279 mol dm⁻³ solution of copper sulfate?

Amount of $CuSO_4$ $(n) = c \times V = 0.279$ mol dm⁻³ $\times 0.0173$ dm³ $= 0.00483$ mol

Mass of $CuSO_4.5H_2O = n \times M = 0.00483$ mol $\times 249.7$ g mol⁻¹ $= 1.21$ g

Ionic substances split up into their component ions when dissolved in water. The concentrations of the individual ions will depend on how many of these ions are produced when the substance dissolves. In a 2 mol dm^{-3} solution of aluminium sulfate, for example, the concentration of the aluminium ions is 4 mol dm^{-3} and that of the sulfate ions is 6 mol dm^{-3}, as illustrated by the equation below

$$Al_2(SO_4)_{3(aq)} \Rightarrow \quad 2\ Al^{3+}_{(aq)} \quad + \quad 3\ SO_4^{2-}_{(aq)}$$

1 mole	2 moles	3 moles
2 mol dm^{-3}	4 mol dm^{-3}	6 mol dm^{-3}

A concentrated solution may have solvent added to produce a more dilute one. In such calculations it is important to remember that the total amount of solute remains constant.

EXAMPLE

Calculate the volume to which 20.0 cm^3 of 7.63 mol dm^{-3} hydrochloric acid must be diluted to produce a solution with a concentration of exactly 5.00 mol dm^{-3}.

Amount of HCl $= c \times V = 7.63$ mol dm$^{-3} \times 0.0200$ dm$^3 = 0.153$ mol
Volume of 5.00 mol dm^{-3} acid that would contain this number of moles

$$= \frac{n}{c} = \frac{0.153\ \text{mol}}{5.00\ \text{mol dm}^{-3}} = 0.0305\ \text{dm}^3$$

Therefore the 20 cm^3 of the original acid must be diluted to 30.5 cm^3. Assuming that there is no volume change on dilution 30.5 - 20.0 = 10.5 cm^3 of water must be added.

EXERCISE 1.11

1. How many moles of hydrochloric acid are present in 0.80 dm^3 of a solution with a concentration of 0.40 mol dm^{-3}.

    A   0.32
    B   0.5
    C   0.8
    D   2

2. Sodium phosphate has the formula Na_3PO_4. What is the concentration of sodium ions in a 0.6 mol dm^{-3} solution of sodium phosphate?

    A   0.2 mol dm^{-3}
    B   0.3 mol dm^{-3}
    C   0.6 mol dm^{-3}
    D   1.8 mol dm^{-3}

3. What volume of a 0.5 mol dm^{-3} solution of sodium hydroxide can be prepared from 2 g of the solid?

  A   0.05 litres
  B   0.1 litres
  C   0.4 litres
  D   0.5 litres

4. What are the concentrations of the solutions produced by dissolving

  a)   3.0 moles of nitric acid in 4.0 dm^3 of solution?
  b)   2.81 g of KOH in 2.00 dm^3 of solution?
  c)   5.00 g of magnesium sulfate heptahydrate in 250 cm^3 of solution?

5. How many moles are there in the following?

  a)   7.0 dm^3 of sulfuric acid of concentration 0.30 mol dm^{-3}.
  b)   50 cm^3 of a 0.040 mol dm^{-3} solution of lithium chloride.
  c)   15.0 cm^3 of a solution made by dissolving 5.80 g of zinc chloride in 2.50 dm^3 of solution.

6. What volume of solution could you produce in the following cases?

  a)   1 mol dm^{-3} copper(II) chloride from 0.4 moles of the solid.
  b)   0.0200 mol dm^{-3} NaNO$_3$ starting from 5.00 g of the solid.
  c)   Dilute 0.50 mol dm^{-3} sulfuric acid starting with 20 cm^3 of a concentrated 18 mol dm^{-3} solution.

7. How would you prepare 500 cm^3 of a 0.100 mol dm^{-3} NaCl solution?

8. How would you prepare 1.2 dm^3 of a 0.40 mol dm^{-3} solution of HCl starting from a 2.0 mol dm^{-3} solution?

9. 500 cm^3 of 0.500 mol dm^{-3} NaCl is added to 500 cm^3 of 1.00 mol dm^{-3} Na$_2$CO$_3$ solution. Calculate the final concentration of Na$^+$ ions in solution.

10. When hydrochloric acid is added to aqueous lead nitrate, solid lead chloride is precipitated. If 10 cm^3 of 2 mol dm^{-3} hydrochloric acid is added to 40 cm^3 of 0.5 mol dm^{-3} aqueous lead nitrate, what is the concentration in the final solution of

  a)   nitrate ions   b)   chloride ions   c)   hydrogen ions   d)   lead ions

TITRATION CALCULATIONS

Titration is a technique which involves measuring the volume of one solution which just reacts completely with another solution.

Usually one of the solutions will have an accurately known concentration and this will be used to find the concentration of the other solution. The solution of accurately known concentration is called a **standard solution**. Its concentration can be checked by titrating it against a solution of a **primary standard**, which is prepared by dissolving a precisely known mass of pure solute to make an accurately known volume of solution, using a **volumetric flask**.

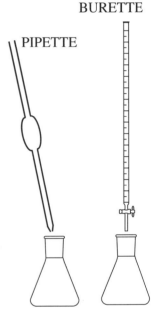

A primary standard must:

- be available in very pure form

- have a relatively high molar mass

- be stable as both the solid and in solution

- be readily soluble in water

- react completely in a known manner

Sodium carbonate and potassium hydrogenphthalate are commonly used as primary standards for acid-base titrations. Although acid-base titrations are the most common, the technique is not restricted to these. Redox, precipitation and compleximetric titrations are also frequently encountered.

An accurately known volume of one of the solutions will be measured out into a conical flask with a **pipette (pipet)**, which is designed to deliver exactly the same volume each time it is used at that temperature. An indicator will usually be added and the second solution run in from a **burette (buret)**, until the indicator just changes colour. The burette is fitted with a tap and is calibrated so as to accurately measure a variable volume of liquid. The volume of the second solution required, called the **titre**, can be found by subtracting the initial burette reading from the final one. A 50 cm^3 burette should be read accurately to 2 decimal places (with an uncertainty of ± 0.01 cm^3).

The amount of solute can be calculated from the volume of the solution of known concentration. The amount of the unknown may then be found using the balanced equation. Finally the concentration of the unknown may be calculated from this and the volume of the second solution used. The three stages involved are closely analogous to those used in reacting mass calculations.

EXAMPLE

It is found that 10.00 cm^3 of 0.200 mol dm^{-3} aqueous sodium carbonate requires 25.00 cm^3 of hydrochloric acid to just neutralise it. What is the concentration of the hydrochloric acid?

SOLUTION

Stage One - Calculate the amount in the solution of known concentration

Amount of sodium carbonate = $c \times V$ = 0.200 mol dm^{-3} × 0.0100 dm^{-3} = 0.00200 mol

Stage Two - Use a balanced equation to calculate the amount of the unknown

Na_2CO_3 +	2 HCl	$\Rightarrow$	2 NaCl	+	CO_2	+	H_2O
1 mol	2 mol						
0.00200 mol	2 × 0.00200 = 0.00400 mol						

Stage Three - Calculate the concentration of the unknown solution

$$[HCl] = \frac{n}{V} = \frac{0.00400 \text{ mol}}{0.02500 \text{ dm}^3} = 0.160 \text{ mol dm}^{-3}$$

A titration technique can also be used to investigate the stoichiometry of an equation by finding out the amounts of the various reagents that react together.

EXAMPLE

It is found that 10.0 cm^3 of iodine solution of concentration 0.131 mol dm^{-3}, just reacts completely with 20.4 cm^3 of aqueous sodium thiosulfate of concentration 0.128 mol dm^{-3}. Calculate the stoichiometry of the reaction between iodine and the thiosulfate ion.

SOLUTION

Calculate the amounts of each of the reagents involved:
Amount of iodine = $c \times V$ = 0.131 mol dm^{-3} × 0.01 dm^3 = 1.31 x 10^{-3} mol
(n.b. 10 cm^3=0.01 dm^3)
Amount of thiosulfate = c × V = 0.128 mol dm^{-3} × 0.0204 dm^3 = 2.61 × 10^{-3} mol
Then calculate the ratio of these:
Ratio of moles I_2 : moles $S_2O_3^{2-}$ = 1.31 × 10^{-3} : 2.61 × 10^{-3} = 1 : 2

EXERCISE 1.12

1. Sulfuric acid from an automobile battery reacts with sodium hydroxide according to the equation

$$2\ NaOH + H_2SO_4 \Rightarrow Na_2SO_4 + 2\ H_2O$$

It is found that 10 cm^3 of the acid is just neutralised by 32 cm^3 of 2.0 mol dm^{-3} aqueous sodium hydroxide. What is the concentration of the battery acid?

A   0.63 mol dm^{-3}
B   1.6 mol dm^{-3}
C   3.2 mol dm^{-3}
D   6.4 mol dm^{-3}

2. The amount of copper(II) ions present in a solution may be estimated by adding excess iodide ions and then titrating the iodine formed with aqueous thiosulfate ions. The equations involved are:

$$2\ Cu^{2+}_{(aq)} + 4\ I^-_{\ (aq)} \Rightarrow 2\ CuI_{(s)} + I_{2\ (aq)}$$

$$2\ S_2O_3^{2-}_{\ (aq)} + I_{2\ (aq)} \Rightarrow S_4O_6^{2-}_{\ (aq)} + 2\ I^-_{\ (aq)}$$

How many moles of thiosulfate will be required for each mole of copper ions?

A   1
B   2
C   4
D   8

3. Which one of the following is not an important property for a primary standard?

A   Purity
B   Stability as a solid
C   Stability in solution
D   Bright colour

4. 20 cm^3 of hydrochloric acid was just neutralised by 25.0 cm^3 of a solution of potassium hydroxide of concentration 0.500 mol dm^{-3}.

a)   How many moles of potassium hydroxide were used in the reaction?
b)   How many moles of hydrochloric acid did this react with?
c)   What was the concentration of the hydrochloric acid?

5. 25.0 cm^3 of saturated calcium hydroxide solution (limewater) required 7.50 cm^3 of 0.0500 mol dm^{-3} nitric acid to just neutralise it.

a)   How many moles of nitric acid were used?
b)   How many moles of calcium hydroxide did this react with?
c)   What is the concentration of the calcium hydroxide in **grams per litre**?

CORE

6. A 0.245 g sample of a mixture of calcium chloride and sodium nitrate is dissolved in water to give 50.0 cm^3 of solution. This solution is titrated with 0.106 mol dm^{-3} aqueous silver nitrate which reacts with the chloride ions present to form insoluble silver chloride. The end point is reached after 37.7 cm^3 of the silver nitrate solution has been added.

a) Write a balanced chemical equation for the reaction, including state symbols.

b) Calculate the amount of silver nitrate used in the titration.

c) Calculate the amount of calcium chloride present in the solution.

d) Calculate the percentage by mass of calcium chloride in the original mixture.

7. The number of moles of water of crystallisation (x) present in hydrated ammonium iron(II) sulfate, $Fe(NH_4)_2(SO_4)_2 \cdot x\,H_2O$, can be determined by oxidising the iron(II) ions with aqueous potassium permanganate in acidified solution. The ionic equation for the reaction is

$$MnO_4^{-}{}_{(aq)} + 5\ Fe^{2+}{}_{(aq)} + 8\ H^+{}_{(aq)} \Rightarrow Mn^{2+}{}_{(aq)} + 5\ Fe^{3+}{}_{(aq)} + 4\ H_2O_{(l)}$$

It is found that when 0.980 g of the compound is dissolved in 25.0 cm^3 of water and titrated with 0.0300 mol dm^{-3} aqueous permanganate, 16.7 cm^3 are required for complete reaction.

a) Calculate the amount of potassium permanganate used in the titration.

b) Calculate the amount of iron(II) ions present in the solution.

c) Given that the molar mass of $Fe(NH_4)_2(SO_4)_2$ is 284 g mol^{-1}, calculate the mass of anhydrous solid that must have been present.

d) Calculate the mass of water present in the crystals and hence the value of x.

8. Concentrated hydrochloric acid has a density of 1.15 g cm^{-3} and contains 30.0% by mass hydrogen chloride.

a) Determine the concentration of the hydrochloric acid.

b) What volume of this must be diluted to 5.00 dm^3 to give a solution of concentration 0.200 mol dm^{-3}.

9. 0.130 g of a sample of impure iron was dissolved in excess dilute sulfuric acid to form iron(II) sulfate. This was then titrated with a 0.0137 mol dm^{-3} solution of dichromate ions $(Cr_2O_7^{2-})$ and was found to be just sufficient to reduce 27.3 cm^3 of the solution to chromium(III) ions (Cr^{3+}).

a) Write a balanced ionic equation for the titration reaction.

b) Calculate the amount of dichromate ion used in the reaction.

c) Calculate the amount of iron(II) ions present in the solution.

d) Calculate the percentage purity (by mass) of the iron.

10. 1.552 g of a pure carboxylic acid (Y-COOH) is titrated against 0.4822 mol dm^{-3} aqueous sodium hydroxide and 26.35 cm^3 are found to be required for complete neutralisation. Calculate the molar mass of the acid and hence deduce its probable formula.

BACK TITRATION

Sometimes reactions occur too slowly for a titration to be employed. This, for example, is usually the case when insoluble solid reagents are used. Back titration is usually employed for quantitative work with substances of this kind. In this technique the sample, say an insoluble base, is reacted with a known excess of one reagent, in this case a known volume of a standard solution of acid. When the reaction with the sample is complete a titration is then carried out, in the example with an alkali of known concentration, to determine how much of the reagent in excess remains unreacted. By knowing the initial amount of the reagent and the amount remaining as excess, then the amount that has reacted with the sample can be calculated. This is clarified by Figure 1.3.

Figure 1.3 - Illustration of the principle of back titration

Amount of standard acid - known from volume and concentration	
Amount of acid reacting with the sample - unknown	Amount of acid reacting with the standard alkali used in the titration - known from vol. & conc.

The total (known) amount of acid must be the sum of the amount that reacted with the alkali (known) and the amount that reacted with the sample (unknown) so the latter can be calculated.

EXAMPLE

0.5214 g of impure calcium hydroxide was dissolved in 50.00 cm^3 of 0.2500 mol dm^{-3} hydrochloric acid. When the reaction was complete, 33.64 cm^3 of 0.1108 mol dm^{-3} aqueous sodium hydroxide was required to just neutralise the excess acid. Assuming that the impurities do not react, what percentage of the sample was calcium hydroxide?

SOLUTION

Amount of alkali in titration $= c \times V = 0.1108$ mol dm$^{-3} \times 0.03364$ dm$^3 = 0.003727$ mol

$$HCl + NaOH \Rightarrow NaCl + H_2O$$

1: 1 reaction therefore 0.003727 moles of HCl react with the NaOH added.

Amount of acid used initially $= c \times V = 0.2500$ mol dm$^{-3} \times 0.05000$ dm$^3 = 0.01250$ mol

Amount of acid reacting with calcium hydroxide = 0.01250 – 0.003727 = 0.008773 mol

$$Ca(OH)_2 + 2HCl \Rightarrow CaCl_2 + 2\ H_2O$$

2:1 ratio therefore $0.004386 (= \frac{1}{2} \times 0.008773)$ moles of calcium hydroxide react with the hydrochloric acid.

Mass of $Ca(OH)_2 = n \times M = 0.004386$ mol $\times$ 74.10 g mol^{-1} = 0.3250 g

Percent of $Ca(OH)_2 = 100 \times \dfrac{0.3250}{0.5214} = 62.34\%$

EXERCISE 1.13

1. Aspirin is a sparingly soluble monobasic acid. 1.0 g of impure aspirin ($C_9H_8O_4$) was added to 10 cm^3 of 1.0 mol dm^{-3} aqueous sodium hydroxide. The excess base was then titrated with 0.20 mol dm^{-3} hydrochloric acid and 25 cm^3 were needed to neutalise the excess alkali.

   a)   How many moles of hydrochloric acid were used?
   b)   How many moles of sodium hydroxide were taken initially?
   c)   How many moles of aspirin were present in the tablet?
   d)   What mass of aspirin does this correspond to?
   e)   What was the percentage purity of the aspirin?

2. A 20.0 g block of marble was dissolved in 250 cm^3 of 2.00 mol dm^{-3} nitric acid. When the block completely dissolved, 25.0 cm^3 of the solution was titrated with 1.00 mol dm^{-3} aqueous sodium hydroxide and 17.0 cm^3 were required for neutralisation. What percent of the marble was calcium carbonate. What assumptions did you make in calculating this?

3. 0.600g of a metal M was dissolved in 200 cm^3 of 0.500 mol dm^{-3} hydrochloric acid. 25.0 cm^3 of 2.00 mol dm^{-3} aqueous sodium hydroxide were required to neutralise the excess acid. Calculate the molar mass of the metal assuming that the formula of its chloride is:

   a)   MCl   b) MCl_2 c) MCl_3

   Which do you consider to be the more likely value? Why?

SCIENTIFIC NOTATION

Scientific notation is a method of expressing large or small numbers as factors of the powers of 10. One can use exponents of 10 to make the expression of scientific measurements more compact, easier to understand, and simpler to manipulate (0.0000000013 m compared with 1.3×10^{-9} m and 7500000 g compared to 7.5×10^{6} g).

To express numbers in scientific notation, one should use the form: $a \times 10^{b}$

where a is a real number between 1 and 10 (but not equal to 10), and b is a positive or negative integer. This form works for 7500000, a large number as follows:

1. Set a equal to 7.5, which is a real number between 1 and 10.

2. To find b, count the places to the right of the decimal point in a to the original decimal point. There are 6 places to the right (+6) from the decimal point in a to the original decimal point, so $b = 6$. The number is expressed as 7.5×10^{6}.

For a large number, the exponent of 10 (b) will be a POSITIVE integer equal to the number of decimal places to the RIGHT from the decimal point in a to the original decimal point.

For 0.0000000013, a small number:

1. *Set $a = 1.3$, which is a real number between 1 and 10.*

2. To find b, count the places to the left of the decimal point in a, finishing up at the original decimal point. There are 9 places from the left (–9) of the decimal point, so b = –9. This is expressed as 1.3×10^{-9}.

For a small number, the exponent of 10 will be a NEGATIVE integer equal to the number of decimal places to the LEFT from the decimal point in a to the original decimal point.

Manipulating numbers in this form is also easier, especially multiplying and dividing. In multiplying the first part of the numbers (the 'a' s) are multiplied, the exponents are added and then the decimal place adjusted.

EXAMPLE
Calculate the number of oxygen molecules in 5.00×10^{-8} moles of oxygen.

SOLUTION
$N = n \times 6.02 \times 10^{23} = 5.00 \times 10^{-8} \times 6.02 \times 10^{23} = 30.1 \times 10^{15} = 3.01 \times 10^{16}$

Similarly, in dividing numbers, the first part of the numbers (the 'a' s) are divided, the exponents subtracted and then the decimal place adjusted.

EXAMPLE

Calculate the mass of a protein molecule that has a molar mass of 1.76×10^4 g mol^{-1}.

SOLUTION

$$m = \frac{M}{6.02 \times 10^{23}} = \frac{1.76 \times 10^4}{6.02 \times 10^{23}} = 0.292 \times 10^{-19} = 2.92 \times 10^{-20} \text{ g}$$

EXERCISE 1.14

1. Which one of the following numbers is in correct scientific notation?

    A 862×10^5
    B 0.26×10^5
    C 4.73×10^5
    D $2.93 \times 10^{5.2}$

2. The number 57230.357 is best shown in scientific notation as

    A 5.7230357×10^{-4}
    B 57230357×10^{-3}
    C 5.7230357×10^4
    D 5.7230357×10^8

3. 2.872×10^{-4} is best written as a normal number in the form

    A   0.0002872
    B   28720
    C   −42.872
    D   −28720

4. Write the following in scientific notation:

    a)   437600   b)   0.00000023   c)   415000000
    d)   0.0372   e)   476.8   f)   3.26

5. Write the following as normal numbers:

    a) 8.2×10^5 b) 6.29×10^{-3} c) 2.7138×10^{11}
    d) 2×10^{-7} e) 4.2×10^1 f) 5.89×10^{-1}

SIGNIFICANT FIGURES

The accuracy of a measurement depends on the quality of the instrument one uses for measuring and on the carefulness of the measurement. When a measurement is reported, the number of **significant figures**, can be used to represent one's own precision and that of the instrument. So significant figures should show the limits of accuracy and where the uncertainty begins.

Measuring with an ordinary meter stick, you might report the length of an object as 1.4 m, which means you measured it as being longer than 1.35 m, but shorter than 1.45 m. The measurement 1.4 has *two* significant figures. If you had a better ruler, or were more careful, you might have reported the length as 1.42 m, which means that you measured the object as being longer than 1.415 m, but shorter than 1.425 m. The measurement 1.42 has *three* significant figures.

The last digit in a significant figure is uncertain because it reflects the limit of accuracy.

A. SIGNIFICANT ZEROS

You'll have to decide whether zeros are significant in three different situations.

1. *If the zeros precede the first non-zero digit, they are not significant.* Such zeros merely locate the decimal point; i.e., they define the magnitude of the measurement. For example, 0.000 14 m has two significant figures, and 0.01 has one significant figure.

2. *If the zeros are between non-zero digits, they are significant.* For example, 103 307 kg has six significant figures while 0.044 03 has four significant figures.

3. *If the zeros follow non-zero digits, there is ambiguity if no decimal point is given.* If a volume is given as 300 cm^3, you have no way of telling if the final two zeros are significant. But if the volume is given as 300. cm^3, you know that it has three significant figures; and if it is given as 300.0 cm^3, it has four significant figures.

Note: You can avoid ambiguity by expressing your measurements in scientific notation. Then if you record your final zeros in *a*, they are significant. So, if you report '300 cm^3' as 3×10^2 cm^3, it has only one significant figure; 3.0×10^2 cm^3 has two significant figures; and 3.00×10^2 N has three significant figures. A number such as 20 700 in which the last two zeros are not significant is probably better written as 2.07×10^4, to avoid ambiguity.

CORE

B. USING SIGNIFICANT FIGURES IN CALCULATIONS

For multiplication and division, a result can only be as accurate as the factor with the least number of significant figures that goes into its calculation.

Note: Integer whole numbers and constants do not alter your calculation of significant figures. For example, the volume of a sphere is $v = 4/3 \pi r^3$. The 4 and 3 are exact whole numbers, while the constant pi can be reported to any desired degree of accuracy (3.14159...). The result for the volume will depend only on the accuracy of the measurement for the radius r.

C. ROUNDING OFF

The rules are simple: If the digit following the last reportable digit is:
* 4 or less, you drop it
* 5 or more, you increase the last reportable digit by one

For addition & subtraction, the answer should contain no more digits to the right of the decimal point than any individual quantity i.e. use the <u>least number of decimal places</u>. **For multiplication & division**, use the <u>least number of significant figures</u>.

Note: You may wonder just when to round off. The answer is, round off when it's most convenient. With calculators and computers, it's as easy to carry six or seven digits as it is to carry three or four. **So, for economy and accuracy, do your rounding off at the last step of a calculation.**

EXERCISE 1.15

1. The number of significant figures in 0.0003701 is

    A   3
    B   4
    C   7
    D   8

2. A calculator display shows the result of a calculation to be 57230.357. If it is to be reported to 4 significant figures, it would be best recorded as

    A   5723
    B   57230
    C 5.723×10^{-4}
    D 5.723×10^{4}

3. If a sample of a metal has a mass of 26.385 g and a volume of 5.82 cm³, its density is best recorded as

    A   4.5 g cm⁻³
    B   4.53 g cm⁻³
    C   4.534 g cm⁻³
    D   4.5335 g cm⁻³

4. A bottle of mass 58.32 g contains 0.373 kg of water and a crystal of mass 3000.6 mg. To how many significant figures should the total mass be recorded?

    A   2
    B   3
    C   4
    D   5

5. Give the results of the following calculations to the appropriate degree of accuracy.

    a) 0.037×0.763 b) $200.1257 \div 7.2$
    c) $3.76 \times 10^5 - 276$ d) $0.00137 + 3.762 \times 10^{-4}$
    e) $3 \times 10^8 \times 7.268$

FURTHER WORKED EXAMPLES

There are only four formulae used in these worked examples, though these formulae may be rearranged or combined together depending on what is required and the data available. These four formulae are:

$$\text{Number of moles} = \frac{\text{Number of particles}}{6.02 \times 10^{23}} \qquad n = \frac{N}{6.02 \times 10^{23}}$$

$$\text{Number of moles} = \frac{\text{Mass of substance}}{\text{Molar mass of substance}} \qquad n = \frac{m}{M}$$

$$\text{Number of moles of gas} = \frac{\text{Volume of gas}}{\text{Molar volume at same T \& P}} \qquad n = \frac{V}{V_m}$$

$$\text{Concentration of solution} = \frac{\text{Moles of solute}}{\text{Volume in litres}} \qquad n = \frac{n}{V}$$

1. **Finding the amount of substance from the number of particles.**

What is the amount of substance in 2.408×10^{21} molecules of ammonia?

    Required - n Known - N (2.408×10^{21} particles)

    Therefore use: $n = \dfrac{N}{6.02 \times 10^{23}}$

    Substituting: $n = \dfrac{N}{6.02 \times 10^{23}} = \dfrac{2.408 \times 10^{21}}{6.02 \times 10^{23}} = 0.004$ moles of ammonia.

CORE

2. Finding number of particles from the amount of substance.

How many molecules are there in 15.0 moles of water?

Required - N Known - n (15.0 moles)

Therefore use: $n = \dfrac{N}{6.02 \times 10^{23}}$

Substituting: $15.0 = \dfrac{N}{6.02 \times 10^{23}}$

Rearranging: $N = 15.0 \times 6.02 \times 10^{23} = 9.03 \times 10^{24}$ molecules of water.

3. Finding the amount of substance from the mass and the molar mass

What is the amount of substance in 12.00 g of barium sulfate?
(Ba = 137.34, S = 32.06, O = 16.00)

Required - n Known - m (12 g) & M (from formula).

Therefore use: $n = \dfrac{m}{M}$.

Molar mass of $BaSO_4$ = 137.34 + 32.06 + (4 × 16.00) = 233.40

Substituting: $n = \dfrac{m}{M} = \dfrac{12.00}{233.40} = 0.0514$ moles of barium sulfate.

4. Finding mass from the amount of substance and molar mass.

What is the mass of 0.500 moles of borax crystals, $Na_2B_4O_7 \cdot 10H_2O$
(Na = 22.99, O = 16.00, B = 10.81, H = 1.01)

Required - m Known - n (0.500 mole) & M (from formula)

Therefore use: $n = \dfrac{m}{M}$

Molar mass of $Na_2B_4O_7 \cdot 10H_2O$ = (2×22.99) + (4×10.81) + (7×16.00) + (10×18.02)

$= 381.42$

Substituting: $0.500 = \dfrac{m}{381.42}$

Rearranging $m = 0.500 \times 381.42 = 191$ g of borax crystals.

5. Finding the molar mass from the mass and amount of substance

5.42 g of a substance is found to contain 0.0416 moles. What is its molar mass?

Required - M Known - n (0.0416 mole) & m (5.42 g)

Therefore use: $n = \dfrac{m}{M}$

Substituting: $0.0416 = \dfrac{5.42}{M}$

Rearranging: $M = \dfrac{5.42}{0.0416} = 130$ g mol^{-1}.

6.   Finding the percentage composition

Gypsum is a naturally occuring form of calcium sulfate ($CaSO_4 \cdot 2H_2O$). What percentage by mass of Gypsum is water?
(Ca = 40.08; S = 32.06; O = 16.00; H = 1.01)

Required - $\%H_2O$

Known - molar masses of Gypsum and water.

Molar mass of Gypsum = $40.08 + 32.06 + (4 \times 16.00) + (2 \times 18.02) = 172.18$

Mass of water in this = $2 \times 18.02 = 36.04$

Percentage of water = $\dfrac{36.04}{172.16} \times 100 = 20.93\,\%$

7.   Finding the empirical formula from mass data

5.694 g of an oxide of cobalt yielded 4.046 g of the metal on reduction. What was the formula of the oxide? (Co = 58.93; O = 16.00)

Required - molar ratio of Co to O.

Known - the masses and molar masses of Co and O.

Amount of cobalt in the oxide $= \dfrac{m}{M} = \dfrac{4.046}{58.93} = 0.06866$ moles.

Amount of oxygen in the oxide $= \dfrac{m}{M} = \dfrac{5.694 - 4.046}{16.00} = 0.1030$ moles

Ratio of cobalt to oxygen = $0.06866 : 0.1030 = 1 : \dfrac{0.1030}{0.06866} = 1.500 = 2 : 3$

Therefore the formula of the oxide is Co_2O_3.

8.   Finding the empirical formula from percentage composition data

Treatment of metallic copper with excess of chlorine results in a yellow solid compound which contains 47.2% copper, and 52.8% chlorine. What is the simplest formula of the compound? (Cu = 63.55; Cl = 35.45)

Required - molar ratio of Cu to Cl.

Known - the percentages by mass and molar masses of Cu and Cl.

In 100.0 g of compound there are 47.2 g of copper and 52.8 g of chlorine.

Amount of Cu = $\dfrac{m}{M}$ = $\dfrac{47.2}{63.55}$ = 0.7427

Amount of Cl = $\dfrac{m}{M}$ = $\dfrac{52.8}{35.45}$ = 1.489

Ratio of amounts of Cu : Cl = 0.7427 : 1.489 = 1 : 2.005 = 1 : 2

The empirical formula is therefore $CuCl_2$.

9. Finding the empirical formula of a hydrate from percentage composition data.

When hydrated strontium hydroxide crystals are strongly heated, they decrease in mass by 54.2% to leave the anhydrous solid. What is the formula of the hydrate?
(Sr = 87.62; O = 16.00; H = 1.01)

Knowing that the strontium ion is Sr^{2+} (in Group 2 of the Periodic Table) and that the hydroxide ion is OH^-, the formula of strontium hydroxide can be calculated as $Sr(OH)_2$. (N.B. positive and negative charges must cancel.)

Required - molar ratio of to H_2O : $Sr(OH)_2$

Known - the molar masses and masses of these in 100 g of the hydrate.

Amount of H_2O = $\dfrac{m}{M}$ = $\dfrac{54.2}{18.02}$ = 3.008

Amount of $Sr(OH)_2$ = $\dfrac{100 - 54.2}{121.64}$ = 0.3765

Ratio of amounts of H_2O : $Sr(OH)_2$ = 3.008 : 0.3765 = 7.989 : 1

The formula of the hydrate must be $Sr(OH)_2 \cdot 8\ H_2O$.

10. The molecular formula from molar mass and combustion data.

Vitamin C, a compound of carbon hydrogen and oxygen only, is found in many fruits and vegetables. The percentages of carbon, hydrogen, and oxygen in vitamin C are determined by burning a sample of vitamin C weighing 2.00 mg. The masses of carbon dioxide and water formed are 3.00 mg and 0.816 mg, respectively. By titration its molar mass is found to be about 180. From these data, determine the molecular formula of vitamin C.
(O = 16.00; C = 12.01; H = 1.01).

Required - molar ratio of C, H and O.

Known - the molar masses and masses of CO_2 and H_2O formed by the combustion of 2.00 mg of the compound and the approximate molar mass.

Firstly calculate that amounts of CO_2 and H_2O:

Amount of $CO_2 = \dfrac{3.00 \times 10^{-3}}{44.01} = 6.816 \times 10^{-5}$ moles.

Amount of $H_2O = \dfrac{m}{M} = \dfrac{8.16 \times 10^{-4}}{18.02} = 4.528 \times 10^{-5}$ moles.

The amounts of C and H in the 2.00 mg of vitamin C must have been 6.816×10^{-5} and 9.056×10^{-5} (as it is H_2O) respectively.

Calculate the mass of oxygen in the sample by subtraction and hence the amount:

Mass of oxygen $= 0.002 - (12.01 \times 6.816 \times 10^{-5}) - (1.01 \times 9.056 \times 10^{-5})$

$= 1.090 \times 10^{-3}$ g.

Amount of oxygen $= \dfrac{m}{M} = \dfrac{1.090 \times 10^{-3}}{16.00} = 6.812 \times 10^{-5}$ moles.

Ratio of amounts of $C : H : O = 6.816 : 9.056 : 6.812 = 1 : 1.33 : 1 = 3 : 4 : 3$

The empirical formula of vitamin C must be $C_3H_4O_3$,

The molar mass of this would be approximately $(3 \times 12) + (4 \times 1) + (3 \times 16) = 88$

The observed molar mass is ~180, so it is composed of $\dfrac{188}{80} \approx 2$ of these units.

The molecular formula of vitamin C is therefore $2 \times (C_3H_4O_3) = C_6H_8O_6$.

11. Reacting mass calculations

When aqueous silver nitrate is added to an aqueous solution containing chromate ions, a brick-red precipitate of silver chromate (Ag_2CrO_4) forms. What mass of silver chromate could be obtained from a solution containing 5.00 g of silver nitrate?
($Ag = 107.87$; $Cr = 52.00$; $O = 16.00$; $N = 14.01$)

Required	mass of silver chromate
Known:	mass and molar mass of, hence the amount of $AgNO_3$.
	equation, hence the amount of Ag_2CrO_4.
	molar mass of Ag_2CrO_4, hence calculate the mass from the amount.

Amount of $AgNO_3 = \dfrac{m}{M} = \dfrac{5.00}{169.88} = 0.02943$ moles.

Equation: $Na_2CrO_4 + 2\,AgNO_3 \implies Ag_2CrO_4 + 2\,NaNO_3$

$\qquad\qquad\qquad\qquad$ 2 moles $\qquad\qquad$ 1 mole

$\qquad\qquad\qquad$ 0.02943 moles $\qquad$ 0.01472 moles

Mass of $Ag_2CrO_4 = n \times M = 0.01472 \times 331.74 = 4.89$ g.

12. The amount of reactant required.

When potassium nitrate is heated, it decomposes to potassium nitrite and oxygen. What mass of potassium nitrate must be heated to produce 10 g of oxygen?
(Potassium nitrite is KNO_2; K = 39.10; O = 16.00; N = 14.01)

Required	mass of potassium nitrate.
Known	mass and molar mass of O_2, hence the amount of O_2.
	equation, hence the amount of KNO_3.
	molar mass of KNO_3, hence calculate the mass from the amount.

Amount of $O_2 = \dfrac{m}{M} = \dfrac{10}{32.00} = 0.3125$ moles.

Equation: $2\ KNO_3 \Rightarrow$ $2\ KNO_2\ +\ O_2$

                2 moles   1 mole

        $0.3125 \times 2 = 0.625$ moles   0.3125 moles

Mass of $KNO_3 = n \times M = 0.625 \times 101.11 = 63.19$ g.

13. Finding the molar mass of a gas from the mass of a sample under standard conditions.

10.4 g of a gas ocuupies a volume of 3.72 dm^3 at standard temperature and pressure. What is the molar mass of the gas?

Required - M Known - m (10.4 g) and V (3.72 dm^3)

Therefore use $n = \dfrac{V}{V_m}$ to find n and then use $n = \dfrac{m}{M}$ to find M.

Moles of gas $= \dfrac{V}{22.4} = \dfrac{3.72}{22.4} = 0.166$ moles

Molar mass $= \dfrac{m}{n} = \dfrac{10.4}{0.166} = 62.7$g mol^{-1}.

14. Finding the volume of gas produced in a reaction.

When hydrogen peroxide is added to a manganese(IV) oxide catalyst it undergoes catalytic decomposition to water and oxygen. What volume of oxygen, measured at room temperature and pressure, can be produced from a solution containing 17 g of hydrogen peroxide?

Required - V Known - m (17 g) and M (34 g mol^{-1})

Therefore use $n = \dfrac{m}{M}$ to find $n(H_2O_2)$, use balanced equation to find $n(O_2)$.

and then use $n = \dfrac{V}{V_m}$ to find V.

Moles of $H_2O_2 = \dfrac{m}{M} = \dfrac{17}{34} = 0.5$ moles.

Balanced equation: $2\,H_2O_2 \;\Rightarrow\; 2\,H_2O + \; O_2$

$\qquad\qquad\qquad\quad$ 2 moles $\qquad\qquad$ 1 mole

$\qquad\qquad\qquad\quad$ 0.5 moles $\qquad\quad$ 0.25 moles

Volume of oxygen $= n \times 24 = 0.25 \times 24 = 6\,dm^3$.

15. Finding the concentration from the amount of substance and the volume.

What is the concentration of the solution produced when 0.02 moles of magnesium sulfate is dissolved to give 40 cm^3 of solution?

$\qquad$ Required - c $\qquad$ Known - n (0.02 mole) and V (0.04 dm^3).

$\qquad$ Therefore use: $\quad c = \dfrac{n}{V}$

$\qquad$ Substituting $\qquad c = \dfrac{n}{V} = \dfrac{0.02}{0.040} = 0.5\;mol\;dm^{-3}$.

16. Volume from concentration and amount of substance

What volume of 0.200 mol dm^{-3} nitric acid contains 5.00×10^{-2} moles of the acid?

$\qquad$ Required - V $\qquad$ Known - n (5×10^{-2} moles) and c (0.2 mol dm^3).

$\qquad$ Therefore use: $\quad V = \dfrac{n}{c}$

$\qquad$ Substituting $\qquad V = \dfrac{n}{c} = \dfrac{5.00 \times 10^{-2}}{0.200}dm^{-3} = 250\;cm^{-3}$.

17. Concentration from mass and volume

What concentration is the solution formed when 2.00 g of solid potassium chloride is dissolved in 250 cm^3 of solution? (K = 39.1, Cl = 35.45).

$\qquad$ Required - c $\qquad$ Known - m (2.00 g), M (39.1 + 35.45) and V (0.250 dm^3).

$\qquad$ Therefore: $\qquad$ first use $n = \dfrac{m}{M}$ to find n and then $c = \dfrac{n}{V}$.

$\qquad$ Substituting: $\quad n = \dfrac{m}{M} = \dfrac{2.00}{74.55} = 0.02683$ moles.

$$c = \frac{n}{V} = \frac{0.02683}{0.250} = 0.107 \text{ mol dm}^{-3}.$$

18. Mass from concentration and volume.

What mass of solid will remain when 2.0 dm^3 of a 0.40 mol dm^{-3} solution of sucrose ($C_{12}H_{22}O_{11}$) is evaporated to dryness? ($O = 16.00$; $C = 12.01$; $H = 1.01$).

Required - m Known - c (0.40 mol dm^3), M (342.34) and V (2 dm^3).

Therefore: first use $n = c \times V$ to find n and then $m = n \times M$.

Substituting: $n = c \times V = 0.40 \times 2.0 = 0.80$ moles.

$\qquad\qquad m = n \times M = 0.80 \times 342.34 = 270$ g.

19. Calculating concentration from titration results.

It is found that 33.7 cm^3 of hydrochloric acid just neutralises 20 cm^3 of aqueous sodium carbonate with a concentration of 1.37 mol dm^{-3}. What is the concentration of the acid?

Required - c

Known - c_{alkali} (1.37 mol dm^{-3}), V_{alkali} (0.02 dm^{-3}), V_{acid} (0.0337 dm^{-3})

Therefore: first use $n = c_{alkali} \times V_{alkali}$ to find the amount of alkali used;

then use the balanced equation to calculate the amount of acid required.

finally use $c = \dfrac{n}{V_{acid}}$ to calculate the concentration of the acid.

$n = c_{alkali} \times V_{alkali} = 1.37 \times 0.02 = 0.0274$ moles

$$2\,HCl + Na_2CO_3 \quad \Rightarrow \quad 2\,NaCl + H_2O + CO_2$$

    2 moles   1 mole

    0.0548   0.0274

$$c = \frac{n}{V_{acid}} = \frac{0.0548}{0.0337} = 1.63 \text{ mol dm}^{-3}.$$

20. Diluting an acid.

250 cm^3 of hydrochloric acid with a concentration of exactly 0.1 mol dm^{-3} is to be prepared using the hydrochloric acid above. What volume of this must be diluted?

Required - $V_{starting}$

Known - $c_{starting}$ (1.63 mol dm^{-3}), c_{final} (0.1 mol dm^{-3}) and V_{final} (0.25 dm^3)

Therefore: first use $n = c_{final} \times V_{final}$ to find the amount required

$$\text{then } V_{starting} = \frac{n}{c_{starting}} \text{ to calculate the volume of the acid}$$

required.

$$n = c_{final} \times V_{final} = 0.1 \times 0.25 = 0.025 \text{ moles.}$$

$$V_{starting} = \frac{n}{c_{starting}} = \frac{0.025}{1.63} = 0.0154 \text{ dm}^3 = 15.4 \text{ cm}^3.$$

21. Finding the concentration of the solution produced by a reaction.

'Iron tablets', to prevent anaemia, often contain hydrated iron(II) sulfate ($FeSO_4 \cdot 7H_2O$). One such tablet weighing 1.863 g was crushed, dissolved in water and the solution made up to a total volume of 250 cm^3. When 10 cm^3 of this solution when added to 20 cm^3 of dilute sulfuric acid and titrated with aqueous 0.002 mol dm^{-3} potassium pemanganate, was found on average to require 24.5 cm^3 to produce a permanent pink colouration. Given that the equation for the reaction between iron(II) ions and permanganate ions is

$$MnO_4^- + 5 \text{ Fe}^{2+} + 8 \text{ H}^+ \Rightarrow Mn^{2+} + 5 \text{ Fe}^{3+} + 4 \text{ H}_2O$$

calculate the percentage of the tablet that was iron(II) sulfate.
(Fe = 55.85; S = 32.06; O = 16.00)

Required - the mass of iron(II) sulfate in the tablet, hence the percentage by mass
Known - the volume of permanganate solution reacting with a fraction of the tablet.

Therefore: Find amount of permanganate used.

Hence find amount of iron reacting.

Hence find amount of iron in total tablet.

Hence find the mass of the iron(II) sulfate and the percentage.

Amount of permanganate = $c \times V = 0.002 \times 0.0245 = 4.90 \times 10^{-5}$ moles.

$$MnO_4^- + 5 \text{ Fe}^{2+} + 8 \text{ H}^+ \Rightarrow Mn^{2+} + 5 \text{ Fe}^{3+} + 4 \text{ H}_2O$$

1 mole   5 moles

4.90×10^{-5} 2.45×10^{-4}

There are 2.45×10^{-4} moles of iron(II) in 10 cm^3 of solution,

so in 250 cm^3 there are $2.45 \times 10^{-4} \times \frac{250}{10} = 6.125 \times 10^{-3}$ moles.

Mass of iron(II) sulfate = $n \times M = 6.125 \times 10^{-3} \times 278.05 = 1.703$ g.

Percentage of iron(II) sulfate = $\frac{1.703}{1.863} \times 100 = 91.4\%$

22. Finding the concentration of the solution produced by a reaction.

1.86 g of lead carbonate is added to 50.0 cm³ (an excess) of nitric acid. What is the concentration of lead nitrate in the resulting solution?
($Pb = 207.19$; $O = 16.00$; $C = 12.01$)

Required - c Known - m (1.86 g), M (283.2); V (0.050 dm³)

Therefore   first use $n = \dfrac{m}{M}$ to find the amount of lead carbonate,

then use the balanced equation to find the amount of lead nitrate,

finally use $c = \dfrac{n}{V}$ to find the concentration.

$$n = \frac{m}{M} = \frac{1.86}{267.2} = 0.006961 \text{ moles.}$$

$$
\begin{array}{ccccccc}
PbCO_3 & + & 2\,HNO_3 & \Rightarrow & Pb(NO_3)_2 & + H_2O + CO_2 \\
1 \text{ mole} & & & & 1 \text{ mole} & \\
0.006961 & & & & 0.006961 &
\end{array}
$$

$$c = \frac{n}{V} = \frac{0.006961}{0.050} = 0.139 \text{ mol dm}^{-3}.$$

23. Calculating the limiting reagent.

1.34 g of magnesium are added to 120 cm³ of a 0.200 mol dm⁻³ solution of silver nitrate. What mass of silver will be formed? ($Ag = 107.87$, $Mg = 24.31$)

Required - m_{Ag}

Known c_{Ag} (0.20 mol dm⁻³); V_{Ag} (0.12 dm3); m_{Mg} (1.34 g)

Therefore   use $n = \dfrac{m}{M}$ to find the amount of Mg

then use $n = c \times V$ to find the amount of Ag^+

use balanced equation find the limiting reagent and the amount of Ag

finally calculate the mass using $m = n \times M$.

$$n = \frac{m}{M} = \frac{1.34}{24.31} = 0.05512 \text{ moles of magnesium.}$$

$$n = c \times V = 0.200 \times 0.120 = 0.024 \text{ moles of silver nitrate.}$$

$$
\begin{array}{ccccccc}
 & Mg & + & 2\,Ag^+ & \Rightarrow & 2\,Ag + & Mg^{2+} \\
\text{In theory -} & 1 & & 2 & & & \\
\text{Actually -} & 0.05512 & & 0.024 & & &
\end{array}
$$

Magnesium is in excess as only 0.012 moles are required. The silver is the limiting reagent and therefore it controls the yield of the metal:

$$Mg \quad + \quad 2\,Ag^+ \quad \Rightarrow 2\,Ag + \quad Mg^{2+}$$
$$2 \qquad\qquad 2$$
$$0.024 \qquad 0.024$$

$$m = n \times M = 0.024 \times 107.87 = 2.59 \text{ g.}$$

24. Calculating the number of molecules from the concentration

The concentration of gold in seawater is approximately 10^{-10} mol dm^{-3}. How many gold atoms will there be in the average drop (0.04 cm^3) of seawater?

Required - N Known - c (10^{-10} mol dm^{-3}) and V (4×10^{-5} dm^3)

Therefore   use $n = c \times V$ to find the amount of gold

then use $N = n \times 6.02 \times 10^{23}$ to find the number of gold atoms.

$$n = c \times V = 10^{-10}\ 4 \times 10^{-5} = 4 \times 10^{-15}$$

$$N = n \times 6 \times 10^{23} = 4 \times 10^{-15} \times 6.02 \times 10^{23} = 2.41 \times 10^{9}$$

i.e. each drop has nearly $2\frac{1}{2}$ billion gold atoms in it!

25. Calculating molar mass by back titration.

2.04 g of an insoluble, dibasic organic acid were dissolved in 20.0 cm^3 of 2.00 mol dm^{-3} aqueous sodium hydroxide. The excess alkali required 17.6 cm^3 of 0.50 mol dm^{-3} hydrochloric acid to neutralise it. What is the molar mass of the acid?

Required - moles of acid in known mass and hence molar mass

Known - volumes and concentrations of excess alkali and neutralising acid

Therefore: find amount of excess alkali and neutralising acid

use these to calculate the amount of the organic acid

find the molar mass of the organic acid from the mass and amount

Amount of excess alkali $= c \times V = 2.00 \times 0.020 = 0.040$ moles.

Amount of neutralising acid $= c \times V = 0.50 \times 0.0176 = 0.0088$ moles.

Amount of alkali reacting with organic acid $= 0.040 - 0.0088 = 0.0312$ moles

$$H_2A \quad + \quad 2\,NaOH \quad \Rightarrow \quad Na_2A \quad + \quad 2\,H_2O$$
$$1 \text{ moles} \qquad 2 \text{ mole}$$
$$0.0156 \qquad 0.0312$$

Hence 0.0156 moles of the organic acid has a mass of 2.04 g

Molar mass of the organic acid $= \dfrac{m}{n} = \dfrac{2.04}{0.0156} = 131$

ATOMIC THEORY

2

Chapter contents

2.1 THE NUCLEAR ATOM

2.1.1 State the relative mass and relative charge of protons, electrons and neutrons.

The accepted values are:

	Relative Mass	Charge
Proton	1	+1
Neutron	1	0
Electron	$\dfrac{1}{1840}$	-1

2.1.2 State the position of protons, neutrons and electrons in the atom.

2.1.3 Define the terms mass number (A), atomic number (Z) and isotope.

2.1.4 State the symbol for an isotope given its mass number and atomic number.

Use the notation $^{A}_{Z}X$ *e.g.* $^{12}_{6}C$

2.1.5 Explain how the isotopes of an element differ.

Isotopes have the same chemical properties but different physical properties.

Examples such as $^{1}_{1}H, ^{2}_{1}H, ^{3}_{1}H$ *;* $^{12}_{6}C, ^{14}_{6}C$ *and* $^{35}_{17}Cl, ^{37}_{17}Cl$ *should be considered.*

2.1.6 Calculate and explain non-integer atomic masses from the relative abundance of isotopes.

2.1.7 Calculate the number of protons, electrons and neutrons in atoms and ions from the mass number, atomic number and charge.

© IBO 2001

INTRODUCTION

In 1807 John Dalton proposed his atomic theory - that all matter was made up of a small number of different kinds of atoms, that were indivisible and indestructible, but which could combine in small whole numbers to form compounds.

From the point of view of chemical change this theory remains largely true, i.e. atoms, or most of the atom, remains intact throughout chemical reactions. We now know, however, that atoms are not indivisible and are in fact composed of many smaller sub-atomic particles. Even though much of the atom does not change in chemical reactions, the outermost part of the atom (known as the valence electron shell) is crucial to chemical interactions, so knowing about the atomic structure of atoms allows us to understand how atoms join together to form compounds and why different atoms react in different ways.

ATOMIC STRUCTURE

Three important types of subatomic particles are the **proton**, the **neutron** and the **electron**. The proton and neutron have a much greater mass than the electron and are very tightly bound together to form the **nucleus** of the atom. Hence the nucleus contains all the positive charge and nearly all the mass (>99.9%) of the atom. It is very much smaller than the atom - if the nucleus were 1 metre across, then the electrons would be about 10 kilometres away, so most of the atom is empty space. The electrons occupy shells around the nucleus. The proton and electron carry a single positive and a single negative charge respectively, whilst the neutron is electrically neutral. The characteristics of these subatomic particles are given in Table 2.1.

Table 2.1 - The subatomic particles

Particle	Proton	Neutron	Electron
Relative mass	1	1	$\dfrac{1}{1840}$
Relative electrical charge	+1	0	−1
Where found	In the nucleus	In the nucleus	Shells around the nucleus

The fundamental difference between atoms of different elements lies in the number of protons in the nucleus. An element consists of atoms which have the same number of protons in their nuclei. This is known as the **atomic number** (Z) of the element. Each element has one more proton than the preceding element in the periodic table (see Section 3.1, page 84). The sum of the protons and neutrons in the nucleus is known as the **mass number** (A). The atomic number and mass number of an element may be indicated by a subscript and a superscript respectively, placed before the symbol for the element, e.g. for aluminium:

$$\text{Mass number} \rightarrow 27$$
$$\text{Atomic number} \rightarrow 13 \quad Al$$

This is sometimes written Al-27. The number of neutrons can be found by subtracting the atomic number from the mass number, e.g. in the case of aluminium there are 27–13 = 14 neutrons in the nucleus. For lighter elements, the numbers of protons and neutrons are approximately equal, but elements with a large number of protons require a higher proportion of neutrons because of the greater repulsion between the larger number of protons. Lead, for example, has 82 protons and (207–82) 125 neutrons (p:n approx. 2:3, see Chapter 16).

In order to preserve electrical neutrality, the number of electrons in an atom is equal to the number of protons, so that aluminium has 13 electrons, which exist outside of the nucleus in shells of differing energies, as is discussed in greater detail later in Section 2.3, page 68.

Atoms can gain or lose electrons to form **ions**, which have a net electrical charge because the numbers of protons and electrons are no longer equal. If an atom gains electrons, as non-metals tend to, then it will form a negatively charged ion (or **anion**), because there are now more electrons than protons. The ion will have one negative charge for each electron gained. An atom, especially of a metal, may also lose electrons to form a positive ion (or **cation**), because there are now more protons than electrons. The ion will have one positive charge for each electron lost. In chemical reactions, atoms never gain or lose protons. It is the interactions of the electrons that determine the chemical properties.

Knowing the atomic number (or name of the element), mass number and charge on a particle it is possible to calculate the numbers of protons, neutrons and electrons present.

For example in the ion $^{58}Ni^{2+}$ there will be 28 protons (because the atomic number of nickel must be 28 - see Table 1.2, page 4), 30 neutrons (58 – 28) and 26 electrons (28 in a nickel atom minus 2 to give the +2 charge).

Many elements are composed of slightly differing types of atoms known as **isotopes**. These atoms all have the same number of protons (which makes them still the same element), but differ in the number of neutrons in the nucleus. Isotopes therefore have the same atomic number, but different mass numbers. Chlorine for example occurs naturally as a mixture of two isotopes. Both contain 17 protons, but one contains 18 neutrons and the other contains 20 neutrons, so the symbols for the two isotopes respectively are:

$$^{35}_{17}Cl \text{ and } ^{37}_{17}Cl$$

Both isotopes of chlorine have the same number of electrons and, as it is the number of electrons that determines the chemical properties of a substance, both isotopes have identical chemical properties. Physical properties often also depend on the mass of the particles and so different isotopes will often have *slightly* different physical properties such as density, rate of diffusion etc.

Natural chlorine contains 75% ^{35}Cl and 25% ^{37}Cl. These percentages, known as the **natural abundances** of the isotopes, give the proportions of the different isotopes of chlorine in the element and in all compounds of chlorine. The existence of isotopes must therefore be taken into account in calculating the relative atomic mass of the element, which is the weighted mean. In chlorine, for example, out of 100 chlorine atoms, on average, 75 will have a mass of 35 and 25 will have a mass of 37, so the relative atomic mass of chlorine is:

$$\frac{(75 \times 35) + (25 \times 37)}{100} = 35.5$$

Usually if an element has an atomic mass that is greater than 0.1 from being an integer, it is a sign that it is composed of a mixture of isotopes, though some elements that are composed of isotopes have atomic masses that are almost integers. For example bromine consists of approximately equal amounts of ^{79}Br and ^{81}Br to give an atomic mass of almost exactly 80. Many elements have naturally occurring isotopes, but often these are only present in low percentages. This is the case in the isotopes of hydrogen ($^{2}_{1}H$ - deuterium and $^{3}_{1}H$ - tritium) and carbon ($^{13}_{12}C$ and $^{14}_{12}C$). Radioactive isotopes of all elements can be produced by exposing the natural element to a flux of slow moving neutrons in a nuclear reactor. This results in the nucleus of the atom capturing an additional neutron.

EXERCISE 2.1

1. Which of the following are usually found in the nucleus of an atom?

    A   Electrons and neutrons only.
    B   Neutrons only.
    C   Protons neutrons and electrons.
    D   Protons and neutrons only.

2. The number of neutrons in an atom of $^{138}_{56}Ba$ is

    A   56
    B   82
    C   138
    D   194

3. How many electrons would have about the same mass as a proton or a neutron?

    A   200
    B   500
    C   2000
    D   5000

4. Identify the following subatomic particles:

    a)   The particle that has a much lower mass than the others.
    b)   The particle that has no electrical charge.
    c)   The particle that is not found in the nucleus.
    d)   The number of these in the nucleus is equal to the atomic number.
    e)   The particle that is gained or lost when ions are formed.

5. Calculate the numbers of protons, neutrons and electrons in the following:

Element	Mass No.	Protons	Neutrons	Electrons
Helium	4			
Nitrogen	14			
Aluminium	27			
Manganese	55			
Iodine	127			

6. Boron has atomic number 5. It comprises two isotopes, one with five neutrons, the other with six.

    a)   Explain what is meant by the term "isotope".
    b)   Calculate the mass numbers of the two isotopes and represent them in the form $^{x}_{y}B$.

CORE

c) In naturally occurring boron, 20% of the atoms contain five neutrons and 80% six neutrons. Calculate the relative atomic mass of boron.

7. Naturally occurring copper is a mixture of two isotopes. One of these has 29 protons and 34 neutrons, the other one two more neutrons. Complete the following table for both isotopes:

	No. Protons	No. Neutrons	No. Electrons	Atomic No.	Mass No.
Isotope 1	29	34			
Isotope 2					

If the relative atomic mass of copper is 63.55, calculate the natural abundances of the two isotopes.

8. Give the numbers of protons, neutrons and electrons in the following isotopes:

	Number of		
Isotope	protons	neutrons	electrons
$^{3}_{1}H$			
$^{15}_{7}N$			
$^{57}_{26}Fe$			
$^{90}_{38}Sr$			
$^{235}_{92}U$			

9. Complete the following table:

	Number of		
Species	protons	neutrons	electrons
$^{3}H^{-}$			
$^{24}Mg^{2+}$			
	13	14	10
	16	18	18
4+	22	26	

10. Germanium is composed of 5 isotopes:

^{70}Ge - 20%, ^{71}Ge - 27%, ^{72}Ge - 8.0%, ^{73}Ge - 37% & ^{74}Ge - 8.0%

Calculate the relative atomic mass of germanium.

2.2 THE MASS SPECTROMETER

12.1.1 State the principles of a mass spectrometer and outline the main stages in its operation.

A simple diagram of a single beam mass spectrometer is required. The following stages of operation should be considered: vaporization, ionization, acceleration, deflection and detection.

12.1.2 Describe how the mass spectrometer may be used to determine relative isotopic, atomic and molecular masses using the ^{12}C scale.

Students should be able to calculate the relative atomic mass from the abundance of the isotopes (see 2.1.6). Interpretation of fragmentation patterns is not required. © IBO 2001

A mass spectrometer is an instrument which separates particles according to their masses and records the relative proportions of these. In a mass spectrometer the substance is firstly converted to atoms or molecules in the vapour phase (**A**). These are then turned into positive ions (**B**) and accelerated (**C**). The fast moving ions are deflected (**D**) - the lighter the particle the greater the deflection. Finally particles of a particular mass, which can be adjusted, will be detected (**E**). The body of the instrument must be maintained at a high vacuum by a pump (**F**).

Figure 2.1 - A diagram of a simple mass spectrometer

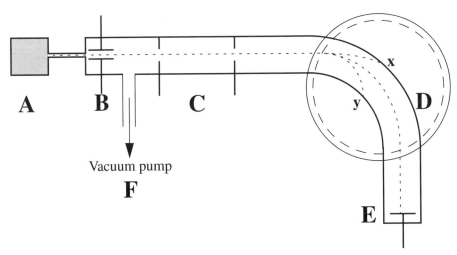

Region **A** contains the vapourised substance. If it is already a gas, then it will contain the gas at low pressure, if the sample is a solid or liquid, it must be heated to produce the vapour. This is connected to the rest of the mass spectrometer by a fine tube, or capillary, so that the transfer of material into the body of the instrument occurs very slowly. This is vital as the body of the mass spectrometer must be kept at a high vacuum for its correct operation, which depends on particles being able to pass through it without colliding with any other particles.

In region B, the particles are converted from neutral atoms or molecules into positive ions. This is usually done by bombarding them with fast moving electrons that are

65

accelerated between the two plates shown. These electrons collide with electrons in the particle knocking them out and leaving a positive ion.

$$X_{(g)} + e^- \Rightarrow X^+_{(g)} + 2\,e^-$$

In region **C**, these positive ions are accelerated by the high electrical potential difference between the two parallel electrodes with holes in their centres. In region **D** these fast moving ions enter a magnetic field produced by an electromagnet. The poles, shown as circles, are above and below the plane of the diagram. This causes the fast moving ions to deflect, as shown. Particles of a certain mass (dependent on the field strength) will continue round the tube and strike the detector plate. Those with a greater mass will not be deflected as much and those with a smaller mass will be deflected more (deflection depends on the charge to mass ratio). These will strike the wall of the instrument at (**x**) and (**y**) respectively. This means that only ions of a certain mass are detected at E, usually by means of the current flow required to neutralise the positive charge that they carry - the greater the number of particles of a given mass that are present, the greater the current.

By varying the strength of the magnetic field, ions of different masses can be brought to focus on the detector. In this way the relative abundances of ions of different masses produced from the sample can be determined. This is known as a mass spectrum. Usually the electron bombardment is adjusted to produce ions with only a single charge. Any doubly charged ions will be deflected more than the singly charged ions and will in fact behave in the same way as a singly charged ion of half the mass. That is why the x-axis is labelled m/z.

To summarise, the main operations are:

A	vapourised sample introduced
B	ionisation by electron bombardment
C	positive ions accelerated by electrical field
D	ions deflected by a magnetic field
E	detector records ions of a particular mass
F	vacuum prevents collisions with gas molecules

The mass spectrometer has many applications, but one of the simplest is to determine the natural abundances of the isotopes of a particular element and hence allow calculation of its atomic mass. If for example a sample of magnesium was vapourised in the mass spectrometer, the resulting mass spectrum would be similar to that shown below.

Figure 2.2 - The mass spectrum of magnesium

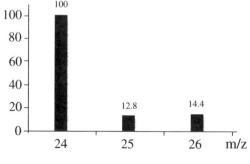

ADVANCED

The relative abundance is recorded so that either the most abundant isotope is given a value of 100 and the others recorded as a proportion of this, or the abundances are given as percentages of the whole.

The natural abundances of the three isotopes of magnesium and hence its relative atomic mass can be calculated from these data:

$$^{24}Mg = 100 \times \frac{100}{127.2} = 78.6\%$$

$$^{25}Mg = 100 \times \frac{12.8}{127.2} = 10.0\%$$

$$^{26}Mg = 100 \times \frac{14.4}{127.2} = 11.3\%$$

Relative atomic mass of magnesium $= (24 \times 0.786) + (25 \times 0.100) + (26 \times 0.113)$
$$= 24.3$$

With molecules, the relative molecular mass of the molecule can be found. The ionisation process often causes the molecule to break into fragments and the resulting 'fragmentation pattern' acts like a fingerprint to identify the compound (see Section 11.2, page 356 and Section 17.6, page 669).

EXERCISE 2.2

1. Describe briefly how in the mass spectrometer

    a)   the atoms are converted into ions.
    b)   the ions of different mass are separated.
    c)   the ions are detected.

2. Germanium (atomic number 32) contains 20% germanium-70, 27% germanium-71, 8% germanium-72, 37% germanium-73 and 8% germanium-74. Draw a graph of the mass spectrum that you would expect germanium to produce. If an atom of germanium-70 lost two electrons to become a doubly charged ion, at what mass would it appear?

3. The graph alongside shows the mass spectrum of the element which contains 76 protons in its nucleus.

    a)   Write down, in the form $^{Z}_{A}X$, the isotopes that it is composed of with their natural abundances (as a %).
    b)   Calculate the relative atomic mass of the element.

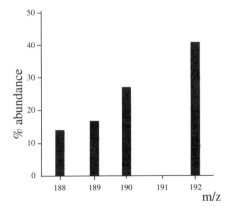

2.3 ELECTRON ARRANGEMENT

2.2.1   Describe and explain the difference between a continuous spectrum and a line spectrum.

2.2.2   Explain how the lines in the emission spectrum of hydrogen are related to the energy levels of electrons.

Students should be able to draw an energy-level diagram, show transitions between different energy levels and recognize that the lines in a line spectrum are directly related to these differences. An understanding of convergence is expected. Series should be considered in the ultraviolet, visible and infrared regions of the spectrum. Calculations, knowledge of quantum numbers and historical references are not required.

2.2.3   Describe the electron arrangement of atoms in terms of main energy levels.

Students should know the maximum number of electrons that can occupy a main energy level (up to Z = 18). No knowledge of sub-levels s, p, d and f is required. The term valence electrons is used to describe the electrons in the highest main energy level.

2.2.4   Determine the electron arrangement up to Z = 20.

For example, 2.8.7 or 2,8,7 for Z = 17.   © IBO 2001

ATOMIC EMISSION SPECTRA

The study of the emission of light by atoms and ions is the most effective technique for deducing the structure of atoms. The electrons in an atom surround the nucleus in certain allowed energy levels, or orbitals. The best evidence for this comes from a study of the emission spectra of elements. When an element is excited it will often emit light of a characteristic colour (e.g. the red of neon signs). In the case of gases this can be achieved by passing an electrical discharge through the gas at low pressure. For many metals the same effect can be observed when their compounds are heated directly in a Bunsen flame. This is the basis of the 'flame tests' for metals. For example, the alkali metals all impart a characteristic colour to the flame: lithium - red, sodium - yellow, potassium - lilac. If the light is passed through a spectroscope, containing a prism or diffraction grating, to separate out the different colours, then what is observed is not a continuous spectrum (like a rainbow) as is observed with normal 'white' light, which contains all frequencies. Instead, it comprises very bright lines of specific colours with black space in between. This is known as a line spectrum and is illustrated in Figure 2.3. Each element has its own characteristic line spectrum that can be used to identify it.

Figure 2.3 - Continuous and line spectra

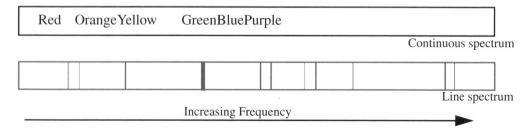

When an atom is excited its electrons gain energy and move to a higher energy level. In order to return to lower energy levels, the electron must lose energy. It does this by giving out light. This is illustrated in Figure 2.4.

Figure 2.4 - The origin of line spectra

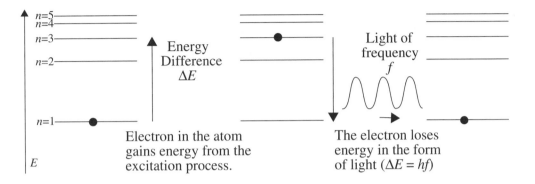

The frequency (f), and hence colour, of the light depends on the amount of energy lost by the electron (ΔE), according to the equation:

$$\Delta E = h f$$

The colour of light is sometimes defined by its wavelength (λ) rather than its frequency (f). The two are related by the equation $c = f.\lambda$ ($c = 3 \times 10^8$ ms^{-1}, the velocity of light) i.e. the greater the frequency, the shorter the wavelength.

Because there are only certain allowed energy levels within the atom, there are a limited number of amounts of energy (ΔE) that the electron can lose. This means that only certain frequencies of light can be emitted, hence the line spectrum. A continuous spectrum would imply that an electron in an atom could have any energy.

By studying the frequencies of the lines in the emission spectrum of an element, the energies of the various energy levels in its atoms may be found. The situation is not quite as simple as has been portrayed because there are sub-levels within the main allowed levels and this makes the spectra significantly more complex, nevertheless they may still be used to determine the allowed energy levels for electrons within an atom. It is found that the energy levels are not evenly spaced, like the rungs of a ladder, but that the higher the energy, the smaller the difference in energy between successive energy levels becomes. This means that the lines in a spectrum will converge (i.e. get closer together) with increasing frequency. The limit of this convergence indicates the energy required to completely remove the electron from the atom (i.e. to ionise it) and so it may be used to determine the ionisation energy (see Section 2.4, page 73).

THE ATOMIC EMISSION SPECTRUM OF HYDROGEN

The emission spectrum of the hydrogen atom is the simplest emission spectrum, because there is no electron-electron repulsion which causes the principal energy levels to split into different sub-levels. When a potential difference is applied across hydrogen gas at low pressure, electromagnetic radiation is emitted. As explained above, this is not uniform but concentrated into bright lines, indicating the existence of only certain allowed electron energy levels within the atom. It was by a study of these lines that the electronic structure of the hydrogen was deduced, though it is simpler to start, as below, with the accepted electronic structure and show how this results in the observed spectrum.

Figure 2.5 - Explanation of the atomic emission spectrum of hydrogen

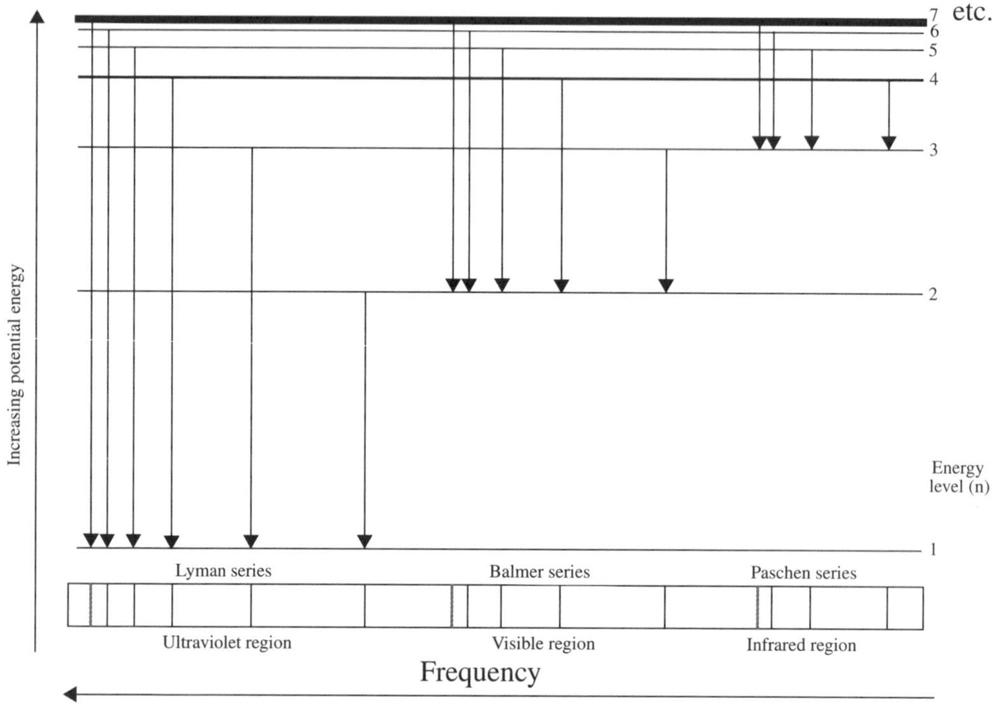

The spectrum is divided into a number of distinct series, named after the people who discovered them, which occur in different spectral regions as shown (there are also further series at longer wavelengths which are not shown). Each series corresponds to transitions in which the electron falls to a particular energy level. The reason why they occur in different spectral regions is that as the energy levels increase, they converge (i.e. get closer together in energy). This means that all transitions to the $n=1$ level include the large $n=1$ to $n=2$ energy difference and so they are all high energy transitions found in the UV region. For similar reasons all transitions to the $n=2$ level are in the visible region etc.

Each series has a very similar structure of lines that become closer together going towards higher frequencies. This is another result of the convergence of energy levels. Each series ends in a brief continuum at the high frequency end where the lines become too close together to be separated. The cut off of this is the energy emitted when an electron completely outside the atom ($n=\infty$) falls to the particular level involved. In the case of the Lyman series, this corresponds to the ionisation energy of the hydrogen atom, which can be found from the high frequency cut off of the continuum.

ELECTRONIC STRUCTURE AND THE PERIODIC TABLE

The most stable energy levels, or shells, are those closest to the nucleus and these are filled before electrons start to fill the higher levels. There is a maximum number of electrons that each energy level can hold. The first can hold up to two electrons, the second up to eight electrons. Beyond this the situation becomes more complex. The number of electrons in each orbital is known as the **electronic structure** of the atom. For example aluminium has 13 electrons so its electronic structure is 2,8,3; i.e. it has 2 electrons in the first level, 8 in the second (so both of these are filled) and the remaining 3 in the third. Different isotopes of an element have the same number of electrons and the same electronic structure, hence they exhibit identical chemical properties.

It is the electrons, especially those in the outermost shell, or **valence shell**, that determine the physical and chemical properties of the element. For example elements with three or less electrons in the valence level, with the exception of boron, are metals, the others non-metals. It is therefore not surprising that the electronic structure of an element is closely related to its position in the periodic table, which can therefore act as a memory aid for electronic structure. The period (horizontal row) gives the number of energy levels that contain electrons and the group (number of vertical columns from the left) gives the number of electrons in the valence level. This is shown in Figure 2.6.

Figure 2.6 - Electronic structure in relation to the periodic table

H							He
1							2
Li	**Be**	**B**	**C**	**N**	**O**	**F**	**Ne**
2,1	2,2	2,3	2,4	2,5	2,6	2,7	2,8
Na	**Mg**	**Al**	**Si**	**P**	**S**	**Cl**	**Ar**
2,8,1	2,8,2	2,8,3	2,8,4	2,8,5	2,8,6	2,8,7	2,8,8
K	**Ca**						
2,8,8,1	2,8,8,2						

Phosphorus, for example is in the third period, so it has electrons in the first three energy levels, and in the fifth group, so it has five electrons in the valence level. Its electronic structure is therefore 2,8,5.

EXERCISE 2.3

1. An atom has an atomic number of 13 and a mass number of 27. How many electrons will it have in its valence level?

A   1
B   2
C   3
D   5

2. Which of the following would produce a line spectrum rather than a continuous spectrum?

A   A yellow (sodium) street light.
B   A normal filament light bulb.
C   Sunlight.
D   A white hot piece of steel.

3. Which of the following colours corresponds to light of the highest energy

A   Yellow.
B   Red.
C   Green.
D   Blue.

4. Which one of the following is **not** a valid electronic structure?

A   2,8,4.
B   2,6
C   2,9,1
D   2,8,8,2

5. Given the atomic numbers of the following elements, write their simple electronic structures:

a)   Beryllium (At. No. = 4)
b)   Aluminium (At. No. = 13)
c)   Fluorine (At. No. = 9)
d)   Argon (At. No. = 18)
e)   Sulfur (At. No. = 16)

6. Two particles have the following composition:

A 37 protons; 38 neutrons, 37 electrons

B 37 protons; 40 neutrons, 37 electrons

a)   What is the relationship between these particles?

b)   These two particles have very similar chemical properties. Explain why.

2.4 ELECTRONIC STRUCTURE OF ATOMS

12.2.1 State and explain how evidence from first and successive ionization energies accounts for the existence of the main energy levels and sub-levels.

Interpretation of graphs of first ionization and successive ionization energies versus atomic number provides evidence for the existence of the main energy levels and sub-levels.

12.2.2 State how orbitals are labelled.

Limit this to n < 5.

12.2.3 State the relative energies of s, p, d and f orbitals.

12.2.4 State the number of orbitals at each energy level.

12.2.5 Draw the shape of an s orbital and the shapes of the p_x, p_y and p_z orbitals.

12.2.6 State the Aufbau principle.

Reference should be made to Hund's rule.

12.2.7 Apply the Aufbau principle to electron configurations.

Apply the Aufbau principle for an atom up to Z = 54, e.g. for Z = 23 the electronic configuration is $1s^2 2s^2 2p^6 3s^2 3p^6 4s^2 3d^3$ or [Ar] $4s^2 3d^3$ or [Ar] $3d^3 4s^2$. Exceptions to this rule are not expected.

12.2.8 Relate the electron configuration of an atom to its position in the periodic table.

Students should be able to label the s, p, d and f blocks of the periodic table.

© IBO 2001

THE ELECTRONIC ORBITALS IN ATOMS

The nucleus of the atom is surrounded by electrons arranged in specific energy levels and sub-levels. The different sub-levels differ in the shape of the electron distribution. Each energy sub-level is divided into orbitals each of which can contain up to two electrons, which must have opposite spins, as a consequence of the Pauli exclusion principle. The evidence to support this model of electronic structure comes mainly from the study of atomic spectra, as described above.

The energy level closest to the nucleus only contains one sub-level and one orbital. This orbital has spherical symmetry and as orbitals of this shape are known as 's' orbitals, it is referred to as the 1s orbital. It can hold two electrons of opposite spins.

The second energy level has two sub-levels. The 's' sub-level has one 's' orbital, with spherical symmetry, and the 'p' sub-level has three 'p' orbitals, which have a "figure of eight" electron distribution. These differ in that one is oriented along the x-axis, a second along the y-axis and the third along the z-axis. Each orbital can again hold two electrons making six p-electrons and a total of eight in the second level. Owing to increased electron-electron repulsion, the p-orbitals are at a slightly higher energy than the s-orbitals in all atoms except hydrogen.

ADVANCED

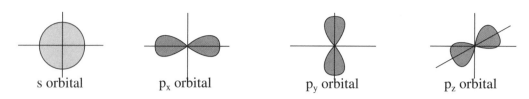

s orbital   p$_x$ orbital   p$_y$ orbital   p$_z$ orbital

The third energy level similarly has three sub-levels. The 's' and 'p' sub-levels contain two s-electrons and six p-electrons respectively. It also has five 'd' orbitals with even more complex shapes. The d-orbitals can therefore hold ten electrons, giving a total of eighteen for the third level. There is however a complication in that the 3d-orbitals are at a higher energy than the 3p-orbitals, and they occur, in most atoms, at a slightly higher energy than the 4s-orbital. In the fourth energy level, as well as the s-orbital, the three p-orbitals and the five d-orbitals, there are also seven 'f'-orbitals. These orbitals (up to and including the 4d) and their relative energies for a typical atom are shown in Figure 2.7 below:

Figure 2.7 - The electron energy levels in a typical atom

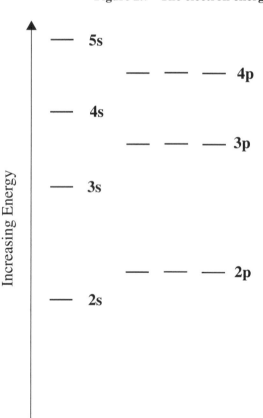

Table 2.2
A summary of energy levels

Energy level	Types of sub-levels	Total orbitals	Electron capacity
1	s	1	2
2	s,p	1+3=4	8
3	s,p,d	1+3+5 =9	18
4	s,p,d,f	1+3+5 +7=16	32
n	n types	n^2	$2n^2$

THE ELECTRONIC STRUCTURE OF ATOMS

The electrons in atoms always adopt the lowest energy configuration possible by filling one sub-level completely before starting to fill the sub-level of next highest energy. This is known as the '*Aufbau*' (building up) principle. In hydrogen therefore, the electron occupies the 1s orbital and in helium this is doubly filled. The electronic structures of these atoms can therefore be written as $1s^1$ and $1s^2$ respectively. The first energy level is now full, so in lithium, the third electron must occupy the s-orbital of the second level, and with beryllium this is doubly filled so that their respective electronic structures are $1s^2 2s^1$ and $1s^2 2s^2$. The fifth electron in boron now occupies one of the 2p orbitals, giving an electronic structure of $1s^2 2s^2 2p^1$. Carbon has six electrons so there is the possibility of these electrons occupying separate p-orbitals, with similar spins (a), separate p-orbitals with opposite spins (b) or the same p-orbital with opposite spins (c):

It turns out that (a) is the most stable configuration (this is known as **Hund's rule**, or the principle of 'maximum multiplicity'; sub-level orbitals are singly occupied as far as possible) and so in carbon the two outer electrons singly occupy two of the p-orbitals and in nitrogen all three p-orbitals are singly occupied, the electronic structures being $1s^2 2s^2 2p^2$ and $1s^2 2s^2 2p^3$ respectively. Going from oxygen, through fluorine to neon, these orbitals are each doubly filled, the electronic structures in this order being $1s^2 2s^2 2p^4$, $1s^2 2s^2 2p^5$ and $1s^2 2s^2 2p^6$.

At sodium the outer electrons start to occupy the third energy level in a manner totally analogous to the filling of the second energy level until argon ($1s^2 2s^2 2p^6 3s^2 3p^6$) is reached. At this point, the 4s level is at a lower energy than the 3d level and so this is the next to be filled in potassium and calcium. With longer electronic structures, the symbol for a noble gas in square brackets indicates filled inner shells as for that gas, so the electronic structure of potassium can be written as either $1s^2 2s^2 2p^6 3s^2 3p^6 4s^1$ or $[Ar] 4s^1$. The electronic structure for calcium can be similarly written as $[Ar] 4s^2$.

Starting at scandium the 3d orbitals are gradually filled, each orbital being first singly occupied (Hund's rule), as far as manganese ($[Ar] 3d^5 4s^2$) and then doubly filled, until at zinc ($[Ar] 3d^{10} 4s^2$) the 3d and 4s sub-levels are both fully filled. From gallium to krypton the 4p orbital is filled in the usual manner. There are two exceptions to the filling of the 3d orbital, both associated with a 4s-electron being used to generate the additional stability associated with a half filled and fully filled 3d orbital. Chromium is $[Ar] 3d^5 4s^1$ rather than $[Ar] 3d^4 4s^2$ and copper $[Ar] 3d^{10} 4s^1$ rather than $[Ar] 3d^9 4s^2$. A peculiarity of these elements with both d and s electrons in the valence shell is that when the elements between scandium and zinc form cations, the first electrons that they lose are the 4s electrons, even though this orbital was filled before the 3d orbitals. This is a consequence of a change in the relative stabilities of the 3d and 4s orbitals which occurs as the 3d orbital starts to fill which means that the ion with the most d-electrons is the more stable. Therefore, for example, the electronic structure of the iron(II) ion, formed by the loss of two electrons from an iron atom ($[Ar] 3d^6 4s^2$) is $[Ar] 3d^6$ not $[Ar] 3d^4 4s^2$. The 3d and 4s sublevels are close in energy, so that once the $4s^2$ electrons are lost, the 3d electrons also behave as valence electrons, for example, Fe^{3+} is $[Ar] 3d^5$. This accounts for many of the unique properties of these elements (see section 3.5, page 103).

Atomic Theory

The electronic structures of the elements are related to the position of the element in the periodic table. In the elements on the far left of the periodic table, the s-orbitals are being filled up, so this is known as the s-block. Similarly in the middle d-block of the periodic table the d-orbitals are being filled and in the right hand p-block, the p-orbitals are being filled. The f-block is traditionally separated from the main table, though it should be placed between the s-block and the d-block, as is found in the "long form" of the table, as shown diagrammatically in Figure 2.8.

Figure 2.8 - The 'long form' of the periodic table

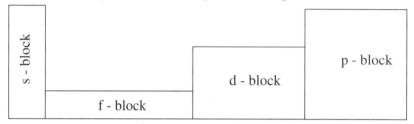

QUANTUM NUMBERS (EXTENSION)

Electrons have a wave as well as a particle nature. Their wave like nature in atoms can be described by the Schrödinger wave equation. This involves four constants, called quantum numbers, and a solution for the equation is only possible if the values of these quantum numbers lie within certain limits. The principal quantum number (n) must be a positive integer. The azimuthal (or subsidiary) quantum number (l) can have integer values from zero to ($n - 1$). The magnetic quantum number (m) can have integer values from $-l$ to $+l$ (including zero), whilst the spin quantum number (s) can be ±1. This interpretation corresponds exactly with the electron orbital concept, the principal quantum number dictating the level, the azimuthal quantum number the sub-level ($l=0$ is an s-sub-level; $l=1$ is a p-sub-level; $l=2$ is a d-sub-level; $l=3$ is an f-sub-level etc.), the magnetic quantum number the particular orbital and the spin quantum number differentiating between the two electrons in that orbital. This correspondence is shown in Table 2.2 below, in which ↑ represents $s=+1$ and ↓ represents $s=-1$:

Table 2.2 - Interpretation of orbitals in terms of quantum numbers

Value of l	0	1			2					3
Value of m	0	−1	0	+1	−1	−1	0	+1	+2	−3 to +3
Value of n 1	1s ↑↓									
2	2s ↑↓	2p ↑↓	↑↓	↑↓						
3	3s ↑↓	3p ↑↓	↑↓	↑↓	3d ↑↓	↑↓	↑↓	↑↓	↑↓	
4	4s ↑↓	4p ↑↓	↑↓	↑↓	4d ↑↓	↑↓	↑↓	↑↓	↑↓	4f 7 x ↑↓

A more precise statement of the Pauli exclusion principle is that no two electrons in a given atom can have the same four quantum numbers.

IONISATION ENERGY

The ionisation energy of an atom is the minimum amount of energy required to remove a mole of electrons from a mole of gaseous atoms to form a mole of gaseous ions, i.e. using Q as the symbol for the element, it is the energy required for the change:

$$Q_{(g)} \Rightarrow Q^+_{(g)} + e^-$$

The second ionisation energy is similarly the energy required to remove a second mole of electrons from the ion produced by the loss of one electron, i.e the energy required for the change:

$$Q^+_{(g)} \Rightarrow Q^{2+}_{(g)} + e^-$$

Note that these are both endothermic changes, energy being required to remove a negatively charged electron from the attraction of a positively charged nucleus. The magnitude of the ionisation energy will depend on the charge on the nucleus. This will be counteracted by the repulsion, or "shielding" of electrons in filled inner orbitals. To a first approximation, each electron in a filled inner shell will cancel one unit of nuclear charge and after these have been subtracted, the remaining nuclear charge is referred to as the *effective nuclear charge*. The third factor that affects the ionisation energy is the repulsion that the electron experiences from other electrons within the valence shell.

SUCCESSIVE IONISATION ENERGIES

The more electrons that have been removed from an atom, the greater the energy required to remove the next electron. Within an energy level this is because of a reduction in the amount of electron-electron repulsion and hence the greater effect of nuclear-electron attraction that results from remaining electrons moving closer to the nucleus. Consider for example the successive ionisation energies for the magnesium atom, shown in Figure 2.10 below. The two outer electrons experience the same effective nuclear charge. The first one to be removed is repelled by the other valence electron, but this force is absent when the second electron is removed. After the first electron is lost, the second electron is attracted closer to the nucleus, hence the higher ionisation energy.

Similarly, from the third to the tenth electron the electrons are being removed from the second energy level. In the case of the third electron the nuclear attraction is counteracted by the repulsion of seven other electrons in the same valence shell, but in the case of the fourth electron there are only six other electrons repelling it, so the remaining valence electrons are now closer to the nucleus and this trend continues as the second shell are removed. The last two electrons have slightly higher ionisation energies than would be anticipated from this trend because they are being removed from the s sub-shell which are slightly more stable than the p sub-shell.

ADVANCED

Sometimes the next electron must be removed from a filled inner energy level, so that this electron will experience a much higher effective nuclear charge (see Fig. 2.9) and there is a sudden large rise in ionisation energy. This is the case for the third and the eleventh electrons to be removed from magnesium. Note the use of the logarithmic scale in Figure 2.10. This makes the shell structure more obvious because, if a linear scale were used, all of the first ten ionisation energies would lie very close to the *x*-axis.

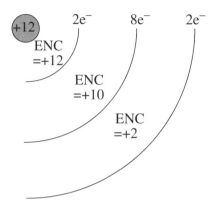

Figure 2.9 - Illustrating the effective nuclear charge (ENC) operating on the electron levels in the magnesium atom

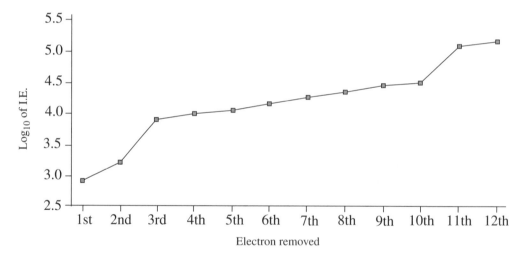

Figure 2.10 - The removal of successive electrons from a magnesium atom.

VARIATION OF IONISATION ENERGY WITHIN THE GROUP

Going down a group of the periodic table, the ionisation energy of the elements decreases. This is because whilst the effective nuclear charge remains approximately constant (the extra nuclear charge being approximately cancelled out by an extra filled electron shell), the electrons that are being lost are in successively higher energy levels and hence further from the nucleus. An example would be the first ionisation energy of the elements of Group 1, the alkali metals:

Element	Li	Na	K	Rb	Cs
I.E. (kJ mol⁻¹)	526	502	425	409	382

In lithium, for example, the electron is lost from the 2s sub-shell at a distance of 152pm from the nucleus. In sodium it is lost from the 3s sub-shell which is 186pm from the nucleus, hence the lower ionisation energy.

This trend can be seen for these elements and perhaps even more clearly for the noble gases, the peak ionisation energies, in Figure 2.11 below.

THE VARIATION OF IONISATION ENERGY ACROSS A PERIOD

The ionisation energies of successive elements (in kJ mol^{-1}) is shown in Figure 2.11 below:

Figure 2.11 - The variation of first ionisation energy with atomic number

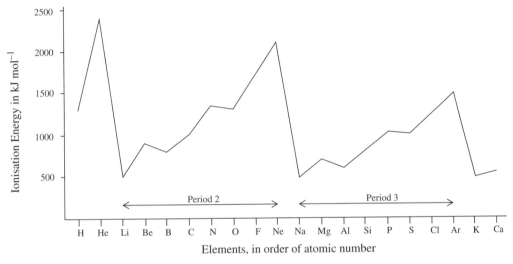

Overall, going across a period (e.g. period 2 from Li to Ne, or period 3 Na to Ar), it can be seen that the ionisation energy increases. This is because of the increase in the charge on the nucleus which, as the electrons being removed are all in the same energy level, increases the effective nuclear charge, and hence the ionisation energy.

The increase is not however a smooth one. Going from the second to the third element in each period (Be to B and Mg to Al) there is a decrease. This is because the electron removed from the third element is in a p-subshell (e.g. B is $1s^2 2s^2 2p^1$) and these are at a higher energy than the s-subshell from which the second element loses its electron (e.g. Be is $1s^2 2s^2$), resulting in a decrease in ionisation energy.

There is also a slight decrease going from the fifth to the sixth element in each period (N to O and P to S). This is because in the fifth element each of the p-orbitals is singly filled (the p level in N is ↑↑↑) whereas with the sixth element one of these must be doubly filled (the 2p level in O is ↑↓↑↑) and this results in greater electron-electron repulsion and hence a lower ionisation energy.

EXERCISE 2.4

1. The electronic structure $1s^2 \, 2s^2 \, 2p^6 \, 3s^2 \, 3p^6$ would be found in

    A   neon atoms
    B   sodium ions
    C   sulfide ions
    D   chlorine atoms

2. Which one of the following elements has the lowest first ionisation energy?

    A   Argon
    B   Magnesium
    C   Sodium
    D   Lithium

3. How many 3d electrons are present in the ground state of a cobalt atom?

    A   6
    B   7
    C   8
    D   9

4. The first three ionisation energies of aluminium (in kJ mol^{-1}) are 584, 1823 & 2751. The fourth ionisation energy (in kJ mol^{-1}) is most likely to be about:

    A   3000
    B   5000
    C   10 000
    D   100 000

5. The first ionisation energy of aluminium is slightly lower than that of magnesium because

    A   magnesium has a higher nuclear charge.
    B   the outer electron in aluminium is in a p-orbital not an s-orbital.
    C   in aluminium the electron is being lost from a doubly filled orbital.
    D   the radius of the aluminium atom is greater than the magnesium atom.

6. Which one of the following atoms would have the highest fourth ionisation energy?

    A   C
    B   N
    C   Si
    D   P

ADVANCED

7. How many unpaired electrons are there in the Cr^{3+} ion?

    A   0
    B   1
    C   3
    D   6

8. Which one of the following would require the most energy for the removal of one more electron?

    A F^-
    B   Ne
    C Na^+
    D Mg^{2+}

9. Write the complete electron configurations of:

    a)   Mn   b)   S   c) Mg^{2+}
    d) Fe^{3+} e)   Cu

10. Arrange the following in order of increasing ionisation energy

        Li   Na   Ne   N   O

11. a)   Sketch a graph to show how you would expect the successive ionisation energies of silicon to vary with the number of electrons removed.

    b)   Explain how this provides evidence that the electrons in atoms are arranged in distinct energy levels.

    c)   Explain why, within one of these levels, the amount of energy required to remove an electron varies with the number of electrons removed.

12. Explain why

    a)   the first ionisation energy of lithium is greater than that of sodium.

    b)   the first ionisation energy of oxygen is less than that of nitrogen.

    c)   the first ionisation energy of beryllium is greater than that of boron.

13. A particular metal cation M^{3+} has the electronic structure [Ar] $3d^2$.

    a)   Identify the metal concerned.

    b)   Write the electronic structure of the metal atom.

ADVANCED

c)   Explain why the electronic structure of the ion could not be the electronic structure of a neutral atom.

14.   The graph alongside shows the logarithm of the successive ionisation energies of a particular element with atomic number less than or eaqual to 20.

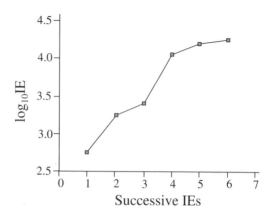

a)   Identify the element.

b)   Predict the approximate value of the logarithm of the seventh ionisation energy.

c)   How would you expect the equivalent successive ionisation energies of the element immediately above it in the periodic table to compare in magnitude?

15.   The table below gives successive ionisation data for a number of elements in kJmol⁻¹.

Element	First IE	Second IE	Third IE	Fourth IE
A	580	1800	2700	11600
B	900	1800	14800	21000
C	2080	4000	6100	9400
D	590	1100	4900	6500
E	420	3600	4400	5900

a)   Which two elements are probably in the same group of the periodic table?

b)   Which element is probably in group 3 of the periodic table? How can you tell?

c)   Which two elements probably have consecutive atomic numbers?

d)   Which element is most probably a noble gas? Give two pieces of evidence for this.

PERIODICITY

3

Chapter contents

3.1 THE PERIODIC TABLE

CORE

3.1.1 Describe the arrangement of elements in the periodic table in order of increasing atomic number.

Names and symbols of the elements are given in the Chemistry Data Booklet. The history of the periodic table is not required.

3.1.2 Distinguish between the terms *group* and *period*.

The numbering system for groups in the periodic table is shown in the data booklet. Students should also be aware of the position of the transition metals in the periodic table.

3.1.3 Deduce the relationship between the electron configuration of elements and their position in the periodic table.

Explanations are only required for the first 20 elements, although general principles can extend to the whole of the periodic table. For example, students should know or be able to predict that K is in group 1 using Z = 19, but need only know that since Cs is in group 1, it has one electron in its outer shell. © IBO 2001

The relationship between electronic structure and chemical properties is one of the key concepts in chemistry. This lies at the heart of the periodic table which is a most valuable arrangement of the elements to which chemical properties can be related.

In the periodic table, the elements are arranged in order of increasing atomic number, reading from left to right, top to bottom (as in reading English). This means that knowing the atomic number, the position of an element can be found by counting down the squares in this way. Try it, using the periodic table in Figure 3.1, for phosphorus (Z=15).

Figure 3.1 – The first twenty elements in the periodic table and their electronic structures

Group →	1	2	3/13	4/14	5/15	6/16	7/17	0
Period								
1	1 H 1							2 He 2
2	3 Li 2,1	4 Be 2,2	5 B 2,3	6 C 2,4	7 N 2,5	8 O 2,6	9 F 2,7	10 Ne 2,8
3	11 Na 2,8,1	12 Mg 2,8,2	13 Al 2,8,3	14 Si 2,8,4	15 P 2,8,5	16 S 2,8,6	17 Cl 2,8,7	18 Ar 2,8,8
4	19 K 2,8,8,1	20 Ca 2,8,8,2						

Elements with very similar characteristics are placed in the same vertical column (known as a **group**). These are numbered above. Originally they were numbered from 0 to 7, but recently the system has been changed to 0 to 17 to include the d–block elements. This is to be preferred, though both are shown. It is then found that going across a horizontal row (known as a **period**) the chemical properties gradually change from those of reactive metals to those of reactive non–metals, with the noble gases in the final group at the far right. Consider this for the first 20 elements shown in Figure 3.1.

It is the electrons, especially those in the outermost shell, or valence shell, that determine the physical and chemical properties of the element. It is therefore not surprising that the position of an element in the periodic table is closely related to its electronic structure, so this can be used as a memory aid. A period is a sequence of elements in which the same electron energy level (or shell) is being filled. Hence the period an element is in gives the number of energy levels that contain electrons. A group is a series of elements that have the same valence shell electron configuration, so that the group number (or the group number –10 in the modern numbering of groups 13 to 17) gives the number of electrons in the valence shell. This is also shown in Figure 3.1. Phosphorus, for example is in the third period, so it has electrons in the first three energy levels, and in the fifth group (or 15–10), so it has five electrons in the valence level. Its electronic structure is therefore 2,8,5.

Hence the first element in each period (e.g. sodium, Na) has only one electron in its outer shell. The elements in this first group are known as the **alkali metals**. The last but one element in the period (e.g. chlorine, Cl) requires one more electron to complete its outer shell. The elements in this last but one group are known as the **halogens**. The final element in the period (e.g. argon Ar) has all its electron shells filled. These elements have little chemical reactivity and are known as the **noble gases**. This pattern, the repetition of similar properties because of similar valence electron configuration, is known as **periodicity**. Physical properties, such as melting points, and chemical properties, such as the reaction with water, both show periodicity and are discussed in section 3.2 and 3.3 respectively.

EXERCISE 3.1

1. In the periodic table, reading from left to right and top to bottom, the elements are arranged in order of

   A   the number of protons in their nucleus.
   B   the number of neutrons in their nucleus.
   C   increasing relative atomic mass.
   D   increasing mass number.

2. An element has 13 electrons orbiting the nucleus. In which group of the periodic table will it be found?

   A   Group 1
   B   Group 2
   C   Group 3
   D   Group 4

3. Find the element chlorine in the periodic table.

    a)   How many electrons will it have in its outer shell?

    b)   How many fully filled electron shells does it have?

    c)   Give the symbol of another element in the same period as chlorine.

    d)   Give the symbol of another element in the same group as chlorine.

    e)   What name is given to the elements in this group?

3.2 PHYSICAL PROPERTIES

3.2.1 Describe and explain the periodic trends in atomic radii, ionic radii, ionization energies, electronegativity and melting points for the alkali metals (Li → Cs), halogens (F → I) and period 3 elements Na → Ar).

Cross reference with topics 2, 4 and 5. Data for all these properties are listed in the data booklet. Explanations for the first four trends should be given in terms of the balance between the attraction of the nucleus for the electrons and the repulsion between electrons. Explanations based on effective nuclear charge are not required.

Ionization energy is defined as the minimum energy required to remove one electron from an isolated gaseous atom. © IBO 2001

Going down a group of the periodic table, for successive elements there are more energy levels filled with electrons, so the outer electrons are farther from the nucleus. The extra charge on the nucleus is approximately cancelled out by additional filled shells of electrons, so the charge experienced by the valence electrons is approximately the same for each element. This means that the size of the atoms and ions increases going down the group. As a result of the valence electrons being further from the nucleus, the ionisation energy (a measure of how much energy is required to remove an electron from the gaseous atom) and the electronegativity (a measure of how strongly the atom attracts the electrons in a chemical bond) both decrease going down the group. These trends are illustrated in Figure 3.2 using as examples, for atomic radius, the alkali metals (Group 1), for ionisation energy the noble gases (Group 0) and the halogens (Group 7/17) for electronegativity.

Figure 3.2 – Some trends in various atomic properties on going down different groups of the periodic table

(a) The trend in atomic radius going down Group 1

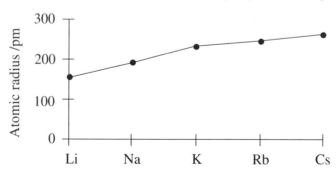

(b) The trend in ionisation energy going down Group 0

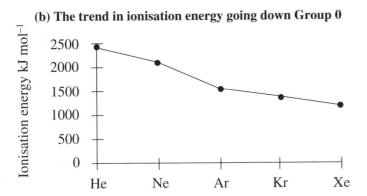

(c) The trend in electronegativity going down Group 17

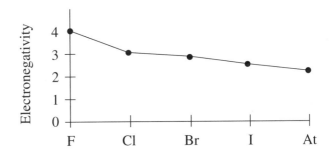

Going across a period of the periodic table, the number of protons in the nucleus and hence the charge on the nucleus increases. This means that going across the period the electrons, which are all in the **same** energy level, are more strongly attracted to the nucleus. The ionisation energy and the electronegativity both increase overall going across the period as the attraction of the nucleus for the electrons increases, although the change in ionisation energy is by no means smooth. The increased attraction of the nucleus causes the electrons to be pulled closer to the nucleus, so the size of the atoms, and ions with the same charges, also decreases going across a period. These trends are illustrated for the elements of period 3 (Na – Ar) on the graphs in Figure 3.3. Note that these variations are much greater than those found within a group.

Figure 3.3 – Variations in some atomic properties on going across the third period of the periodic table

(a) Variation in atomic radius across the third period

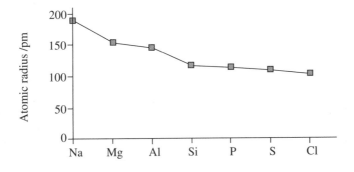

CORE

(b) Variation in ionisation energy across the third period

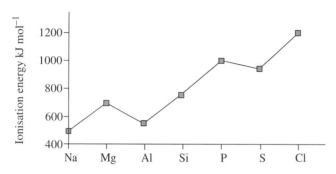

(c) Variation in electronegativity across the third period

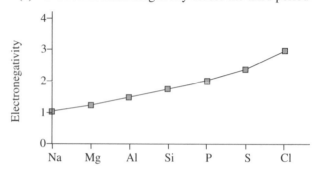

The overall trends in atomic size, ionisation energy and electronegativity are summarised in Figure 3.4 below.

Figure 3.4 – Periodic trends in some atomic properties

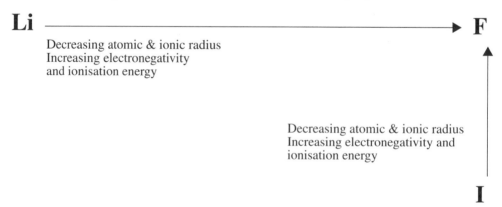

The size of an atom **always decreases** when it is converted into a positive ion (cation). This may be because the whole of an outer shell of electrons has been lost (e.g. when Cs turns into Cs^+) or because there is less electron–electron repulsion between the electrons (e.g. when Mg turns into Mg^+).

Conversely the size of an atom **always increases** when it is converted into a negative ion (anion), because there is an increase in repulsion between the valence electrons (e.g. when F turns into F⁻).

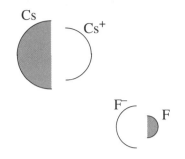

Almost every common cation (i.e. positive ion) is smaller than any anion (i.e. negative ion), the converse only being true for the extremities such as Cs^+ and F^-, illustrated in the scale drawings. H– is also quite small.

Physical properties, such as melting point, boiling point and density also depend on the nature of the bonding between the particles of the element. This is dealt with in much greater detail in Chapter 4, which should be read in conjunction with this section. Clear periodicity patterns are visible in a graph of the melting points of the elements against atomic number, shown in Figure 3.5 below.

Figure 3.5 – The melting points of the first twenty elements

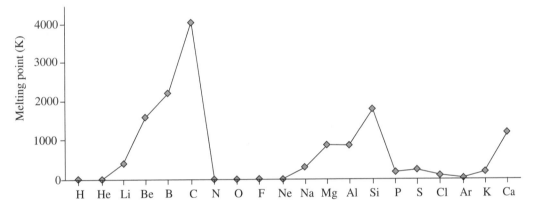

At the left of the period the elements (Li, Na, K) are metallic and going across the period the strength of the metallic bonding increases as the number of valence electrons increases, giving rise to an increase in the melting points. At the centre of each period (C, Si) giant covalently bonded structures occur with very strong bonds between the particles, and hence have very high melting points. Following this the melting points suddenly drop (N, P) as the elements here have molecular covalent structures and there are only weak van der Waals' forces between the molecules. This is further emphasised with the noble gases (He, Ne, Ar), which exist as single atoms.

EXERCISE 3.2

1. Which one of the following has the lowest electronegativity?

A   Boron
B   Beryllium
C   Magnesium
D   Carbon

CORE

2. Which one of the following has the smallest radius?

  A K
  B K^+
  C Ca
  D Ca^{2+}

3.

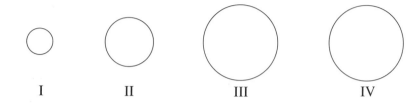

I   II   III   IV

The circles above represent the relative sizes of the F^-, Na^+, Mg^{2+}, K^+ and ions, but not necessarily in that order. Which one of the following would give them in this order?

  A II, I, III, IV
  B III, I, II, IV
  C I, II, III, IV
  D III, II, I, IV

4. Going across a given short period, in which group are you most likely to find the element with the highest melting point?

  A Group 0
  B Group 2
  C Group 4
  D Group 6

5. Arrange the following in order of **increasing** atomic radius

  Mg   Cs   Ca   Al   Ba

6. For each of the following properties, state how you would expect it to change in the direction indicated and give reasons for the change based on concepts such as nuclear charge, shielding, electron–electron repulsion and atomic/ionic radius.

  a) The electronegativity going down a group.
  b) The atomic radius going across a period.
  c) The radius of an anion compared to its parent atom.
  d) The first ionisation energy going down a group.
  e) The radius of a series of isoelectronic species (i.e. species having the same electronic structure, such as Cl^-, Ar, Na^+) with increasing atomic number.

3.3 CHEMICAL PROPERTIES

3.3.1   Discuss the similarities in chemical nature of elements in the same group.

The following reactions should be covered:alkali metals (Li, Na and K) with water and with halogens (Cl_2 and Br_2); halogens (Cl_2, Br_2 and I_2) with halide ions (Cl^-, Br^- and I^-); halide ions (Cl^-, Br^- and I^-) with silver ions.

Reactions of the halogens with alkali and confirmation of the silver halide by reaction with ammonia solution are not required.

3.3.2   Discuss the change in nature, from metallic to non–metallic, of the elements across period 3.

Use the study of the period 3 oxides to illustrate, for example, the change from basic through amphoteric to acidic oxides and their reaction with water. Halides and hydrides are not required.   © IBO 2001

THE ALKALI METALS

Alkali Metals	Li	Na	K	Rb	Cs
Electronic Structure	2,1	2,8,1	2,8,8,1	2,8,8,18,1	2,8,8,18,18,1
Melting Point – K	454	371	336	312	302

Increasing   ⟶
atomic and ionic radius

Decreasing   ⟶
ionisation energy

Decreasing   ⟶
electronegativity

The alkali metals (Li, Na, K, Rb and Cs – Fr has not been included because of its scarcity and nuclear instability) are soft malleable metals with low melting points and low densities. They are very chemically reactive and tarnish rapidly on exposure to air.

The alkali metals all have just one electron in their valence electron shell. This electron is very easily lost and this is the major reason why they are very reactive metals. They always form ions with a single positive charge in their compounds. Physically they are soft, malleable solids with low densities and low melting points. The low density is a result of the atoms of the alkali metals being the largest atoms in their period of the periodic table and the low melting points result from the fact that each atom can only contribute one electron to the metallic bonding, so this is less strong than for many other metals. Both of these properties decrease going down the group as the attraction for the outer electrons becomes less as a result of the increase in the size of the atoms.

They combine directly with reactive non–metals such as oxygen, chlorine and bromine to form ionically bonded compounds:

$$4 \, Li_{(s)} + O_{2(g)} \Rightarrow 2 \, Li_2O_{(s)} \quad [Li^+ \text{ and } O^{2-}] \quad [\text{Na and K form more complex oxides}]$$
$$2 \, Na_{(s)} + Cl_{2(g)} \Rightarrow 2 \, NaCl_{(s)} \quad [Na^+ \text{ and } Cl^-]$$
$$2 \, K_{(s)} + Br_{2(l)} \Rightarrow 2 \, KBr_{(s)} \quad [K^+ \text{ and } Br^-]$$

Going down the group, as the atomic radius increases, the ionisation energy of the elements decreases, the **reactivity of the elements increases**. This is best illustrated by the reaction of the elements with water. All of the metals react with water to form a solution of the metal hydroxide and hydrogen, according to the equation below (M is the alkali metal):

$$2 \, M_{(s)} + 2 \, H_2O_{(l)} \Rightarrow 2 \, M^+{}_{(aq)} + 2 \, OH^-{}_{(aq)} + H_{2(g)}$$

With lithium, the reaction occurs slowly and steadily. In the case of sodium the reaction is vigorous, producing enough heat to melt the sodium which fizzes around on the surface quite vigorously. With potassium the reaction is violent and the heat evolved is enough to ignite the hydrogen evolved, which burns with a purple flame. In all cases the remaining solution is strongly alkaline owing to the formation of hydroxide ions.

THE HALOGENS

Halogens	F	Cl	Br	I
Electronic Structure	2,7	2,8,7	2,8,8,7	2,8,8,18,7
Colour	Pale yellow	Yellow Green	Red Brown	Black/Purple
State at room T & P	Gas	Gas	Liquid	Solid

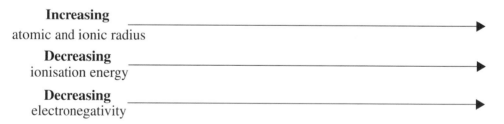

Increasing
atomic and ionic radius

Decreasing
ionisation energy

Decreasing
electronegativity

The halogens (F, Cl, Br and I – At has not been included because of its scarcity and nuclear instability) are very reactive non–metals that occur at the right hand side of the periodic table, hence they all require just one electron to fill their valence shell.

All of the elements exist as diatomic molecules (Cl_2, Br_2, I_2). They are all coloured and going down the group their state, at room temperature and pressure, changes as the strength of the van der Waals' forces between the molecules increases with molar mass. Chlorine is a yellow–green gas, bromine a red–brown liquid and iodine a black solid that forms a purple vapour on heating.

The halogens are only slightly soluble in water as they are non–polar and hence can only bond by weak van der Waals' forces to the polar water molecules. Solutions of chlorine have a green tinge and those of bromine darken from yellow through orange to brown as their concentration increases. In non–polar solvents iodine forms the purple solution that would be expected, but in polar solvents, such as water and ethanol, the solution is a brown colour. In aqueous solution the halogens dissociate slightly to form an acidic solution:

$$X_{2(aq)} + H_2O_{(l)} \rightleftharpoons H^+_{(aq)} + X^-_{(aq)} + HOX_{(aq)} \text{ [where X is the halogen and HOX is a weak acid]}$$

The compound HOX can readily donate its oxygen to other substances, so it acts as an oxidant. Chloric(I)acid (HOCl) will for example oxidise coloured dyes to colourless products. The second stage of the test for chlorine, in which it turns moist blue litmus paper red (the acidic solution) and then bleaches it to colourless, depends on this reaction. As a result HOCl and its conjugate base OCl$^-$ are used as bleaches (e.g. for paper). They are also toxic to microbes, hence chlorine is used in water treatment.

The halogensare are all quite electronegative elements. They require just one electron to complete their valence shell, hence they readily gain electrons to form the singly charged halide ions (Cl$^-$, Br$^-$, I$^-$). The ease with which they gain electrons decreases going down the group, as the electrons gained are further from the nucleus and hence less strongly attracted. This means that, in contrast to the alkali metals, **the reactivity of the elements decreases going down the group**.

The halogens combine with metals to give ionically bonded salts containing the halide ion. These salts are usually white and soluble in water giving colourless solutions. The common insoluble halides are those of lead and silver (though the lead(II) salts are moderately soluble in boiling water). These insoluble salts can be precipitated by adding solutions containing the halide ion to a soluble salt containing the metal ion. Lead(II) iodide (PbI_2) is easily recognised because of its bright yellow colour and this is a convenient test for the iodide ion. The usual test for halide ions is however to add dilute nitric acid (to prevent carbonates etc. giving a precipitate) followed by aqueous silver nitrate to a solution of the unknown substance. The formation of a precipitate (see equation below) indicates that a chloride, bromide or iodide ion is present (note that because AgF is soluble, the fluoride does **not** give a precipitate). Silver chloride (AgCl) is white, but rapidly darkens through purple to black in sunlight through photodissociation to silver and chlorine. Silver bromide (AgBr) is an off–white (or cream) colour and silver iodide (AgI) a pale yellow.

$$Ag^+_{(aq)} + X^-_{(aq)} \Rightarrow AgX_{(s)}$$

The electronegativity and oxidising power of the halogens both decrease going down the group as the size of the atoms increases and the attraction for electrons decreases. As a result, going down the group, the elements become less powerful oxidants. This means that a higher halogen will displace a lower halogen from its salts, e.g. chlorine will oxidise iodide to iodine and this may be detected by the solution changing colour from colourless to brown. A lower halogen cannot however displace a higher halogen from its salts, e.g. iodine will not oxidise chloride to chlorine:

$$Cl_{2(aq)} + 2\,I^-_{(aq)} \Rightarrow I_{2(aq)} + 2\,Cl^-_{(aq)} \checkmark \qquad I_{2(aq)} + 2\,Cl^-_{(aq)} \Rightarrow Cl_{2(aq)} + 2\,I^-_{(aq)} \; ✗$$

Table 3.1 – Summary of reactions of the halide ions

Reagent	F^-	Cl^-	Br^-	I^-
Aqueous Ag^+	No reaction	White precipitate, black in sunlight $Ag^++Cl^-\Rightarrow AgCl\downarrow$	Cream precipitate $Ag^++Br^-\Rightarrow AgBr\downarrow$	Pale yellow precipitate $Ag^++I^-\Rightarrow AgI\downarrow$
Chlorine	No reaction	No reaction	Solution turns yellow then brown Cl_2+2Br^- $\Rightarrow Br_2+2Cl^-$	Solution goes yellow then black precipitate $Cl_2+2I^-\Rightarrow I_2+2Cl^-$
Bromine	No reaction	No reaction	No reaction	Solution goes yellow then black precipitate $Br_2+2I^-\Rightarrow I_2+2Br^-$
Iodine	No reaction	No reaction	No reaction	No reaction

N.B. All of the solutions of the halide ions are clear and colourless (unless with a coloured cation).

TRENDS ACROSS A PERIOD

Table 3.2

Period 3	Na	Mg	Al	Si	P	S	Cl	Ar
Electronic structure	2,8,1	2,8,2	2,8,3	2,8,4	2,8,5	2,8,6	2,8,7	2,8,8
Boiling point – K	1156	1380	2740	2528	553	718	238	87

Decreasing atomic radius   ⟶

Increasing ionisation energy   ⟶

Increasing electronegativity   ⟶

Decreasing metallic character   ⟶

Increasing hydrolysis of chlorides   ⟶

Increasingly acidic oxides   ⟶

Going across a period of the periodic table, the nature of the elements changes. At the left hand side the elements (e.g. Na & Mg) have relatively low ionisation energies and so they bond to other elements to form ionic compounds in which they have lost their valence electrons and exist as cations. This is typical metallic behaviour. The oxides of these elements are ionic and contain the oxide ion. This means that they act as bases dissolving in water to give alkaline solutions and neutralising acids to produce a salt and water:

$$O^{2-}_{(s)} + H_2O_{(l)} \Rightarrow 2OH^-_{(aq)}$$

$$O^{2-}_{(s)} + 2\,H^+_{(aq)} \Rightarrow H_2O_{(l)}$$

Aluminium oxide is amphoteric (i.e. it will dissolve in both acids and alkalis) and hence it shows the properties of both metallic and non–metallic oxides.

Moving towards the middle of the periodic table the ionisation energy becomes too great for cation formation and the elements tend towards non–metallic behaviour. In this region the elements (e.g. C and Si) bond by means of covalent bonds.

Most of these oxides of non–metallic elements react with water to form acidic solutions, e.g.

$$CO_{2(g)} + H_2O_{(l)} \rightleftharpoons H^+_{(aq)} + HCO_3^-{}_{(aq)}$$

At the far right of the period this behaviour continues (except for the noble gases), but gaining an additional electron also becomes energetically feasible. This means that these elements (e.g. S and Cl) also have the option of combining with metals to form ionic compounds in which they exist as anions (e.g. S^{2-} and Cl^-).

These trends in the properties of the compounds of the elements on going across a period are discussed in considerably more detail in the next section.

EXERCISE 3.3

1. The reactivity of the alkali metals increases in the order

    A   Na, K, Li
    B   K, Na, Li
    C   Li, Na, K
    D   Li, K, Na

2. An aqueous solution of chlorine acts as a bleach. This is because the solution

    A   acts as an oxidant and converts the coloured dye to a colourless product.
    B   acts as a base and converts the coloured dye to a colourless product.
    C   acts as a reductant and converts the coloured dye to a colourless product.
    D   acts as an acid and converts the coloured dye to a colourless product.

3. Going down the halogen group the state of the elements, at room temperature and pressure, changes from gas to liquid to solid. The reason for this is that

A   the strength of the bonds between the atoms increases.
B   the strength of the forces between the molecules increases.
C   the polarity of the molecules increases.
D   the electronegativity of the atoms decreases.

4. On going across a period of the periodic table, the elements tend to become less metallic in character. Which one of the following is **not** an indication of this trend?

A   There is an overall increase in molar mass.
B   There is an increase in electronegativity.
C   There is an overall increase in ionisation energy.
D   There is a change in bond type from ionic to covalent.

5. Which one of the following is **not** true of the alkali metals?

A   They have a high density.
B   They form ionic compounds.
C   Their chlorides dissolve to give neutral solutions.
D   Their oxides dissolve to give alkaline solutions.

6. a)   Write a balanced equation for the reaction of sodium with water.
b)   What would be seen as this reaction occurred?
c)   To what class of chemical reactions does this belong?
d)   Describe how the change in the character of this reaction can be used to compare the reactivity of sodium with those of lithium and potassium.

7. Give the colours of the following:

a)   Iodine vapour.

b)   The precipitate initially formed when barium chloride reacts with silver nitrate.

c)   The colour this changes to when exposed to light for a long time.

d)   The colour of the solution when chlorine is bubbled through aqueous sodium bromide.

e)   The precipitate formed by the reaction of aqueous solutions of lead(II) nitrate and potassium iodide.

8. When aqueous silver nitrate is added to a colourless aqueous bromide solution, in the presence of excess nitric acid, an off–white precipitate forms. The experimenter assumes that this shows the presence of bromide ions in the solution.

    a) If this is the case, write a balanced ionic equation for the formation of the precipitate.

A colleague suggests that this would also be the expected result that if the solution had contained a mixture of chloride and iodide ions.

    b) How could the experimenter test his colleague's hypothesis? Describe what he should do and give the results you would expect for both the bromide ion and the mixture of chloride and iodide ions. Write balanced equations for any reactions that you describe.

9. For each of the following pairs, state whether a reaction would or would not occur on mixing, explaining your reasoning. In cases where a reaction does occur, write an ionic equation for the reaction and state any colour change you would expect to see.

    a) chlorine and aqueous sodium bromide.
    b) bromine and aqueous potassium fluoride.
    c) bromine and aqueous calcium iodide.
    d) iodine and aqueous magnesium bromide.

10. Properties of the elements and their compounds often show regular variations with respect to their position in the periodic table.

    a) Describe the general trend in acid–base character of the oxides of the elements in the third period (Na to Ar). Give one example each of an acidic oxide and a basic oxide and show with equations how these oxides react with water.

    b) How does the oxidising strength of the halogens vary down the group? Account for this trend.

    c) How does the reducing strength (i.e. the ability to donate electrons) of the alkali metals vary down the group? Account for this trend.

3.4 PERIODIC TRENDS IN PERIOD 3 (Na → Ar)

13.1.1 Explain the physical properties of the chlorides and oxides of the elements in the third period (Na → Ar) in terms of their bonding and structure.

Refer to the following oxides and chlorides:

Oxides: Na_2O, MgO, Al_2O_3, SiO_2, P_4O_6 and P_4O_{10}, SO_2 and SO_3, Cl_2O and Cl_2O_7.

Chlorides: $NaCl$, $MgCl_2$, Al_2Cl_6, $SiCl_4$, PCl_3 and PCl_5 and Cl_2 (sulfur chloride is not required).

Limit the explanation to the physical states of the compounds under standard conditions and electrical conductivity in the molten state only.

13.1.2 Describe the chemical trends for the chlorides and oxides referred to in 13.1.1. Include relevant equations.

Limit this to acid–base properties of the oxides and the reactions of the chlorides and oxides with water.   © IBO 2001

The position of the elements in the periodic table affects the type of chemical bonding that occurs in their compounds, which in turn has an effect on the formulae and properties of the compounds.

CHLORIDES OF PERIOD 3

As the number of valence electrons increases, there is a steady increase in the number of electrons available for bond formation and hence in the number of chlorine atoms that each element bonds to – $NaCl$, $MgCl_2$, $AlCl_3$ (more correctly written as Al_2Cl_6 in its gaseous state), $SiCl_4$, PCl_5 (though PCl_3 also exists).

The chlorides of metals, such as sodium chloride and magnesium chloride, are ionically bonded crystalline solids with high melting points. When added to water these chlorides dissolve without chemical reaction, to give solutions in which the component ions can behave independently. Because of the presence of these mobile ions, these compounds conduct electricity when molten or in aqueous solution.

$$NaCl_{(s)} \overset{water}{\Rightarrow} Na^+_{(aq)} + Cl^-_{(aq)}$$

The chlorides of non–metals, such as phosphorus trichloride, have molecular covalent structures. As a result of the weak forces between the molecules these compounds have low melting and boiling points. When added to water a **hydrolysis** (i.e. splitting by the action of water) reaction occurs in which the bonds between the element and chlorine are replaced by bonds between the element and oxygen. The result is an acidic solution containing hydrogen ions, chloride ions and the oxide, or an oxyacid of the element. This oxyacid may then also dissociate. In the case of phosphorus trichloride, for example, the reaction is:

$$PCl_{3\,(l)} + 3\,H_2O_{(l)} \Rightarrow P(OH)_{3\,(aq)} + 3\,H^+_{(aq)} + 3\,Cl^-_{(aq)}$$

$P(OH)_3$ or H_3PO_3 is phosphoric(III) acid which is a weak acid and partially dissociates as shown below.

$$H_3PO_{3\,(aq)} \rightleftharpoons H^+_{(aq)} + H_2PO_3^-{}_{(aq)}$$

These chlorides in the molten state do not conduct electricity, as would be expected for molecular covalent compounds. In aqueous solution however they do conduct electricity because of the ions formed in the chemical reactions above.

Chlorine itself (Cl_2), which may be regarded as chlorine chloride, fits in with this pattern of behaviour, being a molecular covalent substance that reacts with water in an analogous hydrolysis reaction (see page 93).

Even though aluminium is a metal the behaviour of many of its compounds, especially when anhydrous, is more typical of non–metals. This is a result of the small size and high charge of the ion that aluminium forms. Aluminium chloride for example, although a solid, sublimes at the surprisingly low temperature of 178°C to give a vapour consisting mainly of Al_2Cl_6 molecules. Anhydrous aluminium chloride undergoes vigorous hydrolysis when added to water. Even the hydrated chloride produces quite acidic solutions owing to the dissociation of the water molecules associated with the small, highly charged, Al^{3+} ion (see section 9.9, page 315).

OXIDES OF PERIOD 3

The oxides of the elements also show trends across the period, the most noticeable being the change from basic to acidic character. The trend in the formulae of the oxides, an extra half oxygen for each successive element, is more complete than that of the chlorides, extending as far as chlorine – Na_2O, MgO, Al_2O_3, SiO_2, P_4O_{10} (as well as P_4O_6), SO_3 (as well as SO_2), Cl_2O_7 (as well as Cl_2O).

The oxides of the elements on the left of the periodic table (Na and Mg) are ionic solids. They behave as basic oxides and react with water to form an alkaline solution of the hydroxide, though in the case of magnesium hydroxide, the solution is only weakly alkaline owing to its low solubility. The equation for the reaction of sodium oxide with water is:

$$Na_2O_{(s)} + H_2O_{(l)} \Rightarrow 2\,Na^+_{(aq)} + 2\,OH^-_{(aq)}$$

Being basic oxides, they will react with acids to form a salt and water. In the case of magnesium oxide the equation for the reaction is:

$$MgO_{(s)} + 2\,H^+_{(aq)} \Rightarrow Mg^{2+}_{(aq)} + H_2O_{(l)}$$

In the centre of the periodic table the oxides are giant covalent lattices with very high melting and boiling points. This type of bonding could not occur with the chlorides because chlorine only forms a single bond, so it cannot produce an extended lattice. Both aluminium oxide and silicon dioxide, because of their giant covalent structures, are virtually insoluble. With regard to acid–base properties, aluminium oxide is amphoteric, i.e. it will react with and dissolve in both acids and alkalis:

ADVANCED

$$Al_2O_{3\,(s)} + 6\,H^+_{(aq)} \Rightarrow 2\,Al^{3+}_{(aq)} + 3\,H_2O_{(l)}$$

$$Al_2O_{3\,(s)} + 2\,OH^-_{(aq)} + 3\,H_2O_{(l)} \Rightarrow 2\,Al(OH)_4^-_{(aq)}$$

Silicon dioxide has little acid–base activity, but it does show weakly acidic properties by dissolving in hot concentrated alkalis to form silicates.

$$SiO_{2(s)} + 2OH^-_{(aq)} \Rightarrow SiO_3^{2-}_{(aq)} + H_2O_{(l)}$$

To the right of the period, molecular covalent bonding occurs, so that the compounds are gases, liquids or low melting point solids. Often a variety of oxides exist, containing the element in different oxidation states, for example phosphorus can form both P_4O_6 (P is in a +3 oxidation state) and P_4O_{10} (P is in a +5 oxidation state). These non–metal oxides react with water to form acids, which may then dissociate.

$$P_4O_{10(s)} + 6H_2O_{(l)} \Rightarrow 4H_2PO_4^-_{(aq)} + 4H^+_{(aq)}$$

$$SO_{3\,(g)} + H_2O_{(l)} \Rightarrow HSO_4^-_{(aq)} + H^+_{(aq)}$$

$$Cl_2O_{7(l)} + H_2O_{(l)} \Rightarrow 2ClO_4^-_{(aq)} + 2H^+_{(aq)}$$

The trends in the properties of the elements, chlorides and oxides of the elements from sodium to chlorine are summarised in Figure 3.6 below:

Figure 3.6 – The elements of the third period, their chlorides and their oxides

Element	Na	Mg	Al	Si	P	S	Cl
Bonding	Metallic			Giant covalent		Molecular covalent	
Chloride Formula	NaCl	MgCl$_2$	AlCl$_3$	SiCl$_4$	PCl$_5$/PCl$_3$		Cl$_2$
Bonding	Ionic			Molecular covalent			
Oxide Formula	Na$_2$O	MgO	Al$_2$O$_3$	SiO$_2$	P$_4$O$_{10}$ P$_4$O$_6$	SO$_3$ SO$_2$	Cl$_2$O$_7$ Cl$_2$O
Bonding	Ionic			Giant covalent		Molecular covalent	
Acid/base properties	Sol. basic	Insol. basic	Ampho– teric	Insol. acidic		Soluble acidic	

EXERCISE 3.4

1. Going across the third period of the periodic table, there is a steady change in the formulae of the oxides formed. Which one of the following oxides is **not** an example of this trend?

   A Al_2O_3
   B Na_2O
   C SO_2
   D P_4O_{10}

2. Hydrolysis is a reaction in which

   A water adds on to a molecule.
   B water splits up a molecule.
   C water is a product.
   D water acts as a catalyst.

3. a) When sodium chloride is added to water the resulting solution is a good electrical conductor. The same is true of the solution formed when phosphorus trichloride is added to water, but for slightly different reasons. Explain this behaviour, writing equations for any reactions involved.

   b) Given a sample of the two solutions produced by adding these two chlorides to water describe, giving the results that would be observed,
      i   A test to show that both contained the chloride ion.
      ii   A test that would tell which solution was formed from which chloride.

4. The oxides of the elements in the third period show a trend in acid–base properties going across the period. Choose specific examples of three oxides, one basic, one amphoteric and one acidic, then use these examples to illustrate this trend, writing balanced equations for any chemical reactions involved.

5. There is a trend in the chemical character of the elements in the third period (Na to Ar). Describe this briefly with respect to the bonding present in the element and its chloride. Explain these in terms of trends that occur in atomic properties such as nuclear charge, ionisation energy and electronegativity.

ADVANCED

HISTORICAL DEVELOPMENT OF THE PERIODIC TABLE

Although the periodic table, in its modern form, is organised in terms of atomic numbers and electronic structure, it originated from a study of the periodicity of chemical properties. No sooner had theoretical chemistry been put on a sound footing in the early 18th century by the recognition of the elements as fundamental building blocks, through the work of Boyle, Lavoisier and Dalton, and the determination of the relative atomic masses of these, especially by Berzelius and Cannizzaro, than people started to notice that certain elements had very similar chemical properties. Döbereiner noticed that if three elements had similar chemical properties then one element often had a relative atomic mass approximately mid–way between the other two. Examples of this are Li (7), Na (23), K (39) and Cl (35), Br (80), I (127). Döbereiner named these groups 'triads'. Newlands then noticed that every eighth element, when placed in order of increasing relative atomic mass, showed similar chemical properties and referred to these as 'octaves'. The examples given above fit in with this (note the noble gases had not been discovered at this date) as do many others. There were however still many anomalies, for example copper was in the same group as sodium and potassium!

The name most closely associated with the periodic table is undoubtedly that of Mendeléev. He extended and rearranged Newland's table, separating groups into two subgroups that gave better correspondence with chemical properties. Another innovation was that he left gaps in the table to improve the fit, and predicted that elements would be discovered to fit these gaps. The early ones correspond to the elements we now know as scandium, gallium and germanium. Mendeléev gave detailed predictions of the chemistry that he expected these undiscovered elements to have and his predictions proved to be remarkably accurate – a classic example of scientific methodology in action. Mendeléev's periodic table is shown in Table 3.2 below with his gaps marked by stars (*):

Table 3.2 – Mendeléev's periodic table (1871)

Series	Group 1	Group 2	Group 3	Group 4	Group 5	Group 6	Group 7	Group 8
1	H							
2	Li	Be	B	C	N	O	F	
3	Na	Mg	Al	Si	P	S	Cl	
4	K	Ca	*	Ti	V	Cr	Mn	Fe,Co,Ni
5	Cu	Zn	*	*	As	Se	Br	
6	Rb	Sr	Y	Zr	Nb	Mo	*	Ru,Rh,Pd
7	Ag	Cd	In	Sn	Sb	Te	I	
8	Cs	Ba	Dy	Ce	*	*	*	
9	*	*	*	*	*	*	*	
10	*	*	Er	La	Ta	W	*	Os,Ir,Pt
11	Au	Hg	Tl	Pb	Bi	*	*	
12	*	*	*	Th	*	U		

The modern periodic table is similar to that of Mendeléev, except that the elements have been re–ordered according to atomic number (otherwise Ar would be an alkali metal!), the noble gases have been added and the d– and f–block metals have been collected together as separate groups in the centre of the table.

3.5 THE d–BLOCK ELEMENTS (FIRST ROW)

13.2.1 List the characteristic properties of transition elements.

Restrict this to variable oxidation states, complex ion formation, coloured compounds and catalytic properties.

13.2.2 Identify which elements are considered to be typical of the d–block elements.

Sc and Zn are not typical.

13.2.3 Describe the existence of variable oxidation states in d–block elements.

The 4s and 3d sub–shells are close in energy. Students need to know that all d–block elements can show an oxidation state of +2. In addition they should be familiar with the oxidation states indicated for any two of the following: Cr (+3, +6), Mn (+4, +7), Fe (+3) and Cu (+1).

13.2.4 Define the term 'ligand'.

13.2.5 Describe how complexes of d–block elements are formed.

Suitable examples are $[Fe(H_2O)_6]^{3+}$, $[Fe(CN)_6]^{3-}$, $[CuCl_4]^{2-}$, $[Cu(NH_3)_4]^{2+}$, $[Ag(NH_3)_2]^+$. Monodentate ligands only are required.

13.2.6 Explain why some complexes of d–block elements are coloured.

Students need only know that in complexes the d orbitals are split into two sets at different energy levels and the electronic transitions that take place between them are responsible for their colours.

13.2.7 Outline the catalytic behaviour of d–block elements and their compounds.

Limit this to: MnO_2 in the decomposition of hydrogen peroxide; V_2O_5 in the Contact process; Fe in the Haber process; Ni in the conversion of alkenes to alkanes. The mechanisms of action are not required. © IBO 2001

1st row of the d–block	Sc	Ti	V	Cr	Mn	Fe	Co	Ni	Cu	Zn
Electronic structure	[Ar] $3d^14s^2$	[Ar] $3d^24s^2$	[Ar] $3d^34s^2$	[Ar] $3d^54s^1$	[Ar] $3d^54s^2$	[Ar] $3d^64s^2$	[Ar] $3d^74s^2$	[Ar] $3d^84s^2$	[Ar] $3d^{10}4s^1$	[Ar] $3d^{10}4s^2$

Decreasing ⟶
stability of maximum oxidation state

Increasing ⟶
stability of +2 oxidation state

The d–block elements are those that occur in the central block of the periodic table, i.e the groups headed by the elements scandium to zinc, in which the d–subshell of an atom is being filled with electrons. A subset of these elements, known as the "transition metals", are those in which the element has a partially filled d–electron shell in one of its common oxidation states.

The elements of the d–block are all dense, hard metallic elements. The electronic structures essentially vary in the number of d–electrons present, but note the two exceptional electronic structures (Cr and Cu) associated with the additional stability of the half filled and fully filled d–orbital. Because the 3d electrons quite effectively shield the outer 4s electrons, the ionisation energy required to remove these remains relatively constant. As a result the d–block elements have many similar chemical and physical characteristics. The ease with which the 3d electrons are lost decreases as the nuclear charge increases, resulting in a trend from the maximum oxidation state to the +2 oxidation state being the most stable. Because of their partially filled d–orbital, the transition metals have certain properties in common, which are not generally shared by other metals (including Sc and Zn), some of these are:

- a variety of stable oxidation states
- the ability to form complex ions
- the formation of coloured ions
- catalytic activity

VARIABLE OXIDATION STATES

The s–block metals, such as sodium and calcium, have s–electrons that are easily lost, but the ionisation energies for the inner electrons are so high that these are never lost in chemical reactions, as shown in Figure 3.7 for calcium. For this reason they always have the same oxidation states in their compounds +1 for sodium and +2 for calcium. Transition metals have slightly higher effective nuclear charges and so their first ionisation energies are a little higher, but there is no large increase in successive ionisation energy in the same way as there is with the s–block elements as can be seen for chromium in Figure 3.7. This is because the 3d and 4s electrons have similar energies. The oxidation state of transition metals therefore depends on how strongly oxidising the environment is, i.e. the presence of species that readily gain electrons.

Figure 3.7 – The relative ionisation energies of calcium and chromium

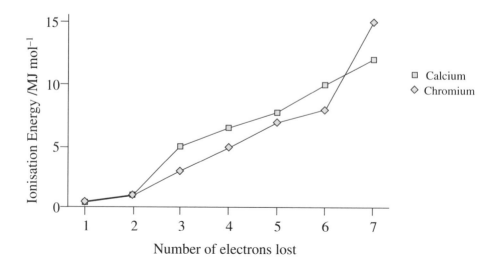

One of the most commonly found oxidation states of transition metals is the +2 state which corresponds to the loss of the two 4s electrons. This is a very stable state on the right of the d–block where the high nuclear charge increases the difference in energy between the 3d and 4s electrons, but becomes an increasingly powerful reductant going to the left. Ti^{2+}, for example, does not exist in aqueous solution because it reduces water to hydrogen. The second commonly found oxidation state, going as far as manganese, is that which corresponds to the loss of all the 3d and 4s valence electrons (+3 for Sc; +4 for Ti etc.). These are stable on the left of the d–block, but become increasingly powerful oxidants going across the period as the energy required to produce these states becomes quite high (see Fig. 3.7). The highest oxidation states usually occur as oxyanions, such as dichromate(VI) ($Cr_2O_7^{2-}$) and permanganate (also referred to as manganate(VII), MnO_4^-). There are also a few other commonly encountered states, such as Cr^{3+} and Fe^{3+}, which do not fit into this pattern. The common oxidation states are summarised in Table 3.3.

Table 3.3 – Common oxidation states of the d–block elements

	Sc	Ti	V	Cr	Mn	Fe	Co	Ni	Cu
+7					X				
+6				X	X				
+5			X						
+4		X	X		X				
+3	X	X	X	X		X			
+2			X	X	X	X	X	X	X
+1									X

Increasing stability of +2 state $\longrightarrow$

$\longleftarrow$ Increasing stability of maximum state

ADVANCED

Note that the variety of oxidation states increases to a maximum at manganese and in the second half of the d–block far fewer oxidation states are found. The stability of the half–filled and fully filled 3d level (encountered before in the unusual electronic structures of Cr and Cu) also affects the stability of oxidation states. In manganese the +2 state, which has a half filled shell ($[Ar]3d^5$), is much more stable than the +3 ($[Ar]3d^4$) state and the +4 ($[Ar]3d^3$) state (usually encountered as manganese(IV) oxide, MnO_2), which are therefore quite strong oxidants. With iron however the reverse is true because it is the +3 state that has the half filled shell ($[Ar]3d^5$) and the +2 state ($[Ar]3d^6$) is quite reducing. In copper, the existence of the +1 state is due to the stability of the filled shell ($[Ar]3d^{10}$). Note that because this has a full 3d sub–shell, like Zn^{2+}, it is not coloured.

THE FORMATION OF COMPLEX IONS

The ions of d–block metals and those in the lower section of the p–block (e.g. lead) have low energy unfilled d– and p–orbitals. These orbitals can accept a lone pair of electrons from some species, known as **ligands**, to form a dative bond between the ligand and the metal ion. This behaviour, in which one species donates an electron pair whilst another accepts it, is Lewis acid–base behaviour (see Section 9.7, page 305). These species which contain ligands bonded to a central metal ion are known as **complex ions**, a common example being the deep blue complex ion $[Cu(NH_3)_4]^{2+}$ formed when excess aqueous ammonia is added to a solution of a copper(II) salt. Note that the complex ion is written in square brackets. The charge is the sum of the charges on the central metal ion and the ligands.

Ligands are species that can donate a pair of non-bonding electrons to the central metal ion and the most common examples are water, ammonia and the chloride ion. Most complex ions have either six ligands arranged octahedrally around the central atom (usually found with water and ammonia ligands), or four ligands arranged tetrahedrally (usually found with chloride ion ligands). This is illustrated in Figure 3.8.

Figure 3.8 – Illustration of tetrahedral and octahedral complex ions

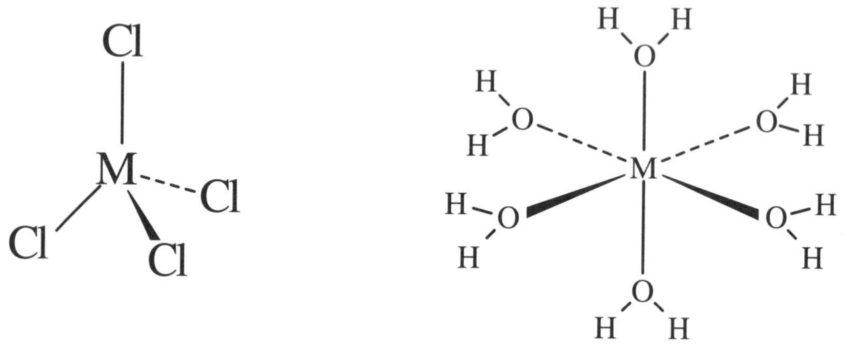

Tetrahedral chloroanion

Octahedral aqua ion

The number of particles around the central particle is known as the **coordination number**. Hence the coordination number of the metal ion in the chloroanion is 4 and in the aqua ion is 6. This concept is also used in crystal structures.

The formation of complex ions stabilises certain oxidation states and often affects the solubility of compounds. The formation of a complex ion can also have a major effect on the colour of the solution of a metal ion. Aqueous cobalt(II) salts, for example contain the hexaaquacobalt(II) ion, which is a pink colour. If concentrated hydrochloric acid is added to this, the solution turns blue owing to the formation of the tetrachlorocobalt(II) ion:

$$[Co(H_2O)_6]^{2+}_{(aq)} + 4\,Cl^-_{(aq)} \rightleftharpoons [CoCl_4]^{2-}_{(aq)} + 6\,H_2O_{(l)}$$

Pink

Blue

Other examples of complex ions and their colours are given Table 3.4:

Table 3.4 – Some common complex ions and their colours

Metal ion	Water Octahedral	Ammonia Octahedral/Sq. planar	Chloride ion Tetrahedral
Cobalt(II)	Pink – $[Co(H_2O)_6]^{2+}$	Straw – $[Co(NH_3)_6]^{2+}$	Blue – $[CoCl_4]^{2-}$
Nickel(II)	Green $[Ni(H_2O)_6]^{2+}$	Blue – $[Ni(NH_3)_6]^{2+}$	Yellow–green $[NiCl_4]^{2-}$
Copper(II)	Blue – $[Cu(H_2O)_6]^{2+}$	Deep blue – $[Cu(NH_3)_4]^{2+}$	Yellow – $[CuCl_4]^{2-}$

ISOMERISM IN COMPLEX IONS

Complex ions exhibit many types of isomerism analogous to those found with organic compounds (see sections 11.4, page 367 and 11.5 page 371). Firstly there is formula isomerism (analogous to structural isomerism) associated with which species are acting as ligands and hence directly bonded to the metal ion. There are for example three forms of chromium(III) chloride hexahydrate that vary in the way the chloride ions are bonded. Because the bonding of the ligand to the metal ion is very stable in this case, the number of chloride ions present as free Cl^- ions can be found by titration with aqueous silver nitrate. These isomers are summerised in Table 3.5 below:

Table 3.5 – Isomers of hydrated chromium(III) chloride hexahydrate

Formula	Colour	Moles of chloride precipitated by $Ag^+_{(aq)}$
$[Cr(H_2O)_4Cl_2]^+Cl^- \cdot 2H_2O$	Dark green	One
$[Cr(H_2O)_5Cl]^{2+}(Cl^-)_2 \cdot H_2O$	Light green	Two
$[Cr(H_2O)_6]^{3+}(Cl^-)_3$	Grey–blue	Three

Stereoisomerism also occurs in complex ions. The simplest examples of geometric isomerism occurs in square planar transition metal complexes such as $Pt(NH_3)_2Cl_2$ (note that as it contains Pt^{2+}, this is an electrically neutral complex), which exists in both cis– and trans– forms:

Cis–complex   Trans–complex

Geometric isomerism can also occur in six coordinate octahedral complexes such as $[Co(NH_3)_4Cl_2]^+$ depending on whether the two chloride ligands occupy adjacent (cis) or opposite (trans) sites.

The ligands considered up to now can only form one bond to the metal ion, they are **monodentate ligands**. With **bidentate ligands** (i.e. those that can form two rather than one bond to a metal ion) such as diaminoethane ($H_2N-CH_2-CH_2-NH_2$ shown as

N⌒N below) non–superimposable mirror image forms can occur, giving rise to enantiomerism. An example is the complex ion $[Co(H_2N-CH_2-CH_2-NH_2)_3]^{3+}$, shown below:

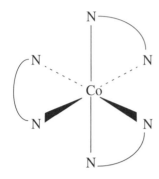 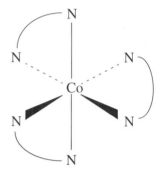

COLOURED IONS

In an isolated atom all of the d–orbitals have exactly the same energy, but if an atom or ion is surrounded by charged ions or polar molecules, the effect of the electric field from these has a different effect on the different d–orbitals. Because of their symmetry the orbitals are often split up into two different groups. With octahedral ligands three orbitals are at low energy and two orbitals at higher energy. The difference in energy between these two groups of orbitals varies slightly with the nature of the species surrounding the metal ion, but the frequency of the light corresponding to this (linked by the formula $\Delta E = h.f$) occurs in the visible region. This means that when white light passes through a compound of a transition metal, light of a particular frequency is absorbed and an electron is promoted from a lower energy orbital to a higher energy orbital, as shown in the Figure 3.9 below.

Figure 3.9 – Illustrating the interaction between transition metal ions and light

The light that passes through therefore appears coloured because some of the frequencies have been absorbed. In the case of most copper(II) compounds, red and yellow light are absorbed so that they look a blue–green colour, i.e. we see the transmitted light which is the complementary colour of the absorbed light. The exact shade depends slightly on the species surrounding the copper, so that the hexaaquacopper(II) ion is light blue but the tetraamminecopper(II) ion is dark blue.

If there are no electrons in the d–orbitals, as is the case for Sc^{3+} and Ti^{4+}, then there are no d-electrons to move and the compounds are colourless. If the d–orbitals are all completely filled, as is the case with Zn^{2+}, then there are no vacant orbitals for the electrons to move into and again the compounds are colourless.

CATALYTIC ACTIVITY

The catalytic behaviours of transition metals and their ions are mainly caused by a combination of two properties already mentioned. Firstly they form complex ions with species that can donate lone pairs of electrons. This results in close contact between the different ligands, as well as between the metal and the ligand. Secondly transition metal ions have a wide variety of relatively stable oxidation states, so they can readily gain and lose electrons in redox reactions.

d–block element catalysts can either be **heterogeneous** or **homogeneous**, though the former are more common. Many enzymes involved in catalysing redox reactions also contain transition metal ions near the active site (see Chapter 13). In a heterogeneous catalyst the surface of the metal or compound provides an active surface on which the reaction can occur with a reduced activation energy. A common example of heterogeneous catalysis is manganese(IV) oxide which catalyses the decomposition of hydrogen peroxide to water and oxygen.

$$2H_2O_{2(aq)} \overset{MnO_2}{\Rightarrow} 2H_2O_{(l)} + O_{2(g)}$$

Another example is nickel catalysing the reaction between hydrogen and an alkene to produce an alkane.

Here bonding to the metal surface not only brings the molecules into close contact, but also electrons from the bonds are used to bond to the metal atoms. This weakens the bonds in the molecules and lowers the activation energy.

Many other important industrial catalysts involve transition metals, such as iron in the Haber process and vanadium(V) oxide in the Contact process.

$$\text{Haber process: } N_{2(g)} + 3H_{2(g)} \overset{Fe}{\rightleftharpoons} 2NH_{3(g)}$$

$$\text{Contact process: } 2SO_{2(g)} + O_{2(g)} \overset{V_2O_5}{\rightleftharpoons} 2SO_{3(g)}$$

In homogeneous catalysis, the catalyst is in the same phase as the reactants. In these reactions a particular metal ion is oxidised in one stage and then reformed by being reduced in a second stage. A good example is the role of iron(II)/(III) in catalysing the slow reaction between acidified hydrogen peroxide and iodide ions. The iron(II) is oxidised by the peroxide to iron(III).

$$H_2O_{2(aq)} + 2H^+_{(aq)} + 2Fe^{2+}_{(aq)} \Rightarrow 2H_2O_{(l)} + 2Fe^{3+}_{(aq)}$$

This is then reduced by the iodide ions to reform iron(II).

$$2I^-_{(aq)} + 2Fe^{3+}_{(aq)} \Rightarrow I_{2(s)} + 2Fe^{2+}_{(aq)}$$

These reactions occur more rapidly than the direct reaction because they both have lower activation energies than the direct reaction.

ADVANCED

THE CHEMISTRY OF SOME INDIVIDUAL D–BLOCK ELEMENTS

Chromium has an electronic structure [Ar] $3d^5 4s^1$ (n.b. like copper an exception in only having one 4s electron). Its common oxidation states are +3 and +6. Compounds of chromium(III), such as Cr_2O_3 and the hexaaquachromium(III) ion, $Cr(H_2O)_6^{3+}$, are usually a dark green colour. Dark green chromium(III) hydroxide is precipitated when aqueous alkali is added to solutions of chromium(III) salts. Like aluminium hydroxide, it is amphoteric and redissolves in high concentrations of hydroxide ions to give a dark green solution:

$$Cr^{3+}_{(aq)} + 3OH^-_{(aq)} \Rightarrow Cr(OH)_{3(s)}$$

$$Cr(OH)_{3(s)} + OH^-_{(aq)} \Rightarrow Cr(OH)_4^-_{(aq)}$$

The common compounds of chromium(VI) are the dark red–brown oxide, CrO_3 – which in many ways resembles SO_3, as well as the yellow chromate(VI), CrO_4^{2-}, and orange dichromate(VI), $Cr_2O_7^{2-}$, ions derived from it.

$$2CrO_{3(s)} + H_2O_{(l)} \Rightarrow 2H^+_{(aq)} + Cr_2O_7^{2-}_{(aq)}$$

The chromate(VI) and dichromate(VI) ions are in an acid–base equilibrium. If acid is added to the yellow chromate, then the equilibrium shifts to the right to give the orange dichromate. This change can be reversed by adding an alkali:

$$2\ H^+_{(aq)} + 2\ CrO_4^{2-}_{(aq)} \rightleftharpoons Cr_2O_7^{2-}_{(aq)} + H_2O_{(l)}$$
$$\quad\text{Yellow} \qquad\qquad \text{Orange}$$

The dichromate(VI) ion is a strong oxidant in acidic solution, being reduced to the green chromium(III) ion:

$$Cr_2O_7^{2-}_{(aq)} + 14\ H^+_{(aq)} + 6\ e^- \Rightarrow 2Cr^{3+}_{(aq)} + 7\ H_2O_{(l)}$$
$$\text{Orange} \qquad\qquad\qquad\qquad \text{Green}$$

Manganese has an electronic structure [Ar] $3d^5 4s^2$. Its common oxidation states are +2, +4, +6 and +7. The most common manganese(VII) compound is the permanganate ion (or manganate(VII) ion), MnO_4^-, which has a very intense purple colour. It is a very powerful oxidant and the other common oxidation states can be formed by its reduction under various conditions, depending on the pH at which the reaction occurs. In very strongly alkaline conditions, the dark green manganate(VI) ion is the product:

$$MnO_4^-_{(aq)} + e^- \Rightarrow MnO_4^{2-}_{(aq)}$$

In approximately neutral solution, a brown precipitate of manganese(IV) oxide forms:

$$MnO_4^-_{(aq)} + 4\ H^+_{(aq)} + 3e^- \Rightarrow MnO_{2(s)} + 2\ H_2O_{(l)}$$

In acidic solution the almost colourless manganese(II) ion is the product. This reaction is frequently used in titrations to determine the concentrations of some easily oxidised species.

$$MnO_4^-_{(aq)} + 8\ H^+_{(aq)} + 5\ e^- \Rightarrow Mn^{2+}_{(aq)} + 4\ H_2O_{(l)}$$

Manganese(IV) oxide is itself a powerful oxidant, for example oxidising concentrated hydrochloric acid to chlorine:

$$MnO_{2(s)} + 4\ HCl_{(aq)} \Rightarrow MnCl_{2(aq)} + 2\ H_2O_{(l)} + Cl_{2(g)}$$

It is most commonly encountered because of its ability to catalyse the decomposition of hydrogen peroxide (see page 109).

When aqueous alkali is added to solutions of manganese(II) salts a flesh coloured precipitate of manganese(II) hydroxide is formed. This rapidly darkens in the presence of air as manganese(II) hydroxide is oxidised to manganese(III) hydroxide by oxygen:

$$Mn^{2+}_{(aq)} + 2\ OH^-_{(aq)} \Rightarrow Mn(OH)_{2\ (s)}$$

$$4\ Mn(OH)_{2\ (s)} + 2\ H_2O_{(l)} + O_{2\ (g)} \Rightarrow Mn(OH)_{3\ (s)}$$

Iron has an electronic structure [Ar] $3d^6\ 4s^2$. Its two common oxidation states are +2 and +3. Iron(II) compounds are usually pale green in colour. Iron(III) compounds usually vary from yellow to brown in colour. The two oxidation states are readily interconverted ($E° = 0.77V$) so that iron(II) acts as a mild reductant and iron(III) as a mild oxidant:

$$Fe^{3+}_{(aq)} + e^- \rightleftharpoons Fe^{2+}_{(aq)}$$

Oxygen in the air will oxidise iron(II) to iron(III), the higher the pH the faster the reaction. As a result iron(II) compounds are often contaminated with traces of iron(III).

The oxidation state of iron in aqueous solution can be readily detected by adding aqueous alkali until a precipitate of the hydroxide forms. Iron(II) hydroxide is green, though it turns brown on standing as a result of aerial oxidation, and iron(III) hydroxide is red–brown:

$$Fe^{2+}_{(aq)} + 2\ OH^-_{(aq)} \Rightarrow Fe(OH)_{2(s)} \qquad \text{Green precipitate}$$

$$Fe^{3+}_{(aq)} + 3\ OH^-_{(aq)} \Rightarrow Fe(OH)_{3(s)} \qquad \text{Red–brown precipitate}$$

When thiocyanate (SCN^-) ions are added to a solution of an iron(III) compound an intense blood–red coloured complex ion is formed. Iron(II) salts, if pure, give no reaction.

Copper has an electronic structure [Ar] $3d^{10}\ 4s^1$ (again note that this is an exception, having only one s–electron). The most common oxidation state of copper is the Cu^{2+} state. Copper(II) compounds are usually blue coloured though some, such as the carbonate, are green and both copper(II) oxide and copper(II) sulfide are black. Most copper(II) compounds are soluble and contain the pale blue hexaaqua ion, but the hexaaquacopper(II) ion is readily converted into other complex ions. Adding concentrated hydrochloric acid produces the yellow tetrachlorocopper(II) anion, whilst adding aqueous ammonia, initially produces a pale blue precipitate of copper(II) hydroxide, but this readily redissolves in excess of the reagent to give a dark blue solution containing the tetraamminecopper(II) cation:

$$[Cu(H_2O)_6]^{2+}_{(aq)} + 4\ Cl^-_{(aq)} \rightleftharpoons [CuCl_4]^{2-}_{(aq)} + 6\ H_2O_{(l)}$$

Pale blue   Yellow

$$[Cu(H_2O)_6]^{2+}_{(aq)} + 4\ NH_{3(aq)} \rightleftharpoons [Cu(NH_3)_4]^{2+}_{(aq)} + 6\ H_2O_{(l)}$$

Pale blue   Dark blue

The reaction to precipitate copper(II) hydroxide also occurs when other aqueous alkalis are added to solutions of copper(II) salts:

$$Cu^{2+}_{(aq)} + 2OH^-_{(aq)} \Rightarrow Cu(OH)_{2(s)}$$

Copper can also exist in a +1 oxidation state. This state has a completely filled d–subshell (like Ag^+ and Zn^{2+}), so that its compounds are colourless. The ion is unstable in aqueous solution, forming copper metal and copper(II) ions:

$$2\ Cu^+_{(aq)} \Rightarrow Cu_{(s)} + Cu^{2+}_{(aq)}$$

Note that in this reaction the copper(I) is simultaneously oxidised and reduced. Reactions of this type are known as **disproportionation reactions**.

Insoluble copper(I) salts are stable however, the most common being copper(I) iodide, which is a white solid formed by the reduction of copper(II) compounds with iodide ions. The iodine, formed at the same time, can be removed by adding excess aqueous thiosulfate.

$$2\ Cu^{2+}_{(aq)} + 4\ I^-_{(aq)} \Rightarrow 2\ CuI_{(s)} + I_{2\ (aq)}$$

Copper(I) oxide is a red–brown solid that is formed when copper(II) compounds are reduced under alkaline conditions, for example in Fehling's solution where tartrate ions complex the copper(II) ions to prevent copper(II) hydroxide precipitating:

$$2\ Cu^{2+}_{(aq)} + 2\ OH^-_{(aq)} + 2\ e^- \Rightarrow Cu_2O_{(s)} + H_2O_{(l)}$$

Transition metals form a number of quite small highly charged ions such as Cr^{3+} and Fe^{3+}. In aqueous solution these hydrated ions behave in a similar way to Al^{3+}, the water ligands dissociate to make the solution acidic:

$$[M(H_2O)_6]^{3+}_{(aq)} \rightleftharpoons [M(H_2O)_5OH]^{2+}_{(aq)} + H^+_{(aq)}$$

EXTENSION

EXERCISE 3.5

1. The oxidation state that occurs for the greatest number of the transition metals is

     A   +1
     B   +2
     C   +3
     D   +4

2. The high oxidation states of transition metals are

    A   usually found to the right hand side of the transition series.
    B   usually found to involve simple ions.
    C   usually powerful oxidants.
    D   usually colourless.

3. Transition metal ions are frequently coloured because

    A   they absorb infrared radiation and re–emit it as visible light.
    B   of the vibrations of the ligands surrounding them.
    C   of the movement of electrons between d–orbitals.
    D   light causes them to spontaneously change their oxidation state.

4. The colour of the complex ion formed between cobalt(II) ions and chloride ions is

    A   green.
    B   yellow.
    C   pink.
    D   blue.

5. Which one of the following elements would **not** usually be classified as a transition metal?

    A   Cu
    B   Zn
    C   Mn
    D   Ti

6. Explain briefly why

    a)   Potassium always occurs as a +1 ion in its compounds and calcium as a + 2 ion, but compounds of manganese are known in which the oxidation state of the manganese varies from +2 to +7.
    b)   There is a slight change in the shade of green of an aqueous solution of nickel(II) sulfate, when concentrated hydrochloric acid is added.
    c)   Ammonia forms complex ions with cobalt(II) ions, but methane does not.

7. Describe what would be seen during the following:

    a)   A few drops of aqueous ammonia are added to aqueous copper(II) sulfate and then a large excess is added.
    b)   Sulfur dioxide gas (a strong reducing agent) is bubbled through acidified potassium dichromate(VI).
    c)   Aqueous iron(II) sulfate is warmed with excess aqueous hydrogen peroxide and then aqueous sodium hydroxide is added to the product.
    d)   Solid manganese(IV) oxide is added to aqueous hydrogen peroxide.

ADVANCED

8. Catalysts containing transition metals or their compounds, are important in many industrial processes. Choose **two** examples of this and in each case:

 a) Name the catalyst.
 b) Write a balanced equation for the reaction that it catalyses.

 Explain the difference between homogeneous and heterogeneous catalyst and state which category your chosen examples belong to.

9. Give the formulae of the complex ion(s) or oxyanion(s) of the first row of d–block elements (Sc to Zn) corresponding to each of the following:

 a) A blue solution that turns green then yellow when concentrated hydrochloric acid is added.
 b) The ion formed when excess aqueous ammonia is added to aqueous copper(II) sulfate.
 c) A blue solution that turns pink when water is added to it.
 d) An orange solution that turns yellow when alkali is added to it.
 e) A purple solution that goes dark green when concentrated alkali and a reductant are added.

10. The cyanide ion (CN^-) can form two complex ions with iron ions. The formulae of these are $Fe(CN)_6^{4-}$ and $Fe(CN)_6^{3-}$.

 a) What shape would you expect these to have?
 b) What is the oxidation state of the iron in the two complex ions?
 c) What feature of CN^- allows it to form complex ions with transition metals?

11. Account for the following observations:

 a) Ti^{2+} will reduce water to hydrogen, but Ca^{2+} will not.
 b) V^{3+} compounds are coloured but Sc^{3+} compounds are not.
 c) V^{3+} can act as both an oxidising agent and a reducing agent, whilst Sc^{3+} is neither.
 d) Cu^+ has colourless compounds but Cu^{2+} compounds are coloured.
 e) $Co(NH_3)_3Cl_3$ exists in a number of isomeric forms.

12. The complex ion $[Co(H_2NCH_2CH_2NH_2)_2Cl_2]^+$ is octahedral and exists as two different geometric isomers.

 a) Draw these isomers so as to illustrate how the geometric isomerism arises.

 One of these two isomers can also exist in two enantiomeric forms.

 b) Draw these isomers so as to illustrate how the enantiomerism arises and explain why enantiomers of the other geometric isomer do not occur.

BONDING

4

Chapter contents

4.1 IONIC BONDING

A chemical bond is a strong electronic interaction between atoms. The reason atoms form bonds is that this decreases their potential energy and so makes the system more stable. In some cases bonding results in small groups of atoms being held tightly together. If they are electrically neutral, these small groups are known as molecules.

Chemical bonding between atoms involves the interaction of the electrons in the valence shells of the atoms. There are three fundamental types of chemical bond, namely ionic, covalent and metallic, though there are examples of bonds intermediate between these. The bond type depends on the attraction for electrons of the atoms involved, i.e. their electronegativity. If the elements have very different electronegativities then ionic bonding results. If they both have quite high electronegativities then the bonding will be covalent, whereas if they both have low electronegativities they form a metallic bond. Each type of bonding gives rise to distinctive physical properties of the substance formed.

4.1.1 Describe the ionic bond as the result of electron transfer leading to attraction between oppositely charged ions.

4.1.2 Determine which ions will be formed when metals in groups 1, 2 and 3 lose electrons.

4.1.3 Determine which ions will be formed when elements in groups 6 and 7 gain electrons.

4.1.4 State that transition metals can form more than one ion.

Restrict examples to simple ions eg Fe^{2+} and Fe^{3+}.

4.1.5 Predict whether a compound of two elements would be mainly ionic or mainly covalent from the position of the elements in the periodic table, or from their electronegativity values.

4.1.6 Deduce the formula and state the name of an ionic compound formed from a group 1, 2 or 3 metal and a group 5, 6 or 7 non-metal.   © IBO 2001

Ionic bonding occurs between an atom with a low electronegativity (i.e. a metal) and an atom with a high electronegativity (i.e. a non-metal). This means that we can predict that the bonding in BaSe is ionic because Ba is a metal (in group 2) and Se is a non-metal (in group 6). Almost all metal compounds are ionic. Ionic bonding usually occurs when there is a large difference in electronegativity between the elements involved. They are made up of a regular array of positively and negatively charged particles, called **ions**, held together by electrostatic attraction. In simple cases these ions are **isoelectronic** (i.e. have the same electronic structure) as the noble gases.

In ionic bonding the metal atom loses electrons to form a positively charged ion, or **cation**. The number of electrons lost varies from metal to metal, but the elements in the s-block of the periodic table lose all of the electrons in their valence level. Sodium, which has an electronic structure 2,8,1, therefore loses just its one outer electron to give a sodium ion, with an electronic structure 2,8 (isoelectronic with Ne). This carries a single positive charge because it has one more proton than electron (11 p$^+$ compared to 10 e$^-$).

$$Na \Rightarrow Na^+ + e^-$$
$$(2,8,1) \quad (2,8)$$

Similarly calcium has two valence electrons (2,8,8,2) and so it forms an ion (with an electronic structure 2,8,8) that has two positive charges.

The number of electrons lost by metals outside of the s-block is less easy to predict and, particularly in the case of the transition metals, a particular metal can form ions with different charges, for example iron can form both Fe^{2+} (the iron(II) ion) and Fe^{3+} (the iron(III) ion). This means that the charges on the ions must be learnt and those most commonly met are given in Table 4.1, from which it can be seen that a +2 charge is by far the most common.

Non-metals gain electrons to form negatively charged ions, or **anions**. The number of electrons gained usually fills the valence level of the atom. Chlorine therefore, with an electronic structure 2,8,7, requires one electron to fill its valence level, so it forms an ion with an electronic structure 2,8,8 (isoelectronic with Ar), which carries a single negative charge because it has one more electron than proton (18 e$^-$ compared to 17 p$^+$).

$$Cl + e^- \Rightarrow Cl^-$$
$$(2,8,7) \quad (2,8,8)$$

Similarly oxygen (2,6) requires two electrons to fill its valence level and so it forms an ion (with an electronic structure 2,8) that has two negative charges.

Hence in forming sodium chloride the sodium atom can be considered to have **transferred** an electron to the chlorine atom. Similarly in forming calcium oxide the calcium atom transfers two electrons to the oxygen atom. No electron sharing occurs between the ions in ionic bonding.

Groups of atoms, joined together by covalent bonds (see Section 4.2, page 121) can also have an electrical charge and so form compounds with ions of the opposite charge by ionic bonding. The sulfate ion ($SO_4{}^{2-}$) consists of a sulfur atom and four oxygen atoms, joined by covalent bonds, which has gained two extra electrons to give a charge of -2. Table 4.1 gives the electrical charges carried by common anions and cations.

Table 4.1 - The charges on common anions and cations

Anions			Cations		
−1	−2	−3	+1	+2	+3
Fluoride F^-	Oxide O^{2-}	Nitride N^{3-}	Hydrogen H^+	Magnesium Mg^{2+}	Aluminium Al^{3+}
Chloride Cl^-	Sulfide S^{2-}	Phosphide P^{3-}	Sodium Na^+	Calcium Ca^{2+}	Chromium(III) Cr^{3+}
Bromide Br^-			Potassium K^+	Manganese Mn^{2+}	Iron(III) Fe^{3+}
Iodide I^-			Copper(I) Cu^+	Iron(II) Fe^{2+}	
			Silver Ag^+	Cobalt Co^{2+}	
				Nickel Ni^{2+}	
				Copper(II) Cu^{2+}	
				Zinc Zn^{2+}	
				Lead Pb^{2+}	
				Tin Sn^{2+}	
Hydroxide OH^-	Carbonate CO_3^{2-}	Phosphate PO_4^{3-}	Ammonium NH_4^+		
Nitrate NO_3^-	Sulfate SO_4^{2-}				

- Simple anions change the ending of the names of the atoms to -ide, e.g. chlorine gives the chloride ion.

- Anions that contain oxygen have an -ate ending, e.g. sulfate.

Ionically bonded compounds are simply named according to the names of the two ions involved, the cation being given first, so that $Cr(OH)_3$ is chromium(III) hydroxide. Note that the bracketed Roman numeral gives the oxidation number of the metal (usually equal to the charge on the ion). Going from the name to the formula requires a knowledge of the ratio that the ions combine in. Ionic compounds must contain cations and the anions in such a ratio that their charges cancel each other to give a neutral compound. If they have equal, but opposite charges, as for example with zinc and sulfide, then this requires just an equal number of each, so the formula of zinc sulfide is simply ZnS. In other cases the formula must give the ratio of the different ions, so that copper(II) fluoride is CuF_2, because for each doubly charged copper(II) there must be two singly charged fluorides. When multiplying groups of atoms, they must be enclosed in brackets, so that ammonium sulfate has the formula $(NH_4)_2SO_4$. A simple way of predicting the formula of an ionic compound is to 'swap' the numbers of the charges on the ions involved. For example, the formula of calcium phosphate can be predicted as $Ca_3(PO_4)_2$, by 'swapping' the **bold** numbers of the charges on the ions - Ca^{2+} and PO_4^{3-} i.e. the '2' charge for the calcium becomes the phosphate superscript and vice versa. The formulae of acids can be predicted by combining the hydrogen ion (H^+) with the appropriate anion, hence nitric acid (H^+ & NO_3^-) has the formula HNO_3.

The anions and cations have opposite electrical charges and are attracted together into a crystal lattice in which each anion is surrounded by cations and *vice versa*. A single layer of such a lattice, formed by ions of equal charge, is shown in Figure 4.1.

Figure 4.1 - A layer of an ionic lattice

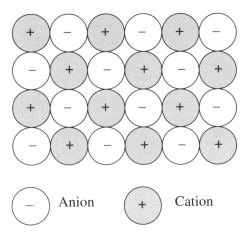

The lattice naturally extends in three dimensions, so that there would be an anion above and below each cation and *vice versa*. The whole of the substance is therefore held together by strong electrostatic attractions in all three dimensions. This means that there are no molecules present in ionic substances. Because of the way in which bonding occurs, ionic compounds have distinctive physical properties:

* Hard, brittle solids.

* Quite high melting and boiling points.

* Do not conduct electricity when solid, but do when molten or in solution.

* Are more soluble in water than other solvents.

EXERCISE 4.1

1. An element has an atomic number of 16. What will be the charge on the ions that it forms?

    A   +2
    B   +1
    C   -1
    D   -2

2. The electronic structure of five elements is given below. Which one of these will form an ion with a charge of +2?

    A   2,1
    B   2,4
    C   2,6
    D   2,8,2

Bonding

CORE

3. Which one of the following elements is most likely to be capable of forming cations with different charges?

A   Be
B   V
C   Sr
D   Cs

4. Name the following compounds:

a)   KBr   b) Li_3N c)   BaS
d) AlI_3 e)   BeO

5. The table below gives the electronic structures of pairs of elements, A and B. On the basis of these electronic structures, predict the ions that these elements would form amd hence the formula of the compound that would result.

	Element A	Element B
a)	2,1	2,8,7
b)	2,6	2,8,8,2
c)	2,8,1	2,8,6
d)	2,8,3	2,7
e)	2,5	2,8,2

4.2 COVALENT BONDING

4.2.1 Describe the covalent bond as the result of electron sharing.

The electron pair is attracted by both nuclei leading to a bond which is directional in nature. Both single and multiple bonds should be considered. Dative covalent bonds are not required.

4.2.2 Draw the electron distribution of single and multiple bonds in molecules.

Examples should include O_2, N_2, CO_2, C_2H_4 (ethene) and C_2H_2 (ethyne).

4.2.3 State and explain the relationship between the number of bonds, bond length and bond strength.

The comparison should include bond lengths and bond strengths of: two carbon atoms joined by single, double and triple bonds; the carbon atom and the two oxygen atoms in the carboxyl group of a carboxylic acid.

4.2.6 Draw and deduce Lewis (electron dot) structures of molecules and ions for up to four electron pairs on each atom.

A pair of electrons can be represented by dots, crosses, a combination of dots and crosses or by a line. © IBO 2001

Covalent bonding occurs between atoms that have quite high electronegativities, i.e. between non-metals. In covalent bonding the two atoms involved **share** some of their valence electrons. The attraction of the two positively charged nuclei for these shared electrons results in the two atoms being bonded together as illustrated in Figure 4.2.

Figure 4.2 - Covalent bonding as a result of electron sharing

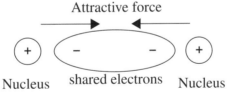

A single covalent bond consists of a shared pair of electrons, a double bond two shared pairs and a triple bond three. Usually each atom involved contributes one electron, but in some circumstances one atom can donate both electrons. In this case the bond is known as a **dative** covalent bond (also sometimes referred to as a coordinate bond, or as a donor-acceptor bond), but it is equivalent to a normal bond in every other way. When forming covalent bonds, the atoms involved usually fill their valence level, so that the number of bonds formed is equal to the number of electrons needed for this. As a result the noble gases, which have filled valence shells, rarely form compounds. This means that atoms in compounds (except for hydrogen) usually have eight electrons in their valence shell. This is sometime known as the octet rule. Carbon has an electronic structure of 2,4 and so requires four more electrons to fill its valence level. It therefore forms four bonds, as shown in Figure 4.3.

Similarly fluorine, which has an electronic structure 2,7 and hydrogen (1) both require just one electron to fill their valence levels and so form just one bond. Oxygen (2,6) requires two electrons and normally forms 2 bonds, whilst nitrogen (2,5) forms 3 bonds.

Figure 4.3 - The valence level in carbon, showing vacancies

x - electron in valence shell

o - vacancy in valence shell

If carbon and fluorine form a compound, because carbon forms four bonds and fluorine only forms one, four fluorines are required for each carbon and so the formula is CF_4. This can be represented as a structural formula, in which each covalent bond is shown as a line joining the atoms involved, or as a Lewis diagram (electron dot diagram), which shows all the valence electrons of the atoms involved, or as a hybrid of these in which each electron pair is represented by a line. These representations of CF_4 are given in Figure 4.4. The Lewis diagram and hybrid show that the atoms involved all have filled valence levels in the molecule.

Figure 4.4 - The bonding in CF_4 illustrated as both a structural formula (left), a hybrid diagram (centre) and a Lewis diagram (right)

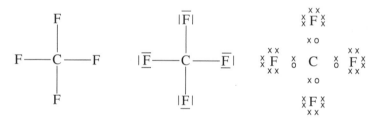

In some cases two atoms can share two pairs of electrons. This forms a double bond, which joins the atoms more tightly and closer together than a single bond. Carbon forms four bonds and oxygen forms two bonds, so that two oxygens are needed for each carbon, giving carbon dioxide. The oxygen and carbon atoms are joined by double bonds, which are represented as double lines in the structural formula. The diagrams for these are given in Figure 4.5.

Figure 4.5 - The bonding in CO_2 illustrated as both a structural formula (left), a hybrid diagram (centre) and a Lewis diagram (right)

$$O = C = O \qquad \overline{O} = C = \overline{O}$$

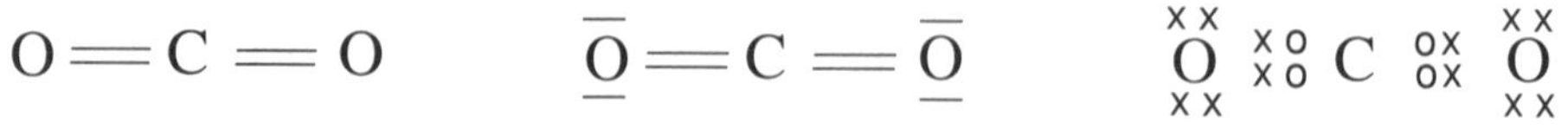

Again notice that the valence shells of both the carbon and oxygen are filled. Ethene is an example of an organic molecule that contains a double bond. Its structural formula is given in Table 4.2, (page 128).

Two atoms can also share three pairs of electrons giving an even stronger triple bond. A nitrogen atom has five electrons in its valence level (electronic structure 2,5) and so requires three more electrons to fill it. In nitrogen gas therefore, the two nitrogen atoms are held together by a triple bond to form a nitrogen molecule, as shown in Figure 4.6.

Figure 4.6 -The bonding in N_2 illustrated as both a structural formula (left), a hybrid diagram (centre) and a Lewis diagram (right)

$$N\equiv N \qquad |N\equiv N| \qquad {}^{x}_{x}N\ {}^{x\,o}_{x\,o}\,N\,{}^{o}_{o}$$

Again note that the valence shells of both nitrogen atoms are filled. Ethyne is an example of an organic molecule containing a triple bond (see Table 4.2, page 125).

The types of diagrams above represent three of the stages involved in drawing a Lewis diagram:

1   Decide how many bonds each atom involved forms. (For many simple molecules this equals the number of electrons required to fill the outer electron shell, for more complicated cases see "Molecules with LESS than four electron pairs" on page 128).

2   Decide on which is the central atom(s) (i.e. the one that can form most bonds) and join the atoms together with bonds, so that all the atoms have the required number of bonds - this gives the structural formula. (n.b. if more than one structural formula is possible then the species most likely displays delocalised bonding, see Section 4.7, page 142).

3   Each bond will involve one electron from each of the atoms it joins (unless it is a dative bond). Subtract these from the total number of electrons in the valence shell of each atom to calculate the number of electrons present as non-bonding electrons. Draw a line to represent each of these pairs - this gives the hybrid formula. If the species is an ion, then show the charge on the atoms with unpaired electrons.

4   Replace each bond and each line by an electron pair. The electrons may be all represented by 'x's, or preferably a mixture of 'x's and 'o's can be used to indicate which atom the electron originally came from.

5   If the species is an ion rather than a molecule then one electron needs to be added for each negative charge and one removed for each positive charge. Usually these species will have unpaired electrons and under-filled or over-filled valence shells. The electrons should be added/removed so as to give full valence shells of paired electrons. It may be useful to indicate such electrons by a '□'.

This can be illustrated considering hydrogen cyanide (HCN) and the methanoate ion (HCO_2^-):

Hydrogen cyanide	**Methanoate ion**
Carbon (2,4) forms four bonds, nitrogen (2,5) three and hydrogen (1) one in order to complete their valence shells.	Carbon (2,4) forms four bonds, oxygen (2,6) two and hydrogen (1) one in order to complete their valence shells.

Hydrogen cyanide

The carbon will be the central atom. As hydrogen can only form one bond to the carbon, there must be three bonds (i.e. a triple bond) between the carbon and the nitrogen. The structural formula is therefore:

$$H-C\equiv N$$

The structural formula accounts for all of the carbon and hydrogen valence electrons, as the carbon has eight in its valence shell and the hydrogen one. The structural formula however only accounts for three of nitrogen's five valence electrons, so it must have a non-bonding pair. The hybrid formula is therefore:

$$H-C\equiv N|$$

There is one pair of electrons in the C-H bond and three pairs of electrons in the triple C≡N bond, so the Lewis structure is:

$$H \overset{x}{\underset{o}{}} C \overset{x\ o}{\underset{x\ o}{x\ o}} N \overset{o}{\underset{o}{o}}$$

Hydrogen cyanide is a neutral molecule so there is no need to add or remove electrons.

Methanoate ion

The carbon will be the central atom and it will bond to both of the oxygens and the hydrogen. If the carbon-oxygen bonds were both double there would be five bonds to the carbon, so one must be single. We note the charge that will complete the octet around this oxygen. The structural formula is therefore:

$$\overset{O}{\underset{||}{H-C-O^-}}$$

[Note that it would be possible to exchange the double bond and the negative charge between the two oxygens, an indication that delocalisation occurs in this ion]

The structural formula accounts for two electrons around the hydrogen and eight electrons around the carbon. The double bonded to the oxygen only accounts for two of its six electrons so there must also be two non-bonding pairs. The single bond to the other oxygen only accounts for one of its electrons so there are five more valence electrons to account for, two pairs and an unpaired electron. The hybrid formula is therefore:

$$\overset{|O|}{\underset{||}{H-C-\overline{O}^-}}$$

Replacing each bond by a pair of electrons, replacing the lines by non-bonding pairs and taking into account the unpaired electron on the oxygen, is the first stage in producing the Lewis structure.

Finally the electron that causes the negative charge needs to be shown in the Lewis structure and the overall charge shown outside the square brackets:

$$\left[H \overset{x}{\underset{o}{}} C \overset{x}{\underset{o}{}} \overset{x\,o\,x}{\underset{x\,x}{O}} \overset{xx}{\underset{xx}{O}} \right]^-$$

Organic molecules, such as ethane, ethene and ethyne show the effect of single, double and triple bonding on the length and strength of the carbon-carbon bond:

Table 4.2 - Some simple hydrocarbons

	Ethane (single C-C bond)	Ethene (double C-C bond)	Ethyne (triple C-C bond)
Structural formula	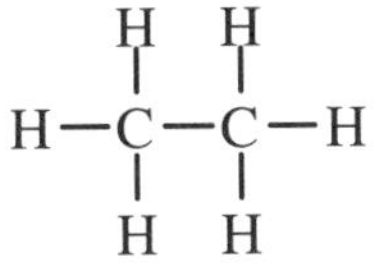 H—C—C—H with H H above and H H below (each C)	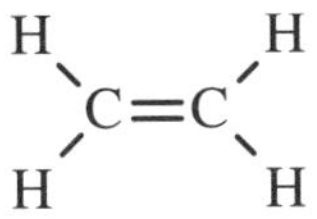 C=C with H H on left C and H H on right	H—C≡C—H
Lewis diagram	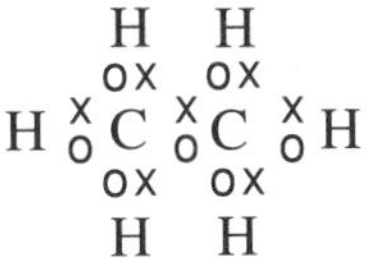 H H / OX OX / H ⊗ C ⊗ C ⊗ H / OX OX / H H	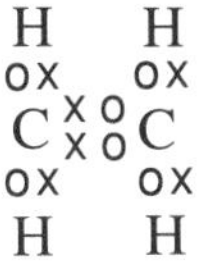 H H / OX OX / C ⊗ C / OX OX / H H	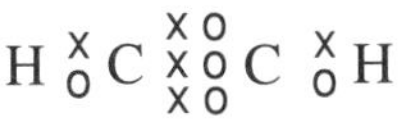 H ⊗ C ⊗ C ⊗ H (with XO dots)
C-C bond length /pm	154	134	121
C-C bond energy /kJ mol^{-1}	346	598	837

Covalent bonding can lead to two types of structures. Usually, as in all the examples so far considered the covalent bonds hold a small number of atoms together to form discrete units called molecules. Although the covalent bonds holding the molecule together are strong, the forces between molecules are much weaker (see section 4.8, page 146), so that individual molecules are easily separated from each other. As a result molecular covalent solids have characteristic physical properties, such as being quite soft in the solid state, not conducting electricity, being more soluble in non-polar solvents than in water and having low melting and boiling points (often liquids or gases at room temperature and pressure). This is discussed in more detail in section 4.8, page 146.

Sometimes, the whole lattice of a solid can be held together by strong covalent bonds. These 'covalent network', or 'giant covalent' structures are very different, being very hard and having very high melting and boiling points (see Section 4.10, page 152).

EXERCISE 4.2

1. An element forms a covalently bonded compound with hydrogen, that has the formula XH_3, where X is the element. In which group of the periodic table would you expect to find X?

A   Group 1
B   Group 14
C   Group 15
D   Group 17

2. "Two atoms each provide two electrons that are shared by the two atoms". This is a description of a

A   single covalent bond.
B   double covalent bond.
C   triple covalent bond.
D   quadruple covalent bond.

3. A non-metal usually forms two covalent bonds in its compounds. How many electrons will it have in its valence level?

A   2
B   4
C   6
D   8

4. The noble gases do not usually form chemical compounds because

A   they have very stable nuclei.
B   the bonds between their atoms are very strong.
C   they already have complete valence electron levels.
D   they are not polar.

5. Which one of the following compounds contains **both** ionic and covalent bonds?

A SiO_2
B BaF_2
C Na_2CO_3
D Cl_2O

6. From the electronic structures of the following elements deduce the numbers of covalent bonds, if any, that they would normally form, and hence predict the formulae of the compound you would expect to result.

a)   helium and sulfur   b)   chlorine and hydrogen
c)   nitrogen and chlorine   d)   silicon and fluorine
e)   phosphorus and oxygen

7. From the electronic structures of the pairs of elements given, predict the type of bonding that you would expect in the compound they form.

a)   2,4 and 1   b)   2,8,5 and 2,8,7   c)   2,1 and 2,8,6
d)   2,6 and 2,7   e)   2,8 and 3,2,6

8. Draw Lewis diagrams of the following molecules:

a)   HCl   b) O_2 c) PH_3
d) F_2O e) H_2CO

4.3 SHAPES OF MOLECULES AND IONS

4.2.7   Predict the shape and bond angles for molecules with four charge centres on the central atom.

Use the valence shell electron pair repulsion (VSEPR) theory to predict the shapes and bond angles of molecules and ions having four pairs of electrons (charge centres) around the central atom. Suitable examples are NH_3, H_2O and alkanes (e.g. CH_4).

4.2.8   Identify the shape and bond angles for species with two and three negative charge centres.

Examples should include species with non-bonding as well as bonding electron pairs, e.g. CO_2, SO_2, C_2H_2, C_2H_4, CO_3^{2-} and NO_2^-.   © IBO 2001

MOLECULES WITH 4 ELECTRON PAIRS

Covalent molecules all have distinct shapes. The shape of a molecule is determined by repulsion between the electron pairs in the valence shell. This is known as Valence Shell Electron Pair Repulsion (VSEPR) theory. Most common molecules have filled valence levels that contain four pairs of electrons. In order to be as widely separated as possible and hence minimise their potential energy, these electron pairs distribute themselves so that they are pointing towards the corners of a tetrahedron, i.e. a regular triangular based pyramid. If all of the electron pairs are bonding pairs, as for example in methane, CH_4, then this is also the shape of the molecule (see Table 4.3, page 128).

Some molecules also contain non-bonding, or 'lone', pairs of electrons and these still affect the shape of the molecule. In order to determine this it is vital to draw a correct Lewis structure for the species before any attempt is made to predict its shape. In ammonia, NH_3, if there were only the three pairs of bonding electrons, then these would point to the corners of an equilateral triangle with the nitrogen atom at its centre. The pair of electrons on the nitrogen that is not involved in the bonding (the lone pair or non-bonding pair), repels the bonding electrons so the molecule has the shape of a triangular pyramid. Similarly, if it were not for the non-bonding electrons, the water molecule would be linear and not bent. The basic shapes that these common molecules have is summarised in Table 4.3.

In all of these structures, the angles between all of the bonds would be expected to be the tetrahedral angle of 109.5° and this is the angle that is found in methane and other molecules that contain just four bonding pairs. The repulsion between a lone pair and a bonding pair is greater than that between two bonding pairs. As a result the presence of a lone pair distorts the geometry, causing a slight reduction in the bond angle. If there is just one lone pair, as in ammonia, the bond angle is about 107°, whilst the presence of two lone pairs, as in water, reduces the bond angle to about 104°.

Note that in describing the shape of the molecule only the atoms and not the lone pairs are considered so that even though water has four regions of high electron density that have approximate tetrahedral orientation, its shape is given as non-linear because that is the orientation of the atoms.

Table 4.3 - The shapes of common molecules

No. non-bonding electron pairs	Example	Lewis diagram	Shape and bond angle
None	Methane	H $\overset{\times\times}{\underset{\times\times}{\times\text{C}\times}}$ ... (see diagram)	Tetrahedral 109.5°
One	Ammonia	(see diagram)	Trigonal pyramidal 107°
Two	Water	(see diagram)	Non-linear ('bent') 104° 'angular' or 'V-shaped'.

MOLECULES WITH LESS THAN FOUR ELECTRON PAIRS

As discussed above, the shape of a molecule is determined by repulsion between the regions of high electron density in the valence level, i.e. covalent bonds and non-bonding (or 'lone') electron pairs. This theory (VSEPR) is still valid in systems that have less or more than the four regions of high electron density discussed above. The former arises when elements in groups 2 and 3/13 form covalent bonds, or when elements in the later groups form multiple bonds and hence have a reduced number of electron dense regions close to the nucleus. Ethene and ethyne (see Table 4.2 page 125) are good examples of this.

If there are two regions of high electron density, then the result will be a linear molecule, as is found in gaseous beryllium chloride and in carbon dioxide. If there are three regions of high electron density then these will point towards the corners of an equilateral triangle. If they are all bonding pairs then a trigonal planar molecule results, such as boron trifluoride. If one is a non-bonding pair, as in sulfur dioxide, then a bent (V-shaped; angular) molecule results. As would be expected the presence of the lone pair in sulfur dioxide reduces the bond angles to ~117°. These structures are given in Table 4.4.

Table 4.4 - The shapes of common molecules with less than four regions of high electron density

No. of regions of high e⁻ density	No. of non-bonding electron pairs	Example	Shape and bond angle
Two	None	Carbon dioxide	Linear $O=C=O$ 180°
Three	None	Boron trifluoride	Trigonal planar 120° 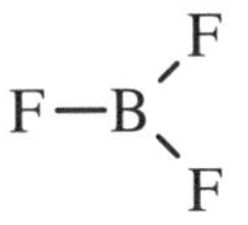 F—B with F (top) and F (bottom)
Three	One	Sulfur dioxide	Non-linear (V-shaped) 117°  S with O (double bonds)

As will be seen later, quite a number of molecules and ions involve π-bonds (see Section 4.6, page 140) and delocalised bonds (see Section 4.7, page 142). When predicting the shape of these, exactly the same theory applies. The shape is dictated by the σ-bonds and the non-bonding electron pairs. π-bonds do not affect the shape of the molecule and hence it does not matter whether the delocalised structure or one of the resonance structures derived from a Lewis diagram is considered, as both give identical answers. This is illustrated below for the nitrate ion, which has three regions of high electron density (charge centres, or centres of negative charge) around the nitrogen and hence is trigonal planar.

Resonance structure   Delocalised

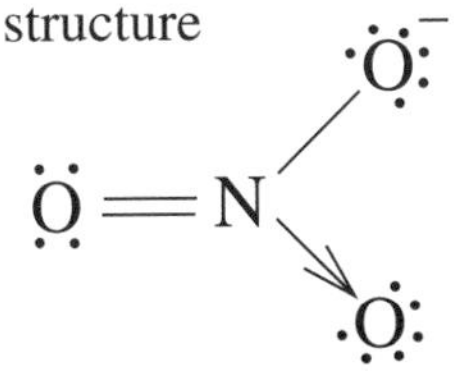

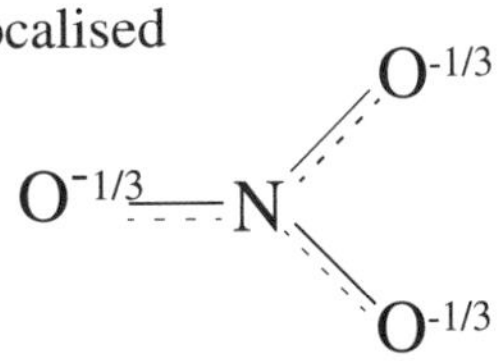

$O=N$ with O^- and O groups $O^{-1/3}$—N with $O^{-1/3}$ and $O^{-1/3}$ groups

Consider for example the shapes of the three species NO_2^+, NO_2 and NO_2^-. Oxygen will normally form two bonds and nitrogen three, so the requirements of simple bonding theory cannot be satisfied in NO_2. Oxygen can however also accept an electron pair to form a dative bond and this does meet the bonding requirements, except that it will be noted that there is a single unpaired electron on the nitrogen atom. (Species with unpaired valence electrons are called free radicals and are usually very reactive. NO_2 by being relatively stable is a notable exception. Further details of free radicals are given in Section 11.6, page 374). In NO_2^+ this unpaired electron is lost and in NO_2^- an additional electron has been gained to give a non-bonding electron pair on the nitrogen. The Lewis structures are therefore:

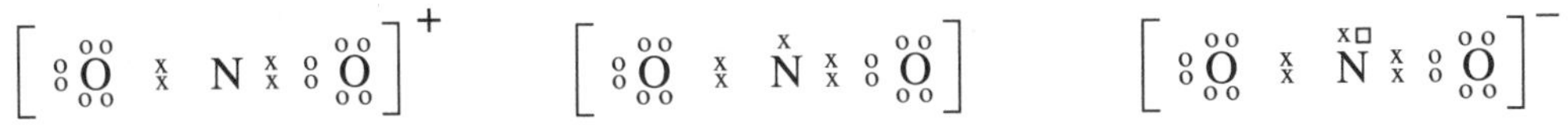

$$\left[O\ N\ O \right]^+ \qquad \left[O\ N\ O \right] \qquad \left[O\ N\ O \right]^-$$

It can therefore be seen that NO_2^+ will be linear with a bond angle of $180°$ and that NO_2^- will be trigonal planar with a bond angle of $120°$. In the case of NO_2, because there is only a single lone electron rather than a lone pair, it is likely that it will be non-linear, but because of the lower repulsion the bond angle will be between $120°$ and $180°$ (it is in fact $134°$). It is an arbitrary decision in all of these structures which of the oxygen atoms to join with a single bond and which with a double. This gives a clear indication that they are resonance structures, so that the actual species will involve delocalised π-bonds and be resonance hybrids of the possible resonance structures (see Section 4.8, page 146). Similar considerations show that the carbonate ion (CO_3^{2-}) is trigonal planar.

MOLECULES WITH MORE THAN FOUR ELECTRON PAIRS

14.1.1 State and predict the shape and bond angles using the VSEPR theory for 5- and 6-negative charge centres.

The shape of the molecules/ions and bond angles if all pairs of electrons are shared, and the shape of the molecules/ions if one or more lone pairs surround the central atom, should be considered. Examples such as PCl_5, SF_6 and XeF_4 can be used.

© IBO 2001

Molecules with more than four negative charge centres arise because elements in the third (Al to Ar) and lower periods of the p-block can 'promote' one or more electron from a doubly filled s- or p-orbital into an unfilled low energy d-orbital. This increases the number of unpaired electrons available, and hence the number of bonds that can be formed, by two for each electron promoted. Phosphorus ([Ne] $3s^23p^3$) for example usually has three unpaired electrons and forms the chloride PCl_3. By promoting one of its s-electrons it can take on the electron configuration ([Ne] $3s^13p^33d^1$) which has five unpaired electrons and can form the chloride PCl_5. Molecules of this kind have more than eight outer electrons and so are said to have an expanded valence shell. This usually occurs only when the extra bonds formed are strong bonds (which in practice means to very electronegative elements) to small atoms (so that they can fit around the central atom). As a result in many molecules with expanded valence shells the central atom is bonded to fluorine, oxygen or chlorine, especially fluorine.

In some molecules with expanded valence shells, there may be five or six regions of high electron density, giving shapes based on the trigonal bipyramid and the octahedron respectively. The trigonal bipyramid has two types of electron rich regions, two axial ones (each at $90°$ to three other pairs and at $180°$ to the fourth) and three equatorial ones (each at $90°$ to two other pairs and at $120°$ to the remaining two). Non-bonding electron pairs always occupy the equatorial positions. In the octahedral configuration, all of the positions are equal, but if there are two non-bonding pairs in an octahedral arrangement then these take positions opposite to each other to give a square planar shape. It is of course vital to draw correct Lewis structures to determine the geometry of a molecule or ion, so as to find the number of lone pairs. As with tetrahedral based shapes, the presence of a lone pair causes slight distortion of the bond angles. These basic shapes and some common examples are summarised in Table 4.5.

Table 4.5 - The shapes of common molecules with more than four regions of high electron density

No. of regions of high e⁻ density	No. of non-bonding electron pairs	Example	Shape and bond angle
Five	None	Phosphorus pentafluoride	Trigonal bipyramidal 90°& 120°
Five	One	Sulfur tetrafluoride	'Saw horse' 90° & ~117°
Five	Two	Iodine trichloride	T-shaped 90°
Five	Three	Xenon diflouride	Linear 180°
Six	None	Sulfur hexafluoride	Octahedral 90°
Six	One	Bromine pentafluoride	Square pyramid ~88°
Six	Two	Xenon tetrafluoride	Square planar 90°

ADVANCED

EXERCISE 4.3

1. Which one of the following molecules would you **not** expect to be planar?

A SCl_4
B C_2H_4
C BCl_3
D XeF_4

2. If a molecule has a trigonal pyramid shape, how many non-bonding pairs of electrons are there in the valence level of the central atom?

A 1
B 2
C 3
D 4

3. What shapes would you predict for the following molecules?

a) SiF_4 b) PCl_3 c) H_2S
d) NF_3 e) CCl_4

4. Draw Lewis diagrams for and hence predict the shape, giving approximate bond angles, for CH_3^+, CH_3^- and $\bullet CH_3$ (i.e. a methyl radical).

5. Sketch the shapes and predict the bond angles in each of the following species:

a) H-CO-OH   b) CH_3-NH_2
c) H-CN   d) ICl_2^-

ADVANCED

4.4 POLARITY

4.2.4   Compare the relative electronegativity values of two or more elements based on their positions in the periodic table.

Precise values of electronegativity are not required.

4.2.5   Identify the relative polarity of bonds based on electronegativity values.

In a covalent bond, electron distribution may not be symmetrical and the electron pair may not be equally shared.

4.2.9   Predict molecular polarity based on bond polarity and molecular shape.

The polarity of a molecule depends on its shape and on the electronegativities of its atoms, eg CO_2, H_2O.   © IBO 2001

CORE

POLARITY IN COVALENT BONDING AND MOLECULES

In covalent bonding, the bonds consist of electrons **shared** between the atoms. This sharing is not equal, unless the two atoms involved are identical (e.g. the two chlorine atoms in a Cl_2 molecule), because different atoms have different electronegativities, i.e. different attraction for electrons in a covalent bond. The more electronegative atom will attract the electrons more strongly than the less electronegative and that will result in it having a slight negative charge. The less electronegative atom will therefore be slightly deficient in electrons and so will have a slight positive charge. A covalent bond in which the atoms have slight electrical charges (shown as δ+ and δ-) is known as a **polar bond**. In hydrogen chloride, for example, the chlorine atom is more electronegative than the hydrogen, which has the lowest electronegativity of all the common non-metals, and so the chlorine attracts the shared electrons more strongly. The hydrogen therefore has a slight positive charge and the chlorine a slight negative charge, as illustrated in Figure 4.7.

Figure 4.7 - Illustrating a polar bond in hydrogen chloride

$H^{\delta+}$ $Cl^{\delta-}$

The electronegativity of an element can be judged from its position in the periodic table. All of the elements involved in covalent bonds have quite high electronegativities, otherwise they would bond in a different way. The electronegativity of atoms increases across a period of the periodic table and also increases going up a group (see Figure 3.4, page 88), so that the electronegativities fall into a series:

B & Si < P & H < C & S & I < Br < Cl & N < O < F
High   Very high   Extremely high

The greater the difference in electronegativity of the atoms involved, the greater the polarity of the bond and hence the electrical charges on the atoms involved. In the extreme case the electron can be considered to have been transferred, hence giving ionic bonding.

Bonding

In some cases, such as hydrogen chloride, the polar bonds result in the molecule having a resultant **dipole**, i.e. there is a positive and a negative end to the molecule. In carbon dioxide, even though the carbon-oxygen bonds are polar, their effects cancel out because of the symmetry of the molecule. The centres of positive and negative charge are in the same place, so that there is no overall dipole. In other molecules, such as water, because the shape is not so symmetrical, the effects of the polar bonds do not cancel, so that the molecule does have an overall dipole. Carbon dioxide and water are compared in Figure 4.8.

Figure 4.8 - Comparing a non-polar molecule (carbon dioxide) with a polar molecule (water)

$$O^{\delta-} = C^{\delta+} = O^{\delta-}$$

In summary, for a molecule to be polar:

*   it must contain polar bonds

and

*   its shape must be such that the centres of positive and negative charges are not in the same place.

The dipole moment is a measure of the polarity of a molecule. Non-polar molecules have a zero dipole moment. For other molecules the more polar the molecule, the greater the dipole moment. Methane for example has a dipole moment of zero, hydrogen iodide has a value of 0.42 debye and hydrogen fluoride a value of 1.91 debye.

Another way to represent the polarity of a bond is by means of arrows drawn next to the bond. Similarly molecular polarity can be indicated by an arrow drawn next to the molecule. By convention the head of the arrow points in the direction of the partial negative charge. If because of symmetry the arrows on the various bonds in a molecule cancel each other out (i.e. their vector sum is zero) then the molecule will be non-polar (think of CO_2). If they do not then the molecule will be polar and the vector sum of the polar bonds will give the molecular dipole (think of H_2O). This concept is illustrated below for trichloromethane ($CHCl_3$) and tetrachloromethane (CCl_4), both of which are tetrahedral:

Figure 4.9 - Using bond polarity vectors to predict molecular polarity

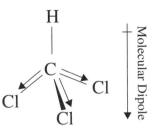

Trichloromethane, polar bonds
do not cancel, so it is a polar
molecule.

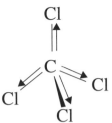

Tetrachloromethane, polar bonds
cancel (equal and symmetrical) so
it is a non-polar molecule.

Similar consideration of the polar bonds in symmetrical molecules such as methane (CH_4) and ethene (C_2H_4) will indicate that these are non-polar, whereas less symmetrical molecules such as ammonia (NH_3), chloromethane (CH_3Cl) and dichloromethane (CH_2Cl_2) are polar.

Experimentally, it is easy to tell if a liquid is polar or not by bringing an electrostatically charged rod close to a jet of liquid running out of a burette. If it is polar (e.g. $CHCl_3$) the stream of liquid will be attracted to the rod, if non-polar (e.g. CCl_4) it will be unaffected. This occurs because, in the electrical field produced by the rod, the molecules orientate themselves so that the end closest to the rod has the opposite charge to the rod. This means the electrostatic force of attraction is greater than the force of repulsion.

EXERCISE 4.4

1. Which one of the following bonds would be the most polar?

A C-N
B S-O
C Si-F
D P-Cl

2. Carbon and chlorine form a series of compounds: CH_4; CH_3Cl; CH_2Cl_2; $CHCl_3$; CCl_4. Which of these will be polar molecules?

A CCl_4 only
B CH_3Cl and $CHCl_3$ only
C CH_3Cl, CH_2Cl_2 and $CHCl_3$ only
D CH_3Cl, CH_2Cl_2, $CHCl_3$ and CCl_4 only

3. State whether you would expect the molecules below to be polar or non-polar.

a) SiF_4 b) PCl_3 c) H_2S
d) NF_3 e) CCl_4

4. Which atom in the following bonds would you expect to carry a partial negative charge?

a)   H—N   b)   O—P   c)   C—F
d)   S—S   e)   B—O

5. Two molecules are shown below

a)   In the molecules there are three kinds of bonds (C=C, C-Cl and C-H). Which would you expect to be the most polar and which the least?

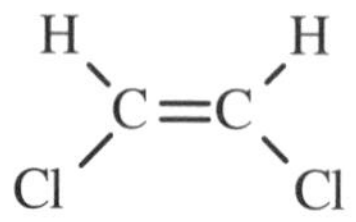

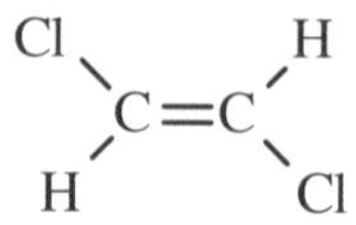

b)   Which one of these molecules would you expect to be polar and which non-polar? Explain why.

c)   Given unlabelled samples of the two liquids, how could you use this property to identify them. Say exactly what you would do and what result you would expect in each case.

6. For each of the following species :

i)   draw the Lewis structure, including all non-bonding electrons.
ii)   give a sketch of the shape (including bond angles) of the molecule.
iii)   state whether it would be polar or non-polar.

a) $BeCl_{2 (g)}$ b) H_2CO c) N_2F_2 (2 forms possible)
d) ICl_4^- e) PF_4^-

4.5 HYBRIDIZATION

When carbon and hydrogen form methane (CH_4), a perfectly tetrahedal molecule in which carbon bonds to four hydrogens results. How can this be explained when carbon has only two unpaired electrons with which to form bonds in its ground state? Firstly one of the pair of electrons in the s-orbital is 'promoted' to the vacant p-orbital to produce a carbon atom in an excited state, so as to produce four unpaired electrons (see below, this is similar to the electron promotion in valence shell expansion). One of these is however an s-electron and the others are p-electrons, and it seems most unlikely that these would produce four entirely equivalent bonds with hydrogen atoms. The theory used to explain this is **hybridization** which states that when an atom bonds the atomic orbitals involved in forming the σ-bonds, or accommodating the lone pairs of electrons interact with each other to form an equal number of highly directional **hybrid orbitals** of equal energy. This results in four equivalent sp^3 hybrid orbitals for carbon, shown in the diagram below:

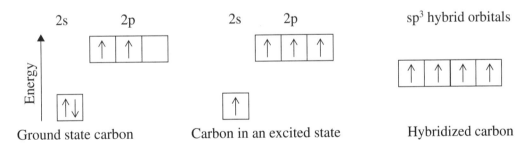

| 2s | 2p | | 2s | 2p | | sp^3 hybrid orbitals |

Ground state carbon   Carbon in an excited state   Hybridized carbon

Note that the total energy has not changed, it has just been redistributed equally amongst the four new hybrid orbitals. Because of electron-electron repulsion these hybrid orbitals are directed towards the corners of a regular tetrahedron.

In other words, when atoms join together to form molecules (except in the case of hydrogen), their outer atomic orbitals interact with each other to produce hybrid orbitals. This process of hybridization gives the same number of hybrid orbitals as the atomic orbitals involved, but these orbitals are all of the same energy, are symmetrically arranged around the atom and are more directional so as to produce greater interaction with the orbitals of the other atom. The precise type of hybridization that occurs depends on the number of σ-bonds and non-bonding electron pairs that have to be accommodated about the atom. If there are two of these, then the hybridization will involve one s-orbital and one p-orbital and so is known as sp hybridization. This produces two hybrid orbitals at 180° to each other. If three electron pairs are to be accommodated, then it involves one s-orbital and two p-orbitals to give sp^2 hybridization, with a trigonal planar symmetry, and if four such regions then an s-orbital and three p-orbitals interact to give four tetrahedrally orientated sp^3 hybrid orbitals. These hybrid orbitals are shown in Table 4.6:

Table 4.6 - The shapes of hybrid orbitals

No. of orbitals	Hybridization	Shape	
2	sp	Linear 	
3	sp^2	Trigonal planar 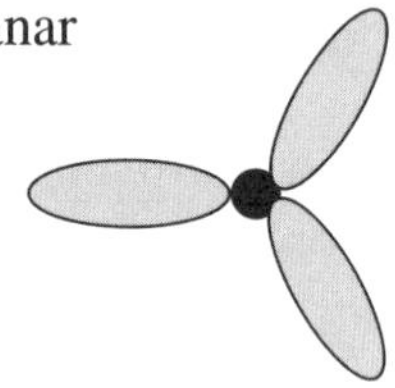	
4	sp^3	Tetrahedral 	

It can be seen that the shapes of these hybrid orbitals correspond to the shapes found for molecules according to electron repulsion theory (VSEPR) and the best way to determine the hybridization around an atom is by considering the shape of the molecule.

In ethyne for example, we can conclude that the carbon atoms are sp hybridized because of the linear shape of the molecule.

$$H-C\equiv C-H \qquad \text{Linear}$$

Note that hybrid orbitals can just form σ-bonds; π-bonds are only produced by unhybridized p-orbitals. (For an explanation of σ- and π-bonds see Section 4.7, page 142) The hybridization process of the carbons in this case can be represented as:

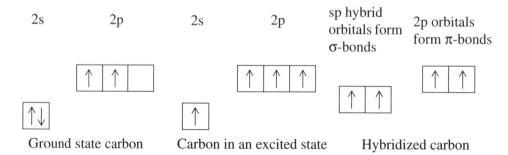

Another example is ammonia, which has sp^3 hybridization because its trigonal pyramid shape can only result from a tetrahedral geometry. In this case however the sp^3 hybrid orbitals are not all used for bonding as one accommodates a lone pair of electrons. The hybridization can be represented as:

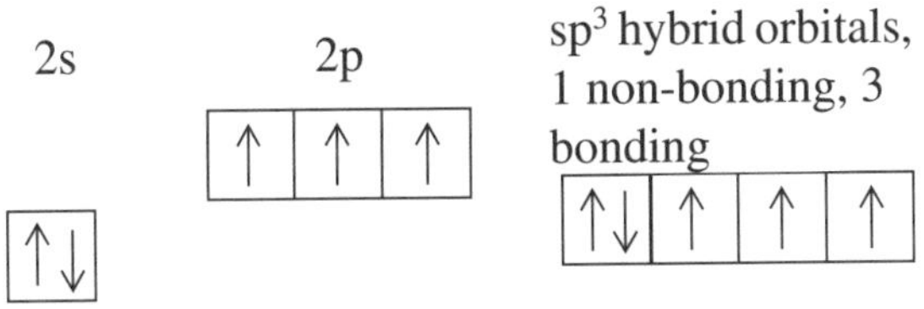

2s   2p   sp³ hybrid orbitals,
                        1 non-bonding, 3
                        bonding

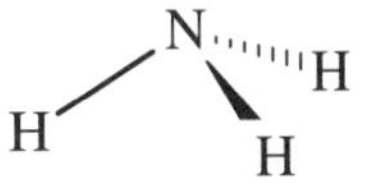

Ground state nitrogen   Hybridized nitrogen   Trigonal pyramid shape

Another way to predict the hybridization present is from the Lewis structure. In this case the number of orbitals required around the central atom will be equal to the sum of the number of bonds (single, double or triple as each only involves one σ-bond) and the number of lone pairs. In water for example, there are two bonds and two lone pairs so the four orbitals are required, hence the hybridization will be sp³. A second example would be the carbon atom in ethene which must be sp² hybridized in order to form bonds to three other atoms with no lone pairs.

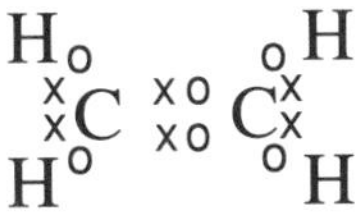

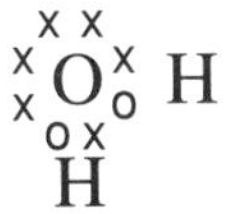

EXERCISE 4.5

1. The carbon atoms in ethane (C_2H_6), ethene (C_2H_4) and ethyne (C_2H_2) provide examples of the three common types of hybridization. In the order given above the type of hybridization corresponds to

A   sp, sp², sp³
B   sp, sp³, sp²
C   sp³, sp², sp
D   sp³, sp, sp²

2. The hybridization of the boron atom in boron trifluoride is described as sp².

a)   Use this example to explain what is meant by the term 'hybridization'.
b)   Why may we conclude that this kind of hybridization occurs in boron trifluoride?
c)   Boron trifluoride can react with a fluoride ion to give the tetrahedral BF_4^- ion. What type of hybridization would you expect the boron in this to have?

ADVANCED

4.6 MULTIPLE BONDS

14.2.1 Describe σ and π bonds.

> *Treatments should be restricted to; σ bonds - electron distribution has axial symmetry around the axis joining the two nuclei; π bonds resulting from the combination of parallel p orbitals; double bonds formed by a σ and a π bond, and triple bonds formed by a σ and two π bonds.* © IBO 2001

When a double bond forms between two atoms, the two bonds are not identical. The first bond is formed by the interaction of electrons in s-orbitals, one of the p-orbitals or more commonly hybrid orbitals (see Section 4.5, page 137). When they interact they produce a bond in which the electron density is at its greatest on the internuclear axis (an imaginary line joining the two nucleii) and is symmetrical about it. Bonds of this type are called σ (pronounced sigma) bonds.

The second bond in a double bond is formed by the interaction of electrons in p-orbitals at right-angles to the internuclear axis. This bond has a low electron density on the internuclear axis, but regions of high electron density on opposite sides of it. Bonds of this type are called π (pronounced pi) bonds. The formation of sigma and pi bonds is shown in Figure 4.10.

**Figure 4.10 - The formation of σ-bonds and π-bonds
from the interaction of atomic orbitals**

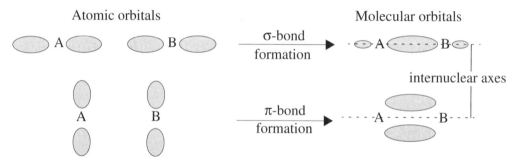

Single bonds are always σ-bonds, **double bonds** are always made up of one σ-bond plus one π-bond, whereas **triple bonds** are one σ-bond plus two π-bonds, with the π-bonds being at 90° to each other (i.e. one with high electron density above and below the internuclear axis, the other with high electron density in front of and behind it as you view the page.)

Because there are more electrons between the two nuclei, double and triple bonds result in them being more strongly bonded than single bonds, so pulling the atoms closer together. This means that going from single to double to triple bonds the bond energies increase and the bond lengths decrease, as shown in Table 4.7 using carbon-carbon bonds as examples.

Table 4.7 - The bond energies and bond lengths of carbon-carbon bonds

Bond type	Bond energy - kJ mol^{-1}	Bond length - pm
Single (C-C)	348	154
Double (C=C)	612	134
Triple (C≡C)	837	120

This is also true for other types of bond. For example ethanoic acid contains two carbon-oxygen bonds, one single and one double, and it is found that the double bond is significantly shorter than the single. Similarly in the second period of the periodic table, the bond energy decreases going from nitrogen (N≡N, 944 kJmol^{-1}, one of the strongest covalent bonds), through oxygen (O=O, 496 kJmol^{-1}) to fluorine (F-F, 158 kJmol^{-1}, one of the weakest covalent bonds).

EXERCISE 4.6

1. Which one of the following correctly describes a π-bond?

A   It is formed by the interaction of s-orbitals and has a high electron density on the internuclear axis.

B   It is formed by the interaction of s-orbitals and has a low electron density on the internuclear axis.

C   It is formed by the interaction of p-orbitals and has a high electron density on the internuclear axis.

D   It is formed by the interaction of p-orbitals and has a low electron density on the internuclear axis.

2. Carbon and oxygen can bond either by a single bond (as in CH_3-OH), a double bond (as in O=C=O), or a triple bond (as in C≡O).

a)   Describe these three types of bonds in terms of σ-bonds and π-bonds.

b)   How would you expect the length of the carbon-oxygen bond to vary in the three examples given?

ADVANCED

4.7 DELOCALIZATION

14.3.1 State what is meant by the delocalization of π electrons and explain how this can account for the structures of some substances.

Examples such as NO_3^-, NO_2^-, CO_3^{2-}, O_3, $RCOO^-$ and benzene can be used. (These could also be dealt with through a resonance approach).   © IBO 2001

A π-bond results from the interaction of p-orbitals on two atoms, each containing one electron. On some occasions this interaction can involve more that two atoms and the p-orbitals on these atoms may contain differing numbers of electrons. This results in what is known as a **delocalized π-bond**. This concept can be used to explain observations that are not readily accounted for in other ways.

The best known occurrence of delocalization is in benzene, C_6H_6, which is a planar, regular hexagonal shaped molecule, in which all of the carbon-carbon bond lengths and angles are equal. Simple bonding theory would predict that the carbon-carbon bonds in the ring would be alternately double and single (see Figure 4.11 a). This however would not lead to a regular hexagonal shape, as double bonds are shorter than single ones. The description involving delocalization is that each carbon atom in benzene is sp^2 hybridized. One of these orbitals forms a σ-bond to the hydrogen atom it is attached to, the other two form σ-bonds to the carbons on either side. The remaining electron (carbon has four valence electrons, three of which have been used to form the three σ-bonds) is in a p-orbital perpendicular to the plane of the σ-bonds. These p-orbitals on each carbon atom interact to produce a delocalized π-bond, which gives rings of high electron density above and below the ring of carbon atoms (see Figure 4.11 b).

Figure 4.11 - Some descriptions of the bonding in benzene

(a) Possible structures in terms of single and double bonds

(b) Delocalized description

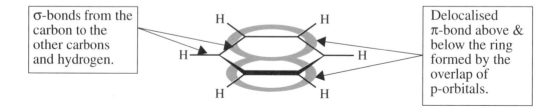

| σ-bonds from the carbon to the other carbons and hydrogen. | | Delocalised π-bond above & below the ring formed by the overlap of p-orbitals. |

An alternative approach is to consider the bonding in relation to the structures that are possible on a simple bonding model (i.e. Lewis structures). If there are two or more equivalent structures that can be drawn for a molecule, as shown for benzene in Figure 4.11 (a), then what actually occurs will be mid-way between these various possibilities. The equivalent simple structures are called **resonance structures** and the actual molecule that exists is referred to as a **resonance hybrid** of these structures. This resonance hybrid is more stable than any of the resonance structures, the difference in stability being known as the **resonance energy** (delocalisation energy and stabilisation energy are also sometimes used). This means that, for example, thermochemical calculations based on resonance structures give incorrect results.

Figure 4.12 - The thermochemistry of the hydrogenation of benzene

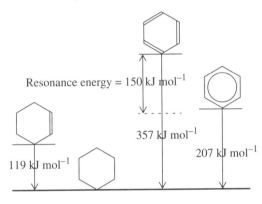

Resonance energy = 150 kJ mol^{-1}

357 kJ mol^{-1}

207 kJ mol^{-1}

119 kJ mol^{-1}

Cyclohexene reacts with hydrogen to form cyclohexane and this reaction releases 119 kJ mol^{-1} of heat energy. If benzene contained three double bonds (i.e. it was cyclohexatriene) then it would be reasonable to expect it to release three times this amount of energy (i.e. 357 kJ mol^{-1}). In fact only 207 kJ mol^{-1} of heat energy is released so that the delocalisation of the double bonds results in benzene being more stable by about 150 kJ mol^{-1}. This is illustrated in Figure 4.12.

Graphite, an allotrope of carbon, has bonding that is very similar to that in benzene. The hydrogens on benzene are replaced by other carbons, so that each carbon is bonded to three other carbons by σ-bonds, formed by sp^2 hybrid orbitals, and the p-orbitals on the carbon atoms interact to form a delocalised π-bond that extends in two dimensions throughout the graphite crystal. This gives a carbon-carbon **bond order** (the average of the bonds between the atoms) of $1\frac{1}{3}$. The structure of graphite is shown in Figure 4.24.

Another example of delocalized bonding is the carbonate ion shown in Figure 4.13. There are three equivalent resonance structures that can be drawn for this. Note the use of the double headed arrow ($\leftrightarrow$) used to join resonance structures. This should never be confused with, or substituted for, the equilibrium arrow $\rightleftharpoons$. The resonance hybrid has all the carbon-oxygen bonds part way between single and double bonds (specifically, the bond order is $1\frac{1}{3}$ as each is a double bond in 1 of the three resonance structures), with the negative charge equally distributed over all of the oxygens (to be more precise each oxygen has a $\frac{2}{3}$– charge as it carries a negative charge in 2 of the 3 resonance structures). The description of the carbonate ion in terms of delocalized bonding would be that the central carbon is sp^2 hybridized and that it forms σ-bonds to the three oxygens. There is then a delocalised π-bond formed by the p-orbitals on the carbon and the oxygens that also accommodates the extra electrons which give the ion its negative charge.

ADVANCED

Figure 4.13 - Delocalization in the carbonate ion

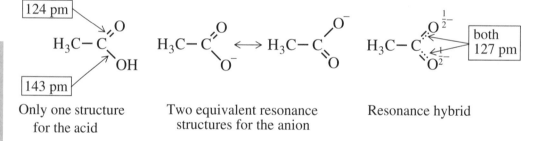

Resonance structures

Resonance hybrid   Delocalised description

It is sometimes difficult deciding exactly when delocalisation is likely to occur. Ethanoic acid and its anion, the ethanoate ion are very similar, however, delocalisation occurs in the anion, but not in the acid. The way that this may be predicted is from the fact that only one valid Lewis structure can be drawn for the acid, but there are two valid equivalent Lewis structures for the anion. The evidence that this interpretation is correct is that in the acid the two carbon-oxygen bond lengths are different, but in the anion the two bonds are equal and their length is between the lengths of the bonds in the acid.

Figure 4.14 - Bonding in ethanoic acid and the ethanoate ion

124 pm

143 pm

Only one structure
for the acid

Two equivalent resonance
structures for the anion

both
127 pm

Resonance hybrid

Two other examples of common species in which delocalisation occurs are ozone (O_3) and the nitrite ion (NO_2^-, also known as the nitrate(III) ion). In ozone the contributing resonance structures each have the central atom forming a dative single bond to one oxygen and a double bond to the other. A delocalised π-bond description would be that the oxygens all have sp^2 hybridization and the p-orbitals perpendicular to this interact to form a delocalised π-bond above and below the plane of the oxygen atoms.

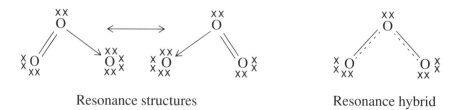

Resonance structures   Resonance hybrid

This predicts that the oxygen-oxygen bond length will be part way between the single bond found in hydrogen peroxide (HO-OH, 146 pm) and the double bond in the oxygen molecule (O=O, 121 pm). The empirically determined value of 128 pm fits with this prediction. Lewis diagrams for the possible resonance structures for the nitrite ion, which is isoelectronic with ozone, are shown below along with the resonance hybrid:

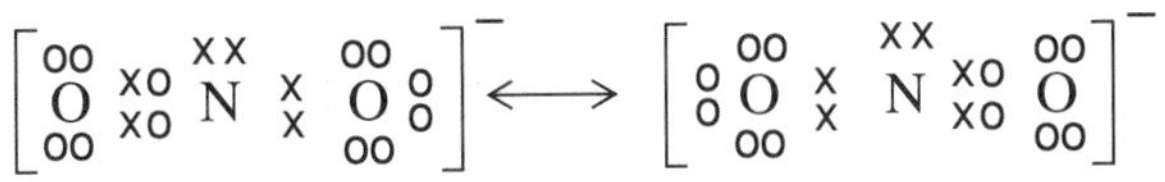

Resonance structures 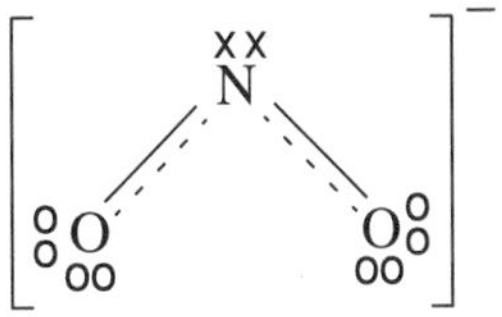   Resonance hybrid

Note that the predicted nitrogen-oxygen bond order is $1\frac{1}{2}$ and that the charge is shared equally over the two oxygen atoms. A similar approach can be used to predict the bonding in the nitrate(V) ion (see question 2 below).

EXERCISE 4.7

1. Which one of the following species cannot be adequately described by a single Lewis diagram?

    A NH_4^+
    B HCO_3^-
    C C_2H_2
    D OH^-

2. a)   Draw a Lewis diagram for the nitrate(V) ion.

    b)   Explain how this fails to adequately describe the shape of the nitrate(V) ion.

    c)   How is the bonding better described using the concept of delocalisation?

    d)   Describe how the atomic orbitals interact to produce a delocalised bond.

    e)   What bond order would you expect for the N-O bond in the nitrate(V) ion and what charge would you expect each oxygen atom to carry?

    f)   How would you expect the lengths of the N-O bonds in nitric(V) acid to compare with those in the nitrate(V) ion?

ADVANCED

4.8 INTERMOLECULAR FORCES

CORE

4.3.1 Describe the types of intermolecular force (hydrogen bond, dipole-dipole attraction and van der Waals' forces) and explain how they arise from the structural features of molecules.

All these intermolecular forces are weaker than covalent bonds. For substances of similar molar mass, hydrogen bonds are stronger than dipole-dipole attractions which are stronger than van der Waals' forces. Van der Waals' forces arise from the electrostatic attraction between temporary induced dipoles in both polar and non-polar molecules.

4.3.2 Describe and explain how intermolecular forces affect the boiling points of substances.

The hydrogen bond can be illustrated by comparing physical properties of: H_2O and H_2S; NH_3 and PH_3; C_3H_8, CH_3CHO and C_2H_5OH.   © IBO 2001

Covalent bonding between atoms can result in either a giant structure such as diamond, or in a molecular structure such as methane. In the latter weak forces exist **between** the molecules. If it were not for these then they would never condense to liquids and solids when cooled. There are three types of these **intermolecular forces** that will be dealt with in order of increasing strength.

a)   van der Waals' Forces

These forces are also sometimes referred to as London (after the Polish physicist Fritz London), or dispersion forces. They exist between all species as a result of the fact that a temporary dipole on one molecule resulting from the random movements of the electrons, especially in the valence shell, has an inductive effect on the neighbouring molecules. Thus, if one end of a molecule has an instantaneous positive charge then the electrons in a neighbouring molecule will be attracted to that end of the molecule. The net result is that the attractive forces between molecules are on average stronger than the repulsive forces.

The strength of these forces increases with the molar mass of the molecule, owing to an increase in the number of electrons and hence the size of the instantaneous dipoles. This effect can be seen, for example in the noble gases (helium boils at 4 K, xenon at 165 K) and the alkanes (methane boils at 111 K, hexane at 341 K). Another example of this trend is the halogens which all exist as non-polar diatomic molecules. As the molar mass of the molecules increases, so does the boiling point as shown in Figure 4.15:

Figure 4.15 - The variation of boiling point of the halogens with molar mass

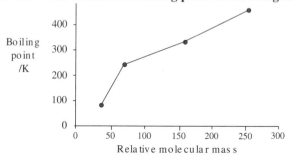

146

These forces are also only effective over a short range and so they are dependent on the surface area of the molecules that come into close contact with each other. The more elongated the molecule, the stronger the van der Waals' forces and the higher the boiling point. Pentane [CH_3-CH_2-CH_2-CH_2-CH_3] boils at 309 K, whereas its almost spherical isomer, dimethylpropane [$(CH_3)_4C$] boils at 283 K. Under certain circumstances van der Waals' forces can become quite strong, such as those between polymer chains in some common plastics, such as polythene. These long thin molecules have both a high molar mass and a very large surface area.

b)   Dipole-Dipole Forces

These occur because of the electrostatic attraction between molecules with permanent dipoles.

Electrostatic attraction

$$H^{\delta+}\!\!-\!Cl^{\delta-} ||||||||||||||||||||| \; H^{\delta+}\!\!-\!Cl^{\delta-}$$

These are significantly stronger than van der Waals' forces in molecules of a similar size, so that, even though both have similar molar masses, the boiling point of polar hydrogen chloride (188 K) is significantly higher than that of non-polar fluorine (85 K). Similarly, as shown in Figure 4.15, the boiling points of the non-polar noble gases (Ar, Kr and Xe) are considerably lower then the polar hydrogen halides of a similar molar mass (HCl, HBr and HI), because both will have van der Waals' forces between their molecules, but in addition to these the hydrogen halides will have dipole-dipole forces:

Figure 4.16 - A comparison of the boiling points of polar and non-polar substances

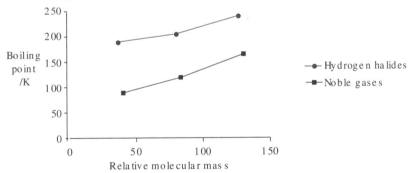

c)   Hydrogen Bonding

This occurs in molecules that contain **hydrogen** bonded to **nitrogen, oxygen** or **fluorine**. It occurs as a result of the interaction of a non-bonding electron pair on one of these atoms with a hydrogen atom that is carrying a high partial positive charge, as a result of being bonded to another of these small very electronegative atoms. As such it may be thought of as being part way between a dipole-dipole bond and a dative covalent bond. In the hydrogen bond, for maximum strength, the two atoms and the hydrogen should all be in a straight line. The hydrogen bonding interaction is illustrated in Figure 4.17 (in which X & Y are N, O or F).

Figure 4.17 - An illustration of hydrogen bonding

$$X^{\delta-} : \quad \boxed{\begin{array}{c}\text{Hydrogen} \\ \text{bond}\end{array}} \quad H^{\delta+}\!\!-\!Y^{\delta-}$$

Hydrogen bonding is usually considerably stronger than other intermolecular forces and has a large effect on the physical properties of the substances in which it occurs (see Section 4.10, page 152). Hydrogen peroxide (H_2O_2), of a similar molar mass to fluorine and hydrogen chloride mentioned above, has a boiling point of 431 K (158°C) - an increase of >250° over hydrogen chloride. Another set of examples is that propane C_3H_8 ($M_r = 44$), which has only van der Waals' force, boils at 231 K, ethanal CH_3-CO-H ($M_r = 44$) which is polar but cannot hydrogen bond, boils at 294 K, whereas ethanol CH_3CH_2OH ($M_r = 46$), which has intermolecular hydrogen bonds, boils at 352 K.

Hydrogen bonding has a profound effect on the boiling points of the hydrides of nitrogen (NH_3), oxygen (H_2O) and fluorine (HF) when compared to those of other elements in the same group of the periodic table. This is shown in Figure 4.18.

Figure 4.18 - The effect of hydrogen bonding on the boiling points of some hydrides

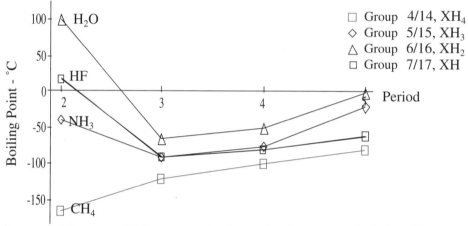

In the case of the group 4/14 compounds, the molecules are tetrahedral and hence non-polar, so that the only forces between them are van der Waals' forces. As a result they are always the compounds with the lowest boiling points. All of the other hydrides are less symmetrical and so will have some resultant dipole and hence a degree of dipole-dipole interaction as well as the van der Waals' forces. It can be seen that going from period 5 to period 4 to period 3 the boiling points decrease in all of the groups, because of the reduction in the strength of the van der Waals' forces with decreasing molar mass. In group 4/14 this trend continues into period 2, but in the other groups there is a sharp increase in boiling point on going from period 3 to period 2. This is explained by the existence of hydrogen bonding between molecules of ammonia (NH_3), water (H_2O) and hydrogen fluoride (HF), as well as van der Waals' forces. The deviation is most marked for water because each water molecule has two hydrogen atoms and two non-bonding electron pairs. This allows it to form two hydrogen bonds per molecule. Ammonia has only one non-bonding electron pair and hydrogen fluoride has only one hydrogen atom, so in both cases they can form only one hydrogen bond per molecule.

Water is one of the most strongly hydrogen bonded substances and this affects many other physical properties, such as the molar enthalpy of fusion (6.0 kJmol^{-1} for H_2O and only 2.4 kJmol^{-1} for H_2S) and molar enthalpy of vapourisation (41 kJmol^{-1} for H_2O and only 19 kJmol^{-1} for H_2S). It also accounts for many of its anomolous physical properties, such as ice having a density less than that of water. Because each water molecule can form four hydrogen bonds, ice has a structure in which each water molecule is hydrogen bonded to four others with tetrahedral symmetry. This produces a structure very similar to the diamond structure (see Figure 4.23), but with hydrogen bonds instead of covalent bonds. This is a very open structure with large empty spaces enclosed in it, hence the low density. Even when ice melts, this structure persists to some extent, which is why the density of liquid water increases when heated from 0°C to 4°C, the exact opposite of the effect of temperature on density in almost all other liquids.

The properties of many organic compounds are affected by the fact that hydrogen bonding can occur between their molecules, for example ethanoic acid (CH_3-CO-OH, $M_r = 60$, b.p. 391 K) is a liquid at room temperature and pressure, whereas butane (CH_3-CH_2-CH_2- CH_3, $M_r = 58$, b.p. 273 K) is a gas. Even in the gaseous state or in non-aqueous solution, the hydrogen bonding between pairs of ethanoic acid molecules persists, as shown below, so that its relative molecular mass appears to be ~120.

$$H_3C-C \overset{\displaystyle O \quad \text{H-bond} \quad H-O}{\underset{\displaystyle O-H \quad \text{H-bond} \quad O}{}} C-CH_3$$

Butane is insoluble in water, because its presence would disrupt the hydrogen bonding between water molecules, whereas ethanoic acid can form its own hydrogen bonds to water and hence is fully miscible. Water solubility even extends to compounds such as propanone (CH_3-CO-CH_3), which cannot form hydrogen bonds to other propanone molecules (it has no suitable hydrogen), but which can bond to water molecules (the oxygen bonds to the H-atom of a water).

Hydrogen bonding is also of great biological importance. It provides the basis for the pairing of bases in DNA (see Chapter 13) and the α-helix and β-sheet structures of protein molecules. The α-helix is in fact an example of **intramolecular hydrogen bonding**, i.e. hydrogen bonding within a molecule. This type of bonding can also occur in much simpler molecules and explains why the boiling point of 2-nitrophenol (216°C), which mainly bonds intramolecularly, and hence has weaker intermolecular forces, is significantly lower than that of 4-nitrophenol (279°C), which mainly bonds intermolecularly, as shown below.

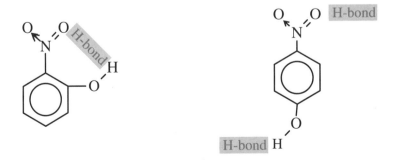

EXERCISE 4.8

1. In which one of the following compounds would hydrogen bonding occur?

A $COCl_2$

B PH_3

C H_2CO

D CH_3OH

2. Which one of the following molecules would you expect to have the highest boiling point?

A $CH_3- CH_2- CH_2- CH_2- CH_2- CH_3$

B $CH_3- CH(CH_3)- CH_2- CH_2- CH_3$

C $CH_3- CH_2- CH(CH_3)- CH_2- CH_3$

D $CH_3- C(CH_3)_2-CH_2- CH_3$

3. In which of the following substances would there be the strongest forces between the molecules?

A SiH_4

B $H_2C=O$

C CH_3-CH_3

D O_2

4. Which one of the following usually produces the weakest interaction between particles of similar molar mass?

A Hydrogen bonding

B Covalent bonds

C Dipole-dipole forces

D Van der Waals' forces

5. In which one of the following substances is hydrogen bonding **not** significant?

A Ice

B Polythene (polyethene)

C DNA

D Protein

6. Explain the following in terms of the intermolecular forces that exist.

a) At room temperature and pressure chlorine is a gas, bromine a liquid and iodine a solid.

b) Water is a liquid at room temperature and pressure, but hydrogen sulphide is a gas.

c) Ethanol (CH_3CH_2OH) has a much higher boiling point than its isomer methoxymethane (CH_3OCH_3).

d) Pentan-1-ol boils at 137°C, whereas pentan-3-ol boils at 116°C.

e) The boiling point of sulfur dioxide is 24°C higher than that of chlorine.

7. Explain why the boiling points of hydrogen fluoride, water and ammonia are significantly higher than those of the analogous compounds in the next period. What other effects on physical properties occur as a consequence of the bonding you describe? Give specific examples.

CORE

4.9 METALLIC BOND

4.4.1 Describe metallic bond formation and explain the physical properties of metals.

- *Metallic bonding is explained in terms of a lattice of positive ions surrounded by delocalized valence electrons. The delocalized electrons should be related to the high electrical conductivity, malleability and ductility of metals.* © IBO 2001

Metallic bonding occurs between atoms which all have low electronegativities. In a metal the atoms are all packed together as closely as possible in three dimensions - like oranges packed into a box. A regular arrangement of this type is known as a **lattice**. Because the metal atoms have many low energy unfilled orbitals, the valence electrons are delocalized amongst (i.e. shared by) all the atoms, so that no electron belongs to any particular atom and they are free to move throughout the metal. The atoms, having lost their valence electrons, are positively charged and are therefore better described as being cations. The attraction of these positive ions for the mobile electrons provides the force which holds the structure together. Thus a metallic structure is often described as consisting of a close packed lattice of positive ions with a mobile 'sea' of electrons, as illustrated in Figure 4.19.

Figure 4.19 - An illustration of the bonding in metals

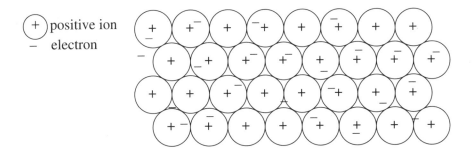

$\left(+\right)$ positive ion
$-$ electron

CORE

The attraction is between the ions and the mobile electrons and not between the ions themselves, so that the layers of ions can slide past each other without the need to break the bonds in the metal. This means that metals are malleable and ductile. If an atom of a different size is introduced (eg. carbon in steel) then it is less easy for the planes to slide, hence alloys (metals containing more than one type of atom) are usually harder than pure metals.

The delocalised electrons are free to move from one side of the lattice to the other when a potential difference is applied, so that they can carry an electric current. Metals are therefore good conductors of electricity. These mobile electrons also make them good conductors of heat and the interaction of these electrons with light produces the lustre characteristic of metals, at least when freshly cut.

The strength of the bond between the metal atoms depends on how many electrons each atom shares with the others. For example, the melting point of potassium (one e^-) is 337 K, calcium (two e^-s) is 1123 K and scandium (three e^-s) is 1703 K. It also depends on how far from the positive nucleus the electrons in the 'sea' are (i.e. depends on the ionic radius). For example, going down group 1 the melting point decreases from lithium (454 K), through sodium (371 K) to potassium (337 K). In some cases, such as sodium, the bonding is quite weak, so that the substance is soft and has low melting and boiling points. In most cases however metallic bonding is strong, so that the solid is quite hard, though still malleable, and has high melting and boiling points. Mercury, a metal that is one of two elements that is a liquid at room temperature and pressure (bromine is the other) is an obvious exception.

EXERCISE 4.9

1. Use the commonly accepted model of metallic bonding to explain why:

    a)   the boiling points of the metals in the third period increase from sodium to magnesium to aluminium.

    b)   metals are malleable.

    c)   metals conduct electricity in the solid state.

4.10 PHYSICAL PROPERTIES

4.5.1   Compare and explain the following properties of substances resulting from different types of bonding: melting and boiling points, volatility, conductivity and solubility.

Consider melting points, boiling points and volatility of similar substances, such as F_2, Cl_2, Br_2 and I_2, and substances with different types of bonding and different intermolecular forces. Students should be aware of the effect of impurities on the melting point of a substance.

The solubilities of compounds in non-polar and polar solvents should be compared and explained. Consider also the solubilities of alcohols in water as the length of the carbon chain increases.

4.5.2 Predict the relative values of melting and boiling points, volatility, conductivity and solubility based on the different types of bonding in substances. © IBO 2001

The physical properties of a substance depend on the forces between the particles that it is composed of. The stronger the bonding between these particles, the harder the substance and the higher the melting and boiling points, though the melting point is also very dependent on the extent to which the bonding depends on the existence of a regular lattice structure. The presence of impurities in a substance disrupts the regular lattice that its particles adopt in the solid state, weakening the bonding. Hence the presence of impurities always lowers the melting point of a substance. For this reason, melting point determination is often used to check the purity of molecular covalent compounds. Similarly, alloys have lower melting points than the weighted mean of their component metals. The volatility, i.e. how easily the substance is converted to a gas, also depends on the strength of these forces. Electrical conductivity depends on whether the substance contains electrically charged particles that are free to move through it. Solubility involves the intimate mixing of the particles of two substances (the solute and solvent). In order for it to take place the forces between the two types of particles in the mixture must be as strong, or stronger, than that between the particles in the two pure substances, though entropy changes (see Section 6.7, page 207) also play an important role in solubility.

In metals the hardness, volatility, melting point and boiling point all depend upon the number of valence electrons that the individual metal contributes to the delocalized electrons. It is the mobility of these delocalized electrons that allow metals to conduct electricity in all states. The malleability and ductility of metals results from the fact that the bonding is between the metal ions and these electrons, and not between the ions themselves. This allows one layer of the lattice to slide over another without the need to break the bonding. The forces between metal atoms are often quite strong and metal atoms cannot form bonds of comparable strength to substances that are held together by bonding of a different type (i.e. ionic or covalent). As a result metals do not dissolve in other substances unless they react with them chemically (e.g. sodium in water). Metals can however dissolve in other metals to form mixtures of variable composition called alloys, for example brass is an alloy of copper and zinc. To a limited extent non-metals can also be dissolved into metals to form alloys, the most common example being steel, which is iron with a small percentage of dissolved carbon. Alloys usually retain metallic properties, though an alloy is generally less malleable and ductile than the pure metal because the varying size of atoms in the lattice means that it is less easy for the layers to slide over each other.

The ions in an ionic compound are held together by strong electrostatic forces in all three dimensions, so that they are non-volatile, with high melting points and high boiling points. Hence they are all solids at room temperature and pressure. If one layer moves a fraction then ions of the same charge will come next to each other and so repulsion rather than attraction will result. This causes the substance to break, hence ionic solids as well as being hard, are also brittle.

The particles that make up an ionic solid are electrically charged ions. In the solid however, these are firmly held in place and cannot move to carry an electric current.

When the substance is molten, or in solution, the ions can move freely and carry an electric current. Ionic compounds therefore conduct when molten and in solution, but not in the solid state.

The strong forces between the ions mean that ionic substances are insoluble in most solvents. Water however is a very polar molecule hence water molecules can bond to both anions and cations because of the attraction between the partial charge on the atoms of the water molecule and the charge on the ion. The interaction between ions and the polar water molecules is illustrated in Figure 4.20.

Figure 4.20 - The hydration of anions and cations by polar water molecules

● The oxygen atoms carry a slight negative charge

○ The hydrogen atoms carry a slight positive charge

As a result of this hydration of the ions, ionic substances are more soluble in water than in non-polar solvents. If however the forces between the ions are very strong, then the ionic substance will not even dissolve in water. There are definite patterns to the solubility of ionic compounds and the solubility of most ionic substances can be correctly predicted using a few simple solubility rules:

• All nitrates are soluble.

• All sodium, potassium and ammonium compounds are soluble.

• All sulphates are soluble, except $BaSO_4$. $CaSO_4$ is only sparingly soluble.

• All chlorides, bromides and iodides are soluble, except those of silver. Lead halides are sparingly soluble in cold water, but quite soluble in boiling water.

• All other compounds are insoluble, though some, such as $Ba(OH)_2$ and $Ca(OH)_2$ are sparingly soluble.

The hydration energy (ie. the strength of the interaction of the water molecule with the ion) increases with the charge on the ion and decreases with the size of the ion. It is also greater for cations than for anions as a result of their smaller size and the angular shape of the water molecule giving better packing. As a result the hydration energy is greatest for small, highly charged cations such as Al^{3+}.

In the substances of the two kinds described above the bonding is uniform throughout the substance and this kind of structure is described as a 'giant' structure. Covalent bonding can lead to two very different structures. The first of these is a **giant covalent** structure (also known as network covalent or macromolecular structure). In this all of the atoms in a substance are joined to each other by strong covalent bonds, so that giant covalent substances are very hard and have very high melting and boiling points. The strong forces holding the substance together also means that giant covalent substances are solids at room temperature and pressure, and insoluble in all solvents. All of the electrons are usually firmly held in the covalent bonds so the substance does not conduct electricity (with the exception of graphite).

By contrast, in the second type of covalent structure, known as a **molecular covalent** structure, there are strong covalent bonds (**intra**molecular forces) between the atoms making up the molecule, but only weak **inter**molecular forces between these molecules (see Section 4.8, page 146). Because the bonds between one molecule and another are so weak, molecular covalent substances are often liquids or gases at room temperature and pressure, whereas the other structure types almost always give rise to solids. The state depends on the strength of the intermolecular forces. In the case of the halogens, as the molar mass and hence the strength of the van der Waals' forces increases (see Section 4.8, page 146) the state of the element (at room T & P) changes from gas (F_2 & Cl_2) to liquid (Br_2) to solid (I_2). Molecular covalent substances are usually quite soft as a result of the weak forces between the molecules of the solid. They will often dissolve in non-polar solvents, such as hexane, which also have weak van de Waals' forces between the molecules, but are insoluble in very polar solvents like water. This is because water is very strongly hydrogen bonded, so that inclusion of a non-polar molecule into its structure would require the breaking of these bonds. As with giant covalent substances, the electrons in molecular covalent substances are firmly held in the bonds and so they do not conduct electricity. The bonding in a molecular covalent substance is illustrated in Figure 4.21.

Figure 4.21 - An illustration of molecular covalent bonding

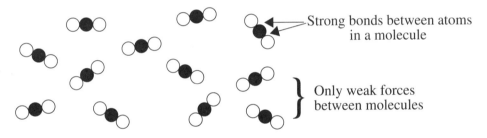

Strong bonds between atoms in a molecule

Only weak forces between molecules

Hydrogen bonding can however have a large effect on the properties of molecular covalent substances. These forces are much stronger than other intermolecular forces so that hydrogen bonded substances have much higher melting and boiling points than molecules of a similar molar mass that cannot hydrogen bond. For example, at room temperature and pressure ethanol (CH_3-CH_2-OH) is a liquid (b.p. = 351 K), whereas its isomer methoxymethane (CH_3-O-CH_3), which is unable to form hydrogen bonds, is a gas (b.p. = 248 K). In solids, hydrogen bonding can often result in the crystals being harder, and more brittle, than those solids with other types of intermolecular forces. Sucrose (sugar) would be a good example of such a substance. Molecules that can hydrogen bond, such as ethanol and sucrose, are usually quite soluble in water. This is because the molecule can form hydrogen bonds to the water to compensate for the water-water hydrogen bonds broken. In alcohols the hydroxyl (-OH) group forms hydrogen bonds, but the hydrocarbon chain disrupts the hydrogen bonding in the water. This means that as the length of the hydrocarbon chain increases, the solubility of the alcohol in water decreases. This also explains why ethanoic acid (CH_3-CO-OH) is fully miscible with water, but benzoic acid (C_6H_5-CO-OH) is only sparingly soluble.

The physical properties associated with different types of structure are summarised in Table 4.8, along with some typical examples.

Table 4.8 - structural types and physical properties - a summary

Structure type Property	Giant Metallic	Giant Ionic	Giant Covalent	Molecular Covalent
Hardness and malleability	Variable hardness, malleable rather than brittle	Hard, but brittle	Very hard, but brittle	Usually soft and malleable unless hydrogen bonded
Melting and boiling points	Very variable, dependent on No. of valence electrons	High - m.p. usually over 500 °C	Very high - m.p. usually over 1000 °C	Low - m.p. usually under 200 °C. Liquids and gases are molecular covalent
Electrical and thermal conductivity	Good in all states	Do not conduct as solids, but do conduct when molten or in solution	Do not conduct in any state (graphite is an exception).	Do not conduct in any state
Solubility	Insoluble except in other metals to form alloys	More soluble in water than other solvents	Insoluble in all solvents	More soluble in non-aqueous solvents, unless they can hydrogen bond to water
Examples	Iron, copper, lead	Sodium chloride, calcium carbonate	Carbon (diamond) silicon dioxide (sand)	Carbon dioxide, ethanol, iodine

14.4.1 Describe and explain the structures and properties of diamond, graphite and fullerene.

Students should recognize the type of hybridization present in each allotrope and the delocalization of electrons in graphite and C$_{60}$ fullerene. © IBO 2001

Diamond is the most common example of a substance that has a giant covalent structure. Each carbon atom in diamond is sp^3 hybridised and is joined to four others arranged tetrahedrally, so that there is strong bonding in all three dimensions. The arrangement of carbon atoms in diamond is illustrated in Figure 4.22. Diamond is probably the best example of a giant covalent structure.

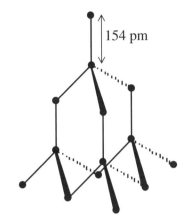

Figure 4.22 - The arrangement of carbon atoms in diamond

154 pm

Silicon dioxide (SiO$_2$, sometimes called silica), which occurs commonly as quartz and (in a less pure form) sand, has a very similar structure to diamond, except that each carbon is replaced by a silicon and the C–C bonds are replaced by an oxygen 'bridging' between the silicon atoms. A two dimensional diagram of the bonding is shown in Figure 4.23 below.

Figure 4.23 - A two dimensional representation of the bonding in silicon dioxide

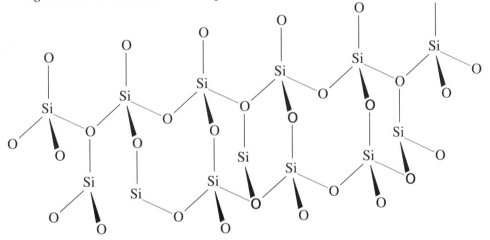

Graphite is a second allotrope of carbon. (Allotropes are different forms of an element that exist in the same physical state, ozone and normal diatomic oxygen molecules are another example of allotropes.) It is unusual in that it comprises a giant covalent network in two dimensions, but has only weak van der Waals' forces between these sheets of carbon atoms, see Figure 4.24 below. There is a delocalised π-bond between all of the sp^2 hybridised carbon atoms in a given sheet, so that the bond order of the carbon-carbon bonds is $1\frac{1}{3}$, hence the carbon-carbon bond length is slightly less than that found in diamond. The distance between the sheets is quite large and the forces between them quite small, hence they can easily slide over each other. This results in graphite being a soft solid used as a lubricant and, as layers of carbon are easily rubbed off on to paper, it

ADVANCED

is used in 'lead' pencils. The delocalised electrons between the layers are free to move so that graphite is a good conductor of electricity in two dimensions.

Figure 4.24 - The structure of graphite

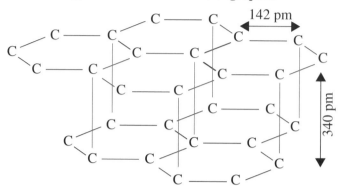

The **fullerenes** are a recently discovered allotrope of pure carbon. They contain approximately spherical molecules made up of five- and six-membered carbon rings. The fullerene that has been most completely investigated is C_{60}, illustrated in Figure 4.25. In fullerenes each sp^2 hybridised carbon is bonded by sigma bonds to three other carbons , but because the surface of the sphere is not planar, there is little delocalisation of the unpaired bonding electrons (contrast to graphite). Chemically C_{60} behaves as an electron deficient molecule readily accepting electrons from reducing agents to form anions with a variety of charges. Addition reactions, similar to those

Figure 4.25 - Skeletal structure of fullerene–60 (C_{60})

found in alkenes, can also occur. Unlike diamond and graphite fullerenes are molecular, hence they will dissolve in non-polar solvents and have comparitively low melting points. For example C_{60} is moderately soluble in non-polar solvents, such as methylbenzene, and sublimes at about 800 K. Fullerenes have interesting compressibility properties and some of their derivatives have unusual electrical properties. Closely related to the fullerenes are the nanotubes, which comprise capped cylinders of carbon atoms bonded in a very similar manner to the fullerenes.

A SUMMARY OF CHEMICAL BONDING

Chemical bonding is the interaction of valence electrons that results in atoms, of the same or different kinds, binding together. The number of bonds an atom forms depends mainly on the number of valence electrons. The type of bonding that occurs depends mainly on how strongly the valence electrons are attracted by the nucleus, i.e. on the electronegativity of the elements.

Ionic bonding involves electron transfer between different atoms of very different electronegativities. The atom with low electronegativity loses electron(s) to form a positively charged cation. The atom of high electronegativity gains electron(s) to form a negatively charged anion. Because of the strong electrostatic attraction between opposite charges these ions come together to form a regular array known as an ionic crystal lattice. Because there are strong forces throughout the whole solid, the solid is hard and brittle, with a high m.p. and b.p.. The ions allow it to conduct electricity when molten or in solution, but not as a solid. They are often soluble in water because the ions can bond to the polar water molecules.

Covalent bonding involves the sharing of electrons between two atoms of high electronegativity. This can result in single bond (1 shared e- pair), double bond (2 shared e- pairs), or triple bond (3 shared e- pairs). [Single σ-bond; double σ- + π-bond; triple σ- + 2 π-bonds. σ-bonds generally formed by hybrid orbitals, π-bonds by perpendicular p-orbitals. Delocalised π-bonds involve more than two atoms and do not have one electron pair per bond.] If the covalent bond is between two different types of atoms the electrons will not be evenly shared and the bond will be a polar bond. Covalent bonding results in two kinds of structures, giant covalent and molecular covalent.

Giant covalent structures are totally joined together by covalent bonds. As a result they are very hard, have very high m.p. and b.p., do not dissolve in solvents and do not conduct electricity.

Molecular covalent structures contain small groups of atoms joined by covalent bonds to form molecules. Molecules have a definite shape that results from the repulsion between electron pairs, both in the bonds [σ-bonds only] and in non-bonding electron pairs. If the molecule contains polar bonds then in very symmetrical molecules their polarity will cancel to give a non-polar molecule, but if less symmetrical they will not cancel, resulting in a polar molecule.

Between molecules there are only weak intermolecular forces. There are three kinds of these. The weakest are van der Waal's forces, which exist between all species as a result of the inductive effect of instantaneous dipoles. Next strongest are the dipole-dipole forces that result from the electrostatic attraction between polar molecules. The strongest kind is hydrogen bonding, which occurs in molecules containing a hydrogen atom bonded to N, O or F. The properties of molecular covalent substances are dictated by the intermolecular forces. As these are weak they are gases, liquids or soft, low melting solids. They do not conduct electricity and are generally soluble in non-polar solvents rather than water, unless they can hydrogen bond to water. Hydrogen bonding increases the hardness, m.p. and b.p.

Metallic bonding occurs between atoms of low electronegativity. The valence electrons are completely shared by all atoms, so they can be regarded as a close packed lattice of cations in a 'sea' of mobile electrons. Hence metals conduct electricity even in the solid state. There are no specific bonds so the layers can slide over each other making metals malleable and ductile. The bond strength increases with the number of valence electrons, but generally the bonds are strong giving a high m.p. and b.p.

ADVANCED

EXERCISE 4.10

1. A substance that is a gas is likely to

    A   have a molecular covalent structure.
    B   be a compound of a metal.
    C   have a giant covalent structure.
    D   have its atoms held together by metallic bonds.

2. If an element in group 2 of the periodic table formed a compound with an element in group 7/17 of the periodic table, the compound formed is likely to

    A   conduct electricity in the solid state.
    B   have a low boiling point.
    C   dissolve in non-polar solvents.
    D   be a crystalline solid.

3. Ethanol (C_2H_5OH) is a molecular covalent compound. When pure ethanol boils the gas consists of

    A   a mixture of carbon dioxide and water.
    B   carbon, hydrogen and oxygen.
    C   water and ethanol.
    D   ethanol only.

4. Which one of the following substances would you expect to have the lowest boiling point?

    A $CsCl$
    B $SrSO_4$
    C Sc_2O_3
    D $AsCl_3$

5. Which one of the following would **not** conduct an electric current?

    A   Solid sodium chloride
    B   Liquid sodium chloride
    C   Aqueous sodium chloride
    D   Solid mercury

6. Which one of the following substances would you expect to be most soluble in water?

    A $CH_3 - CH_2 - CH_2 - CH_2 - CH_2 - CH_3$
    B $H_2N - CH_2 - CH_2 - CH_2 - CH_2 - NH_2$
    C $Cl - CH_2 - CH_2 - CH_2 - CH_2 - Cl$
    D $CH_3 - CH_2 - CH_2 - O - CH_2 - CH_2 - CH_3$

7. Molten lead and molten lead(II) bromide both conduct electricity. Which one of the following statements relating to this is true?

   A Both undergo a chemical change when they conduct.
   B Both conduct by the movement of charged particles.
   C Both will also conduct in the solid state.
   D Both contain mobile electrons.

8. Rubidium chloride is an ionic compound, naphthalene is a molecular covalent solid, scandium is a metal and silicon carbide has a giant covalent structure.

   a) Which of these substances would you expect to have the highest melting point?

   b) Which of these substances would you expect to have the lowest melting point?

   c) Which of these substances would you expect to be soluble in water?

   d) Which of these substances would you expect to conduct electricity as a solid?

   e) Which of these substances would you expect to be soluble in a non-polar solvent, such as hexane?

   f) Which of these substances would you expect to conduct electricity only when molten, or in solution?

   g) Which of these substances would you expect to be malleable?

   h) Which of these substances is an element rather than a compound?

   i) Which of these substances would you expect to be the hardest solid?

   j) Which of these substances contains charged particles?

9. Magnesium is a silver-grey metal, iodine a black crystalline non-metal. Under suitable conditions, they will react together to form a white compound, magnesium iodide.

   a) Give two physical properties that you would expect to be different for magnesium and iodine.

   b) How would the appearance of a mixture of magnesium and iodine compare with that of their compound?

   c) What is the formula of the compound that they form? What kind of bonding is present in it?

   d) How would you expect the behaviour of magnesium iodide to compare with that of a mixture of magnesium and iodine if both were shaken with water?

   e) Describe how a non-polar solvent, such as tetrachloromethane could be used to separate the mixture of magnesium and iodine into its components.

10. In cookery class Anita expresses surprise that sugar melts so much more easily than salt, when in many other ways they are similar. Her friend Jenny, wanting to show off the fact that she is taking science, says

"That's because sugar has covalent bonds and salt has ionic bonds. Ionic bonds are stronger than covalent ones"

As is often the case, there is some truth in what Jenny says. Using suitable examples, explain why this statement as it stands is not accurate and then express more accurately what Jenny was meaning.

11. Ethanoic acid (CH_3-CO-OH) reacts with sodium hydroxide to form sodium ethanoate (CH_3-CO-O⁻ Na⁺) and with ethanol to form ethyl ethanoate (CH_3-CO-O-CH_2-CH_3). Explain why ethanoic acid and sodium ethanaote both dissolve in water, but ethyl ethanoate does not.

12. The graph below shows the melting points of representative oxides of the elements in the third period of the periodic table. Explain how the type of bonding present in these compounds varies across the period and how this is reflected in the graph.

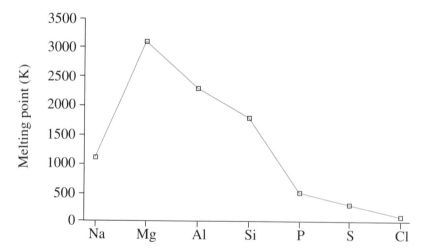

STATES OF MATTER

5

Chapter contents

5.1 THE STATES OF MATTER

5.1.1   Describe and compare solids, liquids and gases as the three states of matter.

The movement of particles, the attractive forces between particles and interparticle spacing should be described. A molecular level description of what happens when evaporation, boiling, condensing, melting and freezing occur should be given. Students should understand what is meant by the term diffusion.

5.1.2   Describe kinetic theory in terms of the movement of particles whose average energy is proportional to absolute temperature.

Kinetic theory should be interpreted in terms of ideal gases consisting of point masses in random motion whose energy is proportional to absolute temperature. Students should be able to describe what happens when the temperature is changed.

5.1.3   Describe the Maxwell-Boltzmann energy distribution curve.

5.1.4   Draw and explain qualitatively Maxwell-Boltzmann energy distribution curves for different temperatures.

© IBO 2001

There are three states of matter that are commonly encountered - solid, liquid and gas. These may be differentiated by their physical properties. Solids have an almost fixed volume and a fixed shape, liquids have an almost fixed volume, but they take on the shape of their container, whereas the volume and the shape of gases can vary, so that they completely fill the container that they are in.

Kinetic theory proposes that all matter is composed of particles in continual motion and it seeks to explain the properties of the different states in terms of the interaction of these particles. The absolute temperature (i.e. in Kelvin, K) of a substance is considered to be proportional to the mean kinetic energy of its particles, so that at 0 K the particles are motionless, and at 200 K they have twice as much kinetic energy as they do at 100 K. The nature of the forces between the particles depends on the type of bonding present, as discussed in Chapter 4.

In a solid the bonding results in the particles having fixed positions, but the particles can vibrate around these positions. Each particle is strongly bonded to its nearest neighbours, giving the solid a fixed shape. The particles are closely packed together so solids have quite high fixed densities, ie. they are not easily compressed. If the positions of the particles form a regular lattice, then the solid is crystalline and said to have long range order, otherwise it is described as amorphous.

In liquids the forces between particles are still quite strong, but less dependent on position, so the attractive forces are continually breaking and reforming, hence it only has short range order. This means that the particles continually 'jostle' each other, but they can move slowly at random throughout the body of the liquid which has no fixed shape. The particles are however still quite closely packed together, so that the density and compressibility of the solid and liquid states are usually quite similar to each other.

In a gas the forces between the particles are unable to keep them together. This means that there is rapid random motion which causes the gas to completely fill its container.

The volume, and hence the density, of a gas is variable and depends upon the pressure and temperature. The density of a gas is however typically much less (at room temperature and pressure ~1000 times less) than those of liquids and solids, hence collisions occur as separate events. The properties of the states of matter, and their explanation in terms of kinetic theory, are summarised in Table 5.1.

Table 5.1 - Solids, liquids and gases

State	Shape	Density	Inter-particle forces	Particle movement	Particle separation	Illustration
Solid	Fixed - has a definite shape	Fixed and quite high	Greater than average K.E.	Vibrate around fixed point	Close together	
Liquid	Variable - fills container to a given level	Fixed and quite high	Similar to average K.E.	Random motion - continual jostling	Close together	
Gas	Variable - totally fills container	Variable and quite low	Much less than average K.E.	Random motion - separated collisions	Widely separated	

In a solid the kinetic energy of the vibrating particles is not enough to allow them to overcome the forces between them, so that they remain in fixed positions. As the temperature is increased the vibrational kinetic energy also increases and eventually the the vibration will start to overcome the forces maintaining a regular order, allowing random motion, so that the solid will melt to a liquid. The opposite changes occur when a liquid freezes, i.e. the particles will cease to have enough kinetic energy to allow attractive forces to be continually broken and reformed. Note therefore that melting is an endothermic change and freezing an exothermic one (see Section 6.1, page 180). The melting/freezing point is the temperature at which the solid and liquid are in equilibrium. As the temperature of the liquid increases, the particles will have greater and greater kinetic energy and so eventually they will have enough energy to overcome all attractive forces and escape from the liquid to become a gas. Evaporation can occur at any temperature and in this process it is just the faster moving particles near the surface that escape. The mean kinetic energy of the remaining particles is of course reduced by the loss of the most energetic particles, so that the temperature of the liquid falls. Boiling only occurs at a particular temperature, dependent on pressure, and energy has to be supplied to maintain this temperature. The boiling point is the temperature at which a gas (at a particular pressure) is in equilibrium with the liquid. In this case the change of state occurs throughout the body of the liquid, forming bubbles. In condensing, particles that come close to each other no longer have enough energy to totally break free from other particles. Boiling and evaporation require energy to overcome attractive forces and are therefore endothermic processes. Conversely, condensation is exothermic.

The pressure of a gas is a result of the particles of the gas colliding with the walls of the container. The more frequent the collisions and the greater the impact when they strike the wall, then the greater the pressure. If a gas is compressed, then there are more particles within a given volume and so there are more collisions with the wall, hence the pressure increases. Similarly as the temperature is increased, the speed of the molecules increases, so collisions again occur more frequently and there are also greater impacts from each collision. These again cause the pressure to increase. If an increase in pressure is to be avoided when a gas is heated, then it must be allowed to expand, thus reducing the collision frequency, so as to compensate. Similarly a decrease in temperature results in a decrease in pressure and/or volume. The properties of gases are dealt with in much greater detail in Section 5.2, page 170.

In kinetic theory, a gas is considered to be made up of a large number of point masses with no attractive forces between them, in rapid random motion. Support for this comes from **Brownian motion**, the jerky movement of smoke particles ascribed to the continual random bombardment of these by sub-microscopic particles in the air. As stated above, the average kinetic energy is proportional to the absolute temperature. Not all particles have the same energy so there is a distribution of kinetic energy, and hence velocity, amongst the particles of the gas, known as the Maxwell-Boltzmann distribution, shown in Figure 5.1 below. As with cars on a freeway, some are moving more rapidly and others more slowly. There is a mean speed, though because the curve is asymmetric, this does not coincide with the most probable speed. This distribution of kinetic energy is of great importance in considering the rates of chemical reactions (see section 7.6, page 239).

Figure 5.1 - The distribution of speeds amongst particles of a particular gas at various temperatures

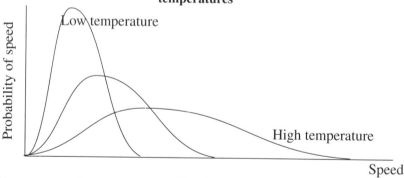

Because all gases have the same average kinetic energy at a given temperature, the average speed of the particles of a gas (v) will depend on the mass of the particle (as K.E. $= \frac{1}{2}mv^2$), the greater the mass the lower the speed. If a gas is released, from say a bottle of perfume, then it will slowly spread out to fill the space that it is in. This is a process known as **diffusion** (movement from a region of high concentration to one of low concentration). It occurs only slowly because, even though the particles are moving very rapidly, they are continually colliding with one another, resulting in changes in direction and a slowing down of the diffusion process. As a result, diffusion in liquids is much slower than in gases. Lowering the pressure decreases the number of collisions between gas molecules and hence increases the rate of diffusion. Also, because diffusion depends on the speed of movement of a gas, it is faster at higher temperatures. As heavier gas particles move more slowly than light ones, the rate of diffusion of a gas decreases as its molar mass increases.

[EXTENSION: A more mathematical statement of this, known as Graham's law of diffusion, states that.

$$\text{Rate of diffusion} \propto \frac{1}{\sqrt{M_r}}; \quad \text{therefore:} \quad \text{Rate of diffusion} = Q \times \frac{1}{\sqrt{M_r}}$$

or

$t \propto \sqrt{M_r}$; therefore $t = Q \times \sqrt{M_r}$ (t is the time taken for a given volume to diffuse)

By measuring the rate of diffusion, or time for diffusion, with a known gas the constant of proportionality (Q) may be found and hence by repeating the procedure, under identical conditions, with an unknown gas, the molar mass of that gas may be found.]

EXERCISE 5.1

1. In which one of the following elements, at room temperature and pressure, are the particles quite close together, disordered and moving in a random manner?

    A   Lead
    B   Chlorine
    C   Sulfur
    D   Mercury

2. Which one of the following changes in conditions would give the greatest increase in the frequency with which gas particles collide with the walls of the container?

    A   Raising the temperature of the gas and increasing the volume of the gas.
    B   Raising the temperature of the gas and decreasing the volume of the gas.
    C   Lowering the temperature of the gas and decreasing the volume of the gas.
    D   Lowering the temperature of the gas and increasing the volume of the gas.

3. When a bicycle tyre is pumped up at constant temperature, assuming any change in its volume can be neglected, the pressure increase comes from the fact that

    A   the gas particles are moving faster.
    B   the collisions with the wall occur at a greater frequency.
    C   each collision has a greater impact on the wall than before.
    D   two or three of the changes mentioned in A, B and C occur simultaneously.

4. 'Floating' balloons are filled with helium. Explain why these always deflate more quickly than those blown up with air.

5. Explain why your hand feels cold when alcohol is wiped on the back of it.

6. The graph shows the distribution of molecular speeds in three gas samples. Explain how the samples must differ if

a) They are all the same gas, but under different conditions.

b) They are all under the same conditions, but they are for different gases.

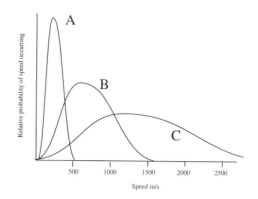

7.

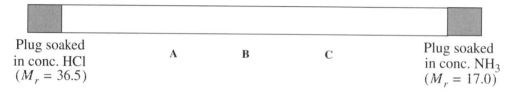

Plug soaked in conc. HCl ($M_r = 36.5$)

A   B   C

Plug soaked in conc. NH_3 ($M_r = 17.0$)

The apparatus above is set up and left to stand for about half an hour. At this time a white smoke of ammonium chloride, formed by the reaction of the ammonia and hydrochloric acid, is observed to form in a part of the tube.

a) Write a balanced equation for the reaction that occurs.

b) Explain how the reagents reach the point where the reaction occurs.

c) What name is given to this process?

d) At which point (A, B or C) does the smoke form?

e) Explain why the reaction occurs at this point.

f) If the process were carried out at a higher temperature, how would this affect the time taken for the reaction to occur?

g) Explain why temperature has this effect.

8.

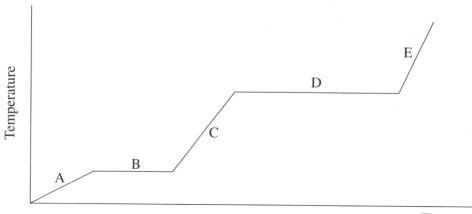

The graph above shows the variation of temperature with time that occurs when a solid is heated with a constant power heater .

a) What states are represented by the regions A, C and E?

b) What processes are represented by the two horizontal sections (B and D)?

c) Explain why during these horizontal periods the input of energy does not produce any increase in temperature.

d) What is the **major** change in the arrangement of the particles that occurs during B? What is the major change during D?

e) The process is repeated using an impure sample of the solid. What change will there be in the temperature at which B occurs.

f) When the same amount of another substance was used under identical conditions, the length of time needed for process D to occur was much shorter. What may be deduced from this?

5.2 THE GASEOUS STATE

5.1.5 Describe qualitatively the effects of temperature, pressure and volume changes on a fixed mass of an ideal gas.

5.1.6 State the ideal gas equation, $PV = nRT$.

5.1.7 Apply the ideal gas equation in calculations.

Use the relationship between P, V, n and T for gases. Students should be familiar with $\dfrac{P_1 V_1}{T_1} = \dfrac{P_2 V_2}{T_2}$ *and be able to calculate molar volume.* © IBO 2001

Ideal gases are those in which the volume of the particles and the attractive forces between them can be neglected under the prevailing conditions and the kinetic energy of the particles is proportional to the absolute temperature.

Consider n moles of particles in random motion contained within a volume V. According to the kinetic theory of gases, when these particles collide with the wall, their impact on the wall produces the pressure (P).

- If the volume is halved then the collision rate will double because the particles have on average only half the distance to travel between collisions with the wall, i.e. $P \propto \dfrac{1}{V}$.

- If the number of moles of particles (n) is doubled, then the number of collisions will double, so the pressure doubles, i.e. $P \propto n$.

- If the absolute temperature (T) doubles then the average kinetic energy doubles, so the average speed increases by $\sqrt{2}$. [The kinetic energy is given by the expression $E_k = \frac{1}{2}mv^2$. If the absolute temperature is doubled, the average kinetic energy doubles, but the average speed of the particles is only increased by $\sqrt{2}$, owing to the v^2 term in the expression.] The greater average speed does however increase both the collision rate (by $\sqrt{2}$) and the impact of each collision (also by $\sqrt{2}$), so that the overall effect is to double the pressure, i.e. $P \propto T$.

Combining these three proportionalities:

$$P \propto \frac{nT}{V} \text{ or } P = R\frac{nT}{V}$$

where R is a constant, known as the gas constant. This is known as the **ideal gas equation** and it is more commonly written in the form:

$$PV = nRT$$

The value of R will depend on the units used to measure P, n, T and V, but if P is in kPa, n is in moles, T is in Kelvin and V is in dm^3, then R has a value of 8.314 J K^{-1} mol^{-1}.

A corollary of this is that the same volumes of different gases at the same temperature and pressure contain the same number of moles (or molecules) - this is known as Avogadro's law. In other words, the pressure exerted by the gas is independent of the mass of the gas particles. This is because at a given temperature a heavier gas particle, whilst having a greater impact each time it collides with the walls, has a lower average speed (because the kinetic energy must be the same) and hence collides less frequently and at a lower speed. These two effects exactly cancel each other out and so the expression holds for all ideal gases.

The ideal gas law only holds for 'ideal gases', i.e. those in which the particles have zero volume, there are no attractive forces between the particles and the kinetic energy of the particles is proportional to the absolute temperature. For many real gases this approximation holds good at low pressures and high temperatures, but it tends to break down at low temperatures and high pressures, especially for substances with strong intermolecular forces, such as hydrogen bonding. At low temperature and high pressure (when the separation between the molecules is smaller) attractive forces become significant so the observed pressure is less than that predicted because these attractive forces cause the particles to decelerate as they are about to strike the wall. Also under these conditions the total volume of the gas is less, so that occupied by the particles becomes significant. The free volume for the particles to move in is less than the total volume.

The ideal gas equation may be used to find any one of the terms, provided that the others are known or remain constant. For example we can calculate the volume occupied by 1 mole of a gas (so $n = 1$) at room temperature (say $20.0°C = 293.0$ K, note that this conversion to K is vital!) and pressure (101.3 kPa):

$$V = \frac{nRT}{P}$$

$$= \frac{1 \times 8.314 \times 293}{101.3}$$

$$= 24.05 dm^3$$

Hence the volume of gas under known conditions may be used to calculate the amount of gas. Similarly, if the volume of a known mass of gas is measured at a particular temperature and pressure, then the ideal gas equation may be used along with the formula $n = \frac{m}{M}$ to calculate the molar mass of the gas.

EXAMPLE

3.376 g of a gas occupies 2.368 dm^3 at 17.6°C and a pressure of 96.73 kPa, what is its molar mass?

CORE

SOLUTION

$$n = \frac{PV}{RT}$$

$$= \frac{96.73 \times 2.368}{8.314 \times 290.6} \quad \text{(n.b. temperature is in K)}$$

$$= 0.09481$$

$$M = \frac{m}{n}$$

$$= \frac{3.376}{0.09481}$$

$$= 35.61 \text{ g mol}^{-1}$$

If the density of a gas under known conditions is given, then the same method may be used substituting the standard volume (usually 1 dm³) for V and the density for the mass m. This technique may also be used to determine the molar mass of a volatile liquid by making the measurements at a temperature above the boiling point of the liquid. One common technique is to inject a weighed sample into a heated gas syringe and measuring the volume of the vapourising sample.

In order to convert the volume, pressure and temperature of a **given amount** of gas (so n and R are both constant) from one set of conditions (1) to another set of conditions (2), when the third variable remains constant, the ideal gas equation simplifies to:

Boyle's law $P_1 V_1 = P_2 V_2$ (at constant T)

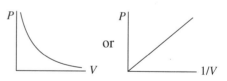

Charles' Law $\dfrac{V_1}{T_1} = \dfrac{V_2}{T_2}$ (at constant P)

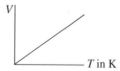

Pressure Law $\dfrac{P_1}{T_1} = \dfrac{P_2}{T_2}$ (at constant V)

These may be combined into the expression:

$$\frac{P_1 V_1}{T_1} = \frac{P_2 V_2}{T_2}$$

In this and the preceding equations, T must be in Kelvin, but P and V may be in any units, provided these units are used throughout.

EXAMPLE

A syringe contains 50 cm³ of gas at 1.0 atm pressure and 20°C. What would the volume be if the gas were heated to 100°C, at the same time compressing it to 5.0 atm pressure?

SOLUTION

$$\frac{P_1V_1}{T_1} = \frac{P_2V_2}{T_2}$$

$$\therefore \frac{1.0 \times 50}{293} = \frac{5.0 \times V_2}{373}$$

$$V_2 = 50 \times \frac{1.0}{5.0} \times \frac{373}{293}$$

$$= 13 \text{cm}^3$$

In mixtures of gases, the particles behave independently of each other and this leads to Dalton's law which states that the total pressure of a gaseous mixture is equal to the sum of the pressures of the individual gases (known as partial pressures).

$$P_{total} = P_A + P_B + P_C + \ldots$$

This also means that the partial pressure of any gas will be equal to the total pressure of the gas multiplied by the fraction of that gas in the mixture (either by moles or volume, because of Avogadro's law).

$$P_A = P_{total} \times \frac{n_A}{n_{total}} \quad \text{or} \quad P_A = P_{total} \times \frac{V_A}{V_{total}}$$

EXAMPLE

If 20 cm³ of oxygen is mixed with 60 cm³ of hydrogen at a total pressure of 300 kPa, find the partial pressure of the oxygen.

SOLUTION

$$P_{O_2} = P_{total} \times \frac{V_{O_2}}{V_{total}} \quad \left(\text{or} \quad \frac{n_{O_2}}{n_{total}} \right)$$

$$= 300 \times \frac{20}{20 + 60}$$

$$= 75 \text{ kPa}$$

The concept of partial pressures can also be used to correct the volume of a gas collected over water for the water vapour present.

EXAMPLE

$100 cm^3$ of hydrogen is collected over water at standard atmospheric pressure (101.3 kPa) and at a temperature at which the vapour pressure of water is 7.30 kPa. What volume of pure hydrogen (at standard atmospheric pressure) is present?

SOLUTION

$$P_{H_2} = P_{total} - P_{H_2O} = 101.3 - 7.30 = 94.0 \text{ kPa}$$

The temperature is constant, so:

$$P_1 V_1 = P_2 V_2$$

$$\therefore 94.0 \times 100 = 101.3 \times V_2$$

$$V_2 = \frac{94.0 \times 100}{101.3}$$

$$= 92.8 \text{ cm}^3$$

EXERCISE 5.2

1. A flask contains $250 cm^3$ of gas at $65°C$ and atmospheric pressure. The flask is then heated to $650°C$. The pressure of the gas will increase by a factor of about

A   2
B   10
C   250
D   585

2. The pressure on $600 cm^3$ of gas is increased from 100 kPa to 300 kPa at constant temperature. What will the new volume of gas be?

A $200 cm^3$
B $300 cm^3$
C $1200 cm^3$
D $1800 cm^3$

3. A gas cylinder contains compressed air at a pressure of 50 MPa. Assuming that the air contains 20% oxygen by volume, what is the partial pressure of the oxygen in the cylinder?

A   50 MPa
B   40 MPa
C   20 MPa
D   10 MPa

4.   Which one of the following is **not** a property of an ideal gas?

A   The particles have negligible volume.
B   The particles have zero mass.
C   The particles have no attractive forces between them.
D   The mean kinetic energy of the particles is proportional to the absolute temperature.

5.   1 dm³ of gas in a container at –73°C is allowed to expand to 1.5 dm³. What must the temperature be so that the pressure remains constant?

A   -36°C
B   0°C
C   27°C
D   73°C

6.   4.00 dm³ of air at 0°C and a pressure of 2.00 atmospheres, is heated to 273°C and the pressure increased to 8.00 atmospheres. What will the new volume of the gas be?

A   1.00 dm³
B   2.00 dm³
C   8.00 dm³
D   32.00 dm³

7.   2.00 dm³ of a gas at a pressure of 1000 kPa is allowed to expand at constant temperature until the pressure drops to 300 kPa. What will the new volume of the gas be?

A   3.00 dm³
B   3.33 dm³
C   6.00 dm³
D   6.66 dm³

8.   What volume is occupied by 0.0200 g of oxygen gas at 27°C and a pressure of 107 kPa?

A   0.466 dm³
B   0.029 dm³
C   0.015 dm³
D   0.002 dm³

9.   A sample of air at a pressure of 97 kPa was analysed and the mole fractions of the major constituents were determined as nitrogen 0.78, oxygen 0.21 and argon 0.01. Calculate the partial pressure of each gas in the sample.

10. A container is filled with 0.20 moles nitrogen and 0.10 moles carbon dioxide to give a total pressure of 1.0 atmosphere. Calculate the partial pressure of the nitrogen.

11. In a particular experiment aluminium was reacted with dilute hydrochloric acid according to the equation:

$$2\ Al_{(s)} + 6\ HCl_{(aq)} \Rightarrow 2\ AlCl_{3\ (aq)} + 3\ H_{2\ (g)}$$

355 cm^3 of hydrogen was collected over water at 25.0°C (at which temperature the vapour pressure of water is 3.20 kPa) and a total pressure of 100.0 kPa.

a) What was the partial pressure of hydrogen in the sample?
b) How many moles of hydrogen were collected?
c) If 0.300 g of aluminium was used with excess acid, what was the percentage yield of hydrogen?

12. a) Give a brief account of the kinetic theory of gases and the way in which it predicts the dependence of pressure on temperature, volume and amount of gas.
b) Use this theory to explain the fact that different gases diffuse at different rates.
c) Explain why at s.t.p. one mole of hydrogen and one mole of sulfur hexafluoride occupy almost the same volume.
d) Under what conditions would you expect one mole of these two compounds, though gaseous, to occupy significantly different volumes? Explain why this occurs.

13. A steel cylinder contains 32 dm^3 of hydrogen at 4.0×10^6 Pa and 39°C. Calculate:

a) the volume that the hydrogen would occupy at s.t.p. (0°C and 101.3 kPa).
b) the mass of hydrogen in the cylinder.

14. The following readings were taken during the determination of the molar mass of a gas by direct weighing. If the experiment was carried out at 23.0°C and 97.7 kPa, calculate the molar mass of the gas.

Mass of evacuated flask	183.257 g
Mass of flask and gas	187.942 g
Mass of flask filled with water	987.560 g

15. 50 cm^3 of propane and 50 cm^3 of butane are mixed.

    a)   What is the percentage of propane in the mixture
            i)   by mole?   ii)   by mass?

    b)   If the total pressure of the gas is 150 kPa, calculate the partial pressures of the two gases in the mixture.

    c)   If there were a hole in the container, which of the two gases would leak out faster? Give reasons for your choice.

CORE

16. Two 5 dm^3 flasks of equal volume are connected by a narrow tube of negligible volume. Initially the two flasks are both at 27°C and contain a total of 2 moles of an ideal gas at a pressure of 100 kPa. One flask is heated to a uniform temperature of 127°C while the other is kept at 27°C. Assuming the volume of the flasks does not alter, calculate the final pressure of the gas and the number of moles in each flask.

5.3 PHASE DIAGRAMS

Phase diagrams show the way in which the stable state of a substance is affected by changes in temperature and pressure. A typical phase diagram is shown in Figure 5.2 below. The regions in which a state is stable are labelled and the solid lines are called phase boundaries:

Figure 5.2 - A phase diagram for a typical substance

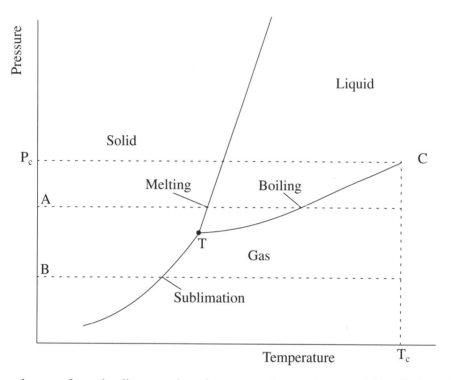

As can be seen from the diagram, there is one set of conditions at which all three phases are stable. This point (T) is called the triple point. As the diagram shows, if a substance is heated at a constant pressure (dotted line A) above the triple point, then it first of all melts and then boils. If it is heated at a pressure below the triple point (dotted line B) then it will sublime (i.e. change straight from a solid to a gas). If the pressure is standard atmospheric (101.3 kPa) this will be the normal melting/boiling/sublimation point. The line dividing the liquid and gas stops at a point (C) called the critical point. At this point density of the liquid and gas are equal so that it is no longer possible to discriminate between them. One consequence of this is that it is not possible to liquefy a gas by simply compressing it if the temperature is above that of the critical point. This temperature is known as the critical temperature (T_c) and the pressure required to liquefy the gas at this temperature is the critical pressure (P_c). Strictly speaking, at temperatures below the critical temperature, gases should be referred to as vapours. Note that for most substances increasing the pressure very slightly increases the melting point of a solid. Water is different, because ice is less dense than liquid water at the melting point, and in this case that phase boundary would slope slightly backwards.

ENERGETICS

6

Chapter contents

6.1 EXOTHERMIC AND ENDOTHERMIC REACTIONS

6.1.1 Define the terms exothermic reaction, endothermic reaction and standard enthalpy change of reaction (ΔH^θ).

Standard enthalpy change is heat transferred under standard conditions- pressure 101.3 kPa, temperature 298 K. Only ΔH can be measured, not H for the initial or final state of a system.

6.1.2 State the relationship between temperature change, enthalpy change and whether a reaction is exothermic or endothermic.

Combustion of organic compounds are good examples of exothermic reactions.

6.1.3 Deduce, from an enthalpy level diagram, the relative stabilities of reactants and products and the sign of the enthalpy change for the reaction.

If the final state is more stable (lower on the enthalpy level diagram), this implies that $H_{final} < H_{initial}$ and ΔH must be negative. Energy must be released in going to a more stable state.

6.1.4 Describe and explain the changes which take place at the molecular level in chemical reactions.

Relate bond formation to the release of energy and bond breaking to the absorption of energy.

6.1.5 Suggest suitable experimental procedures for measuring enthalpy changes of reactions in aqueous solution.

Explore different reactions operating at constant pressure (open containers). Use of the bomb calorimeter is not required. © IBO 2001

Thermochemistry is the study of energy changes associated with chemical reactions. Most chemical reactions absorb or evolve energy, usually in the form of heat, though chemical reactions can also produce light and mechanical energy. Thermochemistry studies the amounts of energy associated with these changes. The energy evolved or absorbed in a reaction is totally unrelated to the rate at which it occurs.

Enthalpy (*H*, also known as heat content) is the total energy of a system, some of which is stored as chemical potential energy in the chemical bonds. In chemical reactions, bonds are made and broken, but the energy absorbed in breaking bonds is never exactly equal to that released in making new bonds. As a result, all reactions are accompanied by a change in the potential energy of the bonds and hence an enthalpy change. There is no 'absolute zero' for enthalpy, so absolute enthalpies for particular states cannot be measured, but the change in enthalpy that occurs during a reaction can be measured. This enthalpy change, known as the enthalpy of reaction, can be measured and is given the symbol ΔH. It is equal to the difference in enthalpy between the reactants and the products (see Figure 6.1) assuming that the reaction occurs with no change in temperature or pressure, or that these conditions are restored to their initial values. If this is the case and any other factors affecting a system's enthalpy do not change, then ΔH is equal to the change in the energy of the chemical bonds. Strictly speaking the term enthalpy change only applies to reactions that occur at **constant pressure**, but in the laboratory using open beakers and test tubes, this is most often the case.

A useful comparison may be made with gravitational potential energy. If an object gains gravitational potential energy, then it must absorb energy from its surroundings (e.g. from the muscles of the person lifting it) and if this is in the form of heat energy, heat is lost from the surroundings and they cool down. Similarly if a chemical reaction leads to an increase in enthalpy (i.e. the total enthalpy of the products is less than the total enthalpy of the reactants, so the enthalpy change, ΔH, is positive), then heat energy is absorbed from the surroundings and either they get cooler or heat from an external source must be provided. This is described as an **endothermic reaction**. If the chemicals lose enthalpy (i.e. the enthalpy change, ΔH, is negative), then the heat energy lost by the chemicals is gained by the surroundings and they get hotter. This is described as an **exothermic reaction**. A comparison would be that a falling object loses gravitational potential energy and this is converted into sound (and a little heat) when it hits the floor. Most spontaneous reactions (i.e. ones that occur, without heating, on mixing the reagents and hence are capable of doing useful work) are exothermic, but spontaneous endothermic reactions do occur (e.g. dissolving ammonium chloride). This is summarised in Table 6.1:

Table 6.1 – Summary of exothermic and endothermic changes

Type of reaction	Heat energy change	Temperature change	Relative enthalpies	Sign of ΔH
Exothermic	Heat energy evolved	Becomes hotter	$H_p < H_r$	Negative (−)
Endothermic	Heat energy absorbed	Becomes colder	$H_p > H_r$	Positive (+)

Enthalpy changes during the course of a reaction may also be represented by energy level diagrams. In an exothermic reaction the products are more stable than the reactants (bonds made are stronger than bonds broken), so that ΔH is negative. In an endothermic reaction the opposite is true. This is shown in Figure 6.1 below for both an exothermic and an endothermic reaction. In these energy level diagrams, the horizontal axis (x–axis) signifies the transition from reactants to products and hence is sometimes referred to as the reaction coordinate.

Figure 6.1 – Energy level diagrams of reactions

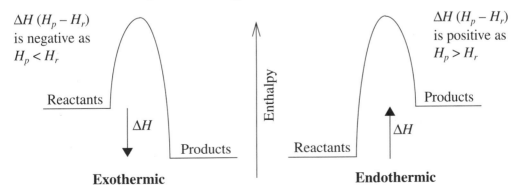

ΔH $(H_p - H_r)$ is negative as $H_p < H_r$

Reactants

ΔH

Products

Exothermic

Enthalpy

ΔH $(H_p - H_r)$ is positive as $H_p > H_r$

Products

Reactants

ΔH

Endothermic

The enthalpy change for a reaction is best shown by writing the balanced chemical equation for the reaction, with the enthalpy change written alongside it. It is vital to include state symbols in all thermochemical equations because changes of state have their own enthalpy changes associated with them. The enthalpy change will of course vary with the amount of the limiting reagent, so by convention it is given for molar amounts in the equation as it is written. The units may therefore be given as kJ mol^{-1} (to indicate that it refers to molar quantities) or simply as kJ (because it may not be for one mole of all the species involved). The former convention is used throughout this book. Using the thermal decomposition of sodium hydrogencarbonate as an example, a thermochemical equation would be:

$$2\ NaHCO_{3\ (s)} \Rightarrow Na_2CO_{3\ (s)} + H_2O_{(l)} + CO_{2\ (g)}\ \Delta H = +91.6\ kJ\ mol^{-1}$$

Note that ΔH is positive, indicating the reaction is endothermic. It is advisable to actually put in the '+' sign rather than just assuming that its absence indicates a positive quantity, as this concentrates the mind on whether the sign should be positive or negative. It is however also correct, though perhaps less common to write:

$$NaHCO_{3\ (s)} \Rightarrow \tfrac{1}{2}Na_2CO_{3\ (s)} + \tfrac{1}{2}H_2O_{(l)} + \tfrac{1}{2}CO_{2\ (g)}\ \Delta H = +45.8\ kJ\ mol^{-1}$$

so as to focus on the amount of sodium hydrogencarbonate. Hence the need to always quote an equation. Note that the basic unit of enthalpy is the Joule (J), but the quantities involved in chemical enthalpy changes are quite high, so that it is more convenient to use kilojoules (kJ, 1 kJ = 10^3 J).

By definition an enthalpy change must occur at constant pressure, but the exact numerical value will depend slightly on the exact conditions, such as the pressure and the temperature at which the reaction is carried out. For convenience thermochemical standard conditions have been defined as 25°C (298 K), standard atmospheric pressure (101.3 kPa) and the concentration of all solutions being 1 mol dm^{-3}. Note that the temperature is different from standard temperature and pressure (s.t.p.), which is 0°C (273 K). Thermochemical quantities that relate to standard conditions are often indicated by a 'standard' sign ($\ominus$) as a superscript after the quantity (e.g. $\Delta H^{\ominus}$), or even more correctly by also including the temperature as a subscript (e.g. $\Delta H^{\ominus}_{298}$). Frequently however, as in this text, standard conditions are simply assumed.

EXERCISE 6.1

1.   If a reaction is endothermic

   A ΔH is negative and heat is absorbed.
   B ΔH is positive and heat is absorbed.
   C ΔH is positive and heat is evolved.
   D ΔH is negative and heat is evolved.

2. A reaction gives out heat. This means that

A   the reaction only involves making new bonds.
B   the reaction only involves breaking existing bonds.
C   the bonds made are stronger than the bonds broken.
D   the bonds broken were stronger than the bonds made.

3. In the enthalpy level diagram shown

A   the reactants are more stable than the products and the reaction is endothermic.
B   the products are more stable than the reactants and the reaction is endothermic.
C   the reactants are more stable than the products and the reaction is exothermic.
D   the products are more stable than the reactants and the reaction is exothermic.

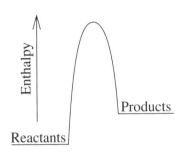

4. When magnesium is added to dilute sulfuric acid, the temperature of the acid rises.

a)   Write a balanced equation for the reaction of magnesium with sulfuric acid.
b)   Is the reaction exothermic or endothermic?
c)   Explain what this implies in terms of the chemical potential energy contained in the reactants and the products.
d)   Draw an energy level diagram for this reaction, clearly label on this the enthalpy of reaction.

5. Consider the formation of chlorine monoxide (Cl_2O) from its elements

a)   What bonds must be broken? Does this process absorb or release energy?
b)   What bonds are made? Does this process absorb or release energy?
c)   Explain what is meant by the term "enthalpy change".
d)   In this case the bonds made are less strong than those broken, will the enthalpy change be positive or negative ?
e)   Will the formation of (Cl_2O) from its elements be an endothermic or exothermic change?

6.2 CALCULATION OF ENTHALPY CHANGES

6.2.1   Calculate the heat change when the temperature of a pure substance is altered.

Students should be able to calculate the heat change for a substance given the mass, specific heat and temperature change.

6.2.2   Explain that enthalpy changes of reaction relate to specific quantities of either reactants or products.

Enthalpy changes are measured in joules (J) and are often quoted in kJ mol^{-1} of either a reactant or a product.

6.2.3   Analyse experimental data for enthalpy changes of reactions in aqueous solution.

6.2.4   Calculate the enthalpy change for a reaction in aqueous solution using experimental data on temperature changes, quantities of reactants and mass of solution.

Enthalpy change of an acid-base reaction could be investigated.   © IBO 2001

When the temperature of a substance increases, heat energy must be absorbed from the surroundings. The amount of heat required will depend on how much of the substance there is to heat (i.e. its mass, m), what the substance is made of (i.e. its specific heat capacity, s) and the amount by which its temperature is being increased (ΔT). The amount of heat energy released when a substance cools can be calculated in the same way:

$$\text{Heat energy} = m.s.\Delta T$$

For example the energy required to heat 50.0 g of water (specific heat = 4.18 J g^{-1} K^{-1}) from 20.0°C to 60.0°C ($\Delta T = 40.0$°C) is:

$$
\begin{aligned}
\text{Heat energy} \ &= \ ms\Delta T \\
&= \ 50.0 \times 4.18 \times 40.0 \\
&= \ 8360 \text{J} \\
&= \ 8.36 \text{kJ}
\end{aligned}
$$

The heat capacity of an object is the amount of energy required to increase its temperature by 1°C (i.e. m.s). Thus heating a calorimeter with a heat capacity of 50 J K^{-1} by 12°C will require $50 \times 12 = 600$ J of energy.

Heat changes are usually measured by a technique known as calorimetry. In this the temperature change of a liquid inside a well insulated container, known as a calorimeter, is measured before and after the change. For many chemical reactions a styrofoam (i.e. expanded polystyrene) cup is a convenient calorimeter because it has a very low (i.e. for most purposes negligible) heat capacity and it is a good insulator. If calorimeters made of other materials are used, for example in a combustion experiment, then the heat absorbed by the calorimeter must be added to that absorbed by the liquid:

$$\text{Heat absorbed} = (m.s.\Delta T)_{\text{liquid}} + (m.s.\Delta T)_{\text{calorimeter}}$$

Calorimetry depends on the assumption that all the heat involved changes the temperature of the calorimeter and its contents, i.e. that no heat is gained from/lost to the surroundings. That is why it is important that calorimeters are well insulated. Nevertheless heat exchange with the surroundings is the major source of error in all thermochemistry experiments in school laboratories. It may be minimised by increasing the insulation, especially by fitting an insulated lid, but significant errors are inevitable, especially in reactions where a gas is evolved. Errors in combustion experiments, where a hot gas is being used to heat liquid in a calorimeter, are even greater. This source of error always leads to ΔH values that are numerically less than literature values. Thermometers used often only read to $\pm 0.1°C$ or even worse, so that uncertainty in the value of the temperature change can also be a major source of inaccuracy.

The enthalpy change that occurs in a reaction is quoted for molar amounts in the chemical equation as it is usually written, so for example the equation

$$2\ Mg_{(s)} + O_{2\ (g)} \Rightarrow 2\ MgO_{(s)} \quad \Delta H = -1200\ kJ\ mol^{-1}$$

means that 1200 kJ of heat are evolved (as ΔH is negative) when 2 moles of magnesium react completely with 1 mole of oxygen. Thus if 0.600 g of magnesium $= \dfrac{0.600}{24.3}$ moles) is burnt, then the amount of heat produced is:

$$\frac{1}{2} \times \frac{0.600}{24.3} \times 1200 = 14.8\ kJ$$

Often chemical reactions occur in aqueous solution and the energy evolved or absorbed alters the temperature of the water the reactants are dissolved in. Water is usually in excess and has a very high specific heat capacity, so that to a first approximation, the heat energy required to change the temperature of the other substances present may be ignored, in comparison to that needed to heat the water.

If for example 20.0 cm³ of exactly 2 mol dm⁻³ aqueous sodium hydroxide is added to 30.0 cm³ of hydrochloric acid of the same concentration, the temperature increases by 12.0°C. The total volume of aqueous solution is 50.0 cm³ (20 + 30) and the density of water (also assumed for dilute aqueous solutions) is 1.00 g cm⁻³, hence the mass of the aqueous solution is 50.0g. The amount of heat required to heat the water can be calculated:

$$\begin{aligned}
\text{Heat required} &= ms\Delta T \\
&= 50.0 \times 4.18 \times 12.0 \\
&= 2508\,J \\
&= 2.51\,kJ
\end{aligned}$$

This heat is equal to the heat energy evolved by the reaction

$$H^+_{(aq)} + OH^-_{(aq)} \Rightarrow H_2O_{(l)}$$

The hydroxide ion was the limiting reagent (amount of NaOH $= c.V = 2 \times 0.0200 = 0.0400$ moles, amount of HCl $= 2 \times 0.0300 = 0.0600$ moles), so the reaction of 0.0400 moles evolved this amount of heat energy. The enthalpy of reaction can therefore be calculated as:

$$\Delta H = 2.51 \times \frac{1}{0.0400}$$

$$= 62.7$$

But as the reaction is exothermic the sign of ΔH must be negative, therefore

$$\Delta H = -62.7 \text{ kJ mol}^{-1}.$$

EXERCISE 6.2

In this section, assume the specific heat capacity of water and all dilute aqueous solutions to be 4.18 kJ $dm^{-3}K^{-1}$ (equivalent to 4.18 J $g^{-1}K^{-1}$).

1. How much heat energy is required to increase the temperature of 10 g of nickel (specific heat capacity 440 J kg^{-1} K^{-1}) from 50°C to 70°C?

    A   4.4 J
    B   88 J
    C   4400 J
    D   88000 J

2. Copper has a specific heat capacity of 400 J kg^{-1} K^{-1}. If a 50 g cylinder of copper absorbs 800 J of energy, by how much will its temperature rise?

    A   5°C
    B   20°C
    C   40°C
    D   320°C

3. The enthalpy of combustion of ethanol (C_2H_5OH) is 1370 kJ mol^{-1}. How much heat is released when 0.200 moles of ethanol undergo complete combustion?

    A   30 kJ
    B   274 kJ
    C   1370 kJ
    D   6850 kJ

4.
$$H_{2(g)} + \tfrac{1}{2}O_{2(g)} \Rightarrow H_2O_{(l)}$$

ΔH for the reaction above is –286 kJ mol^{-1}. What mass of oxygen must be consumed to produce 1144 kJ of energy?

    A   4 g
    B   32 g
    C   64 g
    D   128 g

5. When 4.0 g of sulfur is burnt in oxygen, 40 kJ of heat is evolved. What is the enthalpy change for the combustion of sulfur?

A   10 kJ
B   40 kJ
C   160 kJ
D   320 kJ

6. In thermochemistry experiments carried out in a school laboratory the major source of error is usually

A   heat losses to the surroundings.
B   accurate measurement of the volumes of liquids.
C   innacuracies in the concentrations of the solutions.
D   impurities in the reagents.

7. When 25 cm^3 of 2 mol dm^{-3} aqueous sodium hydroxide is added to an equal volume of hydrochloric acid of the same concentration, the temperature increases by 15°C. What is the enthalpy change for the neutralisation of sodium hydroxide by hydrochloric acid?

A $25 \times 2 \times 15 \times 4.18$ kJ mol^{-1}

B $50 \times 2 \times 15 \times 4.18$ kJ mol^{-1}

C $\dfrac{25 \times 15 \times 4.18}{2}$ kJ mol^{-1}

D $\dfrac{50 \times 15 \times 4.18}{2 \times 25}$ kJ mol^{-1}

8. When 8.00 g of ammonium nitrate completely dissolved in 100 cm^3 of water, the temperature fell from 19.0°C to 14.5°C. Calculate the enthalpy of solution of ammonium nitrate.

9. In cooking 'Crepe Suzette' a tablespoon of brandy is poured over the pancakes and then it is ignited.

a)   If the volume of brandy in a tablespoon is 10 cm^3 and the brandy is 30% ethanol by volume, what volume of ethanol is present?

b)   The density of ethanol is 0.766 g cm^{-3}. What mass of ethanol is there in the tablespoon of brandy?

c)   The molar mass of ethanol is 46 g mol^{-1}. How many moles of ethanol were there in the tablespoon?

d)   Write a balanced equation for the complete combustion of one mole of ethanol.

e)   The standard enthalpy change for this reaction is –1350 kJ mol^{-1}. How much heat is given out when the brandy on the Crepe Suzette burns?

10. A camping stove, burning butane, was used to heat 500 g of water from 20°C until it was boiling. Heating this amount of water from 20°C to boiling with an electrical heater requires 168 kJ of energy.

a) If the pot was made out of aluminium and it weighed 100 g, how much heat energy was required to heat the pot (the specific heat capacity of aluminium is 875 J kg^{-1} K^{-1})?

b) What is the total energy required to heat the pot and water?

c) When the water started to boil, the stove weighed 14.5 g less than it had initially. How many moles of butane (C_4H_{10}) were used to heat the pot and water?

d) What is the enthalpy of reaction, in kJ mol^{-1}, of butane with air?

e) The accepted value for the enthalpy of combustion of butane is 2874 kJ mol^{-1}. Explain why you think the two values are so different.

6.3 HESS'S LAW

6.3.1 Determine the enthalpy change of a reaction which is the sum of two or more reactions with known enthalpy changes.

Use examples of simple two- and three-step processes. Students should be able to construct simple enthalpy cycles, but will not be required to state Hess's law.

© IBO 2001

The principle of conservation of energy states that energy cannot be created or destroyed. In chemistry terms this means that the total change in chemical potential energy (i.e. enthalpy change) must be equal to the energy lost or gained by the system. It also means that the total enthalpy change on converting a given set of reactants to a particular set of products is constant, irrespective of the way in which the change is carried out. This is known as **Hess's Law**. This principle holds irrespective of whether a particular reaction could actually be carried out in practice.

For example sodium hydrogencarbonate can be directly reacted with hydrochloric acid to produce sodium chloride, carbon dioxide and water:

$$NaHCO_{3\,(s)} + HCl_{(aq)} \Rightarrow NaCl_{(aq)} + CO_{2(g)} + H_2O_{(l)} \qquad \Delta H_1$$

The reaction, to give exactly the same products, could also be carried out by first heating the sodium hydrogencarbonate and then reacting the sodium carbonate produced with the hydrochloric acid:

$$2\,NaHCO_{3(s)} \Rightarrow Na_2CO_{3(s)} + CO_{2(g)} + H_2O_{(l)} \qquad \Delta H_2$$
$$Na_2CO_{3(s)} + 2\,HCl_{(aq)} \Rightarrow 2\,NaCl_{(aq)} + CO_{2(g)} + H_2O_{(l)} \qquad \Delta H_3$$

If these equations are added together, the Na_2CO_3 cancels and the result is equal to twice the overall equation given.

$$2\,NaHCO_{3(s)} + 2\,HCl_{(aq)} \Rightarrow 2\,NaCl_{(aq)} + 2\,CO_{2(g)} + 2\,H_2O_{(l)}$$

Hess's Law states that the total enthalpy change for the two stage reaction must be equal to the single stage process, i.e.

$$2\,\Delta H_1 = \Delta H_2 + \Delta H_3$$

Note the factor of two occurs because the equation for the direct reaction, as usually written involves only one mole of $NaHCO_3$ being converted to one mole of $NaCl$, whereas the route via Na_2CO_3 would usually be written for the conversion of two moles.

This may also be shown in the form of an **enthalpy cycle**.

$$2\,NaHCO_{3\,(s)} + 2\,HCl_{(aq)} \xrightarrow{\quad 2\Delta H_1 \quad} 2\,NaCl_{(aq)} + 2\,CO_{2(g)} + 2\,H_2O_{(l)}$$

$$\Delta H_2 \searrow \qquad \nearrow \Delta H_3$$

$$Na_2CO_{3(s)} + CO_{2(g)} + H_2O_{(l)} + 2\,HCl_{(aq)}$$

Energetics

The use of Hess's Law is particularly important in determining enthalpy changes for reactions for which direct measurement is difficult (i.e. not easy in practice) or impossible (i.e. the reaction in question does not occur). In the example considered above, ΔH_2 would be difficult to measure in practice because it involves heating the substance. Both ΔH_1 and ΔH_3 can be easily determined by standard calorimetric methods, and values of -140 kJ mol^{-1} and -370 kJ mol^{-1} can be found respectively. Hence ΔH_2 can be calculated as

$$\Delta H_2 = 2\Delta H_1 - \Delta H_3 = 2(-140) - (-370) = +90 \text{ kJ mol}^{-1}$$

Another important example is the enthalpy change for the formation of compounds, such as the alkanes, which cannot be formed by the direct combination of the elements. This is discussed in more detail in Section 6.7 page 203.

EXERCISE 6.3

1. Below are four reactions, or series of reactions. Which of these would have an **overall** enthalpy change different from the others?

    A $NaOH_{(s)} + HCl_{(aq)} \Rightarrow NaCl_{(aq)} + H_2O_{(l)}$
    B $NaOH_{(s)} + H_2O_{(l)} \Rightarrow NaOH_{(aq)}$ and $NaOH_{(aq)} + HCl_{(aq)} \Rightarrow NaCl_{(aq)} + H_2O_{(l)}$
    C $NaOH_{(s)} + CO_{2(g)} \Rightarrow NaHCO_{3(s)}$
        and $NaHCO_{3(s)} + HCl_{(aq)} \Rightarrow NaCl_{(aq)} + H_2O_{(l)} + CO_{2(g)}$
    D $HCl_{(aq)} + \frac{1}{2}MgO_{(s)} \Rightarrow \frac{1}{2}MgCl_{2(aq)} + \frac{1}{2}H_2O_{(l)}$

        and $\frac{1}{2}MgCl_{2(aq)} + NaOH_{(s)} \Rightarrow NaCl_{(aq)} + \frac{1}{2}Mg(OH)_{2(s)}$

2. Given the enthalpy changes of the reactions below

    $2 H_2O_{2(aq)} \Rightarrow 2 H_2O_{(l)} + O_{2(g)}$ $\Delta H = -200$ kJ mol^{-1}
    $2 H_{2(g)} + O_{2(g)} \Rightarrow 2H_2O_{(l)}$ $\Delta H = -600$ kJ mol^{-1}
    what will be the enthalpy change for $H_{2(g)} + O_{2(g)} \Rightarrow H_2O_{2(aq)}$?

    A -200 kJ mol^{-1}
    B -400 kJ mol^{-1}
    C -600 kJ mol^{-1}
    D -800 kJ mol^{-1}

3. Iron and chlorine react directly to form iron(III) chloride, not iron(II) chloride, so that it is not possible to directly measure the enthalpy change for the reaction

$$Fe_{(s)} + Cl_{2(g)} \Rightarrow FeCl_{2(s)}$$

The enthalpy changes for the formation of iron(III) chloride from the reaction of chlorine with iron and with iron(II) chloride are given below. Use these to calculate the enthalpy change for the reaction of iron with chlorine to form iron(II) chloride.

$$2\,Fe_{(s)} + 3\,Cl_{2(g)} \Rightarrow 2\,FeCl_{3(s)} \quad \Delta H = -800 \text{ kJ mol}^{-1}$$
$$2\,FeCl_{2(s)} + Cl_{2(g)} \Rightarrow 2\,FeCl_{3(s)} \quad \Delta H = -120 \text{ kJ mol}^{-1}$$

4. The enthalpies of combustion of ethene, ethane and hydrogen are -1390 kJ mol^{-1}, -1550 kJ mol^{-1} and -286 kJ mol^{-1} respectively. Use these data to calculate the enthalpy of hydrogenation of ethene.

5. The decomposition of calcium carbonate to calcium oxide and carbon dioxide only takes place at very high temperatures, making the direct measurement of ΔH for this reaction difficult. Both calcium carbonate and calcium oxide react readily with dilute hydrochloric acid at room temperature.

a) Describe an experiment to find out the enthalpy change of these reactions, describing what you would do and stating what measurements you would make.

b) Which of these two experiments is likely to give the more accurate result? Why?

c) What further piece of data would you need so that you could use your results to find the enthalpy change for the decomposition of calcium carbonate?

d) Given this further information, describe how you would calculate the enthalpy change for this decomposition.

6.4 BOND ENTHALPIES

6.4.1   Define the term average bond enthalpy.

Bond enthalpies are quoted for the gaseous state and should be recognized as average values obtained from a number of similar compounds. Cross reference with 11.2.6.

6.4.2   Calculate the enthalpy change of a reaction using bond enthalpies.   © IBO 2001

Bond enthalpies are a measure of the strength of a covalent bond and the stronger the bond, the more closely the atoms are joined together. The **breaking** of a chemical bond requires energy and is therefore an **endothermic** process. Conversely the **formation** of chemical bonds is an **exothermic** process. The amount of energy associated with the formation/breaking of a particular covalent bond is to a large extent independent of the bonding in the rest of the molecule, i.e. the energy bonding a carbon atom to a hydrogen atom is about 413 kJ mol^{-1} in both methane and ethanol. This means that **approximate** enthalpy changes for reactions may be calculated by considering the bonds being broken and the bonds being made in a reaction:

ΔH = the sum of the energy of bonds broken – the sum of the energy of bonds made

i.e. if the bonds being broken are weaker than those being made the reaction will be exothermic (ΔH is negative) and vice versa.

Bond enthalpies are given for the conversion of a **gaseous molecule** (not necessarily the normal state of the compound) into **gaseous atoms** (not the element in its standard state), i.e. the H–Cl bond energy is the enthalpy change for the reaction:

$$HCl_{(g)} \Rightarrow H_{(g)} + Cl_{(g)} \textbf{ NOT } H_{2\,(g)} \text{ and } Cl_{2\,(g)}$$

The fact that they refer to gases, coupled with the fact that bond enthalpy values are the average of that bond in a range of compounds and hence are only approximately constant, means that enthalpy changes calculated using bond energies are less precise than those obtained by other methods. Nevertheless, apart from a few exceptional cases such as benzene (see Section 4.7, page 140), the values are within about 10% of other more accurate values and hence this is a useful way of calculating approximate enthalpy changes.

Consider the formation of ammonia from nitrogen and hydrogen:

$$N_{2\,(g)} + 3\,H_{2\,(g)} \Rightarrow 2\,NH_{3\,(g)}$$

The enthalpies of the bonds involved are:

$$N{\equiv}N \;\; 945 \text{ kJ mol}^{-1}; \;\; H–H \;\; 436 \text{ kJ mol}^{-1}; \;\; N–H \;\; 391 \text{ kJ mol}^{-1}$$

The bonds broken are: (N≡N) + 3 (H–H) = 945 + (3 × 436) = 2253 kJ mol^{-1}
The bonds made are: 6 (N–H) = 6 × 391 = 2346 kJ mol^{-1}

Taking into account that bond breaking is endothermic and bond making is exothermic:

$$\Delta H = 2253 - 2346 = -93 \text{ kJ mol}^{-1}$$

The bond enthalpy concept can be used to explain various observations. For example the enthalpies of combustion of successive alkanes, which form a homologous series (see Section 11.1, page 352) increase in a regular manner with the number of carbon atoms as shown in Figure 6.2 below.

Figure 6.2 – The enthalpies of combustion of the alkanes

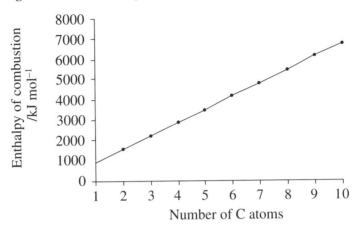

This can be explained by the fact that each successive member of the series contains one more ($-CH_2-$) group than the next one. When it is burnt there will be one extra C–C bond (347 kJ mol^{-1}) and two extra C–H bonds (2×413 kJ mol^{-1}) and $1\frac{1}{2}$ extra O=O bonds (for the extra oxygen required; $1\frac{1}{2} \times 499$ kJ mol^{-1}) to break. There will however be two more C=O bonds (2×805 kJ mol^{-1}) and two more O–H bonds (2×464 kJ mol^{-1}) made from the extra carbon dioxide molecule and water molecule formed respectively. This means, taking into account that bond breaking is endothermic (positive ΔH) and bond making is exothermic (negative ΔH), that the difference in enthalpy of combustion between successive hydrocarbons will be:

$$(347) + (2 \times 413) + (1\tfrac{1}{2} \times 499) - (2 \times 805) - (2 \times 464) = -616 \text{ kJ mol}^{-1}$$

approximately in keeping with the values in the graph.

A knowledge of bond enthalpies is also useful in the prediction of some reaction mechanisms, because the fission of a weak covalent bond (e.g. O–O or F–F) will often be the initiation step of a chain reaction, such as the halogenation of the alkanes (see Section 11.8, page 394).

Apart from a few simple molecules, such as H–Cl, it is not possible to determine bond enthalpies directly, so they must be determined indirectly. This can be done applying Hess's Law to the fundamental stages involved (see Section 6.7, page 207).

EXERCISE 6.4

1. For which of the following equations is the value of ΔH equivalent to the bond enthalpy for the carbon–oxygen bond in carbon monoxide?

A $\quad CO_{(g)} \Rightarrow C_{(g)} + O_{(g)}$

B $\quad CO_{(g)} \Rightarrow C_{(s)} + O_{(g)}$

C $\quad CO_{(g)} \Rightarrow C_{(s)} + \frac{1}{2}O_{2(g)}$

D $\quad CO_{(g)} \Rightarrow C_{(g)} + \frac{1}{2}O_{2(g)}$

2. The bond enthalpy of the bond between nitrogen and oxygen in nitrogen dioxide is $305\ kJ\ mol^{-1}$. If those of the bonds in the oxygen molecule and the nitrogen molecule are $496\ kJ\ mol^{-1}$ and $944\ kJ\ mol^{-1}$ respectively, what will be the enthalpy change for the reaction?

$$N_{2(g)} + 2O_{2(g)} \Rightarrow 2NO_{2(g)}$$

A $\quad +716\ kJ\ mol^{-1}$

B $\quad +1135\ kJ\ mol^{-1}$

C $\quad +1326\ kJ\ mol^{-1}$

D $\quad +1631\ kJ\ mol^{-1}$

3. Given that the bond enthalpy of the carbon–oxygen bonds in carbon monoxide and carbon dioxide are $1073\ kJ\ mol^{-1}$ and $743\ kJ\ mol^{-1}$ respectively, and that of the bond in the oxygen molecule is $496\ kJ\ mol^{-1}$, calculate the enthalpy change for the combustion of 1 mole of carbon monoxide.

4. Given that the enthalpy change for the reaction

$$N_{2(g)} + 3Cl_{2(g)} \Rightarrow 2NCl_{3(g)}$$

is $+688\ kJ\ mol^{-1}$, calculate the bond enthalpy of the N–Cl bond, given that the bond enthalpies in the nitrogen molecule and the chlorine molecule are $944\ kJ\ mol^{-1}$ and $242\ kJ\ mol^{-1}$ respectively.

5. Use bond enthalpy data to calculate the enthalpy change when cyclopropane reacts with hydrogen to form propane. The actual value found is $-159\ kJ\ mol^{-1}$. Give reasons why you think this differs from the value you have calculated.

[Bond enthalpies in $kJ\ mol^{-1}$: C–C 348; C–H 412; H–H 436]

6.5 STANDARD ENTHALPY CHANGES OF REACTION

15.1.1 Define and use the terms standard state and standard enthalpy change of formation ($\Delta H_f^\ominus$).

15.1.2 Calculate the enthalpy change of a reaction using standard enthalpy changes of formation.

© IBO 2001

Just as in comparing altitudes it is useful to assign an arbitrary zero point for comparison (i.e. mean sea level), so in considering enthalpies it is useful to assign an arbitrary zero. This is taken as the elements in their standard states under standard conditions. The enthalpy of formation of any element in its standard state is therefore zero by definition.

The **standard enthalpy change of formation** (ΔH_f) is the amount of energy evolved or absorbed in the formation of one mole of the compound in its standard state from its constituent elements in their standard states. **Standard state** refers to the form normally found at a temperature of 25°C (298 K) and a pressure of 101.3kPa (normal atmospheric pressure). If allotropes exist, then one of these is agreed on as the standard state. For example the standard state of oxygen is $O_{2\,(g)}$, not $O_{3\,(g)}$. The superscript $\ominus$ is sometimes placed after a quantity to indicate that its value refers to standard conditions, though this is often omitted, as has been done in this text.

Under standard conditions, sodium chloride is a solid formed from solid sodium and gaseous chlorine. The enthalpy of formation of sodium chloride (-411 kJ mol^{-1}) is therefore the enthalpy change for the reaction:

$$Na_{(s)} + \tfrac{1}{2}Cl_{2\,(g)} \Rightarrow NaCl_{(s)} \quad \Delta H = -411 \text{ kJ mol}^{-1}$$

The sum of the enthalpies of formation of the reactants will give the total enthalpy change to form the reactants from the component elements in their standard states. Similarly the sum of the enthalpies of formation of the products will give the total enthalpy to form the products. The enthalpy change of the reaction is therefore the difference between these, so that the enthalpy change for any reaction can be calculated using the equation:

$$\Delta H = \Sigma\Delta H_f(\text{products}) - \Sigma\Delta H_f(\text{reactants})$$

This same formula also results from a consideration of the appropriate enthalpy cycle:

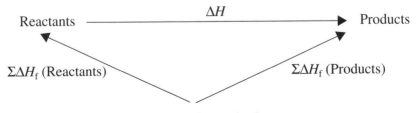

Consider for example the reaction of ethanol and ethanoic acid to form ethyl ethanoate and water:

ADVANCED

Energetics

(1) $C_2H_5OH_{(l)} + CH_3COOH_{(l)} \Rightarrow CH_3COOC_2H_{5\ (l)} + H_2O_{(l)}$ $\qquad\qquad \Delta H_1$

This could be thought of as the result of two hypothetical reactions, going via the elements:

(2) $C_2H_5OH_{(l)} + CH_3COOH_{(l)} \Rightarrow 4\ C_{(s)} + 5\ H_{2\ (g)} + 1\tfrac{1}{2}\ O_{2\ (g)}$ $\qquad\qquad \Delta H_2$

followed by

(3) $4\ C_{(s)} + 5\ H_{2\ (g)} + 1\tfrac{1}{2}\ O_{2\ (g)} \Rightarrow CH_3COOC_2H_{5\ (l)} + H_2O_{(l)}$ $\qquad\qquad \Delta H_3$

ΔH_2 is obviously $-[\Delta H_f(C_2H_5OH_{(l)}) + \Delta H_f(CH_3COOH_{(l)})]$ as it is the reverse of the formation of the compounds from the elements, and ΔH_3 is even more obviously $[\Delta H_f$ $(CH_3COOC_2H_{5\ (l)}) + \Delta H_f(H_2O_{(l)})]$, as it is the formation of the elements from their compounds. Applying Hess's Law:

$\Delta H_1 = \Delta H_2 + \Delta H_3$
$\qquad = -[\Delta H_f(C_2H_5OH_{(l)}) + \Delta H_f(CH_3COOH_{(l)})] + [\Delta H_f(CH_3COOC_2H_{5\ (l)}) + \Delta H_f(H_2O_{(l)})]$

Substituting in appropriate values $[\Delta H_f(C_2H_5OH_{(l)}) = -1367\ kJ\ mol^{-1}$;
$\Delta H_f(CH_3COOH_{(l)}) = -874\ kJ\ mol^{-1}$; $\Delta H_f(CH_3COOC_2H_{5\ (l)}) = -2238\ kJ\ mol^{-1}$;
$\Delta H_f(H_2O_{(l)}) = -286\ kJ\ mol^{-1}]$:

$\Delta H_1 = -[(-1367) + (-874)] + [(-2238) + (-286)] = 2241 - 2524 = -283\ kJ\ mol^{-1}$

It is simpler however just to substitute in the equation relating ΔH and ΔH_f values. Consider as a second example the decomposition of ammonium nitrate:

$$NH_4NO_{3(s)} \Rightarrow N_2O_{(g)} + 2\ H_2O_{(l)}$$

The enthalpies of formation of the compounds involved are:

$NH_4NO_{3\ (s)}$ $-366\ kJ\ mol^{-1}$; $N_2O_{(g)}$ $+82\ kJ\ mol^{-1}$; $H_2O_{(l)}$ $-285\ kJ\ mol^{-1}$

Substituting in the equation:

$\Delta H = \Sigma\Delta H_f(products) - \Sigma\Delta H_f(reactants)$
$\qquad = [\Delta H_f(N_2O_{(g)}) + 2\times\Delta H_f(H_2O_{(l)})] - [\Delta H_f(NH_4NO_{3\ (s)})]$
$\qquad = [(+82) + 2(-285)] - [(-366)] = (-488) - (-366) = -122\ kJ\ mol^{-1}$

Notice the care taken not to make mistakes with signs!

EXTENSION
Two other commonly encountered enthalpy terms are:
Standard enthalpy change of combustion (ΔH_{comb}) – the enthalpy change when one mole of the compound undergoes complete combustion in excess oxygen under standard conditions. For example the standard enthalpy change of combustion for methane is ΔH for the reaction:

$$CH_{4\ (g)} + 2\ O_{2\ (g)} \Rightarrow CO_{2\ (g)} + 2\ H_2O_{(l)}\quad \Delta H = -891\ kJ\ mol^{-1}$$

The standard enthalpy change of combustion is always exothermic. Note that the enthalpies of formation of many oxides (e.g. H_2O and CO_2) are equivalent to the enthalpies of combustion of the element, because both refer to the same equation.

Standard enthalpy change of neutralisation (ΔH_{neut}) – the enthalpy change when one mole of the acid (base) undergoes complete neutralisation with a strong base (acid) under standard conditions. For example the standard enthalpy change of neutralisation for ethanoic acid is ΔH for the reaction:

$$CH_3COOH_{(l)} + OH^-_{(aq)} \Rightarrow CH_3COO^-_{(aq)} + H_2O_{(l)} \quad \Delta H = -56.1 \text{ kJ mol}^{-1}$$

This also is always exothermic. Note that the enthalpy of neutralisation of any strong acid by any strong base is always the same because it is equal to the enthalpy change for the reaction:

$$H^+_{(aq)} + OH^-_{(aq)} \Rightarrow H_2O_{(l)} \quad \Delta H = -57.9 \text{ kJ mol}^{-1}$$

EXERCISE 6.5

1. Which one of the following is **not** a 'standard state' condition?

A   A temperature of 298 K
B   A pressure of 101.3 kPa
C   All substances in the gaseous state
D   Elements present as the standard allotrope.

2. The standard enthalpy change of formation for hydrogen chloride is the enthalpy change for

A $H_{2(g)} + Cl_{2(g)} \Rightarrow 2 \, HCl_{(g)}$

B $\frac{1}{2}H_{2(g)} + \frac{1}{2}Cl_{2(g)} \Rightarrow HCl_{(g)}$

C $H_{(g)} + Cl_{(g)} \Rightarrow HCl_{(g)}$

D $H^+_{(g)} + Cl^-_{(g)} \Rightarrow HCl_{(g)}$

3. Given the standard enthalpy of formation data:

$NaHCO_{3 \, (s)} : -948;\ Na_2CO_{3 \, (s)} : -1131;\ CO_{2 \, (g)} : -395;\ H_2O_{(l)} : -286;$ all in kJ mol^{-1}

what is the enthalpy change for the reaction

$2NaHCO_{3(s)} \Rightarrow Na_2CO_{3(s)} + CO_{2(g)} + H_2O_{(l)}$

A $+84 \text{ kJ mol}^{-1}$
B $+864 \text{ kJ mol}^{-1}$
C -864 kJ mol^{-1}
D -84 kJ mol^{-1}

ADVANCED

4. Write balanced equations for the following reactions and use standard enthalpy of formation data to calculate the standard enthalpy change associated with each:

a) Zinc and chlorine reacting to form zinc chloride.
b) Hydrogen sulfide and sulfur dioxide reacting to form sulfur and water.
c) Lead(II) nitrate decomposing to lead(II) oxide, nitrogen dioxide and oxygen.

[Standard enthalpy of formation data, in kJ mol^{-1}: $ZnCl_{2\,(s)}$ –416; $H_2S_{(g)}$ –21; $SO_{2\,(g)}$ –297, $H_2O_{(l)}$ –286; $Pb(NO_3)_{2\,(s)}$ –449; $PbO_{(s)}$ –218; $NO_{2\,(g)}$ +34.]

5. Depending on whether you consider the chlorine to be converted to the element or to hydrogen chloride, it is possible to write two different equations for the combustion of dichloromethane (CH_2Cl_2). Use enthalpy of formation data to calculate the enthalpy changes of these two reactions. If the experimental value is –578 kJ mol^{-1}, what conclusions can you draw?

[Standard enthalpy of formation data, in kJ mol^{-1}: $CH_2Cl_{2\,(l)}$ –121; $HCl_{(g)}$ –92; $CO_{2\,(g)}$ –395; $H_2O_{(l)}$ –286]

6. In the Apollo project, the engines of the lunar module mixed methylhydrazine (CH_3-NH-NH_2) and dinitrogen tetroxide (N_2O_4), which ignite spontaneously, as fuel for the rocket.

a) Write the most probable equation for the reaction. (It forms common simple molecules).
b) Use enthalpy of formation data to calculate the enthalpy change for this reaction.
c) What factors, apart from the reaction being highly exothermic, would have made this combination of fuels suitable for this application?

[Standard enthalpy of formation data, in kJ mol^{-1}: $CH_3NHNH_{2\,(l)}$ +13.0; $N_2O_{4\,(g)}$ +9; $H_2O_{(g)}$ –244; $CO_{2\,(g)}$ –395]

ADVANCED

7. a) How could you attempt to measure the enthalpy change for the hypothetical isomerisation of butan–1–ol (C_4H_9OH) to ethoxyethane ($C_2H_5OC_2H_5$) experimentally?
b) Use bond energy data to calculate a value for this enthalpy change.
c) Use enthalpy of formation data to calculate a value for this enthalpy change.
d) Which would you expect to give the best agreement with your experimental value? Why?

[Standard enthalpy of formation data, in kJ mol^{-1}: $H_2O_{(l)}$ –286; $CO_{2\,(g)}$ –395; $C_4H_9OH_{(l)}$ –327; $C_2H_5OC_2H_{5\,(l)}$ –280.
Bond energies in kJ mol^{-1}: C–C 346; C–H 413; H–H 436; C–O = 358; O–H 464]

6.6 LATTICE ENTHALPY

15.2.1 Define the term lattice enthalpy.

The sign of $\Delta H_{lattice}$ indicates whether the lattice is being formed or broken.

15.2.2 Compare the effect of both the relative sizes and the charges of ions on the lattice enthalpies of different ionic compounds.

The relative value of the theoretical lattice enthalpy increases with higher ionic charge and smaller ionic radius due to increased attractive forces.

15.2.3 Construct a Born-Haber cycle and use it to calculate an enthalpy change.

15.2.4 Analyse theoretical and experimental lattice enthalpy values.

A significant difference between the two values indicates covalent character.

© IBO 2001

The formation of an ionic compound can be considered as the sum of a number of individual processes converting the elements from their standard states into gaseous atoms, losing and gaining electrons to form the cations and anions respectively and finally these ions coming together to form the solid compound. The diagrammatic representation of this, shown below in Figure 6.3, is known as the Born–Haber cycle.

Figure 6.3 – The Born–Haber cycle

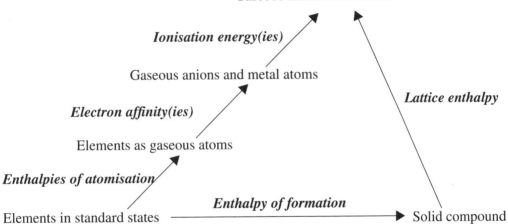

The **enthalpy change of atomisation** is the enthalpy change required to produce one mole of gaseous atoms of an element from the element in the standard state. For example for sodium it is the enthalpy change for:

$$Na_{(s)} \Rightarrow Na_{(g)} \quad \Delta H_{at} = +103 \text{ kJ mol}^{-1}$$

Note that for diatomic gaseous elements, such as chlorine, it is numerically equal to half the bond enthalpy, because breaking the bond between the atoms produces two atoms. Considering chlorine as the example:

$$\tfrac{1}{2}Cl_{2\,(g)} \Rightarrow Cl_{(g)} \quad \Delta H_{at} = \tfrac{1}{2}E\,(Cl-Cl) = \tfrac{1}{2}(242) = +121 \text{ kJ mol}^{-1}$$

The **electron affinity** is the enthalpy change when one mole of gaseous atoms or anions gains electrons to form a mole of negatively charged ions. For example the electron affinity of chlorine is the enthalpy change for

$$Cl_{(g)} + e^- \Rightarrow Cl^-_{(g)} \quad \Delta H = -364 \text{ kJ mol}^{-1}$$

The **ionisation energy**, the enthalpy change for one mole of a gaseous element or cation to lose electrons to form a mole of positively charged gaseous ions, has been met before (see Section 2.4, page 73).

Notice the **lattice enthalpy** is the energy required to convert one mole of the solid compound into gaseous ions. Using sodium chloride as the example it is the enthalpy change for:

$$NaCl_{(s)} \Rightarrow Na^+_{(g)} + Cl^-_{(g)} \quad \Delta H = +771 \text{ kJ mol}^{-1}$$

The lattice enthalpy is therefore very highly endothermic. In fact all of the energy terms in the cycle are endothermic except for the first electron affinities of very electronegative elements, such as nitrogen, oxygen and the halogens.

The Born–Haber cycle is subject to Hess's Law, so that if the magnitude of every term except one is known, then the remaining value may be calculated. The lattice enthalpy of sodium chloride can therefore be calculated knowing the other terms in the cycle:

Enthalpy of formation of NaCl $= -411 \text{ kJ mol}^{-1}$
Enthalpy of atomisation of Na $= +103 \text{ kJ mol}^{-1}$
Enthalpy of atomisation of Cl $= +121 \text{ kJ mol}^{-1}$
Electron affinity of Cl $= -364 \text{ kJ mol}^{-1}$
Ionisation energy of Na $= +500 \text{ kJ mol}^{-1}$

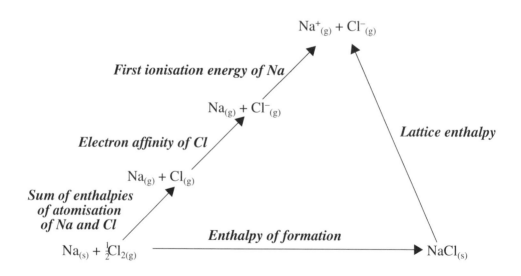

Enthalpies of atomisation + Electron affinity + Ionisation energy

$$= \text{Enthalpy of formation} + \text{Lattice enthalpy}$$

$$(+103) + (+121) + (-364) + (+500) = (-411) + \text{L.E.}$$

$$\text{L.E.} = 411 + 103 + 121 - 364 + 500$$

$$= +771 \text{ kJ mol}^{-1}$$

The magnitude of the lattice enthalpy depends upon the nature of the ions involved. The greater the charge on the ions, the greater the electrostatic attraction and hence the greater the lattice enthalpy. The larger the ions, then the greater the separation of the charges and the lower the lattice enthalpy. These trends are illustrated in Table 6.2, which compares the lattice enthalpies of sodium chloride, magnesium oxide and potassium bromide, all of which crystallise with a similar lattice:

Table 6.2 – Comparison of the lattice enthalpies of some compounds

Compound	Lattice enthalpy – kJ mol^{-1}	Change from NaCl
MgO	3889	Increased ionic charge
NaCl	771	
KBr	670	Larger ions

It is not possible to measure lattice enthalpies directly, but the Born–Haber cycle provides a way in which these can be indirectly measured through experimental techniques (an empirical value). It is also possible to calculate theoretical lattice enthalpies for ionic compounds. This is done by assuming the ionic model (see Section 4.1, page 116), then summing the electrostatic attractive and repulsive forces between the ions in the crystal lattice. As can be seen from Table 6.3, this gives excellent agreement for many compounds, implying that the ionic model is an appropriate one. For others however, such as the silver halides, the agreement is less good. This is interpreted as evidence for a significant degree of covalent character in the bonding of such compounds and this always leads to an increase in the lattice enthalpy. In the case of silver halides this increased lattice enthalpy helps to explain their insolubility and the fact that silver fluoride (the most ionic) is in fact soluble.

ADVANCED

Table 6.3 – Experimental and theoretical lattice enthalpies for some compounds

Compound	Empirical value (kJ mol^{-1})	Theoretical value (kJ mol^{-1})
Sodium chloride	766	766
Potassium bromide	672	667
Potassium iodide	632	631
Silver iodide	865	736

EXERCISE 6.6

1. The lattice energy is dependent on two main factors, the size of the ions and the charge on the ions. Which combination of these would lead to the greatest lattice enthalpy?

	Size of ions	Charge on ions
A	Large	Large
B	Large	Small
C	Small	Large
D	Small	Small

2. Which one of the following quantities is **not** directly involved in the Born–Haber cycle?

A Ionisation energy
B Lattice enthalpy
C Electronegativity
D Enthalpy of formation

3. Which one of the following ionic solids would you expect to have the greatest lattice enthalpy?

A RbCl B CaS C BaI_2 D LiF

4. Use the data below, relating to the formation of barium chloride, to calculate a value of the electron affinity of the chlorine atom.

Data: Enthalpy of atomisation of barium   +175 kJ mol⁻¹
      Enthalpy of atomisation of chlorine $+121$ kJ mol⁻¹
      First ionisation energy of Ba $+502$ kJ mol⁻¹
      Second ionisation energy of Ba $+966$ kJ mol⁻¹
      Lattice enthalpy of $BaCl_2$ $+2018$ kJ mol⁻¹
      Enthalpy of formation of $BaCl_2$ -860 kJ mol⁻¹

5. It would be theoretically possible for calcium to form a fluoride CaF containing Ca^+ ions and the F^- ions in equal numbers. Assuming that the lattice enthalpy of the hypothetical compound is similar to that of NaF (+891 kJ mol⁻¹), use a Born–Haber cycle to calculate its enthalpy of formation using the data below.

Data: Enthalpy of atomisation of calcium   +193 kJ mol⁻¹
      F–F bond enthalpy $+158$ kJ mol⁻¹
      First ionisation energy of Ca $+590$ kJ mol⁻¹
      Electron affinity of fluorine -348 kJ mol⁻¹

The enthalpy of formation of CaF_2 is -1214 kJ mol⁻¹. Use this to explain why it is not possible to produce CaF even if two moles of calcium are reacted with one mole of fluorine gas.

ADVANCED

6.7 OTHER THERMOCHEMICAL CYCLES

There are a number of other circumstances in which it is useful to employ thermochemical cycles similar to the Born–Haber cycle. Some of the more common are discussed in this section. Most bond enthalpies cannot be found by direct empirical methods, so an indirect method must be used. The most common is an enthalpy cycle equating the enthalpy change of formation to the sum of the enthalpy of atomisation of the elements and the sum of the bond enthalpies, assuming a gaseous product (if not then a further enthalpy term for the change of state of the product must be added). This approach is illustrated below for the determination of the carbon–hydrogen bond enthalpy by applying this process to methane.

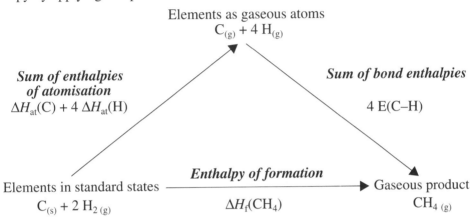

Note that in this the standard state of carbon is defined as solid graphite, rather than the less stable allotrope diamond. Substituting in the enthalpy changes of atomisation ($\Delta H_{at}(C) = +717$ kJ mol^{-1} & $\Delta H_{at}(H) = +218$ kJ mol^{-1}) and the enthalpy change of formation for methane ($\Delta H_f(CH_4) = -75$ kJ mol^{-1}), the bond enthalpy for the carbon hydrogen bond may be calculated:

Enthalpy of formation = Sum of enthalpies of atomisation + Sum of bond enthalpies

$$
\begin{aligned}
\Delta H_f(CH_4) &= \Delta H_{at}(C) + 4\,\Delta H_{at}(H) + 4\,E(C\text{-}H) \\
-75 &= +717 + 4\,(+218) + 4\,E(C\text{-}H) \\
4\,E(C\text{-}H) &= -75 - 717 - 872 = -1664 \\
E(C\text{-}H) &= -416 \text{ kJ mol}^{-1}
\end{aligned}
$$

Note that this is an average value for the four bonds. It does not imply, and it is **not true**, that this is equal to the enthalpy change for the reaction:

$$CH_{4\,(g)} \Rightarrow CH_{3\,(g)} + H_{(g)}$$

This process can be carried out for a variety of bonds over a variety of compounds and it is by this process that the average bond enthalpies given in data books are deduced.

Another important enthalpy cycle is that for the formation of an aqueous solution from a solid ionic compound. The **enthalpy change of solution** (ΔH_{sol}; i.e. the enthalpy change when one mole of the substance is dissolved in water to form a dilute aqueous solution) is equal to the lattice enthalpy of the compound plus the sum of the hydration enthalpies of the component ions. The **enthalpy change of hydration** (ΔH_{hyd}) for an ion is the enthalpy change (always exothermic) when one mole of the gaseous ion is added to water to form a dilute solution - the term solvation is used in place of hydration for solvents other than water. This is illustrated below using calcium chloride as an example:

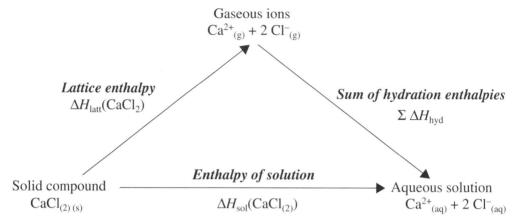

Again, if all the terms are known except one, then this one may be calculated. For example the above cycle will be used to calculate the enthalpy of solution using the lattice enthalpy for calcium chloride ($+2258$ kJ mol^{-1}) and the hydration enthalpies of the ions ($\Delta H_{hyd}(Ca^{2+}) = -1650$ kJ mol^{-1} & $\Delta H_{hyd}(Cl^-) = -364$ kJ mol^{-1}).

Enthalpy of solution = Lattice enthalpy + Sum of hydration enthalpies
$$\Delta H_{sol}(CaCl_2) = \Delta H_{lat}(CaCl_2) + \Delta H_{hyd}(Ca^{2+}) + 2\,\Delta H_{hyd}(Cl^-)$$
$$\Delta H_{sol}(CaCl_2) = +2258 + (-1650) + 2\,(-364) = -120 \text{ kJ mol}^{-1}$$

Note that the enthalpy of solution, being the sum of two very large terms one of which is always endothermic the other always exothermic, is usually quite small and may be either positive (endothermic) or negative (exothermic). If it is large and positive, then the compound in question will almost certainly be insoluble and this is the explanation for the lack of solubility of many inorganic compounds.

Another class of thermochemical cycles that are very important are those relating to the enthalpy change of combustion (ΔH_{comb}). These are very useful to determine the enthalpy of formation of compounds that cannot be formed by direct combination of the elements, for example ethane from carbon and hydrogen:

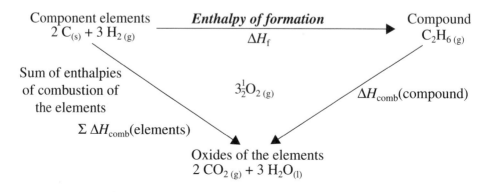

Considering the reactions involved, the formation of ethane is:

(1) $2\,C_{(s)} + 3\,H_{2\,(g)} \Rightarrow C_2H_{6\,(g)}$ ΔH_1

Carbon burns to form carbon dioxide, hydrogen burns to form water and ethane burns to form a mixture of these (n.b. the enthalpy of combustion of the element is related to the enthalpy of formation of its oxide). The enthalpy changes of these reactions can be determined directly and literature values are given:

(2) $C_{(s)} + O_{2\,(g)} \Rightarrow CO_{2\,(g)}$ $\Delta H_2 = -394$ kJ mol^{-1}

(3) $2\,H_{2\,(g)} + O_{2\,(g)} \Rightarrow 2\,H_2O_{(l)}$ $\Delta H_3 = -572$ kJ mol^{-1}

(4) $C_2H_{6\,(g)} + 3\tfrac{1}{2}\,O_{2\,(g)} \Rightarrow 2\,CO_{2\,(g)} + 3\,H_2O_{(l)}$ $\Delta H_4 = -1560$ kJ mol^{-1}

Equation (1) can be created by multiplying equation (2) by 2, equation (3) by $1\tfrac{1}{2}$ and subtracting equation (4), so to calculate ΔH_1, the enthalpy terms must be treated in the same way:

$$\Delta H_1 = 2\,\Delta H_2 + 1\tfrac{1}{2}\,\Delta H_3 - \Delta H_4 = 2(-394) + 1\tfrac{1}{2}(-572) - (-1560) = -86 \text{ kJ mol}^{-1}$$

This technique can also be used to find the enthalpy change of other reactions in which the reactants and products can all be readily converted to the oxides, for example the relative stability of propan–1–ol and propan–2–ol may be determined through measuring their enthalpies of combustion:

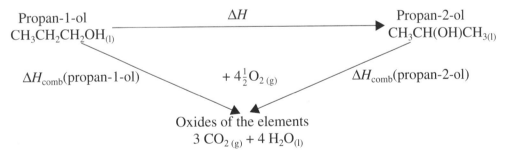

EXERCISE 6.7

1.   Which one of the following enthalpy terms is not required to calculate the enthalpy of the nitrogen–fluorine bond in nitrogen trifluoride?

   A   The electron affinity of fluorine.
   B   The fluorine–fluorine bond enthalpy.
   C   The enthalpy of atomisation of nitrogen.
   D   The enthalpy of formation of nitrogen trifluoride.

2. Calculate the lattice enthalpy of sodium chloride given the following data:

$\Delta H_{sol}(NaCl) = -4$ kJ mol^{-1}

$\Delta H_{hyd}(Na^+) = -406$ kJ mol^{-1}

$\Delta H_{hyd}(Cl^-) = -364$ kJ mol^{-1}

A   +774 kJ mol^{-1}

B   +766 kJ mol^{-1}

C   +46 kJ mol^{-1}

D   +38 kJ mol^{-1}

3. Which one of the following enthalpy terms will always have a different sign to the others?

A   Ionisation enthalpy

B   Enthalpy of hydration

C   Lattice enthalpy

D   Enthalpy of atomisation

4. Given the enthalpies of atomisation of phosphorus and hydrogen (+354 kJ mol^{-1} and +218 kJ mol^{-1} respectively) and the phosphorus-hydrogen bond enthalpy (321 kJ mol^{-1}), calculate then the enthalpy of formation of a hypothetical compound PH$_5$.

5. The theoretical and experimentally determined lattice enthalpies for silver chloride are +833 kJ mol^{-1} and +905 kJ mol^{-1} respectively. Combine these, with the enthalpy of hydration of the component ions ($\Delta H_{hyd}(Ag^+) = -464$ kJ mol^{-1} & $\Delta H_{hyd}(Cl^-) = -364$ kJ mol^{-1}) to calculate two values for the enthalpy of solution of the compound. Use these to explain the fact that silver chloride is insoluble in water, yet sodium chloride is readily soluble.

EXTENSION

6.8 ENTROPY

6.5.1 State and explain the factors which increase the disorder (entropy) in a system.

An increase in disorder can result from the mixing of different types of particles, change of state (increased distance between particles), increased movement of particles or increased numbers of particles. An increase in the number of particles in the gaseous state usually has a greater influence than any other possible factor.

6.5.2 Predict whether the entropy change (ΔS) for a given reaction or process would be positive or negative.

From a given equation, identify a single factor which affects the value of ΔS and predict the sign of ΔS.   © IBO 2001

Some states are inherently more probable than others, in the same way that the probability of rolling '7' on a pair of dice (1+6, 2+5, 3+4, 4+3, 5+2, 6+1) is much greater than that of rolling '12' (6+6 only). The probability of a state existing is known as its entropy and it is given the symbol S. Unlike enthalpy (H), absolute values of the entropy of a substance in a particular state can be measured, the units of entropy being J K^{-1}mol^{-1}. In general terms the less order there is in a state, the greater the probability of the state and the greater its entropy. The entropy of a system is therefore a measure of the degree of order in a system. Thus, other factors being equal, there is an increase in entropy on changing state from solid to liquid to gas, as illustrated by the values for the states of water below:

	solid (ice)	$\Rightarrow$	liquid/solution (water)	$\Rightarrow$	gas. (steam)
Entropy	48.0		69.9		188.7 J K^{-1}mol^{-1}

Therefore in any conversion, as well as the enthalpy change (ΔH), there is also an entropy change (ΔS). This entropy change is likely to be positive if there is a decrease in order through a decrease in the number of moles of solid, or an increase in the number of moles of gas, e.g.

$$NH_4Cl_{(s)} \Rightarrow NH_{3(g)} + HCl_{(g)} \quad \Delta S = +285 \text{ J K}^{-1}\text{mol}^{-1}$$

Conversely if the number of moles of gas decreases, or the number of moles of solid increases there is an increase in order, the change in entropy is likely to be negative, e.g.

$$Pb^{2+}_{(aq)} + 2\ I^-_{(aq)} \Rightarrow PbI_{2(s)} \quad \Delta S = -70 \text{ J K}^{-1}\text{mol}^{-1}$$

An increase in temperature and an increase in the number of particles, especially if some of these are of a different type, also increase entropy. The latter is, for example, the reason why, even if a reaction is slightly endothermic, a small amount of product will exist at equilibrium. This is dealt with more fully in the next section.

EXERCISE 6.8

1. Which one of the following does **not** generally lead to an increase in the entropy of a system?

    A   An increase in the total number of moles of particles.
    B   The formation of a solution.
    C   The formation of gaseous products.
    D   The formation of solid products.

2. What is the entropy change associated with the Haber process?

$$N_{2(g)} + 3H_{2(g)} \Rightarrow 2NH_{3(g)}$$

[Standard entropies in J $K^{-1}mol^{-1}$: $N_{2(g)}$: 191; $H_{2(g)}$: 131; $NH_{3(g)}$: 193]

    A -129 J $K^{-1}mol^{-1}$
    B -198 J $K^{-1}mol^{-1}$
    C $+129$ J $K^{-1}mol^{-1}$
    D $+198$ J $K^{-1}mol^{-1}$

3. For each of the following state what kind of entropy change you would expect and briefly give your reasons.

    a) $Br_{2(l)} \Rightarrow Br_{2(g)}$
    b) $Ag^+_{(aq)} + Cl^-_{(aq)} \Rightarrow AgCl_{(s)}$
    c) $2\ NO_{2(g)} \Rightarrow N_2O_{4(g)}$
    d) $2\ OH^-_{(aq)} + CO_{2(g)} \Rightarrow H_2O_{(l)} + CO_3^{2-}_{(aq)}$
    e) $H_{2(g)} + Cl_{2(g)} \Rightarrow 2\ HCl_{(g)}$

EXTENSION

6.9 SPONTANEITY OF A REACTION

15.3.1 Calculate the standard entropy change for a reaction (ΔS^θ) using values of absolute entropies.

15.3.2 Calculate ΔG^θ for a reaction using the equation $\Delta G^\theta = \Delta H^\theta - T\Delta S^\theta$ or by using values of the standard free energy change of formation, ΔG_f^θ.

© IBO 2001

The exact value of the entropy change can be calculated from absolute entropies using the formula:

$$\Delta S = \Sigma S(\text{Products}) - \Sigma S(\text{Reactants})$$

Consider the complete combustion of methane:

$$CH_{4(g)} + 2\,O_{2(g)} \Rightarrow CO_{2(g)} + 2\,H_2O_{(l)}$$

$S(CH_{4(g)}) = 186$, $S(O_{2(g)}) = 205$, $S(CO_{2(g)}) = 214$, $S(H_2O_{(l)}) = 70$ (all in J K^{-1}mol^{-1})

$$\Delta S = [(2 \times 70) + 214] - [(2 \times 205) + (186)] = -242 \text{ J K}^{-1}\text{mol}^{-1}$$

As expected, because of the decrease in the number of moles of gas (3 to 1), there is an increase in the order of the system so the entropy change is negative. Note that, in contrast to standard enthalpies of formation, the entropy of elements, such as oxygen, is **not** zero.

Any change may occur spontaneously (like water flowing downhill) if the final state is more probable than the initial state, i.e. if the final entropy of the universe is greater than the initial entropy of the universe. The entropy of the universe depends on both the entropy of the system and the entropy of the surroundings. ΔS measures the change in the entropy of the system. The major effect of chemical changes on the entropy of the universe results from the gain and loss of heat energy. If potential energy is converted to heat energy which is then transferred to the universe (i.e. an exothermic change), then this results in an increase in the entropy of the surroundings and vice versa for an endothermic change. The magnitude of this entropy change is $-\Delta H/T$, so that the condition for a spontaneous change to occur is that $\Delta S_{universe}$ is positive, where $\Delta S_{universe}$ is given by:

$$\Delta S_{universe} = \Delta S_{surroundings} + \Delta S_{system} = -\frac{\Delta H}{T} + \Delta S_{system}$$

In other words a change will be spontaneous if:
* the final state has a lower enthalpy than the initial state (ΔH is negative)

and
* the final state is more disordered than the initial state (ΔS is positive).

If only one of these is the case then the outcome will depend on which factor is the dominant one at the temperature being considered.

In chemistry this condition has traditionally been considered in terms of the **Gibbs free energy**, ΔG. The Gibbs free energy is equal to $-T\Delta S_{universe}$ and if this quantity is negative, then $\Delta S_{universe}$ must be positive, so that the process in question may occur spontaneously.

Multiplying through the equation above by $-T$ gives the expression:

$$\Delta G = \Delta H - T\Delta S$$

where T is in Kelvin and ΔS is assumed to be ΔS_{system}. ΔH and ΔS can both be either positive or negative, the results of the various combinations of these on the sign of ΔG, which must be **negative** for a spontaneous change to occur, is given in Table 6.4 below:

Table 6.4 – The effect of ΔH and ΔS on the spontaneity of reaction

ΔH	ΔS	ΔG	Spontaneity
Positive, i.e. endothermic	Positive, i.e. more random products	Depends on T	Spontaneous at high temperatures, when $T\Delta S > \Delta H$
Positive, i.e. endothermic	Negative, i.e. more ordered products	Always positive	Never spontaneous
Negative, i.e. exothermic	Positive, i.e. more random products	Always negative	Always spontaneous
Negative, i.e. exothermic	Negative, i.e. more ordered products	Depends on T	Spontaneous at low temperatures, when $T\Delta S < \Delta H$

This may be illustrated graphically as shown in Figure 6.4 below:

Figure 6.4 – The conditions for spontaneity and the effect of temperature on this

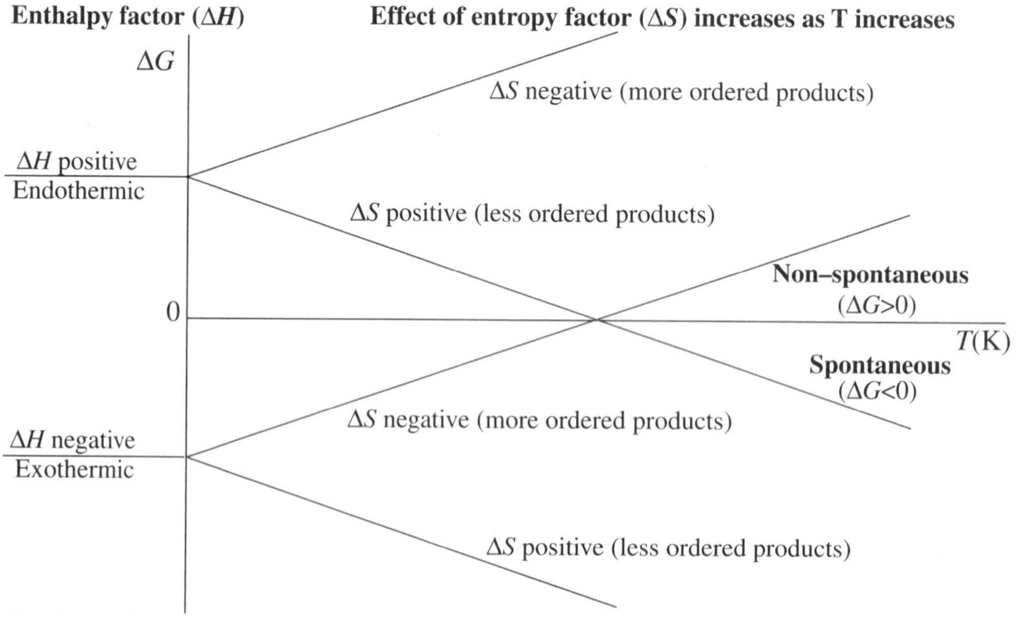

Graphs such as this, which readily show whether a reaction is spontaneous (i.e. below the ΔG axis) at a particular temperature, are closely related to Ellingham diagrams (see Chapter 15). These show the way in which the ΔG for formation of metal oxides and for the reactions of oxygen with a variety of reducing agents, vary with temperature and hence the temperatures at which the reducing agents, could reduce the metal oxide.

Table 6.4 and Figure 6.4 just give the conditions under which a reaction may be spontaneous, they do not actually mean that the reaction will occur spontaneously. If the reaction has a high activation energy, then the rate at which the reaction occurs may be infinitesimally slow, even though it is energetically feasible. For example a mixture of hydrogen and oxygen will not react at room temperature and pressure, even though the reaction to form water is spontaneous, because none of the molecules have sufficient energy to overcome the activation energy for the reaction. This is dealt with in greater detail in Section 7.6, page 239.

The Gibbs free energy (ΔG) for a change is equal to the amount of energy from that system that is available to do useful work. Hence for any system in equilibrium (see Chapter 8) ΔG must be exactly zero, i.e. the system can do no useful work. Thus if ΔG for a reaction is zero, then when stoichiometric amounts of both reactants and products are all mixed together there will be no further change. If ΔG is slightly negative there will be a net reaction to increase the amount of products and decrease the amount of reactants. This will continue until ΔG for any further change will be zero (remember standard values only apply to standard conditions, i.e. stoichiometric amounts), at which point equilibrium will be established. If ΔG is very negative then this position will be so far to the right that the reaction will effectively go to completion. Similarly if ΔG is small and positive then an equilibrium favouring the products will occur, but if ΔG is very negative the reaction will in effect not occur.

The value of ΔG can be calculated at any given temperature from values of ΔH and ΔS for the reaction, which are in turn calculated from data about the reactants and products. Consider for example the thermal decomposition of calcium carbonate at 500K:

$$CaCO_{3(s)} \Rightarrow CaO_{(s)} + CO_{2(g)}$$

The required data are:

Substance	$\Delta H_f - kJ\ mol^{-1}$	$S - J\ K^{-1}mol^{-1}$
$CaCO_{3(s)}$	−1207	93
$CaO_{(s)}$	−636	40
$CO_{2(g)}$	−394	214

Using these data, values of ΔH and ΔS can be calculated for the reaction:

$$\Delta H = \sum H_f(\text{Products}) - \sum H_f(\text{Reactants})$$
$$= [(-636) + (-394)] - [-1207]$$
$$= +177\ kJmol^{-1} = +177\ 000\ J\ mol^{-1}$$

$$\Delta S = \sum \Delta S(\text{Products}) - \sum \Delta S(\text{Reactants})$$
$$= [(40) + (214)] - [93]$$
$$= +161\ JK^{-1}mol^{-1}$$

$$\Delta G = \Delta H - T\Delta S$$
$$= 177000 - (161 \times 500)$$
$$= 96500\ Jmol^{-1}$$
$$= +96.5\ kJmol^{-1}$$

ADVANCED

Energetics

ΔG is positive, therefore at this temperature the reaction is not spontaneous and cannot occur. If the temperature is increased to 2000K however, assuming ΔH and ΔS are both independent of temperature:

$$\Delta G = \Delta H - T\Delta S$$
$$= 177000 - (161 \times 2000)$$
$$= -145000 \text{ Jmol}^{-1}$$
$$= -145 \text{ kJmol}^{-1}$$

The reaction is now spontaneous, provided there is sufficient energy to overcome the activation energy, which is the case for this reaction, so that the process occurs. The temperature at which the system is in perfect equilibrium (i.e. $K_c = 1$) can be calculated knowing that at equilibrium, because $\Delta G = 0$, $\Delta H = T.\Delta S$:

$$177000 = T \times 161$$
$$T = \frac{177000}{161}$$
$$= 1099\text{K}$$

ΔG under standard conditions (298 K and 101.3 kPa) can also be calculated using the standard Gibbs free energy of formation (ΔG_f) data in the same way as data on the standard enthalpy of formation (ΔH_f) data is used to calculate enthalpy changes (ΔH). The Gibbs free energy of elements in their standard state is similarly defined as zero, so that the standard Gibbs free energy change of formation is the free energy change when one mole of a compound is formed from its elements under standard conditions. Therefore:

$$\Delta G_f = \Sigma G_f(\text{Products}) - \Sigma G_f(\text{Reactants})$$

Using this approach for the calcium carbonate example above standard free energy of formation data for the compounds in the appropriate state is:

$\Delta G_f(CaCO_3) = -1120 \text{ kJ mol}^{-1}$; $\Delta G_f(CaO) = -604 \text{ kJ mol}^{-1}$; $\Delta G_f(CO_2) = -395 \text{ kJ mol}^{-1}$

Hence:

$$\Delta G = [(-604) + (-395)] - [-1120] = +121 \text{ kJ mol}^{-1}$$

As might be expected this value, at 298 K, is even more positive than the value at 500 K because the $T\Delta S$ term is even smaller.

ADVANCED

EXERCISE 6.9

1. Which of the following combinations of enthalpy change and entropy change ensures that the position of equilibrium will favour the products under all conditions?

	ΔH	ΔS
A	Positive	Positive
B	Positive	Negative
C	Negative	Positive
D	Negative	Negative

2. For the reaction of liquid phosphorus(III) chloride with chlorine gas to form solid phosphorus(V) chloride at 298K, the entropy change is -85 J mol^{-1}K^{-1} and the enthalpy change is -124 kJ mol^{-1}. What is the approximate value of the Gibbs free energy at this temperature?

A -200 kJ mol^{-1}
B -100 kJ mol^{-1}
C -40 kJ mol^{-1}
D $+40$ kJ mol^{-1}

3. Under certain conditions it is possible for three moles of gaseous ethyne (C_2H_2) to polymerise to form liquid benzene (C_6H_6). Use the data provided to calculate:

a) The entropy change of the system.

b) The enthalpy change of the system.

c) The entropy change of the surroundings that would result from the emission of this amount of heat energy at 25°C.

d) Explain how these factors combine to determine whether spontaneous reaction is possible and predict the optimum conditions for the formation of benzene.

Data:

	ΔH_f / kJ mol^{-1}	ΔS / J mol^{-1}K^{-1}
Ethyne	227	201
Benzene	83	269

ADVANCED

4. Use values of the Gibbs free energy change of formation, given below, to deduce whether the cis– or trans– isomer of but–2–ene is the more stable at 25°C. At what temperature will the two isomers have the same stability?

Data:

	ΔG_f – kJ mol^{-1}	ΔH_f – kJ mol^{-1}	ΔS – J mol^{-1}K^{-1}
cis–but–2–ene	67.1	–5.7	301
trans–but–2–ene	64.1	–10.1	296

5. This question refers to the graph of ΔG against temperature shown. This shows the variation of ΔG for the reaction of the substance indicated with one mole of oxygen to form the most stable oxide.

a) The line for $2Pb + O_2 \Rightarrow 2PbO$ shows two distinct changes of gradient. Explain these.

b) Is carbon or carbon monoxide the more powerful reducing agent?

c) Explain what it shows about the potential use of hydrogen as a reductant for:

    i Al_2O_3 ii   PbO   iii   ZnO

6. For the melting of ice, $\Delta H = +6.00$ kJ mol^{-1} and $\Delta S = 22.0$ J K^{-1} mol^{-1}

a) Calculate ΔG for the process at –10°C.
b) Use this to explain which form of water is stable at this temperature.
c) Repeat this for water at +10°C.
d) Calculate the temperature at which $\Delta G = 0$. What is the significance of this temperature.
e) Suppose that the entropy of liquid water was increased by the presence of a solute. How would this affect ΔS and the temperature at which ΔG is zero? Does this correspond to any common phenomenon?

KINETICS

7

Chapter contents

7.1 RATES OF REACTION

7.1 .1   Define the term rate of reaction and describe the measurement of reaction rates.

Rate of reaction can be defined as the decrease in the concentration of reactants per unit time or the increase in the concentration of product per unit time.

7.1.2   Analyse data from rate experiments.

Graphs of changes in concentration, volume or mass against time should be interpreted qualitatively.

© IBO 2001

Different chemical reactions occur at different rates (i.e. speeds). Some, such as the neutralisation of a strong acid by a strong base in aqueous solution, take place very rapidly whilst others, such as the rusting of iron, take place far more slowly.

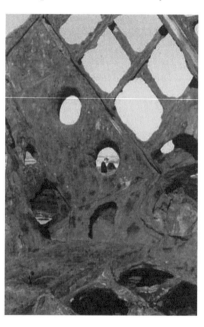

Explosions tend to be rapid, corrosion much slower.

The rate of a chemical reaction is a measure of the rate at which products are formed, which is equal to the rate at which the reactants are consumed. This is taken as the change in concentration divided by the change in time and hence has units of mol dm^{-3}s^{-1}. For a reaction:

$$R \Rightarrow P, \ \text{rate} = \frac{\Delta[P]}{\Delta t} = -\frac{\Delta[R]}{\Delta t}.$$

Note the minus sign for the reactants, which is necessary as the concentrations of reactants decreases with time whereas the concentrations of products increases. Rate is always positive.

The numerical value will vary according to the number of moles of the substance involved in the stoichiometric equation, so that in the reaction:

$$MnO_4^-{}_{(aq)} + 8\ H^+{}_{(aq)} + 5\ Fe^{2+}{}_{(aq)} \Rightarrow Mn^{2+}{}_{(aq)} + 4H_2O_{(l)} + 5\ Fe^{3+}{}_{(aq)}$$

The rate of appearance of Fe^{3+} is five times as great as the rate at which MnO_4^- is consumed. The rate is usually considered to apply to a product that has a coefficient of one as the equation is usually written:

$$\text{Rate} = -\frac{\Delta[MnO_4^-]}{\Delta t} = \frac{1}{5}\frac{\Delta[Fe^{3+}]}{\Delta t}$$

Any property that differs between the reactants and the products can be used to measure the rate of the reaction. The physical properties most commonly used are absorption of coloured light, electrical conductivity and volume/mass/pressure of gas. Another technique is to remove a sample of the solution at different times and titrate it with a reagent that reacts with either a reactant or a product. Whichever property is chosen, a graph is drawn of that property against time and the rate of reaction is proportional to the gradient of the curve or line ignoring the sign. Changes in the gradient of similar graphs illustrate the effect of changing conditions on the rate of reaction, without the need to convert the units to $mol\ dm^{-3}s^{-1}$.

In most cases the rate of reaction decreases with time because the concentration of the reactants decreases with time and the reaction rate usually depends on the reactant concentration. It is most common to compare initial rates, i.e. the gradient of the tangent to the curve at $t = 0$. This is also easiest to draw as this section of the curve is the most linear. Typical curves obtained for the consumption of a reagent and formation of a product are shown in Figure 7.1 below:

Figure 7.1 – Curves illustrating the variation of reaction rate with time

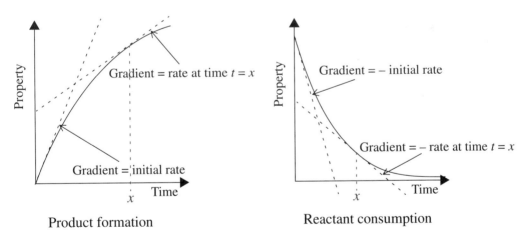

CORE

EXERCISE 7.1

1. The equation for a reaction is: $4 NO_{2 (g)} + 2 H_2O_{(g)} + O_{2 (g)} \Rightarrow 4 HNO_{3 (g)}$

Which one of the following is not numerically equal to the others?

A $\quad -\dfrac{1}{2}\dfrac{\Delta[NO_2]}{\Delta t}$

B $\quad -\dfrac{1}{2}\dfrac{\Delta[O_2]}{\Delta t}$

C $\quad -\dfrac{\Delta[H_2O]}{\Delta t}$

D $\quad \dfrac{1}{2}\dfrac{\Delta[HNO_3]}{\Delta t}$

2. Which of the curves on the following graph shows the greatest initial reaction rate?

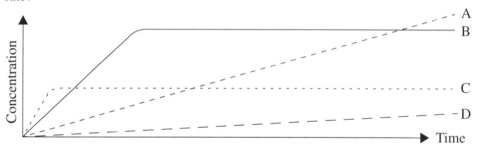

3. Iodate(V) ions oxidise iodide ions in acidic solution to form iodine and water according to the equation

$$IO_3^-{}_{(aq)} + 5 I^-{}_{(aq)} + 6 H^+{}_{(aq)} \Rightarrow 3 I_{2 (aq)} + 3 H_2O_{(l)}$$

If the number of moles of each reactant consumed after one minute was measured, which would have been consumed least?

A $\quad IO_3^-$
B $\quad I^-$
C $\quad H^+$
D They would all have been consumed to the same extent.

4. The rate of reaction between zinc and sulfuric acid is measured by weighing a zinc plate, which is then placed into a beaker of the acid. Every 10 minutes it is removed, rinsed, dried and reweighed. This is continued until all of the acid is consumed.

a) Sketch the graph you would expect for the mass of the zinc plate against time in the acid.

b) At what point is the reaction rate the greatest? How can you tell?

c) Suggest another way that the rate of this reaction could have been measured.

7.2 SOME TECHNIQUES FOR MEASURING RATES

There are a variety of techniques that can be used to measure the rate of a chemical reaction and some of the more common are described below. Anything that changes between the start and end of the reaction can in principle be used. It is however best if this changes by a large amount compared to the limits of accuracy of its measurement. It is also simpler to use quantitatively if the characteristic is directly proportional to the concentration of one or more components. For these reasons monitoring the rate of reaction by observing a pH change is generally not to be recommended, because the pH, being a logarithmic scale (see Section 9.3, page 293), will only change by 0.30 for a change of [H$^+$] by a factor of 2.

In some techniques the time taken for a particular event to occur may be used to measure the reaction rate (e.g. the time taken for a piece of magnesium ribbon to dissolve in a dilute acid). In these techniques it is important to remember that the greater the time the smaller the rate of reaction, i.e. the rate of reaction is **inversely proportional** to the time taken:

$$\text{Rate } \alpha \ \frac{1}{\text{Time}}$$

If the purpose of the investigation is simply to observe the effect of some variable, such as the concentration of a particular species, on the rate of reaction, then a graph of the property proportional to concentration against time, will suffice. If however the reaction rate is required in standard units (mol dm^{-3} s^{-1}) then it will be necessary to calibrate the system so as to produce graphs of concentration against time.

Whichever technique is being used, it is important to keep the reaction mixture at a constant temperature during the reaction, because temperature has a great effect on the rate of reaction. For this reason it is usual to immerse the reaction vessel in a water bath at the required temperature. It is also preferable to immerse the reactants in the water bath, to allow them to reach the required temperature before mixing.

TITRATION

This involves removing small samples from the reaction mixture at different times and then titrating the sample to determine the concentration of either one of the reactants or one of the products at this time. The results can then be used directly to generate a graph of concentration against time. In its simplest form this is only really suitable for quite slow reactions, in which the time taken to titrate the mixture is insignificant compared to the total time taken for the reaction. One common variant that helps to overcome this difficulty is to **quench** the reaction before carrying out the titration. This means altering the conditions so as to virtually stop the reaction. This can be done by rapidly cooling the reaction mixture to a very low temperature or by adding an excess of a compound that rapidly reacts with one of the reactants. If for example the reaction was that of a haloalkane with an alkali, it could be quenched by running the reaction mixture into an excess of a strong acid. This means that the time at which the sample of the reaction mixture was quenched is much easier to determine.

Another example of a reaction that can be readily measured by this technique is the rate of reaction of hydrogen peroxide with iodide ions in acidic solution to produce iodine and water. The amount of iodine produced can be measured by titrating the mixture with aqueous sodium thiosulfate. The reaction mixture can be quenched by adding excess of an insoluble solid base, such as powdered calcium carbonate, to neutralise the acid required for reaction.

$$H_2O_{2\ (aq)} + 2\ H^+_{\ (aq)} + 2\ I^-_{\ (aq)} \Rightarrow 2\ H_2O_{(l)} + I_{2\ (aq)}$$

COLLECTION OF AN EVOLVED GAS/INCREASE IN GAS PRESSURE

The gas produced in the reaction is collected either in a gas syringe, or in a graduated vessel over water. The volume of gas collected at different times can be recorded. This technique is obviously limited to reactions that produce a gas. In addition, if the gas is to be collected over water, this gas must not be water soluble. An alternative technique is to carry out the reaction in a vessel of fixed volume and monitor the increase in the gas pressure. These techniques would be suitable for measuring the rate of reaction between a moderately reactive metal (such as zinc) and an acid (such as hydrochloric acid).

$$Zn_{(s)} + 2\ H^+_{\ (aq)} \Rightarrow Zn^{2+}_{\ (aq)} + H_{2\ (g)}$$

MEASUREMENT OF THE MASS OF THE REACTION MIXTURE

The total mass of the reaction mixture will only vary if a gas is evolved. To be really effective, the gas being evolved should have a high molar mass (i.e. not hydrogen), so that there is a significant change in mass, also the gas should not be significantly soluble in the solvent used. This technique would be suitable for measuring the rate of reaction between a metal carbonate (such as calcium carbonate, marble chips) and an acid (such as hydrochloric acid), by measuring the rate of mass loss resulting from the evolution of carbon dioxide.

$$CaCO_{3\ (s)} + 2\ H^+_{\ (aq)} \Rightarrow Ca^{2+}_{\ (aq)} + H_2O_{(l)} + CO_{2\ (g)}$$

LIGHT ABSORPTION

If a reaction produces a precipitate, then the time taken for the precipitate to obscure a mark made on a piece of paper under the reaction vessel can be used as a measure of reaction rate. For simple work comparison of the times, keeping the total volume of liquid constant will suffice; e.g. if the time taken doubles then the reaction rate is halved. A reaction that is often studied by this technique is the reaction between aqueous thiosulfate ions and a dilute acid which gives sulfur dioxide, water and a finely divided precipitate of sulfur.

$$S_2O_3^{2-}_{\ (aq)} + 2\ H^+_{\ (aq)} \Rightarrow H_2O_{(l)} + SO_{2\ (g)} + S_{(s)}$$

If the reaction involves a coloured reactant or product, then the intensity of the colour can be used to monitor the concentration of that species. In its simplest form this can be done by comparing the colour by eye against a set of standard solutions of known concentration. The technique is far more precise if an instrument that measures the absorbance (which is directly proportional to concentration – see the Beer–Lambert law in Section 17.3, page 660), such as a colorimeter or spectrophotometer is available. If a colorimeter is used then a filter of the complementary colour to that of the coloured species should be chosen – an aqueous solution of a copper salt is blue because it absorbs red light, so that it is the intensity of transmitted red light not blue light that will vary with its concentration. If a spectrophotometer is used, then a wavelength near to the absorption maximum of the coloured species should be selected.

A reaction that is often studied by this technique is the reaction between propanone and iodine to form iodopropanone. The yellow–brown iodine is the only coloured species involved and so the intensity of blue light (or light of wavelength ~450 nm if a spectrophotometer is used) passing through the solution will increase with time as the concentration of the iodine falls. Most instruments, however, give a direct reading of absorbance which has an inverse relationship to the transmitted light (see Section 17.3, page 660), so that absorbance decreases with time.

$$CH_3COCH_{3\,(aq)} + I_{2\,(aq)} \Rightarrow CH_3COCH_2I_{(aq)} + H^+_{(aq)} + I^-_{(aq)}$$

ELECTRICAL CONDUCTIVITY

The presence of ions allows a solution to conduct, so if there is a significant change in the concentration of ions (especially hydrogen and hydroxide ions which have an unusually high conductivity) during the course of a reaction, then the reaction rate may be found from the change in conductivity. This is usually found by measuring the A.C. resistance between two electrodes with a fixed geometry, immersed in the solution. A reaction that is suitable for this technique would be the hydrolysis of phosphorus(III) chloride that produces dihydrogenphosphate(III) ions, hydrogen ions and chloride ions from non–ionic reactants.

$$PCl_{3\,(aq)} + 3\,H_2O_{(l)} \Rightarrow H_2PO_3^-{}_{(aq)} + 4\,H^+_{(aq)} + 3\,Cl^-_{(aq)}$$

CLOCK TECHNIQUES

There are some reactions in which the product can be consumed by further reaction with another added substance. When all of this substance is consumed then an observable change will occur. The time taken for this corresponds to the time for a certain amount of product to have been formed and so is inversely proportional to the rate of reaction. The classic reaction studied in this way is the reaction between hydrogen peroxide and iodide ions, in the presence of acid, to form iodine and water. Thiosulfate ions are added to the system and these initially react rapidly with the iodine produced. When all of the thiosulfate has been consumed, free iodine is liberated and this colours the solution yellow, or more commonly blue–black through the addition of starch solution (which forms an intensely coloured complex with iodine) to the system.

$$H_2O_{2\,(l)} + 2\,H^+_{(aq)} + 2\,I^-_{(aq)} \Rightarrow 2\,H_2O_{(l)} + I_{2\,(aq)}$$

$$2\,S_2O_3^{2-}{}_{(aq)} + I_{2\,(aq)} \Rightarrow S_4O_6^{2-}{}_{(aq)} + 2I^-_{(aq)}$$

The blue colour of the iodine-starch complex suddenly appears when all of the thiosulfate has been consumed. The time taken for this to occur is inversely proportional to the rate.

EXERCISE 7.2

1. The rate of a chemical reaction can sometimes be determined by measuring the change in mass of the reaction flask and its contents with time. For which of the following reactions would this technique be most successful?

A Magnesium oxide and dilute sulfuric acid.
B Aqueous sodium chloride and aqueous silver nitrate.
C Copper(II) carbonate and dilute hydrochloric acid.
D Zinc and aqueous copper(II) sulfate.

2. You wish to carry out an investigation that involves the use of a conductivity meter to monitor the rate of a chemical reaction. Which of the reactions below would be the **least** suitable for this?

A $H_2O_{2\,(aq)} + 2\,H^+_{(aq)} + 2\,I^-_{(aq)} \Rightarrow 2\,H_2O_{(l)} + I_{2\,(aq)}$
B $Ba^{2+}_{(aq)} + SO_4^{2-}_{(aq)} \Rightarrow BaSO_{4\,(s)}$
C $POCl_{3\,(l)} + 3\,H_2O_{(l)} \Rightarrow 4\,H^+_{(aq)} + 3\,Cl^-_{(aq)} + H_2PO_4^-_{(aq)}$
D $2\,H_2O_{2\,(aq)} \Rightarrow 2\,H_2O_{(l)} + O_{2\,(g)}$

3. For which one of the following reactions would a colorimeter be most suitable for monitoring the reaction rate?

A The reaction of acidified permanganate ions (manganate(VII)) ions with ethanedioic acid to form carbon dioxide, manganese(II) ions and water.
B The reaction of magnesium carbonate with a dilute acid to form a soluble magnesium salt, carbon dioxide and water.
C The reaction of bromobutane with aqueous sodium hydroxide to form butanol and aqueous sodium bromide.
D The reaction of lithium with water to form aqueous lithium hydroxide and hydrogen.

4. You wish to measure the rate of reaction of acidified dichromate(VI) ions with aqueous sulfur dioxide to produce aqueous chromium(III) ions and aqueous sulfate ions at 35°C. This reaction involves a colour change from orange to green. Discuss how you might go about doing this, the measurements you would need to take and the precautions required.

5. During your study of chemistry you will most likely have studied the way in which altering certain variables affected the rate of a chemical reaction.

a) What reaction did you study?
b) What technique did you use to study the rate of this reaction? Why do you think this method was appropriate?
c) What variable did you change? How was this carried out?
d) How could you modify the investigation to study another variable. State which variable you are now going to study and outline how you would carry this out along with any precautions you would take.

7.3 COLLISION THEORY

7.2.1 Describe and explain the collision theory.

Students should know that not all collisions lead to a reaction.

7.2.2 Define activation energy (E_a) and explain that reactions occur when reacting species have $E \geq E_a$.

Molecules must have a minimum energy and appropriate collision geometry in order to react. A simple treatment is all that is required. Cross reference with 5.1.3 and 5.1.4.

7.2.3 Predict and explain, using collision theory, the qualitative effect of particle size, temperature, concentration and catalysts on the rate of a reaction.

Increasing the temperature increases the frequency of collisions but, more importantly, the proportion of molecules with $E \geq E_a$ increases.

7.2.4 Explain that reactions can occur by more than one step and that one step can determine the rate of reaction.

Few reactions involve just one step although one step in the reaction, the rate determining step, determines the reaction rate. Orders of reactions and rate laws are not required. © IBO 2001

Collisions are vital for chemical change, either to provide the energy required for a particle to change (e.g. for a bond to break), and/or to bring the reactants into contact.

As particles approach each other there is repulsion between the electron clouds of the particles. In order for reaction to occur, the collision must have sufficient energy to overcome this repulsion. Frequently energy is also required to break some of the bonds in the particles before a reaction can take place. Hence not all collisions lead to a reaction. This minimum amount of energy required for reaction is known as the **activation energy (E_a)** for the reaction. This is illustrated, for an exothermic reaction, in Figure 7.2 below

Figure 7.2 – Illustrating the principle of activation energy

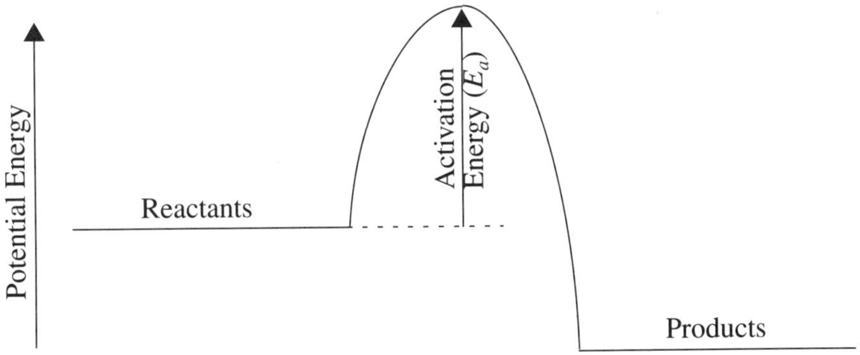

The activation energy involved varies tremendously from reaction to reaction. In some cases (such as the reaction of the hydrogen ion and hydroxide ion) it is so low that reaction occurs on almost every collision even at low temperatures. In other cases (such as sugar and oxygen) it is so high that reaction at room temperature is negligible.

In order to react, the two particles involved must:

- collide with each other

- the collision must be energetic enough to overcome the activation energy of the reaction

- the collision must occur with the correct geometrical alignment, i.e. it must bring the reactive parts of the molecule into contact in the correct way

This final factor, often called the **steric factor**, is particularly important with regard to reactions involving large organic molecules.

If anything increases the collision rate, then the rate of reaction increases, similarly for anything that increases the proportion of the collisions that have an energy equal to or greater than the activation energy. These factors are summarised in Table 7.1 below:

Table 7.1 – Factors affecting the rate of reaction

Factors mainly affecting the collision rate	Factors mainly affecting the proportion with required E_a
Concentration/pressure	Temperature
Surface area	Catalyst

The rate at which particles collide is increased by increasing the **concentration** of the reactants. Thus marble chips react faster with concentrated hydrochloric acid than they do with the dilute acid. For gases, increasing the pressure is equivalent to increasing the concentration. If the reaction involves substances in phases that do not mix (e.g. a solid and a liquid, or a liquid and a gas) then an increase in the **surface area** in contact will increase the collision rate. As a result powdered calcium carbonate reacts faster with hydrochloric acid than lumps of the solid with the same mass.

The number of molecules with the required activation energy is much greater at a higher **temperature** than at a lower one. This means that marble chips react more rapidly with warm hydrochloric acid than with cold hydrochloric acid. Increasing the temperature also has a very slight effect on the collision rate, but in most cases this is insignificant compared to its effect on the proportion with the required activation energy. For many reactions an increase in temperature of 10°C will double the rate of reaction. A **catalyst** is a substance that increases the rate of a chemical reaction without undergoing any overall change. Catalysts achieve this by providing an alternative reaction mechanism with a lower activation energy by which the reaction can take place, so that a greater proportion of collisions will have the required energy. The factors affecting reaction rate are illustrated below and the effects of temperature and catalyst are discussed in much more detail in Section 7.6, page 239.

Figure 7.3 – The factors affecting the rate of a reaction

a)   Concentration – higher concentration, more particles in a given volume, hence more collisions

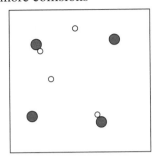 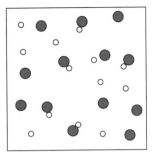

b)   Surface area – greater surface area, so more collisions per second can occur.

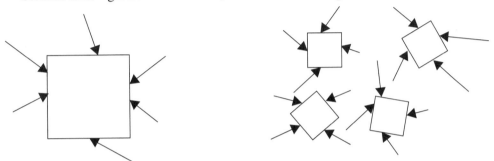

c)   Temperature – higher temperature, more collisions with the required activation energy

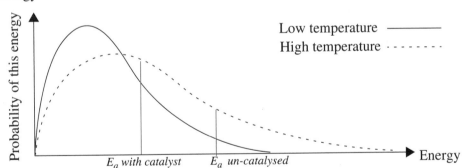

d)   Catalyst – provides an alternative mechanism with a lower activation energy

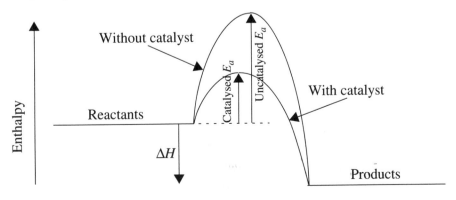

CORE

The chance of more than two particles colliding simultaneously is very small. This means that if there are more than two reactants, the reaction must occur by a number of simpler reaction steps. In addition, many reactions that have apparently simple equations do not occur in this manner, but are the result of a number of steps. The simple stages by which a chemical reaction occurs are known as the **mechanism** of the reaction. The sum of the various steps of the mechanism must equal the balanced equation for the reaction.

The various steps in the reaction mechanism will have the potential to occur at different rates. The products cannot however be formed faster than the slowest of these steps and so this is known as the **rate determining step**. An analogy would be that if people can come off a train at the rate of 20 per second, can travel up the escalator at a rate of 10 per second, and can pass through the ticket barrier into the street at a rate of 50 per second, then they will still only reach the street at a rate of 10 people per second. Making larger doors on the train or putting in an extra ticket barrier will not make this any faster, only a change affecting the escalator (i.e. the slow step) will increase the rate.

EXERCISE 7.3

1. Which one of the following factors does **not** affect the rate of a chemical reaction?

    A   The amounts of the reagents.
    B   The concentration of the reagents.
    C   The temperature of the reagents.
    D   The presence of a catalyst.

2. In most chemical reactions, the rate of reaction decreases as the reaction proceeds. The usual reason for this is that

    A   The energy for the reaction is running out.
    B   The concentrations of the reactants are becoming lower.
    C   The temperature is falling as the reaction proceeds.
    D   The activation energy becomes greater.

3. In which of the following situations would you expect the rate of reaction between marble (calcium carbonate) and nitric acid to be the greatest?

    A   Powdered marble and 2 mol dm^{-3} acid at 40°C.
    B   Powedered marble and 0.5 mol dm^{-3} acid at 40°C.
    C   Powdered marble and 2 mol dm^{-3} acid at 20°C.
    B   Marble chips and 0.5 mol dm^{-3} acid at 40°C.

4. In which one of the following reactions would surface area **not** be a factor affecting the rate?

    A   Zinc and sulfuric acid.
    B   Carbon dioxide gas with limewater (aqueous calcium hydroxide).
    C   Vegetable oil and aqueous sodium hydroxide.
    D   Aqueous oxalic acid and aqueous potassium permanganate.

5. Which one of the following reactions **must** occur by more than one reaction step?

A $H^+_{(aq)} + OH^-_{(aq)} \Rightarrow H_2O_{(l)}$

B $2\,H_2O_{2\,(aq)} \Rightarrow 2H_2O_{(l)} + O_{2\,(g)}$

C $2H_{2\,(g)} + O_{2\,(g)} \Rightarrow 2H_2O_{(l)}$

D $H_{2\,(g)} + O_{3\,(g)} \Rightarrow H_2O_{(l)} + O_{2\,(g)}$

6. Explain briefly why:

a) Increasing the concentration of the reagents usually increases the rate of a chemical reaction.

b) A reaction does not occur every time the reacting species collide.

c) Increasing the temperature increases the rate of reaction.

7. The rate of decomposition of an aqueous solution of hydrogen peroxide can be followed by recording the volume of gas collected over water in a measuring cylinder, against time.

a) Sketch the graph of volume against time you would expect for the complete decomposition of a sample of hydrogen peroxide.

b) On the same axes, use a dotted line to sketch the curve that you would expect to find if the experiment were repeated using a smaller volume of a more concentrated solution of hydrogen peroxide so that the number of moles of hydrogen peroxide remains constant.

c) When lead(IV) oxide is added, the rate at which oxygen is evolved suddenly increases, even though at the end of the reaction, the lead(IV) oxide remains unchanged. Explain this?

d) In what way, apart from altering the concentration or adding another substance, could the rate at which the hydrogen peroxide decomposes be increased?

7.4 RATE EXPRESSION

16.1.1 Define the terms rate constant and order of reaction. [Also A 2.1]

16.1.2 Derive the rate expression for a reaction from data. [Also A 2.2]

Rate = k [A]^m[B]^n, where k=rate constant, [A]=concentration of A in mol dm^{-3} etc., m,n = integers, m + n = overall order of the reaction.

16.1.3 Draw and analyse graphical representations for zero-, first- and second- order reactions. [Also A 2.3]

16.1.4 Define the term half-life and calculate the half-life for first-order reactions only.

The half-life should be calculated from graphs and by using the integrated form of the rate equation. The integrated rate equation for second-order reactions is not required. [Also A 2.4]

Altering the concentration of the reactants usually affects the rate of the reaction, but the way in which the rate is affected is not the same for all substances, nor can it be predicted from the balanced equation for the reaction. The **rate expression** gives the way in which the concentration of the reactants affect the rate. This expression must be determined experimentally, usually by varying the concentration of one species whilst holding those of the other species constant. Consider a reaction involving reactants A, B, etc. The rate expression for this reaction takes the form:

$$\text{Rate of reaction} = -\frac{d[A]}{dt} = k[A]^m[B]^n \text{ etc.}$$

The **order of reaction** is said to be '*m*' in substance A, '*n*' in substance B etc. The **overall order** of the reaction is the sum of these powers, i.e. *m* + *n* etc. The constant '*k*' in the rate expression is known as the **rate constant**.

Note that '*k*' will not vary with concentration, but it will vary greatly with temperature, so it is important to always state the temperature at which the rate constant was measured.

If doubling the concentration of one species (say *A*), whilst the other conditions are held constant, has no effect on the initial rate of reaction, then the reaction is zero order with respect to *A* (as $2^0 = 1$). If doubling the concentration of *A* doubles the rate, then the reaction is first order with respect to A (as $2^1 = 2$). If it increases by a factor of four it is second order with respect to A (as $2^2 = 4$), by a factor of eight then third order with respect to *A* (as $2^3 = 8$) etc. Similar considerations apply to altering the concentrations by other factors.

Table 7.2 gives some data about the effect of varying concentrations upon the rate of a chemical reaction involving three species – A, B and C:

Table 7.2 – Data about the effect of concentration changes on the rate of a reaction

Experiment	[A] mol dm^{-3}	[B] mol dm^{-3}	[C] mol dm^{-3}	Initial rate mol dm^{-3}s^{-1}
1	0.400	1.600	0.0600	4.86×10^{-3}
2	0.800	1.600	0.0600	9.72×10^{-3}
3	0.400	0.800	0.0600	4.86×10^{-3}
4	0.800	1.600	0.1800	87.5×10^{-3}

Comparing experiments 1 and 2, the only change is that the concentration of A has been doubled. The data in the table indicate that the rate has been doubled, so the reaction is first order with respect to A. Comparing 1 and 3, the only change is that the concentration of B has been halved, but there is no effect on the reaction rate, indicating that the reaction is zero order with respect to B (if first order it would be $\frac{1}{2}$ the rate in 1, if second order, then $\frac{1}{4}$ of the rate in 1). Comparing 2 and 4 the only difference is that the concentration of C has been increased by a factor of three. The rate has increased by a factor of nine, so the reaction is second order in C (as $3^2 = 9$ – if it had been first order in C, the rate would only have increased by a factor of 3.). This means that the rate expression for this reaction is:

$$\text{Rate} = k.[A]^1[B]^0[C]^2 \text{ or more simply Rate} = k.[A][C]^2$$

Hence the reaction is third order (1 + 2) overall.

The rate constant for a reaction may be calculated provided that the rate of reaction has been measured in standard units of mol dm^{-3} s^{-1}, at known concentrations of the reagents. Consider the data in Table 7.2 above. The rate constant can be calculated by substituting any set of data in the rate expression. For example using the data from experiment 1:

$$\text{Rate} = k[A][C]^2$$
$$4.86 \times 10^{-3} = k(0.400)(0.06)^2$$
$$k = \frac{4.86 \times 10^{-3}}{0.400 \times 0.06^2}$$
$$= 3.375 \text{ mol}^{-2} \text{ dm}^6 \text{ s}^{-1}$$

Note the units for the rate constant. These only hold for a reaction that is third order overall and other order reactions will have rate constants with different units.
The units can be calculated remembering that the units for rates are mol dm^{-3}s^{-1} and the units for concentrations are mol dm^{-3}. Hence the units of the rate constant are:

Zero order mol dm^{-3}s^{-1}
First order s^{-1}
Second order mol^{-1}dm^{3}s^{-1}
Third order mol^{-2}dm^{6}s^{-1}

In general, (mol dm^{-3})$^{q-1}$s^{-1}
where q is the overall order

The order of reaction can also be found from a graph showing the way in which the initial rate varies with the initial concentration of the reactant, all other factors being equal. This is illustrated in Figure 7.4.

Figure 7.4 – Graphs showing the effect of concentration on rate

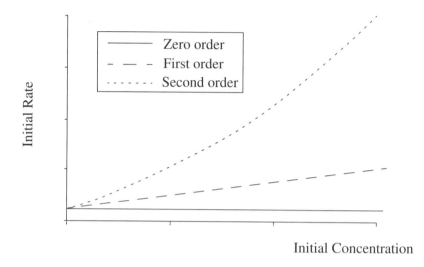

The order of a reaction can also be found from a graph of concentration against time, which shows the effect of the reactants being used up on the rate of reaction. The gradient of the graph at any point gives the rate of reaction. If this is constant (i.e. the graph is a straight line) then the reaction must be zero order in the reactants whose concentrations are undergoing significant change, because the decrease in concentration is not affecting the rate of reaction. If the reaction rate is halved when the concentration is halved, then the reaction is first order. If halving the concentration causes the rate to fall by a factor of 4, the reaction is second order ($(\frac{1}{2})^2 = \frac{1}{4}$) etc. To be really useful such experiments should have all but one reagent in large excess, so that the order in the limiting reagent is what causes the reaction rate to change.

It is easy to recognise a first order reaction from graphs of concentration (or something proportional to concentration) against time. This is because the concentration shows an exponential decrease, i.e. the time for the concentration to fall from its initial value to half its initial value, is equal to the time required for it to fall from half to one quarter of its initial value and from one quarter to one eighth etc. This time is known as the **half life** $t_{(1/2)}$ of the reaction and it is illustrated in Figure 7.5 below. Figure 7.5 shows that the successive half lives of reactions of other orders vary in characteristic ways.

Figure 7.5 – Graphs showing the variation of concentration with time for reactions of different orders

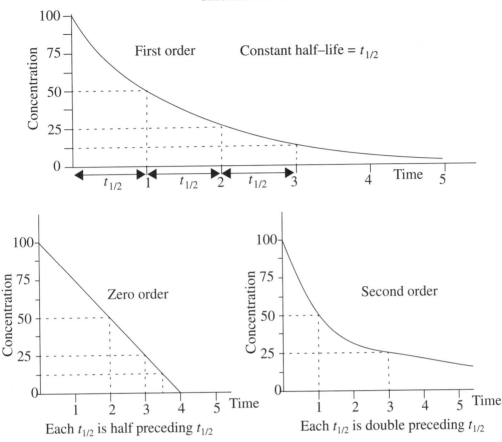

The first order exponential decay is the same as that found in radioactive decay. Because it remains constant, the half-life is an important quantity for these systems and it can be found from an appropriate graph (such as that above) or it may be found from the rate constant (k) by substituting in the equation:

$$t_{\frac{1}{2}} = \frac{\ln 2}{k}$$

This results from the integration of the first order rate expression. Obviously if the half life is known, say from a concentration-time graph, then this equation may be rearranged to find the rate constant.

ADVANCED

OPTION

EXERCISE 7.4

Questions 1 to 4 refer to the rate expression for a chemical reaction given below:

$$Rate = k[A][B]^2[H^+]$$

1. Which one of the following statements is **not** true about this reaction?

A   It is first order in A.
B   It is second order in B.
C   It is first order in H^+.
D   It is third order overall.

2. The units of the rate constant (k) will be:

A $mol\ dm^{-3}\ s^{-1}$
B $mol\ s^{-1}$
C $dm^3\ mol^{-1}\ s^{-1}$
D $dm^9\ mol^{-3}\ s^{-1}$

3. If the concentrations of A and B are both doubled, but the concentration of H^+ remains constant, the rate would increase by a factor of:

A   2
B   4
C   8
D   16

4. Which one of the following would lead to the greatest increase in reaction rate?

A   Doubling the concentration of A only.
B   Doubling the concentration of B only.
C   Doubling the concentration of A and H^+ only.
D   Doubling the concentration of B and H^+ only.

5. Which one of the graphs shown would indicate that a reaction was zero order in the reactant whose concentration was being varied?

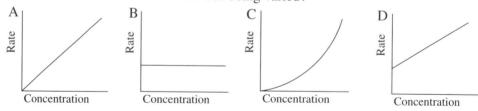

6. The following data refers to the acid catalysed iodination of propanone

$$CH_3-CO-CH_{3\ (aq)} + I_{2\ (aq)} \Rightarrow CH_3-CO-CH_2-I_{(aq)} + H^+_{(aq)} + I^-_{(aq)}$$

Solution	$[CH_3-CO-CH_3]$ mol dm^{-3}	$[I_2]$ mol dm^{-3}	$[H^+]$ mol dm^{-3}	Initial Rate mol dm^{-3} s^{-1}
1	0.2	0.008	1	4×10^{-6}
2	0.4	0.008	1	8×10^{-6}
3	0.6	0.008	1	1.2×10^{-5}
4	0.4	0.004	1	8×10^{-6}
5	0.4	0.002	1	8×10^{-6}
6	0.2	0.008	2	8×10^{-6}
7	0.2	0.008	4	1.6×10^{-5}

a) From the data in the table derive the rate expression for the reaction, explaining the evidence for the dependency on each of the species.

b) Give the order with respect to $CH_3-CO-CH_3$, I_2 and H^+, and the overall order.

c) Use the data from Solution 1 to calculate the value of the rate constant.

7. The data given below refer to the hydrolysis of a 0.002 mol dm^{-3} solution of an ester by 0.2 mol dm^{-3} aqueous sodium hydroxide.

Time (s)	60	120	180	240	300	360	420	480
[ester] (mmol dm^{-3})	1.48	1.10	0.81	0.60	0.45	0.33	0.24	0.18

a) Plot a suitable graph to determine the order of the reaction with respect to the ester, explaining your method.

b) Use your graph to determine the half-life of the reaction and hence determine a value for the apparent rate constant, giving appropriate units.

c) Why does this graph give no indication of the order with respect to the hydroxide ion?

d) How would you modify the experiment to determine the dependence on hydroxide ion?

e) Assuming that it is also first order in hydroxide ion, write a new rate expression. Use this to calculate a value for the rate constant, giving appropriate units. Why does this differ from the value found in b) and how are the two related?

7.5 REACTION MECHANISM

17.2 Define the terms 'rate determining step', 'molecularity' and 'activated complex'.

Describe the relationship between mechanism, order, rate determining step and activated complex.

Examples should be restricted to 1 or 2 step reactions, where the mechanism is known. Students should be able to demonstrate an understanding of what an activated complex (transition state) is and how the order of a reaction relates to the mechanism. [Also A 3.1 & A 3.2]   © IBO 2001

There are only two kinds of fundamental process that can occur to bring about a chemical reaction. More complex changes occur by a series of these fundamental processes, known as the **mechanism** of the reaction. Firstly, a species can break up or undergo internal rearrangement to form products, which is known as a **unimolecular** process. As this only involves one species, a unimolecular step is first order in that species. Radioactive decay, for example, is unimolecular. Secondly, two species can collide and interact to form the product(s) and this is known as a **bimolecular** process. As this involves the collision of the two species then doubling the concentration of either will double the collision rate. Hence, it is first order in each and second order overall. Both unimolecular and bimolecular processes can be either reversible (i.e. lead to equilibrium) or irreversible (i.e. lead to complete reaction) depending on the relative stability of the reactants and products. Whether a particular reaction step is unimolecular or bimolecular, is known as the **molecularity** of that reaction step. In a bimolecular process, the species collide to initially give an **activated complex** (or **transition state**), at a potential energy maximum, which then breaks down to either form the products or reform the reactants.

A $\Rightarrow/\rightleftharpoons$ Products	Unimolecular	Forward rate α [A]
A + B $\Rightarrow/\rightleftharpoons$ Products	Bimolecular	Forward rate α [A][B]

As outlined above, many chemical reactions occur by a series of simple steps known as the mechanism of the reaction. It is possible to write a number of mechanisms (i.e. series of fundamental processes by which the reaction could occur) for any reaction and it is only possible to suggest which model in fact operates by studying the kinetics of the reaction. The overall reaction cannot occur faster than the slowest of these steps and this is known as the **rate determining step**. Only species that are involved in the rate determining step, or in an equilibrium preceding it, can affect the overall rate of reaction. Hence, determining the rate expression for a reaction will help to identify the rate determining step and this will eliminate many possible mechanisms for the reaction.

Consider for example a reaction

$$2A + B \Rightarrow C + D$$

as an illustration of how the rate expression will depend upon the mechanism and upon which step in the mechanism is the rate determining step.

There are three particles involved in the reaction, so it is most unlikely that this occurs as a single step. Many mechanisms for the reaction could be written and these would produce a variety of rate expressions. Some examples are given in Table 7.3 below. Note that adding together the different steps always leads to the overall equation.

Table 7.3 – Some possible mechanisms for the reaction; $2A + B \Rightarrow C + D$

	Mechanism		Rate expression
I	$A + B \Rightarrow X + C$ $A + X \Rightarrow D$	Slow RDS Fast	Rate α [A] [B]
II	$A + B \rightleftharpoons X$ $A + X \Rightarrow C + D$	Fast Slow RDS	Rate α $[A]^2$ [B]
III	$A + A \rightleftharpoons A_2$ $A_2 + B \Rightarrow C + D$	Fast Slow RDS	Rate α $[A]^2$ [B]
IV	$A + A \rightleftharpoons A_2$ $A_2 + B \Rightarrow C + D$	Slow RDS Fast	Rate α $[A]^2$
V	$B \Rightarrow X$ $X + A \Rightarrow Y + C$ $Y + A \Rightarrow D$	Slow RDS Fast Fast	Rate α [B]

Some of these mechanisms involve equilibria, a topic that is dealt with in greater detail in Chapter 8. For the present purposes it is enough to know that for the equilibrium, $A + B \rightleftharpoons X$, the [X] will depend on both the [A] and [B]. Similarly in the equilibrium, $A + A \rightleftharpoons A_2$, the $[A_2]$ will be proportional to $[A]^2$.

In I, the first bimolecular step is rate determining so that the rate will depend on the rate of collisions between A and B, i.e. the rate will be proportional to [A].[B]. In II the second bimolecular step is rate determining so that the rate will depend on the rate of collisions between A and X, i.e. the rate will be proportional to [A] [X], but [X] will depend on both [A] and [B], so that taking this into account the rate depends on $[A]^2$ [B]. In V the rate depends on the unimolecular conversion of B to an intermediate X, so the rate only depends upon [B].

Note that III and IV only differ in which of the two steps is the rate determining step. This is not necessarily fixed, for example at very low [B] the second step could be the RDS (i.e. mechanism III), but at very high [B] the second step will become much faster so that now the first step might be rate determining (i.e. mechanism IV). Because A_2 will react with B as soon as it is formed, the first step is no longer an equilibrium. Note also that both mechanism II and mechanism III lead to the same rate expression and so some other means would have to be used to decide which (if either!) was operating.

Consider as another example the reaction between propanone and iodine:

$$CH_3COCH_{3\,(aq)} + I_{2\,(aq)} \Rightarrow CH_3COCH_2I_{(aq)} + H^+_{\,(aq)} + I^-_{\,(aq)}$$

Kinetics

This would appear to be a simple bimolecular process, but if this were the case, then the rate of reaction would be expected to depend on the concentrations of both the propanone and the iodine, i.e. the rate expression would be:

$$\text{Rate} = k\ [CH_3COCH_3]\ [I_2]$$

In practice it is found that the reaction is catalysed by acids and that the rate is independent of the concentration of iodine, i.e. that the reaction is first order in both propanone and hydrogen ions but zero order in iodine. Hence the rate expression is:

$$\text{Rate} = k\ [CH_3COCH_3]\ [H^+]$$

This means that one molecule of propanone and one hydrogen ion must be involved in the rate determining step, or in equilibria occurring before this. The commonly accepted mechanism for this reaction is:

$$CH_3COCH_3 + H^+ \rightleftharpoons CH_3C(OH^+)CH_3 \qquad\qquad \text{Fast equilibrium}$$

$$CH_3C(OH^+)CH_3 \Rightarrow CH_2{=}C(OH)CH_3 + H^+ \qquad\qquad \text{Slow – rate determining step}$$

$$CH_2{=}C(OH)CH_3 + I_2 \Rightarrow CH_3COCH_2I + H^+ + I^- \qquad \text{Fast (does not affect rate)}$$

This mechanism agrees with the experimentally determined rate expression. The rate expression can never prove that a particular mechanism is correct, but it can provide evidence that other possible mechanisms are wrong.

The species $CH_3C(OH^+)CH_3$ and $CH_2{=}C(OH)CH_3$ are known as **intermediates**, rather than activated complexes, because they occur at a potential energy minimum and are consumed in a later step in the mechanism. In this reaction mechanism there would be a number of activated complexes, firstly (A_1) between CH_3COCH_3 and H^+ before forming $CH_3C(OH^+)CH_3$ secondly (A_2) when $CH_3C(OH^+)CH_3$ starts to break up to form $CH_2{=}C(OH)CH_3$ and H^+ and finally (A_3) in the reaction of this with iodine. This is illustrated in Figure 7.6 below and the differences between intermediates and activated complexes (transition states) are summarised in Table 7.4.

Figure 7.6 - P.E. diagram for the iodination of propanone

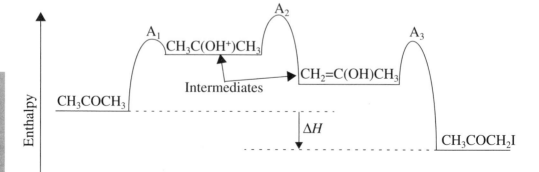

Table 7.4 - Differences between intermediates and activated complexes

Intermediates	Activated Complexes
Exist for a finite time	Have only a transient existence
Occur at a P.E. minimum	Occur at a P.E. maximum
Formed in one step of a reaction and consumed in a subsequent step	Exist part way through every step of a reaction

EXERCISE 7.5

1. Which one of these steps is unimolecular?

A $NH_3 + H^+ \Rightarrow NH_4^+$
B $H^+ + OH^- \Rightarrow H_2O$
C $N_2O_4 \Rightarrow 2\ NO_2$
D $H\bullet + Cl\bullet \Rightarrow HCl$

2. Which one of the following is **not** a difference between an activated complex and an intermediate?

A An activated complex occurs at a potential energy maximum and an intermediate at a minimum.
B An activated complex cannot take part in bimolecular reactions, but an intermediate can.
C An activated complex does not exist for a finite time but an intermediate does.
D An activated complex can reform the reactants, but an intermediate cannot.

3. The rate determining step of a mechanism is the one which

A occurs most rapidly.
B occurs most slowly.
C gives out the most energy.
D gives out the least energy.

4. Which one of the following mechanisms would give a first order dependence on A and zero order on B for the reaction below?

$$A + B \Rightarrow C$$

A	$A + X \rightleftharpoons Y$ (fast)	then	$Y + B \Rightarrow C + X$ (slow)
B	$B \Rightarrow X$ (slow)	then	$X + A \Rightarrow C$ (fast)
C	$2\ A \Rightarrow A_2$ (slow)	then	$A_2 + B \Rightarrow C$ (fast)
D	$A \Rightarrow X$ (slow)	then	$X + B \Rightarrow C$ (fast)

5. A reaction involves two reactants, A and B. The initial reaction rate was measured with different starting concentrations of A and B and the following results were obtained at 25°C:

[A] (mol dm^{-3})	[B] (mol dm^{-3})	Initial rate (mol dm^{-3} s^{-1})
0.2	0.2	3.2×10^{-4}
0.4	0.4	1.3×10^{-3}
0.4	0.8	1.3×10^{-3}

a) Deduce the order of the reaction in A, in B and the overall order. Hence write a rate expression for the reaction.

b) Calculate a value for the rate constant, giving suitable units.

c) What initial rate would you expect if the initial concentrations of both reactants were 0.1 mol dm^{-3}?

d) If the overall equation for the reaction is A + B $\Rightarrow$ C + D, write a mechanism, indicating which step is the rate determining step, that is:
i   consistent with the rate expression found.
ii   inconsistent with the rate expression found.

7.6 ACTIVATION ENERGY

16.3.1 Describe qualitatively the relationship between the rate constant (k) and temperature (T).

16.3.2 Describe how the Arrhenius equation can be used to determine the activation energy and the Arrhenius constant (A).

Arrhenius equation $k = Ae^{\left(-\frac{E_a}{RT}\right)}$. A relates to the geometric requirements of the collisions (see 7.2). Direct substitution using simultaneous equations and a graphical method can be used. The logarithmic form of the Arrhenius equation is: $\ln k = -\dfrac{E_a}{RT} + \ln A$. Both methods should be explained, but actual calculations are not needed.

16.3.3 Draw and explain enthalpy level diagrams for reactions with and without catalysts.

16.3.4 Distinguish between homogeneous catalysts and heterogeneous catalysts.

Homogeneous catalyst-reactants and catalyst are in the same phase. Heterogeneous catalyst-reactants and catalyst are in different phases.

16.3.5 Outline the use of homogeneous and heterogeneous catalysts.

Examples include hydrogenation using metals (see 13.2.7) and acid catalysed formation of esters.   © IBO 2001

In a substance, not all of the particles have exactly the same kinetic energy. Some particles have a greater energy than others. Graphs may be drawn of the distribution of energy amongst the particles at different temperatures. This distribution is known as the Maxwell–Boltzmann energy distribution. Some particles will have very little energy whilst others have high energy and in between there will be the energies that occur most frequently. An analogy would be drawing the distribution of speeds amongst cars travelling along a stretch of road. As the temperature increases, the number of particles with a high energy increases, though there are still some particles with very little energy. The result is a flattening of the distribution curve, because the total area under it must remain constant.

Figure 7.7 - The distribution of kinetic energy at two different temperatures

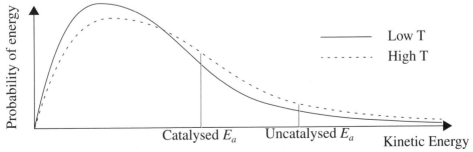

All reactions require a certain minimum energy, the activation energy (E_a), for the reaction to occur. As can be seen from Figure 7.7 above, at the higher temperature a greater proportion of the molecules have an energy greater than the activation energy,

ADVANCED

i.e. there is a greater proportion of the total area under the curve to the right of the E_a line (either the catalysed or uncatalysed) on the higher temperature curve than on the lower temperature curve. It is for this reason that reactions occur more rapidly at higher temperatures.

For many reactions it is found that the effect of temperature on reaction rate is given by the expression:

$$\text{Rate} = Ae^{\left(\frac{-E_a}{RT}\right)}$$

where E_a is the activation energy, T the absolute temperature (in Kelvin), R the gas constant (8.314 J K mol^{-1}; see Section 5.2, page 170) and A is the called the **Arrhenius constant** (or the pre–exponential factor). It is dependent on collision rate and steric factors i.e. any requirements regarding the geometry of the colliding particles). This equation is known as the **Arrhenius equation** after the chemist who first proposed it.

The expression indicates that the rate constant k depends exponentially on temperature, which is why temperature has such a large effect on reaction rate. Rather satisfyingly the expression for the area under the Maxwell–Boltzmann distribution curve in excess of E_a also gives an exponential dependence if $E_a \gg RT$. If we take logarithms to the base e (a mathematical procedure you may possibly not have met) then the Arrhenius equation is converted to:

$$\ln k = \ln A - \frac{E_a}{RT}$$

If the rate constant (k), or a value proportional to it (e.g. rate, with all other factors remaining constant), is known at two different temperatures there is no need to know A because, assuming it remains constant, the equation can be solved for E_a using simultaneous equations. Alternatively, the equation may be rearranged to:

$$\ln k = \ln A - \left(\frac{E_a}{R}\right)\frac{1}{T}$$

This is the equation of a straight line so, as shown in Figure 7.8 below, a graph of $\ln k$ against $\frac{1}{T}$ will be linear with gradient $-\frac{E_a}{R}$ and an intercept on the y–axis of $\ln A$. The activation energy for a reaction can therefore be found by measuring the rate of reaction at different temperatures, with all the other conditions unchanged (so that rate α k), and then plotting the data on a graph of this type.

Figure 7.8 – Determining the activation energy graphically

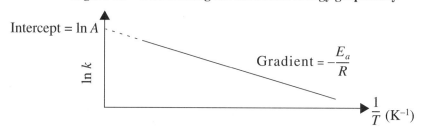

If a catalyst is used in a chemical reaction, it reduces the activation energy required by providing an alternative mechanism for the reaction. This increases the proportion of the reactants that have the required activation energy. This is shown in Figure 7.7 with regard to the Maxwell–Boltzmann distribution and in Figure 7.9 in terms of an energy level diagram.

Figure 7.9 – Illustrating the effect of catalysis on activation energy

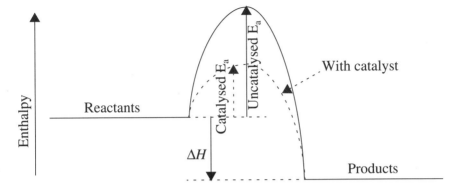

There are two ways in which catalysts can work, known as homogeneous catalysis and heterogeneous catalysis. In **homogeneous catalysis**, the catalyst is in the same phase as the reactants. The catalyst allows the reaction to take place by a different mechanism, which has a lower activation energy than the normal mechanism, thus increasing the rate of the reaction. In this process the catalyst is consumed at one stage in the mechanism and reformed at a later stage. An example is the action of iron(III) salts in catalysing the reaction of hydrogen peroxide and iodide ions in acidified aqueous solution:

$$H_2O_{2\,(aq)} + 2\,H^+_{(aq)} + 2\,I^-_{(aq)} \Rightarrow I_{2\,(aq)} + 2\,H_2O_{(l)}$$

In the presence of iron(III) ions the reaction occurs in two stages, both of which have lower activation energies than the direct reaction:

$$2\,Fe^{3+}_{(aq)} + 2\,I^-_{(aq)} \Rightarrow I_{2\,(aq)} + 2\,Fe^{2+}_{(aq)}$$

$$H_2O_{2\,(aq)} + 2\,H^+_{(aq)} + 2\,Fe^{2+}_{(aq)} \Rightarrow 2\,Fe^{3+}_{(aq)} + 2\,H_2O_{(l)}$$

The role of acid in the formation or hydrolysis of an ester is another example of homogeneous catalysis (see Section 11.7, page 382).

The second type of catalysis is **heterogeneous catalysis**. In this the catalyst is in a different phase to the reactants – most usually a solid catalyst with the reactants being in a liquid or gas phase. In this type of catalysis, the catalyst provides a reactive surface upon which the reaction can take place. The reactants are **adsorbed** onto the surface. This weakens the bonding in the molecules and also brings them into close contact. The reaction occurs on the surface and then the products are desorbed, freeing the surface for further reaction. Most industrial processes involve heterogeneous catalysts, often employing transition metals or their compounds (See section 3.5, page 103). Some common examples are given in Table 7.4 below.

ADVANCED

Table 7.4 – Some common examples of industrial heterogeneous catalysts

Process	Equation	Catalyst
Haber process	$N_{2(g)} + 3\,H_{2(g)} \rightleftharpoons 2\,NH_{3(g)}$	Iron
Contact process	$2\,SO_{2(g)} + O_{2(g)} \rightleftharpoons 2\,SO_{3(g)}$	Vanadium(V) oxide
Hydrogenation of oils	$>C=C<_{(l)} + H_{2(g)} \Rightarrow >CH\!-\!CH<_{(l)}$	Nickel

Enzymes are large protein molecules that catalyse biochemical processes, such as amylases in the conversion of starch to sugars in digestion. They are very efficient and have some characteristics of both homogeneous and heterogeneous catalysts. Like homogeneous catalysts most enzymes occur in the same phase as the reactants, but like heterogeneous catalysts the reactants bind to an active site on the surface of the enzyme molecule. Enzymes are dealt with in much more detail in Chapter 13.

EXERCISE 7.6

1. Which one of the following is **not** true about the activation energy of a reaction?

    A   It is related to the enthalpy change (ΔH) of the reaction.
    B   It is reduced by the addition of a catalyst.
    C   It is the minimum amount of energy that the reactants must have in order to form the products.
    D   The greater the activation energy the lower the rate of reaction.

2. The activation energy of a chemical reaction can be determined by measuring the effect on reaction rate of varying

    A   the temperature.
    B   the concentration of the reagents.
    C   the concentration of the catalyst.
    D   the surface area in contact.

3. Which one of the following is **not** true of **both** heterogeneous and homogeneous catalysts?

    A   They lower the activation energy of the reaction.
    B   They increase the reaction rate.
    C   They provide an active surface on which the reaction occurs.
    D   They remain unchanged at the end of the reaction.

ADVANCED

4. Which one of the following is an example of a homogeneous catalyst?

A Manganese(IV) oxide in the decomposition of hydrogen peroxide.
B Sulfuric acid in the formation of an ester from an alkanoic acid and an alkanol.
C Vanadium(V) oxide in the oxidation of sulfur dioxide to sulfur trioxide.
D Nickel in the hydrogenation of vegetable oils to form margarine.

5. The temperature at which a reaction is carried out is increased from 20°C to 40°C. If the half-life of the reaction was initially t, the half-life at the higher temperature will be:

A $2t$

B $\frac{1}{2}t$

C t^2

D It would depend on the size of the activation energy.

6. The activation energy for the reaction below is 112 kJ mol^{-1} and ΔH is +57 kJ mol^{-1}.

$$2\,NO_{2\,(g)} \rightleftharpoons 2\,NO_{(g)} + O_{2\,(g)}$$

a) Draw an energy level diagram illustrating the energy changes for this reaction. Clearly mark and label the activation energy E_a and the enthalpy change (ΔH).

b) On the same diagram, using dotted lines, show the effect of a platinum catalyst, clearly labelling the change 'With catalyst'. Would the platinum be acting as a homogeneous or heterogeneous catalyst?

c) Is the reaction exothermic or endothermic? When it occurs will the container become hotter, or cooler?

d) If the temperature was increased, how would this affect the rate of reaction? Explain this in terms of the collision theory of reactions (a diagram might help).

e) What other factor (i.e. **not** temperature or catalyst) could be changed to increase the rate of reaction – be precise, remembering that these are all gases.

f) Nitrogen dioxide is a brown gas, whereas nitrogen monoxide is colourless. Suggest how you might be able to measure the rate of reaction.

ADVANCED

7. When aqueous solutions of benzenediazonium chloride decompose, they evolve nitrogen gas. The table below gives the volume of gas obtained at different times for such a decomposition at 70°C.

Time (min)	Volume (cm³)	Time (min)	Volume (cm³)
1	5	7	28
2	9	9	33
3	13	12	40
4	17	16	48
5	21	20	54

a) If, when decomposition was complete, the total volume of gas released was 70 cm³, graphically determine the order of the reaction. What further data, if any, would you need to calculate a value for the rate constant?

b) Draw the apparatus you could use to obtain such data and state what precautions you would take.

c) If you wanted to determine the activation energy for this reaction, what further experiments would you carry out? How would you use the data from these to determine the activation energy?

EQUILIBRIUM

8.1 DYNAMIC EQUILIBRIUM

8.1.1 Outline the characteristics of a system in a state of equilibrium.

Many chemical reactions are reversible and never go to completion. Equilibrium can be approached from both directions. For a system in equilibrium the rate of the forward reaction equals the rate of the reverse reaction and the concentrations of all reactants and products remain constant. The system is closed and macroscopic properties remain constant. Use phase equilibrium as an example of dynamic equilibrium involving physical changes. © IBO 2001

Many chemical reactions go to completion because the products are much more energetically favourable than the reactants (see Section 6.9, page 209) and the activation energy is low enough to allow for a rapid reaction at the ambient temperature (see Section 7.6, page 239), e.g. the neutralisation of aqueous sodium hydroxide by hydrochloric acid. Other potential reactions do not occur either because, though energetically feasible, the activation energy barrier is too great for significant reaction at the ambient temperature (e.g. the combustion of sucrose at room temperature), or because as well as the activation energy being too high, the reactants are much more energetically stable than the products (e.g. the decomposition of water to hydrogen and oxygen). With some chemical systems however the energies of the reactants and products are of a similar order of magnitude so that the reaction is reversible, i.e. it can occur in either direction. An example is the reaction of ammonia and hydrogen chloride to form ammonium chloride. If ammonia gas and hydrogen chloride gas are mixed they react to form a white smoke of solid ammonium chloride. Conversely if ammonium chloride is heated, then some of the solid 'disappears', because it has been converted into ammonia and hydrogen chloride gas. We indicate such a reversible reaction by means of a double arrow as shown below:

$$NH_{3\,(g)} + HCl_{(g)} \rightleftharpoons NH_4Cl_{(s)}$$

If such a system is established in a closed vessel (i.e. so that no gases can escape) and at a constant temperature, then a chemical equilibrium is established.

Chemical equilibrium is the state of **dynamic equilibrium** that occurs in a closed system when the **forward and reverse reactions** of a reversible reaction occur at the **same rate**. If we consider mixing together two reactants A and B in the reversible reaction:

$$A + B \rightleftharpoons C + D$$

then initially the forward reaction occurs rapidly, but as the concentrations of the reactants fall its rate decreases. The reverse reaction initially cannot occur at all, but as soon as C and D start to form, its rate increases. Eventually the rate of the two reactions becomes equal, the concentrations reach constant values and equilibrium is established. This is shown in Figure 8.1 below:

Figure 8.1 – The change of concentration (a) and rate of reaction (b) with time in establishing a chemical equilibrium

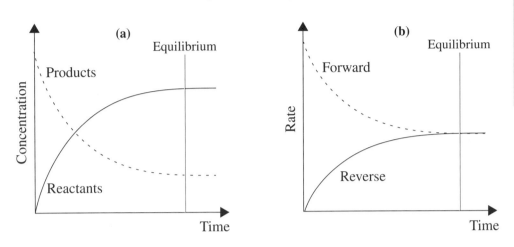

In an equilibrium all of the species involved, both reactants and products, are present at a constant concentration. As a consequence, macroscopic properties of the system, such as its colour, density, pH etc. are constant, even though on a microscopic scale there is continual interconversion of reactants and products. The concentrations of the species at equilibrium will reflect how readily they react on collision. If two species react on every collision, then the concentration required to produce a given rate of reaction will be much less than if they only have a 10% chance of reacting. In Figure 8.1 above, the reactants (A & B) react together far more easily than the products (C & D) because a smaller concentration is required to give the same rate of reaction. A similar equilibrium could obviously be established by mixing together C and D.

A specific example of such a system would be taking one mole of liquid dinitrogen tetroxide and introducing it into an evacuated, sealed one dm^3 flask at ~80°C. The colourless dinitrogen tetroxide would initially vapourise, then it would start to decompose into brown nitrogen dioxide. The rate of this decomposition would fall as the concentration of dinitrogen tetroxide decreases. Initially there is no nitrogen dioxide present to dimerise, but as more is produced the rate of the reverse reaction to form dinitrogen tetroxide will increase. Eventually the two rates would become equal and chemical equilibrium is established as indicated by the fact that the brown colour of the gas does not change any further. Under these conditions equilibrium would occur when about 60% of the dinitrogen tetroxide has been converted to nitrogen dioxide, so that the concentration of dinitrogen tetroxide has fallen to 0.4 mol dm^{-3} and the concentration of nitrogen dioxide has increased to 1.2 mol dm^{-3}, because each dinitrogen tetroxide molecule decomposes to give two nitrogen dioxide molecules. This is shown in the equation below and in Figure 8.2.

	$N_2O_{4 (g)}$	$\rightleftharpoons$	$2\ NO_{2 (g)}$
Initial concentration	1 mol dm^{-3}		0 mol dm^{-3}
Equilibrium concentration	0.4 mol dm^{-3}		1.2 mol dm^{-3}

CORE

Figure 8.2 – The equilibrium established by heating dinitrogen tetroxide

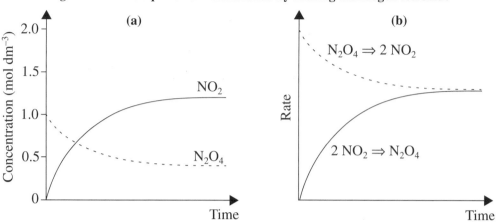

If 2 moles of nitrogen dioxide were cooled to 80°C from a much higher temperature, at which there was no dintrogen tetroxide present, then the brown colour would fade to a constant value, but eventually **exactly the same position of equilibrium** would be reached – see Figure 8.3 below.

Figure 8.3 – The equilibrium established by cooling nitrogen dioxide

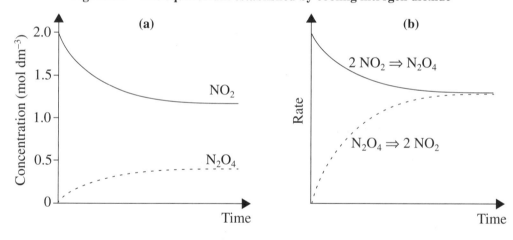

EXERCISE 8.1

1. In a system at equilibrium, which of the following is **not** always true?

    A   There are both reactants and products present.
    B   The forward and reverse reactions occur at the same rate.
    C   The concentrations of reactants and products are equal.
    D   The concentrations of reactants and products remain constant.

2. When solid phosphorus(V) chloride is heated it decomposes to solid phosphorus(III) chloride and chlorine gas. Conversely when phosphorus(III) chloride is shaken in an atmosphere of chlorine, it forms phosphorus(V) chloride.

    a) Write a balanced equation for this reversible reaction, with phosphorus(V) chloride on the left hand side.

    b) Consider warming some phosphorus(V) chloride in an empty, sealed flask:

        i   What will happen to the phosphorus(V) chloride?
        ii   As time passes what will happen to the rate at which this occurs? Why?
        iii   Initially, what is the rate of reaction between phosphorus (III) chloride and chlorine? Why?
        iv   As time passes what will happen to the rate at which this occurs? Why?
        v   Eventually what will happen to the rates of these two processes?
        vi   What name is given to this state?
        vii   At this point what species will be present in the flask? Will their concentrations all be equal?

    c) Would the same thing occur if the phosphorus(V) chloride was heated in an open beaker? If not explain why and predict what would in fact happen.

8.2 THE POSITION OF EQUILIBRIUM

8.2.1 State the equilibrium constant expression (K_c) for a homogeneous reaction.

Consider equilibria involving one phase, gases or species in aqueous solution. The equilibrium constant is specific to a given system and varies with temperature. No calculations are required.

8.2.2 Deduce the extent of a reaction from the magnitude of the equilibrium constant.

When $K_c \gg 1$, the reaction goes almost to completion. When $K_c \ll 1$, the reaction hardly proceeds.

8.2.3 Describe and predict the qualitative effects of changes of temperature, pressure and concentration on the position of equilibrium and the value of the equilibrium constant.

Use Le Chatelier's principle to predict the effects of these changes on the position of equilibrium. The value of the equilibrium constant (K_c) is only affected by temperature. The position of equilibrium may change without the value of K_c changing.

8.2.4 State and explain the effect of a catalyst on an equilibrium reaction.

8.2.5 Describe and explain the application of equilibrium and kinetics concepts to the Haber process and the Contact process.   © IBO 2001

The rate at which a reaction occurs depends upon the concentration of the species involved. If we consider both the forward and reverse reaction in the equilibrium

$$A + B \rightleftharpoons C + D$$

to be first order in each species (the final result can also be proved for a more general case) then the rate expressions for the forward and reverse reactions are:

Forward rate = $k_f[A][B]$ Reverse rate = $k_r[C][D]$

At equilibrium these rates are equal, so

$$k_f[A][B] = k_r[C][D] \qquad \text{which rearranges to} \qquad \frac{k_f}{k_r} = \frac{[C][D]}{[A][B]}$$

As k_f and k_r are constants, at a given temperature, their ratio must also be a constant. This is known as the **equilibrium constant, K_c**. More generally, the equilibrium constant is given by the concentration of the products raised to the power of their stoichiometric coefficients (i.e. the numbers that appear before them in the balanced equation) divided by the concentrations of the reactants also raised to these powers, i.e. for the reaction:

$$a\,A + b\,B + c\,C + ... \rightleftharpoons p\,P + q\,Q + r\,R + ...$$

The equilibrium constant is given by

$$K_c = \frac{[P]^p[Q]^q[R]^r...}{[A]^a[B]^b[C]^c...}$$

For example in the equilibrium between ammonia and oxygen to give nitrogen monoxide and water:

$$4\ NH_{3\ (g)} + 5\ O_{2\ (g)} \rightleftharpoons 4\ NO_{(g)} + 6\ H_2O_{(g)}$$

The equilibrium constant is given by

$$K_c = \frac{[NO]^4[H_2O]^6}{[NH_3]^4[O_2]^5}\ \text{mol dm}^{-3}$$

The equilibrium constant does not have fixed units and it must be calculated in each case from the equation for K_c, using the fact that concentrations have units of mol dm^{-3}.

If the concentrations of the species involved are all 1 mol dm^{-3}, then K_c will have a value of 1. If K_c is greater than one then the concentrations of products are greater than those of the reactants and the equilibrium is said to lie on the right hand side. If K_c **is very large** the reaction can be regarded as going to **completion**. If K_c is less than one the opposite is true and if K_c **is very small**, then the reaction may be considered **not to occur**.

The concentrations of certain substances remain constant, so these are **not** included in the equilibrium constant and omitted from the expression. All solids for example have a constant concentration and a fixed density, and so their concentration is omitted, thus for the equilibrium:

$$NH_4Cl_{(s)} \rightleftharpoons NH_{3\ (g)} + HCl_{(g)}$$

the equilibrium constant is simply given by

$$K_c = [NH_3][HCl]\ \text{mol}^2\ \text{dm}^{-6}$$

because the constant concentration of the solid ammonium chloride is omitted. The concentration of any pure liquid is also constant as it too has a fixed density. This is particularly important for the concentration of water which is taken as constant and omitted for equilibria in dilute aqueous solutions.

The equilibrium constant for the formation of the tetrachlorocobaltate ion in dilute solution is therefore written as shown below:

$$Co(H_2O)_6{}^{2+}{}_{(aq)} + 4\ Cl^-{}_{(aq)} \rightleftharpoons CoCl_4{}^{2-}{}_{(aq)} + 6\ H_2O_{(l)}$$

$$K_c = \frac{[CoCl_4{}^{2-}{}_{(aq)}]}{[Co(H_2O)_6{}^{2+}{}_{(aq)}][Cl^-{}_{(aq)}]^4}$$

If however the concentration of water can vary because the reaction is not in aqueous solution, or the water is in the gas phase, then the water must be included, as for example for the reduction of carbon dioxide shown in (1) below. The value for the equilibrium constants being those found at 1000K.

(1) $\quad H_{2\,(g)} + CO_{2\,(g)} \rightleftharpoons H_2O_{(g)} + CO_{(g)} \qquad K_c = \dfrac{[CO][H_2O]}{[H_2][CO_2]}$

$$= 0.955 \text{ N.B. the units cancel}$$

This equilibrium could easily be written the other way round, as shown in (2) below, and in this case the equilibrium constant is obviously the reciprocal of the value given for (1) above:

(2) $\quad H_2O_{(g)} + CO_{(g)} \rightleftharpoons H_{2\,(g)} + CO_{2\,(g)} \qquad K_c = \dfrac{[H_2][CO_2]}{[CO][H_2O]}$

$$= \dfrac{1}{0.955}$$

$$= 1.05 \text{ the units again cancel}$$

The reactant in one equilibrium could be the product of a previous equilibrium, so that for example the carbon monoxide in (2) could be the product of the reaction of carbon with steam shown in (3) below. The equilibrium constant again being that at 1000K:

(3) $\quad H_2O_{(g)} + C_{(s)} \rightleftharpoons H_{2\,(g)} + CO_{(g)} \qquad K_c = \dfrac{[H_2][CO]}{[H_2O]}$

$$= 4.48 \times 10^{-4} \text{ mol dm}^{-3}$$

These two equilibria can then be combined, as shown in (4) and in this case the equilibrium constant is the product of those for the two separate equilibria:

(4) $\quad 2\,H_2O_{(g)} + C_{(s)} \rightleftharpoons 2\,H_{2\,(g)} + CO_{2\,(g)}$

$$K_c = \dfrac{[H_2]^2[CO_2]}{[H_2O]^2}$$

$$= \dfrac{[H_2][CO_2]}{[CO][H_2O]} \times \dfrac{[H_2][CO]}{[H_2O]}$$

$$= 1.05 \times 4.48 \times 10^{-4}$$

$$= 4.70 \times 10^{-4} \text{ mol dm}^{-3}$$

THE EFFECT OF CONDITIONS ON THE POSITION OF EQUILIBRIUM

If the conditions (such as temperature, pressure, or the concentrations of the species involved) under which the equilibrium is established are changed, then the rates of the forward and reverse reactions will no longer be equal. As a result the equilbrium is disturbed and the concentrations of the species will change until this equilibrium condition is once more established.

Le Chatelier's principle is a way of predicting the direction in which the position of equilibrium will change if the conditions are altered.

It states

> "If a change is made to the conditions of a chemical equilibrium, then the
> position of equilibrium will readjust so as to minimise the change made."

i.e. increasing a concentration of a species will result in a change that will cause that concentration to decrease again; increasing pressure will result in a change that will cause the pressure to decrease again; increasing the temperature will result in a change that will cause the temperature to decrease again. The effects of changes in the conditions of equilibrium are summarised in Table 8.1.

Table 8.1 – The effect of changes in conditions on the position of an equilibrium

Change	Effect on Equilibrium	Change in K_c?
Increase concentration	Shifts to the opposite side	No
Decrease concentration	Shifts to that side	No
Increase pressure	Shifts to side with least moles of gas	No
Decrease pressure	Shifts to side with most moles of gas	No
Increase temperature	Shifts in endothermic direction	Yes
Decrease temperature	Shifts in exothermic direction	Yes
Add a catalyst	No change	No

Note that whilst changes in concentration and pressure affect the position of equilibrium and the amounts of the various species present, they have no effect on the value of the equilibrium constant, K_c, because the values of the rate constants k_f and k_r do not change (see page 250). A change in temperature does however affect the rate constants, so that the value of K_c changes as well as the position of equilibrium.

The presence of a catalyst reduces the activation energy of both the forward and reverse reactions by the same amount. This means that both the forward and reverse reactions are speeded up by the same factor, so even though the equilibrium is established more rapidly, neither the position of equilibrium nor the equilibrium constant are affected.

CONCENTRATION

If the concentration of a species is increased, then the equilibrium moves towards the other side causing the concentration to fall to a value between the original concentration and the increased value. Conversely if the concentration of a species is reduced the equilibrium shifts towards the side of the equilibrium on which it occurs causing its concentration to increase to a value between the original concentration and the reduced value. Consider the equilibrium

$$Fe(H_2O)_6^{3+}{}_{(aq)} + SCN^-{}_{(aq)} \rightleftharpoons [Fe(H_2O)_5SCN]^{2+}{}_{(aq)} + 6\ H_2O_{(l)}$$
$$\text{Yellow-Brown} \qquad \text{Colourless} \qquad\qquad \text{Blood–red}$$

If aqueous thiocyanate ions are added to an aqueous solution of an iron(III) salt, then a blood–red colouration is observed owing to the formation of the complex ion shown. If the concentration of **either** the thiocyanate ion or the iron(III) ion is increased, then the intensity of the colouration increases. This is in keeping with Le Chatelier's principle because the shift of the equilibrium to the right causes the concentration of the added reactant to fall again. It also shows that the reaction has not gone to completion because addition of either reactant causes an increase in the amount of product. If the concentration of iron(III) ions is decreased by adding fluoride ions (which form the very stable FeF_6^{3-} complex ion) then the intensity of the coloration decreases. This is in keeping with Le Chatelier's principle because the shift of the equilibrium to the left produces more aqueous iron(III) ions to counteract the reduction caused by the fluoride ions. It also shows that the reaction is reversible. Note that even though the position of equilibrium is altered, the change in concentrations is such that the value of K_c remains unchanged.

PRESSURE

If the total pressure of a system is increased then the equilibrium shifts to the side with least moles of gas, so causing the pressure to fall to a value between the original pressure and the increased value. Conversely if the total pressure of the system is reduced the equilibrium shifts towards the side with the most moles of gas, causing the pressure to increase to a value between the original pressure and the reduced value. Consider the examples below:

$$2\ SO_{2\ (g)} + O_{2\ (g)} \rightleftharpoons 2\ SO_{3\ (g)}$$
3 moles gas go to 2 moles gas
Increased P $\Rightarrow$; decreased P$\Leftarrow$

$$C_{(s)} + H_2O_{(g)} \rightleftharpoons CO_{(g)} + H_{2\ (g)}$$
1 mole gas goes to 2 moles gas
(n.b. carbon is a solid)
Increased P $\Leftarrow$; decreased P$\Rightarrow$

$$H_{2\ (g)} + I_{2\ (g)} \rightleftharpoons 2\ HI_{(g)}$$
2 moles gas go to 2 moles gas
Changing P has no effect

Note that even though the position of equilibrium is altered, the changes in the concentrations that result from the changes in pressure are such that the value of K_c remains unchanged.

TEMPERATURE

If the temperature of a system is increased then the equilibrium shifts in the direction of the endothermic change, so absorbing heat and causing the temperature to fall to a value between the original temperature and the increased value. Conversely if the temperature of the system is reduced the equilibrium shifts in the direction of the exothermic change, so releasing heat and causing the temperature to increase to a value between the original temperature and the reduced value. Consider the examples below:

$$N_{2\ (g)} + O_{2\ (g)} \rightleftharpoons 2\ NO_{(g)}$$
$\Delta H = +180$ kJ mol^{-1}
(i.e. forward reaction endothermic)
Increased T, K_c increases, equilibrium $\Rightarrow$;

$$2 \, SO_{2 \, (g)} + O_{2 \, (g)} \rightleftharpoons 2 \, SO_{3 \, (g)}$$

Decreased T, K_c decreases, equilibrium $\Leftarrow$

$\Delta H = -197 \text{ kJ mol}^{-1}$ (i.e. forward reaction exothermic)

Increased T, K_c decreases, equilibrium $\Leftarrow$;

Decreased T, K_c increases, equilibrium $\Rightarrow$

Note that changes in temperature affect the rate constants of the forward and reverse reactions to different extents, so the actual value of K_c changes.

EXPLANATIONS

Le Chatelier's principle only helps us to predict the effect that a change in conditions will have on the position of an equilibrium. It does not explain why these changes occur. This comes from a consideration of the effect of the change in conditions on the rates of the forward and reverse reactions.

Consider the effects of the changes in conditions on the equilibrium between solid phosphorus pentachloride, liquid phosphorus trichloride and gaseous chlorine:

$$PCl_{5 \, (s)} \rightleftharpoons PCl_{3 \, (l)} + Cl_{2 \, (g)} \quad \Delta H = +88 \text{ kJ mol}^{-1}$$

If the **concentration** of chlorine is increased, then the rate of the reverse reaction will increase, but the forward reaction will be unaffected, so that the reaction rates are no longer equal. In order for equilibrium to be restored, the amount of the pentachloride must increase and the amount of the trichloride decrease so that the position of the equilibrium will shift to the left, hence the amount of chlorine decreases to below its new higher level, but still above the original level (see Figure 8.4a). This is in agreement with the predictions of Le Chatelier's principle that the position of equilibrium will shift to the opposite side to the species whose concentration has been increased. Obviously a decrease in the concentration of chlorine has the opposite effect, though neither affects the value of K_c.

If the total **pressure** is increased then the rate of the reverse reaction will again increase, because this is the only one that involves a gas. The more moles of gas involved on the side of the equilibrium, the more a change in pressure will affect the rate. The result of this increase in the rate of the reverse reaction is the same as those explained above and the position of equilibrium will again shift to the left. This results in a reduction in the amount of chlorine and hence the total pressure falls below the new higher value (see Figure 8.4b). A decrease in total pressure will have the opposite effect, but once again the value of K_c is unchanged.

If the **temperature** is increased, then the rates of both the forward and reverse reactions will increase, but they will not do so by the same amount. The higher the activation energy, the greater the effect of temperature on reaction rate (see Section 7.6, page 239), so that an increase in temperature will speed up the reaction in the endothermic direction (which must have the greater activation energy – consider Figure 7.9, page 241) more than the exothermic reaction. In this example the forward reaction is endothermic (ΔH positive), so the reverse reaction is exothermic. The effect of an increase in temperature is therefore to increase the rate of the forward reaction more than that of the reverse reaction. Therefore, the value of K_c increases and the reaction shifts to the right, producing more chlorine and phosphorus trichloride until the reaction rates again become equal (see Figure 8.4c). This endothermic change absorbs heat energy and causes the temperature of the system to fall to below its new higher value. A decrease in temperature will have the opposite effect and the value of K_c will decrease.

The effects of these changes in conditions on the relevant concentrations and rates is shown in Figure 8.4 below:

Figure 8.4 – The effect of changes in conditions on the equilibrium established by heating phosphorus pentachloride

i   Increased concentration of chlorine

(a)

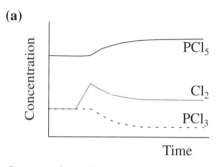

(b)

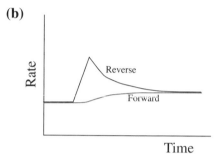

ii   Increased total pressure

(a)

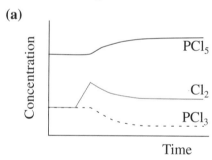

(b)

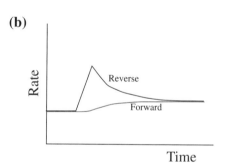

ii   Increased temperature (n.b. the 'flat' sections on the rate graph have been exaggerated to distinguish between the effects of temperatures and concentration changes)

(a)

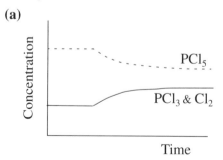

(b)

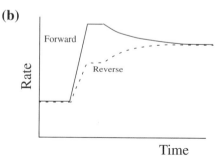

INDUSTRIAL PROCESSES

Many industrial processes involve equilibria. The aim of the process is to produce the desired product as efficiently as possible, i.e. rapidly, but with the minimum amount of waste and the minimum input of energy. This requires a study of both kinetics (i.e. how fast the product is made from the reactants) and equilibrium (i.e. how much of the desired product is present in the mixture produced) considerations. Two processes to which these considerations have been applied are the Haber Process, for the production of ammonia, and the Contact Process, for the production of sulfuric acid. These are considered separately below.

THE HABER PROCESS

The Haber process involves the direct combination of nitrogen and hydrogen to produce ammonia. Firstly it is important to obtain the reactants in an economically viable manner. Hydrogen can, for example be produced by the electrolysis of water and nitrogen by the fractional distillation of liquid air, but both of these would be prohibitively expensive. Instead steam is reacted with excess methane, from natural gas, in a number of stages over various heated catalysts to finally produce a mixture of hydrogen, carbon dioxide and some excess methane.

$$2\,H_2O_{(g)} + CH_{4\,(g)} \rightleftharpoons 4\,H_{2\,(g)} + CO_{2\,(g)}$$

Air is then added with this and the oxygen reacts with the hydrogen to produce more steam, which then reacts (as above) with the excess methane to form more hydrogen and carbon dioxide. The nitrogen, being inert under these conditions, remains unchanged.

$$2\,O_{2\,(g)} + CH_{4\,(g)} \rightleftharpoons 2\,H_2O_{(g)} + CO_{2\,(g)}$$

The final result is a mixture of nitrogen, hydrogen and carbon dioxide. The carbon dioxide is then removed by scrubbing with saturated, aqueous potassium carbonate.

$$CO_{2\,(g)} + K_2CO_{3\,(aq)} + H_2O_{(l)} \rightleftharpoons 2\,KHCO_{3\,(aq)}$$

This reaction can be reversed by heating the aqueous potassium hydrogencarbonate, so regenerating the carbonate. The result of all of these reactions is to provide a mixture of nitrogen and hydrogen in a 1:3 ratio. This is compressed and passed over a heated iron catalyst where the following equilibrium is established.

$$N_{2\,(g)} + 3\,H_{2\,(g)} \rightleftharpoons 2\,NH_{3\,(g)} \quad \Delta H = -92 \text{ kJ mol}^{-1}$$

The choice of conditions for this equilibrium is critical. It can be seen that the reaction goes from 4 moles of gas to 2 moles of gas, hence a high pressure will favour the formation of the product, as Figure 8.5 confirms. The provision of a high pressure is however expensive, both in terms of the capital cost of providing a plant that will resist high pressures and in terms of the operating costs of compressing gases to high pressures. The final choice will therefore be a compromise pressure that takes into account these factors.

It can be seen from the equation above that the forward reaction is exothermic (ΔH negative), hence a low temperature would favour the products, as can be seen from Figure 8.5. Unfortunately low temperatures result in low rates of reaction so that even though there may be a high proportion of ammonia in the product it may take a long time for the conversion to occur. Again a compromise temperature is chosen so as to produce the maximum mass of ammonia per hour. The use of a finely divided catalyst containing iron also increases the reaction rate.

Figure 8.5 – The effect of conditions on the proportion of ammonia at equilibrium

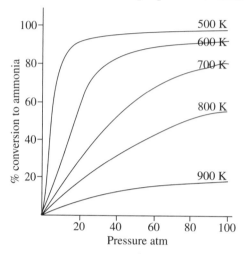

Typical conditions chosen for the Haber process are pressures in the range 200 – 1000 atm (20 – 100 Mpa) and temperatures ~700K. The reaction is however not left for sufficient time for equilibrium to be established (remember the reaction rate will decrease as equilibrium is approached – see Figure 8.1) and typically in the converter only about 20% of the nitrogen and hydrogen is converted to ammonia. It would be very uneconomical to waste the unchanged reactants, so the mixture of gases is cooled causing the ammonia to condense (it can hydrogen bond, unlike the reactants) so that it can be separated and the nitrogen and hydrogen recycled. This is shown schematically in Figure 8.6 below:

Figure 8.6 – Schematic diagram for the commercial production of ammonia

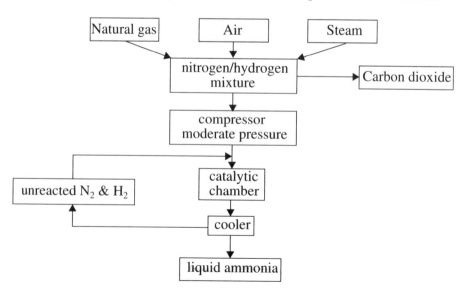

Nitrogen is an element vital for plant growth, so the major use of ammonia is the manufacture of fertilizers, such as ammonium salts and urea. It is also used in the manufacture of nitrogen containing polymers such as nylon. Ammonia can also be oxidised to produce nitric acid (see the equations below), which is used in the production of explosives such as TNT, dynamite etc. and in the dye industry.

$$4\,NH_{3\,(g)} + 5\,O_{2\,(g)} \rightleftharpoons 4\,NO_{(g)} + 6\,H_2O_{(g)}$$

$$2\,NO_{(g)} + O_{2\,(g)} \rightleftharpoons 2\,NO_{2\,(g)}$$

$$4\,NO_{2\,(g)} + 2\,H_2O_{(l)} + O_{2\,(g)} \rightleftharpoons 4\,HNO_{3\,(aq)}$$

THE CONTACT PROCESS

The Contact Process is the production of sulfuric acid by the oxidation of sulfur. Firstly pure sulfur is burnt in air to form sulfur dioxide:

$$S_{(s)} + O_{2\,(g)} \Rightarrow SO_{2\,(g)}$$

The sulfur is either mined from underground deposits of the element, often by injecting superheated steam to melt it, or from the purification of petroleum and natural gas. In addition sulfur dioxide formed in the roasting of sulfide ores of metals may be used as a source of sulfur dioxide. The sulfur dioxide is then mixed with more air and passed over a vanadium(V) oxide catalyst to produce sulfur trioxide:

$$2\,SO_{2\,(g)} + O_{2\,(g)} \rightleftharpoons 2\,SO_{3\,(g)} \quad \Delta H = -196 \text{ kJ mol}^{-1}$$

As with the Haber Process a high pressure would favour the formation of the product (3 moles of gas going to 2), but in this case excellent conversion is achieved without the expense of a high pressure process. Hence the reactants are only compressed to the pressure needed to achieve the desired flow rate in the reactor. Similarly using pure oxygen rather than air would drive the equilibrium to the right, but again it would be an unnecessary expense. Another similarity is that the forward reaction is exothermic, so a low temperature favours the products. As with the Haber Process the temperature cannot be too low otherwise the process becomes uneconomically slow. The result is the choice of a compromise temperature (700 - 800K) and the use of a catalyst (finely divided V_2O_5) to enhance the reaction rate. Also the oxidation to sulfur trioxide is usually done by a number of converters at successively lower temperatures, so as to make use of high temperature to give a fast initial rate of reaction as well as a low temperature to give a high final equilibrium yield. The result is well over 90% conversion to the trioxide. After absorption of the trioxide, the gases are often passed through one more converter to ensure that the waste gases contain so little sulfur dioxide that they can be released directly into the air.

The sulfur trioxide must now be reacted with water to produce sulfuric acid:

$$SO_{3\,(g)} + H_2O_{(l)} \Rightarrow H_2SO_{4\,(l)}$$

The sulfur trioxide is not reacted directly with water because this produces a slow settling mist of sulfuric acid. Instead it is firstly dissolved in sulfuric acid to produce a solution known as 'oleum'. This solution is then mixed with water so that the above reaction takes place using sulfuric acid as the solvent.

Sulfuric acid has numerous uses in the chemical industry – indeed the tonnage of it used annually gives a good indication of the extent of a country's chemical industry. These uses include manufacture of fertilizers (especially converting insoluble phosphate rock to soluble 'superphosphate'), polymers, detergents, paints and pigments. It is also widely used in the petrochemicals industry and in the industrial processing of metals. One of its minor, though possibly most familiar uses, is as the electrolyte in automobile batteries.

EXERCISE 8.2

1. The equilibrium constant for a reaction that occurs totally in the gas phase is given below. What is the chemical equation for this equilibrium?

$$K_c = \frac{[CO_2][CF_4]}{[COF_2]^2}$$

A $\quad CO_{2\,(g)} + CF_{4\,(g)} \rightleftharpoons COF_{2\,(g)}$

B $\quad CO_{2\,(g)} + CF_{4\,(g)} \rightleftharpoons 2\,COF_{2\,(g)}$

C $\quad 2\,COF_{2\,(g)} \rightleftharpoons CO_{2\,(g)} + CF_{4\,(g)}$

D $\quad COF_{2\,(g)} \rightleftharpoons CO_{2\,(g)} + CF_{4\,(g)}$

2. Which one of the following will increase the rate at which a state of equilibrium is attained without affecting the position of equilibrium?

A $\quad$ Increasing the temperature.

B $\quad$ Increasing the pressure.

C $\quad$ Decreasing the concentration of the products.

D $\quad$ Adding a catalyst.

3. In the manufacture of methanol, hydrogen is reacted with carbon monoxide over a catalyst of zinc and chromium oxides and the following equilibrium is established:

$$2\,H_{2\,(g)} + CO_{(g)} \rightleftharpoons CH_3OH_{(g)} \qquad \Delta H = -128.4 \text{ kJ mol}^{-1}$$

Which one of the following changes would increase the percentage of carbon monoxide converted to methanol at equilibrium?

A $\quad$ Decreasing the total pressure.

B $\quad$ Increasing the temperature.

C $\quad$ Increasing the proportion of hydrogen in the mixture of gases.

D $\quad$ Increasing the surface area of the catalyst.

4. When heated in a sealed vessel, ammonium chloride is in equilibrium with ammonia and hydrogen chloride according to the equilibrium:

$$NH_4Cl_{(s)} \rightleftharpoons NH_{3\,(g)} + HCl_{(g)}$$

Increasing the temperature increases the proportion of the ammonium chloride that is dissociated. The best explanation of this is that:

A   this increases the rate of both reactions, but the forward reaction is affected more than the reverse reaction.

B   this increases the rate of both reactions, but the reverse reaction is affected more than the forward reaction.

C   this increases the rate of the forward reaction, but decreases the rate of the reverse reaction.

D   this decreases the rate of both reactions, but the reverse reaction is affected more than the forward reaction.

5.   When methane and steam are passed over a heated catalyst the equilibrium below is established.

$$CH_{4\,(g)} + H_2O_{(g)} \rightleftharpoons CO_{(g)} + 3\,H_{2\,(g)}$$

Which one of the following will result in a change in the value of the equilibrium constant (K_c)?

A   Increasing the pressure.
B   Adding more methane (CH_4).
C   Decreasing the concentration of steam.
D   Increasing the temperature.

6.   When 0.1 mol dm^{-3} aqueous solutions of silver nitrate and iron(II) nitrate are mixed, the following equilibrium is established:

$$Ag^+_{(aq)} + Fe^{2+}_{(aq)} \rightleftharpoons Fe^{3+}_{(aq)} + Ag_{(s)}$$

Which of the following changes would produce more silver?

A   Adding some iron(III) nitrate solution.
B   Adding more iron(II) nitrate solution.
C   Removing some of the Ag^+ ions by forming insoluble silver chloride.
D   Increasing the total pressure.

7.   In the conversion of nitrogen to ammonia using the Haber process, the main reason why the temperature is limited to about 450°C is because

A   a higher temperature would cause the catalyst to break down.
B   a higher temperature would cause the reaction to occur too slowly.
C   a higher temperature would decrease the amount of ammonia present at equilibrium.
D   a higher temperature would cost too much money to maintain.

8.   In the Haber process, the hydrogen is obtained

A   by reacting natural gas with steam.
B   by reacting zinc and hydrochloric acid.
C   from the air.
D   by the electrolysis of water.

9. The central reaction in the Haber process is the equilibrium between nitrogen, hydrogen and ammonia.

a) Write a balanced equation for this equilibrium.

b) The enthalpy change in this reaction is –92.6 kJ mol^{-1} and the activation energy is +335 kJ mol^{-1}. Draw an energy level diagram for this equilibrium.

c) The reaction usually takes place in the presence of an iron catalyst. On the diagram from b), mark the reaction pathway for the catalysed reaction with a dotted line.

d) Would you expect the iron to be present as solid lumps or in a finely divided state? Explain why.

e) The reaction is usually carried out at a pressure well above atmospheric pressure. How would you expect this to affect the rate of reaction? Explain why it has this effect.

10. Nitrogen monoxide and oxygen react together in a reversible reaction to form nitrogen dioxide.

a) Describe, in terms of the rates of the reactions and the concentrations of the species present, the way in which equilibrium is established if nitrogen monoxide and oxygen are suddenly mixed in an empty flask.

b) Write a balanced equation for this equilibrium.

c) Nitrogen dioxide is brown, whereas nitrogen monoxide is colourless. If the oxygen is replaced with an equal volume of air, the mixture of gases becomes lighter coloured. Explain why this occurs.

11. For each of the following equilibria, state:

I   whether change (i) would shift the position of equilibrium to the right or the left.
and
II how you could change the second factor (ii) so as to shift the position of equilibrium in the opposite direction.

a) $C_{(s)} + H_2O_{(g)} \rightleftharpoons CO_{(g)} + H_{2(g)}$ Forward reaction endothermic
(i)   increasing the total pressure. (ii)   changing the temperature.

b) $Br_{2\,(aq)} + H_2O_{(l)} \rightleftharpoons HOBr_{(aq)} + H^+_{(aq)} + Br^-_{(aq)}$
(i)   adding potassium bromide. (ii)   changing the pH.

c) $N_2O_{4(g)} \rightleftharpoons 2\,NO_{2(g)}$ Forward reaction endothermic
(i)   decreasing the temperature. (ii)   changing the total pressure.

d) $CO_{(g)} + Cl_{2(g)} \rightleftharpoons COCl_{2(g)}$ Forward reaction exothermic
    (i)   adding more chlorine.   (ii)   changing the temperature.

e) $NH_4HS_{(s)} \rightleftharpoons NH_{3(g)} + H_2S_{(g)}$
    (i)   reducing the pressure.   (ii)   changing the concentration of ammonia.

12. A gaseous mixture of hydrogen, iodine and hydrogen iodide are in equilibrium according to the equation:

$$H_{2\,(g)} + I_{2\,(g)} \rightleftharpoons 2\,HI_{(g)} \quad \Delta H = +56 \text{ kJ mol}^{-1}$$

State how the position of equilibrium will be affected by the following changes and explain your reasoning:

a)   Decreasing the temperature.
b)   Adding more hydrogen at constant pressure.
c)   Increasing the total pressure.

13. A flask contains iodine monochloride, a brown liquid, iodine trichloride, a yellow solid, and chlorine gas in equilibrium according to the equation:

$$ICl_{(l)} + Cl_{2(g)} \rightleftharpoons ICl_{3(s)}$$

a)   If the volume of the flask was reduced so as to increase the total pressure, explain what you would expect to happen to the amounts of brown liquid and yellow solid?

b)   When the flask is cooled in iced water the amount of yellow solid increases and there is less brown liquid. Explain what this shows about the equilibrium?

14. Sulfuric acid is manufactured by the reaction between sulfur trioxide and water. The sulfur trioxide is formed by the reaction of sulfur dioxide and oxygen from air in the presence of a catalyst. This is known as the Contact process and establishes an equilibrium in which the forward reaction is exothermic.

a)   Write a balanced equation for the equilibrium.

b)   What effect does the catalyst have upon:
    i)   the rate of the forward reaction?
    ii)   the rate of the reverse reaction?
    iii)   the proportion of sulfur dioxide converted to sulfur trioxide?

c)   If a high pressure was used, what effect would this have on the relative proportions of sulfur dioxide and sulfur trioxide? Explain.

d)   Much greater reaction rates could be achieved if the temperature was increased. Explain why this is not done.

8.3 THE EQUILIBRIUM LAW

17.2.1 Solve homogeneous equilibrium problems using the expression for K_c.

Calculate K_c given all equilibrium concentrations. Given K_c and other appropriate concentrations, find an equilibrium concentration. The quadratic formula is not required. K_p and K_{sp} are not required, nor is use of the quadratic expression.
© IBO 2001.

A homogeneous equilibrium is one in which all the reactants and products are in the same phase. If there are two or more phases then it is a heterogeneous equilibrium. The concentrations, when substituted into the equilibrium constant formula, will only equal the equilibrium constant if the system is in fact at equilibrium. For other situations the value produced by treating the concentrations in the same way as the equilibrium constant (sometimes referred to as the reaction quotient, Q_c) will indicate which way the reaction needs to shift in order to attain equilibrium. If $Q_c > K_c$, then the value of Q_c must fall, hence products must be converted to reactants and the system must shift to the left. Conversely if $Q_c < K_c$, then the system must shift to the right. Consider the reaction:

$$CO_{2\,(g)} + H_{2\,(g)} \rightleftharpoons CO_{(g)} + H_2O_{(g)} \quad K_c = 0.955 \text{ at } 1000K$$

If equal amounts of the gases are mixed at 1000K then $Q_c = 1$, which is greater than K_c at this temperature, so the system must shift to the left to achieve equilibrium. In other words, some of the water and carbon monoxide will turn into carbon dioxide and water, altering the concentrations so that $Q_c = K_c$.

As with any mathematical expression, if all of the terms except one in the equilibrium expression are known, the unknown term may be calculated by substitution. This is best illustrated by means of examples.

EXAMPLE

When a mixture initially containing 0.0200 mol dm^{-3} sulfur dioxide and an equal concentration of oxygen is allowed to reach equilibrium in a container of fixed volume at 1000K, it is found that exactly 80% of the sulfur dioxide is converted to sulfur trioxide. Calculate the value of the equilibrium constant at that temperature.

SOLUTION

$$2\,SO_{2\,(g)} + O_{2\,(g)} \rightleftharpoons 2\,SO_{3\,(g)}$$

As 80% of the sulfur dioxide turns into the trioxide:

Equilibrium $[SO_3] = 0.0200 \times 0.8 = 0.0160$ mol dm^{-3}

Each sulfur trioxide is formed from one sulfur dioxide, so:

Equilibrium $[SO_2] = 0.0200 - 0.0160 = 0.0040$ mol dm^{-3}

Each sulfur trioxide requires only half an oxygen molecule, so:

Equilibrium $[O_2] = 0.0200 - (\tfrac{1}{2} \times 0.0160) = 0.0120$ mol dm^{-3}

Substituting into the equilibrium constant expression, the value of the equilibrium constant may be calculated:

$$K_c = \frac{[SO_3]^2}{[SO_2]^2[O_2]} = \frac{0.0160^2}{0.0040^2 \times 0.0120} = 1333 \text{ mol}^{-1} \text{ dm}^3$$

Similarly if the equilibrium constant is known, then given appropriate information the equilibrium or starting concentration of one of the reactants may be found, the best technique usually being to substitute 'x' for the unknown quantity. In many cases though the resulting equation may contain powers of 'x' and hence require special techniques for their solution. This is not however the case with the example given below:

EXAMPLE

In the gas phase at 730 K, the equilibrium constant for the reaction of hydrogen and iodine to form hydrogen iodide has a value of 490. If the initial concentration of iodine is 0.0200 mol dm^{-3}, what concentration of hydrogen is required for 90% of the iodine to be converted to hydrogen iodide?

SOLUTION

$$H_{2\,(g)} + I_{2\,(g)} \rightleftharpoons 2\,HI_{(g)}$$

$$K_c = \frac{[HI]^2}{[H_2][I_2]}$$

Initial $[I_2] = 0.0200$, so at equilibrium, if 90% converted $[I_2] = 0.00200$

Concentration of I_2 converted $= 0.0200 - 0.00200$
$= 0.0180$ mol dm^{-3}

$\therefore$ Concentration of HI formed $= 2 \times 0.0180$ (1 mole of I_2 forms 2 moles of HI)
$= 0.0360$ mol dm^{-3}

If the initial concentration of $H_2 = x$,
then equilibrium concentration $= x - 0.0180$
Substituting:

$$490 = \frac{0.0360^2}{(x - 0.0180) \times 0.00200}$$

$$x - 0.0180 = \frac{0.0360^2}{490 \times 0.00200}$$

$$= 0.00132$$

$$x = 0.00132 + 0.0180$$

$$= 0.0193 \text{ mold m}^{-3}$$

ADVANCED

EXERCISE 8.3

1. At a particular temperature, a mixture of nitrogen monoxide and oxygen is allowed to reach equilibrium according to the equation:

$$2 \, NO_{(g)} + O_{2(g)} \rightleftharpoons 2 \, NO_{2(g)}$$

The equilibrium concentrations of the gases are 0.03 mol dm^{-3} nitrogen monoxide; 0.04 mol dm^{-3} oxygen and 0.02 mol dm^{-3} nitrogen dioxide. What is the value of the equilibrium constant, K_c?

A $-\dfrac{0.3 \times 0.04}{0.02}$ mol dm^{-3}

B $\dfrac{0.02}{0.03 \times 0.04}$ mol^{-1} dm^{3}

C $\dfrac{0.02}{0.03 \times 0.04^2}$ mol^{-2} dm^{6}

D $\dfrac{0.02^2}{0.03^2 \times 0.04}$ mol^{-1} dm^{3}

2. When 0.01 moles of iodine are added to 1 dm^3 of 0.2 mol dm^{-3} aqueous potassium iodide, 99% is converted to the triiodide ion according to the equilibrium

$$I_{2 \, (aq)} + I^-_{(aq)} \rightleftharpoons I_3^-{}_{(aq)}$$

What is the approximate value of the equilibrium constant?

A   500 mol^{-1} dm^3
B   100 mol^{-1} dm^3
C   2 mol^{-1} dm^3
D   0.002 mol^{-1} dm^3

3. The equilibrium constant for the dissociation of hydrogen iodide into its elements, according to the equation below, at 900 K is 0.04.

$$2 \, HI_{(g)} \rightleftharpoons H_{2(g)} + I_{2 \, (g)}$$

If the equilibrium concentration of hydrogen iodide is 0.2 mol dm^{-3}, what is the approximate equilibrium concentration of iodine?

A   0.3
B   0.04
C   0.008
D   0.0016

4. When ammonium hydrogensulfide is heated it dissociates according to the equilibrium below. The value of K_c for this equilibrium at a particular temperature is 0.00001 mol^2 dm^{-6}.

$$NH_4HS_{(s)} \rightleftharpoons NH_{3(g)} + H_2S_{(g)}$$

a) Explain the units of the equilibrium constant.
b) Calculate the concentration of ammonia at equilibrium.
c) If some ammonia gas was injected at constant pressure and temperature, how would this affect
  i the mass of solid present?
  ii the concentration of hydrogen sulfide?
  iii the value of K_c?

5. When nitrogen and hydrogen react together in the presence of a catalyst, they produce ammonia. The following table gives the percent of ammonia in the mixture when a 3:1 H_2:N_2 mixture reaches equilibrium under various conditions:

Pressure – MPa Temperature – °C	10	20
400	25%	36%
500	10%	17%

a) What do these data show about the equilibrium?
b) At 10 MPa and 400°C, the equilibrium concentrations of the species present are:
  $[N_2] = 0.335$ mol dm^{-3}, $[H_2] = 1.005$ mol dm^{-3}, $[NH_3] = 0.450$ mol dm^{-3}.
  Calculate a value for the equilibrium constant and give appropriate units.

6. For the gaseous equilibrium: $CO_{(g)} + Cl_{2\,(g)} \rightleftharpoons COCl_{2\,(g)}$

a) Write the expression for the equilibrium constant K_c.

b) The concentrations of the various species at a particular temperature are given below. Calculate the value of the equilibrium constant K_c, giving appropriate units.

  $[CO] = 0.800$ mol dm^{-3}; $[Cl_2] = 0.600$ mol dm^{-3}; $[COCl_2] = 0.200$ mol dm^{-3}

c) If the pressure of the system is suddenly increased so that the volume halves, calculate the new concentrations.

d) If these are substituted into the equilibrium constant expression, what is the numerical result.

e) Is the system still at equilibrium? If not in which direction will the reaction proceed? How did you deduce this?

f) Is this consistent with Le Chatelier's principle? Explain.

ADVANCED

8.4 PHASE EQUILIBRIUM

17.1.1 State and explain the equilibrium established between a liquid and its own vapour.

Liquid-vapour equilibrium is a dynamic equilibrium established when the rate of condensation equals the rate of vaporization. The vapour pressure is independent of the volume of the container, liquid or vapour.

17.1.2 State and explain the qualitative relationship between vapour pressure and temperature.

Students should be able to show the relationship graphically and explain it in terms of kinetic theory.

17.1.3 State and explain the relationship between enthalpy of vaporization, boiling point and intermolecular forces.

Students should be able to predict the relative strength of intermolecular forces of different liquids when given the physical properties, or vice versa. Cross reference with 4.3. © IBO 2001

Consider an evacuated container with a layer of a volatile liquid in the bottom of it. Molecules of the liquid will escape from the surface and enter the vapour phase. These molecules in the vapour phase will collide with the walls of the container and exert a pressure. Some of the molecules will also strike the surface of the liquid and condense back into the liquid phase. Initially this rate of return will be low, but as more and more molecules escape into the vapour phase and the pressure increases, the rate of return also increases until it becomes equal to the rate at which the particles vapourise from the surface so that

Rate of vapourisation = Rate of condensation

At this point the system is in a state of dynamic equilibrium, similar to a chemical equilibrium, and the pressure exerted by the particles in the vapour phase is known as the vapour pressure of the liquid. Altering the surface area of the liquid affects both of the rates equally, so that it has no overall effect on the vapour pressure, though it will affect the time taken to reach equilibrium - the greater the surface area, the more rapidly equilibrium is achieved.

Molecules on the surface need a certain minimum amount of kinetic energy before they can escape from the attractive forces of the other surface molecules. This will depend on the strength of the intermolecular forces and is similar to the concept of activation energy for a chemical reaction. Vapourisation is an endothermic process, as it requires the overcoming of the attractive forces between the particles. The amount of energy required for this phase change is known as the enthalpy of vapourisation.

More precisely the enthalpy of vapourisation is the amount of energy required to convert one mole of the substance from the liquid to the gaseous state, e.g. for water it is the enthalpy change associated with the transition:

$$H_2O_{(l)} \Rightarrow H_2O_{(g)} \qquad \Delta H = +40.7 \text{ kJ mol}^{-1} \text{ (at 373K and 101.3 kPa)}$$

This energy is mainly required to overcome intermolecular forces, though a little is required to do work against the atmosphere. When a substance boils its temperature does not increase (i.e. there is no increase in kinetic energy), so that the energy absorbed is involved in increasing potential energy by overcoming attractive forces between the particles.

In general the stronger the forces between the particles, the greater the enthalpy of vapourisation, the lower the vapour pressure at a given temperature, and the higher the boiling point.

This is illustrated by the data in Table 8.2:

Table 8.2 - Enthalpy of vapourisation and boiling point data of some compounds

Compound	Enthalpy of vapourisation /kJ mol^{-1}	Boiling point /K	Intermolecular forces
Methane	9.0	109	Van der Waals' only
Methoxymethane	27.2	248	Van der Waals' and dipole-dipole
Ethanol	38.6	352	Van der Waals', dipole-dipole, and hydrogen bonds

At a higher temperature, more molecules will have the required kinetic energy to escape into the vapour phase and the rate of vapourisation will increase (see Figure 7.7, page 239). This means that more molecules are required in the gas phase for the rate of condensation to equal this, hence an increase in temperature results in an increase in vapour pressure, as shown in Figure 8.6. A liquid will boil when its vapour pressure is equal to the pressure on the surface of the liquid, because this allows bubbles of vapour to form in the body of the liquid. The normal boiling point is the temperature at which the vapour pressure is equal to standard atmospheric pressure (101.3 kPa), as shown on Figure 8.6. A liquid will, however, boil at a lower temperature if the external pressure is reduced, as would be the case on top of a mountain. Similarly if the external pressure is increased, as in a pressure cooker, the boiling point of the liquid increases.

ADVANCED

Figure 8.6 – The relationship between temperature, vapour pressure and boiling point

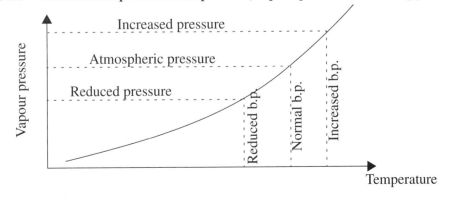

If the system contains two components that do not mix, they will each exert their own vapour pressure, provided it is shaken so both come into contact with the vapour phase. In other words the total vapour pressure is the sum of the individual vapour pressures. The situation is just the same as if one side of the container contained one component and the other side the other component, because particles of a particular substance can only leave from, and return to their own surface.

If the system contains two substances that do mix, then the vapour pressure of both will be lower in the mixture than in the pure liquids. This is because there will be less molecules of each component near the surface, reducing the rate of escape, but all of the surface is available for particles in the gas phase to return to, hence the rate of return is unaffected. If both of the liquids are volatile, then the total vapour pressure is the sum of these reduced vapour pressures and this provides the basis for fractional distillation (see below). If however one of the components is non-volatile, as is usually the case for a solid dissolved in a liquid, then the total vapour pressure of the system will be reduced, as shown in Figure 8.7, and this is the basis for the elevation of boiling point and depression of freezing point (see section 8.5, page 276).

Figure 8.7 - Illustrating the effect of a dissolved solid on the vapour pressure of a solvent

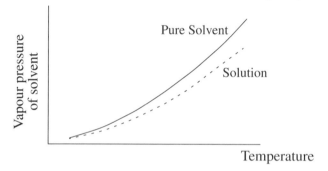

DISTILLATION AND FRACTIONAL DISTILLATION

A volatile liquid can be separated from a non–volatile solute by simple distillation. The apparatus for this is shown in Figure 8.8. The vapour from the heated flask passes over into the condenser, where it is cooled by the circulating cold water and turns back into a liquid, which is collected in the receiver. If necessary, to reduce thermal decomposition, the process can be carried out at a lower temperature by reducing the pressure in the apparatus so as to reduce the boiling point of the liquid (see Figure 8.6).

Figure 8.8 - Typical simple distillation apparatus

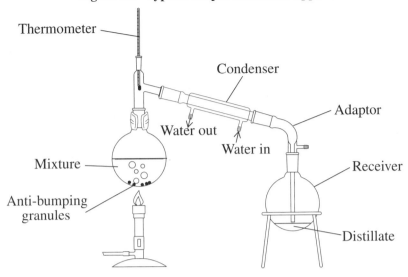

A mixture of two miscible, volatile liquids, will boil when the sum of the vapour pressures of the two components equals the external pressure. The vapour will always contain a greater proportion of the more volatile component than the liquid phase does. If the liquid contained an equal number of moles of two liquids, at the boiling point of the mixture, the more volatile component will be contributing more than 50% of the vapour pressure. For example the vapour above an equimolar mixture of benzene (b.p. = 353 K) and methylbenzene (b.p. = 384 K) will contain more than 50% benzene, but it is not possible to obtain pure benzene by simple distillation as there would still be significant amounts of methylbenzene vapour. Such a mixture could however be more completely separated by successive distillations – the greater the difference in boiling points the easier the separation.

Returning to the equimolar mixture of benzene and methylbenzene, the vapour pressures of the two components over the mixture at various temperatures are shown in Figure 8.9. At a particular temperature (~370 K) the total vapour pressure over the mixture equals atmospheric pressure and the mixture boils. The vapour evolved will contain the two components in the ratio of their vapour pressures at that temperature (~70% benzene and ~30% methylbenzene).

Figure 8.9 - The vapour pressures in an equimolar benzene-methylbenzene mixture

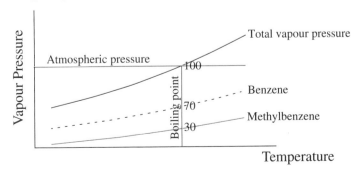

If this 70-30 mixture is now distilled, it will boil at a lower temperature (~365 K), as it is richer in the more volatile component, and the vapour that distils off will be even richer in benzene (~85% benzene and ~15% methylbenzene). This can again be distilled giving a product still richer in benzene and this process continued until the required degree of purity is obtained. This is best illustrated in the form of a boiling point composition graph for the system, shown in Figure 8.10 below. This indicates the boiling point of mixtures of differing compositions (liquid curve) and the composition of the vapour that will distil from this (vapour curve). The result of successive distillations can be seen by drawing lines (sometimes called 'tie lines') parallel to the axes, as shown:

Figure 8.10 - The boiling point-composition graph for benzene-methylbenzene mixtures

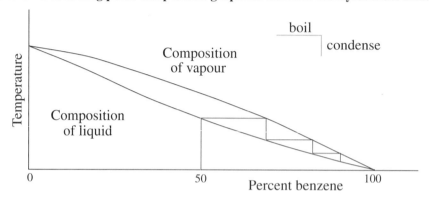

In fractional distillation, the vapour from the liquid rises up the fractionating column, cools and condenses. It then runs down the column and meets hot vapours rising up, causing it to boil again. Thus as it rises up the column the liquid undergoes a number of vapourisation–condensation–vapourisation cycles, equivalent to having been distilled a number of times – the longer the column the more distillations. If a suitable column is used, the liquid distilling over will be the more volatile component of the mixture and eventually, in theory, the distillation flask will contain the less volatile component. Fractional distillation is carried out using apparatus similar to that shown in Figure 8.11. Fractional distillation is used in many industrial processes such as the separation of liquid air and of petroleum (see Chapter 15).

Figure 8.11 - Typical fractional distillation apparatus

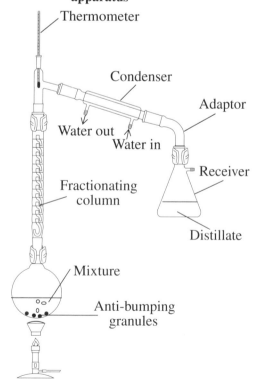

RAOULT'S LAW AND DEVIATIONS FROM IDEALITY (EXTENSION)

The vapour pressure above a mixture of two miscible liquids is predicted by Raoult's law. This assumes that the forces between particles of the two components in the mixture (i.e. A-B forces) are identical to those present in the pure components (i.e. A-A and B-B forces), hence the vapour pressure of the component over the mixture (P_a) is equal to the vapour pressure of the pure component P_A^0 multiplied by its mole fraction:

$$P_A = P_A^0 \times \frac{\text{moles of A}}{\text{total moles}}$$

In many cases when the molecules only have weak van der Waals' forces between them, such as the cases of benzene and methylbenzene above, the situation approximates well to this ideal and the total vapour pressure varies in a linear manner with composition (see a in Figure 8.12 below). In other cases only minor deviations from ideality occur and the vapour pressure/composition graph is a smooth curve (see b in Figure 8.12). In some cases however, where strong inter-particle forces occur, as a result of hydrogen bonding or dissociation of one of the species, there are major deviations from ideality.

If the inter-particle forces are weaker than in the pure liquids, then it is easier for the particles to escape from the mixture, increasing the vapour pressure above the value predicted by Raoult's law. In extreme cases of a **positive deviation** from Raoult's Law, the vapour pressure/composition graph will pass through a maximum, and as a result the boiling point/composition diagram will pass through a minimum (see c in Figure 8.12). In such cases separation of both components by fractional distillation is not possible because the liquid that distils over is not a pure component, but the mixture with the minimum boiling point. The mixture with this composition is known as an **azeotrope**. An example of this type of behaviour is a mixture of ethanol and water, where the azeotropic mixture (96% ethanol, 4% water) boils at a temperature of 78.2°C, whereas the boiling point of pure ethanol is 78.5°C.

If the inter-particle forces are stronger than in the pure liquids, then it is more difficult for the particles to escape from the mixture, decreasing the vapour pressure below the value predicted by Raoult's law. In extreme cases of a **negative deviation** from Raoult's Law the vapour pressure/composition graph will pass through a minimum, and as a result the boiling point/composition diagram will pass through a maximum (see d in Figure 8.12 below). Again it is not possible to separate the mixture into the two components because the liquid that remains in the flask is the mixture with the maximum boiling point. This mixture is also known as an azeotrope. An example of this type of behaviour is a mixture of nitric acid and water, where the azeotropic mixture (68% nitric acid, 32% water) boils at a temperature of 121°C, whereas the boiling point of pure nitric acid is 83°C.

ADVANCED

Figure 8.12 - Vapour pressure/composition and boiling point/composition graphs for ideal and non-ideal solutions

a) An ideal mixture

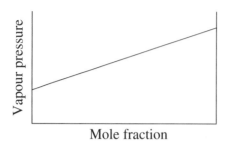
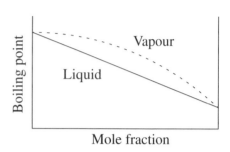

b) A slight positive deviation from Raoult's law

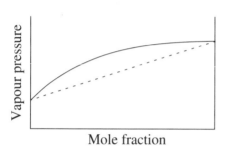
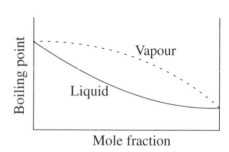

c) A major positive deviation from Raoult's law (e.g. ethanol-water)

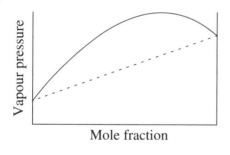
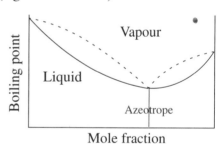

d) A major negative deviation from Raoult's law (e.g. nitric acid-water)

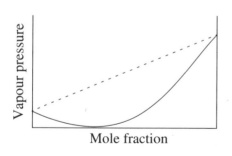
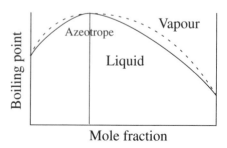

ADVANCED

EXERCISE 8.4

1. As the temperature increases, the vapour pressure of a liquid increases because

    A   the intermolecular forces become weaker.

    B   expansion causes the surface area of the liquid to increase.

    C   a greater proportion of the molecules have the kinetic energy required to escape from the surface.

    D   the number of molecules in the gas phase is constant, but they are moving at a greater velocity.

2. At 50°C, which one of the following would you expect to have the greatest vapour pressure?

    A   Ethanol

    B   Lubricating oil

    C   Mercury

    D   Water

3. Which one of the following does **not** affect the boiling point of a liquid?

    A   The strength of the intermolecular forces.

    B   Its surface area.

    C   The external pressure.

    D   The presence of dissolved impurities.

4. A mixture containing equal numbers of moles of hexane (b.p. 69°C) and cyclohexane (b.p. 81 °C) is heated.

    a)   What conditions determine the temperature at which the liquid boils?

    b)   What do the relative boiling points show about the relative strengths of the intermolecular forces in the two substances?

    c)   Would you expect this mixture to boil below 69°C, between 69°C and 81°C, or above 81°C? Explain why.

    d)   How would you expect the composition of the vapour to compare with that of the liquid? Explain why this is so.

    e)   If the vapour is condensed and then further distilled a number of times, what will happen to the proportions of the two components in the distillate?

    f)   What separation technique depends on this principle?

    g)   Give one industrial application of the separation method.

ADVANCED

8.5 COLLIGATIVE PROPERTIES OF SOLUTIONS (EXTENSION)

As was discussed previously, the addition of a non–volatile solute to a solvent lowers its vapour pressure and this will affect both its freezing point and its boiling point. As a liquid boils when its vapour pressure is equal to the external pressure, by lowering the vapour pressure, a solute will increase the temperature required for this to occur, i.e. it **elevates the boiling point**, as shown in Figure 8.13 below.

At the freezing point of a substance the vapour pressure of both the liquid and the solid states must be equal. If this were not the case then, if both the liquid and solid were placed in an evacuated container at the freezing point, equilibrium would not exist. Normally when a solution freezes it is the pure solvent that separates from the solution, leaving the solute in the liquid phase. Hence, the vapour pressure of the solid state is unaffected, so lowering the vapour pressure of the liquid state means that it is not equal to that of the solid until a lower temperature, i.e. it **depresses the freezing point**, as shown in Figure 8.13 below.

Figure 8.13 – The effect of a non–volatile solute on freezing point and boiling point

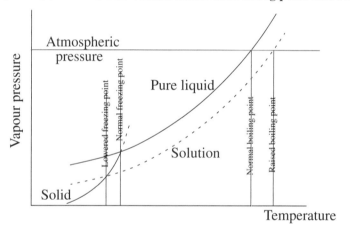

An alternative explanation depends on the fact that when one phase is in equilibrium with another $\Delta G = 0$, i.e. $\Delta H = \Delta S.T$. Adding the non–volatile solute to the liquid phase increases the entropy of the liquid phase without affecting that of either the solid or vapour. This decreases ΔS for the phase change into the vapour (as the vapour has a greater entropy than the liquid $\Delta S = S_{vap} - S_{liq}$ gets smaller), hence a greater temperature is required for $\Delta S.T$ to equal ΔH. It will however increase ΔS for the phase change from solid to liquid (in this case the solid has a lower entropy than the liquid so $\Delta S = S_{liq} - S_{sol}$ gets greater), so that it requires a lower temperature for $\Delta S.T$ to equal ΔH.

The decrease in the vapour pressure of a particular solvent is proportional to the concentration of solute particles because they occupy spaces on the surface and hence reduce the surface available for solvent molecules to escape from. It is the concentration of such particles rather than the nature of the particles that is important, i.e. in aqueous solution one mole of sodium chloride (which dissociates into Na^+ and Cl^-) will have twice the effect of one mole of sucrose (which does not dissociate) and aluminium sulfate will have five times the effect ($2 \times Al^{3+}$ and $3 \times SO_4^{2-}$). The magnitude of the effect varies from solvent to solvent, dependent mainly on its molar mass, but constants (cryoscopic constants for freezing and ebullioscopic constants for boiling) have been measured for most common solvents. These usually give the change in boiling/freezing point when one mole of particles is dissolved in 1 kg of the solvent, and if this is the case, the change in boiling/freezing point can be calculated using the formula:

$$\Delta T = K \times \frac{n \times m_{st}}{M_{st}} \times \frac{1000}{m_{sv}}$$

Where K is the relevant constant (units K mol^{-1} kg), n the number of particles the solute dissociates into, m_{st} the mass of the solute, m_{sv} the mass of the solvent (both masses in g) and M_{st} the molar mass of the solute.

EXAMPLE
The freezing point depression constant for water is 1.86 K mol^{-1} kg. By how much will dissolving 5.00 g of sodium chloride in 100 g of water lower the freezing point?

SOLUTION

$$\Delta T = K \times \frac{n \times m_{st}}{M_{st}} \times \frac{1000}{m_{sv}} = 1.86 \times \frac{2 \times 5.00}{58.5} \times \frac{1000}{100} = 3.18 \text{ K}$$

Because their magnitude is proportional to the number of moles of solute particles and is not dependent on the nature of these particles, **reduction in vapour pressure**, **elevation of boiling point** and **depression of freezing point** are all known as **colligative properties** of solutions. One other property that also varies in this way, and hence is also counted as a colligative property, is the **osmotic pressure** of a solution, discussed below. In all cases, the direct proportionality to the concentration of solute particles is only an approximation, the accuracy of which decreases as the concentration increases.

If a solvent and a solution are separated by a selectively permeable membrane (i.e. one that allows solvent molecules to pass through, but not solute particles) then, if the pressure on both sides of the membrane is equal, the rate at which solvent molecules pass into the solution will be greater than the rate at which they pass out of it. This is because on the solution side, some of the collisions between particles and the membrane involve solute particles that cannot pass through (i.e. the pressure of the solvent is less than the total pressure), whereas on the solvent sides the pressure is totally generated by the collision of solvent molecules. The result is the net transfer of solvent molecules from the pure solvent to the solution – a process known as **osmosis**. The system may be brought into equilibrium and the transfer of solvent stopped by applying additional pressure to the solution side. The additional pressure required is known as the osmotic pressure. The osmotic pressure of a solution may be calculated from the expression:

$$\Pi V = nRT$$

Where Π is the osmotic pressure in kPa, V the volume of solvent in dm^3, n the number of moles of solute **particles**, R the gas constant $(8.314 \text{ J K}^{-1} \text{ mol}^{-1})$ and T the absolute temperature.

EXAMPLE

What is the osmotic pressure of a solution of 2.64 g of ammonium sulfate in 250 cm^3 of water at 300 K?

Amount of ammonium sulfate $= \dfrac{m}{M} = \dfrac{2.64}{132} = 0.0200$ moles.

Moles of solute particles $= 3 \times 0.0200$

$\qquad\qquad\qquad\qquad\quad = 0.0600$ (as $(NH_4)_2SO_4$ dissociates into $2 \times NH_4^+$ and $1 \times SO_4^{2-}$)

$P = \dfrac{nRT}{V} = \dfrac{0.0600 \times 8.314 \times 300}{0.250} = 599$ kPa (nearly six times atmospheric pressure!)

Historically all of the colligative properties were important ways of determining the molar mass of a substance.

EXAMPLE

When 1.00 g of a natural oil is dissolved in 50.0 g of tetrachloromethane (boiling point elevation constant 5.02 K mol^{-1} kg), the boiling point is increased by 0.500°C. What is the molar mass of the oil?

SOLUTION

$$\Delta T = K \times \dfrac{n \times m_{st}}{M_{st}} \times \dfrac{1000}{m_{sv}}$$

$$= 5.02 \times \dfrac{1 \times 1.00}{M_{st}} \times \dfrac{1000}{50}$$

$$= 0.500$$

$$M_{st} = 5.02 \times \dfrac{1 \times 1.00}{0.500} \times \dfrac{1000}{50}$$

$$= 200.8 \text{ g mol}^{-1}$$

Since the appearance of modern techniques, such as the mass spectrometer, their importance has been somewhat diminished, but osmotic pressure methods, which produce relatively large effects for low concentrations of solute, are still of value with substances of high molar mass.

EXTENSION

EXERCISE 8.5

1. Which one of the following is **not** a colligative property of a solution?

   A Vapour pressure
   B Elevation of boiling point
   C Depression of freezing point
   D Osmotic pressure

2. Which of the following will have approximately the same effect on the freezing point of water as 0.1 mole of sodium chloride?

   A 0.3 mole of sodium sulfate
   B 0.1 mole of glucose
   C 0.1 mole of copper(II) nitrate
   D 0.05 mole of aluminium chloride

3. When 1.50 g of naphthalene is dissolved in 50.0 g of cyclohexane (freezing point depression constant 20.1 K mol^{-1} kg), the freezing point is decreased by 4.70°C. What is the molar mass of naphthalene?

4. When 0.0135 moles of a non-volatile solute is added to 20.0 g of a solvent in which it does not dissociate, the boiling point of the solvent increases by 1.20°C. Calculate the ebullioscopic constant of the solvent, giving appropriate units.

5. When 5.00 g of a non–volatile solute of molar mass 150 g mol^{-1} is dissolved in 500 cm^3 of water at 25°C, the osmotic pressure is found to be 330 kPa. What can you deduce about the substance from this information?

EXTENSION

8.6 OTHER EQUILIBRIUM CONSTANTS
IN TERMS OF PARTIAL PRESSURES – K_p

The concentration of a gas is proportional to its partial pressure (see Section 5.2, page 170) and it is sometime more convenient to write the equilibrium constant for a gas phase equilibrium in terms of this. This equilibrium constant is differentiated from that in terms of concentration by using the subscript 'p' rather than the subscript 'c'. Therefore for a general equilibrium

$$a\,A + b\,B + c\,C + ... \rightleftharpoons s\,S + t\,T + u\,U + ...$$

in which all the components are in the gas phase, the equilibrium constant in terms of partial pressures is given by

$$K_p = \frac{p(S)^s p(T)^t p(U)^u ...}{p(A)^a p(B)^b p(C)^c ...}$$

Where $p(A)$ represents the partial pressure of A, which can be calculated from the total pressure (P_{tot}) and the amount of A in the mixture using the expression:

$$p(A) = P_{tot} \times \frac{\text{moles of A}}{\text{total moles}}$$

For example in the equilibrium between ammonia and oxygen to give nitrogen monoxide and water:

$$4\,NH_{3\,(g)} + 5\,O_{2(g)} \rightleftharpoons 4\,NO_{(g)} + 6\,H_2O_{(g)}$$

The equilibrium constant is given by $K_p = \dfrac{p(NO)^4 p(H_2O)^6}{p(NH_3)^4 p(O_2)^5}$

As with K_c, K_p does not have fixed units and they must be calculated in each case.

The concentration of a gas is linked to its partial pressure using the ideal gas equation:

$$[A] = \frac{n_a}{V} = \frac{p(A)}{RT}$$

This relationship can be used to inter–convert K_p and K_c values, by substituting in the relevant equation. This leads to $K_p = K_c(RT)^{\Delta n}$ where Δn is the change in the number of moles of gas.

It will have been noted by many students that the equilibrium constant and the free energy change for a reaction (ΔG) are both measures of the extent to which the reactants are converted to the products in a chemical reaction at equilibrium. It is not surprising therefore that the two quantities are linked. The exact relationship is:

$$\Delta G^\theta = -R.T.\ln K_p$$

THE SOLUBILITY PRODUCT – K_{sp}

The solubility product is the name given to the equilibrium constant (K_c) for an ionic solid in equilibrium with its aqueous ions (remembering that the concentrations of solids are omitted from such expressions). For example for a saturated solution of lead(II) chloride, the equilibrium and the solubility product is:

$$PbCl_{2\,(s)} \rightleftharpoons Pb^{2+}_{(aq)} + 2\,Cl^-_{(aq)} \qquad K_{sp} = [Pb^{2+}] \times [Cl^-]^2 \ mol^3 \ dm^{-9}$$

It is really only a useful concept for sparingly soluble electrolytes as concentrated ionic solutions exhibit significant deviations from ideal behaviour. The solubility product can be calculated from the solubility of a substance and vice versa.

EXAMPLE

The solubility of lead(II) chloride at 298 K is 3.9×10^{-4} mol dm^{-3}, what is the solubility product for lead chloride at this temperature?

SOLUTION

From the equation above, each formula unit of lead(II) chloride forms one lead ion and two chloride ion, therefore:

$[Pb^{2+}] = 3.9 \times 10^{-4}$ mol dm^{-3} and $[Cl^-] = 2 \times 3.9 \times 10^{-4} = 7.8 \times 10^{-4}$ mol dm^{-3};

substituting:

$K_{sp} = [Pb^{2+}] \times [Cl^-]^2 = 3.9 \times 10^{-4} \times (7.8 \times 10^{-4})^2 = 2.37 \times 10^{-10}$ mol^3 dm^{-9}

Ions behave independently in solution and hence, in the above example, the chloride ions need not necessarily come from the lead chloride, they could also come from some other solute, for example hydrochloric acid. This means that an ionic solid is significantly less soluble in a solution that already contains one of its component ions, than it is in pure water. This is known as the **common ion effect**.

EXAMPLE

What is the solubility of lead(II) chloride, in g dm^{-3}, in 0.1 mol dm^{-3} hydrochloric acid, given its solubility product calculated above?

SOLUTION

$[Cl^-] = 0.1$ mol dm^{-3}, (assuming any ions from the lead(II) chloride are negligible), therefore

$K_{sp} = [Pb^{2+}] \times [Cl^-]^2 = [Pb^{2+}] \times (0.1)^2 = 2.37 \times 10^{-10}$ mol^3 dm^{-9}

$$[Pb^{2+}] = \frac{2.37 \times 10^{-10}}{0.01} = 2.37 \times 10^{-8} \ mol \ dm^{-3} = [PbCl_2]$$

(note this is much less than in water)
$M_r(PbCl_2) = 278$

$m = n \times M_r = 2.37 \times 10^{-8} \times 278 = 6.60 \times 10^{-6}$ g dm^{-3}

The solubility product may be used to predict whether a sparingly soluble salt will be precipitated under particular circumstances. The concentrations of the ions that would be present is calculated and then substituted into the solubility product expression. If the result of this is greater than the solubility product, then the solid will be precipitated.

EXAMPLE

The solubility product for silver sulfate is 1.60×10^{-5} mol^3 dm^{-9}. Would silver sulfate be precipitated when 20 cm^3 of 0.01 mol dm^{-3} aqueous silver nitrate is mixed with 30 cm^3 of 2.00 mol dm^{-3} sulfuric acid?

$[Ag^+] = 0.01 \times \dfrac{20}{50} = 0.004$ mol dm^{-3}; $[SO_4^{2-}] = 2.00 \times \dfrac{30}{50} = 1.20$ mol dm^{-3}; substituting:

$K_{sp} = [Ag^+]^2 \times [SO_4^{2-}] = (0.004)^2 \times 1.20 = 1.92 \times 10^{-5}$ mol^3 dm^{-9}

This is just greater than the solubility product (1.60×10^{-5} mol^3 dm^{-9}), so a small quantity of solid silver sulfate would be precipitated.

EXERCISE 8.6

1. For which one of the following would K_p and K_c have the same numerical value at the same temperature?

A $2\,SO_{2\,(g)} + O_{2\,(g)} \rightleftharpoons 2\,SO_{3\,(g)}$
B $C_{(s)} + H_2O_{(g)} \rightleftharpoons CO_{(g)} + H_{2\,(g)}$
C $N_{2\,(g)} + 3\,H_{2\,(g)} \Rightarrow 2\,NH_{3\,(g)}$
D $H_{2\,(g)} + I_{2\,(g)} \rightleftharpoons 2\,HI_{(g)}$

2. In which of the following solutions will silver chloride be least soluble?

A   0.1 mol dm^{-3} sodium chloride
B   0.1 mol dm^{-3} glucose
C   0.1 mol dm^{-3} copper(II) nitrate
D   0.1 mol dm^{-3} aluminium chloride

EXTENSION

3. When air (assume 20% oxygen, 80% nitrogen) is heated to 2000K at a pressure of 100 kPa, 3.0% of the oxygen is converted to nitrogen monoxide in the equilibrium:

$$N_{2\ (g)} + O_{2\ (g)} \rightleftharpoons 2\ NO_{(g)}$$

Calculate the partial pressures of O_2, N_2 and NO at equilibrium.

4. The solubility of calcium sulfate is 6.34 g dm^{-3}.

    a) Calculate its solubility product, stating the units.

    b) If equal volumes of 0.1 mol dm^{-3} solutions of calcium chloride and sulfuric acid are mixed would you expect a precipitate of calcium sulfate to form. Explain your reasoning.

5. The solubility product of magnesium hydroxide is 2.0×10^{-11} mol^3 dm^{-9}.

    a) Calculate its solubility in g dm^{-3}.

    b) What is the concentration of hydroxide ions in a saturated solution?

    c) How many grams of the solid would dissolve in 50 cm^3 of water?

    d) How many grams would dissolve in 50 cm^3 of 0.010 mol dm^{-3} aqueous sodium hydroxide?

    e) Explain why the two values differ.

6. The solubility products of zinc carbonate and zinc hydroxide are:

1.4×10^{-11} mol^2 dm^{-6} and 2.0×10^{-17} mol^3 dm^{-9} respectively.

    a) Write chemical equations, including state symbols, for the two equations involved.

    b) Write solubility product expressions for these.

    c) Saturated aqueous solutions are made of these compounds. Which has the higher concentration of zinc ions?

    d) A solution containing zinc ions is added to a solution that is 0.10 mol dm^{-3} in both hydroxide and carbonate ions. Which solid will precipitate out first and what concentration of zinc ions would be required for this to occur? (Assume negligible change in total volume.)

EXTENSION

ACIDS AND BASES

9

Chapter contents

9.1 PROPERTIES OF ACIDS AND BASES

9.1.1   Outline the characteristic properties of acids and bases in aqueous solution.

The properties that must be considered are: effects on indicators and reactions of acids with bases, metals and carbonates. Bases which are not hydroxides, such as ammonia, soluble carbonates and hydrogencarbonates, should be included. Alkalis are bases that dissolve in water.   © IBO 2001

Acids are corrosive chemicals with a sour taste (N.B. you should never taste chemicals as many are poisonous!). All acids have certain chemical characteristics in common:

* They form solutions with a pH <7, so that indicators which change colour at about this pH give the same reaction with all acids, e.g. they turn blue litmus red.

* They react with reactive metals to give a salt and hydrogen. For example sulfuric acid reacts with magnesium to give magnesium sulfate and hydrogen:

$$\underset{\text{Acid}}{H_2SO_{4\,(aq)}} \quad + \quad \underset{\text{Metal}}{Mg_{(s)}} \quad \Rightarrow \quad \underset{\text{Salt}}{MgSO_{4(aq)}} \quad + \quad \underset{\text{Hydrogen}}{H_{2\,(g)}}$$

* They react with bases, such as metal oxides and hydroxides to form a salt and water. For example nitric acid reacts with copper oxide to form copper nitrate and water: Phosphoric acid reacts with sodium hydroxide to form sodium phosphate and water:

$$\underset{\text{Acid}}{2\,HNO_{3\,(aq)}} \quad + \quad \underset{\text{Metal oxide}}{CuO_{(s)}} \quad \Rightarrow \quad \underset{\text{Salt}}{Cu(NO_3)_{2(aq)}} \quad + \quad \underset{\text{Water}}{H_2O_{(l)}}$$

$$\underset{\text{Acid}}{H_3PO_{4(aq)}} \quad + \quad \underset{\text{Metal hydroxide}}{3\,NaOH_{(aq)}} \quad \Rightarrow \quad \underset{\text{Salt}}{Na_3PO_{4(aq)}} \quad + \quad \underset{\text{Water}}{3\,H_2O_{(l)}}$$

* They react with metal carbonates and hydrogencarbonates to give a salt, water and carbon dioxide, which appears as effervescence (i.e. bubbles appear). For example hydrochloric acid will react with zinc carbonate to form zinc chloride, water and carbon dioxide:

$$\underset{\text{Acid}}{2\,HCl_{(aq)}} + \underset{\text{Metal carbonate}}{ZnCO_{3\,(s)}} \Rightarrow \underset{\text{Salt}}{ZnCl_{2(aq)}} + \underset{\text{Water}}{H_2O_{(l)}} + \underset{\text{Carbon dioxide}}{CO_{2(g)}}$$

Ethanoic acid reacts with sodium hydrogencarbonate to form sodium ethanoate, water and carbon dioxide.

$$\underset{\substack{\text{Acid}}}{CH_3COOH_{(aq)}} + \underset{\substack{\text{Metal}\\\text{hydrogencarbonate}}}{NaHCO_{3(aq)}} \Rightarrow \underset{\text{Salt}}{NaCH_3COO_{(aq)}} + \underset{\text{Water}}{H_2O_{(l)}} + \underset{\text{Carbon dioxide}}{CO_{2(g)}}$$

Originally a **base** was considered to be any substance that reacted with an acid to neutralise it, but now the term has more precise meanings (see Section 9.6, page 302). The most common bases are the oxides, hydroxides and carbonates of metals, but a number of other compounds, such as ammonia and amines also act as bases. Solutions of bases, known as **alkalis**, have a slippery feel and a bitter taste (though, again, you should not taste them). As with acids, all bases have certain chemical reactions in common:

- If they are soluble in water they give a solution with pH>7, so that they will all have a similar effect on indicators that change colour at about this pH, e.g. they turn red litmus blue.

- They react with acids to form a salt, e.g. calcium oxide will react with hydrochloric acid to form calcium chloride and water:

$$CaO_{(s)} \quad + \quad 2\,HCl_{(aq)} \quad \Rightarrow \quad CaCl_{2\,(aq)} \quad + \quad H_2O_{(l)}$$
$$\text{Base} \qquad\qquad \text{Acid} \qquad\qquad \text{Salt} \qquad\qquad \text{Water}$$

Some species, like water and the hydrogensulfate ion, can act as both acids and bases and are therefore described as **amphiprotic**:

$$H_3O^+ \Leftarrow \textbf{gain of H}^+ \Leftarrow H_2O \Rightarrow \textbf{loss of H}^+ \Rightarrow OH^-$$
$$H_2SO_4 \Leftarrow \textbf{gain of H}^+ \Leftarrow HSO_4^- \Rightarrow \textbf{loss of H}^+ \Rightarrow SO_4^{2-}$$

Most acids and bases only lose or gain one hydrogen ion and so are said to be **monoprotic**, but other acids and bases that can gain and that can lose more hydrogen ions and are said to be **polyprotic**. Sulfuric acid for example, is **diprotic** in aqueous solution because it can lose two hydrogen ions forming first the hydrogensulfate ion and then the sulfate ion:

$$H_2SO_{4\,(aq)} \Rightarrow H^+_{\,(aq)} + HSO_4^-{}_{(aq)} \rightleftharpoons 2\,H^+_{\,(aq)} + SO_4^{2-}{}_{(aq)}$$

Similarly phosphoric(V) acid, found in cola drinks, is **triprotic**:

$$H_3PO_{4\,(aq)} \rightleftharpoons H^+_{\,(aq)} + H_2PO_4^-{}_{(aq)} \rightleftharpoons 2\,H^+_{\,(aq)} + HPO_4^{2-}{}_{(aq)} \rightleftharpoons 3\,H^+_{\,(aq)} + PO_4^{3-}{}_{(aq)}$$

Polyprotic acids and bases may be recognised because they form anions with more than one charge. Carbonic acid (aqueous carbon dioxide), for example, must be diprotic because it forms the carbonate ion, which has a charge of −2 (i.e. CO_3^{2-}).

One of the first theories to explain the fact that all acids had similar reactions, was that proposed by Arrhenius. This proposed that in aqueous solution all acids, to some extent (dependent on the strength of the acid, see Section 9.3, page 293), split up to form a hydrogen ion and an anion when dissolved in water, i.e. for an acid HX:

$$HX_{(aq)} \Rightarrow H^+_{\,(aq)} + X^-_{\,(aq)}$$

The hydrogen ion is hydrated, like all ions in aqueous solution, but some chemists prefer to show this action more explicitly with the water molecule forming a dative covalent bond to the hydrogen ion, to produce the H_3O^+ ion (variously called the hydronium ion, hydroxonium ion or oxonium ion). In these terms the above equation becomes

$$HX_{(aq)} + H_2O_{(l)} \Rightarrow H_3O^+_{\,(aq)} + X^-_{\,(aq)}$$

This also emphasises the fact that water is not an inert solvent, but is necessary for acid–base activity. Indeed solutions of acids in many non–aqueous solvents do not show acidic properties. For example a solution of hydrogen chloride in methylbenzene does not dissociate and hence, for example, it will not react with magnesium. It is useful in discussing some aspects of acid–base theory, such as conjugate acid–base pairs, but apart from this the simpler terminology of the hydrated proton/hydrogen ion, $H^+_{(aq)}$, will be adopted in this book.

The similar reactions of acids can be explained as all being reactions of the hydrogen ion and it is perhaps more accurate to write them as ionic equations, for example the reaction of an aqueous acid with magnesium can be written as:

$$Mg_{(s)} + 2\ H^+_{(aq)} \Rightarrow Mg^{2+}_{(aq)} + H_{2\,(g)}$$

Bases are defined as substances that react with, and neutralise, acids to form water. Soluble bases (alkalis) form the hydroxide ion when dissolved in water, either because they are soluble and contain the hydroxide ion (as with NaOH), or because they react with water to produce one (as with ammonia, carbonates and hydrogen carbonates):

$$NaOH_{(aq)} \Rightarrow Na^+_{(aq)} + OH^-_{(aq)}$$

$$NH_{3\,(aq)} + H_2O_{(l)} \rightleftharpoons NH_4^+_{(aq)} + OH^-_{(aq)}$$

$$CO_3^{2-}_{(aq)} + H_2O_{(l)} \rightleftharpoons HCO_3^-_{(aq)} + OH^-_{(aq)}$$

$$HCO_3^-_{(aq)} \rightleftharpoons CO_{2\,(aq)} + OH^-_{(aq)}$$

Aqueous acids and alkalis contain ions that are free to move, which explains why they conduct electricity to some extent. If an acid and an alkali are mixed the hydrogen and hydroxide ions react exothermically to form water:

$$H^+_{(aq)} + OH^-_{(aq)} \Rightarrow H_2O_{(l)}$$

This leaves the anion from the acid and the cation from the base in solution. If the water is then evaporated these combine to form a solid salt. For example if the acid were hydrochloric acid and the base sodium hydroxide:

$$Na^+_{(aq)} + Cl^-_{(aq)} \Rightarrow NaCl_{(s)}$$

The current Brønsted–Lowry theory (see Section 9.6, page 302) is simply an extension of the Arrhenius theory to other solvent systems so that reactions such as:

$$NH_4^+ + NH_2^- \Rightarrow 2\ NH_3$$

in a non–aqueous solvent are also classified as acid–base reactions. Similarly Lewis theory (see Section 9.7, page 305) further extends the definition to include reactions that do not involve the transfer of a hydrogen ion, such as:

$$BF_3 + F^- \Rightarrow BF_4^-$$

EXERCISE 9.1

1. Which one of the following substances would you **not** expect an acid to react with?

    A   Blue litmus paper
    B   Sodium carbonate
    C   Magnesium ribbon
    D   Silver chloride

2. Which one of the following acids is diprotic?

    A H_3PO_4
    B CH_3COOH
    C H_2SO_4
    D HNO_3

3. When 2 mol dm^{-3} sulfuric acid and 2 mol dm^{-3} aqueous sodium hydroxide are mixed, how can you tell that they react?

    A   A gas is evolved.
    B   The mixture becomes warm.
    C   The solution changes colour.
    D   A solid precipitate is formed.

4. Write balanced equations for the following reactions:

    a)   iron with dilute sulfuric acid.
    b)   lead carbonate with nitric acid.
    c)   zinc oxide with hydrochloric acid.
    d)   calcium hydroxide with nitric acid.
    e)   sodium hydrogencarbonate with sulfuric acid.
    f)   potassium hydroxide with hydrochloric acid (an ionic equation required).

5. In aqueous solution sulfuric acid and 'carbonic acid' (H_2CO_3) are both *diprotic* acids.

    a)   Explain what is meant by *diprotic*.
    b)   The hydrogencarbonate (bicarbonate) ion, HCO_3^- formed from 'carbonic acid' is described as being *amphiprotic*. Describe what you understand by this term and give the formulae of the species formed.
    c)   Name another substance that is amphiprotic and write equations to illustrate this behaviour.

9.2 STRONG AND WEAK ACIDS AND BASES

9.2.1 Describe and explain the differences between strong and weak acids and bases in terms of the extent of dissociation, reaction with water and conductivity.

The term ionization can be used instead of dissociation. Solutions of equal concentration can be compared by pH and/or conductivity.

9.2.2 State whether a given acid or base is strong or weak.

Specified strong acids are hydrochloric acid, nitric acid and sulfuric acid. Specified weak acids are ethanoic acid and carbonic acid (aqueous carbon dioxide). Specified strong bases are all group 1 hydroxides and barium hydroxide. Specified weak bases are ammonia and ethylamine.

9.2.3 Describe and explain data from experiments to distinguish between strong and weak acids and bases, and to determine the relative acidities and basicities of substances.

© IBO 2001

Strong acids are those which are almost **completely dissociated** (ionised) in dilute aqueous solution:

$$HX_{(aq)} \Rightarrow H^+_{(aq)} + X^-_{(aq)}$$
$$\sim 0\% \qquad \sim 100\%$$

This means that such solutions are good conductors of electricity, owing to the presence of mobile ions. A typical example of a strong acid would be hydrochloric acid:

$$HCl_{(aq)} \Rightarrow H^+_{(aq)} + Cl^-_{(aq)}$$

Other common strong acids include sulfuric acid (H_2SO_4) and nitric acid (HNO_3).

Generally speaking, in strong acids the hydrogen is bonded either to a very electronegative element (e.g. HBr and HI) or to an oxygen bonded to a non metal (e.g. H_2SO_4). In these oxyacids the strength of the acid increases with the electronegativity of the non-metal (H_2SO_4 is a strong acid, H_3PO_4 a weak acid) and the number of oxygens present (HNO_3 is a strong acid, HNO_2 a weak acid).

A **weak acid** is one which is only **slightly dissociated** into ions in dilute aqueous solution:

$$HA_{(aq)} \rightleftharpoons H^+_{(aq)} + A^-_{(aq)}$$
$$\sim 99\% \qquad \sim 1\%$$

A typical example of a weak acid is ethanoic acid, where the undissociated acid is in equilibrium with the ions.

$$CH_3COOH_{(aq)} \rightleftharpoons H^+_{(aq)} + CH_3COO^-_{(aq)}$$

Almost all organic acids are weak acids. Similarly aqueous carbon dioxide behaves as a weak acid:

$$CO_{2\,(aq)} + H_2O_{(l)} \rightleftharpoons H^+_{(aq)} + HCO_3^-{}_{(aq)}$$

Other common inorganic weak acids are:

- aqueous sulfur dioxide (analogous to CO_2)
- hydrofluoric acid (HF, due to factors such as the strength of the H–F bond).
- hydrocyanic acid (HCN)

Intermediate ions of polybasic acids (e.g. HSO_4^-), cations formed by weak bases (e.g NH_4^+) and the hydrated ions of small highly charged metal ions (e.g. $Al^{3+}_{(aq)}$, see Section 9.9, page 315) also act as weak acids.

Strong and weak acids can be differentiated by comparing solutions of equal concentrations. The concentration of hydrogen ions in the solution of the weak acid will be considerably lower, giving rise to a number of differences that may be tested experimentally:

- A weak acid has a higher pH than a strong acid of equal concentration.
- Weak acids do not conduct electricity as well as strong acids of equal concentration, but they conduct better than water.
- Weak acids react more slowly in typical acid reactions (e.g. with a carbonate to give carbon dioxide) than strong acids of equal concentration.

In the same way a strong base is one which is completely dissociated into ions in aqueous solution, like sodium hydroxide and barium hydroxide.

$$BaOH_{2\ (aq)} \Rightarrow Ba^+_{(aq)} + 2\ OH^-_{(aq)}$$

With weak bases an equilibrium exists between the base and the hydroxide ions so that for example ammonia is only partially converted to the hydroxide ion in aqueous solution:

$$NH_{3(aq)} + H_2O_{(l)} \rightleftharpoons NH_4^+{}_{(aq)} + OH^-{}_{(aq)}$$

The closely related amines, such as ethylamine ($C_2H_5NH_2$) also act as weak bases (see Section 11.14, page 386). The anions formed by weak acids (such as the carbonate ion, ethanoate and phosphate ions) also act as weak bases, e.g.

$$CO_3^{2-}{}_{(aq)} + H_2O_{(l)} \rightleftharpoons HCO_3^-{}_{(aq)} + OH^-{}_{(aq)}$$

Methods for differentiating strong and weak bases are similar to those for strong and weak acids, i.e. for solutions of equal concentration a strong base will have a higher pH and a greater conductivity.

In chemistry care must be taken to use the terms strong and weak (i.e. fully and partially dissociated) correctly and **not** as synonyms for concentrated and dilute (i.e. a large or small number of moles in a given volume) as is done in everyday speech. The 'chemical' use of the term is also to be found, in 'strong electrolyte' and 'weak electrolyte'. The term electrolyte means forming ions in aqueous solution allowing it to conduct electricity. The former refers to a substance that is completely converted to ions in aqueous solution (such as salts, strong acids and strong bases) whilst the latter refers to those only partially converted to ions (such as weak acids and bases). Note that only a very small fraction (<1 in 10^8) of molecules in pure water is split up into ions, so it is a very weak electrolyte and a poor conductor of electricity.

EXERCISE 9.2

1. A weak acid is best described as one which

    A   only contains a low concentration of the acid.
    B   has a pH only slightly less than 7.
    C   is only partially dissociated in aqueous solution.
    D   reacts slowly with magnesium ribbon.

2. Which one of the following aqueous solutions would you expect to have a pH significantly different from the rest?

    A   0.001 mol dm^{-3} CO_2
    B   0.001 mol dm^{-3} HNO_3
    C   0.001 mol dm^{-3} H_2SO_4
    D   0.001 mol dm^{-3} HCl

3. Equal volumes of aqueous solutions of 0.1 mol dm^{-3} sodium hydroxide and 0.1 mol dm^{-3} ethylamine could be told apart by three of the following methods. Which one would **not** work?

    A   Comparing the volume of hydrochloric acid required for neutralisation.
    B   Comparing the reading they give on a pH meter.
    C   Comparing the electrical conductivities of the two solutions.
    D   Comparing their effect on universal indicator paper.

4. Ammonia behaves as a weak base in aqueous solution.

    a)   Write a balanced equation for the interaction of this substance with water and explain why it produces an alkaline solution.

    b)   Using ammonia as an example, explain what is meant by the terms **weak** and **base**.

    c)   Would you expect a 0.1 mol dm^{-3} solution of ammonia to have a higher or lower pH than a 0.1 mol dm^{-3} solution of sodium hydroxide? Explain.

5. Hydrochloric acid is a strong acid whereas ethanoic acid is a weak acid.

    a)   Write equations that show the way in which these two acids interact with water and explain how they differ.

    b)   If you had solutions of these two acids with concentrations of 1 mol dm^{-3}, explain how you would expect their electrical conductivities to compare?

    c)   Using a chemical reaction, how could you tell which solution contained the strong acid and which the weak?

9.3 THE pH SCALE

9.3.1 Distinguish between aqueous solutions that are acidic, neutral or basic using the pH scale.

9.3.2 Identify which of two or more aqueous solutions is more acidic or basic, using pH values.

Measure pH using a pH meter or pH paper. Students should know that pH paper contains a mixture of indicators. The theory of pH meters is not required.

9.3.3 State that each change of one pH unit represents a tenfold change in the hydrogen ion concentration $[H^+_{(aq)}]$.

Relate integral values of pH to $[H^+_{(aq)}]$ expressed as powers of ten. Calculation of pH from $[H^+_{(aq)}]$ is not required.

9.3.4 Deduce changes in $[H^+_{(aq)}]$ when the pH of a solution changes by more than one pH unit.

© IBO 2001

Water dissociates to a very slight extent to produce both hydrogen and hydroxide ions, so that in aqueous solutions an equilibrium exists between these ions and the undissociated water molecules:

$$H_2O_{(l)} \rightleftharpoons H^+_{(aq)} + OH^-_{(aq)}$$

In pure water the concentration of hydrogen ions and hydroxide ions that results from this are equal, hence it is described as neutral. An acidic solution has an excess of hydrogen ions, whilst an alkaline solution has an excess of hydroxide ions.

In pure water at 25°C, the concentration of both hydrogen and hydroxide ions from the dissociation above is 10^{-7} mol dm^{-3}, i.e. less than one molecule in 10 million is dissociated. The pH (which stands for **p**ower of **H**ydrogen) of a solution depends upon the concentration of hydrogen ions and is equal to power of 10 with the sign reversed. Hence the pH of water under these conditions is 7 as $[H^+_{(aq)}] = 10^{-7}$ mol dm^{-3}.

If the concentration of hydrogen ions in aqueous solution is increased by adding an acid, then the equilibrium that exists in water will shift to the left (Le Chatelier) and the concentration of hydroxide ions will be reduced. If the concentration of hydrogen ions is increased by a factor of ten (for example, from 10^{-4} to 10^{-3} mol dm^{-3}) then the pH decreases by one unit (in this case 4 to 3). Similarly adding a base to an aqueous solution will reduce the concentration of hydrogen ions. If the concentration of hydroxide ions is increased by a factor of ten (for example, from 10^{-6} to 10^{-5} mol dm^{-3}) the concentration of hydrogen ions is decreased by a factor of ten (from 10^{-8} to 10^{-9} mol dm^{-3}) and the pH increases by one unit.

The pH of a solution can be determined either by using a pH meter, or by using universal indicator. This contains a number of indicators that change colour at different pH values, so that the colour of the mixture will vary with the pH of the solution. The indicators used are chosen so that the colour changes occurs in a 'rainbow' sequence. The relationship between pH, [H⁺], [OH⁻], the colours that universal indicator turns and the acidity of the solution are given in Table 9.1.

Table 9.1 – The relationship between [H⁺], [OH⁻] and pH

pH	0	4	7	10	14
[H⁺]	$1(\times10^0)$	1×10^{-4}	1×10^{-7}	1×10^{-10}	1×10^{-14}
[OH⁻]	1×10^{-14}	1×10^{-10}	1×10^{-7}	1×10^{-4}	$1(\times10^0)$
Universal Indicator	Red	Orange	Green	Blue	Purple
Description	Very Acidic	Slightly Acidic	Neutral	Slightly Basic	Very Basic
Common Example	Laboratory dilute acid	Vinegar, acid rain	Pure water	Milk of magnesia, household ammonia	Laboratory dilute alkali

EXERCISE 9.3

1. 10 cm^3 of an aqueous solution of a monoprotic strong acid is added to 90 cm^3 of water. This will cause the pH of the solution to

    A   increase by ten.
    B   increase by one.
    C   decrease by one.
    D   decrease by ten.

2. Approximately what pH would you expect for a 0.1 mol dm^{-3} solution of ethanoic acid?

    A   1
    B   3
    C   10
    D   13

3. What colour would you expect universal indicator paper to turn when dipped in aqueous sodium hydroxide?

    A   Red
    B   Orange
    C   Green
    D   Purple

4. Calculate the hydrogen ion concentration in solutions of the following pH:

a)   3   b)   11   c)   0

5. Calculate the pH of the following aqueous solutions of strong acids:

a) 10^{-4} mol dm^{-3} hydrochloric acid

b)   0.01 mol dm^{-3} nitric acid

c) 10^{-9} mol dm^{-3} sulfuric acid

6. 0.01 mol dm^{-3} ethanoic acid and 5×10^{-4} mol dm^{-3} hydrochloric acid both have a very similar effect on universal indicator. Explain why this is so.

7. A solution of nitric acid, which is a strong acid, contains 0.63 g of the pure acid in every 100 cm^3 of solution.

a)   What is the concentration of the nitric acid, in mol dm^{-3}?

b)   What is the pH of the solution?

c)   What will the concentration of hydroxide ions be in this solution?

Nitrous acid, HNO_2, in contrast is a weak acid.

d)   Write an equation to show the equilibrium that exists in a solution of this acid.

e)   Would you expect a solution of nitrous acid, of equal concentration to that of the nitric acid calculated above, to have the same pH as the nitric acid, a higher pH or a lower pH. Explain.

8. The pH of 0.01 mol dm^{-3} hydrochloric acid is 2, the pH of 0.01 mol dm^{-3} sulfuric acid is 1.7 and the pH of 0.01mol dm^{-3} ethanoic acid is 3.4. Explain why these three acids, that all have the same concentrations, have different pH values.

9.4 BUFFER SOLUTIONS

9.4.1   Describe a buffer solution in terms of its composition and behaviour.

A buffer resists change in pH when a small amount of a strong acid or base is added. Suitable examples include ammonium chloride/ammonia solution and ethanoic acid/sodium ethanoate. Blood is an example of a buffer solution.

9.4.2   Describe ways of preparing buffer solutions.   © IBO 2001

If a small volume of a strong acid or base is added to water, then the pH of the water will change significantly, for example 0.1 cm^3 (~2 drops) of 1 mol dm^{-3} hydrochloric acid added to a litre of water will change the pH from 7 to 4. If the acid were added to a mixture of a weak acid and its conjugate base rather than water, then the change in pH is much less. Similarly, adding a small volume of a strong base to such a mixture has little effect on its pH. Such solutions, which resist a change of pH, are known as **buffer solutions**.

Consider the equilibrium:

$$HA_{(aq)} \rightleftharpoons H^+_{(aq)} + A^-_{(aq)}$$

If a small amount of a strong acid is added, the additional H^+ displaces the equilibrium to the left (Le Chatelier's principle) and the $[H^+]$ falls to near its original value, so the pH is little changed. Similarly if a small amount of a strong base is added, the OH^- reacts with the H^+ to form water. The equilibrium is therefore displaced to the right until $[H^+]$ increases to near its original value and again the pH is virtually unchanged. In order to behave as an effective buffer the concentration of both the acid/base and its salt must be much greater than the strong acid/base added. The greater the concentration, the better the buffering action.

In order to be effective a buffer solution must contain a significant concentration of both the acid and the conjugate base. Buffer solutions may be prepared in a number of ways. The simplest way is to mix solutions of the weak acid (HA, e.g. ethanoic acid) and a salt of the weak acid, (A^-, e.g. sodium ethanoate will provide ethanoate ions). Similarly solutions of a weak base (e.g. ammonia) and a salt of a weak base (e.g. ammonium chloride) may be used. Alternatively, adding a little strong base to an excess of weak acid (e.g. adding sodium hydroxide to excess ethanoic acid), or a little strong acid to excess weak base (e.g. adding hydrochloric acid to excess ammonia) produces similar buffer solutions.

One common example of a buffer solution is blood. It is vital that the pH of blood remains quite constant as enzymes only function effectively over a limited pH range. The buffering equilibrium is:

$$CO_{2\,(aq)} + H_2O_{(l)} \rightleftharpoons H^+_{(aq)} + HCO_3^-{}_{(aq)}$$

EXERCISE 9.4

1. 10 cm^3 of each of the following is prepared and divided equally between two test tubes. 10 drops of 1 mol dm^{-3} hydrochloric acid is added to one and 10 drops of 1 mol dm^{-3} aqueous sodium hydroxide to the other. For which solution will the difference in pH of the two solutions be least?

    A   0.1 mol dm^{-3} aqueous ethanoic acid mixed with an equal volume of 0.1 mol dm^{-3} aqueous sodium ethanoate.

    B   1 mol dm^{-3} aqueous ethanoic acid mixed with an equal volume of 1 mol dm^{-3} aqueous sodium ethanoate.

    C   0.1 mol dm^{-3} aqueous sodium hydroxide mixed with an equal volume of 0.1 mol dm^{-3} hydrochloric acid.

    D   1 mol dm^{-3} aqueous sodium hydroxide mixed with an equal volume of 1 mol dm^{-3} hydrochloric acid.

2. You wish to turn a solution containing X moles of hydrochloric acid into a buffer solution. Which one of the following should you add?

    A   X moles of sodium hydroxide.

    B   X moles of ammonia.

    C $\frac{X}{2}$ moles of ammonia.

    D   2X moles of ammonia.

3. An aqueous mixture of ammonia and ammonium chloride form a buffer solution with pH~9.

    a)   Explain what is meant by the term *buffer solution*?

    b)   Describe what changes take place within the solution when a small volume of sulfuric acid is added. Repeat this for the addition of a small volume of aqueous sodium hydroxide.

9.5 ACID–BASE TITRATIONS

9.5.1   Draw and explain a graph showing pH against volume of titrant for titrations involving strong acids and bases.   © IBO 2001

Consider gradually adding a 0.1 mol dm^{-3} strong monoprotic base, such as sodium hydroxide, to a 0.1 mol dm^{-3} strong monoprotic acid, such as hydrochloric acid. The pH will change from about 1, when the acid is in excess, to about 13 when the base is in excess. The change between these limits is not a gradual one, but is most rapid close to the equivalence point, as shown in Figure 9.1 below. When 90% of the required base has been added, 10% of the acid will remain and so its concentration, neglecting dilution effects, will be 0.01 mol dm^{-3} therefore the pH will be about 2. 99% of the way to the equivalence point, only 1% remains and the pH of the ~0.001 mol dm^{-3} acid is about 3 and so on. After the equivalence point, 1% of excess base will give a hydroxide ion concentration of 0.001 mol dm^{-3} and a pH of 11. This means that there is a very rapid change of pH in the region of the equivalence point (when moles of acid = moles of base). This is centred around pH7 as a salt of a strong acid and a strong base forms a neutral solution.

Figure 9.1 – The change in pH during titrations

Strong acid – Strong base
    (e.g. HCl + NaOH)

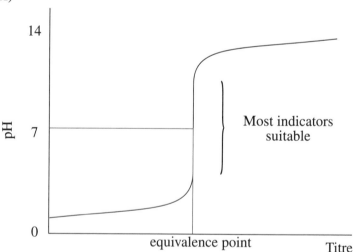

18.5.1   Draw and explain the general shapes of graphs of pH against volume of titrant for titrations involving monoprotic acids and bases.

All combinations should be covered: strong acid + strong base, strong acid + weak base, weak acid + strong base and weak acid + weak base.   © IBO 2001

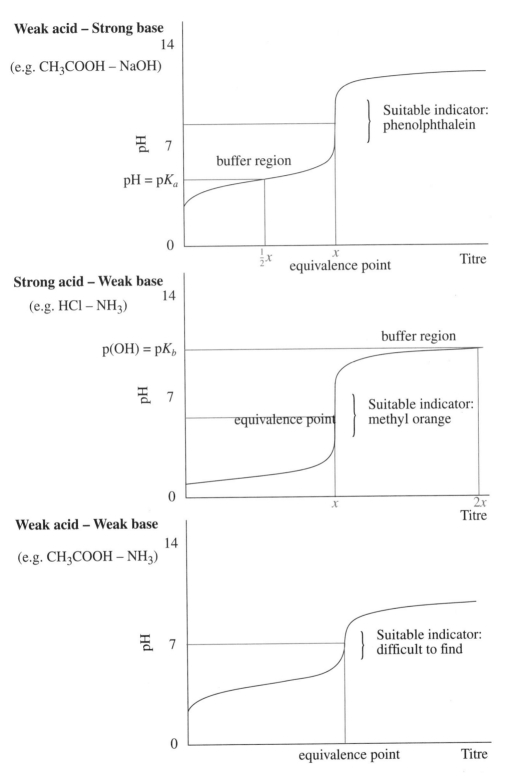

Weak acid – Strong base

(e.g. $CH_3COOH – NaOH$)

Suitable indicator: phenolphthalein

buffer region

$pH = pK_a$

$\frac{1}{2}x$ x equivalence point   Titre

Strong acid – Weak base

(e.g. $HCl – NH_3$)

buffer region

$p(OH) = pK_b$

equivalence point

Suitable indicator: methyl orange

x $2x$ Titre

Weak acid – Weak base

(e.g. $CH_3COOH – NH_3$)

Suitable indicator: difficult to find

equivalence point   Titre

ADVANCED

A study of the titration curve of a weak acid with a strong base, or a weak base with a strong acid, allows the dissociation constant of the weak acid/base (K_a/K_b) to be determined. In order to understand the following discussion you should have already studied Section 9.8.

If the acid is a weak acid, the $[H^+]$ is given by the expression: $[H^+] = K_a \times \dfrac{[HA]}{[A^-]}$

As a strong base is added the reaction that occurs is

$$HA_{(aq)} + OH^-_{(aq)} \Rightarrow H_2O_{(l)} + A^-_{(aq)}$$

so that HA is gradually converted to A^-. This means that the pH gradually increases, as shown on the graph. This region is sometimes referred to as the buffering region because it is indeed a buffer solution (see Section 9.4, page 296) and adding small amounts of acid or alkali has little effect on the pH. At the equivalence point, when all the acid is consumed the pH rapidly increases to that of the strong base.

When half of the amount of base required to neutralise the acid has been added, half of the weak acid (HA) will have been converted into its conjugate base (A^-), so that their concentrations are equal. At this point:

$$[HA] = [A^-] \quad \text{therefore } K_a = [H^+] \quad \text{and} \quad pK_a = pH$$

Note that at the equivalence point the pH of the solution is >7, which corresponds to the fact that at this point the solution is an aqueous solution of a salt of a weak acid and strong base. Salts of this type form slightly alkaline solutions (see Section 9.9, page 315) and knowing the K_a of the acid (or the K_b of the conjugate base) the precise pH can be calculated (see Section 9.8, page 307).

If the acid is a strong acid, but the base is a weak base, then as in the first case, the excess hydrogen ions from the strong acid ensure that the pH remains very low until the equivalence point, when all the base has been converted into its conjugate acid by the reaction:

$$B_{(aq)} + H^+_{(aq)} \Rightarrow BH^+_{(aq)}$$

At the equivalence point the solution is the salt of a weak base and a strong acid, hence the pH of the solution is <7 (see Section 9.9, page 315) and the exact pH can be calculated knowing the K_b of the base, or the K_a of the conjugate acid (see Section 9.8, page 307).

As the concentration of free base starts to increase, the concentration of hydroxide ions, and hence the pH, is governed by the equation:

$$[OH^-] = K_b \times \dfrac{[B]}{[BH^+]}$$

There is therefore a gradual increase in pH as the concentration of the base increases. When the total volume added is double that required to reach the equivalence point, then:

$$[B] = [BH^+] \quad \text{therefore} \quad K_b = [OH^-] \quad \text{and} \quad pK_b = p(OH)$$

In a titration between a weak acid and a weak base, there is only a small change in pH at the equivalence point, making it difficult to detect.

Obviously if in the titration the acid is added to a solution of the base, then the same considerations apply and the shapes of the pH curves are those shown in Figure 9.1, but reflected in a vertical line passing through the equivalence point.

EXERCISE 9.5

1. 1 mol dm^{-3} nitric acid is being titrated with aqueous sodium hydroxide. When 99.9% of the acid has been neutralised, the pH of the solution, ignoring changes in the total volume, will be:

    A   3
    B   6
    C   6.900
    D   6.999

2. During the titration of a weak acid with a strong base, the pH of the solution will equal the pK_a of the weak acid

    A   at the start of the titration.
    B   when half the volume required to reach the end point has been added.
    C   at the end point.
    D   when twice the volume required to reach the end point has been added.

3. During the titration of a weak acid using a strong base, at the end point there will be a rapid change in pH between

    A   4 and 10
    B   3 and 7
    C   7 and 11
    D   6 and 8

4. When 20 cm^3 of a solution of aqueous ammonia is titrated with 0.20 mol dm^{-3} hydrochloric acid, 15 cm^3 of the acid were needed to reach the equivalence point.

    a)   What is the concentration of the aqueous ammonia?

    b)   Given that pK_a for the ammonium ion is 9.3, calculate the pH of the solution (this part requires a knowledge of Section 9.8).

        i   at the start.

        ii   when 7.5 cm^3 of acid has been added.

        iii   at the equivalence point.

    c)   Bearing these values in mind, sketch the shape of the graph of pH against titre you would expect for this titration.

    d)   Which section of this curve is known as the 'buffering region' and why is it so called?

    e)   Identify two important ways in which the curve would differ if the titration were carried out with aqueous barium hydroxide of the same concentration as the ammonia.

ADVANCED

9.6 BRØNSTED–LOWRY ACIDS AND BASES

18.1.1 Define acids and bases according to the Brønsted-Lowry theory.

18.1.2 Identify whether or not a compound could act as a Brønsted-Lowry acid or base.

18.1.3 Identify the conjugate acid-base pairs in a given acid-base reaction.

18.1.4 Determine the structure for the conjugate acid (or base) of any Brønsted-Lowry base (or acid).

The members of a conjugate acid-base pair always differ by a single proton (H^+). Structures of conjugate acid-base pairs should always make clear the approximate location of the proton transferred, eg CH_3COOH/CH_3COO^- rather than $C_2H_4O_2/C_2H_3O_2^-$).

© IBO 2001

The usual contemporary definition of an acid is the Brønsted-Lowry definition, i.e. that an acid is a substance that acts as a donor of hydrogen ions (A hydrogen ion of course consists of just a proton, so acids are also often referred to as 'proton donors'). This means that when it dissolves in water it produces a solution containing hydrogen ions (sometimes written as $H_3O^+_{(aq)}$). When hydrogen chloride dissolves in water to form hydrochloric acid, for example, the hydrogen chloride dissociates into hydrogen ions and chloride ions.

$$HCl_{(aq)} \Rightarrow H^+_{(aq)} + Cl^-_{(aq)} \text{ or}$$

$$HCl_{(aq)} + H_2O_{(l)} \Rightarrow H_3O^+_{(aq)} + Cl^-_{(aq)}$$

According to the same definition, a base is a substance that acts as an acceptor of hydrogen ions. If a base is soluble in water, it is described as an alkali and it produces a solution containing hydroxide ions ($OH^-_{(aq)}$). When, for example, sodium hydroxide dissolves in water it dissociates into sodium ions and hydroxide ions:

$$NaOH_{(aq)} \Rightarrow Na^+_{(aq)} + OH^-_{(aq)}$$

For a species to act as an acid it must contain a hydrogen atom attached by a bond that is easily broken – in many cases this hydrogen is attached to an oxygen atom. For a substance to act as a base, it must have a non–bonding electron pair that can be used to form a bond to a hydrogen ion. Usually this lone pair is on an oxygen or nitrogen atom.

When an acid loses **one** hydrogen ion, the species produced is referred to as the **conjugate base** of the acid, so that, for example, the conjugate base of H_2SO_4 is HSO_4^-. Similarly the species formed when a base gains one hydrogen ion is referred to as the **conjugate acid** of that base. The ammonium ion, NH_4^+, is therefore the conjugate acid of ammonia, NH_3. Acid–base reactions, which can be recognised because they involve the transfer of a hydrogen ion, therefore always involve two such acid–base pairs. Consider ethanoic acid dissolving in water in these terms:

$$CH_3COOH_{(aq)} + \quad H_2O_{(l)} \quad \rightleftharpoons \quad H_3O^+_{(aq)} \quad + CH_3COO^-_{(aq)}$$

Acid 1   Base 2   Acid 2   Base 1

It can be seen that the acid and its conjugate base in these two pairs (CH_3COOH/CH_3COO^- and H_3O^+/H_2O) differ only in the loss of a single hydrogen ion.

If an acid is a strong acid (e.g. HCl), then its conjugate base (Cl⁻) will be such a weak base that it can be considered non–basic, i.e. the equilibrium below will lie fully to the right. As the strength of an acid (HB) decreases however the position of the equilibrium below shifts to the left, which is equivalent to an increase in the strength of its conjugate base (B⁻). Eventually with a strong base (e.g. OH⁻) the equilibrium lies so far to the left that the conjugate acid (H_2O) may be regarded as non–acidic:

Strong conjugate acid ⟶

$$H–B \rightleftharpoons H^+ + B^-$$

⟵ Strong conjugate base

Table 9.2 - The relative strengths of acids and their conjugate bases is shown below:

Conjugate acid	pK_a/pK_b (See section 9.6)	Conjugate base
$HClO_4$	Strong acid	ClO_4^-
H_2SO_4	Strong acid	HSO_4^-
HCl	Strong acid	Cl^-
HNO_3	Strong acid	NO_3^-
'H_2SO_3'	1.8/12.2	HSO_3^-
HSO_4^-	2.0/12.0	SO_4^{2-}
H_3PO_4	2.1/11.9	$H_2PO_4^-$
$ClCH_2COOH$	2.9/11.1	$ClCH_2COO^-$
HF	3.3/10.7	F^-
HNO_2	3.3/10.7	NO_2^-
$C_6H_5NH_3^+$	4.6/9.4	$C_6H_5NH_2$
CH_3COOH	4.8/9.2	CH_3COO^-
'H_2CO_3'	6.4/7.6	HCO_3^-
H_2S	7.1/6.9	HS^-
HSO_3^-	7.2/6.8	SO_3^{2-}
$H_2PO_4^-$	7.2/6.8	HPO_4^{2-}
HCN	9.3/4.7	CN^-
NH_4^+	9.3/4.7	NH_3
C_6H_5OH	9.9/4.1	$C_6H_5O^-$
HCO_3^-	10.3/3.7	CO_3^{2-}
HPO_4^{2-}	12.4/1.6	PO_4^{3-}
H_2O	strong base	HO^-
C_2H_5OH	strong base	$C_2H_5O^-$
NH_3	strong base	NH_2^-

Increasing acid strength →

Increasing base strength →

ADVANCED

EXERCISE 9.6

1. Which one of the following statements about acids is **untrue**?

    A   Acids are proton donors.

    B   Acids dissociate to form H^+ ions when dissolved in water.

    C   Acids produce solutions with a pH greater than 7.

    D   Acids will neutralise bases to form salts.

2. In which one of the following reactions is the species in **bold** type behaving as a base?

    A $2\mathbf{NO} + O_2 \rightleftharpoons 2NO_2$

    B $\mathbf{CO_3^{2-}} + H^+ \rightleftharpoons HCO_3^-$

    C $\mathbf{NH_4^+} + H_2O \rightleftharpoons NH_3 + H_3O^+$

    D $\mathbf{Cu^{2+}} + 2OH^- \rightleftharpoons Cu(OH)_2$

3. Which one of the following is the conjugate base of the hydrogensulfite ion (HSO_3^-)?

    A H_2SO_3

    B $H_2SO_3^+$

    C SO_3^{2-}

    D SO_3^-

4. Which one of the following species, many of which are unstable, would you expect to be capable of acting as a base?

    A CH_4

    B $CH_3\bullet$

    C CH_3^+

    D CH_3^-

5. a)   Give the conjugate acids of Cl^-; PO_4^{3-} ; C_5H_5N; $H_3N\text{-}NH_2^+$; $^-OOC\text{-}COO^-$

    b)   Give the conjugate bases of HNO_3; HI; HSO_4^-; NH_4^+; $HONH_3^+$

    c)   From the species listed, select two species that are *amphiprotic*.

    d)   Write the formula of another amphiprotic species and give its conjugate base and its conjugate acid.

6. In a mixture of concentrated nitric and sulfuric acids, the nitric acid acts as a base and the sulfuric acid as a monoprotic acid.

    a)   Give the Brønsted–Lowry definition of i) an acid and ii) a base.

    b)   Write an equation for this reaction and explain how your equation shows that the sulfuric acid is acting as an acid.

    c)   On your equation link together with lines the two conjugate acid–base pairs

    d)   What is meant by the term '***conjugate***'?

ADVANCED

9.7 LEWIS THEORY

18.2.1 Define and apply the terms Lewis acid and Lewis base.

A Lewis acid-base reaction involves the formation of a new covalent bond in which both electrons are provided by one species. Such bonds are called dative covalent bonds. The formation of complexes (see 13.2.4 and 13.2.5) is usually a Lewis acid-base reaction.   © IBO 2001

When a base accepts a proton from an acid it forms a covalent bond to the proton, but this differs from most covalent bonds in that both of the electrons come from the base, as the proton has no electrons to contribute to the bond. Covalent bonds of this sort are known as 'dative' or 'co–ordinate' covalent bonds, but are identical to other covalent bonds in every way but the origin of the electrons. Dative bonds are indicated in structural formulae by an arrow rather than a line, the arrow pointing in the direction that the electrons are donated.

Lewis pointed out that an acid could be defined as 'a species that accepts a pair of electrons to form a dative bond'. All Brønsted–Lowry acids are in fact Lewis acids, but the term 'Lewis acid' is usually reserved for a species that is not also a Brønsted–Lowry acid. The substance that donates the electron pair to form the bond to these is known as a 'Lewis base'. This extended the range of acid-base reactions beyond those involving the transfer of a hydrogen ion to include all reactions involving the formation of a dative bond.

A common example of a Lewis acid is boron trifluoride, in which boron has only six electrons in its valence shell. This reacts with ammonia (which acts as a Lewis base) to give a compound containing a dative bond (note the arrow in the structural formula), in which the lone pair from the nitrogen completes the valence shell of the boron:

$$\begin{array}{ccc}
\overset{\displaystyle F}{\underset{\displaystyle F}{F-B}} & + & \overset{\displaystyle H}{\underset{\displaystyle H}{:N-H}} \quad \Longrightarrow \quad \overset{\displaystyle F}{\underset{\displaystyle F}{F-B}} \blacktriangleleft \overset{\displaystyle H}{\underset{\displaystyle H}{N-H}}
\end{array}$$

Other common Lewis acids are compounds of elements in group 3 of the periodic table, such as aluminium chloride ($AlCl_3$) in which the element forms three covalent bonds, leaving a vacancy for two electrons in the valence shell. Any species that can accept an electron pair into its incomplete valence shell (e.g. CH_3^+) is, however, capable of acting as a Lewis acid. Similarly any species with a non-bonding electron pair (i.e. all anions and indeed all molecules that are not hydrides, group 3 and group 4 elements) is capable of acting as a Lewis base. All interactions to form 'complex ions' (see Section 3.5, page 103) are also Lewis acid–base reactions. In these the ligand acts as the Lewis base by donating a pair of electrons that is accepted by the central metal ion, which hence acts as a Lewis acid. For example:

$$Fe^{3+}_{(aq)} \quad + \quad :SCN^{-}_{(aq)} \quad \Rightarrow \quad [FeSCN]^{2+}_{(aq)}$$
$$\text{Lewis acid} \qquad \text{Lewis base} \qquad \text{complex ion}$$

ADVANCED

EXERCISE 9.7

1. Which one of the following species, many of which are unstable, would you expect to act as a Lewis acid?

    A CH_4

    B $CH_3 \bullet$

    C CH_3^+

    D CH_3^-

2. Anhydrous aluminium chloride can act as a *Lewis acid*. It will for example react with chloride ions in non-aqueous solution to form the complex ion $AlCl_4^-$.

    a)   Explain what is meant by the term *Lewis acid*.

    b)   Draw Lewis diagrams to represent the interaction between $AlCl_3$ (consider it to be a covalent molecule) and the chloride ion to form the complex ion.

    c)   What kind of bond exists between the chloride ion and the aluminium? In what way does its formation differ from other covalent bonds?

    d)   What shape would you predict for i) $AlCl_3$ and   ii) $AlCl_4^-$?

3. For each of the following species, state whether it is most likely to behave as a Lewis acid or a Lewis base. Explain your answers.

    a) PH_3

    b) BCl_3

    c) H_2S

    d) SF_4

    e) Cu^{2+}

ADVANCED

9.8 CALCULATIONS INVOLVING ACIDS AND BASES

Note: A proton in water can be written as $H^+_{(aq)}$ or $H_3O^+_{(aq)}$ and the former is adopted here.

18.3.1 State the expression for the ionic product constant of water K_w.

$K_w = [H^+_{(aq)}][OH^-_{(aq)}] = 1.0 \times 10^{-14}\ mol^2 dm^{-6}$ *at 298K, but this varies with temperature.*

18.3.2 Deduce $[H^+_{(aq)}]$ and $[OH^-_{(aq)}]$ for water at different temperatures given K_w values.

18.3.3 Define pH, pOH and pK_w.

18.3.4 Calculate $[H^+_{(aq)}]$, $[OH^-_{(aq)}]$, pH and pOH from specified concentrations.

The values of $[H^+_{(aq)}]$ and $[OH^-_{(aq)}]$ are directly related to the concentration of the acid or base.

18.3.5 State the equation for the reaction of any weak acid or weak base with water, and hence derive the ionization constant expression.

In general $HA_{(aq)} \rightleftharpoons H^+_{(aq)} + A^-_{(aq)};$

$B_{(aq)} + H_2O_{(l)} \rightleftharpoons BH^+_{(aq)} + OH^-_{(aq)};$

Then $K_a = \dfrac{[H^+_{(aq)}][A^-_{(aq)}]}{[HA_{(aq)}]}$ *and* $K_b = \dfrac{[BH^+_{(aq)}][OH^-_{(aq)}]}{[B_{(aq)}]}$

Examples used should only involve the transfer of one proton.

18.3.6 Derive the expression $K_a \times K_b = K_w$ and use it to solve problems for any weak acid and its conjugate base and for any weak base and its conjugate acid.

18.3.7 State and explain the relationship between K_a and pK_a and between K_b and pK_b.

18.3.8 Determine the relative strengths of acids or their conjugate bases from K_a or pK_a values.

18.3.9 Apply K_a or pK_a in calculations.

Calculations can be performed using various forms of the acid ionization constant expression (see 18.3.5). Students should state when approximations are used in equilibrium calculations. Use of the quadratic expression is not required.

18.3.10 Calculate the pH of a specified buffer system.

Calculations will involve the transfer of only one proton. Cross reference with 9.4.

[This section is also Syllabus section A.5.1-9]   © IBO 2001

In aqueous solutions molecular water is in equilibrium with hydrogen ions and hydroxide ions:

$$H_2O_{(l)} \rightleftharpoons H^+_{(aq)} + OH^-_{(aq)}\ \Delta H = +57\ kJ\ mol^{-1}$$

In pure water at 25°C (298 K) the concentration of hydrogen and hydroxide ions are both equal to $10^{-7}\ mol\ dm^{-3}$. Hence in an aqueous solution at this temperature, the product of the concentrations of hydrogen and hydroxide ions is always $10^{-14}\ mol^2\ dm^{-6}$. This is known as the **dissociation constant of water** and given the symbol K_w:

$$K_w = [H^+][OH^-] = 1 \times 10^{-14} \text{ mol}^2 \text{ dm}^{-6}$$

The forward reaction of this equilibrium is endothermic so that as the temperature is raised the equilibrium shifts to the right and the equilibrium constant increases. This means that at higher temperatures $[H^+] > 10^{-7}$ mol dm^{-3}, so the pH of pure water is <7, even though it is still neutral (i.e. $[H^+] = [OH^-]$).

If the concentration of hydrogen ions in an aqueous solution is 1×10^{-4} mol dm^{-3} then the concentration of hydroxide ions will be 1×10^{-10} mol dm^{-3} $\left(\text{i.e. } \dfrac{1 \times 10^{-14}}{1 \times 10^{-4}} \right)$. The pH of a solution depends on the concentration of hydrogen ions in the solution and it is defined by the equation:

$$pH = - \log [H^+]$$

This means that the pH of a solution in which $[H^+]$ is 1×10^{-5} mol dm^{-3} is 5. For non–integer values a calculator must be used, so if $[H^+]$ is 5×10^{-4} mol dm^{-3} then the pH is 3.3 and if the pH is 11.7, then $[H^+]$ is 2×10^{-12} mol dm^{-3}.

This can be combined with the K_w expression above to calculate the pH of alkaline solutions. In a 0.001 mol dm^{-3} solution of sodium hydroxide, the $[OH^-]$ is 1×10^{-3} mol dm^{-3}, so that $[H^+]$ will be 1×10^{-11} mol dm^{-3} hence the pH of the solution is 11.

pOH is similarly defined as: $pOH = - \log [OH^-]$
This means that the sum of the pH and pOH of any solution is 14, so the pOH of the solution above is 3.

Consider a weak acid in equilibrium with its ions in aqueous solution:

$$HA_{(aq)} \rightleftharpoons H^+_{(aq)} + A^-_{(aq)}$$

for the general case or, in the specific case of ethanoic acid:

$$CH_3COOH_{(aq)} \rightleftharpoons H^+_{(aq)} + CH_3COO^-_{(aq)}$$

The equilibrium constant for this reaction, known as the **acid dissociation constant** (K_a), is a measure of the strength of the acid – the greater its value the stronger the acid.

$$K_a = \frac{[H^+][A^-]}{[HA]} \quad \text{so for ethanoic acid } K_a = \frac{[H^+][CH_3COO^-]}{[CH_3COOH]} \text{ mol dm}^{-3}$$

The value of K_a is often expressed as a pK_a, the relationship being similar to that between $[H^+]$ and pH:

$$pK_a = - \log K_a$$

The K_a of ethanoic acid, for example, is 1.74×10^{-5} mol dm^{-3} at 298K, so that its pK_a is 4.76. The greater the pK_a value, the weaker the acid. Note that K_a varies with temperature and so calculations involving it only apply to a particular temperature.

The expression for the equilibrium constant above relates together the acid dissociation constant (which may be found from the pK_a), the concentration of the acid and the concentration of hydrogen ions/conjugate base (which must be equal in a solution of the acid and may therefore be found from the pH). Knowing any two of these quantities, the third may be found. Consider the equilibrium:

$$HA \rightleftharpoons H^+ + A^-$$

	HA	H⁺	A⁻
Initial Concentrations	a	0	0
Equilibrium concentrations	$a{-}x$	x	x

Substituting in the equilibrium expression:

$$K_a = \frac{[H^+][A^-]}{[HA]} = \frac{x.x}{a-x} = \frac{x^2}{a-x}$$

Calculations involving this expression will often involve solving a quadratic equation, but in the case of a weak acid, because it is only slightly dissociated, $x \ll a$, so that $a{-}x$ is almost equal to a. Making this approximation the equation becomes:

$$K_a = \frac{x^2}{a-x} \approx \frac{x^2}{a}$$

This much simpler equation can be used in calculations. When the result has been obtained, the values of x and a can be checked to see if the approximation is valid. Note that a second assumption made is that $[H^+] = [A^-]$, i.e. that H^+ from the dissociation of water molecules may be neglected, which can be checked when [H+] is known. It can generally be regarded as valid if pH<6.

Examples of typical calculations are given below:
1. **Calculating K_a**

EXAMPLE

A 0.0100 mol dm^{-3} solution of a weak acid has a pH of 5.00. What is the dissociation constant of the acid?

SOLUTION

If pH = 5.00, then $[H^+] = [A^-] = 1.00 \times 10^{-5}$ mol dm^{-3}.

$$K_a = \frac{x^2}{a-x} \approx \frac{x^2}{a} = \frac{(1.00 \times 10^{-5})^2}{0.0100} = 1.00 \times 10^{-8} \text{ mol dm}^{-3}$$

2. **Calculating pH**

EXAMPLE

Benzoic acid has a pK_a of 4.2. What is the pH of a 0.10 mol dm^{-3} solution of this acid?

SOLUTION

If $pK_a = 4.2$, $K_a = 10^{-4.2} = 6.31 \times 10^{-5}$ mol dm^{-3}.

$$K_a = \frac{x^2}{a-x} \approx \frac{x^2}{a} = \frac{x^2}{0.10} = 6.31 \times 10^{-5}$$

$$x = \sqrt{6.31 \times 10^{-6}}$$

$$= 2.51 \times 10^{-3} \text{ mol dm}^{-3}$$

$$pH = -\log(2.51 \times 10^{-3}) = 2.6$$

3. Calculating concentration

EXAMPLE

What concentration of hydrofluoric acid is required to give a solution of pH 2.00, if the dissociation constant of the acid is 6.76×10^{-4} mol dm^{-3}?

SOLUTION

If pH = 2.00, $[H^+] = [F^-] = 1.00 \times 10^{-2}$ mol dm^{-3}.

$$K_a = \frac{x^2}{a-x} \approx \frac{x^2}{a} = \frac{(1.00 \times 10^{-2})^2}{a} = 6.76 \times 10^{-4}$$

$$a = \frac{10^{-4}}{6.76 \times 10^{-4}} = 0.148 \text{ mol dm}^{-3}$$

Note that here the validity of the approximation is marginal as x is ~7% of a. In this case solving the equation without the approximation is only slightly more difficult and gives a more accurate value of 0.158 mol dm^{-3}.

When a weak base is dissolved in water, the equilibrium established can be dealt with in terms of the dissociation of its conjugate weak acid, using the equations above. Alternatively it can be considered in terms of the equilibrium between the base and water:

$$B_{(aq)} + H_2O_{(l)} \rightleftharpoons BH^+_{(aq)} + OH^-_{(aq)}$$

For this equilibrium making similar assumptions to those above for weak acids:

$$K_b = \frac{[BH^+][OH^-]}{[B]} = \frac{y \cdot y}{b-y} = \frac{y^2}{b-y} \approx \frac{y^2}{b}$$

where K_b is known as the **base dissociation constant**. Similarly:

$$pK_b = -\log K_b$$

Calculations can be carried out using these equilibrium expressions in a similar manner to those for acids.

4. A calculation involving a weak base

EXAMPLE

What is the pH of a 0.050 mol dm^{-3} solution of ethylamine (pK_b = 3.4)?

SOLUTION

$$10^{-3.4} = 3.98 \times 10^{-4} = K_b = \frac{[BH^+][OH^-]}{[B]} = \frac{y.y}{0.050}$$

$$y^2 = 0.050 \times 3.98 \times 10^{-4} = 1.99 \times 10^{-5}$$

$$[OH^-] = y = \sqrt{1.99 \times 10^{-5}} = 4.46 \times 10^{-3}$$
$$pOH = -\log[OH^-] = -\log(4.46 \times 10^{-3}) = 2.4$$
$$pH = 14 - pOH = 11.6$$

Consider a weak acid (HA) and its conjugate base (A$^-$). The equilibria established when they are added to water are:

$$HA_{(aq)} \rightleftharpoons H^+_{(aq)} + A^-_{(aq)} \qquad A^-_{(aq)} + H_2O_{(l)} \rightleftharpoons HA_{(aq)} + OH^-_{(aq)}$$

$$K_a = \frac{[H^+][A^-]}{[HA]} \qquad\qquad K_b = \frac{[HA][OH^-]}{[A^-]}$$

Multiplying these two expressions:

$$K_a \times K_b = \frac{[H^+][A^-]}{[HA]} \times \frac{[HA][OH^-]}{[A^-]} = [H^+][OH^-] = K_w$$

Hence for any conjugate acid–base pair

$$K_a \times K_b = K_w = 10^{-14} \qquad \text{or} \qquad pK_a + pK_b = 14$$

This means that the stronger the acid (i.e. the greater K_a), the weaker the base (i.e. the smaller K_b) and vice versa, as may be seen in Table 9.2, page 303.

The concentration of hydrogen ions, and hence the pH, of buffer solutions (see Section 9.4, page 296) may be calculated using the formula for the acid dissociation constant, which may be rearranged into the slightly more convenient form where [HA] is approximated to the concentration of the acid and [A$^-$] to that of the conjugate base:

$$[H^+] = K_a \times \frac{[HA]}{[A^-]} \quad \text{or, taking logarithms} \quad pH = pK_a - \log\frac{[HA]}{[A^-]}$$

The pH of the buffer solution will therefore depend on the K_a of the weak acid and also on the ratio of the concentrations of the acid and its conjugate base, so that a buffer solution of any desired pH can be prepared. Note that the dependence is only on the **ratio** of these concentrations and not on their actual values. In order to be effective however, both must be present in reasonable concentrations, so in practice the effective buffer range of any weak acid/base is in the range pK_a ±1. The pH of a buffer may be

ADVANCED

OPTION

calculated knowing the K_a value of the acid and the concentrations of the conjugate acid and base. Similarly, if the composition of the buffer and its pH is known, then the dissociation constant of the acid may be found. In the case where $[HA] = [A^-]$, then $pH = pK_a$. The formula chosen for the calculation is a matter of personal preference, taking into consideration the data provided.

4.   A calculation involving a buffer solution

EXAMPLE

Solid sodium ethanoate is added to 0.200 mol dm^{-3} ethanoic acid until its concentration is 0.0500 mol dm^{-3}. Given that K_a for ethanoic acid is 1.74×10^{-5} mol dm^{-3}, and assuming no volume change on dissolving the solid, calculate the pH of the buffer solution formed.

SOLUTION

$$[H^+] = K_a \times \frac{[HA]}{[A^-]} = 1.74 \times 10^{-5} \times \frac{0.200}{0.0500} = 6.96 \times 10^{-5} \text{ mol dm}^{-3}$$

$$pH = -\log[H^+] = -\log(6.96 \times 10^{-5}) = 4.16$$

or

$$pH = pK_a - \log\frac{[HA]}{[A^-]} = \log(1.74 \times 10^{-5}) - \log\left(\frac{0.200}{0.0500}\right)$$

$$pH = 4.76 - 0.6 = 4.16$$

EXERCISE 9.8

1.   Hydrochloric acid is a strong acid. In a 0.01 mol dm^{-3} solution, what is the pH and the hydroxide ion concentration?

A	pH = 0.01	$[OH^-]$ = 0.01 mol dm^{-3}
B	pH = 0.01	$[OH^-]$ = 12 mol dm^{-3}
C	pH = 2	$[OH^-]$ = 0.01 mol dm^{-3}
D	pH = 2	$[OH^-]$ = 10^{-12} mol dm^{-3}

2.   Approximately what proportion of water molecules are dissociated into hydrogen ions and hydroxide ions?

A	One in 10^3
B	One in 10^6
C	One in 10^9
D	One in 10^{14}

3. A 0.01 mol dm^{-3} solution of a weak acid has a pH of 4. What is K_a for the acid?

A 1×10^{-4} mol dm^{-3}
B 1×10^{-5} mol dm^{-3}
C 1×10^{-6} mol dm^{-3}
D 1×10^{-8} mol dm^{-3}

4. The pK_b for a base is 5. What is the pH of a 0.1 mol dm^{-3} solution of the base?

A   8
B   9
C   10
D   11

5. Some weak acids and their pK_a values are given below. Which one of these acids will have the strongest conjugate base?

A   Methanoic acid 3.75
B   Bromorthanoic acid2.90
C   Phenol   10.00
D   Methylpropanoic acid4.85

6. A solution that is 0.10 mol dm^{-3} in fluoroethanoic acid and 0.050 mol dm^{-3} in sodium fluoroethanoate has a pH of 3.0. What is the acid dissociation constant of fluoroethanoic acid?

A 1×10^{-3} mol dm^{-3}
B 5×10^{-4} mol dm^{-3}
C 2×10^{-3} mol dm^{-3}
D 5×10^{-3} mol dm^{-3}

7. A weak monoprotic acid (HA) has an acid dissociation constant of 4×10^{-5} mol dm^{-3}. Which one of the solutions containing the acid and its sodium salt (NaA) will have a pH of exactly 5?

A   [HA] = 0.25 mol dm^{-3}; [NaA] = 0.1 mol dm^{-3}
B   [HA] = 0.4 mol dm^{-3}; [NaA] = 0.1 mol dm^{-3}
C   [HA] = 0.1 mol dm^{-3}; [NaA] = 0.4 mol dm^{-3}
D   [HA] = 0.1 mol dm^{-3}; [NaA] = 0.25 mol dm^{-3}

8.   a)   What is the pH of a solution containing 0.0721 mol dm^{-3} hydrogen ions?
      b)   What is the pH of a soluion containing 4.6×10^{-9} mol dm^{-3} hydrogen ions?
      c)   What is the concentration of hydrogen ions in a solution of pH 5.83?
      d)   What is the concentration of hydroxide ions in a solution of pH 11.64?
      e)   What is the pH of a solution containing 0.135 mol dm^{-3} hydroxide ions?

ADVANCED

OPTION

9. An aqueous solution that is 0.10 mol dm^{-3} in ammonia and 0.10 mol dm^{-3} in ammonium chloride acts as a *buffer solution* with a pH of 9.3.

a) Use the information given to calculate the base dissociation constant (K_b) of ammonia.

b) A buffer with a pH of exactly 9.0 is required. Must more ammonia or more ammonium chloride be added to achieve this? Explain.

c) Calculate the new concentration of the species whose concentration is increased to reduce the pH of the solution.

d) Name two substances that could be mixed to produce a buffer solution of pH~4.

10. Sodium hydroxide is a strong base. In a 0.0010 mol dm^{-3} solution of this:

a) What would the hydroxide ion concentration be?

b) What would the hydrogen ion concentration be?

c) Would the pH be the same, greater or less for 0.0010 mol dm^{-3} solution of barium hydroxide? Why?

11. The K_a for 2–nitrophenol is 6.17×10^{-8} mol dm^{-3}. Use this information to calculate:

a) The pK_a of 2–nitrophenol.

b) The pH of a 0.020 mol dm^{-3} solution of 2–nitrophenol.

c) K_b for the conjugate base of 2–nitrophenol.

12. A 0.28 mol dm^{-3} solution of a weak acid has a pH of 4.67.

a) Calculate K_a for the acid.

b) Is it a stronger or weaker acid than ethanoic acid (pK_a = 4.76)?

c) What concentration of the acid would give a solution with a pH of exactly 5?

13. Hydrocyanic acid (HCN) is a very weak acid (pK_a = 9.3).

a) Write an equation for its interaction with water.

b) What would be the pH of a 0.010 mol dm^{-3} solution of this acid? How does this compare with the value that would be expected for a strong acid, such as hydrochloric, of a similar concentration?

c) In this solution, what percentage of the hydrogen cyanide is present as ions? If the solution were diluted, would this percentage increase or decrease?

d) What pH would you expect a 0.10 mol dm^{-3} solution of sodium cyanide (NaCN) to have?

9.9 SALT SOLUTIONS

18.4.1 State and explain whether salts form acidic, alkaline or neutral aqueous solutions.

Examples should include salts formed from the four possible combinations of strong and weak acids and bases. The effect of the charge density of the cations in groups 1, 2, 3 and d-block elements should also be considered,
e.g. $[Fe(H_2O)_6]^{3+} \rightleftharpoons [Fe(OH)(H_2O)_5]^{2+} + H^+.$ © IBO 2001

The ions contained in salts can act as acids or bases in aqueous solution. Cations act as acids and anions as bases. The stronger the conjugate acid/base they are derived from, then the weaker the acid–base activity of the ion (If K_a is very large then K_b for the conjugate base will be very small and vice versa, see Table 9.2, page 303). The cations derived from strong bases, such as sodium hydroxide and barium hydroxide, have little acid–base activity and the same is true of the anions derived from strong acids, such as sulfuric, nitric and hydrochloric acids. Salts, such as sodium chloride therefore form neutral aqueous solutions.

If however the anion is derived from a weak acid, such as ethanoic acid, then the anion will act as a weak base so that a solution of the salt of a strong base and a weak acid such as sodium ethanoate, will have a pH>7:

$$CH_3COO^-_{(aq)} + H_2O_{(l)} \rightleftharpoons CH_3COOH_{(aq)} + OH^-_{(aq)}$$

Similarly if the cation is derived from a weak base, as is the case with ammonium salts, then the cation will act as a weak acid in aqueous solution, so that the pH of solutions of a weak base and a strong acid such as ammonium chloride, is <7:

$$NH_4^+{}_{(aq)} \rightleftharpoons NH_{3\,(aq)} + H^+{}_{(aq)}$$

With salts formed from a weak acid and a weak base (e.g. ammonium ethanoate) the pH of the solution formed will reflect the relative strengths of the acid and base.

With small, highly charged hydrated cations, such as $[Al(H_2O)_6]^{3+}$ and $[Fe(H_2O)_6]^{3+}$, the electron attracting power of the ion weakens the O–H bonds in the water molecules bonded to it and stabilises the hydroxide ion by dissociation. As a result these hydrated ions dissociate when dissolved in water to produce quite acidic solutions:

$$[Fe(H_2O)_6]^{3+}{}_{(aq)} \rightleftharpoons [Fe(OH)(H_2O)_5]^{2+}{}_{(aq)} + H^+{}_{(aq)}$$

ADVANCED

EXERCISE 9.9

1. Which one of the following salts would produce the most neutral aqueous solution?

    A NH_4NO_3
    B $FeCl_3$
    C Na_2SO_4
    D CH_3COOK

2. Many metal cations in aqueous solution interact with the water to make the solution acidic. Which combination of cation characteristics will lead to the most acidic solution?

    A   Small size and low charge.
    B   Small size and high charge.
    C   Large size and low charge.
    D   Large size and high charge.

3. Which one of the following solutions could you distinguish from the others using universal indicator paper?

    A   Aqueous ammonia
    B   Aqueous sodium carbonate
    C   Aqueous ammonium chloride
    D   Aqueous calcium hydroxide

4. For each of the following salts, state whether you would expect them to form aqueous solutions that were neutral, slightly alkaline or slightly acidic and give reasons for your predictions.

    a)   Ethylammonium sulfate   b)   Barium chloride
    c)   Aluminium nitrate   d)   Sodium carbonate

9.10 INDICATORS

18.6.1 Describe qualitatively how an acid-base indicator works.

    Use $HIn_{(aq)}$ $\rightleftharpoons$ $H^+_{(aq)} + In^-_{(aq)};$ *or similar explanation.*
            Colour A   *Colour B*

18.6.2 State and explain how the pH range of an acid-base indicator relates to its pK_a value.

18.6.3 Determine an appropriate indicator for a titration, given the equivalence point of the titration and K_a (or pK_a) values for possible indicators.   © IBO 2001

An indicator is a substance (often an organic dye) that has a different colour in acidic and alkaline solutions and hence can be used to detect the end point of a titration. An indicator is simply a weak acid/base in which the two forms have different colours and are in equilibrium with each other, i.e.:

                     $HIn_{(aq)}$ $\rightleftharpoons$ $H^+_{(aq)}$ $+$ $In^-_{(aq)}$
For litmus: Red   Blue

In the presence of an acid, the equilibrium is driven to the left (Le Chatelier's principle) so the indicator turns to the HIn form (red for litmus); whereas in the presence of a base the shift is to the right and the indicator changes into its In⁻ form (blue for litmus). The weak acid is governed by the usual equation:

$$K_a = \frac{[H^+][In^-]}{[HIn]}$$

so rearranging this the ratio of the two coloured forms is given by:

$$\frac{[HIn]}{[In^-]} = \frac{[H^+]}{K_a}$$

The colour of the indicator therefore depends not only on the pH, and hence $[H^+]$, but also on the value of K_a, so that different indicators change colour over different pH ranges. Two of the most commonly met indicators are methyl orange and phenolphthalein, the characteristics of which are summarised in Table 9.3 below.

Table 9.3 – The properties of phenolphthalein and methyl orange

Property	Phenolphthalein	Methyl orange
pK_a	9.6	3.7
pH Range	8.3 to 10.0	3.1 to 4.4
Colour in acid	Colourless	Red
Colour in alkali	Pink	Yellow
Useful for	Titrations involving strong bases	Titrations involving strong acids

If the concentration of one form (say HIn) is ten times greater than that of the other form (In⁻), then the colour of the indicator will effectively be that of the predominant species. The pH of the solution at this point will be:

$$[H^+] = K_a \times \frac{[HIn]}{[In^-]} = K_a \times \frac{10}{1} = 10K_a \text{ or } pH = pK_a - 1$$

Hence many indicators change colour over a region of 2 pH units centred on the pK_a value, though this needs to be modified according the the relative intensities of the two colours, as is particularly obvious for phenolphthalein in the above table.

In order to be an effective indicator, the **end point** (i.e. the colour change) must occur rapidly at the **equivalence point** (i.e. when the reagents have just reached their stoichiometric ratio). If a weak acid (e.g. ethanoic acid) is being used in a titration with a strong base, then phenolphthalein should be used as the indicator because the sudden change in pH at the equivalence point is from ~7 to 10 (see Figure 9.1, page 298). Methyl orange conversely is used for titrations involving a weak base (e.g. ammonia or sodium carbonate) and a strong acid when the sudden pH change at the equivalence point is between 3 and 7 (see Figure 9.1, page 298).

ADVANCED

EXERCISE 9.10

1. For which one of the following titrations, would phenolphthalein be the least appropriate indicator?

    A   Nitric acid with sodium hydroxide.
    B   Sulfuric acid with ammonia.
    C   Ethanoic acid with barium hydroxide.
    D   Hydrochloric acid with potassium hydroxide.

2. Hydrochloric acid (in the flask) is to be titrated with aqueous sodium carbonate (in the burette).

    a)   Would you choose methyl orange or phenolphthalein for this titration?
    b)   Explain the reasons for your choice.
    c)   What colour change would you expect to see at the end point?
    d)   Explain why the addition of too much indicator could lead to an inaccurate titration result.
    e)   The laboratory has run out of both methyl orange and phenolphthalein. Below are listed some indicators that are available. Which would you use to replace your original choice? Explain your reasons.

Indicator	pK_a	Colour change
Bromophenol blue	4.0	Yellow to blue
Bromothymol blue	7.0	Yellow to blue
Thymol blue	8.9	Yellow to blue

3. The graph shows the pH changes when 0.1 mol dm^{-3} ethanoic acid is titrated against 0.1 mol dm^{-3} aqueous sodium hydroxide (Curve a) and against 0.1 mol dm^{-3} aqueous ammonia (Curve b).

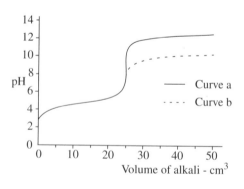

    a)   Why is the pH of 0.1 mol dm^{-3} ethanoic acid just under 3, when the pH of 0.1 mol dm^{-3} hydrochloric acid is 1?

    b)   Would methyl orange or phenolphthalein be a more appropriate indicator to detect the end point in the titration of 0.1 mol dm^{-3} ethanoic acid with 0.1 mol dm^{-3} aqueous sodium hydroxide (Curve a)?

    c)   No indicator is really suitable to detect the end point in the titration of 0.1 mol dm^{-3} ethanoic acid with 0.1 mol dm^{-3} aqueous ammonia (Curve b)? Explain why this is the case.

    d)   Explain how the above graph could be used to determine the base dissociation constant (K_b) of ammonia.

4. The diagram shows the variation in pH when 1 mol dm^{-3} hydrochloric acid is added to 20 cm^3 of 1 mol dm^{-3} aqueous sodium hydroxide.

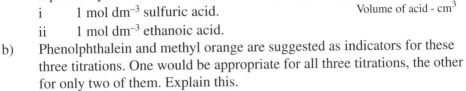

a) Explain how and why the curve would differ in shape if the hydrochloric acid had been replaced by

    i   1 mol dm^{-3} sulfuric acid.

    ii   1 mol dm^{-3} ethanoic acid.

b) Phenolphthalein and methyl orange are suggested as indicators for these three titrations. One would be appropriate for all three titrations, the other for only two of them. Explain this.

5. Hydrogen sulfide (H$_2$S) can act as a weak acid in aqueous solution.

a) What is the conjugate base of hydrogen sulfide?

b) Write an equation for the equilibrium that exists in an aqueous solution of hydrogen sulfide.

c) The solubility of hydrogen sulfide at room temperature and pressure is 3.4 g per litre. What is the concentration of this solution? [A_r values: H – 1; S – 32].

d) The acid dissociation constant of hydrogen sulfide is 9.55×10^{-8} mol dm^{-3}. Calculate the pH of a saturated solution.

e) When 11.0 g of solid sodium hydrogensulfide (NaHS) is dissolved in a litre of this saturated solution, a *buffer solution* is formed. What is meant by the term *buffer solution*?

f) Describe, in terms of the effect on the equilibrium, what the result of adding a little aqueous sodium hydroxide to this solution would be.

g) What is the concentration of hydrogensulfide ions in the solution?

    [A_r values: H – 1; Na – 23; S – 32]

h) Calculate the pH of the buffer solution that is formed.

i) What concentration of hydrogensulfide ions would be required to give a buffer of pH 3? Why would this not be a very effective buffer?

j) Bromothymol blue is an indicator that is yellow in acid and blue in alkali. It changes colour at about pH 7. Methyl yellow is an indicator that is red in acid and yellow in alkali, which changes colour at about pH 3.1. If a saturated solution of hydrogen sulfide is tested with each indicator, what colour will result in each case?

k) Explain how indicators work and why different indicators change colour at different pH values.

l)   Which of these would be the more suitable for titrating hydrogen sulfide solution with aqueous sodium hydroxide? Explain why.

The sulfide ion S^{2-}, acts as a weak base in aqueous solution.

m)   Write an equation for the equilibrium that is established in aqueous solution.

n)   What term can be used to describe the behaviour of the hydrogensulfide ion in this equilibrium and those above?

o)   A 0.100 mol dm^{-3} solution of sodium sulfide has a pH of 12.95. Calculate the concentration of hydroxide ions in this solution.

p)   Use this to determine pK_a for the hydrogensulfide ion.

q)   What two things could you add to sodium sulfide solution to prepare a buffer solution with a pH of 12.5?

ADVANCED

REDUCTION AND OXIDATION

10

10.1 OXIDATION AND REDUCTION

10.1.1 Define oxidation and reduction in terms of electron loss and gain.

Introduce the concept of the half-equation.

10.1.2 Calculate the oxidation number of an element in a compound.

Oxidation numbers should be shown by a sign (+ or -) and a number, eg +7 for Mn in KMnO$_4$.

10.1.3 State and explain the relationship between oxidation numbers and the names of compounds.

Oxidation numbers in names of compounds are represented by Roman numerals, eg iron(II) oxide, iron(III) oxide.

10.1.4 Identify whether an element is oxidized or reduced in simple redox reactions, using oxidation numbers.

Appropriate reactions to illustrate this can be found in topics 3 and 11. Possible examples include: iron(II) and (III), manganese(II) and (VII), chromium(III) and (VI), copper(I) and (II), oxides of sultur and oxyacids, halogens and halide ions.

10.1.5 Define the terms oxidizing agent and reducing agent.   © IBO 2001

Oxidation and reduction are most commonly defined in terms of the loss and gain of electrons. **Oxidation is the loss of electrons**, so if an iron(II) ion (Fe^{2+}) is converted to an iron(III) ion (Fe^{3+}), then the iron(II) ion has lost an electron and so has been oxidised.

$$Fe^{2+}_{(aq)} \Rightarrow Fe^{3+}_{(aq)} + e^-$$

Conversely **reduction is the gain of electrons**, so if hydrogen ions (H^+) are converted to hydrogen gas (H_2) the hydrogen has gained electrons and is therefore reduced.

$$2\,H^+_{(aq)} + 2\,e^- \Rightarrow H_{2\,(g)}$$

Note that in these equations the charge as well as the numbers of atoms must balance.

A useful mnemonic (memory aid) for this is:

LEO (the lion) goes GER

Loss of Electrons is Oxidation; Gain of Electrons is Reduction.

Consider the reaction between zinc and iodine:

$$Zn_{(s)} + I_{2\,(aq)} \Rightarrow Zn^{2+}_{(aq)} + 2\,I^-_{(aq)}$$

In this the zinc has lost two electrons to form the zinc ion and so is oxidised. The iodine has gained two electrons to form the iodide ion and so is reduced. This is most clearly shown by splitting the overall equation into two 'half equations', i.e.

$$Zn_{(s)} \Rightarrow Zn^{2+}_{(aq)} + 2\,e^- \quad \& \quad I_{2\,(aq)} + 2\,e^- \Rightarrow 2\,I^-_{(aq)}$$

The full equation can be produced by combining the appropriate half equations in such a way that the electrons cancel.

There are occasions when the atoms in the species change and so the definition above is difficult to apply. For example nitrogen is reduced in the conversion of nitrogen gas (N_2) to ammonia (NH_3), even though there is no obvious gain of electrons. Even worse, when nitrogen dioxide (NO_2) is converted to the nitrate ion (NO_3^-) it is oxidised even though it gains a negative charge (i.e. electrons = reduction)! These problems are removed by the use of oxidation numbers.

The **oxidation number**, or oxidation state, of an atom is the charge which that atom would have if all covalent bonds were broken so that the more electronegative element kept all the electrons in the bond, hence the sign (+ or –) is always given.

In practice, rather than having to consider the breaking of every covalent bond in a molecule to find the oxidation number, it is easier to calculate this using a number of rules:

1. The total oxidation state of the atoms in a species is equal to the electrical charge it carries. Hence all elements in the elemental state have an oxidation state of zero and simple ions have an oxidation state equal to the charge.

2. Some elements almost always have the same oxidation state in their compounds, with a few exceptions. In order of decreasing numbers of exceptions:

    a)   **fluorine is –1** (no exceptions)

    b)   **hydrogen is +1** (except in the hydride ion, H^-)

    c)   **oxygen is –2** (except +1 in hydrogen peroxide and related compounds)

    d)   **the halogens (group 7 elements Cl, Br, & I) are –1** (except when bonded to oxygen or a halogen that is higher in the group)

Elements which commonly change their oxidation states are carbon, nitrogen, phosphorus, sulfur and the transition metals. The rules above are best illustrated by examples:

Hydrogen in H_2 is 0 — In their elemental state the oxidation state of elements is always zero.

Iron in Fe^{2+} is +2 — The total oxidation number is equal to the charge, and in this case there is only one element present.

Carbon in CH_4 is –4 — There is no charge on CH_4, so the total must be zero. Hydrogen is +1, so that four hydrogens are +4. The carbon is therefore –4.

Sulfur in H_2SO_4 is +6 — The total is again zero. The four oxygens are –8 (–2 each) and the two hydrogens are +2 (+1 each) so that sulfur must be +6.

Phosphorus in PCl_4^+ is +5 — The total is +1 (equal to the electrical charge). The four chlorines are –4 (–1 each) so phosphorus must be +5.

Iodine in IO_4^- is +7 — The total is –1 (charge) and the four oxygens are –8 (–2 each) so that iodine must be +7. (Note that this is one of the exceptions mentioned in rule 2d.)

In terms of oxidation number, oxidation is an increase in oxidation number and reduction is a decrease in oxidation number. If the oxidation number does not change, then that element has not been oxidised or reduced. This covers the definition in terms of electrons, as well as many other cases.

Returning to the dilemmas at the start of the section it can be seen that in going from N_2 to NH_3, the oxidation number of nitrogen has changed from 0 to –3, so it has been reduced. Similarly in going from NO_2 to NO_3^- the oxidation number has increased from +4 to +5 so it is an oxidation.

Consider the **redox** reaction (i.e. one in which **red**uction and **ox**idation occurs) below:

$$2\,MnO_4^-\,_{(aq)} + 5\,SO_{2\,(aq)} + 2\,H_2O_{(l)} \Rightarrow 2\,Mn^{2+}_{(aq)} + 5\,SO_4^{2-}_{(aq)} + 4\,H^+_{(aq)}$$

In order to determine which elements have been oxidised and which reduced, the appropriate oxidation numbers must be calculated. If none of the elements change their oxidation number then the reaction is not a redox reaction. It is unusual for the oxidation state of hydrogen and oxygen to change (unless the reaction involves the elements or hydrogen peroxide). Application of the rules above to manganese and sulfur shows that:

Manganese is reduced as its oxidation number decreases – $MnO_4^- = +7$, $Mn^{2+} = +2$

Sulfur is oxidised as its oxidation number increases – $SO_2 = +4$, $SO_4^{2-} = +6$

A species which causes another to be oxidised is known as an **oxidising agent** (or oxidant), hence in the equation above, the permanaganate(VII) ion acts as an oxidising agent. In the same way a species that causes another species to be reduced is known as a **reducing agent** (or reductant), so that sulfur dioxide is the reducing agent in the reaction above because it reduces the permanganate(VII) ion to the manganese(II) ion. Note the use of Roman numerals in the name to specify the oxidation state of the element, hence iron(II) chloride is $FeCl_2$ and iron(III) chloride is $FeCl_3$.

EXERCISE 10.1

1. Which one of the following reactions is **not** a redox reaction?

    A $CH_4 + 2\,O_2 \Rightarrow CO_2 + 2\,H_2O$
    B $CuO + H_2SO_4 \Rightarrow CuSO_4 + H_2O$
    C $2\,Al + Fe_2O_3 \Rightarrow Al_2O_3 + 2\,Fe$
    D $PbO + CO \Rightarrow Pb + CO_2$

2. In which one of the following reactions is the first reagent reduced?

A $Fe + Pb(NO_3)_2 \Rightarrow Fe(NO_3)_2 + Pb$
B $NaOH + HNO_3 \Rightarrow NaNO_3 + H_2O$
C $H_2 + CuO \Rightarrow H_2O + Cu$
D $CO_2 + C \Rightarrow 2CO$

3. In which of the following changes has the oxidation number of sulfur increased?

A $H_2SO_4 \Rightarrow SO_2$
B $H_2S \Rightarrow S_8$
C $SO_2 \Rightarrow H_2S$
D $SO_2 \Rightarrow S_8$

4. The three reactions below could all be used to prepare iron(II) sulfate:

Reaction I $FeCl_2 + Ag_2SO_4 \Rightarrow FeSO_4 + 2\,AgCl$
Reaction II $Fe_2(SO_4)_3 + SO_2 + 2\,H_2O \Rightarrow 2\,FeSO_4 + 2\,H_2SO_4$
Reaction III $Fe + H_2SO_4 \Rightarrow FeSO_4 + H_2$

Which of the following best summarises what is happening to the iron in each of these reactions?

	Reaction I	**Reaction II**	**Reaction III**
A	reduction	neither	neither
B	neither	oxidation	reduction
C	neither	reduction	oxidation
D	reduction	reduction	oxidation

5. In which one of the following reactions is the species in **bold** type acting as an oxidising agent?

A $\textbf{FeCl}_3 + 3\,AgNO_3 \Rightarrow Fe(NO_3)_3 + 3\,AgCl$
B $Fe + 2\,\textbf{Ag}^+ \Rightarrow Fe^{2+} + 2\,Ag$
C $2\,\textbf{H}^+ + Mg \Rightarrow Mg^{2+} + H_2$
D $2\,Fe^{2+} + \textbf{Cl}_2 \Rightarrow 2\,Fe^{3+} + 2\,Cl^-$

6. Give the oxidation number of the stated element in each of the following species:

a)   Iron in Fe^{2+};   b)   Phosphorus in P_4;   c)   Silicon in SiO_2;

d)   Sulfur in SCl_4 e)   Nitrogen in N_2O;   f)   Carbon in CH_3OH;

g)   Vanadium in VO^{2+} h)   Bromine in BrO^-;   i)   Iodine in IF_6^-;

j)   Chromium in $Cr_2O_7^{2-}$

7.   Give one example of the following:

a)   An iron compound with an oxidation state of +2.
b)   A nitrogen compound with an oxidation state of –3.
c)   A manganese compound with an oxidation state of +7.
d)   A carbon compound with an oxidation state of 0.
e)   A phosphorus compound with an oxidation state of +5

8.   For each of the following transformations, give the initial and final oxidation number of the element in **bold** type and hence state whether it has been oxidised, been reduced, or neither.

a) $\mathbf{Cu^{2+} \Rightarrow CuI}$;   b) $\mathbf{NO_2 \Rightarrow N_2O_4}$;
c) $\mathbf{PH_3 \Rightarrow HPO_2{}^{2-}}$;   d) $\mathbf{CH_3OH \Rightarrow HCOOH}$;
e) $\mathbf{S_2O_3{}^{2-} \Rightarrow S_4O_6{}^{2-}}$

9.   Hydrazine (N_2H_4) and dinitrogen tetroxide (N_2O_4) react violently to form nitrogen as a product from both reactants.

a)   Explain why this is considered to be a redox reaction stating, with reasons, what is being oxidised and what is being reduced.

b)   Write a balanced equation for this reaction.

c)   It has been suggested that this reaction is a very 'environmentally friendly' source of energy. Explain this.

10.   In any redox reaction, the total increase in oxidation number must equal the total decrease in oxidation number. When ammonium dichromate(VI) is heated, it decomposes in a spectacular redox reaction.

a)   Write the formula for ammonium dichromate(VI).

b)   What is the significance of the (VI) in the name ammonium dichromate(VI)?

c)   The chromium is reduced to chromium(III) oxide, a green powder. What is the **total** decrease in oxidation number of chromium in each ammonium dichromate(VI)?

d)   What is the initial oxidation state of the nitrogen in the ammonium ion?

e)   Taking into account the total number of nitrogens in ammonium dichromate(VI), by how much must the oxidation number of each nitrogen increase?

f)   What must the final oxidation state of the nitrogen in the product be?

g)   Suggest a substance containing nitrogen in this oxidation state.

h)   What colour change would you see during this reaction?

i)   The reaction gives out heat and a shower of sparks. What does this show about the reaction?

10.2 REDOX EQUATIONS

19.1.1 Balance redox equations in acid solution.

Half-equations and oxidation numbers may be used. H$^+$$_{(aq)}$ and H$_2$O should be used where necessary to balance half-equations.   © IBO 2001

With many substances, the oxidation or reduction that occurs during redox reactions in aqueous solution is independent of the particular oxidant or reductant that is causing the change. It is therefore convenient to write an equation for this change in terms of the loss or gain of electrons. For example, whenever the purple permanganate ion is reduced in acidic solution the almost colourless manganese(II) ion is formed, so the change occurring is:

$$MnO_4^-{}_{(aq)} + 8\ H^+{}_{(aq)} + 5\ e^- \Rightarrow Mn^{2+}{}_{(aq)} + 4\ H_2O_{(l)}$$

These equations are known as half equations and for a redox reaction the half equations for the substance being oxidised and the substance being reduced can be combined in such a way that the electrons cancel out, so as to give a balanced equation for the redox reaction.

Half equations must balance in the same way as normal equations, the only difference being that they contain electrons. When constructing a half equation it is easiest to follow a sequence of steps. This will be illustrated using the half equation for the reduction of the orange dichromate(VI) ion to the green chromium(III) ion in acidic aqueous solutions, as an example:

$$Cr_2O_7^{2-}{}_{(aq)} \Rightarrow Cr^{3+}{}_{(aq)}$$

1)   balance the number of atoms of the element being oxidised or reduced on the two sides:

$$Cr_2O_7^{2-}{}_{(aq)} \Rightarrow \mathbf{2\ Cr^{3+}{}_{(aq)}}$$

2)   add water molecules to balance the number of oxygen atoms on the two sides:

$$Cr_2O_7^{2-}{}_{(aq)} \Rightarrow 2\ Cr^{3+}{}_{(aq)} + \mathbf{7\ H_2O_{(l)}}$$

3)   add hydrogen ions to balance the number of hydrogen atoms on the two sides:

$$Cr_2O_7^{2-}{}_{(aq)} + \mathbf{14\ H^+{}_{(aq)}} \Rightarrow 2\ Cr^{3+}{}_{(aq)} + 7\ H_2O_{(l)}$$

4)   add electrons so that the electrical charges on both sides balance:

$$Cr_2O_7^{2-}{}_{(aq)} + 14\ H^+{}_{(aq)} + \mathbf{6\ e^-} \Rightarrow 2\ Cr^{3+}{}_{(aq)} + 7\ H_2O_{(l)}$$

Because this is a reduction, the electrons appear on the left hand side of the equation (GER) and their number is equal to the total change in oxidation number (two chromiums changing in oxidation state from +6 to +3 requires a total of 6 electrons). In an oxidation, the electrons would appear on the right hand side of the equation (LEO). For example the half equation for the oxidation of iron(II) to iron(III) is:

$$Fe^{2+}{}_{(aq)} \Rightarrow Fe^{3+}{}_{(aq)} + e^-$$

ADVANCED

To write a balanced equation for a redox reaction, the two half equations involved must be multiplied by suitable factors so that when added together the number of electrons lost by one equals the number gained by the other so that they cancel. In the case of the oxidation of iron(II) to iron(III) by the reduction of dichromate to chromium(III), the equation for the oxidation of the iron(II) must be multiplied by six because six electrons are involved in the reduction of the dichromate, so that the half equations involved become:

$$Cr_2O_7^{2-}{}_{(aq)} + 14\ H^+{}_{(aq)} + 6\ e^- \Rightarrow 2\ Cr^{3+}{}_{(aq)} + 7\ H_2O_{(l)}$$

$$6\ Fe^{2+}{}_{(aq)} \Rightarrow 6\ Fe^{3+}{}_{(aq)} + 6\ e^-$$

When added together, the electrons cancel and the final balanced equation is:

$$Cr_2O_7^{2-}{}_{(aq)} + 14\ H^+{}_{(aq)} + 6\ Fe^{2+}{}_{(aq)} \Rightarrow 2\ Cr^{3+}{}_{(aq)} + 7\ H_2O_{(l)} + 6\ Fe^{3+}{}_{(aq)}$$

Sometimes it will then be necessary to cancel hydrogen ions and water molecules that appear on both sides of the equation. This is best illustrated by a second example – the half equation for the oxidation of sulfur dioxide to the sulfate ion is:

$$SO_{2\ (aq)} + 2\ H_2O_{(l)} \Rightarrow SO_4^{2-}{}_{(aq)} + 4\ H^+{}_{(aq)} + 2\ e^-$$

If this is to be combined with the half equation for the reduction of the permanganate ion, given at the start of this section, then it is necessary to multiply the permanganate half equation by 2 and the sulfur dioxide half equation by 5, so that both involve 10 electrons:

$$2\ MnO_4^-{}_{(aq)} + 16\ H^+{}_{(aq)} + 10\ e^- \Rightarrow 2\ Mn^{2+}{}_{(aq)} + 8\ H_2O_{(l)}$$

$$5\ SO_{2\ (aq)} + 10\ H_2O_{(l)} \Rightarrow 5\ SO_4^{2-}{}_{(aq)} + 20\ H^+{}_{(aq)} + 10\ e^-$$

When these are initially combined, the equation is:

$$2\ MnO_4^-{}_{(aq)} + 16\ H^+{}_{(aq)} + 5\ SO_{2\ (aq)} + 10\ H_2O_{(l)} \Rightarrow 2\ Mn^{2+}{}_{(aq)} + 8\ H_2O_{(l)} + 5\ SO_4^{2-}{}_{(aq)} + 20\ H^+{}_{(aq)}$$

By cancelling the waters and hydrogen ions that appear on both sides, this simplifies to give the final balanced equation, which is:

$$2\ MnO_4^-{}_{(aq)} + 5\ SO_{2\ (aq)} + 2\ H_2O_{(l)} \Rightarrow 2\ Mn^{2+}{}_{(aq)} + 5\ SO_4^{2-}{}_{(aq)} + 4\ H^+{}_{(aq)}$$

ADVANCED

EXERCISE 10.2

1. Which one of the following is the correct half equation for the iodate ion changing to iodine in acidic solution?

A $IO_3^- + 6\,H^+ \Rightarrow I + 3\,H_2O + 5e^-$

B $IO_3^- + 6\,H^+ + 5\,e^- \Rightarrow I + 3\,H_2O$

C $IO_3^- + 6\,H^+ + 5\,e^- \Rightarrow I_2 + 3\,H_2O$

D $2\,IO_3^- + 12\,H^+ + 10e^- \Rightarrow I_2 + 6\,H_2O$

2. In the half equation for a substance acting as a reductant (reducing agent)

A   the oxidation number increases and the electrons are on the right hand side.

B   the oxidation number increases and the electrons are on the left hand side.

C   the oxidation number decreases and the electrons are on the right hand side.

D   the oxidation number decreases and the electrons are on the left hand side.

3. The overall equation for nitric acid oxidising iron(II) ions to iron(III) ions is

$$HNO_3 + 3Fe^{2+} + 3H^+ \Rightarrow NO + 3Fe^{3+} + 2H_2O$$

The half equation for the reduction of the nitric acid must therefore be

A $HNO_3 + 4\,H^+ + 4\,e^- \Rightarrow NO + 2\,H_2O$

B $HNO_3 + 3\,H^+ + 3\,e^- \Rightarrow NO + 2\,H_2O$

C $HNO_3 + 3\,H^+ \Rightarrow NO + 2\,H_2O + 3\,e^-$

D $HNO_3 + H^+ \Rightarrow NO + H_2O + e^-$

4. Write balanced half equations for the following changes:

a)   Zinc metal being oxidised to the zinc ion.

b)   Bromine being reduced to the bromide ion.

c)   Hydrogen sulfide being oxidised to sulfur.

d)   Nitric acid being reduced to nitrogen dioxide.

e)   The vanadate(V) ion (VO_3^-) being reduced to the vanadium(III) ion.

5. Below are given some half equations for redox reactions. Combine these, as indicated, to produce balanced equations for the redox reactions involved.

Equation I $Co^{3+} + e^- \Rightarrow Co^{2+}$

Equation II $PbO_2 + 4\,H^+ + 2\,e^- \Rightarrow Pb^{2+} + 2\,H_2O$

Equation III $ClO_3^- + 6\,H^+ + 6\,e^- \Rightarrow Cl^- + 3\,H_2O$

Equation IV $Sn^{2+} \Rightarrow Sn^{4+} + 2\,e^-$

Equation V $NO_2^- + H_2O \Rightarrow NO_3^- + 2\,H^+ + 2\,e^-$

ADVANCED

a)   Equations II and IV.
b)   Equations I and IV.
c)   Equations II and V.
d)   Equations III and IV.
e)   Equations III and V.

6.   Use the half equation method to write balanced equations for the following reactions:

a)   Magnesium reducing lead ions to lead metal.

b)   Sulfur dioxide being oxidised to sulfate, whilst reducing iodine to iodide ions.

c)   Hydrogen peroxide oxidising iron(II) to iron(III) in acidic solution.

d)   Zinc reducing acidified dichromate ions to chromium(III).

e)   Acidified permanganate ions oxidising methanol to carbon dioxide and water.

7.   A disproportionation reaction is one in which a single species is both oxidised and reduced in the same reaction. An example of this occurs when potassium chlorate(V) ($KClO_3$) is heated to just above its melting point. The chlorate ion is oxidised to the perchlorate [chlorate(VII)] ion (ClO_4^-) and reduced to the chloride ion (Cl^-).

a)   What is the oxidation state of the chlorine in these various species?

b)   Write a half equation for the oxidation of the chlorate(V) ion to the perchlorate(VII) ion in aqueous solution.

c)   Write a half equation for the reduction of the chlorate(V) ion to the chloride ion in acidic solution.

d)   Write a balanced chemical equation for the disproportionation of **potassium** chlorate(V).

e)   Why is there no need for the substances to be in aqueous solution for this reaction to occur?

8.   If wine is left in an open bottle it often tastes 'vinegary' a few days later. This is because of the oxidation of the ethanol to ethanoic acid by atmospheric oxygen.

a)   Write the half equation for the oxidation of ethanol to ethanoic acid.

b)   What is the initial and final average oxidation number of the carbons in this change?

c)   Write the half equation for the reduction of oxygen in acidic solution.

d)   Combine these to produce an overall equation for the reaction.

e)   Normally, oxygen is a poor oxidant in aqueous solution. This change only occurs in the presence of bacteria which produce enzymes. Why is oxygen a poor oxidant and how do the enzymes affect this?

ADVANCED

10.3 SOME COMMON OXIDANTS AND REDUCTANTS

Certain species are known as oxidants or oxidising agents, because they accept electrons very readily, so that the substance that they react with is oxidised. Other species are known as reductants, or reducing agents, because they donate electrons very readily, reducing the species they react with. Note that in these reactions the oxidant is itself reduced and similarly the reductant undergoes oxidation. This sometimes causes confusion. Some of the more common oxidants and reductants are given below along with their half equations and other characteristics.

OXIDANTS

Oxygen

Not a very effective oxidant for substances in aqueous solution as a result of the high activation energy associated with breaking the O=O double bond. It will however oxidise many substances when they are heated in a stream of air or oxygen, the reaction being described as burning, or combustion, e.g.

$$2\,Mg_{(s)} + O_{2\,(g)} \Rightarrow 2\,MgO_{(s)}$$

Chlorine and the other halogens

Strong oxidants both in aqueous solution and when the substance is heated with the element. Going down Group 7 the halogens become less powerful oxidants. The usual colour change with bromine and iodine is from brown to colourless, though if iodide ions are completely oxidised to iodine it appears as a black solid. Using X as the symbol for the halogen, the half equation is:

$$X_{2\,(aq)} + 2e^- \Rightarrow 2\,X^-_{(aq)}$$

Iron(III) ion

The yellow–brown iron(III) ion acts as a mild oxidant and is reduced to the pale green iron(II) ion. The oxidation state of the iron can best be demonstrated by adding aqueous sodium hydroxide and observing the colour of the precipitate.

$$Fe^{3+}_{(aq)} + e^- \Rightarrow Fe^{2+}_{(aq)}$$

Hydrogen peroxide

A moderate strength oxidant which in aqueous solution is reduced to water. The reactants and products are all colourless.

$$H_2O_{2\,(aq)} + 2\,H^+_{(aq)} + 2\,e^- \Rightarrow 2\,H_2O_{(l)}$$

[n.b. very powerful oxidants, such as the permanganate(VII) ion can oxidise hydrogen peroxide to oxygen: $H_2O_{2\,(aq)} \Rightarrow O_{2\,(g)} + 2\,H^+_{(aq)} + 2\,e^-$].

Permanganate(VII) ion

This very powerful oxidant is usually used in acidic solution when the purple permanganate(VII) ion is reduced to the almost colourless manganese(II) ion.

$$MnO_4^-{}_{(aq)} + 8\,H^+_{(aq)} + 5\,e^- \Rightarrow Mn^{2+}_{(aq)} + 4\,H_2O_{(l)}$$

At other pHs the product can be manganese(IV) oxide (a brown solid) or the manganate(VI) ion (a dark green solution) – see section 3.5, page 103.

Dichromate(VI) ion

This too is a powerful oxidant that is usually used in acidic solution. The orange dichromate(VI) ion is reduced to the green chromium(III) ion.

$$Cr_2O_7^{2-}{}_{(aq)} + 14\ H^+{}_{(aq)} + 6\ e^- \Rightarrow 2\ Cr^{3+}{}_{(aq)} + 7\ H_2O_{(l)}$$

REDUCTANTS

Hydrogen

This is not an effective reductant for aqueous solutions owing to a high activation energy. When passed over the heated oxides of metals below zinc in the reactivity series however, it reduces the oxide to the metal:

$$MO_{(s)} + H_{2\ (g)} \Rightarrow M_{(s)} + H_2O_{(g)}$$

Carbon and carbon monoxide

Like hydrogen, activation energy considerations prevent being it effective in aqueous solution, but when heated with the oxide of zinc or metals lower in the reactivity series, they reduce the oxide to the metal:

$$2\ MO_{(s)} + C_{(s)} \Rightarrow M_{(s)} + CO_{2\ (g)}$$

$$MO_{(s)} + CO_{(g)} \Rightarrow M_{(s)} + CO_{2\ (g)}$$

These are very important reactions for obtaining metals from their ores (see Chapter 15).

Metals

The more reactive the metal the stronger it is as a reductant, so that metals such as magnesium, zinc and iron are very effective reductants. The metal is oxidised to the aqueous cation, so that if this is divalent, using M as the symbol for the metal, the half equation is:

$$M_{(s)} \Rightarrow M^{2+}{}_{(aq)} + 2\ e^-$$

Iron(II) ion

The pale green iron(II) ion acts as a mild reductant in aqueous solution, being oxidised to the red–brown iron (III) ion:

$$Fe^{2+}{}_{(aq)} \Rightarrow Fe^{3+}{}_{(aq)} + e^-$$

Iodide ion

The colourless iodide ion acts as a mild reductant in aqueous solution, being oxidised to iodine, which appears as a brown solution if excess iodide is present:

$$2\ I^-{}_{(aq)} \Rightarrow I_{2\ (aq)} + 2\ e^-$$

Thiosulfate ion

The thiosulfate ion is a mild reductant that reacts readily with iodine in aqueous solution according to the equation:

$$2\ S_2O_3^{2-}{}_{(aq)} + I_{2\ (aq)} \Rightarrow S_4O_6^{2-}{}_{(aq)} + 2\ I^-{}_{(aq)}$$

Starch forms a very intense blue-black coloured complex with iodine and the sudden

EXTENSION

colour change from blue-black to colorless is used to determine the end point in redox titrations involving iodine.

Sulfur dioxide

Sulfur dioxide is a moderately powerful reductant in aqueous solution, being oxidised to the sulfate ion:

$$SO_{2\,(aq)} + 2\,H_2O_{(l)} \Rightarrow SO_4^{2-}{}_{(aq)} + 4\,H^+{}_{(aq)} + 2\,e^-$$

The reactants and products are all colourless.

The colour changes that accompany some of these redox changes are summarised in Table 10.1 below:

Table 10.1 – Colour changes for some redox systems

	Oxidised form			Reduced form	
Permanganate	MnO_4^-	Purple	Manganese(II)	Mn^{2+}	Colourless
Dichromate	$Cr_2O_7^{2-}$	Orange	Chromium(III)	Cr^{3+}	Green
Iron(III)	Fe^{3+}	Red–brown	Iron(II)	Fe^{2+}	Pale green
Iodine	I_2	Brown, if excess I⁻; blue-black if starch is present	Iodide	I^-	Colourless

EXTENSION

EXERCISE 10.3

1. Which one of the following is least likely to oxidise iron(II) ions to iron(III) ions in aqueous solution?

   A   Magnesium
   B   Chlorine
   C   Hydrogen peroxide
   D   Dichromate ions

2. Which one of the following redox changes would not give rise to a change in colour of the solution?

   A   Iron(II) being oxidised by acidified permanganate.
   B   Sulfur dioxide being oxidised by hydrogen peroxide.
   C   Dichromate ions being reduced by zinc.
   D   Iodide ions being oxidised by chlorine.

3. Which one of the reactions below, to reduce metal oxides, is least likely to occur?

A $PbO + H_2 \Rightarrow Pb + H_2O$

B $Fe_2O_3 + 2\,Al \Rightarrow Al_2O_3 + 2\,Fe$

C $MgO + CO \Rightarrow Mg + CO_2$

D $2\,CuO + C \Rightarrow 2\,Cu + CO_2$

4. The concentration of copper ions in aqueous solution can be determined by adding an excess of potassium iodide, when the following reaction occurs:

$$2\,Cu^{2+}_{(aq)} + 4\,I^-_{(aq)} \Rightarrow 2\,CuI_{(s)} + I_{2\,(aq)}$$

The iodine liberated is then titrated with standardised aqueous sodium thiosuiphate.

a)   In the above equation, what is the initial and final oxidation state of the copper.

b)   Given that CuI is a white solid, what colour change would be seen when the above reaction occurs?

c)   Write a balanced equation for the reaction of iodine with sodium thiosulfate.

d)   Calculate the initial and final average oxidation states of the sulfur in this reaction.

e)   What indicator is usually used and what is the colour change at the end point?

f)   In such a titration it is found that 20 cm³ of a solution containing copper(II) sulfate required exactly 15 cm³ of aqueous sodium thiosulfate of concentration 0.2 mol dm³ to react with the iodine formed. What was the concentration of the copper(II) sulfate solution?

5. A 2.00 g iron nail is dissolved in excess sulfuric acid. The resulting solution is then titrated with 0.200 mol dm³ aqueous potassium permanganate(VII).

a)   What colour change would occur at the end point of the titration?

b)   What volume of aqueous permanganate would be required if the nail were pure iron?

10.4 REACTIVITY

10.2.1 Deduce a reactivity series based upon the chemical behaviour of a group of oxidizing and reducing agents.

Displacement reactions of metals and halogens (see 3.3.1) provide a good experimental illustration of reactivity. Standard electrode potentials or reduction potentials are not required.

10.2.2 Deduce the feasibility of a redox reaction from a given reactivity series.

© IBO 2001

Usually a certain species will give a particular product as a result of gaining/losing electrons – this pair of species is referred to as a redox couple. (There are however a few exceptions, such as the permanganate ion where the product depends on other conditions such as the pH.) If one species in the couple is a powerful oxidising agent (i.e. has a great attraction for electrons) then it follows that the other half of the couple, that it forms when it has gained this electrons, will not readily give them up again, i.e. it will be a very weak reducing agent. [n.b. This is similar to the relationship that exists between the strengths of a conjugate acid–base pair (see Section 9.6, page 302), though in that case a hydrogen ion rather than an electron is being exchanged.] This allows us to arrange redox pairs as a reactivity series in order of increasing oxidising/reducing power. A very simple reactivity series, showing some common metals and the halogens, is shown in Table 10.2.

Table 10.2 – A simple redox reactivity series

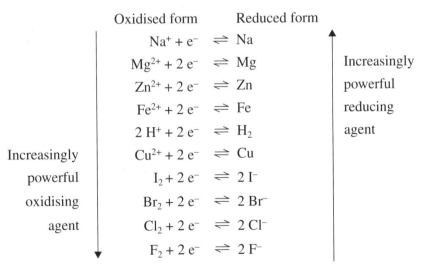

Redox Couple

Oxidised form		Reduced form	
$Na^+ + e^-$	$\rightleftharpoons$	Na	
$Mg^{2+} + 2\,e^-$	$\rightleftharpoons$	Mg	Increasingly
$Zn^{2+} + 2\,e^-$	$\rightleftharpoons$	Zn	powerful
$Fe^{2+} + 2\,e^-$	$\rightleftharpoons$	Fe	reducing
$2\,H^+ + 2\,e^-$	$\rightleftharpoons$	H_2	agent
$Cu^{2+} + 2\,e^-$	$\rightleftharpoons$	Cu	
$I_2 + 2\,e^-$	$\rightleftharpoons$	$2\,I^-$	
$Br_2 + 2\,e^-$	$\rightleftharpoons$	$2\,Br^-$	
$Cl_2 + 2\,e^-$	$\rightleftharpoons$	$2\,Cl^-$	
$F_2 + 2\,e^-$	$\rightleftharpoons$	$2\,F^-$	

Increasingly powerful oxidising agent

The **gain of electrons** to complete valence shells is behaviour that is typical of **non–metals**, hence non–metals tend to be **oxidants** and occur in the left hand column of the table. Going down the left hand column the elements become more reactive (note the relationship to the order of the elements in Group 7 – see Section 3.3, page 91), so that an element lower in the table can oxidise the ion formed from an element higher in the table, but the reverse cannot occur. For example chlorine (Cl_2) attracts electrons more strongly than iodine (I_2), so that chlorine can oxidise iodide ions to iodine, but iodine cannot oxidise chloride ions to chlorine:

$$Cl_{2\,(aq)} + 2\,I^-_{\,(aq)} \Rightarrow I_{2\,(aq)} + 2\,Cl^-_{\,(aq)} \qquad ✔$$

$$I_{2\,(aq)} + 2\,Cl^-_{\,(aq)} \Rightarrow Cl_{2\,(aq)} + 2\,I^-_{\,(aq)} \qquad X$$

Conversely the **loss of electrons** to empty valence shells is behaviour that is typical of **metals**, so metals behave as **reductants** and occur in the right hand column of the table. The most reactive metals are at the top and the reactivity decreases going down the table. A metal higher in the series will displace a metal lower in the series from its salts, but the reverse reaction cannot occur. For example iron will displace copper from copper(II) salts (i.e. iron is a powerful enough reductant to reduce copper ions to copper), but copper will not displace iron from iron(II) salts (i.e. copper is not a powerful enough reductant to reduce iron ions to iron):

$$Fe_{(s)} + Cu^{2+}_{\,(aq)} \Rightarrow Cu_{(s)} + Fe^{2+}_{\,(aq)} \qquad ✔$$

$$Cu_{(s)} + Fe^{2+}_{\,(aq)} \Rightarrow Fe_{(s)} + Cu^{2+}_{\,(aq)} \qquad X$$

The position of a metal in the series relative to hydrogen can also be used to predict whether a metal will liberate hydrogen from dilute acids. Metals above hydrogen are powerful enough reductants to reduce hydrogen ions to hydrogen, e.g. for magnesium

$$Mg_{(s)} + 2\,H^+_{\,(aq)} \Rightarrow H_{2\,(g)} + Mg^{2+}_{\,(aq)}$$

Metals below hydrogen, such as copper, are not strong enough reducing agents to reduce hydrogen ions and hence will not react with dilute acids.

EXERCISE 10.4

1. Which one of the following metals is the most powerful reductant (reducing agent)?

    A   Copper
    B   Magnesium
    C   Iron
    D   Zinc

2. In which one of the following would you expect a reaction to occur?

    A   Copper placed in zinc chloride
    B   Zinc placed in copper sulfate
    C   Iron placed in magnesium sulfate
    D   Magnesium placed in sodium chloride

3. Zinc reacts with dilute acids to liberate hydrogen. This is because

    A   the zinc ion is a more powerful oxidising agent than the hydrogen ion.
    B   the hydrogen ion is a more powerful oxidising agent than the zinc ion.
    C   the zinc ion is a more powerful reducing agent than the hydrogen ion.
    D   the hydrogen ion is a more powerful reducing agent than the zinc ion.

4. a) What would you see when chlorine is bubbled through aqueous sodium bromide?

    b) What would you see when bromine is added to aqueous sodium chloride?

    c) Interpret these results in terms of the reactions that are occurring and explain what this shows about the relative oxidising power of chlorine and bromine.

5. You have a sample of a metal M and an aqueous solution of its sulfate, MSO_4. Describe some simple experiments that you could do to try and determine the reactivity of M relative to other common metals such as copper, zinc and magnesium. Explain how you would interpret the results of these experiments.

10.5 STANDARD ELECTRODE POTENTIALS

10.2.3 Describe and explain how a redox reaction is used to produce electricity in a voltaic cell.

Students should be able to draw a diagram of a simple half-cell, and show how two half-cells can be connected by a salt bridge to form a whole cell. Suitable examples of half-cells are Mg, Zn, Fe and Cu in solutions of their ions. © IBO 2001

Consider a metal in contact with an aqueous solution of its ions. A redox equilibrium will be established and the metal will acquire an electrical charge:

$$M_{(s)} \rightleftharpoons M^{n+}_{(aq)} + n\ e^-$$

In the case of a reactive metal, the equilibrium will tend to the right, a little of the metal will dissolve and the remaining metal will become negatively charged because of the excess of electrons. The opposite may be true for an unreactive metal. It is not possible to measure these electrode potentials directly, but an electrical circuit can be constructed to compare the potentials of two such electrodes, using apparatus such as that illustrated in Figure 10.1:

Figure 10.1 – Apparatus for comparing electrode potentials

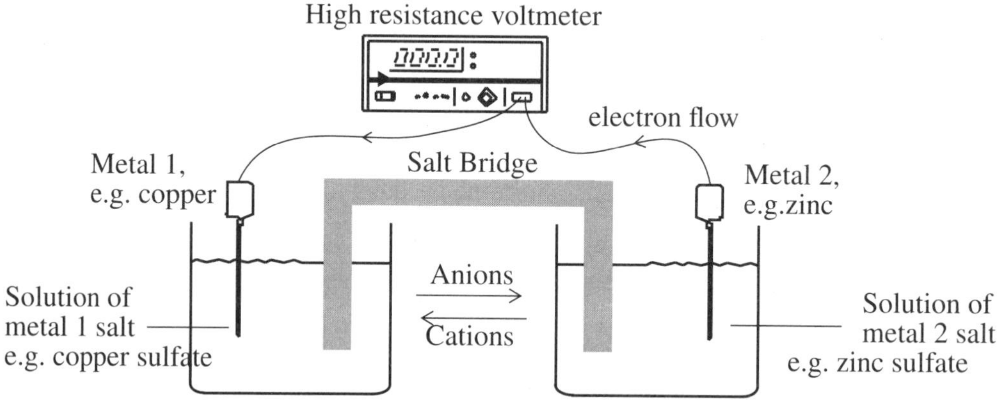

To save drawing, the cell can be represented by a shorthand notation, where "/" represents a phase boundary and "||" a salt bridge. In the above case this is:

$$Cu_{(s)}|Cu^{2+}_{(aq)}||Zn^{2+}_{(aq)}|Zn_{(s)}\ E^\theta = -1.10\ V$$

Note the negative sign of E^θ which indicates that the right hand (i.e. zinc) electrode is the negative electrode. The more reactive metal will be the negative electrode and the greater the difference in reactivity of the metals, the greater the reading on the voltmeter.

The wire allows electrons to flow from the more negative electrode (in this case the zinc) to the less negative electrode and the voltmeter measures the potential difference between the metals. At the more negative electrode, the metal will slowly dissolve as these electrons are removed. In this case the reaction is:

$$Zn_{(s)} \Rightarrow Zn^{2+}_{(aq)} + 2\ e^-$$

As oxidation occurs at this electrode, it may be regarded as the anode (see Section 10.6, page 345). At the less negative electrode, the electrons react with the metal ions to form a layer of the metal. In this case the reaction is:

$$Cu^{2+}{}_{(aq)} + 2\ e^- \Rightarrow Cu_{(s)}$$

As reduction occurs at this electrode, it may be regarded as the cathode.

Overall the cell reaction is:

$$Zn_{(s)} + Cu^{2+}{}_{(aq)} \Rightarrow Cu_{(s)} + Zn^{2+}{}_{(aq)}$$

The energy produced in this reaction is converted to electrical energy rather than heat and this is the basis of commercial electrochemical cells (batteries) - see Chapter 16. The cell will therefore continue to generate electricity until the zinc or the copper sulfate is all consumed.

The salt bridge allows the movement of ions between the solutions, thus completing the circuit and maintaining electrical neutrality. This is frequently a piece of filter paper dipped in a solution of a strong electrolyte, such as potassium nitrate. At the right hand electrode in Figure 10.1 positive ions are being produced and at the left hand one they are being consumed. For this reason positive ions move from right to left in the salt bridge and negative ions from left to right.

Note: In 19.2.1 to 19.2.4 half equations can be used to introduce redox couples, including H^+/H_2 and a selection of common couples from the electrochemical series. The Daniell cell provides a good illustration of the principles under consideration here.

19.2.1 Describe the standard hydrogen electrode.

Laboratory work using the standard hydrogen electrode is not required.

19.2.2 Define the term standard electrode potential and explain the measurement of standard electrode potentials to produce the electrochemical series.

19.2.3 Define the term cell potential and calculate cell potentials using standard electrode potentials.

19.2.4 Predict whether a reaction will be spontaneous using standard electrode potential (E^θ) values.

Students should be able to predict the direction of electron flow in an external circuit and the reaction taking place in a cell. Relate positive E^θ values for spontaneous reactions to negative ΔG^θ values (see 6.6).   © IBO 2001

The potential of any two electrodes can be compared using the apparatus shown in Figure 10.1, but conventionally electrodes are measured relative to the standard hydrogen electrode, which is defined as having a potential of zero. The potential differences of electrodes relative to this are known as **standard electrode potentials** (E^θ). Standard electrode potentials also refer to a temperature of 298K, normal atmospheric pressure (101.3 kPa) and the concentration of all solutions being

1 mol dm^{-3}. The construction of the standard hydrogen electrode is shown in Figure 10.2 below:

Figure 10.2 – The standard hydrogen electrode

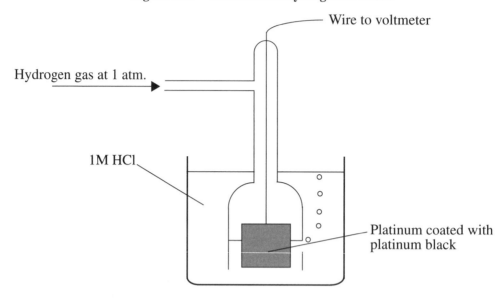

'Platinum black' is very finely divided platinum, which catalyses the electrode equilibrium:

$$2\,H^+_{(aq)} + 2\,e^- \rightleftharpoons H_{2(g)}$$

The electrode potential concept can be extended to redox couples that do not involve metals, for example iodine and the iodide ion. In this case the electrode consists of an inert metal, such as platinum, dipped into a solution containing both the oxidised and reduced form of the couple, so that the redox reaction can occur on the surface of the metal.

Reactive metals, that lose electrons easily have large negative electrode potentials (e.g. –2.71 V for Na$^+$/Na) and reactive non–metals, that gain electrons easily, have large positive electrode potentials (e.g. +2.87 V for F$_2$/2 F$^-$). The greater the E^θ, the stronger the oxidant (on the left hand side of the equation as written below) and the weaker the reductant (on the right hand side). For example fluorine is a very powerful oxidant, but the fluoride ion is a very weak reductant. Conversely species with a very negative E^θ are weak oxidants, but strong reductants. Electrode potentials are always quoted for the oxidised form gaining electrons and being converted to the reduced form. Some species commonly involved in redox reactions and their E^θ values are given in Table 10.3.

Table 10.3 – The standard electrode potentials of common species in aqueous solution

Half equation In standard form: Oxidised + electrons $\rightleftharpoons$ Reduced	E^θ in Volts
$Li^+ + e^- \rightleftharpoons Li$	−3.03
$K^+ + e^- \rightleftharpoons K$	−2.92
$Ca^{2+} + 2\ e^- \rightleftharpoons Ca$	−2.87
$Na^+ + e^- \rightleftharpoons Na$	−2.71
$Mg^{2+} + 2\ e^- \rightleftharpoons Mg$	−2.36
$Al^{3+} + 3\ e^- \rightleftharpoons Al$	−1.66
$Mn^{2+} + 2\ e^- \rightleftharpoons Mn$	−1.18
$H_2O + e^- \rightleftharpoons \frac{1}{2}\ H_2 + OH^-$	−0.83
$Zn^{2+} + 2\ e^- \rightleftharpoons Zn$	−0.76
$Fe^{2+} + 2\ e^- \rightleftharpoons Fe$	−0.44
$Ni^{2+} + 2\ e^- \rightleftharpoons Ni$	−0.23
$Sn^{2+} + 2\ e^- \rightleftharpoons Sn$	−0.14
$Pb^{2+} + 2\ e^- \rightleftharpoons Pb$	−0.13
$H^+ + e^- \rightleftharpoons \frac{1}{2}\ H_2$	0.00
$SO_4^{2-} + 4\ H^+ + 2\ e^- \rightleftharpoons SO_2 + 2\ H_2O$	+0.17
$Cu^{2+} + 2\ e^- \rightleftharpoons Cu$	+0.34
$\frac{1}{2}\ O_2 + H_2O + 2\ e^- \rightleftharpoons 2\ OH^-$	+0.40
$Cu^+ + e^- \rightleftharpoons Cu$	+0.52
$I_{2(s)} + 2\ e^- \rightleftharpoons 2\ I^-$	+0.54
$I_{2(aq)} + 2\ e^- \rightleftharpoons 2\ I^-$	+0.62
$Fe^{3+} + e^- \rightleftharpoons Fe^{2+}$	+0.77
$Ag^+ + e^- \rightleftharpoons Ag$	+0.80
$Br_2 + 2\ e^- \rightleftharpoons 2\ Br^-$	+1.09
$\frac{1}{2}\ O_2 + 2\ H^+ + 2\ e^- \rightleftharpoons H_2O$	+1.23
$Cr_2O_7^{2-} + 14\ H^+ + 6\ e^- \rightleftharpoons 2\ Cr^{3+} + 7\ H_2O$	+1.33
$Cl_2 + 2\ e^- \rightleftharpoons 2\ Cl^-$	+1.36
$MnO_4^- + 8\ H^+ + 5\ e^- \Rightarrow Mn^{2+} + 4\ H_2O$	+1.51
$F_2 + 2\ e^- \rightleftharpoons 2\ F^-$	+2.87

More powerful oxidising agent

More powerful reducing agent

ADVANCED

The electrode potentials allow predictions to be made about which reactions can theoretically occur. For example chlorine is a more powerful oxidant than bromine, as it has a more positive E^θ, so chlorine could oxidise bromide to bromine (because it 'wants the electrons more'), but bromine could not oxidise chloride to chlorine. Similarly considering zinc and copper, zinc is the more powerful reductant, so it can reduce copper(II) ions to copper, but copper could not reduce zinc(II) ions to zinc.

A more formal way of considering this is to calculate the **cell potential** that would be generated by a particular redox reaction. Consider the question of whether acidified potassium dichromate(VI) will oxidise iron(II) to iron(III). The equation for the reaction can be produced by combining the two half equations. That for the iron(II)/iron(III), as well as being multiplied by six, needs to be reversed to give the required equation, so the sign of its electrode potential is changed – note that the fact that the iron(III)/iron(II) equation needed multiplying by a factor, does **not** affect the magnitude of the electrode potential.

Half equations:
$$Cr_2O_7^{2-} + 14\ H^+ + 6\ e^- \rightleftharpoons 2\ Cr^{3+} + 7\ H_2O \qquad E^\theta = +1.33\ V$$
$$6\ Fe^{2+} \rightleftharpoons 6\ Fe^{3+} + 6\ e^- \qquad E^\theta = -0.77\ V$$

Cell equation:
$$Cr_2O_7^{2-} + 14\ H^+ + 6\ Fe^{2+} \rightleftharpoons 2\ Cr^{3+} + 7\ H_2O + 6\ Fe^{3+} E^\theta_{cell} = +0.56\ V$$

The cell potential is calculated by adding the electrode potentials. If the cell potential is positive, as in the above case, then the reaction could occur spontaneously, if negative then it could not. As a further example, consider whether copper metal can reduce hydrogen ions to hydrogen gas:

Half equations:
$$Cu \rightleftharpoons Cu^{2+} + 2\ e^- \qquad E^\theta = -0.34\ V$$
$$2\ H^+ + 2\ e^- \rightleftharpoons H_2 \qquad E^\theta = 0.00\ V$$

Cell equation:
$$Cu + 2\ H^+ \rightleftharpoons Cu^{2+} + H_2 \qquad E^\theta_{cell} = -0.34\ V$$

In this case the cell potential is negative so spontaneous reaction cannot occur, which fits in with the experimental observation that copper does not dissolve in dilute acids.

Predictions about whether a reaction can occur or not can also result from calculating ΔG for a reaction (see Section 6.9, page 209). There is actually a relationship between E^θ_{cell} and ΔG^θ:

$$\Delta G^\theta = -nFE^\theta_{cell}$$

Where n is the number of electrons transferred and F the Faraday constant (965 000 C mol^{-1} - see Section 10.6, page 347). From this it can be seen that if E^θ_{cell} is positive then ΔG^θ will be negative so a spontaneous reaction is possible and vice versa. Using the above examples:

Iron(II)-dichromate(VI) $E^\theta_{cell} = +0.56\ V$ $\quad \Delta G^\theta = -6 \times 96\ 500 \times 0.56 = -324\ kJ\ mol^{-1}$
Copper - dilute acid $\quad E^\theta_{cell} = -0.34\ V$ $\quad \Delta G^\theta = -2 \times 96\ 500 \times (-0.34) = +66\ kJ\ mol^{-1}$

The greater the value of E^θ_{cell}, the more negative will be the value of ΔG^θ and the more spontaneous the reaction.

It must be remembered that predictions made using electrode potentials give no indication of the activation energy and so even the most favourable reaction may not occur in practice if it has a very high activation energy. These predictions, made either by considering which species is the more powerful oxidant/reductant, or by calculating E_{cell}, only give predictions about the reaction under standard conditions, i.e. $T = 298$ K, $P = 101.3$ kPa and the concentration of all species being 1 mol dm^{-3}. If the electrode potentials are quite close (<0.2 V different) then an equilibrium rather than complete reaction will result. It may then be possible to produce some product from an unfavourable reaction by altering the conditions in accordance with Le Chatelier's principle (see Section 8.2, page 250).

Consider the general equilibrium:

$$Ox + n\,e^- \rightleftharpoons Red$$

Increasing [Ox], or decreasing [Red] will shift the position of equilibrium to the right, reducing the number of electrons and hence making E^θ more positive. Similarly E^θ will become more negative if [Ox] is decreased or [Red] increased. In the case of metal/metal ion electrodes, the reduced form is the solid metal and so its concentration is fixed, the equilibrium being:

$$M^{n+} + n\,e^- \rightleftharpoons M$$

This means that increasing the concentration of the metal ions will make E^θ more positive and decreasing the concentration will make it more negative, and hence a better reducing agent.

EXERCISE 10.5

1. Which one of the following is not a condition for the standard hydrogen electrode?

   A The temperature must be 298K.
   B The pressure of hydrogen must be 101.3 kPa.
   C The concentration of hydrogen ions in solution must be 1 mol dm^{-3}.
   D The concentration of hydrogen gas in solution must be 1 mol dm^{-3}.

2. The standard electrode potentials of nickel and lead are:

   $Ni^{2+} + 2e^- \rightleftharpoons Ni \quad E^\theta = -0.23$ V
   $Pb^{2+} + 2e^- \rightleftharpoons Pb \quad E^\theta = -0.13$ V

   What is the cell potential for the reaction $Ni^{2+} + Pb \rightleftharpoons Ni + Pb^{2+}$?

   A +0.36 V
   B +0.1 V
   C −0.1 V
   D −0.36 V

3. A number of possible oxidising agents are suggested to oxidise bromide ions to bromine. Given the information below, which is the most likely to suceed?

$$\tfrac{1}{2} Br_2 + e^- \rightleftharpoons Br^- \qquad E^\theta = +1.09 \text{ V}$$

A Iodate(V) ions $(2 IO_3^- + 12 H^+ + 10 e^- \rightleftharpoons I_2 + 6 H_2O \, E^\theta = +1.19 \text{ V})$

B Copper ions $(Cu^{2+} + 2 e^- \rightleftharpoons Cu \, E^\theta = +0.34 \text{ V})$

C Phosphoric acid $(H_3PO_4 + 2 H^+ + 2 e^- \rightleftharpoons H_3PO_3 + H_2O \, E^\theta = -0.28 \text{ V})$

D Hydrogen gas $(H_2 + 2 e^- \rightleftharpoons 2 H^- \, E^\theta = -2.25 \text{ V})$

4.

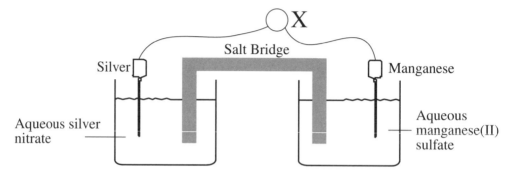

The apparatus above can be used to compare the electrode potentials of silver and manganese. According to reference sources, the standard electrode potentials of these metals are:

$$Mn^{2+} + 2e^- \rightleftharpoons Mn \, E^\theta = -1.18 \text{ V} \qquad Ag^+ + e^- \rightleftharpoons Ag \, E^\theta = +0.80 \text{ V}$$

a) In order for the comparison to be of standard electrode potentials, what conditions must be imposed?

b) If the experiment was to determine the standard electrode potential of manganese, what must replace the silver/silver nitrate electrode?

c) What instrument is the instrument labelled 'X' in the diagram?

d) What could be used as a 'salt bridge'?

e) Supposing the silver and manganese electrodes are joined directly with a wire:

i In which direction will the electrons flow?
ii Describe the changes that will take place at the silver electrode.
iii Describe the changes that will take place at the manganese electrode.
iv In what direction will the anions and cations in the salt bridge move?
f) Give the shorthand notation for the cell.
g) What would you expect the cell potential to be? (Ensure that the sign corresponds to your notation in f). What is the corresponding cell reaction?

h) Calculate ΔG^θ for this reaction and state what this indicates about the spontaneity of the reaction.

i) If the silver nitrate solution were diluted, would you expect the cell potential to increase or decrease? Explain your answer.

ADVANCED

10.6 ELECTROLYSIS OF A MOLTEN SALT

CORE

10.3.1 Draw a diagram showing the essential components of an electrolytic cell.

An electrolytic cell converts electrical energy to chemical energy. The diagram should include the source of electric current and conductors, positive and negative electrodes and the electrolyte.

10.3.2 Describe how current is conducted in an electrolytic cell.

10.3.3 Deduce the products for the electrolysis of a molten salt.

Equations showing the formation of products at each electrode should be given.

10.3.4 Distinguish between the use of a spontaneous redox reaction to produce electricity in a voltaic cell and the use of electricity to carry out a non-spontaneous redox reaction in an electrolytic cell.

10.3.5 Describe and explain the use of electrolysis in electroplating.

Restrict this to copper plating. © IBO 2001

Electrolysis is the passage of electricity through a liquid containing ions, known as an **electrolyte**. In contrast to metals, the current in electrolytes is carried by the movement of ions rather than the movement of electrons. The solid conductors inserted into the liquid are called **electrodes**, the one with a positive charge being the **anode** (because it attracts anions) and the negative one the **cathode**. The energy from the electric current is used to bring about non-spontaneous chemical reactions.

During electrolysis when the anions reach the **anode** they lose electrons and are therefore **oxidised**. If, for example, the electrolyte was molten sodium chloride, the negative chloride ions would be attracted to the positive anode, where they would lose electrons and be oxidised to chlorine gas:

$$2\ Cl^-_{(l)} \Rightarrow Cl_{2\ (g)} + 2\ e^-$$

The cations move towards the **cathode**. When they reach it they gain electrons and are therefore **reduced**. If, for example, the electrolyte was molten sodium chloride, the sodium ions would be attracted to the cathode, where they would gain electrons and be reduced to sodium metal:

$$Na^+_{(l)} + e^- \Rightarrow Na_{(l)}$$

This process is illustrated in Figure 10.3 below:

Figure 10.3 – A diagrammatic representation of electrolysis

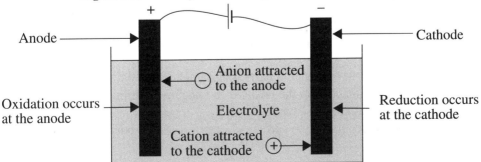

345

Electrolysis of a molten electrolyte is often used to obtain reactive metals from their ores. More details are given in Chapter 15. It can also be seen that a metal is often deposited at the cathode and electrolysis is therefore used to electroplate items. If, for example, the electrolyte contains copper ions, the cathode will become copper plated.

EXERCISE 10.6

1. Which one of the following statements about electrolysis is correct?

    A   Oxidation always occurs at the anode because oxygen is often given off here.
    B   Oxidation always occurs at the anode because it removes electrons from the electrolyte.
    C   Oxidation always occurs at the cathode because hydrogen is often given off here.
    D   Oxidation always occurs at the cathode because it donates electrons to the electrolyte.

2. By what means is an electrical current carried in a molten salt?

    A   By the movement of anions only.
    B   By the movement of cations only.
    C   By the movement of both anions and cations.
    D   By the movement of electrons.

3. When molten lead(II) bromide is electrolysed,

    A   the lead ions gain electrons at the anode to form lead.
    B   the lead ions gain electrons at the cathode to form lead.
    C   the lead ions lose electrons at the anode to form lead.
    D   the lead ions lose electrons at the cathode to form lead.

4. This question concerns the passage of electricity through sodium chloride.

    a)   Is the bonding in sodium chloride metallic, ionic or covalent?
    b)   State whether the following would conduct electricity.
         i)   Solid sodium chloride
         ii)   Molten sodium chloride
         iii) Aqueous sodium chloride

    c)   What names are given to the following?
         i)   Passing an electric current through a solution containing ions.
         ii)   The liquid containing ions.
         iii) The solid conductors put into the liquid.

    d)   A D.C. current is used and particular names are given to the solid conductors attached to the positive and negative terminals of the power supply. What are these names?
    e)   Oxidation occurs on the surface of one of the solid conductors. Which one?

5. This question concerns the electrolysis of copper chloride.

   a) Solid copper chloride does not conduct electricity? Explain why.
   b) Give two ways in which it can be made to conduct.
   c) Write a balanced equation for the reaction that occurs at the anode.
   d) What would be observed on the surface of this electrode?
   e) Write a balanced equation for the reaction that occurs at the cathode.
   f) What would be observed on the surface of this electrode?
   g) Does e) represent an oxidation or a reduction reaction? Explain why.

10.7 ELECTROLYSIS OF AQUEOUS SOLUTIONS

19.3.1 List and explain the factors affecting the products formed in the electrolysis of aqueous solutions.

Factors to be considered are position in the electrochemical series, nature of the electrode and concentration. Suitable examples for electrolysis include water, aqueous sodium chloride and aqueous copper(II) sulfate.

19.3.2 List the factors affecting the amount of product formed during electrolysis.

Factors are charge on the ion, current and duration of electrolysis.

19.3.3 Determine the relative amounts of the products formed during the electrolysis of aqueous solutions. © IBO 2001

When a molten salt is electrolysed the cations are attracted to the cathode where they undergo reduction and the anions are attracted to the anode where they undergo oxidation. If the electrolyte is an aqueous solution, then the water present can also be oxidised or reduced.

At the cathode, the water can be reduced to hydrogen gas and this will occur unless the electrolyte contains the ions of a metal low in the electrochemical series (i.e. with $E^\theta > 0$), such as silver and copper (electrolysis is widely used to electroplate these metals onto cathodes made of more reactive metals, or other easily reduced cations).

$$2\,H_2O_{(l)} + 2\,e^- \Rightarrow H_{2\,(g)} + 2\,OH^-_{(aq)}$$

Similarly at the anode the water can be oxidised to oxygen gas and this will occur unless the electrolyte contains easily oxidised anions, such as bromide and iodide ions, with $E^\theta < 1.23$ V, the E^θ for the oxidation of water.

$$2\,H_2O_{(l)} \Rightarrow O_{2\,(g)} + 4H^+_{(aq)} + 4\,e^-$$

If the anode is made from a metal that is not inert (e.g. copper) then the anode itself may be oxidised and dissolve into the solution.

$$Cu_{(s)} \Rightarrow Cu^{2+}_{(aq)} + 2\,e^-$$

Hence, if aqueous copper sulfate is electrolysed between copper electrodes, copper is in effect transferred from the anode to the cathode. This process is used to purify copper for use as an electrical conductor.

These possibilities are illustrated by the examples of the products from the electrolysis of aqueous solutions given in Table 10.4 below:

Table 10.4 – The products from the electrolysis of some aqueous solutions

Aqueous electrolyte	Product at the cathode	Product at the anode
Copper(II) bromide	Copper	Bromine
Sodium iodide	Hydrogen	Iodine
Silver nitrate	Silver	Oxygen
Potassium sulfate	Hydrogen	Oxygen
Copper sulfate	Copper	Copper(II) ions (if Cu anode)

Pure water cannot of course be electrolysed because the concentration of ions is too low to allow it to conduct the current. If, however, an electrolyte producing ions that are the same as those of water, or less easily oxidised/reduced (such as aqueous sulfuric acid, aqueous sodium hydroxide or potassium sulfate - see Table 1.3) is added, then hydrogen is produced at the cathode and oxygen at the anode. The volume of hydrogen produced is twice that of oxygen. In effect the energy from the electric current is being used to split water into its component elements.

$$2\ H_2O_{(l)}\ \Rightarrow\ 2\ H_{2\ (g)}\ +\ O_{2\ (g)}\qquad \Delta G^\theta = +474\ \text{kJ mol}^{-1}$$
$$\qquad\qquad\quad 2\ \text{vol.}\qquad 1\ \text{vol.}$$

ADVANCED

In some cases, when there is little difference in the ease of discharge of the ion and water, the concentration of the electrolyte may be the determining factor. In dilute aqueous sodium chloride for example, the major product at the anode on electrolysis is oxygen. If however a saturated solution is used then chlorine predominates. The electrolysis of sodium chloride, both molten and aqueous, is very important industrially and is covered in considerable detail in Chapter 15.

The quantity of product that results from electrolysis will depend upon the magnitude of the current and the time for which the current is passed. Hence the amount of product is proportional to the charge passed and calculations can be carried out to find the amount of product that results. The standard unit of electrical charge is the Coulomb (C). The number of Coulombs passed during electrolysis may be calculated by multiplying the current passing (in Amps) by the length of time for which it is passed (in seconds)

$$\text{Charge (in Coulombs)} = \text{Current (in Amps)} \times \text{Time (in seconds)}$$

The charge carried by one mole of electrons can be found by multiplying the charge on the electron (1.60×10^{-19} C) by the Avogadro constant (6.02×10^{23} mol^{-1}). The result (96500 C mol^{-1}) is known as the Faraday constant. Knowing the charge passed and this constant, the number of moles of electrons may be calculated:

$$\text{Moles of electrons} = \frac{\text{Charge passed (in C)}}{96500}$$

The amount of product formed, which will also depend on the number of electrons involved in the electrode reaction, can the be calculated from the balanced equation.

EXAMPLE

Find the mass of copper produced at the cathode by passing a current of 3.00 A through aqueous copper(II) sulfate for exactly 2 hours.

SOLUTION

Charge (in C) = Current (in Amps) × Time (in sec) = $3.00 \times (2 \times 60 \times 60) = 21600$ C

$$\text{Moles of electrons} = \frac{\text{Charge passed (in C)}}{96500} = \frac{21600}{96500} = 0.2238$$

$$Cu^{2+} + 2\,e^- \Rightarrow Cu$$

Amount of Cu $= \frac{1}{2} \times$ Moles of electrons $= \frac{1}{2} \times 0.2238 = 0.1119$ moles

Mass of Cu $= n \times M = 0.1119 \times 63.55 = 7.11$ g

EXERCISE 10.7

1. Which one of the following salts would give the same products irrespective of whether the molten salt or the aqueous solution is electrolysed?

    A   Magnesium bromide
    B   Copper sulfate
    C   Magnesium sulfate
    D   Copper bromide

2. An electric current is passed through two electrolysis cells in series. In the first, copper is deposited on the cathode from aqueous copper sulfate. In the second, silver is deposited on the cathode from aqueous silver nitrate. After a certain length of time the mass of the copper cathode has increased by 1 g. Given that the relative atomic mass of silver and copper are 107.87 and 63.55 respectively, what will the increase in mass of the silver electrode be?

    A $\dfrac{2 \times 107.87}{63.55}$

    B $\dfrac{2 \times 63.55}{107.87}$

    C $\dfrac{107.87}{2 \times 63.55}$

    D $\dfrac{63.55}{2 \times 107.87}$

ADVANCED

3. When an aqueous solution of a metal salt is electrolysed so that the metal is deposited on the cathode, which one of the following will **not** affect the increase in mass of the cathode, if the other variables are fixed?

A   The charge on the ion.
B   The molar mass of the metal.
C   The charge passed.
D   The potential difference applied.

4. With aqueous solutions containing ions, the water may be oxidised or reduced in preference to the ions present. Consider a concentrated aqueous solution of calcium chloride.

a)   Which ion will be attracted to the anode?

b)   Does oxidation or reduction occur at the anode?

c)   Which will be changed most easily, the ion from the calcium chloride or the water?

d)   Write a balanced equation for the reaction at the anode.

e)   What would be seen at the anode?

f)   Describe how diluting the electrolyte may affect the product at the anode

g)   Which ion will go to the cathode?

h)   Which ion will be changed most easily, the ion from the calcium chloride or the water?

i)   Write a balanced equation for the reaction at the cathode.

j)   What would be seen at the cathode?

k)   What would the aqueous solution eventually change into?

l)   As electrolysis is required for this change, what is the probable sign of ΔG^θ for the reaction?

5. When aqueous copper sulfate is electrolysed using copper electrodes, copper is transferred from the anode to the cathode. A current of 0.200 A is passed through such a cell for exactly 5 hours.

a)   The value of the Faraday constant is 96500 C mol^{-1}. What does the Faraday constant represent?

b)   What is the total charge passed through the cell?

c)   Given that the molar mass of copper is 63.55, calculate the increase in mass of the cathode.

ORGANIC CHEMISTRY

11

Chapter contents

11.1 HOMOLOGOUS SERIES

11.1.1 Describe the features of a homologous series.

Features include a general formula and neighbouring members differing by CH_2, with similar chemical properties and with a gradation in physical properties.

11.1.2 Predict and explain the trends in boiling points of members of a homologous series.

In a homologous series there is a gradual increase in boiling point as the number of carbon atoms increases. Cross reference with 4.3.

11.3.4 Discuss the volatility, solubility in water and acid-base behaviour of the functional groups aldehyde, ketone, carboxylic acid, alcohol, amide, amine, ester and halogenoalkane.

For example, use functional groups to explain the higher boiling point of methanol compared with methane. Cross reference with 4.3. © IBO 2001

Organic chemistry is the chemistry of carbon compounds. Carbon is in group 4 of the periodic table and it always forms covalent bonds. As carbon has four electrons in its valence level (2,4 or $1s^2 2s^2 2p^2$) it forms four covalent bonds. When these are all single bonds, they have a tetrahedral arrangement. In organic compounds carbon **always** forms four bonds, oxygen two, hydrogen and the halogens one (see Section 4.2, page 121).

Carbon atoms can combine with each other and with other atoms of non–metals (especially H and O) to form millions of compounds. Compounds of this kind are the basis of all known life, hence the term 'organic'. The existence of such a large number of stable compounds is due to the strength and stability of the C–C and C–H bonds. The former ensure that carbon can form long chains (a process known as catenation) and rings of carbon atoms. The latter that these structures are relatively stable and unreactive. Multiple bonds can also be formed between carbon atoms, but the presence of these usually leads to an increase in chemical reactivity. Similarly **functional groups** containing other atoms, such as oxygen, nitrogen and the halogens (see Table 11.4, page 365), can be attached to the hydrocarbon chain and result in greater reactivity. The reactions of these functional groups are the dominant feature of organic chemistry. Organic compounds may therefore be usefully regarded as comprising a hydrocarbon skeleton to which functional groups are inserted and/or attached:

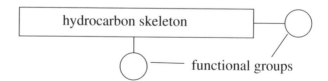

The ability of carbon atoms to form chains leads to the existence of a series of compounds that only differ from each other by the presence of an additional carbon atom and its two associated hydrogen atoms in the molecule. A series of compounds related in this way is said to form a **homologous series**. The alkanes (see below) are the simplest example of such a series, but others would include the alkenes, the alcohols and the carboxylic acids. These series can be thought of as different 'families' of organic compounds. In these families:

- successive compounds differ from each other by a CH_2 unit (known as a methylene group)
- the compounds can all be represented by a general formula (in the case of the alkanes C_nH_{2n+2}, e.g. C_3H_8)
- the compounds have similar chemical properties
- successive compounds have physical properties that vary in a regular manner as the number of carbon atoms present increases.

The point about chemical properties is best illustrated by the sections that follow, on different homologous series. The changes in physical properties are a result of the changes that occur in the strength of van der Waals' forces with increasing molar mass and in some cases a change in molecular polarity (see Section 4.4, page 133). The simplest illustration of the effect of chain length on physical properties is the variation of the boiling point of the alkanes with the number of carbon atoms in the chain, as illustrated in Figure 11.1:

Figure 11.1 – The variation of the boiling points of the straight chain alkanes

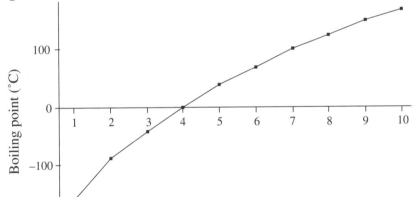

This curve is initially quite steep because, for small molecules, the addition of an extra carbon has a proportionally large effect on the molar mass (e.g. from CH_4 to C_2H_6 there is an increase of 97.5%) and hence on the van der Waals' forces. As the length of the chain increases, the percentage change in molar mass becomes progressively smaller (e.g. there is a 10.9% increase in molar mass from C_9H_{20} to $C_{10}H_{22}$) and so the curve flattens. Similar regular variation would be found in graphs of other physical properties, such as density and viscosity, against the number of carbon atoms.

The physical properties, especially the melting and boiling point of a compound, depend on the intermolecular forces present (see Section 4.8, page 146). All other factors being unchanged, the greater the molar mass of a molecule the stronger the intermolecular forces, hence the trend in the boiling points of the alkanes illustrated above. Some functional groups (such as $>^{\delta+}C=O^{\delta-}$, in aldehydes and ketones, and the presence of halogens) give rise to polarity within molecules, and this can result in slightly higher melting and boiling points than would otherwise be expected. Other functional groups, such as alcohol (–OH), carboxylic acid (–COOH), amine (–NH$_2$) and amide (–CONH$_2$) can result in hydrogen bonding between the molecules. Compounds containing these tend to have significantly higher melting and boiling points than would otherwise be expected. These points are illustrated by the examples below:

H H | | H—C—C—H | | H H	O || H—C—H	H | H—C—O—H | H
Ethane	Methanal	Methanol
$M_r = 30$	$M_r = 30$	$M_r = 32$
Non–polar	Polar	Hydrogen bonds
b.p. = –89°C	b.p. = –21°C	b.p. = 65°C

Most organic compounds are non–polar and hence tend to be insoluble in water owing to the strong hydrogen bonds between the water molecules. If however the functional groups can hydrogen bond to the water (i.e. those that hydrogen bond to themselves, plus those containing the >C=O group which can hydrogen bond to water), then the substance will be water soluble, as long as the hydrocarbon chain is quite short. Some functional groups interact with the water and hence affect the pH of the resulting solution. Carboxylic acids, for example behave as weak acids (see Section 9.2, page 290) and so reduce the pH. Amines act as weak bases in a similar manner to ammonia (see Section 9.2, page 290) and so increase the pH:

EXERCISE 11.1

1. Which of the following is correct about the number of bonds formed by atoms of different elements in organic compounds?

	Carbon	Hydrogen	Oxygen
A	4	2	2
B	4	1	2
C	4	1	3
D	3	2	3

2. The alcohols, methanol, ethanol, propanol, butanol etc., form a homologous series. This means that they:

A   have similar chemical properties, but gradually changing physical properties.

B   have similar physical properties, but gradually changing chemical properties.

C   have the same molecular formula, but different physical properties.

D   have similar physical properties and the same structural formula.

These structural formulae are required for questions 3 & 4:

$$H_3C-CH_2-CH_3$$
A

$$H_3C-CH_2-CH_2-CH_2-CH_3$$
B

$$H_3C-CH_2-CH_2-CH_2-Br$$
C

$$H_3C-CH_2-CH_2-NH_2$$
D

3. Which one of the above compounds would have the lowest boiling point?

4. Which one of the above compounds would be the most soluble in water?

5. Which one of the following lists the alkanes in order of decreasing boiling point?

A	Octane	Methane	Butane	Ethane
B	Methane	Ethane	Propane	Butane
C	Hexane	Octane	Propane	Methane
D	Hexane	Pentane	Propane	Ethane

6. The formulae of a group of closely related molecules are given below.

$$CH_3NO_2; \quad C_2H_5NO_2; \quad C_3H_7NO_2; \quad C_4H_9NO_2; \quad C_5H_{11}NO_2$$

a) What name is given to a group of compounds related in this way.

b) Write a general formula for this group of compounds.

c) How would you expect the boiling points of these compounds to change with increasing numbers of carbon atoms? Explain.

d) Compared to alkanes of a similar molar mass, would you expect these compounds to be

   i   more or less soluble in water.

   ii   more or less volatile.

   Explain your answers.

e) CH_3NO_2 can be reduced to CH_3NH_2 by reacting it with hydrogen over a nickel catalyst. What product would you expect when $C_5H_{11}NO_2$ was treated in the same way? On what do you base your prediction?

11.2 DETERMINATION OF STRUCTURE

20.1.1 State that the structure of a compound can be determined using information from a variety of spectroscopic and chemical techniques.

Students should realize that information from only one technique is usually insufficient to determine or confirm a structure. [Also A.1.1].

20.1.2 Describe and explain how information from an infrared spectrum can be used to identify functional groups in a compound.

Restrict this to using infrared spectra to show the presence of the functional groups: OH, COOH, C=O, CHO, C=C and C≡C, and to match the fingerprint region to a known spectrum. [Also A.1.2].

20.1.3 Describe and explain how information from a mass spectrum can be used to determine the structure of a compound.

Restrict this to using mass spectra to determine the relative molecular mass of a compound and to identify simple fragments, for example: $(M_r-15)^+$ loss of CH_3; $(M_r-29)^+$ loss of C_2H_5 or CHO; $(M_r-31)^+$ loss of CH_3O; $(M_r-45)^+$ loss of COOH. [Also A.1.3].

20.1.4 Describe and explain how information from a ^1H NMR spectrum can be used to determine the structure of a compound.

Restrict this to using NMR spectra to determine the number of different environments in which hydrogen is found and the number of hydrogen atoms in each environment. Splitting patterns are not required. [Also A.1.4]. © IBO 2001

Having discussed the structure of organic compounds it is interesting to consider the way in which the structural formula of a substance may be determined. What techniques can the chemist use to find out the nature of the molecules in a white powder or a pale yellow liquid?

Classically a known mass of the compound was burnt in an excess of air and the mass of the water vapour and carbon dioxide produced was determined. The percentage of carbon present can be found from the mass of carbon dioxide produced and similarly the percentage of hydrogen from the mass of water. Assuming that the only other element present is oxygen, its percentage may be found by subtraction (see Exercise 1.6, question 18, page 20). This elemental analysis leads to the empirical formula and, if the molar mass was determined by some method such as the density of its vapour (see Section 5.2, page 170) or measuring a colligative property of its solution (see Section 8.5, page 276) then, the molecular formula of the substance could be found. The nature of the functional groups present was then deduced from the chemical reactivity of the compound.

These methods have now been mainly supplanted by modern instrumental methods. Three of these techniques are described below and each provides slightly different information about the molecule. Used in combination, these techniques will usually enable a chemist to elucidate the structural formula of a substance. Care must be exercised to ensure that the proposed structural formula fits all the evidence provided by the different techniques and often simple chemical tests, such as determining whether

ADVANCED

the compound decolourises bromine water (and hence contains a double or triple carbon-carbon bond), still have their place.

Most of these techniques produce a graphical output known as a spectrum, in which the way that intensity changes as a result of gradually varying another quantity, such as the frequency of the radiation, is recorded.

INFRARED SPECTROSCOPY

The vibrational motion of molecules (i.e. the bending and stretching of bonds) causes them to absorb energy in the infrared region of the spectrum, where the radiation has a lower frequency and hence less energy per quantum, than visible light. This means that when infrared light is passed through a sample, some frequencies will be strongly absorbed whereas others will hardly be absorbed at all. The result is an infrared absorption spectrum (See Figure 11.2) showing the percentage transmission at different frequencies (traditionally referred to as the wavenumber, with units of cm^{-1}).

Bonds in a molecule absorb infrared radiation of a characteristic frequency and so the presence of an absorption band at this particular frequency indicates the presence of such a bond in the molecule. The frequency depends on the difference in energy between the normal vibrational level and the next highest state. The absorbed infra-red energy increases the amplitude of the vibrational motion. Table 11.1 gives some of the more common bonds with characteristic infrared absorption bands and the frequency of these bands.

Table 11.1 – Characteristic infrared absorption bands of some bonds

Bond	Frequency – cm^{-1}
C – Cl	700 to 800
C – O	1000 to 1300
C = C	1610 to 1680
C = O	1680 to 1750
C ≡ C	2070 to 2250
O – H, in carboxylic acids	2500 to 3300
C – H	2840 to 3095
O – H, in alcohols and phenols	3230 to 3550
N – H	3350 to 3500
O – H, if no H–bonding	3580 to 3670

Some bands, such as the C=O band around 1700 cm^{-1}, because they are very specific to a limited number of compounds and occur in a tightly defined region of the spectrum, tend to be very useful. Similarly the O–H group in aldehydes, phenols and carboxylic acids gives rise to a strong, broad, absorption band at high frequencies. Others, such as the C–H of which there are many in most organic compounds, have only limited use. The region in which carbon–carbon bonds absorb is often complex owing to the number of these bonds, but this region can be used as a "fingerprint" of the molecule, i.e. if a

ADVANCED

known substance and an unknown sample have the same absorption spectrum in region between 900 cm⁻¹ and 1400 cm⁻¹, known as the 'fingerprint region' of the infrared spectrum, they will almost certainly be the same compound. Figure 11.2 shows the infrared spectrum of propanone, with some absorption bands and the 'fingerprint region' labelled.

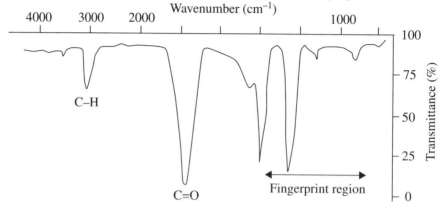

Figure 11.2 – The infrared absorption spectrum of propanone

MASS SPECTROMETRY

In the mass spectrometer molecules are converted to positive ions and these ions, after being accelerated through an electric field, are deflected by a magnetic field (see Section 2.2, page 65). The lower the mass of the ion, the greater the deflection and so, by varying the strength of the magnetic field, ions of differing mass can be brought to focus on the detector. The mass spectrum records the relative abundances of the fragments of different mass reaching the detector.

The inside of the mass spectrometer is at high vacuum so that the ions cannot collide, hence the ion with the greatest mass will usually correspond to a molecule that has only lost a single electron – the **molecular ion**. The mass of the molecular ion gives the relative molecular mass of the molecule, which can be combined with data from elemental analysis to calculate the molecular formula of the substance. In some modern instruments the mass of the molecular ion can be found to such precision that, using the fact that relative atomic masses of isotopes are not precise integers (e.g. ^{16}O is 15.995) the molecular formula can be calculated directly as, for example, to this precision CO (27.995) and C_2H_4 (28.032) have different relative molecular masses.

The excess energy from the impact of the electron forming the molecular ion will often cause it to break down, or 'fragment', inside the mass spectrometer giving rise to a 'fragmentation pattern' of lower molecular mass ions. This fragmentation pattern can be used for 'fingerprint' purposes (see i.r spectra above), but the mass of the units that have broken off the molecule will frequently give clues as to the structure of the molecule. Sometimes only a hydrogen will break off, giving a peak at one mass number less than the main peak. If two fragments differ in mass by 15 then this probably corresponds to the loss of a methyl (CH_3-) group. Similarly a loss of 29 corresponds to the loss of C_2H_5- or $H-CO-$, 31 to the loss of CH_3-O- and 45 to the loss of $-COOH$. Figure 11.3 shows the mass spectrum of butane with the molecular ion and some fragments labelled.

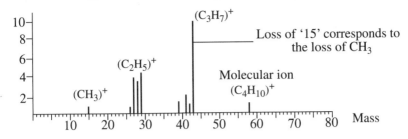

Figure 11.3 – The mass spectrum of butane

NMR SPECTROSCOPY

Nuclear Magnetic Resonance (NMR) spectroscopy is arguably the most powerful single tool for investigating the structure of a molecule. It is found that as a result of changes that occur in the nucleus, atoms with an odd mass number, when placed in a strong magnetic field, absorb radiation of radio frequency. The precise frequency varies slightly with the electron density around the nucleus and hence its chemical environment. Most commonly this is applied to the hydrogen atoms in a molecule. The NMR spectrum indicates the bonding of all of the hydrogen atoms in the molecule and also, from the relative intensities of the signals, the number of hydrogen atoms that are bonded in each of these environments. Table 11.2 gives the common bonding situations of hydrogen atoms in organic molecules and the region of the NMR spectrum (called the chemical shift, δ, and measured in ppm, relative to tetramethylsilane, TMS, which is taken as zero) that these absorb in. Knowing the way in which all of the hydrogen atoms are bonded, along with the relative numbers of these (given by the integration trace), will frequently allow the structure of the molecule to be determined.

Table 11.2 – Characteristic ^{1}H NMR absorptions

Bonding situation (R – alkyl group, ⬡ – benzene ring)	Chemical shift, δ ppm
$R – CH_3$	0.9
$R – CH_2 – R$	1.3
$R_3C – H$	2.0
$CH_3 – CO – O – R$	2.0
$CH_3 – CO – R$	2.1
⬡ $– CH_3$	2.3
$R – C≡C – H$	2.6
$R – CH_2 – F/Cl/Br/I$	3.2 to 3.7
$R – O – CH_3$	3.8
$R – CO – O – CH_2 – R$	4.1

Bonding situation (R – alkyl group, ⬡ – benzene ring)	Chemical shift, δ ppm
⬡ –CO – O – CH$_3$	4.0 to 4.2
R – O – H	4.5
R – CH = CH$_2$	4.9 to 5.9
⬡ – O – H	7
⬡ – H	7.3
R – CO – H	9.7
R – CO – O – H	11.5

The height of the peak (or, more precisely, the area under it) is proportional to the number of hydrogen atoms in that chemical environment. Often NMR spectra include an 'integration curve' that gives the relative areas under each peak.

Figure 11.4 below shows the low resolution NMR spectrum of ethanol with an interpretation of the various peaks in it. In high resolution spectra (see Figure 16.5 page 667 for the high resolution NMR spectrum of ethanol) these broad peaks appear as groups of separate sharp peaks.

Figure 11.4 – The low resolution NMR spectrum of ethanol

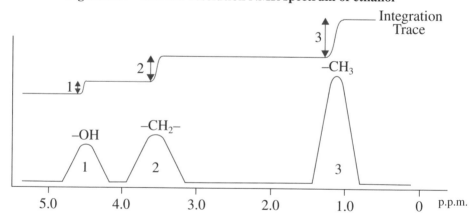

EXERCISE 11.2

1.   The vibration of a C=O bond is responsible for the signal in a

A   mass spectrum.
B   UV–visible spectrum.
C   infrared spectrum.
D   NMR spectrum.

2. Which one of the following nuclei may be detected using NMR spectroscopy?

A ^{1}H

B ^{12}C

C ^{14}N

D ^{16}O

3.

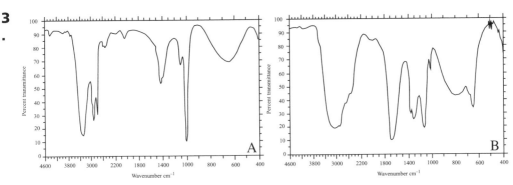

One of the IR spectra above is that of methanol, the other is that of methanoic acid. Deduce which is which and assign two peaks in each spectrum.

4. Consider the IR spectrum shown.

a) Identify the bonds causing the absorptions at 750 and 3000 cm^{-1}.

b) Given the additional information that the 1200 cm^{-1} absorption is caused by C-C the molar mass of the compound is about 130 and it only has a single peak in its NMR spectrum, attempt to identify it.

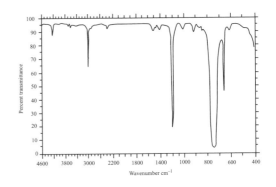

ADVANCED

5.

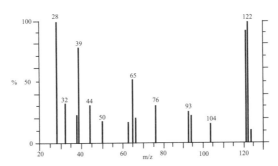

The mass spectrum above has the molecular ion peak at 122. Explain the origin of peaks at:

a) 121   b) 104   c) 93

6.

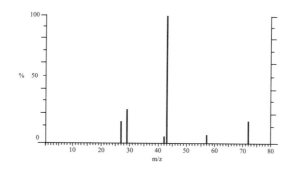

a)   In the mass spectrum above, at what mass is the peak resulting from the molecular ion?

b)   Explain what fragments have been lost from the molecular ion to produce peaks at 57, 43 and 29.

c)   From this information, attempt to deduce the structure of the molecule, which contains carbon, hydrogen and oxygen only.

7.   In the ^{1}H NMR spectrum above the peaks occur in four groups at $\delta = 0.9$, 1.3, 2.0 and 4.1.

a)   Attempt to identify the chemical environment of the hydrogen atoms responsible for each group of peaks.

b)   What is the ratio of the number of hydrogen atoms in each of these environments?

c)   Use this information to try to deduce the structural formula of the molecule.

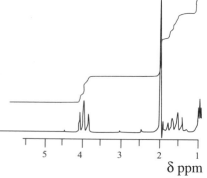

8.   Consider the ^{1}H NMR spectrum shown.

a)   At what chemical shift do the groups of peaks occur?

b)   Attempt to identify the chemical environment of the hydrogen atoms responsible for each group of peaks.

c)   What is the ratio of the number of hydrogen atoms in each of these environments?

d)   Use this information to try and deduce the structural formula of the molecule.

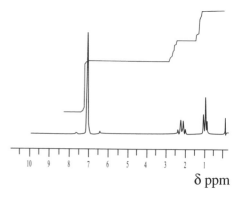

ADVANCED

9.

Attempt to deduce the
structural formula of
the unknown
compound whose IR
spectrum, mass
spectrum and NMR
spectrum are shown.
Explain how you
deduced this structure.

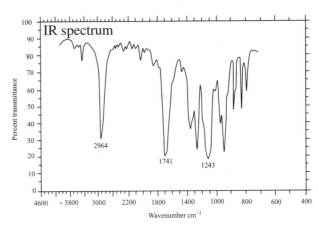

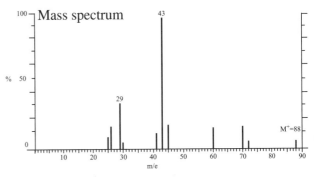

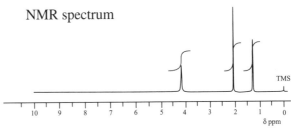

10. The structure of a particular substance is suspected as being

$$Cl - CH_2 - CH = CH - CH_2 - Cl$$

Describe the features that you might expect to observe in its:

a)   mass spectrum.
b)   infrared spectrum.
c)   NMR spectrum.

[For more problems on structure determination using these techniques, see Chapter 17]

ADVANCED

11.3 NAMING ORGANIC COMPOUNDS

11.3.1 Draw and state the names of compounds containing up to five carbon atoms with one of the following functional groups: aldehyde, ketone, carboxylic acid, alcohol, amide, amine, ester and halogenoalkane.

Functional groups in full and condensed forms are required, e.g. aldehyde:

$$R-C=O$$ *or RHCO; carboxylic acid; either* $$R-C=O$$ *or RCOOH.*
$$\quad\quad |$$ $$\quad\quad\quad\quad\quad\quad\quad\quad\quad\quad\quad\quad\quad\quad\quad |$$
$$\quad\quad H$$ $$\quad\quad\quad\quad\quad\quad\quad\quad\quad\quad\quad\quad\quad\quad\quad OH$$

© IBO 2001

There is a systematic scheme for naming organic compounds known as the IUPAC (International Union of Pure and Applied Chemists) system, but many compounds also have 'trivial' names used before the introduction of this system, hence many organic compounds have two names. In this book IUPAC names will be used consistent with the names used in the syllabus.

From the point of view of IUPAC naming, organic compounds are considered to comprise a hydrocarbon 'backbone' to which side chains and functional groups are attached. The backbone is considered to be the **longest continuous chain of carbon atoms** in the molecule and this **supplies the stem** of the name.

Note, it pays to inspect the formula carefully as the most obvious carbon chain is not always the longest one:

e.g.
$$H$$
$$|$$
$$H_3C-C-CH=CH_2$$
$$|$$
$$CH_2$$
$$|$$
$$CH_3$$

$CH_3–CH(C_2H_5)–CH=CH_2$ has a principal chain 5 carbons long, not 4 carbons long.

The prefix 'cyclo' can also be added to indicate that the carbon atoms are arranged in a ring. Hydrocarbon side chains may be attached to this longest chain and they are named in a similar manner. The first six of these are given in Table 11.3.

Table 11.3 – The naming of hydrocarbon chains

No. of C atoms	Stem	Side chain
1	meth	methyl
2	eth	ethyl
3	prop	propyl
4	but	butyl
5	pent	pentyl
6	hex	hexyl

If the compound is an alkane (i.e. no functional groups are present) the ending '-ane' is added to the stem.

Hence:

$$H_3C—CH_2—CH_3$$

Propane

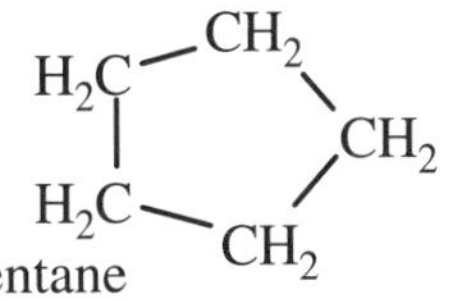

Cyclopentane

$$H_3C—CH_2—CH—CH_3$$ with CH_3

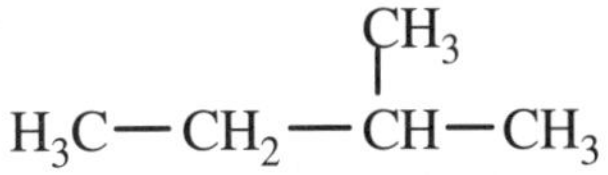

Methylbutane

The **functional groups** present in the molecule are indicated by **prefixes** or **suffixes** attached to the stem. These and a specific example of each class of compound are given in Table 11.4. In some cases a prefix is used if another functional group is already providing the ending – these alternatives are shown in brackets. There are also, in many cases, two ways of writing the functional group depending on whether a full structural formula or a condensed (single line) formula is being written. In formulae written this way, brackets are used to denote side chains.

Table 11.4 – The naming of functional groups

Name	Functional group	Prefix/ suffix	Example
Alkane	None	–ane	CH_4; methane
Alkene	$C = C$	–ene	$CH_2= CH_2$; ethene
Alcohol	–O – H or –OH	–anol (or hydroxy–)	$CH_3–CH_2–OH$; ethanol
Aldehyde	$-\overset{\overset{\displaystyle O}{\|}}{C}-H$ or -CHO	–anal	$CH_3–CHO$; ethanal
Ketone	$-\overset{\overset{\displaystyle O}{\|}}{C}-$ or –CO–	–anone	$CH_3–CO–CH_3$; propanone
Carboxylic acid	$-\overset{\overset{\displaystyle O}{\|}}{C}-O-H$ or –COOH	–anoic acid	$CH_3–COOH$; ethanoic acid
Amine	$-\overset{\overset{\displaystyle H}{\|}}{N}-H$ or –NH$_2$	–ylamine (or amino–)	$CH_3–CH_2–NH_2$; ethylamine
Amide	$-\overset{\overset{\displaystyle O}{\|}}{C}-N\overset{H}{\underset{H}{}}$ or –CONH$_2$	–anamide	$CH_3–CONH_2$; ethanamide
Halogenoalkane (chloro, bromo, or iodoalkane)	–X (i.e. –Cl, –Br, –I)	Halogeno– (i.e. chloro–, bromo–, or iodo–)	$CH_3–CH_2–Cl$; chloroethane

Note that the naming of **esters** is slightly different in that they are named as if they were salts of the carboxylic acid, as explained in Section 11.7, page 382.

- If there is more than one functional group or side chain present then a principal functional group defines the ending and the other functional groups and side chains are indicated as prefixes, arranged in alphabetical order. A double or triple bond may be indicated by changing the first vowel in the ending.

    e.g. $HO-CH_2-C(CH_3)=CH-COOH$ is 4-hydroxy-3-methylbut-2-enoic acid

- If there are a number of identical side chains or substituents, then this is indicated by placing the prefixes di– (2), tri– (3), tetra– (4) etc. immediately in front of the prefix/suffix.

    e.g. $Cl_3C-CH(CH_3)-COOH$ is 3.3.3–trichloromethylpropanoic acid

- If there is more than one possible position for the side chain or functional group to attach itself, then this is indicated by numbers identifying the carbon atoms in the principal chain. If there is a functional group which must occur at the end of a carbon chain (e.g. COOH), then the carbon in this group is taken as the first carbon in the chain.

    e.g. $CH_3-CH_2-CHCl-COOH$ is 2–chlorobutanoic acid

In other cases, the numbering starts from the end of the chain which gives the lowest sum of numbers for the substituents present.

    e.g. $CH_3-CH_2-CHCl-CH_2-OH$ is 2–chlorobutan–1–ol, **not** 3–chlorobutan–4–ol

Comprehensive IUPAC nomenclature is a very complex subject, but this brief summary should enable you to cope with most of the compounds commonly encountered.

EXERCISE 11.3

1. To which series of compounds does the molecule $CH_3-CH_2-\overset{\overset{\displaystyle O}{\|}}{C}-CH_3$ belong?

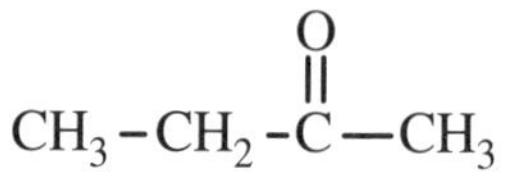

    A   Ketone
    B   Alcohol
    C   Carboxylic acid
    D   Aldehyde

2. Which of the following is the structure of but–1–ylamine?

    A $CH_3-CH_2-CH_2-CH_2-CH_2-NH_2$
    B $CH_3-CH_2-CH_2-CH_2-NH_2$
    C $CH_3-CH_2-CH_2-CO-NH_2$
    D $CH_3-CH_2-CH_2-CH_2-CO-NH_2$

3. Draw structural formulae of the following compounds:

    a)   Pentane   b)   3–ethylhexane
    c)   Bromoethane   d)   2–methylbut–1–ene
    e)   3.3–dichloro–2–methylbutanoic acid

4. Name the following compounds:

a) $CH_3-C=CH_2$
  $\quad\quad\quad\;\; |$
  $\quad\quad\;\; CH_3$

b) $CH_3-CH_2-CH-Cl$
  $\quad\quad\quad\quad\quad\; |$
  $\quad\quad\quad\quad\; CH_2-CH_3$

c) $CH_3-CHI-CH_2-CH_2-OH$

d) $HO-C(CH_3)_2-CH_2-CH_2-COOH$

11.4 ISOMERISM

11.3.2 Explain that functional groups can exist as isomers.

Examples include: ethanoic acid (CH$_3$COOH) and methyl methanoate (HCOOCH$_3$), propanal (CH$_3$CH$_2$CHO) and propanone (CH$_3$COCH$_3$).

11.3.3 Outline the existence of optical isomers.

Restrict this to the fact that, if a carbon atom has four different substituents, the molecule exists in two enantiomeric forms that rotate the plane of polarized light in opposite directions. Students should be able to identify a chiral (asymmetric) centre.   © IBO 2001

Isomers are different compounds that have the same molecular formula. Different compounds means that they have different physical properties (melting point, boiling point etc.). They may also have very different chemical properties depending on the type of isomerism present. Isomers may be divided into:

• **structural isomers**, in which the atoms are joined in a different order so that they have different structural formulae, and

• **stereoisomers**, in which the order in which the atoms are joined is the same, but the molecules have a different spatial arrangement of atoms and hence different three dimensional shapes.

Structural isomers can be further sub–divided into positional isomers, hydrocarbon chain isomers and functional group isomers; stereoisomers into geometrical isomers and enantiomers or optical isomers. The relationship between the different types of isomerism is illustrated in Figure 11.5 below.

Figure 11.5 – The relationship of different types of isomers

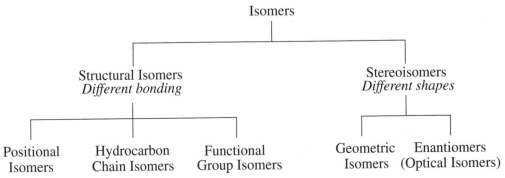

Positional isomers have the same hydrocarbon skeleton and the same functional group, it is just that the functional group is joined to a different part of the skeleton. A simple example of this kind of isomerism is propan–1–ol and propan–2–ol:

$$CH_3-CH_2-CH_2-OH$$

Propan–1–ol

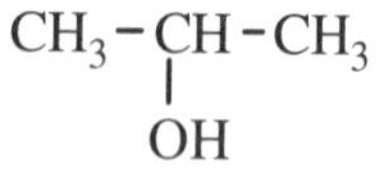

$$CH_3-CH-CH_3$$
$$\quad\quad\;\; |$$
$$\quad\quad\; OH$$

Propan–2–ol

Hydrocarbon chain isomers have, as the name would imply, different hydrocarbon skeletons that the functional group is attached to. Butane and methylpropane illustrate this kind of isomerism:

$$CH_3-CH_2-CH_2-CH_3$$

Butane

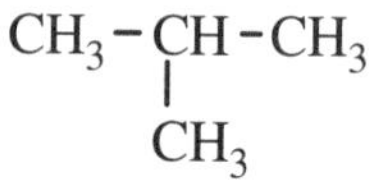

$$CH_3-CH-CH_3$$
$$\quad\quad\;\; |$$
$$\quad\quad\; CH_3$$

Methylpropane

Because of their nature, some functional groups will usually have isomers containing another functional group. For example **alcohols**, such as ethanol, usually have an **alkoxyalkane** that is isomeric to them, in this case methoxymethane:

$$CH_3-CH_2-OH$$

Ethanol

$$CH_3-O-CH_3$$

Methoxymethane

Other common pairs of functional groups that frequently display functional group isomerism with each other are:

Alkene – Cycloalkane

Hex–3–ene

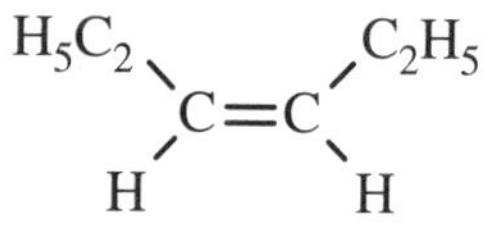

Cyclohexane

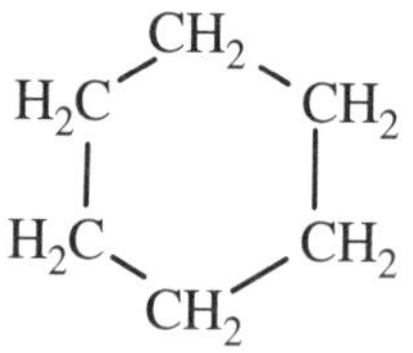

Aldehyde – Ketone

Propanal

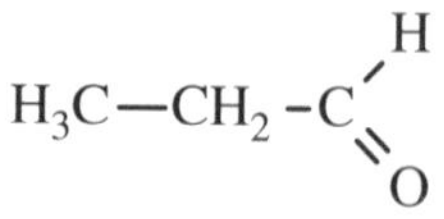

Propanone

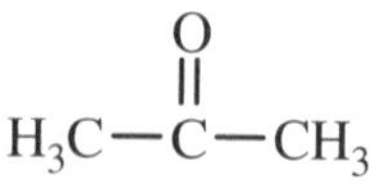

Carboxylic acid – Ester

Ethanoic acid

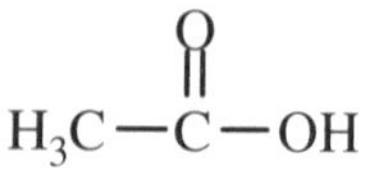

Methyl methanoate

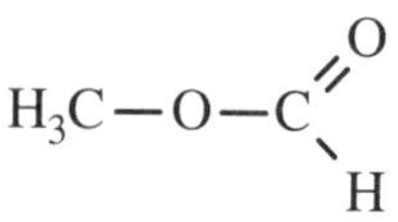

In the case of positional and hydrocarbon chain isomers the functional group, which usually dictates the reactivity of the molecule, is unchanged therefore they have quite similar chemical properties. With functional group isomerism the change in the functional group can have a profound effect on both the physical and chemical properties of the molecule. In the previous example ethanol is a liquid (at room T and P) that will react with sodium. Methoxymethane is a gas (at room T and P – no H–bonding) that does not react with sodium. Similarly methyl methanoate is a sweet smelling liquid that forms neutral solutions, whereas ethanoic acid has a sharp smell (vinegar) and forms acidic solutions.

If a carbon atom has **four different groups attached** to it then there are two different ways in which these groups can be arranged around this carbon atom, which is known as an **asymmetric carbon atom** or a **chiral centre** (from the Greek word for 'hand'). The two forms of the molecule, which are known as **enantiomers** or optical isomers, are mirror images of each other, but cannot be superimposed on each other (like a pair of gloves). This is illustrated below using the amino acid alanine (2–aminopropanoic acid) as an example. The asymmetric carbon atom has a * on it:

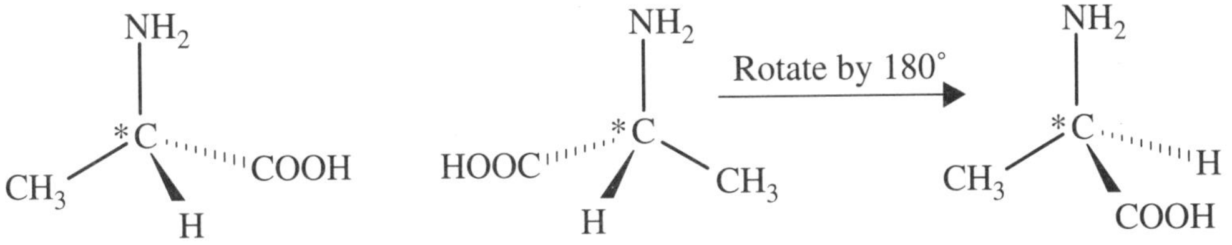

Mirror images

Note that all four groups must be different for this to occur so that glycine (H_2N-CH_2-COOH), in which the methyl group in alanine has been replaced by a second hydrogen atom, does not exist as enantiomers. All other 2–amino acids exist as two enantiomeric forms. Because these molecules are so similar, there is very little difference in their physical and chemical properties. In fact the only difference is that they have differing effects on polarised light, one isomer rotating the plane of polarisation clockwise, the other anticlockwise. This can be detected using an instrument known as a polarimeter. Biological systems are much more sensitive to the shape of the molecule and so they tend to form only one of the pair of enantiomers and have different effects (see Chapter 13).

EXERCISE 11.4

1. Which one of the following formulae could represent more than one compound?

    A C_3H_8
    B $CH_3CH=CH_2$
    C $CH_3(CH_2)_3CH_3$
    D C_4H_{10}

2. How many isomers are there of the molecular formula C_3H_7Cl?

    A   2
    B   3
    C   4
    D   8

3. The structural formula of 1–methoxybutane is

$$CH_3 - O - CH_2 - CH_2 - CH_2 - CH_3$$

Draw structural isomers of this compound that illustrate:

    a)   positional isomerism
    b)   hydrocarbon chain isomerism
    c)   functional group isomerism

4. Write abbreviated structural formulae and name all the structural isomers of the compound with molecular formula C_6H_{14}.

5.   a)   Draw the structural formulae of and name the four structurally isomeric alcohols represented by the molecular formula $C_4H_{10}O$.

        b)   Identify which one of these can exist as a pair of enantiomers (optical isomers) and explain why it is only this isomer that can exist as enantiomers.

        c)   Given two pure enantiomeric samples, how could you determine whether these were the same or different enantiomers.

        d)   If this alcohol were to be synthesised by a biochemical process, catalysed by enzymes, what would you most likely discover about the proportions of the two enantiomers in the product.

        e)   In what way would this differ if the sample was produced by a normal chemical synthesis? Explain.

        f)   Draw the structural formula of a molecule that also has the molecular formula $C_4H_{10}O$, but that is not an alcohol.

        g)   Would you expect this to be more or less soluble in water than the alcohols? Explain.

11.5 STEREOISOMERISM

H.1.1 Describe and explain geometrical isomerism in non-cyclic alkenes.

The existence of geometric (cis-trans) isomers is the result of restricted rotation around the C=C bond.

H.1.2 Explain the difference in physical and chemical properties of geometrical isomers.

Include different boiling points, e.g. cis- 1,2-dichloroethene and trans-1,2-dichloroethene and different reactions when heated, eg cis- and trans-but-2-ene-1,4-dioic acid.

H.1.3 Describe geometrical isomerism in C_3 and C_4 cyclo-alkanes.

Use dichloro-derivatives of cyclopropane and cyclobutane as examples. Rotation is restricted because the C–C bond is now part of a cyclic system.

H.1.4 Define plane-polarized light and describe how it interacts with enantiomers.

Cross reference with 11.3.3. Include the use of a polarimeter.

H.1.5 Define the term racemic mixture.

H.1.6 Compare the physical and chemical properties of enantiomers. © IBO 2001

Double bonds comprise a σ–bond and a π–bond. Because the π–bond involves two regions of high electron density on opposite sides of σ–the bond (see Section 4.6, page 140), atoms joined by a double bond are not free to rotate because rotation would involve breaking this π–bond. This means that in a molecule containing a double bond, if the form produced by rotating one end of the bond by 180° relative to the other is not identical to the original, then there can be two separate forms of the molecule.

These are known as geometric isomers and this form of isomerism is illustrated using 1.2-dichloroethene (ClCH=CHCl) as an example. The form which has two similar groups on the same side of the double bond is known as the **cis–isomer**, the other the **trans–isomer**:

$$\underset{H}{\overset{Cl}{\diagdown}}C=C\underset{H}{\overset{Cl}{\diagup}} \qquad \underset{H}{\overset{Cl}{\diagdown}}C=C\underset{Cl}{\overset{H}{\diagup}}$$

cis–1.2–dichloroethene   trans–1.2–dichloroethene

Frequently, as in this case, the cis–isomer will be polar, whilst the more symmetrical trans–isomer will not. This affects physical properties such as the boiling points, the cis–isomer boiling at 60°C the trans–isomer at 48°C. Usually the chemical properties are similar, but in some cases the proximity of the functional groups allows interaction in the cis–isomer more easily than in the trans–isomer. For example cis–butenedioic acid dehydrates at under 200°C to form the anhydride (see below). The trans–isomer sublimes unchanged at ~200°C. Dehydration of the trans–isomer requires a much higher temperature so as to achieve the activation energy required for rotation about the double bond and hence the product has the same form as the cis–isomer.

$$\begin{array}{c} H-C-CO-OH \\ \| \\ H-C-CO-OH \end{array} \Rightarrow \begin{array}{c} H-C-CO \\ \| \quad\quad >O \\ H-C-CO \end{array} + H_2O$$

OPTION

Cycloalkanes also display geometrical isomerism because being part of a ring prevents rotation of carbon–carbon single bonds as well, so for example, 1.2 dichlorocyclopropane can exist as both cis– and trans– isomers:

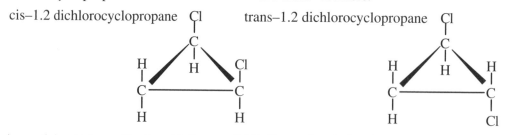

As explained above (Section 11.3, page 367), if a molecule has four different groups attached to a single carbon atom, then the compound can exist as a pair of enantiomers. The only difference in the properties of these compounds is in their interaction with plane polarised light. Plane polarised light can be considered to be light in which the oscillation of the wave is restricted to one plane, say the vertical. This can be achieved by passing the light through a polarising filter. If the light is now passed through a second polarising filter orientated in the same direction (e.g. vertical) then there is virtually 100% transmission (see Figure 11.6). If the second polarising filter has its axis at right angles to the first (e.g. horizontal) then no light will pass. A pure enantiomer placed between the two filters will rotate the plane of polarisation in one direction (say clockwise) so that maximum transmission is no longer when the second filter is aligned with the first one. The second enantiomer will rotate the plane of polarisation by exactly the same amount but in the opposite direction (anticlockwise). Substances that affect polarised light in this way are said to be **optically active**. An instrument containing two polarising filters that can be rotated relative to each other, allowing the angle between the two filters measured is called a **polarimeter**.

Figure 11.6 – Illustrating plane polarised light and the effect of optically active compounds

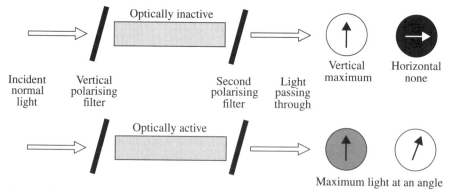

Apart from this the physical properties of enantiomers are identical. Chemically, the behaviour of the enantiomers is identical unless the reaction also involves another pure enantiomer. Chemical reactions that produce an asymmetric carbon atom in a molecule usually give rise to a mixture containing exactly equal amounts of the two enantiomers. Such a mixture is known as a **racemic mixture**. The effects of the two enantiomers in a racemic mixture cancel each other out and so it is not optically active. In contrast almost all natural products, produced by enzyme catalysed biochemical processes, result in just one pure enantiomer and hence produce optically active material. Natural turpentine (produced from pine tree resin) can, for example, be differentiated from white spirit (a substitute produced by the chemical industry) because turpentine is optically active and will rotate the plane of polarised light, whereas white spirit will not.

EXERCISE 11.5

1. Which one of the following compounds will exhibit geometrical isomerism?

    A $CH_3CH = CH_2$
    B $CH_3CCl = CH_2$
    C $CH_3CH = CHCl$
    D $CH_3CH = CCl_2$

2. Counting from the left hand end of the principal chain, which carbon atom in the following molecule is an asymmetric one? $ClCH_2 - C(CH_3)_2 - CHCl - CHCl_2$

    A   The first
    B   The second
    C   The third
    D   The fourth

3. 3–bromopent–1–ene can exist in many isomeric forms. Draw a full structural formula of the molecule and then draw structural formulae of isomers that only differ from it in the manner given:

    a)   A hydrocarbon chain isomer.

    b)   An enantiomer (optical isomer).

    c)   A positional isomer.

    d)   An isomer which displays geometric isomerism.

    e)   An isomer **not** containing a double bond.

4. Lactic acid [$CH_3CH(OH)COOH$] can either be extracted from sour milk, or it may be produced synthetically by the addition of water to propenoic acid ($CH_2=CHCOOH$).

    a)   Explain what is meant by the terms ‘*optically active*’ and ‘*racemic mixture*’.

    b)   How would you expect samples from these two sources to differ.

    c)   In practice, how could you determine whether a sample of lactic acid was of natural or synthetic origin?

5.   a)   Samples of 2–bromobutane may exhibit optical activity. Explain why.

    b)   2–bromobutane may be produced by the reaction of hydrogen bromide with but–2–ene. Would you expect a sample prepared in this way to be optically active? Explain why.

OPTION

11.6 HYDROCARBONS

11.2.1 Draw structural formulas for the isomers of the non-cyclic alkanes up to C_6.

11.2.2 State the names of alkanes up to C_6.

11.2.3 Explain the relative inertness of alkanes.

11.2.4 Draw structural formulas and state the names for straight-chain alkenes (C_nH_{2n}, where n is between 2 and 5).

Geometric (cis-trans) isomers are not required.

11.2.5 Describe complete and incomplete combustion of hydrocarbons.

The formation of CO and C during incomplete combustion should be related to environmental impacts and oxidation-reduction.

11.2.6 State that the combustion of hydrocarbons is an exothermic process.

See 6.3 and 6.4.

11.3.5 Outline the reaction of symmetrical alkenes with hydrogen, bromine, hydrogen halides and water.

A double bond is relatively reactive, therefore molecules such as $H_2C=CH_2$ are important starting materials in organic synthesis.

11.3.6 Outline the uses of reactions of alkenes.

Hydrogenation is used in the production of margarine, hydration of ethene is used in the manufacture of ethanol, and bromination can be used to distinguish between alkanes and alkenes.

Hydrocarbons are compounds containing only carbon and hydrogen. The simplest homologous series of this type is that comprising the straight chain **alkanes**. The first six members of this series, along with their names and structural formulae are given in Table 11.5.

Table 11.5 – The straight chain alkanes

No. of C atoms	Molecular formula	Name	Structural formula
1	CH_4	Methane	$H-\overset{\displaystyle H}{\underset{\displaystyle H}{C}}-H$
2	C_2H_6	Ethane	$H-\overset{\displaystyle H}{\underset{\displaystyle H}{C}}-\overset{\displaystyle H}{\underset{\displaystyle H}{C}}-H$
3	C_3H_8	Propane	$H-\overset{\displaystyle H}{\underset{\displaystyle H}{C}}-\overset{\displaystyle H}{\underset{\displaystyle H}{C}}-\overset{\displaystyle H}{\underset{\displaystyle H}{C}}-H$

No. of C atoms	Molecular formula	Name	Structural formula
4	C_4H_{10}	Butane	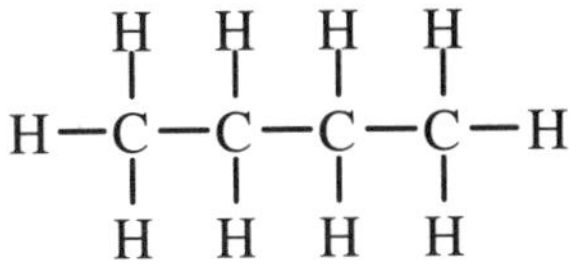 H H H H │ │ │ │ H—C—C—C—C—H │ │ │ │ H H H H
5	C_5H_{12}	Pentane	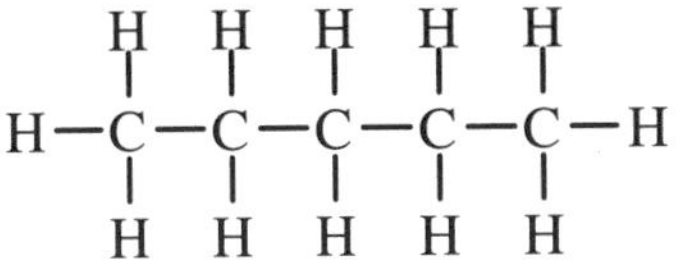 H H H H H │ │ │ │ │ H—C—C—C—C—C—H │ │ │ │ │ H H H H H
6	C_6H_{14}	Hexane	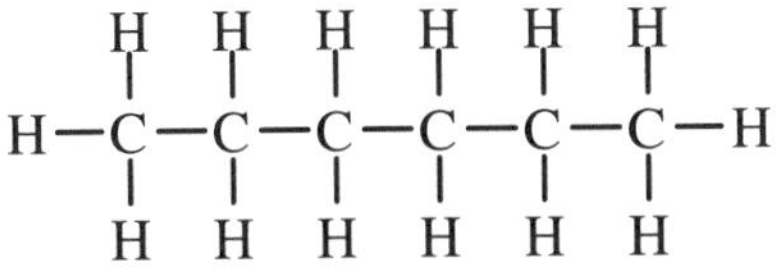 H H H H H H │ │ │ │ │ │ H—C—C—C—C—C—C—H │ │ │ │ │ │ H H H H H H

The compounds shown in Table 11.5 are known as the straight chain alkanes because **isomers** of these compounds exist in which the carbon atoms are not joined in a single chain. Isomers are compounds which have the same molecular formula, but have different structural formulae (see Section 11.4, page 367). The simplest example of isomerism is butane and methylpropane which both have the molecular formula C_4H_{10}. Similarly three isomers exist with the formula C_5H_{12}. The names and structural formulae of these compounds are shown in Figure 11.7 below.

Figure 11.7 – Isomers of C_4H_{10} and C_5H_{12}

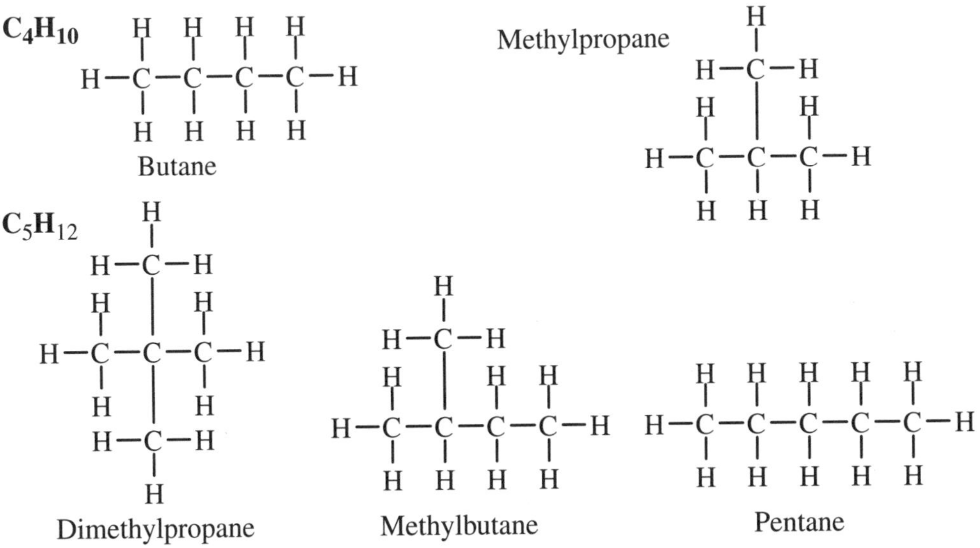

Chemically, the alkanes are fairly unreactive because of the strength and stability of the bonds (C-C = 348 kJ mol^{-1} and C-H = 412 kJ mol^{-1}), their lack of polarity (the electronegativities of C and H only differ by 0.4) and the absence of low energy unfilled orbitals.

The most familiar reaction of the alkanes is combustion. Like almost all organic compounds, the alkanes are flammable and oxidise when burnt in the air to form carbon dioxide and water if sufficient oxygen is present. The combustion of organic compounds is a highly exothermic process and is one of the most common sources of energy in society. Equations for these reactions often involve quite large coefficients, but balancing them is easy provided the following procedure is adopted:

1. All carbon atoms are converted to carbon dioxide fixing this coefficient

2. All hydrogen atoms are converted to water, fixing a second coefficient

3. The number of oxygen molecules on the left must be adjusted to balance the oxygen

Consider applying this to the complete combustion of octane (C_8H_{18}), a component of gasoline:

$$C_8H_{18} + O_2 \Rightarrow CO_2 + H_2O$$

1. There are 8 carbon atoms so these must form 8 carbon dioxide molecules.

2. There are 18 hydrogen atoms so these must form 9 water molecules.

3. There are now 25 oxygen atoms on the right hand side, requiring $12\frac{1}{2} O_2$ molecules.

The final equation is therefore:

$$C_8H_{18} + 12\frac{1}{2} O_2 \Rightarrow 8 CO_2 + 9 H_2O$$

This form is acceptable, but the '$\frac{1}{2}$' can be eliminated by doubling all the coefficients.

Gasoline and many other fuels very rarely burn in this way. If the supply of air/oxygen is limited, as is the case in an automobile engine, then incomplete combustion occurs, so some of the carbon in the fuel, rather than forming carbon dioxide, is converted to carbon monoxide (CO – a colorless, odourless, highly toxic gas) or the element carbon itself (hence black smoke). Note that the hydrogen is still converted to water. These products, along with other minor products of hydrocarbon combustion and the residue of the lead compounds still added to some gasolines, are a major source of air pollution in large cities. Many countries now require the installation of catalytic converters which ensure that the combustion process is more nearly complete. For more details of these pollution problems, see Chapter 14.

The alkanes are said to be **saturated** hydrocarbons because they contain only single bonds, those with multiple bonds are called **unsaturated** hydrocarbons. The simplest compounds of this type are the alkenes, which contain a carbon–carbon double bond. The general formula for this homologous series is C_nH_{2n} and the structural formulae and names of the first five members of the series are given in Table 11.6.

Table 11.6 – The straight chain terminal alkenes

No. of C atoms	Molecular formula	Name	Structural formula
2	C_2H_4	Ethene	
3	C_3H_6	Propene	
4	C_4H_8	But–1–ene	
5	C_5H_{10}	Pent–1–ene	

Though double bonds are stronger than single bonds, they are not twice as strong (C=C 612 kJ mol^{-1}, C–C 348 kJ mol^{-1}). This means that it is energetically favourable for a double bond to be converted into single bonds. The activation energy for these reactions is also relatively low, owing to the high electron density in the double bond. This means that alkenes are considerably more reactive than alkanes and are an important starting point in the synthesis of other organic compounds (see Section 11.9, page 389).

A reaction in which the double bond of an alkene is converted to a single bond is known as an **addition** reaction and they are typical of alkenes and alkynes. The usual test for the presence of a carbon–carbon double or triple bond is to add bromine water to the compound. If a double or triple bond is present, the bromine water changes colour from yellow–brown to colourless. This reaction, which also occurs with chlorine, takes place spontaneously at room temperature and pressure. A similar spontaneous reaction occurs between alkenes and hydrogen halides such as hydrogen chloride. With hydrogen, the activation energy is slightly higher, but if a gaseous mixture of an alkene and hydrogen is passed over a heated nickel catalyst, an addition reaction to form an alkane occurs.

377

This reaction is the basis of the conversion of vegetable oils, which contain a number of C=C double bonds, into margarine, which has fewer double bonds and hence a higher melting point.

With water, the addition reaction is reversible. At ~ 300°C and a high pressure (~7 MPa) the equilibrium shown is driven to the right (Le Chatelier's principle) and this provides the basis for the industrial manufacture of ethanol. At atmospheric pressure the equilibrium lies to the left and alkenes are formed by the dehydration of alcohols. The reaction in both directions is catalysed by either acids (e.g. H_2SO_4 or H_3PO_4) or aluminium oxide.

$$>C=C< + H_2O \rightleftharpoons -\underset{H}{\overset{|}{C}}-\underset{OH}{\overset{|}{C}}-$$

20.2.1 State and explain the low reactivity of alkanes in terms of the inertness of C–H and C–C bonds.

20.2.2 State that alkanes can react with halogens and distinguish between homolytic and heterolytic fission.

Students should be able to define and recognize a free radical. Mechanisms are not required.

20.2.3 Describe and explain the structure of benzene using chemical and physical evidence.

Consider the special stability of the ring system (heat of combustion or hydrogenation of C_6H_6 in comparison to that of cyclohexene, cyclohexadiene and cyclohexatriene), as well as benzene's tendency to undergo substitution rather than addition reactions.

© IBO 2001

Apart from combustion, the major reaction of the alkanes is with chlorine and bromine. This is usually carried out in the presence of ultraviolet (UV) light, which causes the bond between the two halogen atoms to break. This reaction is a **substitution reaction** in which one hydrogen of the alkane is replaced by the halogen, the other product being the hydrogen halide:

$$R-H+X_2 \Rightarrow R-X+HX$$

$$\text{e.g. } CH_4 + Cl_2 \Rightarrow CH_3Cl + HCl$$

The initial product (CH_3Cl) can then react further to produce polysubstituted products (CH_2Cl_2 etc.). The full mechanism of this reaction is given in Section 11.11, page 394, but in brief, the UV light causes the bond between the halogen atoms to break in such a way that each atom takes one of the electrons in the bond, a process known as **homolytic fission**. This produces a species with an unpaired electron.

$$\text{Homolytic fission } X:X \Longrightarrow X\bullet + \bullet Y \quad \text{Produces free radicals}$$

Species of this kind are known as **free radicals** and are usually very reactive. This initiates the reaction.

The other possible way in which bond breaking can occur is **heterolytic fission** in which the more electronegative of the two atoms joined by the bond takes both of the electrons to form an anion, whilst the less electronegative atom forms a cation.

$$\text{Heterolytic fission} \quad X:Y \Longrightarrow X:^- + X^+ \quad \text{Produces a pair of ions}$$

Benzene is a hydrocarbon with the formula C_6H_6. For a long time it was thought to be a cyclic molecule equivalent to 'cyclohexatriene'. There are however many pieces of evidence that lead to the conclusion that this is not in fact the correct structure for benzene. Briefly these are:

cyclohexatriene   benzene

1. Benzene undergoes substitution rather than addition reactions, e.g. it does not decolourise bromine water, a common test for carbon–carbon double bonds.

2. 'Cyclohexatriene' would not be symmetrical owing to the fact that double bonds are shorter than single bonds (C–C = 0.154 nm, C=C = 0.134 nm), yet X-ray crystallography shows that benzene has sixfold rotational symmetry and its bonds are all of an equal intermediate length (0.139 nm).

3. The enthalpy changes for the hydrogenation and for the combustion of benzene are both less exothermic than would be predicted for cyclohexatriene (see Section 4.7, page 142).

The modern interpretation of the bonding in benzene was given in Section 4.7, page 142. The delocalised π–bond makes benzene much more stable than it would be if it contained three isolated π–bonds and this explains the anomalous enthalpy changes. If addition reactions were to take place then the additional stability associated with this delocalised π–bond would be lost, hence substitution reactions are generally preferred. The substitution reactions of benzene are discussed more fully in Section 11.11, page 394.

ADVANCED

EXERCISE 11.6

Questions not applicable to the core are marked *.

1. It is found that natural gas from a particular source decolourises bromine water. From this it can be concluded that

    A   the gas contains some unsaturated hydrocarbons.
    B   the gas contains only unsaturated hydrocarbons.
    C   the gas is an alkene.
    D   the gas contains some saturated hydrocarbons.

2. What is the formula of the organic product of the reaction between propene and bromine?

A $Br–CH_2 – CH = CH_2$

B $CH_3 – CH_2 – CHBr_2$

C $CH_3 – CHBr – CH_2Br$

D $Br–CH_2 – CBr = CH2$

3. Which one of the following molecular formulae does **not** represent an alkane?

A C_3H_6
B C_6H_{14}
C C_8H_{18}
D $C_{12}H_{26}$

4. When propane burns in air, for each mole of propane burnt, how many moles of oxygen are consumed and how many moles of water are formed?

	Moles of oxygen	Moles of water
A	3	8
B	5	8
C	3	4
D	5	4

5. Which one of the following would you **not** expect to find in the exhaust gases of a normal car?

A Nitrogen
B Hydrogen
C Water vapour
D Carbon monoxide

6*. Which one of the following is **not** a consequence of the fact that benzene contains a delocalised π–bond?

A It forms carbon monoxide on incomplete combustion.
B The carbon atoms in the molecule form a regular hexagon.
C It undergoes substitution rather than addition reactions.
D The ring structure is very stable.

7*. A free radical is any substance that:

A is very reactive.
B results from the breaking of a covalent bond.
C is formed by the action of UV light on a molecule.
D contains unpaired electrons.

8. a) Draw the structural formula of pent–2–ene.

b) Write a balanced chemical equation for the complete combustion of pent–2–ene.

c) What is produced during the reaction, other than the chemical products?

d) If the supply of oxygen was reduced, what other chemical product might result from the combustion?

e) Give one reason why the production of this substance is undesirable.

f) Draw a structural isomer, other than pent–1–ene, and name the compound.

9. a) Name and write the structural formula of the organic product formed when ethene reacts with hydrogen bromide.

b) To what class of reactions does this belong?

c) What reagents and conditions are required for the conversion shown below?
$$CH_3 - CH = CH_2 \Rightarrow CH_3 - CH_2 - CH_3$$

d) What test could you carry out on both the starting material and the product that would show that this reaction had occurred?

e) What conditions are required for an alkene to react with steam?

f) Name the alkene $CH_3 - CH = CH - CH_3$.

g) Write the structural formula of the product formed when this alkene reacts with steam.

10[*]. Give three pieces of evidence that lead us to the conclusion that benzene does not contain discrete double bonds.

ADVANCED

11.7 COMPOUNDS OF CARBON, HYDROGEN AND OXYGEN

11.3.8 Outline the condensation reaction of an alcohol with a carboxylic acid to form an ester, and state the uses of esters.

Esters are used as flavouring agents, in plasticizers, as solvents and in perfumes.

11.3.9 Describe the partial and complete oxidation of ethanol.

A suitable oxidizing agent is acidified potassium dichromate(VI). Both oxidation products (ethanal and ethanoic acid) can be obtained by altering the conditions, eg ethanal by distilling off the product as it is formed, and ethanoic acid by heating under reflux.

20.4.1 Describe the dehydration reaction of alcohols to form alkenes.

20.4.2 Determine the products formed by the oxidation of primary, secondary and tertiary alcohols using acidified potassium dichromate(VI) solution. © IBO 2001

The simplest group of organic compounds containing oxygen are the alcohols, which contain the hydroxyl (–OH) group. The best known of this group of compounds is ethanol (C_2H_5OH), the 'alcohol' in alcoholic drinks. For the production of alcoholic drinks ethanol is formed by the **fermentation** of sugars such as glucose, a slow process requiring warm, anaerobic conditions:

$$C_6H_{12}O_6 \Rightarrow 2\ C_2H_5OH + 2\ CO_2$$

This is brought about by **enzymes** (biochemical catalysts) produced by yeast (a microorganism) that grows in the fermenting liquid. Ethanol for industrial purposes is usually produced by the addition reaction of ethene with steam over an acid catalyst (at high pressure (see page 378). If an alcohol is passed over this catalyst or an aluminium oxide catalyst at atmospheric pressure it is dehydrated to an alkene:

$$C_2H_4 + H_2O \xrightleftharpoons[\text{catalyst}]{\text{H}_3\text{PO}_4 \text{ or Al}_2\text{O}_3} C_2H_5OH$$

This reaction is more usually done by heating the alcohol with a dehydrating agent such as concentrated sulfuric acid. Using ethanol as the example:

$$C_2H_5OH \xrightarrow{\text{Excess H}_2\text{SO}_4 \sim 170°C} C_2H_4 + H_2O$$

The mechanism of this dehydration is discussed in more detail later on (see Section 11.11, page 394).

When alcohols are heated with carboxylic acids in the presence of concentrated sulfuric acid, they produce sweet smelling compounds called **esters**. Because of their aroma and taste, esters are often incorporated into artificial perfumes and flavours. They are also used as solvents and plasticisers. A simple reaction of this type is that of ethanol with ethanoic acid to form ethyl ethanoate:

$$CH_3-CO-OH + CH_3-CH_2-OH \xrightleftharpoons[\text{catalyst}]{\text{H}_2\text{SO}_4} CH_3-CO-O-CH_2-CH_3 + H_2O$$

$$\text{ethanoic acid} \qquad\qquad \text{ethanol} \qquad\qquad\qquad\qquad \text{ethyl ethanoate}$$

In these reactions, known as esterification reactions, the sulfuric acid has two functions. Firstly it acts as a catalyst to increase the rate of the reaction and secondly it reacts with the water formed to shift the position of the equilibrium to the right hand side (Le Chatelier's principle) ensuring a good yield of product. Note that unlike the acid and alcohol, an ester does not contain an –OH group and so is much more limited in its ability to hydrogen bond, hence esters tend to be insoluble in water.

It can be seen that the naming of esters is rather different from that of other organic compounds. They are named as if they were salts of the alcohol and the acid. In naming an ester it is important to remember that the –CO– group is part of the carboxylic acid. The molecule below is therefore methyl propanoate (**not** propyl methanoate), because it can be considered as being formed from methanol and propanoic acid

This bond is part of the alcohol ⟍   ⟍ This bond is part of the acid

$$CH_3 - O + CO - CH_2 - CH_3$$

methanol/propanoic acid

Alcohols may be subdivided into three classes according to the number of carbon atoms attached to the same carbon atom as the –OH group (compare with the naming of carbocations, page 397):

$\begin{array}{c} H \\ | \\ C-C-O-H \\ | \\ H \end{array}$	$\begin{array}{c} H \\ | \\ C-C-O-H \\ | \\ C \end{array}$	$\begin{array}{c} C \\ | \\ C-C-O-H \\ | \\ C \end{array}$
Primary	Secondary	Tertiary
(One C atom on -OH carbon)	(Two C atoms on -OH carbon)	(Three C atoms on -OH carbon)

The hydrogen atoms attached to the same carbon as the –OH group are readily oxidised and so these three classes of alcohols behave in rather different ways when they react with oxidising agents such as acidified potassium dichromate(VI). Tertiary alcohols do not have any reactive hydrogen atoms and are not readily oxidised. Secondary alcohols have one reactive hydrogen and so undergo one stage of oxidation to yield ketones. Primary alcohols have two readily oxidised hydrogens and so the oxidation occurs in two stages producing firstly aldehydes and then, on further oxidation, carboxylic acids.

This is summarised below.

Tertiary Alcohol
$$\begin{array}{c} C \\ | \\ C-C-O-H \\ | \\ C \end{array} \longrightarrow\!\!\!\times\!\!\!\longrightarrow \text{Not easily oxidised}$$

Secondary Alcohol
$$\begin{array}{c} H \\ | \\ C-C-O-H \\ | \\ C \end{array} \longrightarrow \underset{\overset{|}{C}}{C-C=O} \; \times\!\!\!\longrightarrow \text{No further oxidation}$$

Ketone

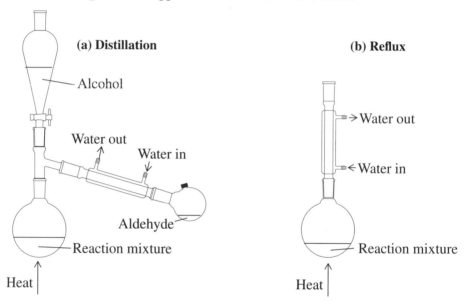

Primary Alcohol → Aldehyde → Carboxylic acid

In practice to obtain the aldehyde, the alcohol is added to the boiling oxidising agent so that as soon as the more volatile aldehyde is formed, it distils off before it can be further oxidised (see Figure 11.8a). In order to obtain the carboxylic acid a more concentrated solution of the oxidising agent is used and the mixture is refluxed so that the aldehyde cannot escape further oxidation (see Figure 11.8b).

Figure 11.8 - Apparatus for distillation and reflux

(a) Distillation

Alcohol

Water out

Water in

Aldehyde

Reaction mixture

Heat

(b) Reflux

Water out

Water in

Reaction mixture

Heat

If dichromate(VI) is used as the oxidising agent, then the orange dichromate(VI) ion ($Cr_2O_7^{2-}$) undergoes a colour change to the green chromium(III) ion (Cr^{3+}). The balanced equation is rather complex (though writing one is a good test of your understanding of half equations - see Section 10.2, page 327) and so in such reactions the convention has arisen to indicate the oxygen from the oxidising agent as an oxygen atom in square brackets. Hence the oxidation of ethanol to its final product can be written as:

Intermediate stage

$$CH_3-CH_2-OH + 2 \,[O] \Rightarrow CH_3-CHO + H_2O + [O] \Rightarrow CH_3-COOH + H_2O$$

ethanol $\quad Cr_2O_7^{2-}/H^+ \quad$ ethanal $\qquad\qquad$ ethanoic acid

Other oxidising agents, such as the permanganate(VII) ion in acidified solution, may also be used, but care must be taken as this more powerful reagent can also oxidise other functional groups (e.g. >C=C<). Ethanoic acid is also produced by bacterial oxidation when alcoholic drinks are left exposed to the air producing vinegar. Carboxylic acids, as their name suggests, act as weak acids in aqueous solution (see Section 9.2, page 290.

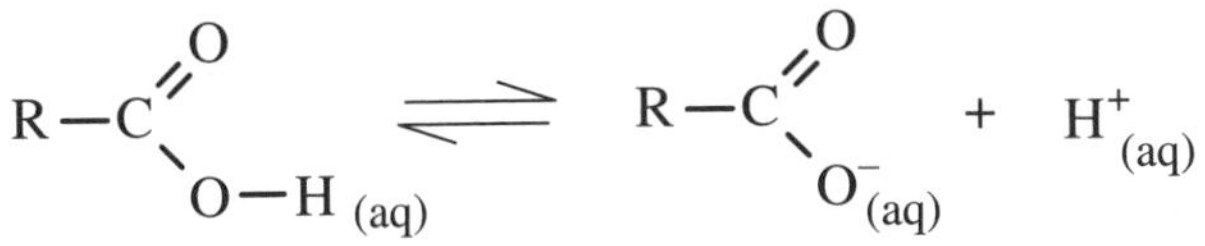

$$R-C\overset{O}{\underset{O-H}{\diagdown}}_{(aq)} \rightleftharpoons R-C\overset{O}{\underset{O}{\diagdown}}_{(aq)} + H^+_{(aq)}$$

EXERCISE 11.7

1.   When ethanol is oxidised to ethanoic acid by heating with acidified potassium dichromate(VI)

     A   the ethanol is reduced and the colour changes from orange to green.
     B   the ethanol is reduced and the colour changes from green to orange.
     C   the ethanol is oxidised and the colour changes from green to orange.
     D   the ethanol is oxidised and the colour changes from orange to green.

2.   Which one of the following compounds would turn moist blue litmus paper red?

     A CH_3OH
     B CH_3CH_2OH
     C CH_3COOH
     D $CH_3COOCH_2CH_3$

3.   The conversion of ethanol to ethene is best described as

     A   substitution
     B   elimination
     C   addition
     D   oxidation

4.   a)   How could you convert butan–1–ol into an alkene?
     b)   Name and write the structural formula of the alkene produced.
     c)   How would you show that the product was an alkene rather than an alkane?

5.   Propan–1–ol can be oxidised to propanoic acid in the same way as ethanol to ethanoic acid.

     a)   What reagents would you use for this oxidation?
     b)   What colour change would you expect to observe during the reaction?
     c)   How would you expect the product to react with sodium carbonate?

6.   When ethanol and ethanoic acid are heated together with a catalyst, a sweet smelling product results.

     a)   Name and draw the structural formula of the product.
     b)   To what class of compounds does this belong?
     c)   What would be a suitable catalyst for the reaction?
     d)   Draw the structural formula of a carboxylic acid that is isomeric with the compound in a).

11.8 HALOGENOALKANES

20.3.1 Distinguish between primary, secondary and tertiary halogenoalkanes. [Also A.4.1].

20.3.2 Describe and explain the S_N1 and S_N2 mechanisms in nucleophilic substitution.

Students must be able to draw a stepwise mechanism. Examples of nucleophiles should include –CN, –OH and NH_3 for each reaction type. [Also A.4.2].

20.3.3 Describe and explain the molecularity for the S_N1 and S_N2 mechanisms.

The predominant mechanism for tertiary halogenoalkanes is S_N1 and for primary halogenoalkanes it is S_N2. Both mechanisms occur for secondary halogenoalkanes. [Also A.4.3].

20.3.4 Describe how the rate of nucleophilic substitution in halogenoalkanes depends on both the identity of the halogen and whether the halogenoalkane is primary, secondary or tertiary. [Also A.4.4].
© IBO 2001

In halogenoalkanes, the polarity of the carbon–halogen bond means that the carbon atom carries a slight positive charge. Because of this it is susceptible to attack by **nucleophiles** (reagents that attack at a centre of positive charge by donating an electron pair), resulting in nucleophilic substitution reactions. These can occur with a wide variety of nucleophiles as indicated below

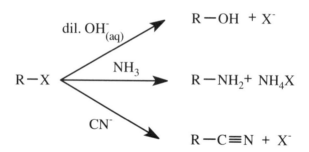

There are two distinct mechanisms for **nucleophilic substitution**. A mechanism is the series of steps by which a reaction occurs (see Section 7.5, page 234 and Section 11.11, page 394). The first of these is known as S_N1 (S for substitution, N for nucleophilic, 1 for first order/unimolecular). In this there is a slow, unimolecular, rate determining, heterolytic fission of the carbon–halogen bond to yield an intermediate carbocation. This then reacts rapidly with any nucleophile present (represented as Nu^-) to yield the final product.

Because the rate determining step is unimolecular (i.e. it only involves one molecule), the rate of this reaction depends only upon the concentration of the halogenoalkane and hence is first order overall:

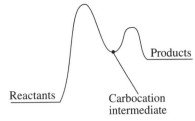

$$Rate = k.[R–X]$$

It does not depend on the concentration of the nucleophile because this is not involved in the rate determining step. The two maxima on the energy profile clearly shows the two steps in the reaction. This mechanism is usually found for halogenoalkanes that yield the more stable tertiary carbocations (see page 397).

The second mechanism is known as S_N2 – the 2 being for second order/bimolecular. In this mechanism, the attack of the nucleophile on the halogenoalkane is rate determining. The reaction passes through a transition state (or activated complex) in which the bond to the nucleophile is starting to form at the same time as the bond to the halogen breaks, i.e. the substitution occurs in one concerted step:

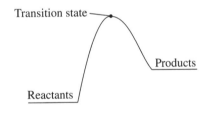

The rate of this reaction depends on the concentration of both the nucleophile and the halogenoalkane and so it gives a second order rate expression:

$$Rate = k.[R–X].[Nu]$$

The energy profile of the reaction has only one maximum.

Like alcohols (see page 383), halogenoalkanes can be divided into primary, secondary and tertiary according to the number of groups bonded to the same carbon as the halogen:

H		H		C	
C—C—X		C—C—X		C—C—X	
H		C		C	
Primary		Secondary		Tertiary	

Primary halogenoalkanes that would yield a relatively unstable carbocation in an S_N1 mechanism usually react by an **S_N2 mechanism**. **Tertiary halogenoalkanes** yield much more stable tertiary carbocations and are sterically hindered for an S_N2 attack and usually react by an S_N2 mechanism. With secondary halogenoalkanes ($R_2CH–X$) the reaction may occur by either or both mechanisms. S_N1 reactions generally occur faster than S_N2 reactions so that the rate of hydrolysis of halogenoalkanes is

tertiary > secondary > primary.

The nature of the halogen also affects the rate of reaction. There are two factors. Firstly, as the halogen changes from chlorine to iodine, the polarity of the carbon–halogen bond decreases and this would be expected to decrease the rate of reaction. Secondly, the strength of the carbon–halogen bond decreases in this direction and it would be expected to have the opposite effect. In practice it is found that the rate of hydrolysis is greater for iodoalkanes than it is for chloroalkanes, implying that the bond strength is the dominant factor:

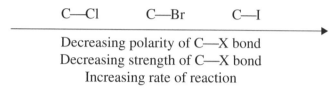

C—Cl   C—Br   C—I

Decreasing polarity of C—X bond
Decreasing strength of C—X bond
Increasing rate of reaction

Nucleophilic substitution reactions are considered in greater detail in Section 11.11, page 394.

EXERCISE 11.8

1. When a halogenoalkane reacts with ammonia, the product is:

    A   a nitrile
    B   an amine
    C   an carboxylic acid
    D   an amide

2. In a nucleophilic substitution reaction of a halogenoalkane that occurs by an S_N2 mechanism,

    A   the reaction rate is independent of the concentration of nucleophile.
    B   the bond forming and bond breaking occur in a single step.
    C   the reaction involves a slow heterolytic fission reaction.
    D   the reaction occurs via a carbocation intermediate.

3. 2–Bromo–2–methylpropane reacts with aqueous alkali via an S_N1 mechanism. Write out the mechanism, identifying the rate determining step, and explain why it is referred to as S_N1?

11.9 POLYMERS

CORE

11.3.7 Outline the polymerization of alkenes.

Polyethene and polyvinyl chloride should be used as examples of addition polymers. Students should be able to draw the structures of the monomer and the repeating unit of the polymer.

11.3.10 Deduce the condensation polymers formed by amines and by carboxylic acids.

Emphasize the need for two functional groups on the monomers: polyamides (nylons) e.g. hexanedioic acid and 1,6-diaminohexane; polyesters e.g. benzene-1,4-dicarboxylic acid and ethane-1,2-diol.

11.3.11 Outline the formation of peptides and proteins from 2-amino acids.

All 2-amino acids (α-amino acids), except aminoethanoic acid (glycine), can show optical activity (see 11.3.3). Peptides are formed from amino acids, and two functional groups allow for the formation of macromolecules. Students should be familiar with simple primary structures (order of amino acids) for peptides containing up to three amino acids, eg:

$$-CH-\overset{\overset{\displaystyle O}{\|}}{C}-NH-CH-\overset{\overset{\displaystyle O}{\|}}{C}-NH-CH-\overset{\overset{\displaystyle O}{\|}}{C}-NH-$$
$$\quad R_1 \qquad\qquad\quad R_2 \qquad\qquad\quad R_3$$

© IBO 2001

Polymers are long chain molecules that are formed by the joining together of a large number of repeating units, called **monomers**, by a process of **polymerisation**. Polymers, can be made artificially and these are usually referred to as plastics, but there are also a great number of naturally occurring polymers.

This simplest type of polymerisation reaction is known as **addition polymerisation**. In this the monomers contain double bonds and in the addition reaction new bonds (shown coloured below) form between these monomer units. The simplest polymerisation reaction of this type is that of ethene when heated under pressure with a catalyst to form polyethene, commonly known as 'polythene'.

$$H_2C=CH_2 \quad H_2C=CH_2 \quad H_2C=CH_2 \implies -\overset{\displaystyle |}{C}-\overset{\displaystyle |}{C}-\overset{\displaystyle |}{C}-\overset{\displaystyle |}{C}-\overset{\displaystyle |}{C}-\overset{\displaystyle |}{C}-$$

Ethene monomers   Polyethene polymer

This may also be represented by the equation below in which the repeating unit is shown in square brackets.

$$n\ CH_2{=}CH_2 \Rightarrow [CH_2{-}CH_2]_n$$

Another common addition polymer is poly(chloroethene), better known as PVC (short for its old name of PolyVinyl Chloride), formed by the polymerisation of chloroethene

$$n\ CH_2{=}CHCl \Rightarrow [CH_2{-}CHCl]_n$$

$$\begin{array}{cccccc} H & Cl & H & Cl & H & Cl \\ C & C & \quad C & C & \quad C & C \\ H & \quad H & H & \quad H & H & \quad H \end{array} \implies \begin{array}{cccccc} H & Cl & H & Cl & H & Cl \\ -C & C- & C & C- & C & C- \\ H & H & H & H & H & H \end{array}$$

Chloroethene monomers   Poly(chlorethene) [PVC] polymer

A second class of polymers are called **condensation polymers**. In these polymers, two different functional groups are required and for each new bond between the monomer units (shown coloured below), a small molecule (often water) is produced. The monomer must have two functional groups. This can involve two different functional groups on the same monomer or more frequently, as in the examples below, two different monomers which have two identical groups on them. One type of condensation polymer is the polyamides, so called because the bonding depends on the reaction of an amine group with a carboxylic acid to form an amide. These polymers are better known as nylon, though there are actually a whole range of nylons. One of the most common is nylon 6.6, formed by the polymerisation of hexanedioic acid with hexane–1.6–diamine.

$H_2N–(CH_2)_6–NH_2$ $HO–CO–(CH_2)_4–CO–OH$ $H_2N–(CH_2)_6–NH_2$ $HO–CO–(CH_2)_4–CO–OH$
hexane–1.6–diamine   hexanedioic acid

$$\Downarrow$$

$–HN–(CH_2)_6–NH–CO–(CH_2)_4–CO–HN–(CH_2)_6–NH–CO–(CH_2)_4–CO–$
$+ H_2O$ $\qquad\qquad + H_2O$ $\qquad\qquad + H_2O$ $\qquad$ Nylon 6.6

Another group of condensation polymers are the polyesters, so called because the bonding depends on the reaction of an alcohol with a carboxylic acid to form an ester. The best known example of this polymer is Terylene, formed by the reaction of benzene–1.4–dicarboxylic acid with ethane–1.2–diol.

$HO·CH_2CH_2 –OH$ $HOOC —⟨○⟩— COOH$ $HO·CH_2CH_2 - OH$ $HOOC —⟨○⟩— COOH$
ethane–1.2–diol   benzene–1.4–dicarboxylic acid

$–OCH_2CH_2O—CO—⟨○⟩—CO—OCH_2CH_2O—CO—⟨○⟩—CO—$ $\quad + 3\,H_2O$
Terylene

There are many natural polymers, some of the most familiar being peptides and proteins. These are formed by the polymerisation of 2–amino acids which, like nylon, can polymerise because of the presence of both carboxylic acid and amine functional groups, though in this case both occur in the same molecule. Peptides and proteins only differ from each other with regard to the number of amino acids used to form them, peptides having a small number of amino acid residues, proteins a large number.

Naturally occurring peptides and proteins are composed of 20 different amino acids which differ from each other only in the nature of the 'R' group in the structural formula shown:

$$\begin{array}{c} H \\ | \\ H_2N-C-COOH \\ | \\ R \end{array}$$

All 2–amino acids (except glycine) can exist as two enantiomers (see page 371), but only one of these is found in natural products, hence these are optically active. When 2–amino acids polymerise, it is a condensation polymerisation brought about by enzymes (biological catalysts) with a molecule of water being produced for each new bond formed. The equation below represents the formation of a short peptide from three amino acids, with side chains R_1, R_2 and R_3.

$$H_2N-\underset{\underset{R_1}{|}}{\overset{\overset{H}{|}}{C}}-COOH \qquad H_2N-\underset{\underset{R_2}{|}}{\overset{\overset{H}{|}}{C}}-COOH \qquad H_2N-\underset{\underset{R_3}{|}}{\overset{\overset{H}{|}}{C}}-COOH$$

Peptide bond

$$H_2N-\underset{\underset{R_1}{|}}{\overset{\overset{H}{|}}{C}}-CO-HN-\underset{\underset{R_2}{|}}{\overset{\overset{H}{|}}{C}}-CO-HN-\underset{\underset{R_3}{|}}{\overset{\overset{H}{|}}{C}}-COOH$$

$$+\,H_2O \qquad\qquad +\,H_2O$$

Note that because an $-NH_2$ occurs at one end of the chain and a $-COOH$ at the other end, the peptide in which the order of the amino acid side chains is R_3, R_2, R_1 is a different substance to the one shown.

EXERCISE 11.9

1. Which one of the following molecules would be most likely to undergo a polymerisation reaction?

    A $F_2C=CF_2$ B $CH_3-CH_2-CH_2-OH$
    C $Br-CH_2-CH_2-Br$ D $CH_3-CH_2-CO-OH$

2. In the formation of a protein from amino acids, which functional groups are responsible for forming the links between individual monomers?

    A $-COOH$ and $-OH$ B $-COOH$ and $-NH_2$
    C $-OH$ and $-NH_2$ D $>C=C<$ only

3. Most plastics are *polymers* formed from *monomers* produced from oil.

    a) Explain what is meant by the terms in *italics*.
    b) Polythene, which may be produced by heating ethene ($CH_2=CH_2$) at a very high pressure, can be represented by the formula $[-CH_2CH_2-]_n$. Give the equivalent formulae for P.V.C. (polyvinyl chloride; polychloroethene) and also give the formula of the monomer that it is made from.
    c) Propene too can be polymerised to form the polymer "Polypropylene", used in ropes and knitwear. Write the structural formula of a section of "Polypropylene" containing three propene units.

Organic Chemistry

11.10 ACID–BASE REACTIONS

H.9.1 Describe and explain the acidic properties of phenol and substituted phenols in terms of bonding.

Compare the acidity of phenol with alcohols, and the acidity of 2,4,6-trinitrophenol with phenol.

H.9.2 Describe and explain the acidic properties of substituted carboxylic acids in terms of bonding.

Relative acidities can be explained in terms of the ease of dissociation of the hydrogen ion or in terms of the relative stability of the conjugate base.

H.9.3 Compare and explain the relative basicities of ammonia, amines and amides.

Include the formation of salts and the liberation of the amine with NaOH from the salt. Cross reference with topic 18. © IBO 2001

The acidity of a compound to a large extent depends on the stability of the anion formed when it dissociates. This in turn is mainly dependent on the degree to which the charge on the anion formed can be distributed amongst other atoms in the molecule.

In alcohols, if the molecule loses a hydrogen ion, the charge on the resultant anion is concentrated on to a single oxygen atom. In the case of phenols, some of the charge may be distributed on to the benzene ring through interaction of a lone pair of electrons on the oxygen with the delocalised π–electrons. The reduction in charge that this produces is much less than that from the complete delocalisation between two oxygen atoms found in carboxylic acids, so that phenol is only very weakly acidic. Like carboxylic acids, phenols will form salts with strong bases such as sodium hydroxide, but unlike carboxylic acids, simple phenols will not produce carbon dioxide when they react with carbonates because they are weaker acids than 'carbonic acid'.

$$R-O-H \rightleftharpoons R-O^- + H^+$$ No delocalisation so all charge on O-atom, ∴ non-acidic

$$\text{C}_6\text{H}_5-O-H \rightleftharpoons \text{C}_6\text{H}_5-O^- + H^+$$ Some delocalisation of charge into the ring to reduce charge on the O-atom, ∴ very weakly acidic

$$H_3C-C(=O)(O-H) \rightleftharpoons H_3C-C(O^{\frac{1}{2}-})(O^{\frac{1}{2}-}) + H^+$$ Complete delocalisation halves charge on the O-atom, ∴ a weak acid

Increasing acid strength

In the case of a substituted phenol, a group that donates electrons (such as $-CH_3$) will increase the charge density in the ring, making the anion less stable and hence the acid weaker. Conversely groups that withdraw electrons (such as $-Cl$ and $-NO_2$) will further reduce the electron density and hence make the acid stronger, as shown below.

OPTION

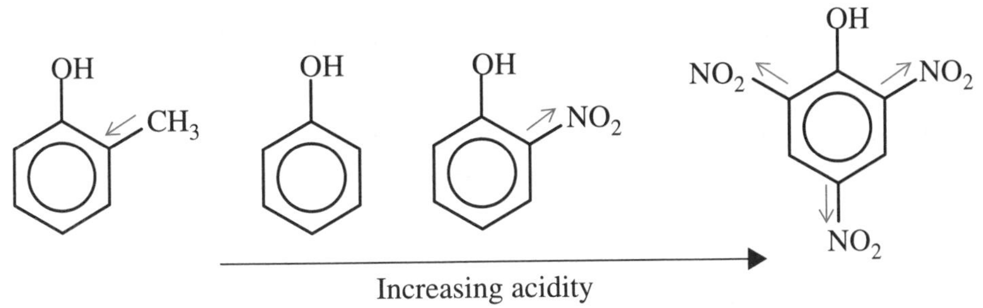
OH
CH3
OH
OH
NO2
OH
NO2
NO2
NO2
Increasing acidity

The same is true for carboxylic acids. Substituents that donate electrons (e.g. $-CH_3$) make the acid weaker, whereas electron withdrawing substituents (e.g. –Cl) make the acid stronger.

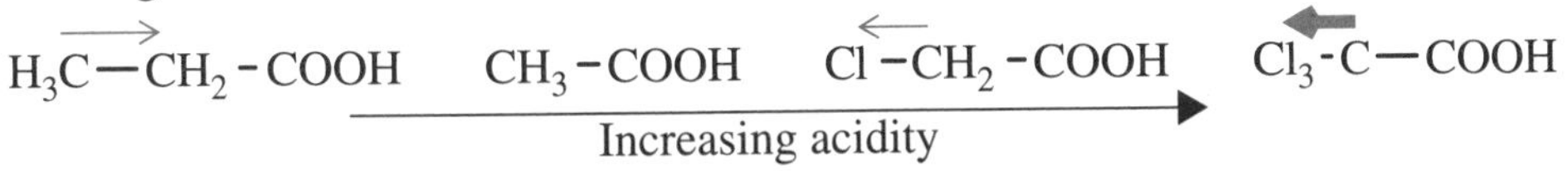
H3C—CH2-COOH
CH3-COOH
Cl—CH2-COOH
Cl3-C—COOH
Increasing acidity

Amines are closely related to ammonia and many of their reactions are analogous to those of ammonia. Like ammonia they have an unpleasant 'fishy' smell. When dissolved in water, like ammonia, they act as weak bases and form an alkaline solution.

$$R\text{-}NH_2 + H_2O \rightleftharpoons R\text{-}NH_3^+ + OH^-$$

Acids drive this equilibrium to the right and convert the amine into a salt, e.g.

$$R\text{-}NH_2 + HCl \Rightarrow R\text{-}NH_3^+ Cl^-$$

These salts are white crystalline solids. When they are warmed with an alkali such as aqueous sodium hydroxide, the equilibrium is driven to the left and the free amine regenerated.

$$R\text{-}NH_3^+ + OH^- \Rightarrow R\text{-}NH_2 + H_2O$$

The principle of reducing the electrical charge on the atom to stabilise the ion also applies to the cations formed when these species act as weak bases. In this case however a positive charge needs minimising, so that electron donating groups, such as alkyl groups, help to stabilise the cation. This means that alkyl amines are stronger bases than ammonia. In amides ($-CO-NH_2$) the lone pair of electrons on the nitrogen is involved in a delocalised π-bond with the electrons in the carbon–oxygen double bond. This means that this pair of electrons is not available to form a bond to a hydrogen ion, hence amides are non–basic. In phenylamine there is some interaction between the lone pair on the nitrogen and the delocalised π-electrons of the benzene rings, but this is incomplete so that it functions as a very weak base.

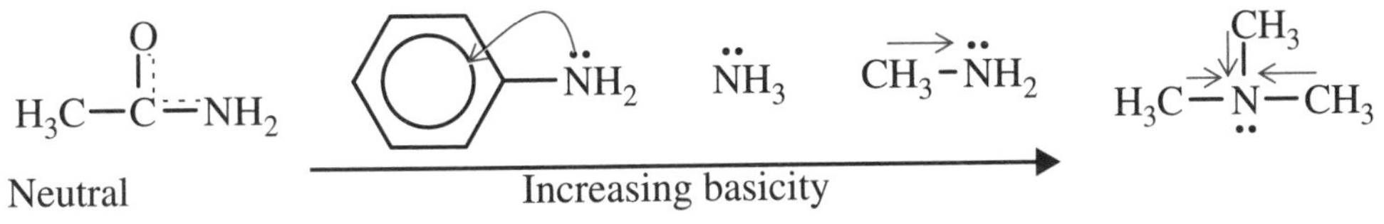
O
H3C—C—NH2
Neutral
NH2
NH3
CH3-NH2
CH3
H3C—N—CH3
Increasing basicity

OPTION

11.11 REACTION MECHANISMS

H.2 Free Radical Substitution Reactions.

H.2.1 Describe the gas phase reactions of alkanes and methylbenzene with halogens.

Consider the free radical mechanism for the reactions of methane and methylbenzene with chlorine, and identify the initiation, propagation and termination steps.

H.2.2 Describe how the gas phase reactions of chloroalkanes affect the level of ozone in the atmosphere.

© IBO 2001

The reaction of an alkane, such as methane, with a halogen is a free radical chain reaction. This process can be split up into three distinct stages, **initiation** (which produces the radicals - species with unpaired electrons), **propagation** (which produces the product and in which the radicals are reformed) and **termination** (which consumes radicals). Note that the initiation stage occurring once can cause the propagation steps to occur many time before the radicals are consumed in a termination step. The details of such a process are given below using the reaction of methane with chlorine as an example.

Initiation

$$Cl-Cl \xrightarrow{\text{UV light}} Cl\bullet + \bullet Cl \quad \text{(homolytic fission)}$$

Propagation

$$Cl\bullet + H-CH_3 \Longrightarrow Cl-H + \bullet CH_3 \quad \text{methyl radical}$$

$$\bullet CH_3 + Cl-Cl \Longrightarrow CH_3-Cl + Cl\bullet$$

Termination

$$Cl\bullet + \bullet Cl \Longrightarrow Cl-Cl$$

$$Cl\bullet + \bullet CH_3 \Longrightarrow CH_3-Cl$$

$$CH_3^\bullet + CH_3^\bullet \Longrightarrow CH_3-CH_3$$

It is traces of this final product, ethane that give a clue as to the nature of the reaction mechanism. Note that hydrogen (H_2) is **not** a product **nor** does the hydrogen atom ($H\bullet$) occur at any stage in the mechanism.

When methylbenzene is reacted with chlorine in UV light (as opposed to in the dark in the presence of a 'halogen carrier', see page 400), then an analogous reaction occurs.

Initiation   UV light

$$Cl-Cl \Longrightarrow Cl\bullet + \bullet Cl \quad \text{(homolytic fission)}$$

Propagation

Cl• + H−CH₂−⬡ ⟹ Cl−H + •CH₂−⬡

(phenylmethyl radical)

⬡−CH₂• + Cl−Cl ⟹ ⬡−CH₂−Cl + •Cl

Termination

Cl• + •Cl ⟹ Cl−Cl

⬡−CH₂• + Cl• ⟹ ⬡−CH₂−Cl

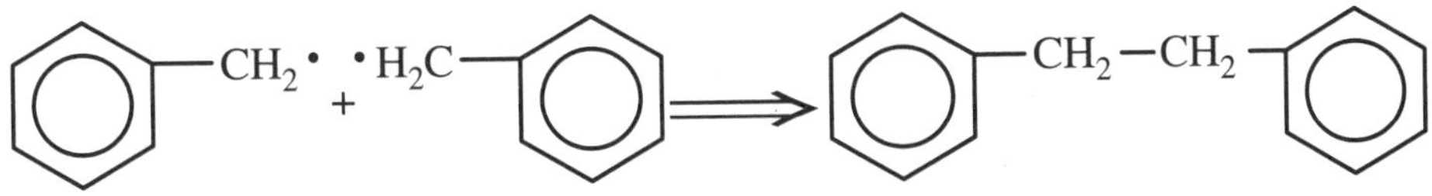

⬡−CH₂• + •H₂C−⬡ ⟹ ⬡−CH₂−CH₂−⬡

Similar radical reactions are responsible for the depletion of the ozone layer by organic chlorine compounds and similar pollutants. The strong UV light in the upper atmosphere leads to homolytic fission of the carbon–halogen bond to produce radicals. Using chloromethane as an example:

$$CH_3-Cl \xrightarrow{\text{UV light}} CH_3{\bullet} + {\bullet}Cl$$

The chlorine atom then reacts with ozone (O_3) to produce an oxychlorine radical (ClO•) and an oxygen molecule (O_2). In a second propagation step, this radical reacts with an oxygen atom to give more oxygen and reforms the original radical:

$$Cl{\bullet} + O_3 \Longrightarrow Cl-O{\bullet} + O_2 \qquad Cl-O{\bullet} + {\bullet}O{\bullet} \Longrightarrow Cl{\bullet} + O_2$$

This can occur many times before a termination reaction removes the radical. The net effect of this is the conversion of ozone back into oxygen and the reduction of the concentration of ozone in the upper atmosphere. Ozone absorbs potentially harmful short wavelength UV radiation from sunlight before it reaches the Earth's surface and a reduction in ozone concentration is likely to lead to problems such as an increase in the incidence of skin cancer. For more detail on ozone depletion, see Chapter 14.

OPTION

ELECTROPHILIC ADDITION REACTIONS

H.3.1   Describe and explain the electrophilic addition reactions of symmetrical alkenes.

A stepwise mechanistic approach is required. Reacting species should include halogens, mixed halogens and hydrogen halides.

H.3.2   Apply Markovnikov's rule to predict the outcome of the electrophilic addition reactions of asymmetrical alkenes.

A stepwise mechanistic approach is required. Reacting species should include mixed halogens and hydrogen halides.

© IBO 2001

The typical reactions that alkenes undergo are addition reactions in which the double bond is converted to a single bond and two new bonds are formed. These reactions occur in two stages and are initiated by species known as **electrophiles**. These are species that will attack a molecule at a region of high electron density, such as a double or triple bond by accepting an electron pair. First the electrophile attacks the double bond. This results in the destruction of the π–bond and the electrons from that bond form a new σ-bond to the electrophile, which itself undergoes **heterolytic fission**. This results in the formation of an **intermediate carbocation** (a species in which the carbon carries a positive charge). If a neutral molecule, such as a halogen, is the electrophile, the approach of the molecule to the double bond causes a movement of electrons in the halogen–halogen bond and hence an **induced dipole** is produced. Using ethene and bromine as the example, the mechanism of the first stage of the addition is

$$
\underset{\substack{\text{electrophilic}\\\text{attack}}}{}\quad
\underset{\substack{H\\ \\H}}{\overset{H\qquad H}{C=C}}\ \underset{\underset{Br^{\delta-}}{Br^{\delta+}}}{}\ \xrightarrow{}\
\underset{\substack{\\Br}}{H-\overset{\overset{H}{|}}{C}-\overset{\overset{H}{}}{C}+}\ \underset{Br^-}{\overset{H}{}}
\qquad
\begin{array}{l}\text{Carbocation}\\\text{Intermediate}\end{array}
$$

'curly arrow'

Then in the second stage, this carbocation will react with an anion present to complete the addition process:

$$
\underset{\substack{\\Br}}{H-\overset{\overset{H}{|}}{C}-\overset{+}{C}}\underset{Br^-}{\overset{H}{\diagdown}H}\ \xrightarrow{}\ \underset{\substack{\\Br\quad Br}}{H-\overset{\overset{H}{|}}{C}-\overset{\overset{H}{|}}{C}-H}
$$

1,2-dibromoethane

Note the use of 'curly arrows' in the equations above. These curly arrows should start at the bond or lone pair initially containing the electrons and should end at the atom the bond is formed to, or where the electron pair creates a lone pair.

The example above involves a symmetrical electrophile, i.e. the two bromine atoms are identical. The reaction can also occur with polar non–symmetrical electrophiles, such as H–Br or I–Cl. In this case, the more positively charged of the two atoms (i.e. the one with the lower electronegativity) will be the one that attacks the alkene. This is important where the alkene is also non–symmetrical so the addition reaction can result in two different products. In these cases, the initial electrophilic attack can produce two different carbocations. These carbocations will have different stabilities and the more stable will always predominate and lead to the major product.

It is found that the lower the electrical charge carried by a particular atom, then the more stable the species is. In the case of carbocations, the inductive effect (i.e. the ability of the covalent bond to polarise and reduce the charge) of the atoms bonded on to the carbon carrying the positive charge must be considered. Empirically it appears that alkyl groups attached to this atom reduce the charge that it carries more than hydrogen atoms do. This means that **tertiary carbocations** (with three carbon atoms attached to the charged one) are more stable than **secondary carbocations** (two carbon atoms) which in turn are more stable than **primary carbocations** (one carbon):

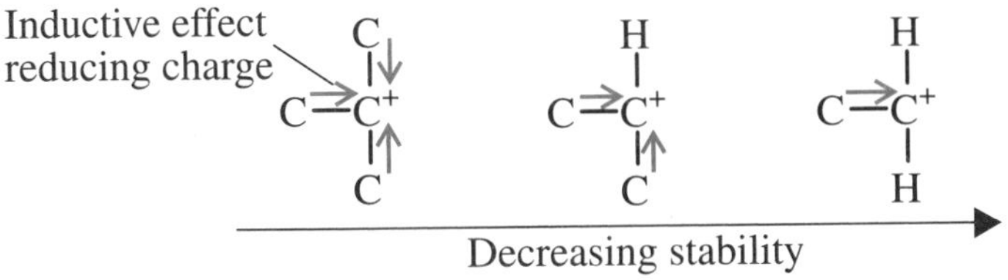

Decreasing stability

Combining a knowledge of the polarity of the attacking electrophile with that of the stability of the intermediate carbocations allows the prediction of the major product from an addition reaction between an asymmetrical electrophile and an asymmetrical alkene. Consider the reaction of iodine monochloride with propene as an example. Iodine is less electronegative than chlorine and so it will have a partial positive charge as a result of the polarity of the chlorine–iodine bond. This means that the iodine atom is the one that attacks the double bond and the carbocation formed is the more stable secondary one rather than the less stable primary carbocation:

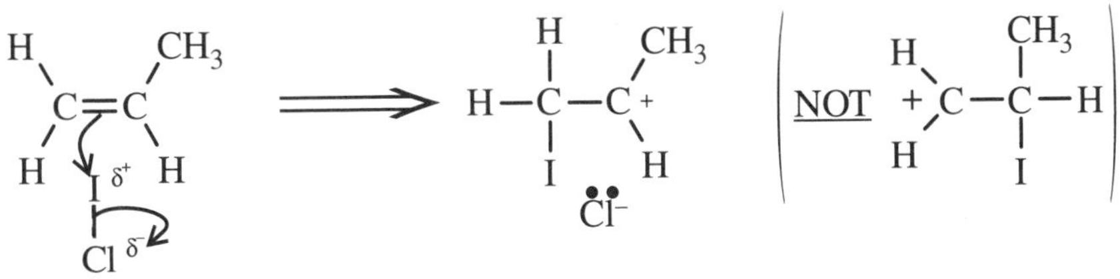

Followed by:

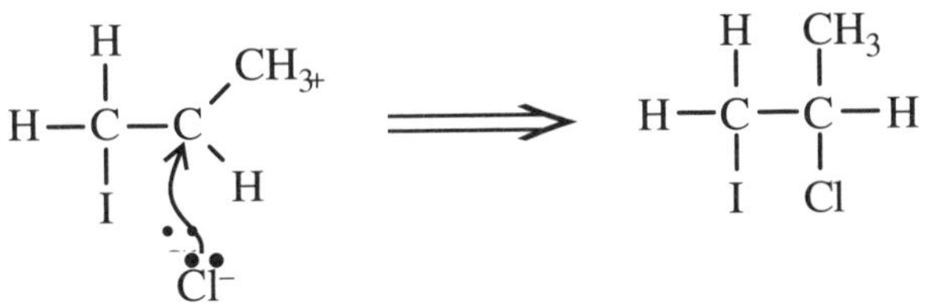

Therefore the major product is CH_3–CHI–CH_2Cl rather than CH_3–$CHCl$–CH_2I. Empirical observation led to the formulation of **Markovnikov's Rule**:

> *"When a molecule H–X adds to a multiple carbon–carbon bond, the hydrogen atom will always attach itself to the carbon atom that already has most hydrogens attached to it"*

This is because in electrophiles that involve hydrogen, then the hydrogen is almost

OPTION

always the atom that carries the partial positive charge owing to its relatively low electronegativity. In addition the carbocation with the least number of hydrogens on the charged carbon is the more stable.

Consider the addition of hydrogen bromide to methylpropene, there are two possible products:

$$CH_3-\overset{\overset{\displaystyle CH_3}{|}}{C}=CH_2 \ + \ HBr$$

A
$$\Longrightarrow \quad CH_3-\overset{\overset{\displaystyle CH_3}{|}}{C}Br-CH_3 \qquad \left(\begin{array}{c} \text{From} \\ \text{Tertiary} \end{array} \quad H_3C-\overset{\overset{\displaystyle CH_3}{|}}{\underset{+}{C}}-CH_3 \right)$$

B
$$\Longrightarrow \quad CH_3-\overset{\overset{\displaystyle CH_3}{|}}{C}H-CH_2Br \qquad \left(\begin{array}{c} \text{From} \\ \text{Primary} \end{array} \quad H_3C-\overset{\overset{\displaystyle CH_3}{|}}{C}H-\underset{+}{CH_2} \right)$$

The reaction, in accordance with Markovnikov's Rule, gives a product that is almost entirely 'A' with very little 'B'. This is in keeping with the explanation in terms of the stability of the intermediate carbocations shown.

ELECTROPHILIC SUBSTITUTION REACTIONS

H.4.1 Describe and explain the mechanism for the nitration of benzene.

A stepwise electrophilic substitution mechanism is required. The formation of NO_2^+ should also be shown.

H.4.2 Describe and explain the chlorination and alkylation reactions of benzene and methylbenzene in the presence of a halogen carrier.

H.4.3 Describe and explain the directing effects and relative rates of reaction of different substituents on a benzene ring.

Examples should be restricted to –CH_3, –OH, –Cl, –NO_2 and –CO_2CH_3. The reaction of phenol with chlorine to form trichlorophenol (TCP) should be covered.

© IBO 2001

The benzene ring, like the double bond, has a high electron density owing to the presence of π–electrons and this means that it too is susceptible to **electrophilic attack** to form a **carbocation intermediate**. In this case however, if it underwent a normal addition reaction, the product would not have a delocalised π–bond and so would lose the added stability that results from this. For this reason the intermediate carbocation loses a hydrogen ion to give a **substitution product**, which retains the delocalised π–electron system. The opposite is true for alkenes, where the addition product is the more stable.

The nitration of benzene is an example of such a reaction. Benzene is warmed with a mixture of concentrated nitric and sulfuric acids. In this mixture there is an equilibrium resulting in the formation of the nitronium ion (NO_2^+):

$$HNO_3 + 2\ H_2SO_4 \rightleftharpoons NO_2^+ + 2\ HSO_4^- + H_3O^+$$

This then acts as the electrophile, attacking the benzene ring to produce an intermediate carbocation in which the delocalised π–electron system is disrupted.

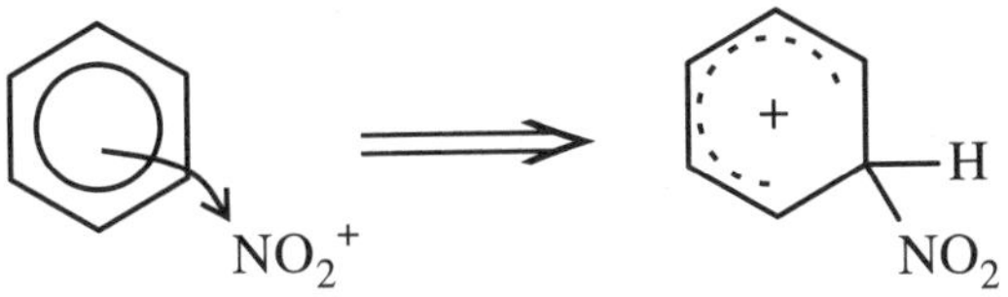

If an anion were now added on to the carbocation to complete the addition reaction, then the additional stability associate with the delocalised π–bond would be permanently lost. Alternatively the carbocation can eliminate a hydrogen ion, restoring the delocalised π–electron system. This latter alternative is much more favourable energetically and results in an overall **electrophilic substitution** reaction:

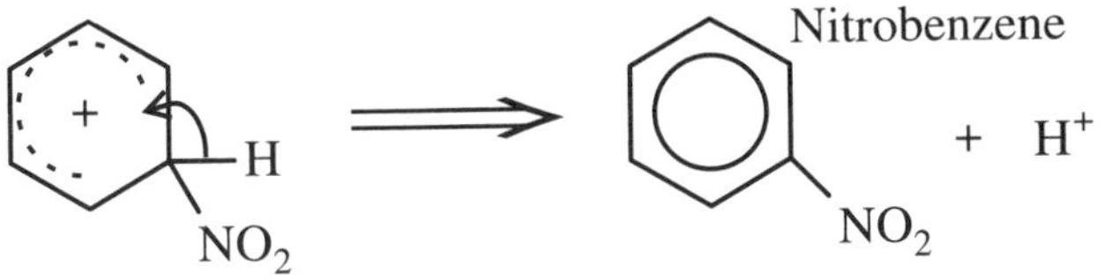

Benzene and related compounds, such as methylbenzene, undergo electrophilic substitution reactions with a range of other electrophiles, some of which are given below:

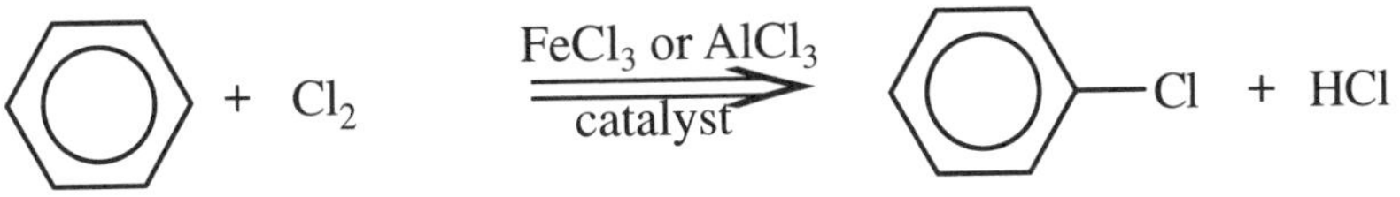

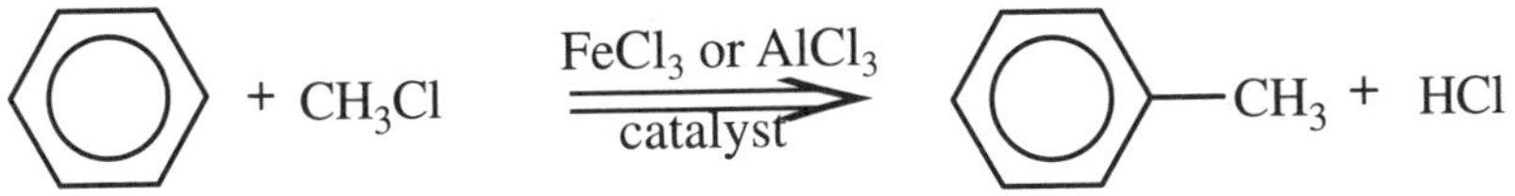

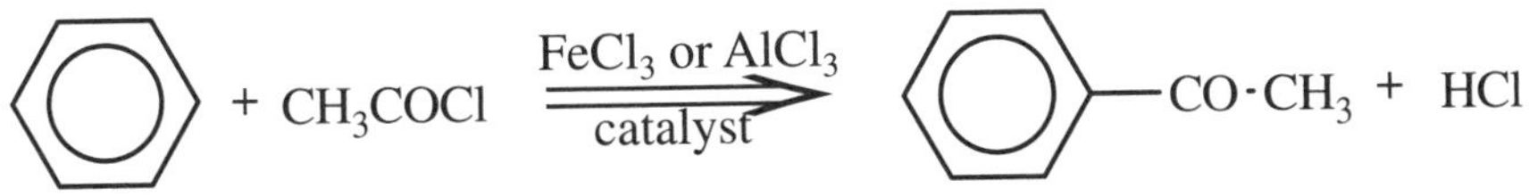

These reactions occur by similar mechanisms to the nitration reaction above. As they all employ similar catalysts these are collectively known as **Friedel Crafts reactions**. In each case the electrophile results from the positive end of the polar species produced by the bonding of the reactant to the trivalent metal chloride catalyst (sometimes referred to as a halogen carrier), e.g.

$$^{\delta+}Cl - Cl{:}^{\delta-} \rightarrow FeCl_3$$

As this complex attacks the benzene ring the Cl–Cl bond breaks heterolytically to form the carbocation and the $FeCl_4^-$ anion breaks free. In the second step of the reaction this acts as a base and accepts the H^+ lost to form HCl and regenerates the MCl_3 catalyst. In bromination the $FeBr_3$ catalyst is often produced 'in situ' by adding iron to the reaction mixture.

The presence of a substituent group on the benzene ring can significantly affect its

OPTION

reactivity with respect to electrophilic substitution reactions. Generally speaking groups which increase the electron density of the π–electron system, either through an inductive effect (e.g. –CH₃) or by donating a pair of electrons to the delocalised π–electron system (e.g. –OH), increase the reactivity of the ring whereas those that withdraw electrons decrease the reactivity. Substituents usually affect the reactivity of the 2,4,6 positions more than that of the 3,5 positions, though the halogens are an exception to this. The effect of the major substituents on the reactivity and position of further substitution is summarised in Table 11.7 below.

Table 11.7 – The effect of substituents on the reactivity and positional preference for electrophilic substitution of the benzene ring

	More reactive than benzene	Less reactive than benzene
2– or 4– substitution	Slightly: –CH₃ Greatly: –OH	–Cl
3– substitution	–	–NO₂ –CO₂CH₃

The substituents that increase the reactivity may be subdivided into those that give a slight increase in reactivity (e.g. –CH₃) and those that produce a very large increase in reactivity (e.g. –OH). Phenol (C₆H₅OH) for example, will react rapidly with aqueous chlorine to produce 2,4,6–trichlorophenol (the antiseptic, TCP) even without a Friedel Crafts catalyst.

It should be noted that with methylbenzene, two possible chlorination reactions are possible. In UV light a free radical substitution of the side chain occurs (see page 395), whereas in the dark with a Friedel Crafts catalyst (i.e. FeCl₃ or AlCl₃) the substitution occurs on the ring.

ELIMINATION REACTIONS

H.7.1 Describe the mechanism for the elimination of water from alcohols.

H.7.2 Describe and explain the mechanism for the elimination of HBr from bromoalkanes.

Under different conditions, the same reactants can undergo either nucleophilic substitution or elimination reactions, eg 1-bromobutane with OH^-.

An elimination reaction is the opposite of an addition reaction. In it a multiple bond is formed between two neighbouring atoms and a small molecule is formed from the groups that were originally attached to these atoms.

When alcohols are heated to a temperature of ~170°C with an excess of concentrated sulfuric acid, they undergo dehydration to form an alkene. For example, ethanol loses water to form ethene.

$$C_2H_5OH \Longrightarrow C_2H_4 + H_2O$$

In this reaction, the sulfuric acid protonates the hydroxyl group, so that in the second elimination step water, a much better leaving group than the hydroxide ion, is lost.

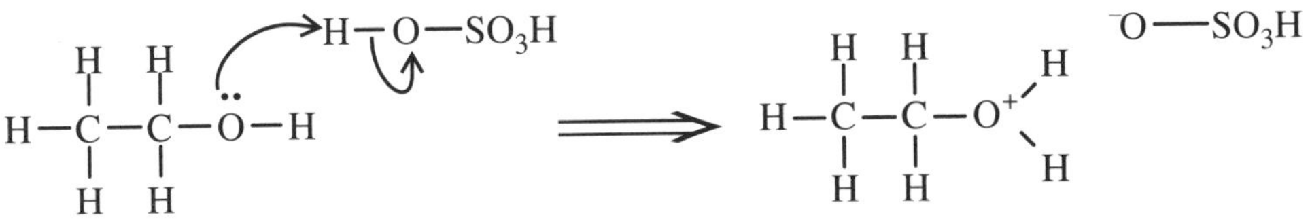

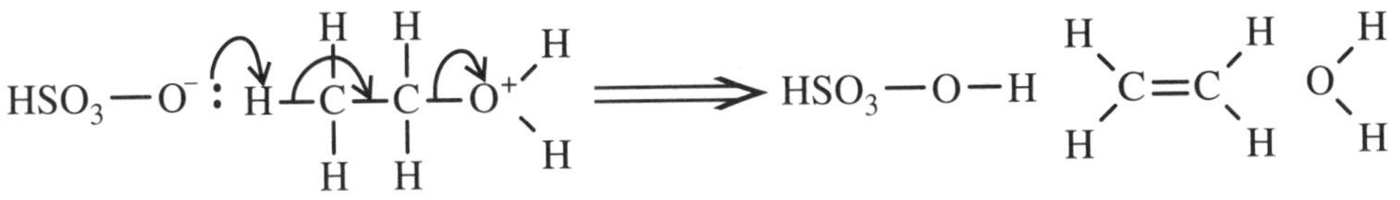

It is interesting to note that the dehydration reaction with sulfuric acid at a slightly lower temperature in the presence of excess ethanol yields ethoxyethane through a nucleophilic substitution reaction (see Section 11.14, page 406):

	Excess H_2SO_4, ~170°C →	$C_2H_4 + H_2O$	(elimination)
C_2H_5OH			
	Excess ethanol, ~140°C →	$\frac{1}{2} C_2H_5OC_2H_5 + \frac{1}{2} H_2O$	(substitution)

Similarly, the reaction of halogenoalkanes with a strong base can yield either the alkene through an elimination reaction at higher temperature or an alcohol through a substitution reaction at lower temperature:

OPTION

$$\text{C}_2\text{H}_5\text{X} \quad \underset{\text{Dilute aqueous OH}^- \text{ at } \sim 60°\text{C}}{\overset{\text{Conc. alcoholic OH}^- \text{ at } \sim 100°\text{C}}{\rightleftharpoons}} \quad \begin{array}{l} \text{C}_2\text{H}_4 + \text{H}^+ + \text{X}^- \quad \text{(elimination)} \\[1em] \text{C}_2\text{H}_5\text{OH} + \text{X}^- \quad \text{(substitution)} \end{array}$$

In the case of the elimination reaction, the hydroxide ion reacts with the ethanol to produce the ethoxide ion:

$$\text{C}_2\text{H}_5\text{OH} + \text{OH}^- \rightleftharpoons \text{C}_2\text{H}_5\text{O}^- + \text{H}_2\text{O}$$

This is a stronger base and weaker nucleophile than the hydroxide ion and so favours the elimination reaction, as does the higher temperature and concentration. The ethoxide ion acts as a base and removes the hydrogen ion from the carbon next to the halogen:

The overall reaction is therefore the elimination of HBr from the bromoalkane. Note that if the halogen (or hydroxyl group) is in the middle, rather than at the end of the hydrocarbon chain then the elimination can occur in more than one direction, hence a mixture of products may result.

NUCLEOPHILIC SUBSTITUTION REACTIONS

H.6.1 Outline how the relative rate of nucleophilic substitution is affected by different nucleophiles.

Consider, for example, the relative rate of reaction using hydroxide or water (polarity differences).

H.6.2 Describe and explain inductive and steric effects of substituents on substitution reaction.

H.6.3 Describe and explain the relative rates of hydrolysis of halogenated benzene compounds.

Compare the inertness of halogenated benzene compounds towards substitution relative to halogenoalkanes. Cross reference with 20.3. © IBO 2001

Nucleophilic substitution reactions can occur by either an S_N1 or an S_N2 mechanism (see Section 11.8, page 386). Which mechanism operates depends on a number of factors relating to the nature of the halogenoalkane, the nucleophile and the solvent.

S_N1 reactions involve the formation of an intermediate carbocation. This mechanism is only likely to occur under circumstances where this carbocation is stable. Generally polar solvents, such as water, will hydrate ions and stabilise them so favouring an S_N1 reaction, whereas non–polar solvents will favour an S_N2 mechanism. Tertiary carbocations are more stable than primary carbocations owing to the inductive effect of the alkyl groups (see page 398). This means that an S_N1 mechanism is more likely to occur if the reaction involves a tertiary halogenoalkane. Finally the bond angle in tetravalent carbon is $109\frac{1}{2}°$ whilst that in the trigonal planar carbocation is $120°$. This means that if the halogenoalkane has a large halogen (i.e. I) and/or bulky substituents resulting in steric stress, then an S_N1 mechanism which goes via the formation of a less stressed carbocation, is likely to occur. Changes in the nature of the nucleophile do not affect the rates of S_N1 reactions because they are not involved until after the rate determining step.

In contrast to S_N1 reactions, the rates at which S_N2 reactions occur depend also on the nature of the nucleophile. The greater the charge on the atom that acts as the nucleophile, the greater the rate at which nucleophilic attack occurs (e.g. reactions occur more rapidly with the hydroxide ion than they do with water) and the more likely the reaction is to occur by an S_N2 mechanism. The attack by the nucleophile occurs at the opposite side of the carbon to the carbon–halogen bond. If the other groups attached to the carbon atom block nucleophilic attack from this side, then the reaction will be slow. If these are alkyl groups, then they will also have the effect of stabilising the carbocation (see above), so that an S_N1 reaction is more likely to occur. These effects are summarised in Table 11.8 below:

Table 11.8 – Factors affecting the mechanism of nucleophilic substitution reactions

Favouring S_N1	Favouring S_N2
Polar solvent	Non–polar solvent
Tertiary halogenoalkane	Primary halogenoalkane
Bulky substituents	No bulky substituents
Weak nucleophile	Strong nucleophile

It is therefore found that an S_N1 mechanism would be likely for the hydrolysis of $(CH_3)_3C\text{-}I$ in water, whereas an S_N2 mechanism would probably occur in the reaction of CH_3Cl with alkali in a less polar solvent.

Attack on a halogenoalkane is from the opposite side to the carbon-hydrogen bond. This means that if the halogenoalkane is optically active (see page 372). then the product is also optically active (but inverted). If it is an S_N1 mechanism then, because the reaction goes via a planar carbocation, which can be attacked from above or below, a racemic mixture results.

In contrast to halogenoalkanes, halogenated benzene derivatives, in which the halogen is attached directly to the benzene ring $\left(\text{e.g. } \langle\bigcirc\rangle\text{-Cl}\right)$, are very resistant to nucleophilic substitution. This is the result of three factors:

- The charge on the carbon atom that is attached to the halogen is much reduced by distortion of the delocalised π–bond.

- Attack of the carbon atom from the side opposite to the carbon–halogen bond, is blocked by the presence of the benzene ring.

- The p–electrons on the halogen interact with the π–bond of the benzene ring to produce a carbon-halogen bond that is stronger than the usual bond.

If the halogen is not directly attached to the benzene ring (e.g. C_6H_5–CH_2–Cl), then the reactivity is similar to halogenoalkanes. Early insecticides, such as DDT, contained chlorine atoms directly bonded on to a benzene ring and their resistance to substitution reactions is part of the reason why they are so persistent in the environment.

NUCLEOPHILIC ADDITION REACTIONS

H.5.1 Describe and explain the mechanism for the addition of hydrogen cyanide to aldehydes and ketones, followed by hydrolysis to give carboxylic acids.

The carbonyl group, found in aldehydes and ketones, is quite polar with the carbon atom being the positive end of the dipole. This carbon atom is therefore susceptible to nucleophilic attack and through this addition to the carbon–oxygen double bond occurs. A nucleophile is a molecule or ion that has a lone pair of electrons that it can use to form a new bond to a centre of positive charge.

A good example of this type of reaction is the addition of hydrogen cyanide to the carbonyl group. This reaction requires a base catalyst to convert the hydrogen cyanide into the more nucleophilic cyanide ion:

$$HCN + OH^- \rightleftharpoons CN^- + H_2O$$

The cyanide ion then acts as a nucleophile and attacks the carbonyl carbon to produce an intermediate anion. This reacts with the water present to generate the hydroxynitrile product (also known as a cyanohydrin) and regenerate the base catalyst:

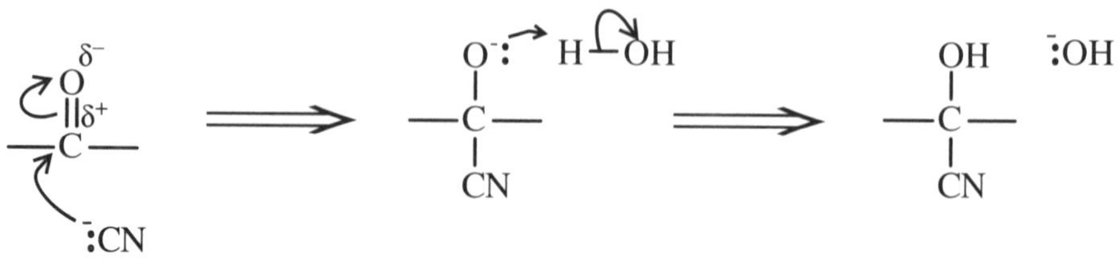

The hydroxynitrile can be hydrolysed by refluxing with either dilute acid or dilute alkali to produce ammonia (or an ammonium salt) and a carboxylic acid (or its anion). This acid contains one more carbon atom than the original aldehyde or ketone and so this is a means of lengthening the carbon chain:

$$\text{HO}-\overset{|}{\underset{|}{\text{C}}}-\text{C}\equiv\text{N} \quad + \quad \text{H}_3\text{O}^+ \Longrightarrow \text{HO}-\overset{|}{\underset{|}{\text{C}}}-\overset{\text{O}}{\overset{\|}{\text{C}}}-\text{OH} \ + \ \text{NH}_4^+ \quad \text{(Acid catalyst)}$$

$$+ \quad \text{OH}^- \Longrightarrow \text{HO}-\overset{|}{\underset{|}{\text{C}}}-\overset{\text{O}}{\overset{\|}{\text{C}}}-\text{O}^- \ + \ \text{NH}_3 \quad \text{(Base catalyst)}$$

NUCLEOPHILIC ADDITION–ELIMINATION REACTIONS

H.8.1   Describe and explain the reactions of 2,4-dinitrophenylhydrazine with aldehydes and ketones.

A detailed mechanism is not required.   © IBO 2001

With some nucleophiles that have a hydrogen atom attached to the same atom that acts as the nucleophile, the initial product can eliminate water (hence they are sometimes called condensation reactions) to reform the double bond resulting in an addition–elimination reaction. The most common reaction of this type is that which occurs between carbonyl compounds and 2.4–dinitrophenylhydrazine (2.4DNP). In this a lone pair on the terminal nitrogen acts as the nucleophile and an addition reaction occurs by a mechanism similar to that given above, followed by the gain and loss of hydrogen ions, to form the intermediate. This then eliminates a hydrogen ion and a hydroxide ion (i.e. H$_2$O) to give the final product.

n.b. In this stage a hydrogen ion is lost by the nitrogen and gained by the oxygen

This final product is an orange–yellow crystalline solid. Its formation is used as a test for aldehydes and ketones. The sharp melting point of these crystalline derivatives was formerly used to identify the aldehyde or ketone that they were formed from.

EXERCISE 11.10

The questions in this exercise are on a broad range of topics in organic chemistry. They have been organised according to the level required.

Questions on the subject specific core.

1. Which one of the following compounds would you expect to have the highest boiling point?

   A $CH_3 – CH_2 – CH_3$
   B $CH_3 – CH_2 – Cl$
   C $CH_3 – OH$
   D $CH_3 – COOH$

2. Which one of the following turns acidified potassium dichromate from orange to green?

   A $CH_3 – CH_2 – OH$
   B C_6H_{14}
   C $CH_3 – COOH$
   D $CH_3 – CH_2 – CH_2Br$

3. Which one of the following does **not** have any isomers?

   A $CH_3 – CHBr – CH_3$
   B $CH_3 – O – CH_3$
   C $CH_3 – CH_2 – CH_3$
   D $H – CO – O – CH_3$

4. You have four colourless liquids that you know are hexane, hexene, ethanol and ethanoic acid. Describe how you would identify these using bromine water and litmus paper.

5. Write the full structural formula of the organic product of the following reactions.

   a)   Adding excess bromine to ethene.
   b)   Reacting ethanoic acid with sodium hydroxide.
   c)   Heating ethanol with ethanoic acid and a little concentrated sulfuric acid.
   d)   Passing ethene and steam over a heated catalyst at high pressure.
   e)   Heating ethanol with acidified potassium dichromate solution.

6. Questions a) to g) refer the the following compounds:

   A $CH_3 – CH_2 – CO – OH$ **B** $CH_3 – CH(CH_3) – CH_3$

   C $C_2H_5 – (CH_2)_2 – OH$ **D** $C_2H_5 – C_2H_5$

   E $CH_2 = CH – CH_3$ **F** $CH_3 – O – CO – CH_2 – CH_3$

   G $CH_3 – CH_2 – CH_2 – CH_2 – O – H$

a) Write the names of compounds A, B, D and E.

b) Which two formulae are different ways of writing the same compound? What is the name of this compound?

c) Which two compounds are isomers of each other? What is the molecular formulae of these compounds?

d) Which compound would decolourise bromine water? Draw the structural formula of the product of this reaction.

e) Which compound would turn moist blue litmus paper red? Explain this behaviour.

f) Compound F can be prepared from one of the other compounds.

    i) Which compound is this?

    ii) What organic compound must be reacted with it?

    iii) What other compound must be present for the reaction to occur?

    iv) What is the name of compound F?

    v) What characteristic would this substance have?

g) Draw an isomer of compound G and name this compound.

7. Write balanced equations for reactions that could be used to produce the compounds below from ethanol giving the reagents and essential conditions required for the reaction:

a) Ethyl ethanoate.

b) Ethanoic acid

c) Ethene.

Questions on Advanced Higher level material and Option A

8. Describe a simple chemical test, i.e. a test tube reaction with clearly visible results, that you could use to differentiate between the pairs of compounds below. In each case give the reagent and the reaction with **both** compounds:

a) Hexene and hexane.

b) Butylamine and ethanamide.

c) 2–methylpropan–1–ol and 2–methylpropan–2–ol.

9. Write balanced equations for the following reactions, giving structural formulae of the organic products:

a) Propanoic acid and methanol.

b) But–1–ene and hydrogen chloride.

Questions on Option H material

10. Which one of the following would make an S_N2 mechanism more likely?

  A   Bulky substituents near the halogen.
  B   A polar solvent.
  C   A tertiary carbocation intermediate.
  D   A reactive nucleophile.

11.

$$CH_3-CH_2-CH_2-\overset{\overset{\textstyle O}{\|}}{C}-H \qquad \text{'X'}$$

  a)   The molecule X above contains a carbonyl group
      i   Identify the carbonyl group.
      ii   Indicate the polarity of the carbonyl group on your drawing.
      iii   What type of attack is the molecule susceptible to as a result of this?
  b)   A number of isomers of compound X exist. Draw the structural formula for, and name, one isomer that could be easily oxidised and one that would not.
  c)   Compound X can be converted to compound Y

$$CH_3-CH_2-CH_2-\overset{\overset{\textstyle O}{\|}}{C}-OH \qquad \text{'Y'}$$

      i   Give one **chemical** test that you could use to distinguish X and Y, stating the result that you would expect in each case.
      ii   Name the reagents would you use to convert X into Y?

12. Describe how altering the conditions can affect the major product of the reaction of:

  a)   ethanol with acidified sodium dichromate(VI).
  b)   bromobutane with potassium hydroxide.

13. Methylpropene can react with hydrogen bromide to produce two isomeric bromoalkanes.

  a)   Draw the structural formulae of the two possible products and state which you would expect to predominate.
  b)   These bromoalkanes can be hydrolysed to give two different alcohols
      i   What reagent and conditions are required for this?
      ii   Give the names of the two alcohols and state whether they are primary, secondary or tertiary alcohols.

14. For each of the following mechanisms, give the balanced equation for a specific example of a reaction that occurs by each mechanism, and then draw the mechanism for the reaction.

Electrophilic addition   Nucleophilic addition
Nucleophilic substitution   Nucleophilic addition–elimination

15. Write the structural formula of the major product from each of the following reactions:

a)   Reacting butan–2–ol with acidified potassium dichromate.
b)   Warming propanal with 2,4–dinitrophenylhydrazine solution.
c)   Heating propan–2–ol and ethanoic acid with a little conc. sulfuric acid.
d)   Refluxing methanol with excess acidified sodium dichromate. (Think carefully!)

16. What would be **seen** in each of the following reactions?

a)   Adding magnesium hydroxide to aqueous ethanoic acid.
b)   Adding 2,4–dinitrophenylhydrazine solution to propanone.
c)   Warming ethanol with acidified potassium permanganate.

17. How could you differentiate between the members of the following pairs using a simple chemical test? In each case give the reagent and state the result that you would expect in **both** cases.

a)   Ethanol and ethanoic acid.
b)   Propanal and propanone.
c)   Butanal and butan–1–ol.
d)   Butanone and butanoic acid.
e)   Hexan–1–ol and cyclohexene.

18. Explain why ethanol is neutral, phenol a very weak acid, ethanoic acid a weak acid, and trichloroethanoic acid a quite strong acid.

19. The hydration of propene to produce propan–2–ol is reversible. Discuss, in terms of Le Chatelier's principle, how the reaction conditions can be varied to favour the forward or reverse reaction. Why is the major product propan–2–ol rather than propan–1–ol?

OPTION

20. 1–Chlorobutane can react with sodium hydroxide to give **two** very different products. Write equations for the two reactions, giving the names and structural formulae of the products. How would you alter the conditions so as to select one or other as the major product?

21. Explain why:

a)   A solution of methylamine in water has a pH ~11.

b)   Chloropropane is almost immiscible with water.

c)   Ethanamide is a crystalline solid

22. 2-hydroxypropanoic acid may be prepared from ethanal by a two stage process via an intermediate compound (X).

a)   Draw the stuctural formulae of these two compounds.

b)   Draw the structure of the probable intermediate (X).

c)   Give the reagents and conditions required to convert ethanal into X.

d)   Outline the mechanism of this reaction.

e)   Give the reagents and conditions required to convert X into hydroxypropanoic acid.

f)   Hydroxypropanoic acid can exist as a pair of enantiomers. Explain why this is and draw diagrams to illustrate how the enantiomers differ.

g)   What is meant by 'optical activity' and how is this related to enantiomers.

h)   In view of this why is the hydroxypropanoic acid produced in the above process optically inactive. Explain in terms of your answer to (d) why this occurs.

MEDICINES AND DRUGS (Option B)

PUBLISHER'S NOTE
This chapter gives general information about drugs. The dosages described are examples only and are not to be interpreted as in an way definitive instructions about medicinal use.

All drugs have dangers and should only be used under the supervision of properly qualified professionals and according to the laws of the country you are in at the time.

12

Chapter contents

The aim of this option is to give students an understanding of how drugs and medicines can influence the functioning of the body. Students should be able to recognize the fundamental structures and relevant functional groups of several classes of drugs and medicines (as listed below or in 11.3.1), and should be able to distinguish between them. Memorizing of complex formulas is not required. Throughout the option, stress the contribution that science has made (and continues to make) toward maintaining and improving the health and well-being of the world's population   © IBO 2001

12.1 PHARMACEUTICAL PRODUCTS

B.1.1   List the effects of drugs and medicines.

Generally a drug or medicine is any chemical which does one or more of the following: alters incoming sensory sensations; alters mood or emotions; alters physiological state, including consciousness, activity level or coordination. Stress the importance of the body's natural healing processes and the placebo effect.

© IBO 2001

The treatment of diseases by use of chemicals is called **chemotherapy**. A **drug** may be defined as any substance used for its effects on bodily processes and is often defined as any substance taken to change the way in which the body or the mind functions. The definitions of drugs and medicines varies across cultures. In some countries the terms drug and medicine are interchangeable. In others drugs are considered harmful and medicines beneficial, though the terms harmful and benficial are open to debate. Generally a drug or medicine is any chemical which does one or more of the following:

- alters incoming sensory sensations

- alters mood or emotions

- alters physiological state, including consciousness, activity level or co-ordination.

Drugs:
- may or may not come from doctors or drug stores/pharmacies

- may or may not have beneficial medicinal properties

- may come from plants or fungi or may be manufactured in laboratories

- can be legal or illegal,

- can be helpful or harmful.

Drugs are divided into categories depending on their effects. These include infection fighters (antiseptics, antibiotics, antivirals), those affecting body chemistry or metabolism (hormones, vitamins), and those affecting the central nervous system (CNS) including the brain (stimulants, depressants, analgesics, anaesthetics).

PLACEBO EFFECT

This refers to a pharmacologically inert substance that produces a significant reaction because of what an individual expects, desires or was told would happen.

A placebo is an inert substance used as a control in an experiment, or given to patients for its probable beneficial effects (i.e. a 'fake' therapy without any side effects). Why a 'sugar pill' should be effective is not completely known, but does suggest the importance of the body's natural healing processes. The word placebo comes from the Latin "to please". Researchers have found asthmatics dilated their own airways when told they were inhaling asthma medicine. The action of placebos implies the power of suggestion, and some believe the placebo effect to be psychological, namely what counts is the reality present in the brain.

OPTION

B.1.2   Outline the stages involved in research, development and testing of new
pharmaceutical products.

*Refer to the Thalidomide case as an example of what can go wrong. The use of
combinatorial chemistry is not required here, but is covered in B.8.4.*   © IBO 2001

RESEARCH, DEVELOPMENT AND TESTING OF NEW DRUGS

This is a lengthy, very costly process which is rigidly controlled by governments in
many countries. In most countries, drugs must be subjected to thorough laboratory and
clinical studies that demonstrate their usefulness and safety. Before studies on humans
are permitted, the drugs are extensively tested on animals and cell cultures. These
include establishment of the range of effective doses, the doses at which side effects
occur and the lethal doses in various animals. Because of differences between species of
animals, at least 3 different species are tested. If a drug is found to be safe when given to
animals, it may be taken to initial clinical trials (phase 1) on volunteers as well as on
patients, aimed at establishing the drug's safety, dose range, and possible problems for
further study. If phase 1 indicates safety, a drug is subjected to thorough clinical
evaluation (phase 2) to eliminate variables such as response and investigator bias.
Statistical validation is critical at this stage. Finally if the drug looks promising, it enters
human studies with extended clinical evaluation (phase 3). Most new drugs never get
approval for marketing! Most drugs on the legitimate market have reasonable risk/
benefit ratios. No drug is completely without risk, but most legal drugs should be
relatively safe.

In 1970, 3620 drugs were tested, 16 came on the market at a cost of $20 million each and
after a six year approval period. In September, 1991, a drug approved for marketing in
the USA was estimated to cost $200 million! According to *New Scientist* (INSIDE
SCIENCE, #65, 16 October 1993, p1) "Bringing a new drug onto the market is a gamble
– it takes on the average 12 years of research and development, and an investment of
£125 million. Fewer than five out of ten thousand potential medicines ever reach a
hospital or chemists' shops".

Thalidomide is an example of what can go wrong. It was marketed outside North
America in the late 1950s and early 60s. It was first introduced in (the then West)
Germany in 1957, and was prescribed to pregnant women to treat morning sickness.
However, its use resulted in the birth of thousands of deformed babies because
thalidomide prevented the proper growth of the fetus. Thalidomide is now approved in
several countries including Brazil, Mexico and the US to treat the painful, disfiguring
skin sores associated with leprosy, and to prevent and control the return of these skin
sores. However, the medicine comes with special warnings about the severe birth defects
or death to an unborn baby. Birth defects include babies with no arms and legs, short
arms and legs, missing bones and intestinal abnormalities.

B.1.3   Describe the different methods of administering drugs.

The four main methods are oral, rectal, inhalation and parenteral (by injection).
Injections may be intravenous, intramuscular or subcutaneous.   © IBO 2001

OPTION

METHODS OF ADMINISTRATION

Transporting a drug into the body is a complex process. Administration of a drug involves introducing a drug into the blood stream. The entire blood volume (approximately 6 litres) circulates in the body about once a minute and drugs are fairly evenly distributed throughout the blood. There are several ways of administering a drug - each has advantages and disadvantages. Also, different effects can be seen depending on the route of administration. The four main methods are: oral, rectal, inhalation and parenteral (by injection).

1. Oral, i.e. by mouth:

This is very convenient. However the effect is variable since the rate of absorption is influenced by, for example, drug concentration and stomach content. Absorption takes place along the entire gastrointestinal tract from the mouth to the intestine. The percentage absorption of a drug in the stomach is generally small, except for alcohol, about one third of which is is absorbed. For most drugs taken orally, the **primary site of absorption** is the small intestines which are also the site of absorption of digested food. A drug that is difficult to dissolve will be absorbed slowly. **Time release capsules** have various coatings to ensure gradual release of the drug over time. The form in which a drug is available, as a tablet or in liquid form, and whether it is taken on an empty stomach or with food determines the rate at which the drug is absorbed.

2. Rectal, i.e. via the rectum:

This method of administration is very effective when patients experience nausea or vomiting or are unable to take medicine orally before or after surgery. Drugs that are pH sensitive and which may be destroyed by the stomach's acidity may be delivered rectally. A drug capable of systemic effect - one that affects any part of the body – can be inserted into the rectum in the form of suppositories. The drug is then absorbed into the bloodstream. Suppositories for the relief of haemorrhoids (enlarged and painful blood vessels in or around the anus) are used for local effect.

3. Inhalation, i.e. breathing in:

Administration is rapid because of the extensive network of blood vessels in the lungs. Drugs can be administered by this route to produce a systemic effect (such as general anaesthesia) in which the drug is absorbed into the blood stream to produce an effect in the brain and the whole body. Patients suffering from asthma achieve quick relief from the use of drugs such as Ventolin™ that dilate the respiratory tract.

4. Parenteral, i.e. by injection:

a.   Beneath the skin (subcutaneous route): Drug absorption is slower than intravenous (directly into a vein). Dental injections are often subcutaneous. The method is also common with illegal drug users.

b.   Into muscles (intra-muscular): For use when immediate response is not required or when a large volume of drug needs to be injected. The method is relatively safe and easy provided a blood vessel is not accidentally penetrated. Many vaccination injections e.g. for overseas travel, are intra-muscular.

c.   Directly into the blood stream (intravenous). This is the most practical; the drug is introduced by injection into a vein and distributed around the body within about a minute, so the effect is virtually instantaneous. An advantage is that it is possible to administer precise amounts of drug since concentration is not affected by stomach acid or content. However, once administered, the drug cannot be retrieved as it can (to some extent) with oral administration.

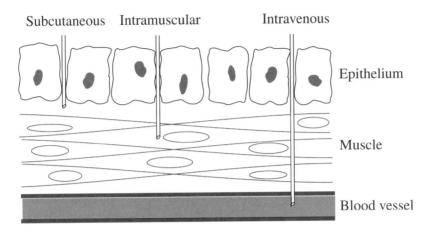

Except for intravenous injections, a drug must be transported across the blood vessels, which contain a fatty or lipid layer. Drugs which dissolve readily in fats are therefore more easily absorbed. Drugs can be absorbed into the blood stream from a region of high to low drug concentration, by osmosis. The capillaries of the brain are denser and prevent diffusion of many substances into the neurons of the brain - this is called the blood-brain barrier and is very important. For example, penicillins do not pass this barrier. This is fortunate since they cause convulsions if injected directly into the brain. Psychoactive drugs have to pass into the brain as these drugs alter behaviour or change consciousness.

Termination of a drug's action takes place when it is broken down by the liver and eliminated by the kidneys. **Half-life** is the time required for half the drug to be eliminated. For example, the half life of cocaine is a few minutes, but marijuana can be detected up to 28 days after use - it is absorbed by fatty tissue and bound to it making diffusion into the blood stream a very slow process.

B.1.4   Discuss the terms lethal dosage (LD_{50}), tolerance, and side effects.

LD_{50} is the lethal dose required for 50% of the population.

A person who develops tolerance requires a larger dose of the drug in order to achieve the effect originally obtained by a smaller dose. Stress that the difference between the main effect and side effects is relative. For example, morphine is often used as a pain killer with intestinal constipation being a side effect. For a person with diarrhoea the constipation induced becomes the main effect, with the pain relief a side effect. The risk:benefit ratio should be considered.

OPTION

A toxic substance (poison) is a chemical that is dangerous or causes illness or death (lethal effect) in small amounts. An example is the nerve gas sarin used in the Tokyo subway incident which was found to be extremely toxic in minute quantities. Substances such as nicotine can be moderately toxic to animals, whereas water is considered almost completely non-toxic. The lethal dose for a toxic substance varies from chemical to chemical and from one individual and/or species to another. Thus, lethal doses of poisons are expressed as milligrams of toxic substance per kilogram of body mass of the animal.

An LD_{50} (lethal dose in 50% of the population) value is used to indicate the dose of a given toxic substance in mg per kg body mass that kills 50% of the laboratory animals under study such as rats, mice and guinea pigs. The smaller the value of LD_{50}, the more toxic the substance. Since different species react differently to various poisons, any application of such data based on animal studies to human beings must be used with caution. Thus, studies are often carried out with different animals before such extrapolation is made. Dosage is an important principle of toxicology.

On the basis of such studies, heroin has a LD_{50} of between 1 and 5 mg/kg. This means that a 75 to 375 mg dose of heroin will be fatal to 50% of average people weighing 75 kg.

Examples of approximate LD_{50} values

Toxic Substance	LD_{50} (mg substance/kg body mass)	Degree of toxicity
Botulism toxin	<0.01	Extremely toxic
Potassium cyanide	between 1 and 5	Highly toxic
Morphine	between 5 and 50	Highly toxic
Aspirin, sulfuric acid	between 50 and 500	Toxic
Amphetamine, nicotine	between 500 and 5000	Moderately toxic
Ethanol, soap	between 5000 and 15000	Slightly toxic

The degree of toxicity is sometimes defined as the mass of substance required for a lethal dose, but this tends to vary between countries. Drugs can be considered hazardous when they pose risks to the physical, mental, or social well-being of the user.

Dependence
Some people use drugs because they have become physically or psychologically dependent on them. When an individual continues to use a certain drug because s/he does not feel 'right' without it, that person can be said to be drug-dependent.

Physical Dependence
Physical dependence occurs when a drug user's body becomes so accustomed to a drug

that it can only function normally if the drug is present. Without the drug, the user may experience a variety of physical symptoms ranging from mild discomfort to convulsions. These symptoms, some of which can be fatal, are referred to as 'withdrawal'. Not all drugs produce physical dependence. Physical dependence is a form of drug addiction. For example, long term use of opiates can lead to physical dependence.

Psychological Dependence

Psychological dependence exists when a drug is so central to a person's thoughts, emotions, and activities that it is extremely difficult to stop using it, or even stop thinking about it. Psychological dependence is marked by an intense craving for the drug and its effects. Like physical dependence, psychological dependence is a form of drug addiction (see Sctions B.3.4, page 423 and B.4.2, page 427).

Tolerance

Tolerance means that, over time and with regular use, a user needs increasing amounts of a drug to get the same physiological effect. For example, long term use of opiates can lead to tolerance. Tolerance increases the health hazards of any drug simply because the amount taken increases over time. Tolerance also increases the risk of dangerous fatal overdose for two reasons:

*   Firstly, with some drugs, the body does not necessarily develop tolerance to the harmful effects of the drug. Long-term barbiturate users, for example, become tolerant to the drug's sedative effect, but not to its side effect on breathing. If the drug is used for too long a time, the dose people need to fall asleep or calm their nerves may be more than enough to stop their breathing.

*   Secondly, if a drug user has not taken the drug in a long time, the expected tolerance may actually have decreased. So after a long period of abstinence, the size of dose the user had previously become accustomed to may actually be enough to cause an overdose.

Drug Side Effects

The desired effect of a drug is considered to be the **main effect**; the unwanted responses are considered **side effects**. This happens because no drug exerts a single effect; usually several different body functions are altered. To achieve the main effect, the side effects must be tolerated which is possible if they are minor but may be limiting if they are more serious. The distinction between main and side effects is relative and depends on the purpose of the drug, e.g. morphine. If pain relieving properties are sought, the intestinal constipation induced is an undesirable side effect. However, it may also be used to treat diarrhoea, so constipation induced is the main effect and any relief of pain is a side effect.

No drug is free of toxic effects, often these may be trivial but can also be serious. Allergies to drugs may take many forms from mild skin rashes to fatal shock caused by such drugs as penicillin. Because drugs are concentrated, metabolized and excreted by the liver and kidney, damage to these is not uncommon, e.g. alcohol causes liver damage and the thalidomide tragedy dramatically illustrated that drugs may adversely influence fetal development.

OPTION

12.2 ANTACIDS

B.2.1 State and explain how excess acidity in the stomach can be reduced by the use of different bases.

Examples should include aluminium and magnesium compounds and sodium hydrogencarbonate. Students should be able to write balanced equations for neutralisation reactions and know that antacids are often combined with alginates (which produce a neutralising layer preventing acid in the stomach from rising into the oesophagus and causing heartburn), and with anti-foaming agents (such as dimethicone). © IBO 2001

Antacids are bases, usually, metal oxides, hydroxides, carbonates or hydrogen carbonates (bicarbonates) that react with excess acid in the stomach to adjust the stomach pH to the desired level. Thus an antacid is a remedy for excess stomach acid.

The walls of the human stomach contain cells that secrete hydrochloric acid. The purposes of this acidic solution are:
- to suppress growth of harmful bacteria, and
- to help in digestion by hydrolysing proteins to amino acids. Over-eating or stress (worrying) stimulates excess production, causing discomfort. (Note that normal pH of gastric juice is in the 1.2 - 0.3 range).

Antacids neutralise excess stomach acid, and thus relieve discomfort. Excess acid can eventually eat away the protective mucus layer that lines the stomach, causing painful ulcers. The active ingredients in 'over-the-counter' antacids include aluminium hydroxide $Al(OH)_3$, magnesium hydroxide $Mg(OH)_2$, calcium carbonate $CaCO_3$, and sodium hydrogen carbonate $NaHCO_3$. The antacids are often combined with chemicals called **alginates** (extracted primarily from brown seaweeds) that produce a neutralising layer that prevents acid reflux. That is, they prevent acid in the stomach from rising into the oesophagus and causing 'heartburn'. Similarly anti–foaming agents such as dimethicone are added that reduce the surface tension of gas bubbles, causing them to coalesce (come together), producing a defoaming action.

Active ingredients of some commercial antacids

Tums: $CaCO_3$, $MgCO_3$, $MgSi_3O_8$ (magnesium trisilicate) for the treatment of ulcers and gastritis.

Rotaids: $AlNa(OH)_2CO_3$.

Malox: $Mg(OH)_2$, $Al(OH)_3$.

Alka Seltzer $NaHCO_3$, citric acid, aspirin. The solid hydrogen carbonate and citric acid react in water ('pop pop fizz fizz') to release carbon dioxide which induces belching and aids in the removal of swollen air in the stomach, thus relieving dicomfort.

Milk of Magnesia $Mg(OH)_2$ (or $MgO/Mg(OH)_2$ mixture).

Amphogel: $Al(OH)_3$.

Di-Gel: $CaCO_3$.

ACTION OF ANTACIDS

1. Magnesium oxide

$$MgO_{(s)} + 2\,HCl_{(aq)} \Rightarrow MgCl_{2\,(aq)} + H_2O_{(l)}$$

2. Magnesium hydroxide

$$Mg(OH)_{2\,(aq)} + 2\,HCl_{(aq)} \Rightarrow MgCl_{2\,(aq)} + 2\,H_2O_{(l)}$$

3. Aluminium hydroxide

$$Al(OH)_{3\,(s)} + 3\,HCl_{(aq)} \Rightarrow AlCl_{3\,(aq)} + 3\,H_2O_{(l)}$$

4. Calcium carbonate

$$CaCO_{3\,(s)} + 2HCl_{(aq)} \Rightarrow CaCl_{2\,(aq)} + H_2O_{(l)} + CO_{2\,(g)}$$

5. Sodium hydrogen carbonate

$$NaHCO_{3\,(aq)} + HCl_{(aq)} \Rightarrow NaCl_{(aq)} + H_2O_{(l)} + CO_{2\,(g)}$$

6. Magnesium trisilicate

$$Mg_2Si_3O_{8\,(s)} + 4\,HCl_{(aq)} \Rightarrow 3\,SiO_{2\,(s)} + 2\,H_2O_{(l)} + 2\,MgCl_{2\,(aq)}$$

Very low antacid doses barely decrease stomach acidity to normal and high doses carry it too far, causing a basic stomach. This also causes discomfort and is often mistaken as being due to an acidic stomach so one takes more antacid making the stomach still more basic, causing more indigestion. This condition is called **alkalosis**. Indigestion is a term which is often used to describe any form of discomfort, usually abdominal, occurring after meals. One problem with neutralising excess stomach acid is that the body tends to respond by producing more acid.

OPTION

12.3 ANALGESICS

B.3.1   Describe and explain the different ways in which analgesics prevent pain.

Mild analgesics function by intercepting the pain stimulus at the source, often by interfering with the production of substances (e.g. prostaglandins) that cause pain, swelling or fever. Strong analgesics work by temporarily bonding to receptor sites in the brain, preventing the transmission of pain impulses without depressing the central nervous system.

© IBO 2001

Pain has been described as 'an unpleasant sensory and emotional experience associated with actual or potential tissue damage'. **Pain receptors** in our bodies are nerves that transmit pain. These are free nerve endings located in various body tissues that respond to thermal, mechanical and chemical stimuli. When stimulated, these pain receptors generate an impulse. Pain results from interaction between various impulses arriving at the spinal cord and the brain. When tissues become injured, they release chemicals called prostaglandins and leukotrienes that make the pain receptors more sensitive. Sensitized receptors react to even gentle stimuli, causing pain.

Analgesics are drugs that relieve pain. These include:
*   mild analgesics used for relief of mild pain (and frequently fever) – examples include aspirin, acetaminophen (metabolic byproduct of phenacetin) also sold as tylenol, paracetamol, etc. phenacetin, ibuprofen (sold as Actiprofen®, Advil®, MotrinIB®, Medipren® etc), NSAIDS (non-steroidal anti-inflammatory drugs). The mild analgesics are considered non-addictive

*   strong analgesics used for the relief of very severe pain include the narcotics (morphine, heroin and codeine). These are controlled substances that are addictive

*   local anaesthetics (pain killers in localised areas) include lidocaine and procaine used in dentistry

*   general anaesthetics (see Section B.9, page 447).

Mild analgesics, such as aspirin, work by indirectly blocking the enzyme-controlled synthesis of prostaglandins. Among their many effects are the constricting of blood vessels. This helps increase the body temperature because less heat can escape from the tissues into the blood. Prostaglandins also have a direct effect on the body's heat regulating centre (the hypothalamus), which produces fever. These chemicals also increase the permeability of capillaries, allowing water to pass out of the capillaries into nearby tissues, thus causing swelling and pain. By lowering the concentration of prostaglandins, mild analgesics reduce pain, fever and inflammation.

Chemical painkillers such as endorphins and enkephalins are produced naturally in the body. Enkephalins are the natural opiates found in the part of the brain and the spinal cord that transmit pain impulses. These are able to bind to neuro-receptors in the brain and produce relief from pain. The temporary loss of pain immediately after an injury is associated with the production of these chemicals. Similarly the strong analgesics (opiates) work by temporarily binding to the opiate receptor sites in the brain, preventing the transmission of pain impulses without depressing the central nervous system.

B.3.2 Describe the use of derivatives of salicylic acid as mild analgesics and compare the advantages and disadvantages of using aspirin and paracetamol (acetaminophen).

Aspirin has been found to be useful in preventing the reccurrence of heart attacks. The disadvantages of aspirin include ulceration and stomach bleeding, allergic reactions and Reye's syndrome in children (a potentially fatal liver and brain disorder). Paracetamol is very safe in the correct dose but can, rarely, cause blood disorders and kidney damage. Overdosage can lead to serious liver damage, brain damage and even death. © IBO 2001

In the past salicylic acid was widely used as a fever reducer (**anti-pyretic drug**) and pain killer (**mild analgesic**). However, salicylic acid is a relatively strong acid so it was unpleasant to take orally and it damaged the membranes lining the mouth, oesphagus and stomach. Thus salicylic acid was chemically modified to overcome these two negative effects of its use. Initially, sodium salicylate, a salt of salicylic acid was used. This is less unpleasant to take by mouth but is, again, highly irritating to the stomach lining where it is changed to salicylic acid. However, the acetate (ethanoate) ester of salicylic acid, called Acetyl Salicylic Acid (ASA) named Aspirin retains the beneficial properties of salicylic acid but is less irritating to the stomach. Addition of the acetyl group reduces the acidity sufficiently to make it relatively non-irritating. Because ASA is relatively tasteless, it can be taken orally. This type of research where a drug is chemically altered to minimise side effects but retain beneficial properties is very common in the modern drug industry.

ASA reacts with water in a hydrolysis reaction to form salicylic acid only after reaching the alkaline (basic) conditions in the small intestines:

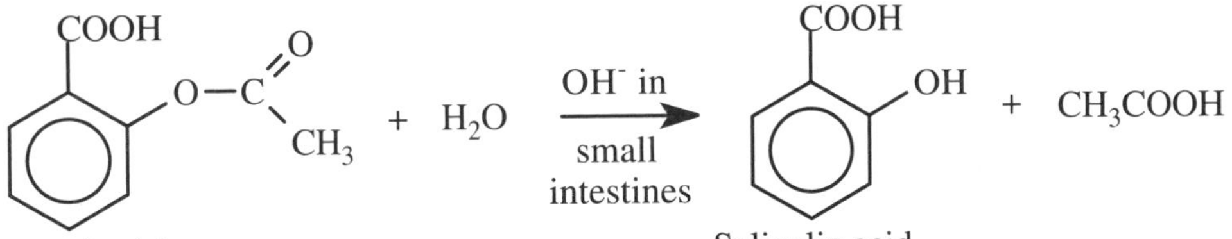

ASA is called a **prodrug** – a less active form of the drug that is converted to the active form sometime after administration. Sometimes it is sold as the sodium salt of ASA for example, in Alka Seltzer®. The sodium salt is ionic and rapidly dissolves in water.

Derivatives of salicylic acid

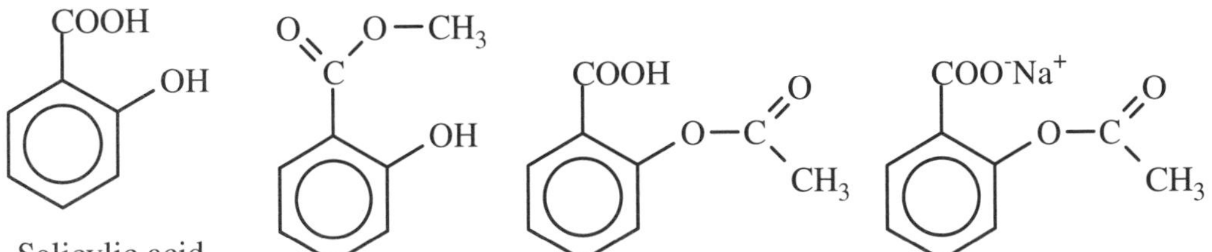

The presence of the carboxylic acid (-COOH) and the hydroxyl group (-OH) on the benzene ring makes salicylic acid a relatively strong acid. Only the sodium salt of ASA is water soluble due to the presence of ionic bonding, the others are virtually insoluble due to the presence of the aromatic ring (and no ionic bonding).

Uses of the derivatives of salicylic acid:
- as a mild analgesic for minor aches and pains, to relieve headaches, sunburn pain and the pain of arthritis.

- as an antipyretic to reduce fever.

- as an anti-inflammatory agent when there is swelling from injuries.

- as an anti-platelet agent in the prevention of abnormal blood clotting and as an anti clotting agent after heart surgery. Aspirin's anti-clotting ability results from the fact that it inhibits the production of prostaglandins. These are hormone–like fatty acids that cause blood platelets to stick together and clot. Moderate doses of ASA have been found to be useful in preventing the recurrence of heart attacks. It has thus been called a 'miracle drug' by heart disease patients.

Disadvantages of aspirin:
- due to its acidic nature in aqueous solution, aspirin can cause stomach upset and internal bleeding; it can cause ulceration and aggravate existing peptic ulcers,

- there is a risk of developing severe gastrointestinal bleeding following use of alcohol,

- about 0.5% who take aspirin (and 3-5% asthmatics) are allergic to aspirin leading to skin rashes, respiratory difficulty, and even shock,

- aspirin is one of the most frequent causes of accidental poisoning in infants.

A large scale study showed there is a small but significant correlation between the use of aspirin and the development of Reye's syndrome in children who took ASA for chicken pox or flu-like symptoms. Reye's syndrome is a potentially fatal liver and brain disorder that can result in coma, brain damage and death.

ASPIRIN SUBSTITUTES
As a result of allergic reactions to aspirin, or for people who experience upset stomachs, substitutes exist. These include phenacetin and acetaminophen (called paracetamol in some countries).

Phenacetin

Acetaminophen

Acetaminophen is the metabolic byproduct of phenacetin and is the active ingredient of many over-the-counter (OTC) drugs.

Uses of acetaminophen

- like aspirin it is an anti-pyretic and reduces fever
- as an analgesic to reduce mild pain.

Unlike aspirin, acetaminophen does not upset the stomach or cause bleeding. It is not, however, an effective anti-inflammatory drug. It is a very safe drug when used in the correct dose but can, very rarely, cause side effects such as blood disorders and kidney damage. An over dose (>20 tablets) can cause serious liver damage, brain damage, coma and even death.

Ibuprofen has many of the same effects as aspirin but seems to cause fewer stomach problems. Unlike acetaminophen, it is an anti-inflammatory drug. It is effective in low doses and has a wide margin of safety. Besides being implicated in kidney problems in large doses, its other side effects are similar to those of ASA.

B.3.3   Compare the structures of morphine, codeine and the semi-synthetic opiate heroin.

Stress the simple modification to the structure of morphine which results in the semi-synthetic drug, heroin.

B.3.4   Discuss the advantages and disadvantages of using morphine and its derivatives as strong analgesics.

Include the social effects as well as physiological effects of both short- and long-term use.   © IBO 2001

STRONG ANALGESICS

The opium alkaloids - morphine, heroin and codeine.
These are refered to as 'opiates', 'narcotics' or 'narcotic analgesics'. The term 'opiate' refers to any natural or synthetic drug that exerts actions on the body similar to those induced by morphine – the major pain relieving substance obtained from the seeds of the opium poppy plant. 'Narcotic' is a term generally used for drugs that have both a narcotic (sleep inducing) and analgesic (pain relieving) action.

Morphine is the principal alkaloid and makes up about 10% by mass of raw opium. Codeine is about 0.5% by mass of raw opium. Heroin does exist in raw opium but is usually synthesised from morphine; heroin is thus a semi-synthetic drug. Heroin is obtained by a relatively simple structural modification of morphine or codeine:

OPTION

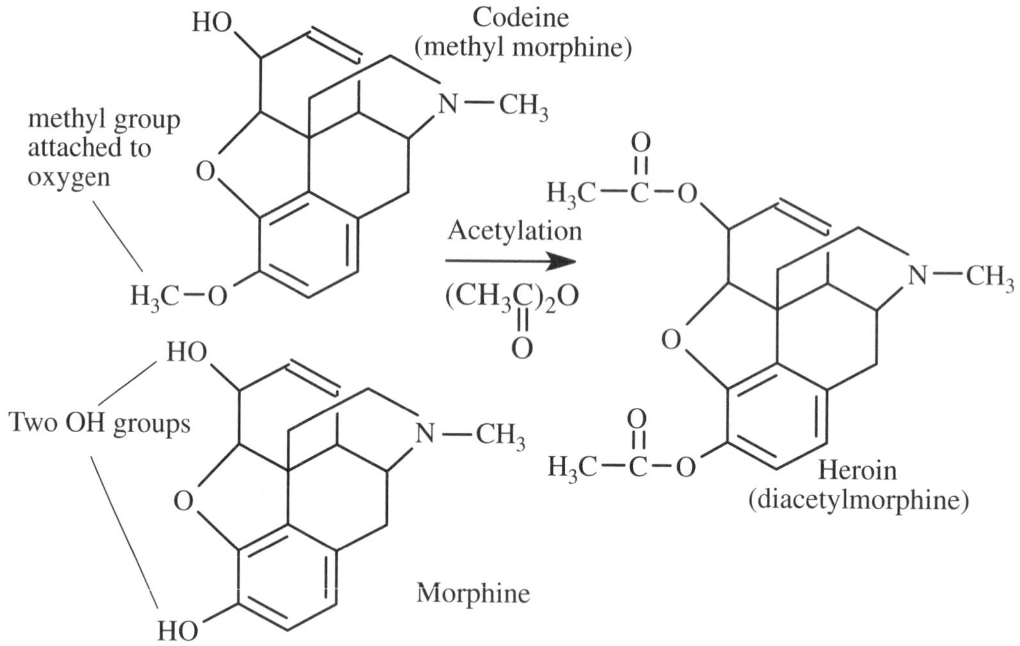

HO

Codeine
(methyl morphine)

N—CH₃ → $N-CH_3$

methyl group
attached to
oxygen

O

H_3C-O

Acetylation

$(CH_3C)_2O$

H_3C-C-O

$N-CH_3$

HO

Two OH groups

$N-CH_3$

O

H_3C-C-O

Heroin
(diacetylmorphine)

HO

Morphine

Besides having the same carbon skeleton, morphine contains two –OH groups. Codeine contains one –OH and one –OCH₃ group and heroin contains two acetyl groups, CH_3COO-. Thus only simple modifications to the structure of morphine result in the semi-synthetic drugs heroin and codeine (also prepared semi-synthetically because of its very small percentage in raw opium).

Several totally synthetic opiates include demerol (meperidine), methadone (dolophine) and fentanyl (sublimaze) that exhibit effects like those of opiates but are produced in the laboratory. Demerol is a synthetic morphine derivative. Methadone blocks the euphoric high of heroin and is used in the treatment of heroin addicts in certain countries where it is a legal drug.

ADVANTAGES AND DISADVANTAGES OF OPIATES
Pharmacological effects:
Opiates exert major effects on:
* the central nervous system

* the eye and

* the gastrointestinal tract (the digestive system).

The prime medical uses of opiates are:
* as a strong analgesic in the relief of severe pain caused by injury, chronic disease such as cancer, prior to and recovery from surgery etc. Heroin is three times as potent as morphine, while codeine is about one sixth as strong as morphine

* in the treatment of diarrhoea by producing a constipating effect

* to relieve coughing by suppressing the 'cough centre' situated in the brain stem.

Because of the addictive nature of opiates, codeine is often replaced by dextromethorphan, a synthetic non-narcotic medication.

Psychological effects of opiates:

Opiates produce analgesia, drowsiness, mood changes and mental clouding. Some individuals experience anxiety, fear, lethargy, sedation, lack of concern, inability to concentrate, nausea and vomiting. Also, users feel a relief from emotional and psychological pain.

Tolerance and dependence:

Tolerance appears due both to the induction of drug metabolising enzymes in the liver and the adaptation of neurons in the brain to the presence of the drug. Cross tolerance – drug users who become tolerant to one opiate will also exhibit a tolerance to all other natural or synthetic opiates, e.g. tolerance to morphine will also lead to tolerance to heroin but not to alcohol or barbiturates which are sedatives (or hypnotics).

Physical Dependence – this is a state in which people do not function properly without a drug. Withdrawal is experienced when the drug is not regularly administered. Symptoms include restlessness, sweating, fever, chills, vomiting, increased rate of respiration, cramping, diarrhoea, unbearable aches and pains. The magnitude of these withdrawal symptoms depend on the dose, frequency of drug administration, the duration of the drug dependence and the opiate used.

The opiates are extremely potent and valuable drugs for the treatment of pain. But they also have the capacity of inducing a state of euphoria and relief from psychological pain, which can lead to a strong compulsion to misuse them. The opiates induce profound tolerance and physiological dependence, the consequencies of which are important both medically and sociologically as the user is difficult to treat and must frequently resort to crime to support the habit and reach a source of supply.

Summary of the effects of narcotics

Usual short - term effects	Typical long - term effects
Sedation and stupor; relief from pain.	Loss of appetite; malnutrition constipation.
Euphoria; impaired functioning and coordination, and temporary impotence.	Sterility.
Reduced tension, worry and fear.	Withdrawal illness, loss of job, crime.
Reduced coughing reflex.	Diversion of energy and money.
Occasional death from overdose.	Risk of dangerous infections (hepatitis, AIDS) due to shared needles.

OPTION

12.4 DEPRESSANTS

B.4.1   Describe the effects of depressants.

At low doses a depressant may exert little or no effect. At moderate doses the compound may induce sedation (soothing, reduction of anxiety). At higher doses it may induce sleep and at extremely high doses it may cause death. Depressants are often described as anti-depressants because they relieve depression.

© IBO 2001

DEPRESSANTS (SOMETIMES CALLED 'DOWNERS')

Depressants (tranquilizers, sedatives and hypnotics) are drugs that calm and relax (that is depress) the central nervous system. These slow down the activity of the brain and other organs (e.g. heart etc.). They reduce the rate of breathing and in general dull emotional responses.

Tranquilizers

Examples include alcohol, valium and librium. These have the property of reducing nervous tension and anxiety but do not produce sleep in normal doses. Librium and valium (diazepam) are two common benzodiazepine tranquilizers used widely for relieving anxiety and tension and are safer than barbiturates.

Sedatives

Examples are certain barbiturates (a class of drugs that are depressants). Sedatives can cause soothing of distress, again without producing sleep in normal doses. The main difference between a tranquilizer and a sedative is one of degree of action. Tranquilizers are mild in their action compared to sedatives.

Hypnotics

An example is chloral hydrate. Hypnotics are a class of drug that produces sleep. Note that phenobarbital (a barbiturate) can behave as a sedative or a hypnotic depending on the dose.

The diagram below shows how increasing the dose of a depressant affects behavior.

Continuum of sedation behaviour

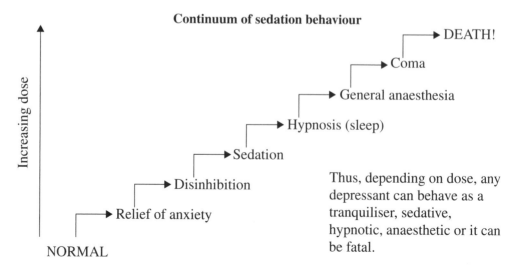

Thus, depending on dose, any depressant can behave as a tranquiliser, sedative, hypnotic, anaesthetic or it can be fatal.

B.4.2   Discuss the social and physiological effects of the use and abuse of ethanol.

Include effects on the family, cost to society and the short and long-term health effects.

B.4.4   Describe the synergistic effects of ethanol with other drugs.

Examples include increased risk of stomach bleeding with aspirin, and increased risk of heavy sedation with any drug that has a sedative effect on the central nervous system.

© IBO 2001

ETHANOL

C_2H_5OH

$$C_2H_5 - \overset{\delta-}{\ddot{O}} \diagdown_{H}{}^{\delta+}$$

The presence of a tiny hydrogen atom attached to a highly electronegative oxygen atom makes it possible for ethanol to form hydrogen bonds with water. Ethanol is also fat-soluble as it is a relatively small organic molecule. Thus it readily penetrates cell and tissue membranes and is therefore completely and easily absorbed from the entire gastrointestinal tract.

Social effects of the use and abuse of alcohol:

The major social costs from alcohol use and abuse are due to sickness and death associated with drinking (see short and long term effects). These costs consist of hospital treatment as well as lost productivity due to ill health and death. It is estimated that in countries such as the US, Australia, Europe, Japan, etc. over 80% of all alcohol-induced costs are borne by society. Other costs attributed to alcohol include crime and motor traffic related costs. These include both property crimes and crimes against people, and the pain and suffering felt by crime and accident victims and their families. Research in the US shows that there is considerable evidence that offenders are often affected by alcohol when committing violent crimes. Organisations such as MADD (mothers against drink drivers) in North America represent some of the victims of excessive alcohol use.

Physiological effects on the use and abuse of alcohol:

Alcohol abuse involves a pattern of drinking associated with failure to fulfill major obligations (at work, school or home), drinking while driving, operating machinery, participating in dangerous situations, physically harming someone or on-going problems in relationships. Alcoholism is characterised by an inability to control intake, that is a craving or compulsion to drink, inability to stop drinking as well as developing physical dependence and tolerance. Physical dependence involves withdrawal symptoms such as nausea, sweating, anxiety, increased blood pressure when alcohol use is stopped. Tolerance involves the need for increasing amounts of the drug to feel the same effects. Alcoholism is a disease which involves a psychological and physical addiction to alcohol as well as genetic factors.

Short–term effects:

As a central nervous system depressant, alcohol reduces tension, anxiety and inhibitions. The extent to which the CNS function is impaired is directly proportional to the concentration of alcohol in the blood.

OPTION

The effects of alcohol

Blood Alcohol concentration (BAC) mg/100 cm³ of blood	Symptoms
10-30	Near normal behaviour.
30-90	Euphoria, sociability, talkativeness, feeling of relaxation, increased self confidence, decreased inhibitions. Impairment of attention, judgement and control. Some loss of sensory-motor efficiency and of finer performance skills.
90-200	Small blood vessels in the skin dilated, leading to feeling of warmth; loss of critical judgement, impairment of perception, memory and comprehension; driving accidents more likely; increased reaction time; drowsiness.
200-300	Violent or aggressive behaviour possible; increased pain threshold, slurred speech; dizziness; double vision, loss of balance; nausea and vomiting.
300-400	Loss of motor functions; general inertia; inability to stand or walk, asleep or in a stupor; impaired consciousness.
350-450	Coma; unconsciousness.
>450	Death from respiratory arrest.

Long–term effects:

These include cirrhosis (due to scar tissue) and cancer of the liver, coronary heart disease, high blood pressure, strokes, gastritis (inflammation of the stomach) and peptic ulcers. Long term heavy drinking leads to physical dependence and tolerance. Alcoholics often suffer from anxiety and depression and poor eating habits. Excess drinking by pregnant women can lead to miscarriage, low birth mass and fetal abnormalities including poor development in infants. Fetal Alcohol Syndrome refers to physical and mental birth defects resulting from a woman drinking too much alcohol during pregnancy

There are few current medical uses for alcohol. It is used as a solvent in tincture of iodine (an antiseptic) and in antiseptics such as mouthwashes. In North America and Europe it is estimated to be used by at least 80% of the adult population.

Interactions with other drugs:

Alcohol produces a synergic effect with other drugs whose performance is enhanced many more times with alcohol than without, sometimes leading to devastating effects. For example, alcohol taken with sedatives like sleeping pills and barbiturates that affect the central nervous system, can produce coma and death. Alcohol taken with aspirin increases the risk of stomach bleeding. If alcohol inhibits the breakdown of a drug (such as some oral antidiabetic drugs), they stay longer in the body with increased effects.

B.4.3   Describe and explain the techniques used for the detection of ethanol in the breath and in the blood or urine.

Include potassium dichromate(VI) in the breathalyser, analysis of blood or urine by chromatography and absorption of infra-red radiation in the intoximeter.

© IBO 2001

The Blood Alcohol Concentration (BAC) is the mass in grams of ethanol per 100 cm^3 of blood. In some countries this is listed as a percentage. For example in many countries drinking with 0.08% blood alcohol level (equal to 80mg alcohol per 100 cm^3 of blood) is the legal limit for driving cars.

Ethanol passes from the stomach into the blood stream, and since it is sufficiently volatile, it passes into the lungs where an equilibrium is established at the body's temperature:

$$C_2H_5OH_{(blood)} \rightleftharpoons C_2H_5OH_{(vapour)}$$

and the concentration of ethanol in the lungs will depend on the concentration of ethanol in the blood.

Breathalyser test:
The roadside breathalyser test done by law enforcement officers involves a redox reaction in which potassium dichromate(VI) $K_2Cr_2O_7$ is used as the oxidising agent. It oxidises any alcohol in the breath to ethanoic acid, CH_3COOH. The Cr(VI) is reduced to Cr(III) with the gain of three electrons per Cr. The two half reactions and the overall reaction are:

$$Cr_2O_7^{2-} + 14 \text{ H}^+ + 6 \text{ e}^- \Rightarrow 2 \text{ Cr}^{3+} + 7 \text{ H}_2O: \text{ reduction half reaction}$$

$$C_2H_5OH + H_2O \Rightarrow CH_3COOH + 4 \text{ e}^- + 4 \text{ H}^+: \text{ oxidation half reaction}$$

$$2 \text{ Cr}_2O_7^{2-} + 3 \text{ C}_2H_5OH + 16 \text{ H}^+ \Rightarrow 4 \text{ Cr}^{3+} + 3 \text{ CH}_3COOH + 11 \text{ H}_2O$$

The redox reaction, involving transfer of electrons generates, an e.m.f. that is converted to a signal in the breathalyser device to indicate the BAC in the sample of breath. Such devices generally suffer from inaccuracy and unreliability when used in legal cases. More accurate analysis is carried out by gas liquid chromatography (glc) and infra-red spectroscopy.

OPTION

GAS LIQUID CHROMATOGRAPHY

Very small samples of gases and volatile liquids such as ethanol can be separated and identified using gas liquid chromatography (glc).

Glc uses a stationary phase such as a non-volatile liquid or solid support and a mobile phase such as an inert carrier gas (eg. N_2). The components of the breath including carbon dioxide, water vapour and alcohol vapour are partitioned between the mobile and stationary phases depending on their boiling points. Thus the components move through a column of the solid phase at differing speeds and exit after intervals of time depending on the substance. These can then be detected and recorded by a detector that can identify the changes in the composition of the carrier gas as it comes out of the column.

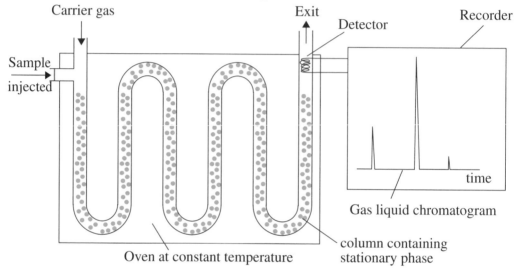

A gas liquid chromatogram displays the time taken for each component to pass through the column, called the **retention time**. A standard ethanol sample is first passed through the column under certain conditions such as the same carrier gas at the same flow rate, the same stationary phase and a constant temperature, to determine its retention time. The sample is then introduced under all the same conditions, and the ethanol is identified by comparing the retention times. Glc not only identifies the compound, but the area under the peak represents the amount of the compound, thus allowing law enforcement officers to determine accurately the blood alcohol concentration (BAC). Blood and urine samples can be analysed using glc.

INFRA-RED SPECTROSCOPY

Use of Infra-red Spectroscopy to detect alcohol levels:

Infra-red (IR) energy is not sufficiently large to excite an electron to a higher energy level, but is sufficient to cause vibrational motions which depend on the mass of the atoms and the length/strength of the bonds within the molecule.

An infra-red spectrum is therefore characteristic of the bonds or functional groups present in a compound and can act as a 'finger print' to identify it. A necessary condition for a bond to absorb infra-red energy is a net change in dipole moment due to vibrational motion, namely a species with a fluctuating dipole moment can absorb IR radiation (see Option G, Modern Analytical Chemistry). Most polyatomic molecules are able to absorb IR radiation as they experience this condition.

IR spectra use the wavenumber scale in cm^{-1} where the wavenumber = $\dfrac{1}{\text{wavelength}}$. The units are cm^{-1} and the IR range is from 667 to 4000 cm^{-1}. The presence of the C-H in alcohol is detected at 2950 cm^{-1} on an IR spectrum, whereas the O-H shows an absorption at 3340 cm^{-1}. However, since water vapour is also present in the breath, the O-H peak cannot be used for the detection of any alcohol and instead the IR absorption at 2950 cm^{-1} is used to detect the presence of the C-H group.

Police use the intoximeter to confirm a road side breathalyser test. This is an IR spectrophotometer in which the IR radiation is passed through the breath sample. If alcohol is present, the frequencies are absorbed by the sample depending on the bands present (such as C-H and O-H) and the rest of the radiation is transmitted. The detector compares the intensity of IR radiation through the sample with the intensity through air. The recorder then produces the IR spectrum as % transmittance (the amount of radiation through the sample) against wavenumber.

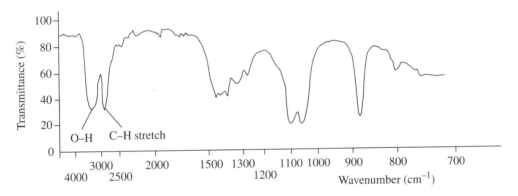

IR spectrum of ethanol showing the C-H stretch used for detection.

A simplified schematic diagram of a double-beam IR spectrophometer

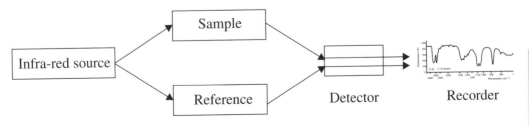

Similar to glc, the size of the peak at 2950 cm^{-1} depends on the amount of radiation absorbed by the breath sample. This depends on the amount of alcohol present, thus allowing accurate determination of the blood alcohol concentration (BAC).

B.4.5 List other commonly used depressants and describe their structures.

> *Limit to a brief mention of the use of diazepam (Valium®), nitrazepam (Mogadon®) and fluoxetine hydrochloride (Prozac®).* © IBO 2001

Valium® (diazepam) is a tranquilizer - sedative drug that is used in the relief of anxiety and tension.

Nitrazepam (Mogadon®) is a hypnotic drug that induces sleep (it is used to control seizures and infantile spasms).

Prozac® (Fluoxetine hydrochloride) is an anti-depressant drug that is used to treat mental depression and is thought to work by increasing the activity of serotonin, a neurotransmitter, in the brain.

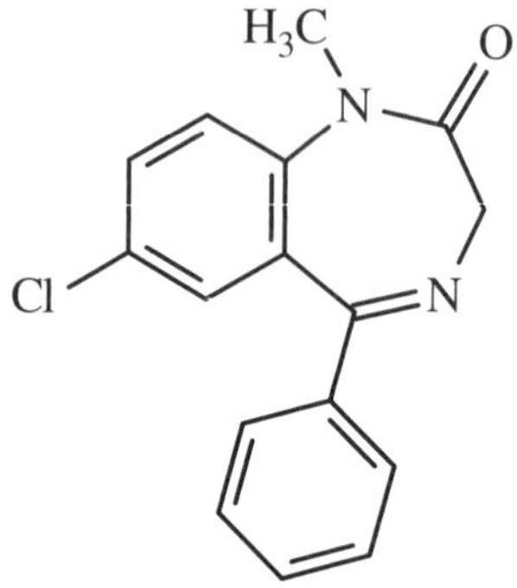

Diazepam

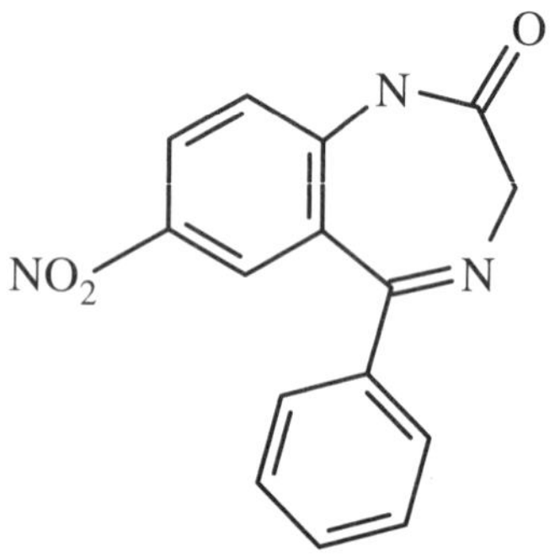

Nitrazepam

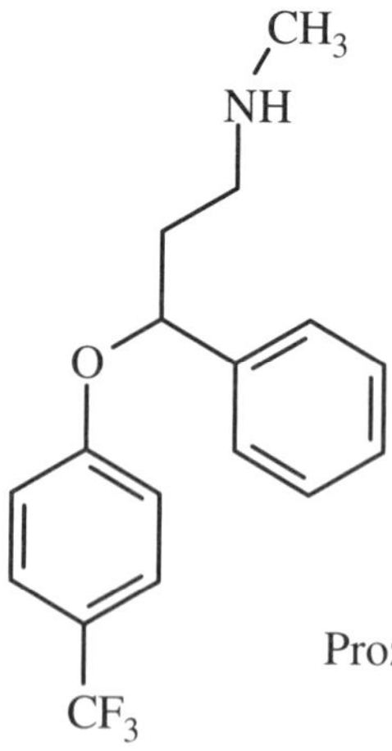

Prozac®

The main carbon skeleton structures of diazepam and nitrazepam are the same, the difference being the side groups. The chemical structure of Prozac® is unlike the other two.

OPTION

12.5 STIMULANTS

B.5.1   List the physiological effects of stimulants.   © IBO 2001

Stimulants (also called 'uppers') are chemicals that stimulate the brain and the central nervous system by increasing the state of mental alertness.

Their effect is opposite to the depressants ('downers'). Stimulants cause increased alertness and wakefulness (and in many cases decrease appetite and are therefore used as diet pills). Amphetamines, nicotine and caffeine are all examples of stimulants.

B.5.2   Compare amphetamines and adrenaline.

Amphetamines and adrenaline are chemically similar in that both derive from the phenylethylamine structure. Amphetamines mimic the effects of adrenaline and are known as sympathomimetic drugs.   © IBO 2001

Amphetamines have chemical structures similar to adrenaline, and both derive from the phenylethylamine structure ($CH_3CH_2NH_2$ is ethylamine):

Phenylethylamine

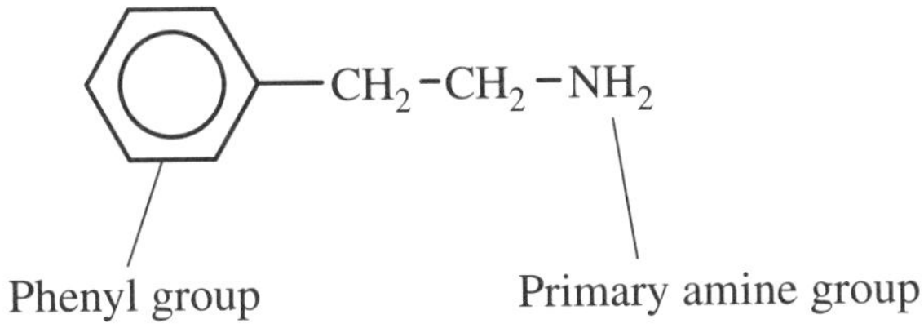

Phenyl group   Primary amine group

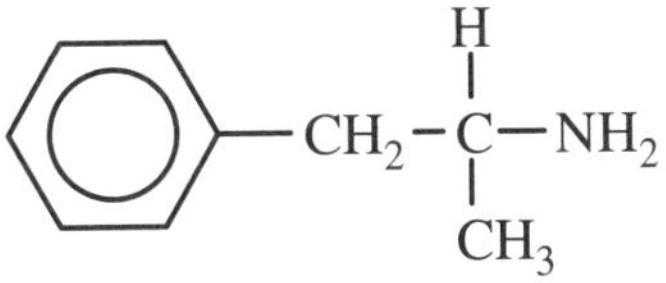

Amphetamine, also drawn as:

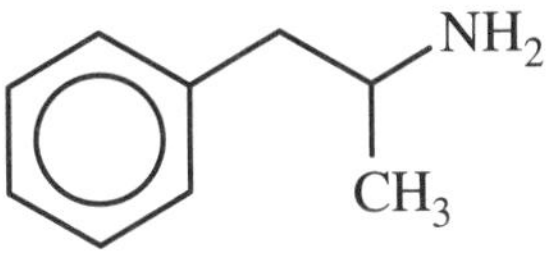

Adrenaline

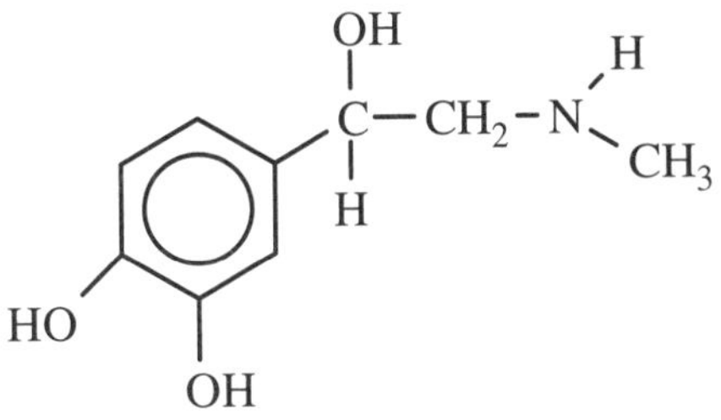

or

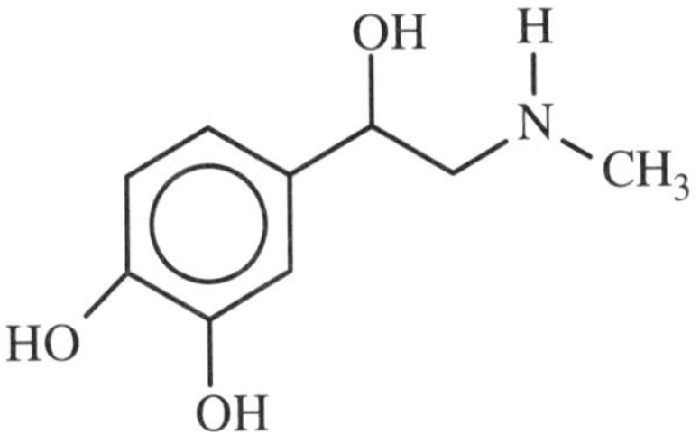

'Speed'

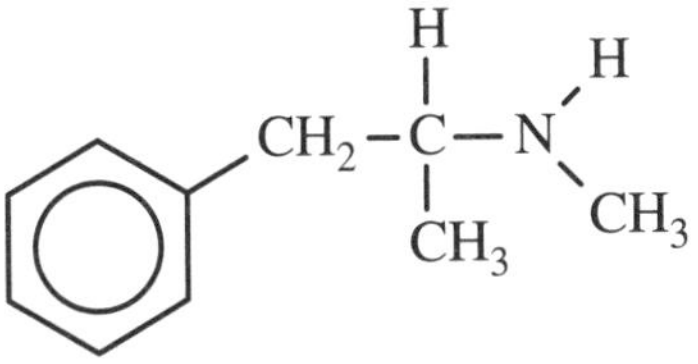

'Speed' (methamphetamine) has a much more pronounced psychological effect than amphetamine.

OPTION

433

Amphetamines mimic the effects of the hormone adrenaline and are known as **sympathomimetic drugs**. They do this by constricting the arteries, increasing sweat production etc. Amphetamines are strong stimulants and act on the central nervous system, mainly the brain. Medical uses of amphetamines include treatment of mild depression, narcolepsy (tendency to fall asleep) and asthma (because these drugs cause broncodilation). Amphetamines increase the heart rate, blood pressure, respiration, wakefulness, restlessness and insomnia. A temporary elevation of mood is produced followed by fatigue, irritability and depression. Amphetamines allow the body to use reserve energy, just like adrenalin. However, use may be followed by sudden exhaustion leading to blackout or collapse.

B.5.3   Discuss the short- and long-term effects of nicotine consumption.

Short-term effects: increased heart rate and blood pressure and reduction in urine output, as well as stimulating effects.

Long-term effects: increased risk of heart disease, coronary thrombosis and peptic ulcers. Discuss also the addictive properties of nicotine and the further risks associated with smoking tobacco.   © IBO 2001

Tobacco is a source of nicotine, a mild stimulant. In fact the effect as a stimulant is rather transient and short-lived. The initial response is followed by depression, which encourages frequent use.

Short term effects of nicotine:
Nicotine increases heart rate and blood pressure and constricts the blood vessels. This puts stress on the heart since it is forced to pump blood harder than normal. This accounts for the greater long-term incidence of heart problems for smokers. Besides causing mild stimulating effects, nicotine reduces urine output.

Long term effects of nicotine:
The ability of nicotine to constrict blood vessels stresses the heart, forcing it to pump harder. This increases the risk of heart disease and coronary thrombosis (formation of blood clots) since it may also cause a rise in fatty acids in the bloodstream. Smoking also produces carbon monoxide which inhibits the ability of the blood to carry oxygen, thus placing more stress on the heart. As a stimulant, it may produce excess acidity in the stomach, thus increasing the risk of peptic ulcers. In addition to nicotine, cigarette smoke contains many other toxic chemicals.

Medical evidence indicates that smoking causes:
- lung cancer,
- cancers of the larynx and mouth,
- heart and blood vessel disease,
- emphysema (a chronic lung condition marked by loss of elasticity of the air sacs or alveoli, causing breathing difficulties),
- chronic bronchitis (inflammation of the bronchial tubes),

- air pollution and
- fires (50% of fires in Canada are caused by careless smoking).

Yellow stained fingers and teeth and bad breath are common amongst regular smokers. It is much easier to become dependent on nicotine than on alcohol or barbiturates. Nicotine produces psychological dependence and builds up tolerance. Many heavy smokers experience physical dependence as well. People who give up smoking can experience withdrawal symptoms such as weight gain, nausea, insomnia, irritability, fatigue, inability to concentrate as well as depression and a craving for cigarettes.

B.5.4 Describe the effects of caffeine and compare its structure with that of nicotine.

Caffeine is a respiratory stimulant. When consumed in large amounts it can cause anxiety, irritability and sleeplessness. It is a weak diuretic. Both caffeine and nicotine contain a tertiary amine group.   © IBO 2001

Caffeine exerts its central nervous system stimulant action by working inside nerve cells to increase their rates of cellular metabolism. This means that the rate at which energy is made available from respiration is increased. Caffeine stimulates the central nervous system, heart, kidneys, lungs and arteries supplying blood to the heart and brain. In moderate doses, caffeine enhances alertness, well-being, energy, motivation and concentration. Thus sustained intellectual effort is made possible. However physical coordination and timing may be adversely affected by higher doses. In small amounts, caffeine is considered relatively harmless. When consumed in large amounts, it can cause sleeplessness. Because it stimulates the kidneys, caffeine is a weak diuretic (a drug that increases the flow of urine).

Caffeine leads to some tolerance, but no physical addiction. It can lead to minor psychological addiction ('morning grouch' symptoms). Because of its ability to stimulate respiration, it finds a medical use to stimulate breathing especially in new born babies with respiratory problems. Caffeine is a vasoconstrictor – it can cause constriction of blood vessels. Since migrane headaches are related to the dilation of blood vessels in the head, caffeine has a potential use in reducing migranes.

Caffeine is a heterocyclic compound in which one or more carbon atoms in the ring are replaced by another atom e.g. nitrogen. Like nicotine it contains a tertiary amine group - in which three organic substituents are attached to nitrogen, fitting the general formula R_3N:

Caffeine   Nicotine

12.6ANTIBACTERIALS

B.6.1　Describe the historical development of penicillins.

Include the discovery by Fleming and the development by Florey and Chain.

B.6.2　Compare broad spectrum and narrow spectrum antibiotics.

B.6.3　Explain how penicillins work and discuss the effects of modifying the side chain.

Penicillins work by interfering with the chemicals that bacteria need to form normal cell walls. Modifying the side chain results in penicillins which are more resistant to the penicillinase enzyme.

B.6.4　Discuss and explain the effect overprescription of penicillins has, and the use of penicillins in animal feedstock.

© IBO 2001

Antibacterials (called antibiotics in many countries) are drugs that inhibit the growth of, or kill, microorganisms that cause infectious diseases. These drugs are **selective**; they act against infecting bacteria much more than they act against human cells. Many diseases can be traced to microorganisms that invade the body and this is the basis of the germ theory of diseases. Microorganisms are usually single celled life forms that are capable of independent life given an adequate supply of nutrients. Infectious diseases occur when the body's natural defences are ineffective, for example when it has no natural immunity to the infection or there are too many microorganisms for the body's immune system to overcome, or when the organism evolves rapidly.

There are two main types of infectious agents; bacteria and viruses. Since antibiotics are ineffective against normal body cells, they cannot combat viral infection. Antibodies produced by the body's defence mechanism protect the body against infection. When bacteria multiply faster than they can be neutralised by the body's defences they produce infectious disease. Antibiotics aid white blood cells by preventing bacteria from multiplying, either by inhibiting cell division (bacteriostatic drugs) or by directly killing bacteria (bacteriocidal drugs).

Examples of bacterial infections include: tetanus, tuberculosis (TB), cholera, typhoid fever, syphilis, gonorrhea. Viral infections include: influenza, the common cold, hepatitis, measles and AIDS.

HISTORICAL DEVELOPMENTS OF PENICILLINS

In the 1890s scientists found that certain fungi killed bacteria. In an experiment, mice were introduced to disease-causing bacteria. Some were also exposed to one of these fungi. Mice exposed only to the bacteria died whereas mice exposed to both the bacteria and the fungus lived. These results were however largely ignored. In 1928 similar observations were made by Alexander Fleming, a bacteriologist working at St Mary's Hospital in Paddington, England. Fleming was working with a bacterium called *staphylococcus aureus* that causes boils and other types of infection. In one of the cultures in a petri dish whose lid had been left off, he found mold (mould) growing, but no bacteria around the mould. He concluded that the mold (*penicillium notatum*) must have inhibited bacterial growth by producing a compound that he called penicillin. However Fleming gave up the project after he found it difficult to isolate and purify the active ingredient in the mold.

In 1940, Florey and Chain, working at Oxford University renewed the research. They injected mice with deadly bacteria; some mice received penicillin and survived. In 1941, penicillin was used for the first time on a human being, a London policeman who had serious blood poisoning from a shaving cut. The effect of penicillin was immediately favourable. In 1941 a massive development program was started in the U.S. where scientists at the Bureau of Agricultural Chemistry in Peoria, Illinois grew strains of penicillin mold in a medium of corn-steep liquor in large fermentation tanks. By 1943 penicillin was available clinically and by 1945 enough supply was present for everyone needing it, thus saving thousands of lives during World War 2. In 1945, Fleming, Florey and Chain received the Nobel Prize for medicine for their work on penicillin.

STRUCTURE OF PENICILLINS AND MODIFICATIONS OF THE SIDE CHAIN

The first penicillin used was penicillin G: after its structure was determined by X-ray crystallography, other penicillins were made. Since penicillin G is deactivated by stomach acid it had to be injected. Acid resistant penicillins such as penicillin V (phenoxymethylpenicillin) were developed by keeping the basic penicillin structure, but modifying the side chains. Also, bacteria were able to deactivate penicillin G by synthesising an enzyme, penicillinase, thus requiring the production of a number of synthetic penicillins. The structural feature common to all the penicillins is 6-APA, 6-aminopenicillanic acid. On its own, this has little effect on the bacterial growth. However, if an extra side-chain is added to its NH_2 amino group, active penicillin is created:

6-aminopenicillanic acid   Penicillin structure with side chain

When R = C_6H_5–CH_2–: benzyl penicillin or penicillin G; not acid resistant.

When R = C_6H_5–CH_2–CH_2–: penicillin V; acid resistant.

When R = cloxacillin; acid and penicillinase resistant.

COMPARISON OF BROAD SPECTRUM AND NARROW SPECTRUM ANTIBIOTICS

A broad spectrum antibiotic is one which is effective against a wide variety of bacteria, whereas a narrow spectrum antibiotic is effective against only certain types of bacteria. Most penicillins (and the sulfa drugs) are examples of narrow spectrum antibiotics (ampicillin on the other hand is a broad-spectrum antibiotic). Tetracyclines are examples of broad spectrum antibiotics – compounds of the tetracycline family get their names from their four-ring structures. Aureomycin® and Terramycin®, both tetracycline

OPTION

antibiotics, are examples of broad spectrum antibiotics; the suffix 'mycin' is used for antibiotics obtained from soil fungi. Repeated use of broad–spectrum antibiotics may wipe out harmless as well as helpful bacteria in the alimentary canal including the oesophagus, stomach and in particular the large intestines. Also, the destroyed bacteria may be replaced by harmful strains.

In the treatment of infection, ideally the bacterium should be identified before prescribing an antibiotic. Since this takes time, usually a day, a physician may prescribe a broad spectrum antibiotic to relieve some of the severe discomfort, followed by an antibiotic more specific for the bacterium identified.

WORKING OF THE PENICILLINS

Cell walls of some bacteria are composed of largely different polysaccharides. The cell wall in the bacteria protects and supports the delicate cell structure and components enclosed within it. The cell wall layers are reinforced by a series of three dimensional chemical **cross-links** connecting one layer to another. Penicillins interfere with this cross link formation, thus weakening the cell walls. The cells can burst easily and the bacteria die. This is why penicillins are called **bacteriocidal drugs**.

Note that cells of animals do not have 'cell walls'. They have external cell membranes which are different in composition and are therefore **not** affected by penicillin. Thus penicillin can destroy some bacteria without harming human cells. Thus penicillins are bacteriocides that destroy bacteria by interferring with cell wall construction. The bacteria can produce the molecular components of their cell walls, but in the presence of penicillin, cannot put them together. Thus it is unable to hold its size and shape. Water enters by osmosis, the cell expands and bursts, thus killing the bacterium.

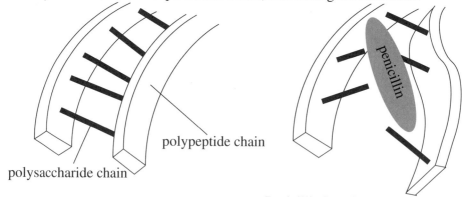

polypeptide chain

polysaccharide chain

Cross-links in a normal
bacterial cell wall

Penicillin interferes with the formation
of cross-links, weakening the cell wall and
causing the bacterial cell to burst and die

EFFECTS OF OVER PRESCRIPTION OF PENICILLINS

Penicillins have had great value in controlling a large number of infectious diseases. However, over prescription can produce disadvantages.

1. Penicillins are usually safe except for a small percentage of the population (about 10%) who experience allergic reactions and suffer side effects ranging from fever and body rash to occasionally shock and death. Repeated use can sometimes lead to allergic reaction.

2. Antibiotics, if used repeatedly, may wipe-out harmless bacteria and helpful ones in the alimentary canal (this is the food canal, or gut, including the oesophagus stomach and intestines). Also, the destroyed bacteria may be replaced by more harmful bacterium.

3. Another serious problem is that of genetic resistance. As antibiotics are used extensively, a few organisms survive and pass on their immunity (resistance) to succeeding generations. For example malaria, typhoid, gonorrhoea, TB and other diseases all have strains that are now resistant to many antibiotics!

A microorganism may also become resistant as a result of mutation. The mutated strain may be able to reproduce on a large scale, with very serious consequences. A mutated strain may develop an enzyme that changes an antibiotic into a harmless substance. Thus continuing research is needed to develop new antibiotics. This is why antibiotics are considered miracle drugs in constant need of renewal. The prime rule for the use of antibiotics is that they should be used only when no other treatment can significantly reduce suffering or save life.

THE USE OF ANTIBIOTICS IN ANIMAL FEEDSTOCK

Antibiotics are used as supplements in animal feedstock for the control of animal diseases and to increase the rate of growth of animals. Feedstock can contain plant and animal pathogens which can be a danger to animal and human health. Thus antibiotics are used in the production of meat and poultry to control these bacteria and hence to increase productivity.

However, routine exposure of bacteria to small amounts of antibiotics allows naturally drug-resistant bacteria to survive, reproduce and spread. Thus, humans may be exposed to drug-resistant salmonella, *E.Coli* etc. that are not killed by the antibiotics in animal feed. The medical profession uses the same antibiotics to treat infectious diseases in humans as are used on livestock. The advent of antibiotic resistant bacteria makes humans vulnerable to life-threatening diseases and increases the cost of treatment. This has clearly raised concerns about the risks to human health resulting from the routine addition of antibiotics to animal feedstock.

OPTION

12.7 ANTIVIRALS

B.7.1   State how viruses differ from bacteria.

B.7.2   Describe the different ways in which antiviral drugs work.

Antiviral drugs may work by altering the cell's genetic material so that the virus cannot use it to multiply. Alternatively they may prevent the viruses from multiplying by blocking enzyme activity within the host cell.

B.7.3   Discuss the difficulties associated with solving the AIDS problem.

Specific proteins on the HIV virus bind to a receptor protein on certain white blood cells (T cells). Because of the ability of the HIV viruses to mutate and because their metabolism is linked closely with that of the cell, effective treatment with antiviral drugs is very difficult, as is vaccine development.

© IBO 2001

Bacteria are single cell microorganisms, measuring between 0.3 and 2.0 microns in diameter. Each cell contains a single chromosome consisting of a circular strand of DNA, which is coiled and which occupies part of the cell. The rigid cell walls are made of protein-sugar (polysaccharide) molecules. Inside the cell membrane is the cytoplasm which contains enzymes to break down food and build cell parts.

Viruses, on the other hand are submicroscopic, non-cellular infectious particles capable of reproduction only inside a living cell using the enzymatic machinery of that cell. Viruses attach themselves to a variety of cells, called host cells, and assume control of them. Viruses have a central core of DNA surrounded by a protein coat known as capsid. However, viruses are not cellular as they have no nucleus, cytoplasm or cell membrane (though some have a membrane outside their protein coats). Viruses do not feed or grow but do reproduce inside the cells of living organisms using the ribosomes of host cells. Viruses are much smaller than bacteria.

DIFFERENT WAYS IN WHICH ANTIVIRAL DRUGS WORK

Antibiotics control bacterial infections. Whether an antibiotic works against viruses depends very much on its mechanism of action. An antibiotic may be effective against viruses if it is able to block the transfer of genetic information. Most antibiotics do not do this and thus control only a few viruses. For the most part viruses are controlled most effectively by innoculations. Polio, smallpox and yellow fever (all caused by viruses) are all prevented by innoculations today, as is influenza caused by several different strains of viruses. The UN Smallpox Innoculation Program has been so successful that the virus is now thought to be extinct in humans. Nonetheless, controlling viral infections remains one of the major challenges for scientists.

Viruses consist of nucleic acid surrounded by a protein coat. They attach themselves to host cells and stimulate the cell to make viral nucleic acid instead of host nucleic acid. The viral nucleic acid is then coated with protein, and the viral particle emerges to infect other cells. A number of enzymes are essential for at least some of these steps, and one of the goals of research into antiviral agents is to find chemical ways to block such enzyme activity within the host cell. Doing so would stop the viruses and prevent replication in host cells. Once replication is stopped, the virus is defeated. Antiviral

OPTION

drugs may also work by altering the cell's ribosomes so that the virus cannot use them to multiply.

A handful of drugs that work against viral infections have been developed. Among them is Acyclovir® (Zovirax®) which is for general topical and oral use against herpes viruses. Acyclovir relieves pain and itching in genital herpes and shortens the duration of the outbreak. It is most effective when used at the time of initial infection but it does not prevent recurrences. Also, while Acyclovir® succeeds in shortening the contagious period, it does not work on all patients.

Some cancers are caused by viruses that don't cause the immediate production of a tumour but insert their genetic material into the genome of an animal or plant cell. The viral genetic material becomes part of the host cell and is duplicated and passed on to new cells at cell division. Latent viruses of this type are very common. A familiar latent virus is the herplex simplex virus which, when stimulated by various factors, leaves its latent state in nerve cells (where it hides), is reproduced, and causes the cell damage known as a 'cold sore'!

PROBLEMS ASSOCIATED WITH SOLVING THE PROBLEMS OF AIDS

AIDS: acquired immunodeficiency syndrome was first reported in the US in 1981 and has since become a major worldwide epidemic. AIDS is caused by the human immunodeficiency virus HIV. By killing or damaging particular cells of the immune system in the body, HIV progressively destroys the body's ability to fight infections, leading to life threatening infections such as pneumonia (called opportunistic infections) that do not generally threaten healthy people. The term AIDS applies to the most advanced stages of HIV infection.

Specific proteins on the surface of the HIV virus bind to a receptor glycoprotein (called CD4) on a certain type of the cell membrane of the white blood cells, namely the T4 lymphocytes. The T4-cells are immune cells that circulate in the blood stream; the crucial T4-cells are disabled by the virus and killed during the course of infection, and are unable to play their central role in the immune response (of signalling other cells in the immune system to perform their functions). The ability of the HIV virus to mutate, together with their similar metabolism to that of the human cell, makes effective treatment with antiviral drugs and vaccine development very difficult.

OPTION

12.8 STEREOCHEMISTRY IN DRUG ACTION AND DESIGN
EXTENSION MATERIAL - HL ONLY

B.8.1 Describe the importance of geometrical isomerism in drug action.

Students should be aware that cis- and trans- isomerism can occur in inorganic complexes and that the two different isomers can have different pharmacological effects. The anti-cancer drug cisplatin is a good example. © IBO 2001

Stereoisomers are isomers with the same molecular formula and the same structural formula, but different arrangement of atoms in space, that is, they differ in spatial arrangement of atoms. In organic chemistry, if a pair of stereoisomers contains a double bond, then it is possible to obtain cis (on the same side) and trans (across/opposite) arrangements of substituents at each end of the double bond. These are referred to as geometric or cis-trans isomers (see Chapter 11).

Properties:

1. Physical properties:

Geometric isomers have different physical properties such as polarity (dipole moment), boiling point, melting point and solubility.

2. Chemical properties:

Geometric isomers can undergo different chemical reactions. Since they contain the same functional groups, they do show some similar chemical properties but not all their chemical properties are identical, and the two different isomers can have different pharmacological effects.

Geometric isomerism is by no means restricted to organic chemistry. A square planar 4-coordinated complex of the form MA_2B_2 will also experience geometric isomerism, for example $Pt(NH_3)_2Cl_2$.

cis-diamminedichloroplatinum(II)

cis-isomer   trans-isomer

The cis-isomer, called cisplatin is an anti-cancer drug which is used in chemotherapy. It is a square planar molecule, making geometric isomerism possible (note that if it was tetrahedral, like a saturated carbon atom, it would not exhibit this isomerism). The trans-isomer is found to be chemotherapeutically inactive. Cisplatin is a heavy metal complex with the two chlorine ligands and two NH_3 groups in the cis position. Because of the cis-arrangement the anticancer ability arises from its ability to enter the nucleus of a cancerous cell and interact with the bases of DNA.

B.8.2 Discuss the importance of chirality in drug action.

The two enantiomers in a racemic mixture of a drug may have very different effects, e.g. Thalidomide. One enantiomer of Thalidomide alleviates morning sickness in pregnant women, whilst the other enantiomer causes deformities in the limbs of the foetus.   © IBO 2001

Optical isomers, differ from geometric isomers in two ways – the molecules are chiral (i.e., asymmetric, containing, for example, 4 different groups on a carbon atom) and optical isomers are non-superimposable mirror images of each other (called a pair of enantiomers). These isomers differ in their optical activity; optical activity is the ability to rotate the plane of polarised light. One optical isomer will rotate plane polarised light clockwise, and its non-superimpossable mirror image will rotate it anti-clockwise by the same amount. 2-butanol, $H_3C-CH-CH_2-CH_3$ is an example of a molecule with a
$\qquad\qquad\qquad\qquad\qquad\quad |$
$\qquad\qquad\qquad\qquad\qquad\ OH$
chiral carbon atom.

An equi-molar mixture of the two enantiomers will not rotate the plane of polarised light and is said to be optically inactive. This is known as a racemic mixture.

Many drugs come from natural sources, often plants, either directly or they are prepared semi-synthetically (i.e. they are chemically modified natural substances). They are usually chiral and are generally found only as single enantiomer in nature rather than as a racemic mixture. Penicillin V which is isolated from penicillium mold is one such example. Its enantiomer does not occur naturally, but can be synthesised and is found to be pharmacologically inactive.

Drugs synthesised entirely in a laboratory, if chiral, are generally formed as racemic mixtures. Ibuprofen, sold as Advil® and Motrin IB® is an example. One of its enantiomers has analgesic and anti-inflammatory properties, the other does not. It is, however, sold as a racemic mixture to reduce costs. However, the 'wrong'/inactive enantiomer may have unintended effects of its own. An example is the thalidomide tragedy. Thalidomide was designed as a mild non-addictive sedative. In the 1950s, it was prescribed to alleviate morning sickness in pregnant women. It was marketed as a racemic mixture of the two enantiomers. One enantiomer alleviates morning sickness, but the other entantiomer causes deformities in the limbs of fetuses and hence birth defects. It is still marketed as a racemic mixture for leprosy patients. Incidentally, the thalidomide molecule does not contain a chiral carbon centre, but a less common chiral nitrogen atom located in a five membered glutamiride ring.

OPTION

B.8.3   Describe the use of chiral auxiliaries to form the desired enantiomer.   © IBO 2001

The separation of racemic mixtures into respective enantiomers can be very difficult since the enantiomers have identical chemical properties in relation to non-chiral reagents but not with other chiral molecules. However, scientists are devising methods of asymmetric synthesis, which allows them to prepare only a single enantiomer rather than a racemic mixture, a so called stereospecific synthesis.

Chiral auxiliaries play a key role in the synthesis of optically active compounds, specifically converting a non-chiral molecule into the desired enantiomer, thus avoiding the need to resolve enantiomers from a racemic mixture (an 'auxiliary' is a 'helping hand'). It works by attaching itself chemically to the non-chiral molecule to create the stereochemical conditions necessary to force the reaction to follow a certain stereo-specific path. Once the new molecule has been formed, the auxiliary can be removed (and recycled) to leave the desired enantiomer. An example is the synthesis of Taxol, an anti-cancer drug, effective against breast cancer.

B.8.4   Explain the use of combinatorial chemistry to synthesise new drugs.

Combinatorial chemistry is used to synthesise a large number of different compounds and screen them for biological activity, resulting in a 'combinatorial library' (ror example the 'mix and split' process whereby polypeptides can be made by every combination of amino acids, using polystyrene resin beads). Stress the importance of solid phase chemistry.   © IBO 2001

As discussed earlier, the research, development and testing of new pharmaceutical drugs is an extremely expensive, time consuming process, akin to finding a needle in the proverbial haystack. Research almost always starts with a potential drug that shows some pharmacological activity. This is called the 'lead' compound. Keeping the main chemical structure of the lead compound, changes are made to its structure to produce more effective drugs in terms of their effectiveness, fewer side effects, etc. Two such simple examples discussed in this chapter include aspirin and penicillin.

Combinatorial chemistry involves a variety of techniques and technologies for creating a large number of molecules and testing them quickly for desirable biological properties. Thus combinatorial chemistry (combi-chem) is considered a much better way of synthesising potential new drugs. Since designing chemicals for biological activity is difficult, this technology allows the testing of thousands of possible chemicals in order to find the right one. Combi-chem basically involves reacting a set of starting materials in all possible combinations. This new and important method is being increasingly used to reduce the time and costs associated with producing effective new drugs.

Combinatorial chemistry uses the same methods as organic synthesis; however, instead of making one compound at a time, combi-chem takes advantage of technology and computerisation to make very large libraries of related chemicals. Larger, more diverse compound libraries can only increase the chances of finding better drugs.

The term 'library' (or compound library or combinatorial library) is used to describe a collection of compounds that are screened to determine their pharmacological activity. Libraries of a very large number of related compounds have been produced by the combi-chem technique. This involves the use of robotics to carry out identical chemical processes between chemicals such as adding fixed volumes of substances using syringes. This technique is called 'parallel synthesis'. The products of such reactions (called 'libraries') are then tested *en masse* for their potential pharmacological activities. Initial testing for many drugs can be achieved in the laboratory rather than on animals by studying the effects of each chemical on enzymes and their ability to bind to receptor sites.

Combinatorial chemistry started with peptides – parts of protein molecules. A condensation reaction between two amino acids produces the dipeptide containing the amide linkage or the peptide bond (and water):

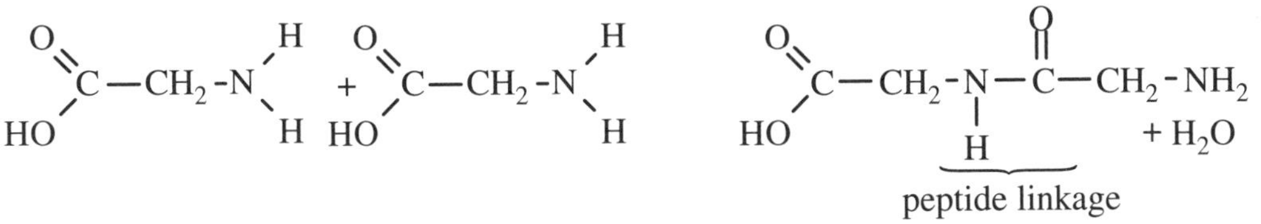

peptide linkage

A method was developed in the 1960's to make peptides by solid-state synthesis; this was followed by a technique to produce a large number of peptides by solid-phase parallel synthesis. The technique of 'mix and split' allows for the synthesis of a very large number of polypeptides by combination of amino acids using solid state chemistry (with resin beads). This is described below and illustrates the importance of solid-phase chemistry in the synthesis of organic molecules.

The formation of a peptide link requires a bond between the N atom on one amino acid (say A) and the C atom containing the acid group of another amino acid (say B). First a 'linking group' is chemically attached to a plastic bead. In vessel 1 (diagram below) a chemical reaction allows amino acid A (via its acid group) to be attached to the linking group on the plastic bead (with the elimination of HCl: H coming from the -OH group of the amino acid, and Cl from the linking group). Vessel 2 contains the amino acid B. The bead from vessel 1 is washed and reacted with amino acid B in vessel 2 to produce the dipeptide A-B attached to the linkage. The linkage to the plastic resin can be broken at any stage or subsequent condensation can be carried out to produce a polypeptide.

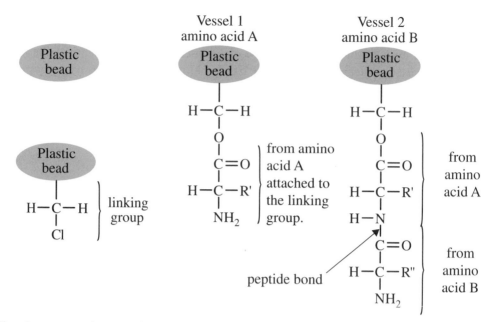

The above procedure can be extended so that the first step commences with reacting two amino acids A and B with the beads through a linking group to give bead-A and bead-B. These can then be split into two containers so that each now contains half of bead-A and half of bead-B. In the second stage, one container is reacted with A and therefore produces bead-A-A and bead-B -A. The second one is reacted with B and will produce bead-A-B and bead-B-B. Thus a two amino acid, two-stage process will provide 4 (2^2) dipeptides A-A, A-B, B-A and B-B. Starting with three different amino acids A, B and C and using three stages would lead to the formation of $3^3 = 27$ tripeptides. A four amino acid, four-stage process would produce $4^4 = 256$ different compounds, leading to the formation of a library of compounds.

Once a compound has been de-inked from the resin bead, mass spectrum and nuclear magnetic resonance spectroscopy can be used to determine its structure.

The linkage to the resin can be broken at any stage or subsequent condensation reactions can be carried out to produce a polypeptide.

EXAMPLE

Consider three aminoacids A, B and C. Calculate the number of dipeptides that could be created from a two stage combi-chem process.

SOLUTION

1st stage:

      bead -A , bead-B, bead -C

2nd stage:

      Divide so that each container now contains $\frac{1}{3}$ bead –A, $\frac{1}{3}$ bead –B and $\frac{1}{3}$ bead-C.

Next, react each one with A, B and C. The first container will have beads with -A-A, -A-B and -A-C, the second container, beads -B-A, -B-B and -B-C and the third container, beads -C-A, -C-B and -C-C for a total of 9 (3^2).

Ten compounds in ten reaction vessels in a four-stage reaction sequence would produce $10^4 = 10 \times 10 \times 10 \times 10 = 10\,000$ compounds with 40 (10+10+10+10) reactions. Scientists realised that this method need not be restricted to making polymeric structures like the polypeptides. Chemicals such as organic heterocyclics can be synthesised – compounds that are often used as starting materials to make drugs. A cyclic compound can often be a very good library starting point to which different branches can be added, eventually leading to new and better drugs.

12.9 ANAESTHETICS

B.9.1   Compare local and general anaesthetics in terms of their mode of action.

© IBO 2001

Local anaesthetics block pain in a specific area when they are injected under the skin or are applied topically (rubbed into the skin). Examples include cocaine (probably the first local anaesthetic used), procaine, used in dental work, benzococaine, used for toothache, and lidocaine which is more potent than procaine and can be applied to the skin. Local anaesthetics block local nerve conduction and cause some decrease in blood supply to the area by constricting blood vessels. A nerve stimulus is transmitted by electrochemical impulses, and a chemical called acetylcholine is frequently involved in transmitting the impulse across tiny gaps between nerve ends called synapses. Local anaesthetics block the action of acetylcholine and thus do not allow impulses to travel along the nerves by blocking the flow of sodium ions across neuron membranes. Procaine and lidocaine do not affect the brain, unlike cocaine, which does, explaining the widespread illegal use of cocaine.

General anaesthetics, on the other hand, act on the brain and produce unconsciousness as well as insensitivity to pain. The unconsciousness induced is readily reversible. Examples include nitrous oxide, N_2O, diethyl ether $C_2H_5-O-C_2H_5$, chloroform $CHCl_3$, cyclopropane C_3H_6 $\left(\triangle \right)$ and halothane $CHClBrCF_3$ (2-bromo-2-chloro-1,1,1-trifluoroethane).

B.9.2 Compare the structures and effects of cocaine, procaine and lidocaine. © IBO 2001

Structures of cocaine, procaine and lidocaine:

Cocaine

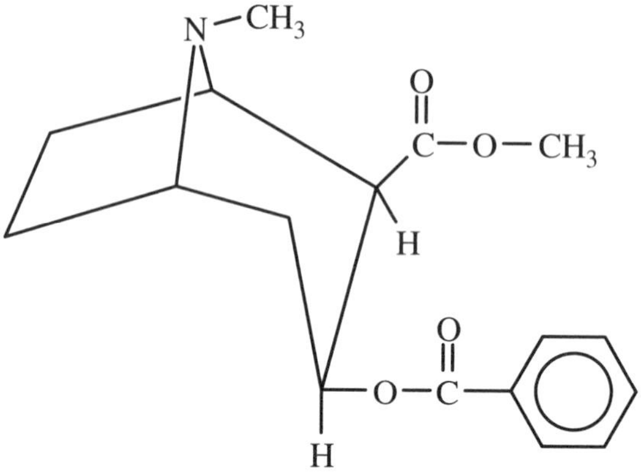

Procaine
(Novacaine)

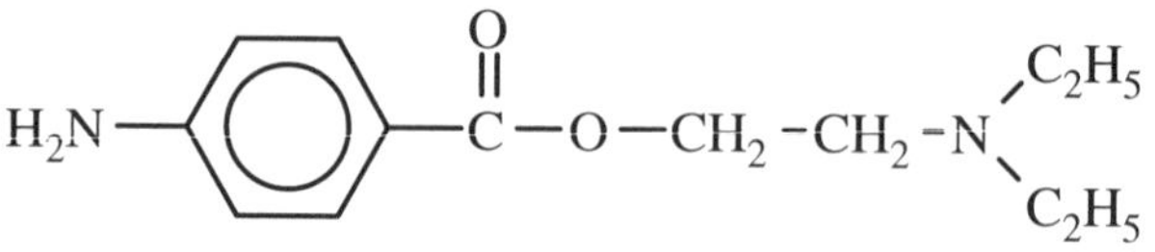

Lidocaine
(Xylocaine)

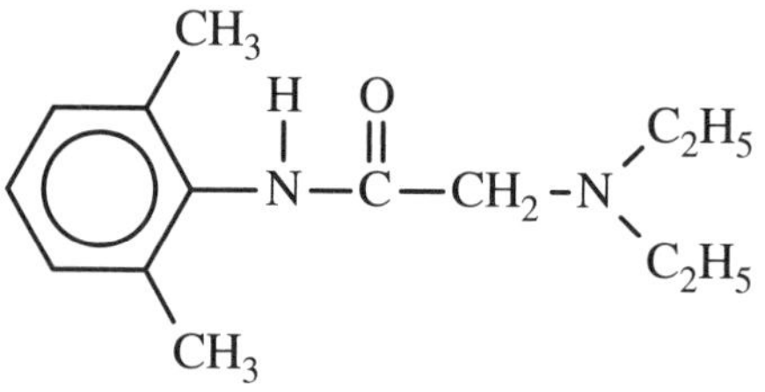

All three contain the benzene ring and the tertiary amine (R_3N) group, where the nitrogen is bonded to three alkyl groups.

EFFECTS OF COCAINE, PROCAINE AND LIDOCAINE

Besides its ability to block pain in a specific area, cocaine also acts as a stimulant of the central nervous system. Its medical use is restricted to surface application in oral surgery. Because it causes a general constriction of blood vessels (it acts as a vasoconstrictor), leading to high blood pressure, it cannot be safely injected for use as a general anaesthetic. Abuse of cocaine has risen rapidly. Although it does not cause physical addiction (no acute withdrawal symptoms) or cause tolerance (i.e. need for an increased dose to produce the same effect) it does produce a strong psychological addiction producing an uncontrollable desire for the drug. An overdose can suppress the heart and respiration, sometimes causing death. In small doses it produces a pleasurable feeling of well being including relief from fatigue, increased mental alertness, physical strength and reduced hunger (thus coca leaves are sometimes chewed by mine workers in South America). Chronic use leads to loss of appetite, severe personality disorders, and increased tendency to violence and anti-social behaviour.

Cocaine has a very short half life in the body (only a few minutes) since it is rapidly metabolized by the liver. Cocaine is poorly absorbed when taken orally, and is extremely dangerous when taken intravenously, as it is a potent drug.

Procaine (also called novocaine) gives prolonged relief from pain, and is very useful in producing loss of feeling immediately prior to surgery or dental procedures. The drug, applied through injection is relatively short acting. It is an effective non-toxic, non-irritant local anaesthetic.

Lidocaine is used topically (rubbed) as a local anaesthetic to produce numbness or loss of feeling before surgery or other painful procedures. It is more potent than procaine, and its side effects include itching and swelling. Lidocaine can be used to decrease the pain of a burn wound itself. Both procaine and lidocaine are used in dentistry and in minor surgery.

B.9.3   Discuss the advantages and disadvantages of nitrous oxide, ethoxyethane, trichloromethane, cyclopropane and halothane.

Nitrous oxide is not very potent, trichloromethane leads to liver damage, ethoxyethane and cyclopropane are highly flammable. Halothane (2-bromo-2-chloro-1,1,1-trifluoroethane) is widely used but is potentially harmful to the ozone layer.   © IBO 2001

A summary of the effects of some anaesthetics

Name	Formula	Structure	Advantages	Disadvantages
Dinitrogen oxide (nitrous oxide, laughing gas)	N_2O	$\ddot{N}{=}N{=}\ddot{O}$ (linear)	Capable of inducing deep levels of anaesthesia (if adequate $[O_2]$ is maintained)	Low potency anaesthetic (not very efficient), induces a state of disinhibition and euphoria and is thus an abused drug
Trichloro-methane (chloroform)	$CHCl_3$	H–C, Cl, Cl, Cl (tetrahedral)	Non-flammable	Leads to liver damage. Not a useful anaesthetic, its toxicity precludes widespread use. It has a narrow safety margin (i.e. a small difference between an anaesthetic and a lethal dose).

OPTION

Name	Formula	Structure	Advantages	Disadvantages
Ethoxy-ethane (ethyl ether)	$(CH_3CH_2)_2O$	H_5C_2 $\overset{..}{\underset{..}{O}}$ C_2H_5 (bent at oxygen)	Alleviates the pain involved in surgical procedures	Highly flammable; (prone to ignite and explode violently), ether has been replaced by safer anaesthetics that result in fewer side effects and are more stable, safe and non-inflammable)
Cyclo-propane	C_3H_6	H C H / \ H–C——C–H H H (Trigonal planar ring)	A very potent general anaesthetic administered by inhalation; used for all types of surgical operations	Forms explosive mixtures with air; highly flammable; can cause nausea vomiting and headaches
2-bromo-2-chloro-1,1,1-trifluoro ethane (Halothane® trade name fluothane®)	$CF_3CBrClH$	F | F–C–F | H–C*–Br | Cl *Chiral carbon, an optically active compound.	Widely used: a potent general anaesthetic for all types of surgical operations; non-flammable; produces rapid recovery; non-irritating to the respiratory tract.	Induction to anaesthesia is slow; prolonged recovery. Potentially harmful to the ozone layer - capable of producing Cl and Br (chlorine and bromine free radicals) that can destroy the ozone layer; $O_3 + \bullet Cl \Rightarrow ClO\bullet + O_2$ See Option D.9

B.9.4 Calculate the partial pressures of component gases in an anaesthetic mixture.

Knowledge of how to use Dalton's law of partial pressures is required. Students are not expected to state the law.
© IBO 2001

In the Ideal Gas Law $PV=nRT$, no quantity depends in **any way** on the chemical; constitution of the gas molecules (see Chapter 5). If several gases (say A, B and C) are present, we can use the Ideal Gas Law provided the number of moles of different gases is accounted for. If A, B and C are confined in a container of Volume V, and n_t is the total number of moles of gas, then:

1. $P_tV=n_tRT$ where P_t is total pressure and n_t = total number of moles of gas.

    $n_t = n_A + n_B + n_C$ and the 3 gases each contribute to the total pressure so that $P_t = P_A + P_B + P_C$. Thus:

2. $P_A = \dfrac{n_A RT}{V}, P_B = \dfrac{n_B RT}{V}$ and $P_C = \dfrac{n_C RT}{V}$

P_A, P_B and P_C are called the **partial pressures** of A, B and C respectively. P_A is the pressure exerted if only A occupied the container at that temperature. Similarly for P_B and P_C.

DALTONS LAW OF PARTIAL PRESSURES

The total pressure in a container is equal to the sum of the partial pressures of the component gases. From the equations (1) and (2) above, consider the ratio $\dfrac{P_A}{P_t}$.

$$\frac{P_A}{P_t} = \frac{\dfrac{n_A RT}{V}}{\dfrac{n_t RT}{V}} = \frac{n_A}{n_t} = \frac{n_A}{n_A + n_B + n_C}$$

Therefore: $\dfrac{P_A}{P_t} = \dfrac{n_A}{n_t}$ or $\dfrac{\text{Partial pressure of A}}{\text{Total pressure}} = \dfrac{\text{Amount of A}}{\text{Total amount}} = \dfrac{\text{Volume of A}}{\text{Total volume}}$

MOLE FRACTION

For a mixture of gases , say A, B and C:

X_A the mole fraction of A = $\dfrac{n_A}{n_A + n_B + n_C} = \dfrac{n_A}{n_t}$, $X_B = \dfrac{n_B}{n_t}$ and $X_C = \dfrac{n_C}{n_t}$ and

$X_A + X_B + X_C = 1$.

From Dalton's Law: $\dfrac{P_A}{P_t} = \dfrac{n_A}{n_t}$; $P_A = P_t\dfrac{n_A}{n_t} = P_t X_A$ therefore $P_A = X_A P_{\text{total}}$

Partial Pressure of each gas = total pressure of mixture × mole fraction of each gas.

OPTION

EXAMPLE

Calculate the partial pressure of each gas in a sample of air at 97 kPa pressure that contains 0.78 mol N_2, 0.21 mol O_2 and 0.01 mol Ar.

SOLUTION

$$P_{N_2} = \frac{n_{N_2}}{n_{total}} P_{total} = \frac{0.78}{1.00} \times 97 = 76 \, kPa, \text{ similarly:}$$

$P_{O_2} = 0.21 \times 97 = 20 \, kPa$ and $P_{Ar} = 0.01 \times 97 = 1 \, kPa.$

(Check: $P_{total} = P_{N_2} + P_{O_2} + P_{Ar} = 76 + 20 + 1 = 97 \, kPa$).

GASEOUS ANAESTHESIA AND PARTIAL PRESSURES

When anaesthetic gases and vapors are inhaled, the patient must also be given life sustaining oxygen gas. Consider nitrous oxide, N_2O which is often abused as an illegal drug for its euphoric effect. If it is not administered with at least 20% O_2 (by volume), it can induce hypoxia (decreased $[O_2]$ in the blood). In order to achieve a euphoric effect, concentrations of 50% (by volume) or more are required. When such a concentration is mixed with atmospheric air, the concentration of O_2 can drop sufficiently to produce hypoxia leading to brain damage.

EXAMPLE

Isoflurane, a halogenated volatile anaesthetic is used with nitrous oxide to sustain anaesthesia during surgery. If the concentrations of Isoflurane, N_2O and O_2 are 2.0%, 70% and 28% respectively, calculate the partial pressure of each gas in the sample at 25°C and 1.0 atmospheric pressure.

SOLUTION

$$P_{isoflurane} = \frac{2.0}{100} \times 1.0 = 0.020 \, atm.$$

$$P_{N_2} = \frac{70}{100} \times 1.0 = 0.70 \, atm.$$

$$P_{O_2} = \frac{28}{100} \times 1.0 = 0.28 \, atm.$$

(Check: $P_{total} = P_{isoflurane} + P_{N_2} + P_{O_2} = 0.020 + 0.70 + 0.28 = 1.00 \, atm$).

12.10 MIND ALTERING DRUGS

B10.1 Describe the effects of lysergic acid diethylamide (LSD), mescaline, psilocybin and tetrahydrocannabinol (THC).   © IBO 2001

Mind altering drugs are also called psychedelic drugs or psychotomimetics (ie simulating 'madness') or hallucinogens. A hallucination is a mistaken notion, that is a perception or feeling that has no external cause. The word psychedelic means something causing an abnormal stimulation of feeling or consciousness. These 'mind bending' or 'mind altering' drugs produce a qualitative change in thought, perception or mood and can cause vivid illusions and fantasies ('imagination unrestrained by reality'). These drugs can cause remarkable distortions in touch, smell, hearing and vision, thereby causing illusions. For example walls may appear to move, colour may appear brilliant, users may claim to "see" sound and "hear" colours and jumping from a high building may appear safe.

Examples of mind altering drugs include LSD (lysergic acid diethylamide), mescaline (one of the oldest known hallucinogens), psilocybin (from 'magic' or peyote mushrooms) and THC (tetrahydrocannabinol) from marijuana (also called grass, pot,..).

EFFECTS OF MIND ALTERING DRUGS

LSD

LSD is a powerful hallucinogen. An LSD experience is a highly personal one and the effect varies with the dose, physiological condition (state of vital processes) and psychological condition (state of mind) of the user, and the user's expectations. Perception is magnified many fold. It can destroy the sense of judgement (i.e. jumping from a high building). LSD can cause strong opposite emotions at the same time eg. relaxation and tension. It can produce frightening 'bad' trips as well as flash backs without taking LSD. It does not produce physical addiction, but tolerance develops and disappears rapidly. Psychological dependence can appear but not as strong as with other drugs.

Mescaline

Produces 'colour' hallucinations, i.e. it produces vivid colour perceptions. A mescaline trip usually lasts about 12 hours.

Psilocybin

Effects similar to LSD where perception is magnified many fold. In low doses it produces feelings of relaxation similar to those of cannabis. At high doses the effect is closer to that of LSD. Users experience an intensification of colour, hallucinations and a sense of well being. A 'magic mushroom' trip tends to last about 4 hours (as opposed to 8 or more with LSD).

Tetrahydrocannabinol, THC

THC is a mild hallucinogen and has some effects similar to alcohol. At low doses users feel excited and silly. As the dose is increased, it produces changes in perception - the user sees bright colours and has a keener sense of hearing. Still higher doses produce visual hallucinations (objects in odd shapes). The initial feeling of joy can turn to

OPTION

extreme anxiety, depression, uneasiness, panic attack and fearfulness. Decisions become harder to make, and a person is more likely to follow the suggestions of others. Tasks like driving that require thinking and good reflexes become difficult. No tolerance develops, but regular use can lead to moderate psychological dependence.

B.10.2 Discuss the structural similarities and differences between LSD, mescaline and psilocybin.

Stress the similarity of all three drugs and compare them to the indole ring.

© IBO 2001

Indole is an example of a heterocyclic amine compound in which the nitrogen atom is part of a ring. Indole is a fused-ring heterocyclic structure containing a benzene ring and a heterocyclic ring sharing a common C=C bond. The N atom bonded to two carbons and an H atom is a secondary amine.

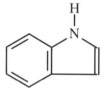

LSD, a fat soluble compound, easily diffuses into the brain. It readily crosses the placental barrier into a foetus. LSD contains the diethylamide side chain.

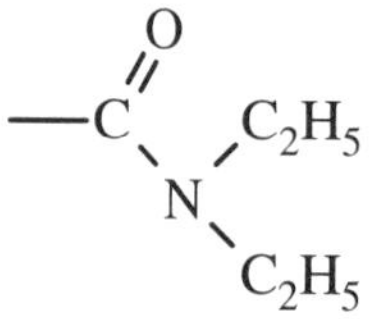

Structure of LSD

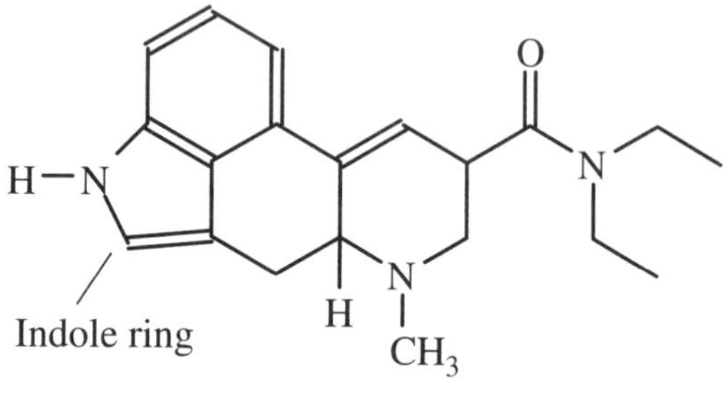

Indole ring

Mescaline contains the benzene ring, but does not contain the fused-ring heterocyclic structure. Instead it contains a primary amine group $-NH_2$ where the N atom is bonded to only one C atom.

Structure of mescaline

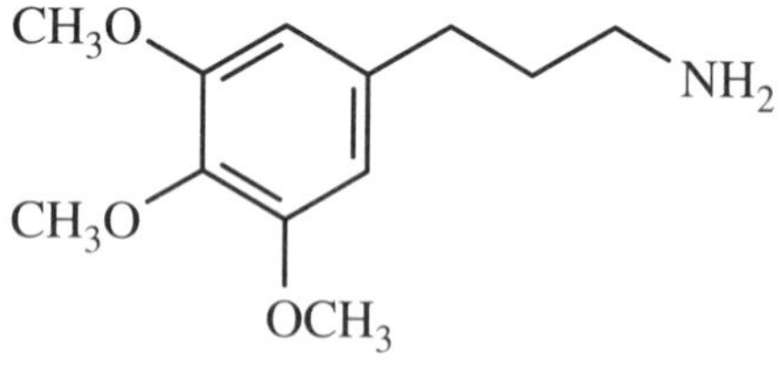

Besides the indole ring, psilocybin also contains the dimethylamine $-N(CH_3)_2$ side chain, as well as the dihydrogen phosphate group on the benzene ring.

Structure of psilocybin

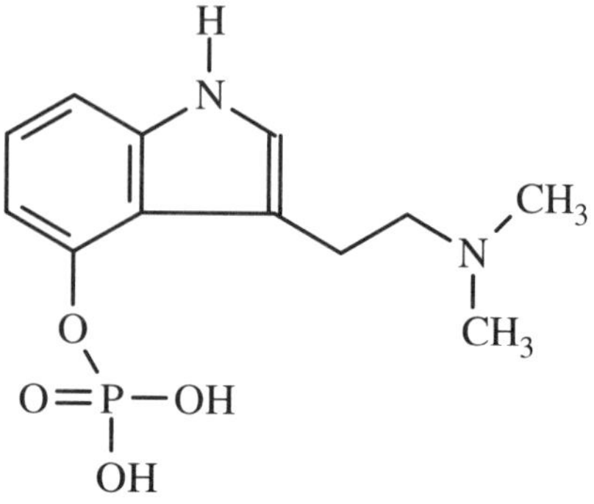

The backbone structure is the same as that of serotonin (a neurotransmitter) but with different side chains.

Structure of serotonin

B.10.3 Discuss the arguments for and against the legalization of cannabis.

Arguments for legalization include the ability of cannabis to offer relief for certain diseases. Arguments against legalization include the possible harmful effects and the possibility of cannabis users moving on to harder drugs. © IBO 2001

The cannabis plant, *cannabis sativa*, contains pharmacologically active compounds, the cannabinoids. Arguments for the legalisation of cannabis include its ability to offer relief from certain diseases and ailments such as AIDS, cancer and glaucoma. The 'wasting syndrome' seen in AIDS patients due to loss of appetite leads to drastic weight loss. The causes of this wasting are not completely known. It is claimed that marijuana use produces beneficial effects from its ability to increase appetite. Treatment using chemotherapy often causes nausea and thus reduces the patient's ability to keep food down. It has been suggested that cannabis relieves nausea, allowing cancer patients to gain weight. It is medically given to terminally ill cancer patients to relieve tension and anxiety. Similarly marijuana is reported to help glaucoma patients by decreasing pressure inside the eyeball which can damage eyes.

Regular smoking of marijuana can lead to respiratory ailments associated with inhaling smoke. It has been suggested that regular use may suppress the body's immune system, thus increasing susceptibility to disease. Also, decreased fertility has been observed in some human males. There is some evidence that marijuana use causes brain damage in rats (to a lesser extent than is caused by alcohol) and some research has reported chromosomal damage which may lead to birth defects. It has also been suggested that cannabis users could possibly move on to 'hard' drugs. This may be true of illegal drug users, but whether medicinal users of cannabis would do the same is considered questionable.

A significant danger in the use of prohibited drugs is that users have to obtain their supplies from criminal sources. Addicts pay much more than the true cost of the drug and are often forced into crime and/or prostitution to support their habit. This produces a very negative impact for society at large and is the main reason why a few governments have decided to supply drugs to addicts under controlled conditions. This does not mean that these drugs (mainly in the 'hard' category) have become, in the strictest sense 'legal'. A case that could be discussed in this context is that of the probition of alcohol in the USA in the early part of the last century. This was widely disobeyed and produced such a spate of organised crime that it had to be scrapped.

OPTION

The issue of how to contain the damage done to both individuals and society at large by the abuse of both legal and illegal drugs remains one of the most challenging issues facing us all.

QUESTIONS
B.1 PHARMACEUTICAL PRODUCTS

1. List the effects of drugs and medicines.

2. Outline the stages involved in research, development and testing of new pharmaceutical products.

3. Describe the different methods of administering drugs.

4. Discuss the terms lethal dosage (LD_{50}), tolerance and side effects.

B.2 ANTACIDS

5. State and explain how excess acidity in the stomach can be reduced by the use of different bases.

B.3 ANALGESICS

6. Describe and explain the different ways that analgesics prevent pain.

7. Describe the use of derivatives of salicylic acid as mild analgesics and compare the advantages and disadvantages of using aspirin and paracetamol (acetaminophen).

8. Compare the structures of morphine, codeine and the semi-synthetic opiate, heroin.

9   Discuss the advantages and disadvantages of using morphine and its derivatives as strong analgesics. Include the social as well as physiological effects of both short- and long-term use.

B.4 DEPRESSANTS

10. Describe the effects of depressants.

11. Discuss the social and physiological effects of the use and abuse of ethanol. Include effects on the family, cost to society and the short- and long-term health effects.

12. Describe and explain the techniques used for the detection of ethanol in the breath and in the blood or urine. Include potassium dichromate(VI) in the breathalyser, analysis of blood or urine by chromatography and absorption of infra-red radiation in the intoximeter.

13. Describe the synergistic effects of ethanol with other drugs.

14. List other commonly used depressants and describe their structures.

B.5 STIMULANTS

15. List the physiological effects of stimulants.

16. Compare amphetamines and adrenaline.

17. Discuss the short- and long-term effects of nicotine consumption.

18. Describe the effects of caffeine and compare its structure with that of nicotine.

B.6 ANTIBACTERIALS

19. Outline the historical development of penicillins. Include the discovery by Fleming and the development by Florey and Chain.

20. Compare broad-spectrum and narrow-spectrum antibiotics.

21. Explain how penicillins work and discuss the effects of modifying the side chain.

22. Discuss and explain the effect overprescription of penicillins has, and the use of penicillins in animal feedstock.

B.7 ANTIVIRALS

23. State how viruses differ from bacteria.

24. Describe the different ways in which antiviral drugs work.

25. Discuss the difficulties associated with solving the AIDS problem.

EXTENSION MATERIAL-HL QUESTIONS ONLY
B.8 STEREOCHEMISTRY IN DRUG ACTION AND DESIGN

26. Describe the importance of geometrical isomerism in drug action.

27. Discuss the importance of chirality in drug action.

28. Describe the use of chiral auxiliaries to form the desired enantiomer.

29. Explain the use of combinatorial chemistry to synthesize new drugs.

B.9 ANAESTHETICS

30. Compare local and general anesthetics in terms of their mode of action.

31. Compare the structures and effects of cocaine, procaine and lidocaine.

OPTION

32. Discuss the advantages and disadvantages of nitrous oxide, ethoxyethane, trichloromethane, cyclopropane and halothane.

33. Explain how you would calculate the partial pressures of component gases in an anesthetic mixture.

B.10 MIND-ALTERING DRUGS

34. Describe the effects of lysergic acid di ethyl amide (LSD), mescaline, psilocybin and tetrahydrocannabinol (THC).

35. Discuss the structural similarities and differences between LSD, mescaline and psilocybin.

36. Discuss the arguments for and against the legalization of cannabis.

OPTION

HUMAN BIOCHEMISTRY (Option C)

13

Chapter contents

The aim of this option is to give students an understanding of the chemistry of important molecules found in the human body and the need for a balanced and healthy diet. Although the role these substances play in the body should be appreciated, the emphasis is placed on their chemistry, and students who have not followed a course in biology will not be at a disadvantage. Students will not be required to memorize complex structures but will be expected to recognize functional groups and types of bonding within molecules. The structures of some important biological molecules are given in the data booklet.

© IBO 2001

13.1 CORE MATERIAL (SL & HL)
DIET

C.1.1 Describe what the human body requires for a healthy diet. Students should recognize the importance of a balanced diet, including minimum requirements and the need for essential minerals.

© IBO 2001

Human Body and its Requirements: The human body requires certain substances to function and grow. Good diet is essential to staying healthy. Food provides energy and replaces molecules used up by bodily processes. **Nutrients are the food components which provide growth, energy and replacement of body tissue.** They are generally divided into **six groups,** namely proteins, carbohydrates, fats/lipids, vitamins, minerals and water; the human body requires different amounts of each nutrient for good health.

Caloric starvation still exists in much of the world and is particularly common in children and infants. It is responsible for weakness, anaemia and muscle wasting. On the other hand, excessive food consumption leads to obesity due to fat storage, and can lead to diabetes, hypertension and cardiovascular disease due to build up of fatty tissue inside blood vessels surrounding the heart. Clearly, moderation and a balanced diet which includes nutrients in the correct amounts is essential.

The four basic food groups are grains from cereals and bread which provide carbohydrates, vitamin B1, iron and niacin (nicotinic acid) for energy and a healthy nervous system; meats including fish and eggs which supply proteins, iron, niacin and vitamins for building muscles, bones and blood cells; milk and cheese which provide calcium, vitamin B2 and protein for strong bones, healthy skin and good vision; and fruits and vegetables which provide vitamins A and C for night vision, to resist infections and provide bulk. Lentils, soybeans and some cereals are protein rich whereas many vegetables contain useful amounts of minerals.

Carbohydrates, Fats and Proteins: Carbohydrates, empirical formula CH_2O, are the main energy source for our bodies and are vital to the synthesis of cells. Only plants synthesise carbohydrates. Potatoes, bread, corn, rice and fruits contain carbohydrates, as do snack foods such as sweets, chips and soft drinks. Important carbohydrates are: starch (a polysaccharide), lactose and sucrose (disaccharides) and glucose and fructose (monosaccharides). Glucose, the most common simple sugar, has the molecular formula $C_6H_{12}O_6$ and is found in all body cells. Fructose, a five–membered ring simple sugar of the same molecular formula as glucose, is found in fruits. Complex sugars are combinations of simple sugars such as maltose, lactose, etc. Cellulose, another polysaccharide, is the major component of plant cells. It cannot be digested by most organisms and is not a source of energy, but makes up an important part of diet called fibre or roughage. Most carbohydrates are changed to glucose, a simple sugar as a result of digestion. Glucose is then carried by the blood to body cells, where it is broken down during respiration and the energy available goes to physical activities, to keeping the body warm and is used for repair and growth of cells. Excess carbohydrates are converted to fats and stored in the body.

Fats which also contain C, H, O, are the most concentrated energy source and provide over twice as much energy per gram as carbohydrates. An average human body contains 15 to 30% fat by mass. Fats are present in milk, butter, cheeses and nuts. An average diet should contain about 30% fats. The most common fats are **esters** made from the reaction of glycerol with long chain carboxylic acids (fatty acids). 98% of fats are triglycerides (glycerol esters) and 2% are complex lipids and cholesterol. Linoleic and linoeic acids are the two most vital fats since they cannot be synthesized in our bodies, but are necessary for its correct functioning.

Proteins, made up of C, H, O, N, (and sometimes S) can also be used as an energy source in the event of starvation. However, their primary use is to provide amino acids which are the building blocks of new proteins in the body. They make up 15% of our bodies and have molar masses of between 6000 to over 1,000,000 g mol^{-1}. Proteins are also natural polymers. Out of some 20 amino acids, there are ten amino acids which our bodies cannot synthesize and cannot store in the same way we do fat, hence they must be found through food consumption. These are called **essential amino** acids – essential because these cannot be synthesized in the body, but no more important than those the body can synthesize.

As part of a healthy diet, foods should contain 20% proteins. These proteins should ideally contain not only the ten amino acids we cannot synthesise, but also in a similar ratio to which our body needs them. Amino acids are used for growth and repair of body tissues as well as to make hormones, enzymes and antibodies. A protein which contains all ten of the amino acids we cannot synthesise and in a ratio similar to that which we need, is called a **complete protein**, such as casein from milk, cheese, eggs and soybeans. Most animal proteins such as those found in meat, fish and eggs are complete. Eggs in particular provide the amino acids in the ratio and amount which human beings require. Approximately 50g of complete protein per day is sufficient to furnish all of the amino acids an adult human body does not synthesize. Incomplete proteins include most plant proteins. For example, wheat protein does not have lysine whereas rice protein does not contain lysine or threonine.

Vegetarians can have a difficult time securing all the proteins they require since plant proteins (except from soy beans) are **incomplete** proteins. However, a combination of legumes (such as peas, beans or corn) and grains can furnish all the proteins humans need and serve to complement each other.

Vitamins, Minerals and Water: Besides protein, fats and carbohydrates, human beings also require vitamins, minerals and water in order to live. Vitamins, needed in small amounts, are the organic requirements that help enzymes regulate changes inside body cells. Vitamin deficiencies lead to diseases such as scurvy due to vitamin C deficiency and rickets due to vitamin D deficiency. A balanced diet provides all the vitamin requirements of humans; however it is common to add vitamins to foods, such as vitamin A to margarine, vitamin B to flour, vitamin C to juices and vitamin D to milk. Minerals are the very small amounts of inorganic ions required by the body for strong bones and teeth (Ca, Mg and P) and for the formation of hormones, enzymes and in the maintaining of fluid levels in the body. Lack of calcium produces osteoporosis, lack of iron causes anemia, lack of iodine produces enlarged thyroid gland (goiter) and lack of sodium ions produces cramps.

OPTION

Option C: Human Biochemistry

Water comprises about 70% of our body mass and is responsible for dissolving most of the chemicals in our system and transporting nutrients and waste. In order to create a balance between our intake and the amount of water we release through sweat, urine, faeces and respiration, humans require about one to one and a half litres of water daily in addition to that obtained from the food consumed.

C.1.2   Calculate the calorific value of a food from enthalpy of combustion data.

The oxidation of fats, carbohydrates and proteins produces carbon dioxide, water and energy. The energy requirements of human beings depend on age, size, sex and daily activity. Metabolism, the chemical reactions in living organisms, converts the food we eat into energy and produces various materials that our bodies require.

The amount of energy stored in food, its calorific value, is obtained indirectly by burning different foods and using the energy released to raise the temperature of a fixed mass of water using a calorimeter. The calorific content or value of a large apple is about 100 Cal (420 kJ). This means that if it were burnt in a calorimeter, the energy produced on combustion would raise the temperature of 1 kg water by 100°C (assuming the calorimeter does not absorb any heat). In any such calculations, any energy absorbed by the calorimeter should be included (see Chapter 6).

EXAMPLE

A large apple weighs 150 g. If a 15.0 g sample of the apple, on complete combustion raises the temperature of 200 g water in a glass container by 45.3 °C, calculate the calorific value of the apple. The heat capacity of the glass calorimeter = 89.1 J °C^{-1} and the specific heat of water = 4.184 J g^{-1} C^{-1}.

SOLUTION

Heat produced = heat absorbed by water + heat absorbed by calorimeter
$$= (m \times c \times \Delta T)_{water} + (m \times c \times \Delta T)_{calorimeter}$$
$$= (200 \text{ g} \times 4.184 \text{ J g}^{-1} \text{ C}^{-1} \times 45.3 \text{ °C}) + (89.1 \text{ J °C}^{-1} \times 45.3 \text{ °C})$$
$$= (37907 + 4036) \text{ J}$$
$$= 41943 \text{ J}$$
$$= 41.9 \text{ kJ (produced by 15.0 g of apple)}$$
Thus the calorific value of the 150 g apple is 419 kJ.

The energy one consumes is expended through activity and the excess energy is stored as fat leading to weight gain. If a person eats less energy containing food than the body needs, the stored fat is broken down for energy, resulting in weight loss. Metabolism of different foods produces different amounts of energy, for example, fats and oils produce approximately 9 Cal per gram, whereas carbohydrates and proteins produce approximately 4 Cal per gram. Thus, a given food containing 10 g of fat, 20 g of carbohydrate and 10 g of protein produces [(10g fat × 9 Cal/g fat) + (20g carb. × 4 Cal/g Carb.) + (10 g protein × 4 Cal/g protein)] = 210 Cal.

Approximate Calorie[*] Content of Typical Foods		Nutritional Values for Breakfast Cereal e.g. 30 g serving of Honey Nut Cheerios			
Food	**Calories[*]**	calories	120 Cal	iron	29% RDA[**]
raw carrot	40	protein	3.1 g	magnesium	10%
2 strips bacon	100	carbohydrate	24 g	phosphorus	8%
large apple	100	fat	1.7 g	zinc	7%
fried egg	110	starch	11.8 g	folic acid	8%
355 ml apple juice	160	sugars	10.7 g	vitamin B1	0%
one slice of pizza	180	sodium	215 mg	vitamin B2	3%
hamburger	350	potassium	80 mg	vitamin B6	10%
milk shake	500	calcium	1% of RDA	vitamin D	0%

[*] 1 Calorie = 1000 calories. 1 calorie is the amount of heat required to raise the temperature of 1 g of water by 1 °C; 1 calorie = 4.184 Joules.

Since requirements vary from person to person and from lifestyle to lifestyle, recommended daily allowances (RDA) are representative of broader ranges. These RDA indicators are, however, useful indicators of nutritional requirements. Half a century ago nutritional concerns revolved around quantity and avoiding vitamin deficiency. Now, in developed nations, interest is directed towards eating less but with greater discrimination and laws in many countries require packaged foods to be labeled with information regarding its nutritional content.

C.1.3   Discuss the benefits and concerns of using genetically modified (GM) foods.

© IBO 2001

A gene is a section of a DNA molecule. Genes control characteristics such as hair colour and, in foods, for example, resistance to pests and diseases. These characteristics are passed from generation to generation. It is possible to insert a gene containing a specific characteristic into a second organism. Such a genetically modified organism (GMO) can sometimes reproduce that characteristic.

Both crops and animals can be modified to provide more food, be more resistant to disease and be more tolerant to toxins. Examples of GM foods include corn modified to be poisonous to some pests, soya beans modified to be herbicide resistant and tomatoes modifed to be denser and drier. The use of herbicide resistant plants allows farmers to reduce the overall use of chemicals.

Concerns over the use of GM foods include the release of genetically modified organisms into the environment where they could spread and compete with naturally occurring crop varieties. Concerns have been raised in the media about possible environmental problems arising from genes escaping from GM crops to produce 'superweeds' (stronger varieties that replace weaker ones). GM crops may also threaten wildlife such as birds and insects.

OPTION

13.2 PROTEINS

C.2.1 State the basic structure of 2-amino acids. There are approximately 20 common 2-amino acids (α-amino acids) found in organisms. 2-amino acids have the following formula.

$$H_2N-\underset{\underset{R}{|}}{\overset{\overset{H}{|}}{C}}-COOH$$

© IBO 2001

Proteins are polymeric substances made up of long molecules formed by sequences of smaller units. Most proteins are globular i.e. 'folded threads'. These smaller nitrogen–containing units are called amino acids. The variety of proteins that are important to human life are made of an assortment of some 20 amino acids.

Amino acids are compounds which contain both a carboxyl group (–COOH) and an amino group (–NH$_2$). Hence, amino acids have the ability to behave both as an acid and as a base in aqueous solution. In the simplest amino acid, glycine (IUPAC name 2-aminoethanoic acid), the methylene group (–CH$_2$–), is bonded to both an acidic carboxyl group (–COOH) and a basic amino group (–NH$_2$):

glycine

There are approximately 20 common 2–amino acids or α–amino acids found in organisms. The R group, called the side chain, can be hydrogen, an alkyl group or a complex substituent. These are called α-amino acids (or 2-amino acids) since the amino acid group is attached to the α–carbon atom, the one next to the carboxylic acid (–COOH) group. If R is –CH$_3$, alanine is formed, (IUPAC name 2-amino propanoic acid).

α–carbon or 2–carbon atom

The general structural formula of a 2-amino acid

The majority of the amino acids contain one acidic and one basic group and are "neutral" amino acids. If the side chain also contains –NH$_2$ group, then the number of –NH$_2$ groups > the number of –COOH, and it is a basic amino acid. If, on the other hand, the number of –COOH groups > the number of –NH$_2$, then it is an acidic amino acid.

Amino acids are colorless, crystalline solids with relatively high melting points for organic compounds (for example, glycine has a melting point of 232 – 236°C), and are generally soluble in water but insoluble in organic solvents. These are characteristic properties of ionic compounds. In the crystalline state and in aqueous solutions, these exist as zwitterions (dipolar ions) and are amphoteric in nature (capable of behaving as acids or bases). The presence of zwitterions explains the high melting points.

The amphoteric nature makes it possible for the amino acids to act as buffers in aqueous solutions. Thus, when a strong acid, H$^+_{(aq)}$, is added to an aqueous solution of an amino acid, the zwitterion accepts the proton, thus minimizing the effect of the acid added:

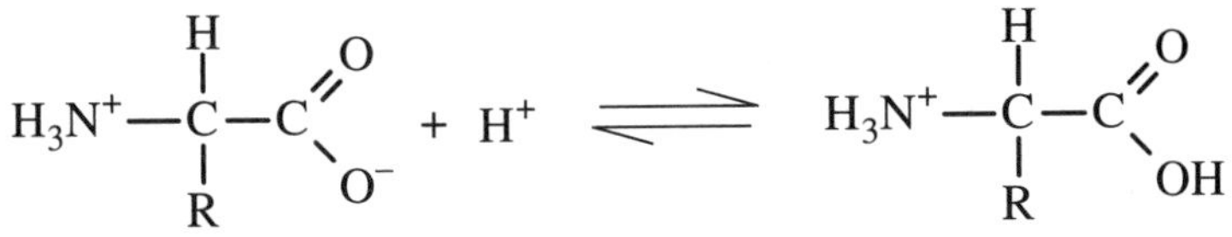

Zwitterion

Similarly, if a strong base OH⁻ is added, the zwitterion donates H⁺ to neutralize the base to form water:

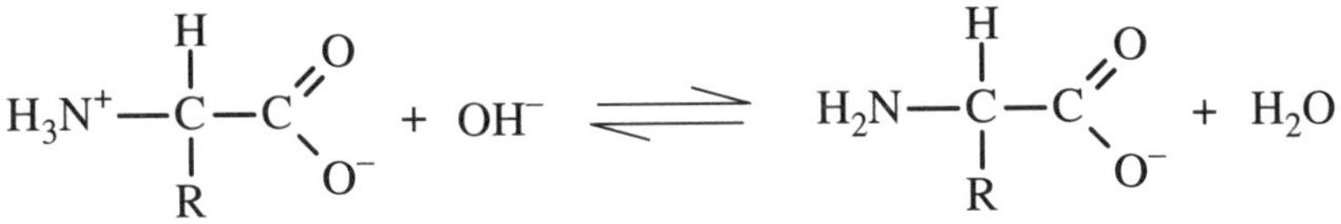

Within the 2–amino acids, when $R \neq H$, the 2–carbon atom is **asymmetric** and gives rise to **optical isomerism**. Thus, all amino acids except glycine where $R = H$ potentially exist as a pair of **enantiomers** (the D or L forms); see Section 11.4, page 371.

The R group side chain affects the 3–dimensional structure of the resulting proteins depending on whether it is non-polar containing mostly C–H bonds (and therefore hydrophobic) or polar containing N–H and O–H bonds (and therefore hydrophilic).

C.2.2   Describe the condensation reaction of amino acids to form polypeptides.

Since all amino acids have both a carboxyl group and an amino group, they are able to undergo condensation reactions to form a substituted amide in the presence of enzymes. For example, glycine and alanine can combine to form two possible dipeptides:

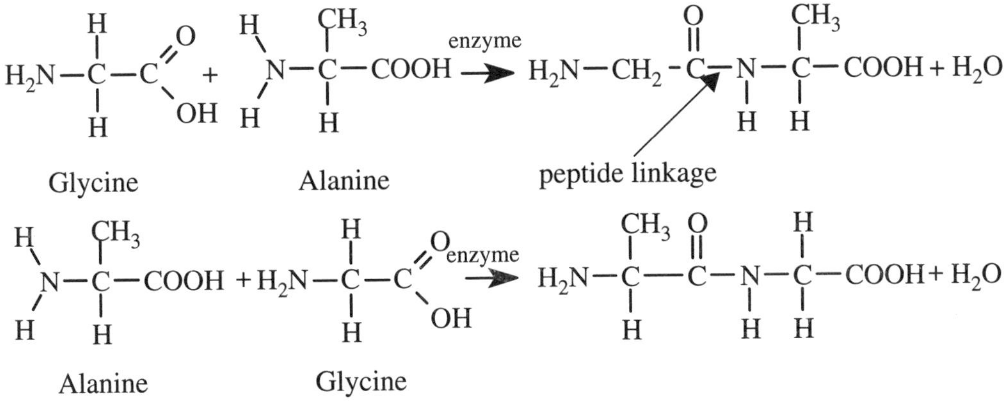

The product, a dipeptide, is a substituted amide made up of two amino acids joined by a peptide bond or peptide linkage. Water is formed in the enzyme controlled process. Six different tripeptides can be formed using three different amino acids, if each amino acid is used only once ($3 \times 2 \times 1$). If a compound contains many of these peptide bonds it is considered to be a polypeptide and, after folding, a protein. The 20 amino acids can undergo condensation reactions to produce a huge number of proteins.

C.2.3   Explain how proteins can be analysed by chromatography and electrophoresis.

To use either of these techniques the peptide bonds in the proteins must first be hydrolysed to release individual amino acids. Include the use of R_f values in paper chromatography. Given isoelectric points, students should be able to determine a suitable pH to achieve good separation in electrophoresis. © IBO 2001

A protein can be analyzed, that is, its amino acid composition can be determined by hydrolyzing the peptide bonds.

The peptide linkage, $-\overset{\overset{\displaystyle O}{\|}}{C}-\underset{\underset{\displaystyle H}{|}}{N}-$ is a strong resonance stabilised bond and complete acid hydrolysis usually requires the use of 6 mol dm^{-3} HCl solution at 110°C for 1 to 3 days. Hydrolysis of the peptide linkages produces individual amino acids which can be identified and the amounts determined using high performance liquid chromatography (hplc) since amino acids are not very volatile. In the laboratory, it is possible to identify individual amino acids using paper chromatography or electrophoresis.

CHROMATOGRAPHY

Chromatography is a very useful method for the separation of mixtures of substances which are otherwise not readily separated. Paper chromatography is suitable for the identification of components of a very small sample of mixture and is particularly suitable for separating hydrophilic substances such as amino acids. The water in the paper fibers acts as the stationary phase as the solvent flows through the paper by capillary action. The principle in paper chromatography is the partition of a solute (the amino acids) between two solvents. One solvent, water (the stationary phase) is adsorbed on the cellulose which makes up the paper (adsorption is the concentration of one substance at the surface of another). The eluting solvent, such as a mixture of 1–butanol (butan–1–ol) and ethanoic acid travels up the paper and is called the mobile phase. The relative solubility of different amino acids varies in the stationary phase (water), and the mobile phase (solvent). Thus, amino acids with greater solubility in the eluting solvent will travel further in the direction of the solvent flow.

Experimentally, a solution of the sample of the mixture of amino acids to be analyzed is placed as a spot on the surface of the chromatographic paper a couple of centimeters from the bottom, marked in pencil and allowed to dry.

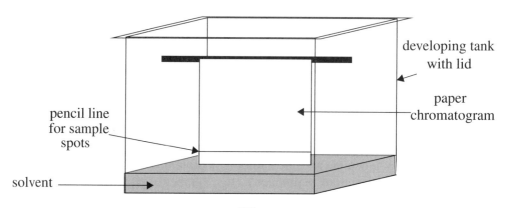

The paper is placed vertically in a developing tank which is then covered and the solvent allowed to rise up due to capillary action. The components of the mixture move with the solvent at different rates depending on their solubility in the stationary and moving phases. Once the solvent reaches near the top of the paper it is removed, the solvent front recorded and the solvent allowed to evaporate. As the amino acids are colorless the plate must be developed by spraying it with a solution of ninhydrin. Glycine, for example, forms a blue/purple compound with ninhydrin, as do 19 of the 20 protein–derived α–amino acids (proline gives an orange color).

A number of spots will be found corresponding to the different amino acids in the protein. The amino acids can be identified by comparing the R_f values of the spots with those for pure amino acids developed at the same time, under the same conditions of solvent and temperature. R_f represents the 'Ratio of fronts' and refers to the ratio of the distance traveled by a compound (d_c) over the distance traveled by the solvent (d_s):

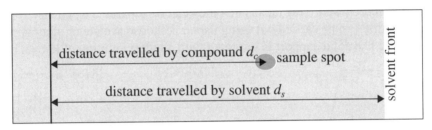

$$R_f = \frac{d_c}{d_s} = \frac{\text{distance travelled by compound}}{\text{distance travelled by solvent}}$$

Different substances have different R_f values under similar experimental conditions, so comparison of R_f values allows for the components of a mixture to be identified. If several components of a mixture have similar R_f values using a particular solvent, thus leading to incomplete separation, it is possible to use two–dimensional chromatography to improve the separation. In this case, the sample spot is placed in one corner of a square piece of chromatography paper, the chromatogram is developed by eluting with one solvent system to allow partial separation. The paper is dried, turned at right angles from its original position and developed using a second solvent system (such as butan–2–ol/ammonia mixture if butan–1–ol/ethanoic acid was the first solvent) to achieve a more complete separation.

ELECTROPHORESIS AND ISOELECTRIC POINTS, PI:

Electrophoresis is the method of separating (similar sized) molecules on the basis of their electric charges. In order to analyse a protein using electrophoresis, the peptide bonds in the protein must first be hydrolysed to release the individual amino acids. The amino acids contain a side chain, R.

Some side chains contain alkyl groups (such as $-CH_3$ in alanine). Others contain basic groups such as the amino group, $-NH_2$, in lysine and still others contain the carboxylic acid group $-COOH$ as in aspartic acid. The presence of the basic and acidic side chains produces positively and negatively charged ions respectively in the amino acids:

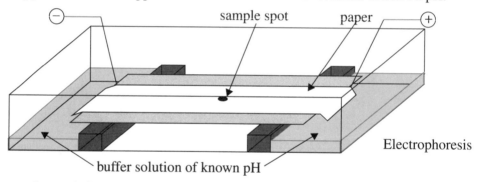

Thus, how an amino acid behaves in the presence of an electric field depends very much on the relative numbers of these charged groups and this is affected by the acidity or basicity of the solution, that is, its pH.

The **isoelectric point**, pI of an amino acid is the pH at which the positive and negative charges are exactly balanced, the molecule has no net charge and it shows no net migration in an electric field at that pH.

Once a protein has been hydrolysed, each amino acid in the mixture produced has a different isoelectric point. This means that they can be separated using electrophoresis. Such a separation can be carried out using paper, cellulose acetate or other appropriate solid supports. The solid support is saturated with a buffer solution of known pH.

The sample consisting of a mixture of amino acids is applied to the center of the paper, the electrodes and ends of the paper are placed in the buffered solution and an electric potential is applied to the electrodes. Any amino acid at its isoelectric point does not move in either direction. However, amino acids with positive charges at that pH move to the cathode and amino acids with negative charges at that pH move to the anode. After sufficient separation is achieved, the paper strip is dried and sprayed with ninhydrin solution to make the components visible. The paper can then be compared with known isoelectric points (standards) to identify individual amino acids.

The table below lists the isoelectric points, pI, of some amino acids (see the IB Chemistry Data Booklet):

Amino acid, Symbol	pI (pH units)
cysteine, Cys	5.1
glutamine, Gln	5.7
glycine, Gly	6.0
histidine, His	7.6
lysine, Lys	9.7

At pH 6.0, glycine exists as the dipolar ion, $H_3N^+-CH_2-COO^-$ and hence will not move if electrophoresis is carried out at this pH. If electrophoresis is carried out with glycine at pH = 7.0, the pH of the buffer is more basic than the isoelectric point of glycine (7.0 compared to 6.0), glycine will have a net negative charge because it largely exists as $H_2N-CH_2-COO^-$ and it will migrate toward the positive electrode. However, if the electrophoresis is carried out at pH = 5.0, the pH of the buffer is more acidic than the isoelectric point of glycine (5.0 compared to 6.0), glycine will have a net positive charge ($H_3N^+-CH_2-COOH$) and migrate to the negative pole.

If electrophoresis of a mixture of the five amino acids listed in the previous table is carried out at a pH of 6.0, glycine will not move from the point of origin as it has a net charge of zero at its isoelectric point of 6.0.

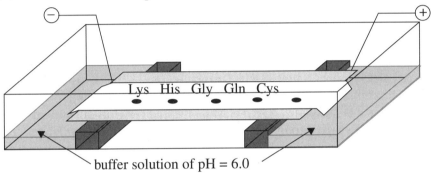

Cysteine (pI = 5.1) and glutamine (pI = 5.7) will have negative charges since the buffer pH of 6.0 is more basic and will move to the positive pole. Histidine (pI = 7.6) and lysine (pI = 9.7) will have positive charges since the buffer of 6.0 is more acidic and will move to the negative pole. Also, the greater the difference between the pI and the pH, the faster the migration.

C.2.4 Describe and explain the primary, secondary, tertiary and quaternary structure of proteins. © IBO 2001

As described (page 465) amino acids can undergo condensation reactions in any order, thus making it possible to form an extremely large number of proteins. Structurally, proteins can be described in four ways. They are: primary, secondary, tertiary and quaternary structures.

Primary Structure: The primary structure is simply the sequence or order of amino acids which form the protein. This is indicated by using the three–letter codes for the amino acids. A tripeptide containing the amino acids lysine, glutamine and leucine would be lys–gln–leu in which the terminal amino acid group of lysine is on the left and the terminal carboxylic acid group of leucine is, by convention, on the right. Thus a different tripeptide leu–gln–lys consisting of the same three amino acids means the amino terminal group leucine is on the left and the acid terminal group lysine is on the right:

$$H_2N-CH-CO-NH-CH-CO-NH-CH-COOH$$

with R₁, R₂, R₃ on the respective CH groups:

$$\begin{array}{ccc} R_1 & R_2 & R_3 \end{array}$$

OPTION

where R_1 is in leucine (containing $-NH_2$), R_2 in glutamine and R_3 in lysine (with $-COOH$).

Each type of protein in a biological organism has its own unique sequence of amino acids. It is this sequence that gives the protein its ability to carry out its characteristic functions.

Primary Structure:

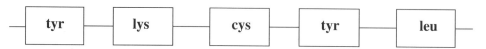

| tyr | lys | cys | tyr | leu |

Secondary Structure: The secondary structure is the manner in which a polypeptide chain folds or aligns itself in certain patterns that repeat themselves, that is, it is the arrangement in space of the polypeptide chain. Usually, a protein's secondary structure can be described as an α–helix or a β pleated sheet. In the α–helix structure, the

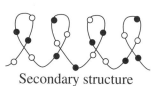

Secondary structure

peptide chain resembles a right handed spiral staircase or coiled spring; this shape is called a helix. This can make the protein elastic or sponge–like as in hair and wool. The α–helix maintains its shape through numerous intramolecular hydrogen bonds. These are between the (δ–) oxygen of the carbonyl group ($-C=O$) and the (δ+) hydrogen of the $-NH$ group that are in just the right position between amino acid residues within the chain (namely the third peptide bond down the chain) to keep its form. The H–bonding in the α–helix structure is found to be parallel to the axis of the helix.

In the beta pleated sheet arrangement, one or several different polypeptide chains are bound together in a secondary structure in which the orderly alignment of protein chains is maintained not by intramolecular bonds (within a molecule) but by those which are intermolecular (between the protein molecules) with the direction of H–bonding being perpendicular to the sheet structure. This hydrogen bonding occurs with neighboring chains of the protein and forms a repeating, pleated pattern. Silk has this arrangement, making it flexible, but strong and resistant to stretching. If a particular part of a polypeptide chain does not exhibit a repeating pattern it is said to contain random coils.

Structures of α–helix and β pleated sheet secondary structures

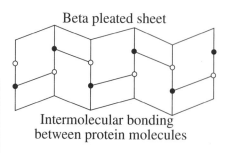

Beta pleated sheet

Intermolecular bonding between protein molecules

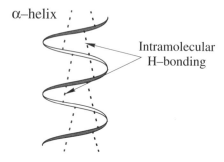

α–helix

Intramolecular H–bonding

Tertiary Structure: It is the tertiary structure that maintains the three dimensional shape of the protein. The amino acid secondary structure in the helical, pleated or random coil form arranges itself to form the unique twisted or folded shape of the protein.

Tertiary structure of myoglobin

About 70% of the amino acid sequence is α–helical secondary structure. The non-helical regions are a major factor that determines its tertiary structure.

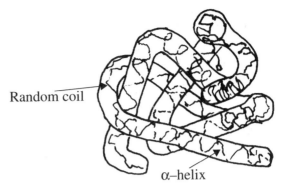

Random coil

α–helix

There are four ways in which parts of the amino acid chains interact to stabilize their tertiary shapes.

These are:

(1)   Covalent bonding, for example disulfide bridges can form between different parts of the protein when two cysteine groups link as their –SH groups are oxidized under enzyme control:

$$\boxed{}\!-\!S\!-\!H + H\!-\!S\!-\!\boxed{} \xrightarrow{\text{[O]}} \boxed{}\!-\!S\!-\!S\!-\!\boxed{} + H_2O$$

For example, the keratin proteins in hair have a large number of cysteines connected by the disulfide bridges which hold the hair in its normal structure. In the artificial hair curling process, the –S–S– disulfide bridges on cysteine residues are reduced to the –S–H groups of cysteine:

$$-S\!-\!S\!- \xrightarrow{\text{[2 H]}} -S\!-\!H + H\!-\!S\!-$$

On using a curler, hair is stretched and the –S–H groups are displaced. Then a solution is used to oxidize the curled hair to form new disulfide linkages to retain the curls.

(2)   Hydrogen bonding between polar groups on the side chain.

(3)   Salt bridges (ionic bonds) formed between $-N^+H_3$ and $-COO^-$ groups and

(4)   Hydrophobic interactions occur when non–polar, hydrophobic side groups tend to clump together on the inside, forcing the protein chain into a tertiary shape with the polar parts of the molecule on the outside. Hydrophobic interactions involve exclusion of water from the non-polar interior of the protein. It is an entropy driven process.

Quaternary Structure occurs only in proteins that are composed of more than one polypeptide chain which are held together by hydrophobic interactions, hydrogen bonding and ionic bonds. When a protein consists of more than one polypeptide chain, each is called a subunit. Quaternary structure is the way in which the polypeptide subunits are held together in a precise structural arrangement such as haemoglobin which consists of two slightly different pairs of polypeptide chains grouped together to form the quaternary structure together with the haem co-factor.

Proteins can be denatured, that is lose their crucial three dimensional structure and hence

OPTION

biological activity, particularly by heating, as is the case when an egg is fried or boiled. Denaturation affects the functioning of a protein since the exact structure is the key to the function of each of the numerous proteins in the body. High energy ionising radiation also leads to denaturation of proteins. Strong acids, bases, urea and concentrated salt solutions can disrupt salt bridges, and, organic solvents and detergents can disrupt hydrophobic interactions. Similarly mercury and lead poisoning are due to the strong interaction of these heavy metal ions with sulfur in the disulfide bridges. In the presence of a chelating agent (polydentate ligands) such as EDTA, the mercury or lead ions can be removed to re-establish the disulfide linkages. This is an example of reversible denaturation. If, however, sufficient bonds are disrupted in the protein, it leads to irreversible or permanent denaturation, as in the case of cooking an egg.

C.2.5 List the major functions of proteins in the body.

These are structure, biological catalysts (enzymes) and energy sources. © IBO 2001

Proteins play very important roles in the human body. They carry out many functions including providing structure, as enzymes (biological catalysts), as transportation proteins, as energy extractors, in providing protection (as immunoglobins) and control (via the action of hormones).

Structural: Fibrous proteins provide structure and strength and are the chief constituents of muscle, cartilage, skin, bones, hair and fingernails. Examples of important structural proteins are collagen (found under the skin) and keratin (found in hair and nails).

Enzymes: Almost every reaction that takes place in the human body is catalyzed by globular proteins called enzymes. Without these enzymes, the reactions important for maintaining life would occur much too slowly. Such catalysts provide an alternate pathway for the reaction to take place, thus lowering the activation energy and speeding up the reaction (see Chapter 7).

Transport: Haemoglobin in the red blood cells carries oxygen from the lungs to the cells and carbon dioxide from the cells to the lungs and behaves as an oxygen transportation protein.

Energy: Proteins play an important role in the human body as energy storage, for example, casein in milk stores nutrients for newborn babies. Cells contain cytochrome proteins which extract energy from food via redox reactions.

Antibodies: Antibodies are proteins produced as a result of the presence of foreign materials in the body and provide immunity to diseases, for example, interferons provide protection against viral infection.

Hormones: Hormones such as insulin are important proteins in humans and animals. Although the insulin from animals such as cattle and sheep is not identical in primary sequence to human insulin, it is similar enough to be used by human beings.

13.3 CARBOHYDRATES

C.3.1 Describe the structural features of monosaccharides.

Monosaccharides contain a carbonyl group (C=O) and at least two –OH groups and have the empirical formula CH₂O.   © IBO 2001

Carbohydrates are composed of three elements: carbon, hydrogen and oxygen, with the empirical formula CH_2O (historically called carbohydrate, i.e., hydrated carbon since hydrogen and oxygen are present in the same relative amounts as water). They serve as food sources for living organisms and provide the structural support for plants. Many of the carbohydrates are large polymeric molecules made of simple sugars.

Monosaccharides, literally meaning 'one sugar' or 'simple sugar' are the smallest molecular units of carbohydrates. They can be combined to form **disaccharides** or **polysaccharides** through condensation reactions. Monosaccharides are alkanals or alkanones containing a carbonyl (>C=O) group and at least two hydroxyl (–OH) groups. Their empirical formula is usually CH_2O. Examples of monosaccharides are glucose, galactose and fructose (a sugar found in fruits and honey). These three simple sugars contain six carbon atoms and are all examples of hexoses. Monosaccharides with five carbon atoms (such as ribose) are given the general name of pentose (see Section 13.8, page 496). Pentoses and hexoses are the most common monosaccharides found in nature.

Monosaccharides (and disaccharides) have low molar masses, are sweet, readily soluble in water and are crystalline substances. Since alkanals are easily oxidized (to alkanoic acids), monosaccharides with alkanal groups such as glucose are strong reducing agents and are called reducing sugars. The general formula of monosaccharides is $(CH_2O)_n$ where $n = 3$ to $n = 9$.

C.3.2 Describe the straight–chain formula of glucose and the structural difference between α–glucose and ß–glucose.   © IBO 2001

The straight chain formula of glucose is shown in I below:

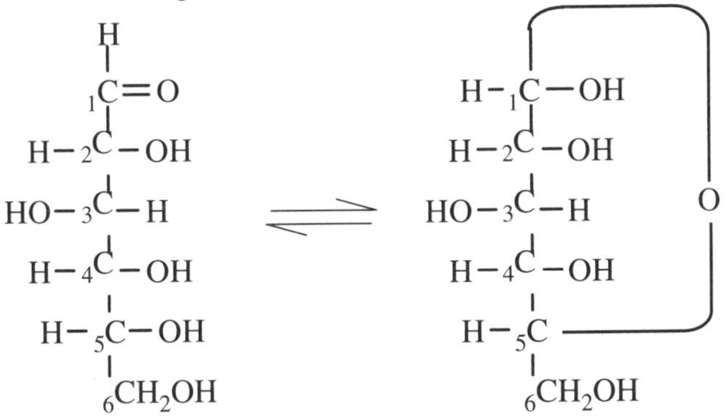

The carbon atoms in glucose are numbered, starting with 1 at the carbonyl group. Note that there are four similar asymmetric C–atoms in the glucose molecule and thus several stereoisomers exist; C_1 and C_6 are not chiral.

OPTION

Option C: Human Biochemistry

Glucose is found almost exclusively in a ring or cyclic (hemiacetal) structure in aqueous solution (structure II) due to an intramolecular reaction between the alkanal group on C_1 and the OH group on the C_5 atom producing an asymmetric carbon atom at C_1. Thus, there are two common ring structure isomers of glucose called α–**glucose where the –OH on C–1 is below the ring and β–glucose where the –OH group on C–1 is above the ring.** The only difference between the two is the side of the C-1 atom the –H and – OH are on (and therefore having different physical and chemical properties):

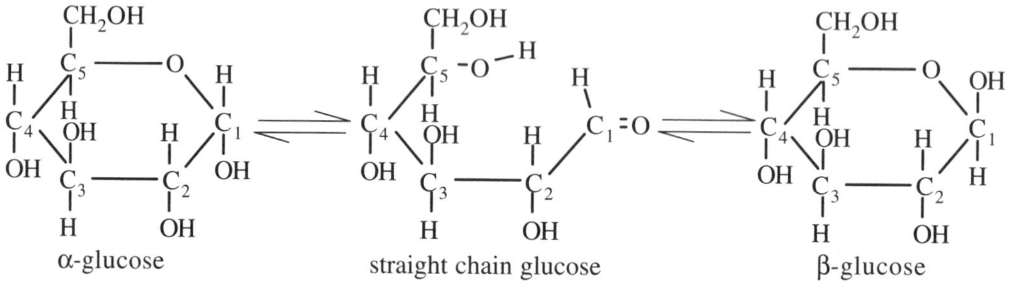

α-glucose   straight chain glucose   β-glucose

The equilibrium between the α and β forms of glucose is called mutarotation and can be followed using a polarimeter.

C.3.3   Describe the condensation of monosaccharides to form disaccharides and polysaccharides.

Limit examples to: disaccharides-lactose and sucrose and polysaccharides-starch.

© IBO 2001

When monosaccharides form disaccharides or when smaller polysaccharides form larger polysaccharides they do so through condensation reactions by eliminating a water molecule to form a C–O–C bond between the rings; this is called the glucoside (glycosidic) linkage. This normally forms between carbon atoms 1 and 4 of neighbouring units and is called a 1,4 or 1→4 bond. When one consumes sucrose, some hydrolysis of the glucoside linkage takes place, (the reverse of the condensation reaction) and produces the two monosaccharides.

The following are some disaccharides formed from monosaccharides:

α–glucose + α–glucose = maltose

α–glucose + β–galactose = lactose

α–glucose + β–fructose = sucrose (table sugar)

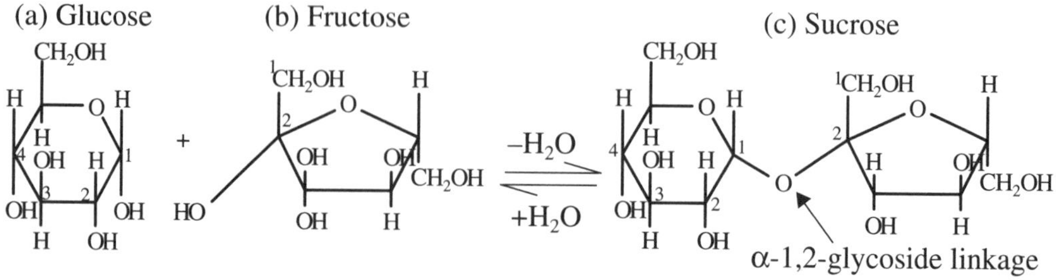

(a) Glucose   (b) Fructose   (c) Sucrose

α-1,2-glycoside linkage

Polysaccharides are complex carbohydrates consisting of numerous monosaccharide units. These have large molar masses, are not sweet, are generally insoluble or only slightly soluble in water and are non–reducing. Starch is the polysaccharide in which glucose is stored by plants for energy in plants and animals. Polysaccharides differ in the nature of their recurring monosaccharide units and their bonds, the length of their chains and the degree of branching. There are two forms of starch; both are polymers of α–glucose. Amylose ($M_r = 10\,000 – 50\,000$) has a straight chain structure consisting of thousands of long chains of α–(1→4) glycosidic linkages, while amylopectin ($M_r = 50\,000 – 100$ million) has these linkages as well as branches consisting of α–(1→6) glycosidic linkages.

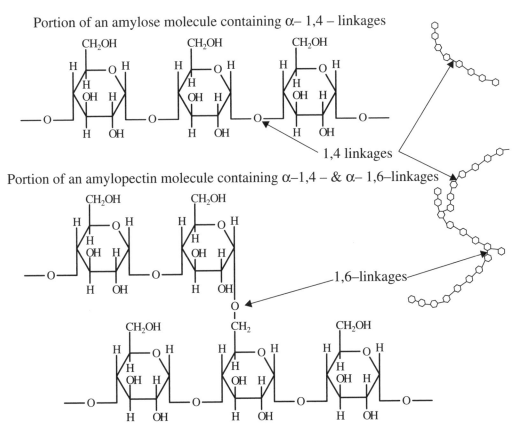

Portion of an amylose molecule containing α– 1,4 – linkages

Portion of an amylopectin molecule containing α–1,4 – & α– 1,6–linkages

C.3.4 List the major functions of polysaccharides in the body.

These are energy sources, energy reserves (e.g. glycogen) and precursors for other biologically important molecules.   © IBO 2001

Polysaccharides are major sources of energy, and energy reserves, in the body. Animals use glycogen as their energy storage polysaccharide. Glycogen is used for energy reserves and can be broken down by enzymes into glucose. Glucose and oxygen are the reactants necessary for aerobic cellular respiration which releases energy. The majority of the body's glycogen is stored in the liver. Polysaccharides are precursors of other biologically important molecules. Heparin is one such example. It occurs in intestinal walls and is used as an anticoagulant.

OPTION

13.4 FATS

C.4.1 Describe the composition of fats and oils. © IBO 2001

Fats, important components in cell structures and metabolism, are a type of lipid. Lipids are defined in terms of their solubility and in general are poorly soluble in water, but soluble in non–polar organic solvents and solvents of low polarity. For this reason, fats cannot dissolve in animal bodies whose chemistry is based upon water (the human body is around 70% water). Although the ester bonds are polar, the very low solubility of fats and oils in water is due to the large R (non–polar hydrocarbon) groups present in such molecules which are water–repellent or hydrophobic ('water–hating') in nature.

Fats are a special type of ester. Esters are formed from the condensation reaction of an organic acid and an alcohol. In fats and oils, the alcohol is glycerol, 1,2,3–propanetriol (propane-1,2,3-triol) and fats and oils are present as esterified glycerol molecules:

$$
\begin{array}{ccc}
\begin{array}{l} CH_2-OH \\ CH-OH \\ CH_2-OH \end{array}
\;+\;
\begin{array}{l} HO-\overset{\overset{O}{\|}}{C}-R_1 \\ HO-C\!\!<^{\;O}_{\;R_2} \\ HO-\underset{\underset{O}{\|}}{C}-R_3 \end{array}
\;\longrightarrow\;
\begin{array}{l} CH_2-O-\overset{\overset{O}{\|}}{C}-R_1 \\ CH-O-C\!\!<^{\;O}_{\;R_2} \\ CH_2-O-\underset{\underset{O}{\|}}{C}-R_3 \end{array}
\;+\;3\,H_2O
\end{array}
$$

glycerol   three fatty acid molecules   triacylglycerol

Since glycerol has three –OH groups, a single molecule of glycerol can have three acid molecules attached to it through ester bonds. Compounds with three acids attached to the glycerol are known as triglycerides or triacylglycerols where R_1, R_2 and R_3 are three fatty acid side chains. The fatty acid, stearic acid, $R = -C_{17}H_{35}$ is an example of a saturated acid, whereas oleic acid, $R = -C_{17}H_{33}$ is unsaturated. Depending on whether it is a solid such as butter or a liquid such as vegetable oil at room temperature, it is classified as a fat or an oil.

Although the R group of the acid component varies, fats and oils have some features in common. These are almost always straight–chain carboxylic acids without any branching present; they contain an even number of carbon atoms (as they are made from a series of ethanoate ions under enzyme control); they usually contain between 10 and 20 carbon atoms in the R group; and besides the carboxylic acid group, no other functional groups are present in the saturated fats and C=C bonds are present in unsaturated fats. Unsaturated acyl groups almost invariably contain double bonds with the cis arrangement.

C.4.2 Describe the difference in structure between saturated and unsaturated fats, and explain the difference in their melting points. © IBO 2001

Saturated and unsaturated fats are terms most commonly used in the context of nutrition. If the chain has no double bonds present between carbon atoms (thus consisting of a maximum number of hydrogens bonded to the carbon atoms in the R groups) it is called a saturated fat. These are common in most animal fats (for example butter) and are usually solids at room temperature. The regular tetrahedral arrangement of carbon atoms in a saturated fat makes it possible for it to pack with parallel chains fairly closely together. Although weak van der Waals' forces are involved, the large surface area in the long R groups produce forces strong enough to make these solids at room temperature.

Closely packed parallel chains of tetrahedral carbon atoms

An unsaturated fatty acid has one or more double bonds formed by the removal of hydrogen atoms. These include vegetable oils and are found to be liquids at room temperature. The change in the bond angle to 120° at the C=C double bonds prevents the oil molecules from packing closely together to solidify. The greater the number of C=C double bonds, the more difficult the hydrophobic packing, the lower the melting points. Oils with one C=C double bond per fatty acid chain are called "monounsaturated oils" and with more than one C=C double bond per fatty acid chain are called "polyunsaturated oils".

Some Fatty Acids found in Dietary Fats and Oils

Name Formula	Structural Formula	Number of C atoms	Number of C=C bonds	Melting Point (°C)
Lauric acid $C_{11}H_{23}COOH$	$CH_3(CH_2)_{10}COOH$	12	0 saturated	44
Myristic acid $C_{13}H_{27}COOH$	$CH_3(CH_2)_{12}COOH$	14	0 saturated	58
Palmitic acid $C_{15}H_{31}COOH$	$CH_3(CH_2)_{14}COOH$	16	0 saturated	63
Stearic acid $C_{17}H_{35}COOH$	$CH_3(CH_2)_{16}COOH$	18	0 saturated	71
Oleic acid $C_{17}H_{33}COOH$	$CH_3(CH_2)_7CH=CH(CH_2)_7COOH$	18	1;monoun-saturated	16
Linoleic acid $C_{17}H_{31}COOH$	$CH_3(CH_2)_4CH=CHCH_2CH=CH(CH_2)_7COOH$	18	2;polyun-saturated	−5

Note the trend in the melting point of the first four acids listed, namely an increase with an increase in the size of the non-polar R group (thus experiencing greater van der Waals' forces). The presence of a one C=C double bond in oleic acid and two double bonds in linoleic acid, correspondingly decreases the melting points of these fatty acids due to the prevention of the close packing possible in the saturated fatty acids. Unsaturated oils can be hydrogenated to solid, saturated fats by the reaction with hydrogen gas in the presence of nickel or platinum as a catalyst and heat.

$$\text{C=C} + H_2 \xrightarrow[\text{heat}]{\text{Ni}} \ -\!\overset{|}{\underset{|}{C}}-\overset{|}{\underset{|}{C}}\!-$$

OPTION

Saturation raises the melting point of the triacylglycerol. For example, the partial hydrogenation of liquid corn oil produces soft margarine.

Unsaturated (particularly polyunsaturated) fats and oils undergo slow aerobic oxidation to form foul smelling and bad tasting alkanals and alkanoic acids. Thus, antioxidants (substances that stop or reduce the oxidation process by themselves being easily oxidized) are added during margarine production. Colors may also be added since fats and oils are colorless compounds. Fats and oils also undergo a hydrolysis reaction to produce fatty acids if exposed to moisture over a period of time. Oxidation and hydrolysis can be substantially reduced by refrigeration.

C.4.3   Calculate the number of C=C double bonds in an unsaturated fat using addition reactions.

The number of C=C bonds can be determined from the number of moles of I_2 which add to one mole of fat.

© IBO 2001

The iodine index or number is the number of grams of iodine (in solution) that adds to 100 g of a triacylglycerol. Addition of iodine solution to an unsaturated molecule will cause the double bonds to break to form single–bonded carbon atoms. Since saturated and unsaturated fats are colorless and iodine is colored, the reaction mixture of an unsaturated fat and iodine will turn from a red–violet to a clear solution as the iodine is used up in the addition reaction. If a fat contains no double bonds and is therefore a saturated fat, it will not react with iodine. Also, the number of moles of iodine reacting with one mole of fat indicates the number of double bonds present in the fat since each mole of double bond requires one mole of I_2:

$$\text{C=C} + I_2 \longrightarrow \text{—C—C—}$$

EXAMPLE

0.010 mol of linoleic acid reacts with 5.1 g iodine. Determine the number of double bonds present in the acid.

SOLUTION

$$n_{I_2} = \frac{5.1 \text{ g}}{254 \text{ g mol}^{-1}} = 0.020 \text{ mol } I_2.$$

Therefore one mol of acid reacts with two mols of I_2 and it therefore contains two C=C double bonds.

Adding the same number of drops of iodine solution to both sunflower oil and peanut oil reveals that the red-violet iodine color in sunflower oil disappears quicker than it does when added to peanut oil. This is because the sunflower oil is more highly unsaturated (that is, contains more C=C bonds per molecule of oil) compared to peanut oil.

Table of iodine numbers and percentage fatty acid composition of common fats and oils

Oil or Fat	Saturated fats	Mono unsaturated fats	Poly unsaturated fats	Iodine Number[*]
Butter fat	67%	29%	4%	30-38
Olive oil	15%	75%	10%	79-95
Peanut oil	18%	49%	33%	85-100
Sunflower oil	10%	13%	77%	119-138

[*] Note that iodine numbers are often quoted as ranges because the fats and oils listed contain variable mixtures of triacylglycerols, whose composition varies according to the mixture of fats and oils in different samples of the foods.

Thus, the more unsaturated oil has a higher iodine number.

EXAMPLE

Calculate the iodine number of linoleic acid, $C_{17}H_{31}COOH$

SOLUTION

$M_{(acid)} = 18(12.0) + 32(1.0) + 2(16.0) = 280$ g mol^{-1}
$M_{(iodine)} = 2 \times 126.9 = 253.8$ g mol^{-1}
Linoleic acid has 2 double bonds and reacts with 2 moles of I_2.
$\therefore$ 280 g of fat reacts with 2×253.8 g of I_2.

$\therefore$ 100 g of fat reacts with $\dfrac{2 \times 253.8}{280} \times 100 = 181$ g of I_2.

$\therefore I_2$ number = 181

C.4.4 Describe the hydrolysis of fats to form soaps and the action of soaps.   © IBO 2001

Base hydrolysis of a fat or oil molecule using a strong base such as aqueous sodium hydroxide produces glycerol and the salt of the fatty acids. The process, called saponification, is used to form soaps. It is the reverse of forming a fat and because a strong base is present, the salts of the fatty acids are produced, (for example, sodium stearate, $C_{17}H_{35}COO^-Na^+$):

Thus, natural soaps are sodium salts of long chain fatty acids. Sodium ions (from strong bases) are neutral cations; however, $RCOO^-$ ions (the conjugate bases of weak acids) are basic in nature and therefore soap solutions are basic, since the conjugate bases can undergo base hydrolysis:

$$RCOO^-_{(aq)} + H_2O_{(l)} \rightleftharpoons RCOOH_{(aq)} + OH^-_{(aq)}$$

The product of base hydrolysis is a weak acid, RCOOH, and a strong base, OH^-, giving rise to a basic solution (see Chapter 7).

Soaps are important cleansing agents in everyday life. Whereas highly polar water molecules wash away polar substances, these do little to non–polar ones. Soaps contain a hydrophilic polar end (the ionic, or charged, head) and a hydrophobic non–polar long chain alkane end (the tail). The hydrophilic end of the soap molecule dissolves in the water and the hydrophobic end dissolves in dirt and grease. This creates a situation where the soap molecules surround the dirt particles in the center with the anionic polar heads pointing outwards which interact with the polar water molecules known as micelles. The long chain hydrocarbon molecules present in grease on the other hand dissolve in the soap by becoming part of the non–polar interior. Thus soap lifts the dirt and grease off the surface of the body at the non–polar end and is washed away by the water.

Hard water containing Ca^{2+} and Mg^{2+} ions precipitate soap anions as insoluble calcium and magnesium salts producing, for example, soap scum in a bath-tub:

$$Ca^{2+}_{(aq)} + 2RCOO^-_{(aq)} \Rightarrow (RCOO)_2Ca_{(s)}$$

Detergents are synthetic soaps containing a long chain non-polar tail, but with phosphate or sulfonate anions whose corresponding calcium and magnesium salts are in fact water soluble and therefore do not precipitate out. Many countries do not allow the use of phosphate detergents because they cause eutrophication in bodies of water.

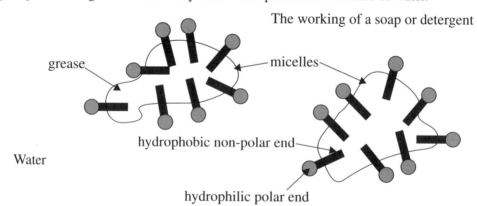

The working of a soap or detergent

C.4.5 **List the major functions of fat in the body.**

These are: energy sources, insulation and cell membrane. © IBO 2001

Fats serve many purposes in the body. Fats are a very efficient way for the body to store energy. Hydrolysis of a fat produces glycerol plus the corresponding fatty acids present in the fat. The fatty acids are oxidized to produce large amounts of energy. Fats have less oxygen atoms than carbohydrate molecules of corresponding molar masses, that is, these are less oxidized and thus more oxidation can take place. Therefore, much more energy is released from the oxidation of fats compared to carbohydrates, hence fats are much better biological fuels.

Since fats provide nearly twice as much energy (more kJ/g) as carbohydrates, the body stores unused carbohydrates as fat. This leads to fat being deposited on the stomach, hips and buttocks when we eat more than we metabolise. Fats are stored in adipose tissue which provides insulation and protective covering for some parts of the body. This is important for regulating the internal temperature of the body.

The membranes of cells in the body are mainly made up of proteins and phospholipids. The latter are esters of glycerol and similar in structure to fats, but with only two fatty acids, the third being a phosphate. This gives rise to two long non–polar hydrocarbon chains attached to a polar head. The phospholipid bilayer forms a stable boundary between two aqueous components, such that the hydrophilic parts face water molecules and protect the hydrophobic parts from water molecules.

13.5 VITAMINS

C.5.1   Define the term *vitamin*.   © IBO 2001

Vitamins are any of the organic compounds required by the body in small amounts (thus called micro–nutrients) for metabolism, to protect health and for proper growth in children. Vitamins also assist in the formation of hormones, blood cells, nervous system chemicals and genetic material. The various vitamins are not chemically related and most differ in their physiological actions. They generally act as catalysts, combining with proteins to create enzymes that produce hundreds of important chemical reactions throughout the body. Without vitamins, many of these reactions would slow down or cease.

C.5.2   Deduce whether a vitamin is water or fat soluble from its structure.   © IBO 2001

Vitamins are classified according to their ability to be absorbed in fat or water. Vitamin A and D, for example, contain only one –OH group and a large hydrocarbon group each, which makes these vitamins more soluble in organic non-polar or slightly polar solvents. The fat–soluble vitamins A, D, E and K are generally consumed along with fat–containing foods and because they can be stored in the body's fat, they do not have to be consumed every day. The water–soluble vitamins—the eight B vitamins and vitamin C—cannot be stored and must be consumed frequently, preferably every day (with the exception of some B vitamins). Vitamin C, which contains 4 –OH groups, is capable of extensive hydrogen bonding with water and is consequently water soluble.

OPTION

C.5.3 Describe the structures and major functions of retinol (vitamin A), calciferol (vitamin D) and ascorbic acid (vitamin C).

Vitamin A - required for the production of rhodopsin (light sensitive material in the rods of the retina). Deficiency can cause night blindness and xerophthalmia.

Vitamin D - required for the uptake of calcium from food. Deficiency can cause weak bones (rickets).

Vitamin C - essential in the production of collagen: the protein of connective tissue. Deficiency: can cause scorbutus (scurvy).

© IBO 2001

Vitamin A (retinol) contains a long carbon chain with many conjugated C=C double bonds and one –OH group (a system of alternate double and single bonds in a carbon chain is called a conjugated system). It is a fat soluble, pale yellow primary alcohol derived from carotene and is stored in the fat cells in the liver. It affects the formation and maintenance of skin, mucous membranes, bones, teeth and most importantly is associated with vision. Vitamin A is light sensitive because it contains many conjugated double bonds. Vitamin A is required for the production of rhodopsin (light sensitive material in the rods of the retina). It is the active material in the process where light impulses change the conformations of the molecules. This is the specific arrangement of atoms, assuming that there is free rotation around a single bond. Conformers are isomers that differ only in rotation around a single bond. The changed conformation of the molecules eventually results in a nerve impulse, which is translated in the cortex of the brain as vision. An early deficiency symptom is night blindness (difficulty in adapting to darkness). Other symptoms are excessive skin dryness; lack of mucous membrane secretion, causing susceptibility to bacterial invasion; and dryness of the eyes due to a malfunctioning of the tear glands, a major cause of blindness in children where the diet is deficient in vitamin A.

Vitamin C, or ascorbic acid, is important in the formation and maintenance of collagen, the protein that supports many body structures such as holding together skin, blood vessels and scar tissues. It also plays a major role in the formation of bones and teeth and enhances the absorption of iron from foods of vegetable origin.

Scurvy is the classic manifestation of severe ascorbic acid deficiency first experienced by sailors on the high seas. Its symptoms of bleeding and weakened gums, tooth decay and teeth falling out and easy bruising of the body are due to loss of the cementing action of collagen. It also produces cellular changes in the bones of children.

Vitamin D is necessary for normal bone formation and for retention of calcium and phosphorus in the body; vitamin D absorbs calcium ions into the blood stream and, in the presence of phosphorus, makes it possible for the calcium ions to be added to the bones and teeth. Thus vitamin D

Vitamin D

protects the teeth and bones against the effects of low calcium intake by making effective use of calcium and phosphorus.

Vitamin D deficiency, or rickets, occurs only rarely in tropical climates where sunlight is abundant, but it was once common among children living in northern and southern climates before the use of vitamin D–fortified milk. Rickets is characterized by deformities of the rib cage and skull and by bowlegs, due to failure of the body to absorb calcium and phosphorus. Excess vitamin D consumption through supplements can cause excessive absorption of calcium and phosphrous and the formation of calcium deposits on major organs such as the kidneys and the heart. Because vitamin D is fat–soluble and stored in the body, excessive consumption can thus cause kidney and heart damage.

C.5.4   Describe the effects of food processing on the vitamin content of food.

Most vitamins are unstable at higher temperatures so will be affected by prolonged cooking.

It is advisable to cook fresh vegetables in the minimum amount of water for short periods of time so as not to lose the important water soluble vitamins. Also, because vitamins such as vitamin A contain C=C bonds and are oxidized, heating these for cooking purposes also speeds up the oxidation process, thus reducing the amounts of vitamins in cooked food. In addition to this, many vitamins are unstable at higher temperatures and tend to be affected or even decomposed by prolonged heating.

13.6 HORMONES

C.6.1   Outline the production and roles of hormones in the body.

Hormones are chemical messengers produced in glands controlled by the pituitary gland which in turn is controlled by the hypothalamus. Limit examples of production and roles to adrenalin, thyroxine, insulin and sex hormones.

Hormones are chemical messengers that are produced by the body's endocrine glands (many of which are controlled by the pituitary gland which in turn is controlled by the hypothalamus). Hormones are released directly into the bloodstream, pass to distant receptor sites such as an organ, tissue or cells where they are absorbed and exert a specific effect. As a result, hormones are much slower chemical messengers compared to nerve impulses. Hormones perform a variety of different functions and vary greatly in their chemical composition and structure. Hormones generally have a negative feedback mechanism whereby a high level of the hormone inhibits its own production. Hormones are effective in minute amounts and only target cells that are equipped to respond to a hormone which can hence affect target cells differently.

Hormone	Production Location	Derived from	Role in the Body
Adrenalin or epinephrine	Adrenal cortex, adjacent to the kidneys	the amino acid tyrosine	Responsible for flight or fight response characterized by goose bumps, increased heart rate/ output and blood pressure. Affects rate of glucagon release into the liver and release of glucose by liver into the blood.
Thyroxine; an iodine containing amino acid.	Thyroid glands	small molecule from amino acids	Responsible for basal metabolic rate in vertebrates: essential for regulating metabolism.
Insulin; a protein of 51 amino acids	Pancreas	protein	Decreases blood glucose level; increases glucose and amino acid uptake and use by cells.
Sex hormones 1. Androgens, principally testosterone	Principally the testes (the ovaries produce very small amounts)		Responsible for development and maintenance of the male reproductive system as well as secondary sexual characteristics.
2. Estrogen, principally estradiol	Principally the ovaries (the ovaries produce very small amounts)	cholesterol	Play a similar role in females.
3. Progestins including progesterone	Principally the ovaries		Prepare and maintain the uterus; important for the developing embryo.

The hypothalamus in the brain sends a releasing hormone to the pituitary gland, which secretes TSH (thyroid stimulating hormone) which stimulates the thyroid gland to secrete thyroxine. The pancreas produces both insulin and glucagon. These two hormones act in a negative feedback mechanism. Thus, the increased blood glucose level caused by eating and digesting, for example, a chocolate bar results in the production of insulin. Body cells take up glucose, as does the liver, which stores it as glycogen and the blood glucose level is lowered. Skipping a meal, for example, lowers blood glucose level and the cells in the pancreas produce glucagon. This stimulates the liver to convert glycogen to glucose and release it into blood and the blood glucose level increases. As a result of this negative feedback mechanism, the blood glucose level remains around a set level, controlled by the hypothalamus.

Human sex hormones (androgens, estrogens and progestins) are found in males and females in differing concentrations.

C.6.2 Compare the structures of cholesterol and the sex hormones.

Stress the common steroid backbone but the difference in functional groups.

© IBO 2001

Steroids, both naturally occurring and synthetically prepared, are a family of polycyclic ring structure chemicals containing a common carbon molecular framework (or backbone). It consists of 17 carbon atoms arranged as 3 cyclohexane rings fused together with a cyclopentane ring on one extremity. The presence of various functional groups such as the methyl and hydroxyl groups results in hormones that give rise to a variety of physiological functions ranging from sexual characteristics (by estrogen and testosterone) to cell membrane components (by cholesterol).

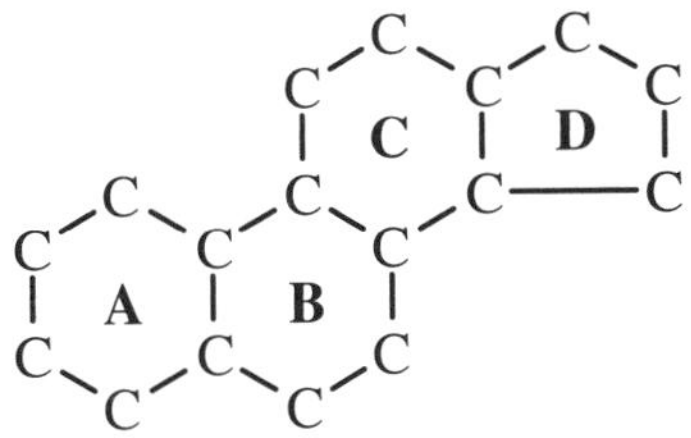

The rings are labelled A, B, C & D.

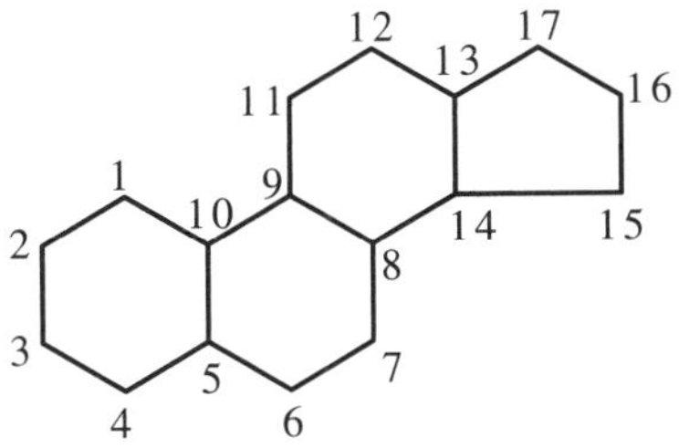

Cholesterol is the most common, important and necessary steroid in the human body. It is multifunctional. It is a component of all tissues and is found in the blood, brain and the spinal cord. It also acts as a building block to create other steroids such as the sex hormones as well as essential substances such as vitamin D. Cholesterol exists in esterified form in fatty acids and in a free form. Cholesterol is synthesised by the liver, but is also available through lipid containing foods.

Sex hormones such as androgens (male sex hormones), estrogens (female sex hormones) and progestins are present in the male and female body. They have a similar backbone to cholesterol. However, the functional groups on the sex hormones are different from those found on cholesterol and these slight differences in their molecular structures give rise to totally different functions.

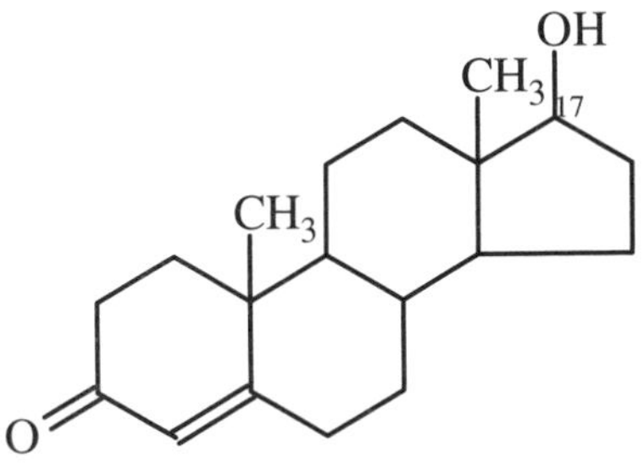

testosterone

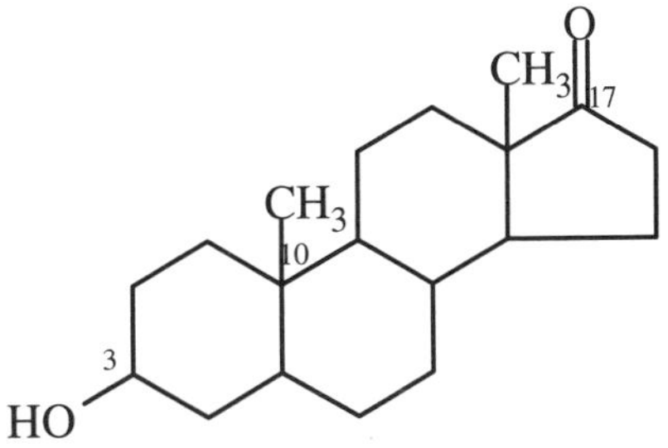

androsterone

OPTION

cholesterol

progesterone

For example, the only difference between testosterone (which promotes the normal growth of male genital organs and is responsible for the regulation of secondary sexual characteristics) and progesterone (responsible for production and control of the reproductive cycle) is the presence of the –OH group on C–17 of the steroid framework for testosterone, compared to the presence of the methyl alkanone on progesterone. Similarly, the difference between cholesterol and androsterone is the presence of a C=C bond between C–5 and C–6 (in the second ring) and a longer chain R group on C17 in cholesterol, compared to just the C=O on C–17 of the framework. Note that besides the common framework, both these molecules contain the secondary –OH group on C3 as well as the methyl groups on C–10 and C–13 atoms.

C.6.3 Describe the mode of action of oral contraceptives.   © IBO 2001

An effective method of birth control is an oral contraceptive (the pill). The most popular version of the pill combines a synthetic progesterone and estrogen. The two hormones act to stop the release of LHRH by the hypothalamus and FSH and LH by the pituitary. This results in the ovaries not being stimulated and thus inhibition of ovulation. In effect, the female reproductive system is fooled because the drug mimics the action of progesterone in a pregnant woman and ovulation is stopped. Because problems were experienced with the use of progesterone such as very high expense, rapid breakdown by the liver and side effects, progesterone–like synthetic chemicals such as norethynodrel and norethindrone are commonly used in birth control pills, combined with an estradiol–like compound to prevent irregular menstrual flow. The molecular framework of the synthetic chemicals in synthetic pills is the same as progesterone, but the –COCH₃ group on the D ring is replaced by the –OH and –C≡CH on C17. The presence of these groups seems to cause the synthetic steroids to tightly bind to their receptor sites. Thus, the rapid breakdown by the liver no longer takes place, making it possible to administer the pill orally.

Norethindrone

Norethynodrel

A second type of oral contraceptive is called the minipill. It contains progestin only (a progesterone–like synthetic chemical). It changes the composition of the cervical mucous from the mucous membrane, thereby preventing the sperm from entering the uterus. This variation of the pill can be inserted underneath the skin and will time release the progestin for a period of 5 years.

C.6.4   Outline the use and abuse of steroids.   © IBO 2001

Besides the development of male secondary sexual characteristics, testosterone promotes muscle growth. Such anabolic (meaning building up) steroids are effective ways to increase muscle mass. Thus for patients suffering from long, debilitating illnesses such as cancer, testosterone–like steroids, which cause minimal side effects, can be used to stimulate muscle growth and increase muscle mass and help such patients recover their body weight. However, athletes have been known to abuse such drugs. Both male and female athletes stand to increase their performances by using these substances. Testosterone is more prevalent in men and is principally responsible for muscle build–up. Women who use anabolic steroids have much to gain because, initially, there is a low concentration of testosterone present in their bodies.

Taking large doses of anabolic steroids causes harmful side effects. In males, the effects of aging are observed including impotence, baldness, problems in urinating, smaller testes, etc. In women, steroids affect secondary sex characteristics, build up muscles and produce facial hair etc. Both men and women also experience violent tempers, increased aggressive behavior as well as diseases such as liver tumors, high blood pressure and heart attacks. As a result, anabolic steroids are strictly forbidden at international athletic competitions. Competitors are given random urine tests (to detect steroids and other banned drugs) and winners are often required to undergo compulsory urine tests for such banned substances.

Anabolic steroids can be taken orally but their muscle building effects can be reduced if the steroid undergoes chemical change before reaching the receptor sites. Hence, they are much more effective when injected as these can reach receptor sites faster through the blood without suffering chemical changes.

OPTION

13.7 ENZYMES (HL ONLY)

C.7.1   Outline the basic characteristics of enzymes.

Include: enzymes are proteins; activity depends on tertiary and quaternary structure; the specificity of enzyme action.   © IBO 2001

Enzymes are protein based biological catalysts that speed up the rate of reactions in the body, without being chemically changed in the process. A catalyst does not alter the enthalpy or free energy change of a reaction. Thus it does not change the position of an equilibrium reaction or the equilibrium constant; it only speeds up the reaction so the equilibrium is reached faster. In other words, a catalyst cannot make a reaction take place that would not usually take place without the catalyst. Rather the same equilibrium is reached but much faster with an enzyme.

The initial amount of energy required to initiate a reaction is called activation energy (E_a) and is usually supplied in the form of heat from its surroundings. A catalyst reduces the activation energy so the reaction occurs faster.

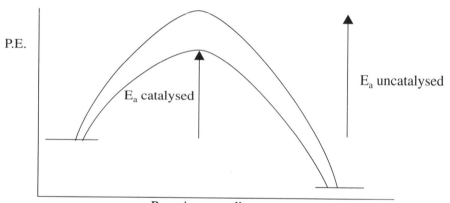

Enzymes are proteins which have four levels of structure (see page 469). It is their tertiary and quaternary structures which determine if the enzyme can act properly. When a protein denatures due to its environment, the tertiary and quaternary structures are altered. For example, the hydrophobic regions in the core of the tertiary structure may be affected when the protein is placed in an organic solvent like ether. Chemicals can also disrupt the hydrogen bonds, ionic bonds and the disulfide bridges in the tertiary structure.

C.7.4   Describe the concept of the active site in enzyme structure.   © IBO 2001

A reactant on which an enzyme reacts is called a substrate and a specific part of the enzyme binds to it for a reaction. This specific part is called the active site. When joined, the catalytic action of the enzyme converts the substrate to the product of the reaction. This product is then released by the enzyme, leaving the active site free for another substrate molecule. The substrate is held to the active site by weak interactions such as hydrogen bonds and ionic interactions.

OPTION

An enzyme can distinguish its substrate from closely related compounds. Hence, enzymes are very specific, each of them speeding up only one particular type of reaction. This is due to the compatible fit between the shape of its active site and the shape of the substrate. For this reason, the reaction between the active site of the enzyme and the substrate is often called the lock and key model. For example, the enzyme urease catalyzes only the hydrolysis of urea but not other amides. Similarly, where steroisomers exist, an enzyme that is effective with one enantiomer is found to be ineffective with the mirror image enantiomer. Thus a very large number of enzymes are needed to perform all the reactions in the human body.

The relationship between enzyme activity and substrate concentration:

If the concentration of an enzyme is increased, while all other factors such as temperature, pH and substrate concentration are held constant, the reaction is found in most cases to be first order with respect to enzyme concentration. That is, the rate is directly proportional to the enzyme concentration when the concentration of the enzyme is much less than the substrate concentration.

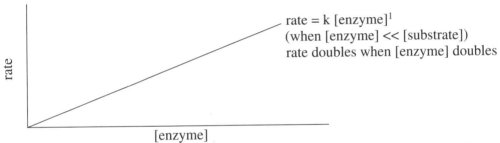

rate = k [enzyme]^1
(when [enzyme] << [substrate])
rate doubles when [enzyme] doubles

Substrates bind to an enzyme's active site to form an enzyme–substrate complex. Once the reaction is finished, the substrate leaves and the enzyme binds to another substrate. Thus the rate at which a given amount of enzyme converts substrate to product is a function of the initial concentration of substrate. More substrate molecules allow more frequent access to active sites of the enzymes. At very low substrate concentrations, the rate generally increases in a linear fashion, because the many active sites of the enzyme molecules have not been used up. Increasing substrate concentration involves more enzyme molecules and the reaction goes faster.

However, a hyperbolic dependence is observed at higher concentrations. This is because once the concentration reaches a certain point, all the active sites are engaged and the rate will not speed up anymore at that enzyme concentration. Eventually the saturation point is reached (V_{max}) and the reaction becomes zero order with respect to the substrate concentration. The observed rate then depends only on the rate at which the enzyme–substrate complex is converted to product. Once a substrate leaves, another takes its place. At this point, the enzyme is said to be saturated and the rate of reaction is dependent on the rate at which the substrate is converted and leaves the active site.

OPTION

Here, the only method of increasing rate is to increase enzyme concentration.

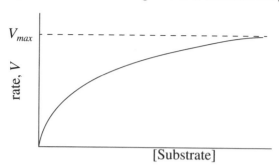

Variation of rate with [substrate] when [enzyme], temperature and pH are constant.

C. 7.2 Determine V_{max} and the value of the Michaelis constant (K_m) by graphical means.

C.7.3 Describe the significance of V_{max} and K_m.

© IBO 2001

The saturation effect led two scientists, Michaelis and Menten, to derive a theory of enzyme kinetics. Here the enzyme E reacts with the substrate S to form ES, the enzyme–substrate complex, which then decomposes to form the product P and the free enzyme E is generated.

$$\underset{k_2}{\overset{k_1}{E + S \rightleftharpoons ES}} \overset{k_3}{\Longrightarrow} P + E$$

In the first equilibrium equation, k_1 is the rate constant of the forward reaction and k_2 is the rate constant of the reverse reaction. k_3 is the rate constant for the second forward reaction. The rate constant of the second reverse reaction is ignored since it is usually too small compared to k_1, k_2 and k_3.

Applying the principles of kinetics, the Michaelis–Menten equation can be derived which provides a means of analyzing enzyme–catalyzed reactions in terms of the rate constants:

$$\text{rate} = v = \frac{V_{max}[S]}{K_m + [S]}$$

V_{max} is the maximum velocity (reaction rate) of the enzyme reaction, that is when the enzyme is fully saturated. [S] is the substrate concentration and K_m, the Michaelis constant (a function of three or more rate constants) in the above equation is equal to $\frac{k_2 + k_3}{k_1}$. The Michaelis–Menten equation accounts for the hyperbolic relationship between the rate, v, and the substrate concentration. Note that in that curve, it is difficult to obtain an accurate value of V_{max} by extrapolation due to the hyperbolic nature of the line. Also, if [S] is much less than K_m, then in the equation the denominator $\approx K_m$ and the equation reduces to $v \approx V_{max}[S]/K_m$ or $v \propto [S]$. This accounts for the linear dependence of rate, v, on [S] at very low substrate concentrations. If $[S] \gg K_m$, then the denominator in the rate equation $\approx [S]$, and $v = V_{max}$.

The Michaelis–Menten equation gives the quantitative relationship between the rate of enzyme reaction, v, and the substrate concentration, [S], if either V_{max}, the maximum velocity, or K_m is known. To understand the significance of the constant, K_m, consider half the maximum velocity, that is, $v = \frac{1}{2}V_{max}$:

According to the Michaelis–Menten equation:

$$\text{rate} = v = \frac{V_{max}[S]}{K_m + [S]} \; ; \text{if } v = \frac{1}{2}V_{max}, \text{then}$$

$$\frac{1}{2} = \frac{[S]}{K_m + [S]}$$

$$K_m + [S] = 2[S]$$

$$\therefore K_m = [S] \text{ when } v = \frac{1}{2}V_{max}$$

Thus K_m is equal to the substrate concentration when the velocity (rate) is equal to half the maximal value. Units of K_m are the same as the units of [S], namely mol dm^{-3}. K_m is an experimentally determined quantity; it is independent of the enzyme concentration [E] and its value varies with the the substrate, as well as temperature and pH. Note that the higher the K_m value, the lower the

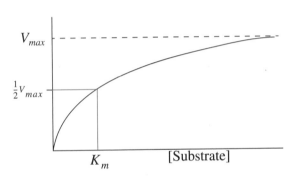

enzyme activity, i.e. K_m is inversely proportional to enzyme activity. A lower value of K_m means a more efficient enzyme because, with the same substrate concentration, there is a higher reaction rate.

Rearrangement of the Michaelis–Menten Equation: $\text{Rate} = \dfrac{V_{max}[S]}{K_m + [S]}$

Taking the inverse of both sides:

$$\frac{1}{v} = \frac{K_m + [S]}{V_{max}[S]}$$

$$= \frac{K_m}{V_{max}[S]} + \frac{[S]}{V_{max}[S]}$$

$$= \left[\frac{K_m}{V_{max}} \times \frac{1}{[S]}\right] + \frac{1}{V_{max}}$$

Option C: Human Biochemistry

$(y = mx + c$ straight line equation)

Thus a graph of $\dfrac{1}{v}$ against $\dfrac{1}{[S]}$ is a straight line with

slope $= \dfrac{K_m}{V_{max}}$ and its intercept is equal to $\dfrac{1}{V_{max}}$.

slope $= \dfrac{K_m}{V_{max}}$

Also, extrapolating the line, when $\dfrac{1}{v} = 0$, then $\dfrac{1}{[S]} = \dfrac{-1}{K_m}$.

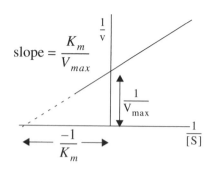

The 'double reciprocal' (Lineweaver–Burke) plot allows for the accurate determination of V_{max}, unlike the rate versus [substrate] plot where the V_{max} value is uncertain due to its asymptotic approach.

C.7.5   Explain competitive inhibition and non–competitive inhibition.   © IBO 2001

Certain chemicals inhibit the action of specific enzymes. If the inhibitor attaches to the enzyme by covalent bonds, inhibition is irreversible and usually involves the destruction or permanent modification of the enzyme structure. If it attaches by weak interactions, the inactivation is reversible and can be treated quantitatively by using the Michaelis–Menten equation.

There are two major types of reversible inhibition: competitive and non–competitive. Inhibitors that resemble the normal substrate molecule and compete for the enzyme's active site are called competitive inhibitors. These reduce the activity of the enzyme as they block the substrate from entering the active site. If inhibition is reversible, an increase of substrate concentration can reduce the impact of the inhibitor.

Consider the enzyme succinate dehydrogenase which catalyzes the reduction (namely the removal of two H atoms) from the two $-CH_2$ groups of the succinate ions:

$$\overset{enzyme}{^-OOC-CH_2-CH_2-COO^- + X \rightleftharpoons {}^-OOC-CH=CH-COO^- + H_2X}$$
succinate ion

The malonate ion, $^-OOC-CH_2-COO^-$, which also has two ionized groups inhibits the action of the enzyme since both compete for the same site as the malonate ion resembles the succinate ion. If the concentration of the succinate ion is increased, the amount of inhibition by the malonate ion is reduced.

Competitive inhibition is recognized in the Lineweaver–Burke double reciprocal plots of $\dfrac{1}{v}$ versus $\dfrac{1}{[S]}$ at varying inhibitor concentrations. In such a case, V_{max} remains the same and is not affected by the competitive inhibitor, I. This is because at any inhibitor concentration, it is still possible to reach the same maximum velocity (that is full enzyme activity) at a substrate concentration, however high.

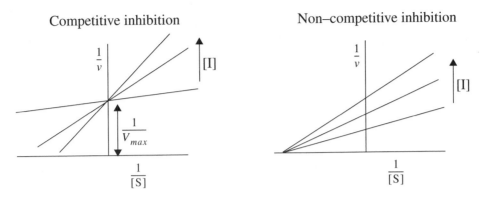

Non–competitive inhibitors impede enzymatic reactions by binding to a part of the enzyme away from the active site. The inhibitor, I, may bind to the free enzyme, E, to the enzyme–substrate complex ES or to both and making EI and ESI inactive, that is this causes the enzyme to alter its shape and the active site can no longer receive its substrate.

$$E + I \rightleftharpoons EI; ES + I \rightleftharpoons ESI$$

Consider the reversible action of a heavy metal ion Hg^{2+} on the –SH group of cysteine residue which is essential for some enzyme catalytic activity:

$$2 E–S–H + Hg^{2+} \rightleftharpoons E–S–Hg–S–E + 2H^+$$

The enzyme is inhibited non–competitively by the formation of the –S–Hg–S– linkage. Thus one would expect V_{max} to be decreased by the inhibitor as the active enzyme concentration is decreased and the velocity cannot be increased by increasing the substrate concentration. Thus in the double reciprocal graphs of $\frac{1}{v}$ against $\frac{1}{[S]}$, the slopes do not have the same intercept on the $\frac{1}{V}$ axis. The higher the inhibitor concentration, the lower the velocity v, the larger the $\frac{1}{v}$ value and therefore the greater the intercept as shown above. Thus the hyperbolic curves for the rate of reaction versus substrate concentration are as follows:

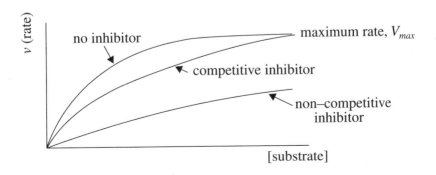

C.7.6 State and explain the effects of heavy metal ions, extremes of temperature and pH changes on enzyme activity.

© IBO 2001

Enzymes and substrates are only effective if they have specific three–dimensional shapes which complement one another, (i.e. the lock and key model). If in any way the enzyme changes its shape or arrangement, the substrate will no longer be able to bind to the active site and the enzyme is rendered non-functional. This denaturation can take place when the surrounding environment changes even slightly. This may be brought about in several ways such as a variation in temperature or pH of the solution, or by the presence of heavy metal ions.

Each enzyme has conditions under which it works optimally as that environment favors the most active conformation for the enzyme. Temperature increases enzymatic reaction rates up to a certain point as the substrates collide with active sites more frequently as the molecules move faster (see Chapter 7). However, the speed of the reaction drops sharply when the temperature reaches a certain point. Here, the thermal agitation of the enzyme disrupts the hydrogen bonds, ionic bonds and other non–covalent interactions that stabilize its active structure. If the three–dimensional structure is changed as a result of temperature, the enzyme activity is affected. All enzymes have an optimum temperature at which they are not yet denatured and the substrates collide fastest with the enzyme. In humans, enzymes have an optimum temperature of about 37°C, about the same as the internal body temperature. Beyond this temperature, the change in the enzyme structure affects the active site (usually irreversibly) and the rate drops sharply.

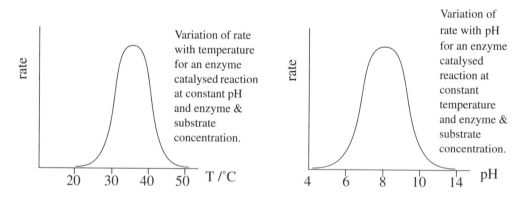

Variation of rate with temperature for an enzyme catalysed reaction at constant pH and enzyme & substrate concentration.

Variation of rate with pH for an enzyme catalysed reaction at constant temperature and enzyme & substrate concentration.

Proteins contain groups such as $-NH_2$ and $-COOH$ and are susceptible to pH changes. Extreme changes in pH values denature such ionisable enzymes rendering them ineffective. For such enzymes, a similar trend is observed to that of the effect of temperature. At low or high pH values, the enzyme is irreversibly denatured and the rate drops sharply. Within a narrow pH range, the enzyme structure changes reversibly and each such enzyme works optimally at a specific pH. Thus the maximum rate for the enzyme chymotrypsin occurs around pH 8 and for pepsin this occurs at pH 2. However, the enzyme invertase which catalyzes the hydrolysis of the neutral sucrose molecule has a constant rate in the pH range 3.3 to 7.5. Thus, if an enzyme is acting on an electrically neutral substrate molecule, or where the charge plays no role in the catalyzed reaction, changes in pH have little effect on the rate of this reaction.

Heavy metal ions can also disrupt some enzyme activity. When a heavy metal ion is present at the active site, substitution of a different metal ion for the original ion causes the enzyme to malfunction and denature, particularly where heavy metal ions can bind or chelate to the –S–H groups in proteins to form –S–M–S– type arrangement (see, for example, page 493).

C.7.7   Describe the uses of enzymes in biotechnology.

Possible examples include proteases in biological detergents, glucose isomerase converting glucose to fructose and streptokinase in breaking down blood clots.

Biotechnology is the application and harnessing of microorganisms (such as bacteria, viruses and fungi) or biological processes to produce desired and useful substances (such as insulin) and facilitate industrial processes. Fermentation is an example of biotechnology. Brewing, baking and manufacture of cheese all involve the fermentation process. The manufacture of wine, for example, involves the fermentation of grape juice, a rich source of glucose, by wild yeasts present on grape skin. The process produces an alcohol content of 8 to 15% by volume which is high enough to kill the yeast. Similarly, the fermentation of sugar by yeast is the basis for the production of other alcoholic drinks:

$$2(C_6H_{10}O_5)_n + nH_2O \xrightarrow{\text{diatstase in malt}} nC_{12}H_{22}O_{11}, \text{maltose}$$

$$C_{12}H_{22}O_{11} + H_2O \xrightarrow{\text{maltase}} 2C_6H_{12}O_6, \text{glucose}$$

$$C_6H_{12}O_6 \xrightarrow{\text{zymase}} 2C_2H_5OH + 2CO_2$$

Better brewing through improving yeast and large scale production are the results of biotechnology. The genes responsible for the yeast enzymes have been cloned and bacteria have been used in the large scale production of the yeast enzymes needed.

Genetic engineering involves the manipulation of genes. It is the term used to describe the modern techniques in molecular biology where genes can be removed from one type of cell to another, altering a cell's properties. Genetic engineering has revolutionized the process of biotechnology and has given rise to the manufacture of important products such as new antibiotics, insulin and biological detergents. Transfer of human insulin genes into bacteria and growth by fermentation has made large scale production of human insulin possible.

Lipolase, an enzyme which is a constituent of biological detergents, consists of fat–digesting (splitting) enzymes. Scientists at Novo Nordisk in Japan have created lipolase by taking a gene coding from a particular species of fungus and transferring it to another microbe, *aspergillus*, that produces enzymes in very high yields. As a result, enzymes are widely used in the soap and detergent industry. Such biological detergents' main environmental benefits are that they save energy (a reduction in washing temperature from 60°C to 40°C). They are rapidly biodegradable thus leaving no harmful residues and produce no negative impact on sewage treatment processes and pose no risk to aquatic life.

OPTION

Similarly scientists working in South America have discovered an enzyme which breaks the glucose chains in cellulose by hydrolysis only when a strand of cellulose comes loose. Thus this has found ready application in detergents used to clean cellulose cotton in which the enzyme is able to break bonds holding loose fibers, making the fabric appear new.

Other applications of genetic engineering have found their way into medicine. Interferons are natural anti–viral proteins that can be used against viral infections. Genes cloned in yeasts are used to produce such proteins and extensive research is under way in this area. Hepatitis B vaccine has been genetically engineered and research is continuing into finding vaccines for AIDS and malaria.

13.8 NUCLEIC ACIDS

C.8.1   Describe the structure of nucleotides and their condensation polymers (nucleic acids).

A nucleotide contains a phosphate group, a pentose sugar group and an organic base. Students should be able to recognize, but need not recall, the structures of the five nucleotide bases: adenine, cytosine, guanine, thymine and uracil.

© IBO 2001

Nucleic acids are essential to protein synthesis. Nucleic acids are high molar mass polymers of fairly simple composition because they are composed of only a few different nucleotide bases compared to proteins which are made of some 20 different amino acids. A nucleic acid is a polymer chain of **nucleotides** and consists of three components, an ionised phosphate group, a pentose sugar group and an organic base. Genetically, the most important components of nucleotides are the nitrogenous bases, since the sequence of the bases in DNA (deoxyribonucleic acid) and RNA (ribonucleic acid) polymer molecules are the key to the storage of genetic information.

There are five possible nitrogenous bases that may be part of a nucleotide, classified into two groups, the **purines** and the **pyrimidines**. Purines have a double ringed structure and consist of adenine (A) and guanine (G), while pyrimidines have a single ringed structure and consist of cytosine (C), thymine (T) and uracil (U). The base thymine is present predominantly in DNA nucleotides (and rarely in RNA, for example, in transfer RNA) while uracil is found only in RNA nucleotides. Thymine differs from uracil only in the presence of $-CH_3$ group on the C–5 position. There are two forms of pentose that may make up a nucleoside. As the name implies, the sugars are either ribose found in RNA or deoxyribose found in DNA nucleotides. These sugars differ only in that the hydroxyl group on the C–2 of ribose is replaced by a hydrogen atom in deoxyribose. Thus deoxysugars, like deoxyribose, do not fit the empirical formula, CH_2O, generally given for carbohydrates.

	Purines	Pyrimidines	Sugars	Phosphates
Present in DNA and RNA	adenine guanine 	cytosine 		phosphate
Present in DNA		thymine 	deoxyribose 	
Present in RNA		uracil 	ribose 	

A nitrogenous base together with a pentose sugar form a **nucleoside.** The condensation reaction occurs through the hydrogen atom present on a N atom of the base combining with the hydroxyl group on the C–1 of the sugar to release water and form a covalent N–C bond between the sugar and the base.

Condensation of adenine with ribose

Nucleoside from uracil and ribose

Option C: Human Biochemistry

A nucleoside combines with a phosphate group to produce a nucleotide. The phosphate group HPO_4^{2-} is an ionized form of phosphoric acid, H_3PO_4 - the reason both DNA and RNA are weakly acidic in aqueous solution. Again, a condensation reaction bonds the $-CH_2OH$ of a nucleoside to the phosphate group, with the hydroxyl group on the C–5 of the sugar reacting with a hydrogen from the phosphate group to release water and form a covalent bond. The bonded phosphate group has a charge of negative two, making the entire nucleotide negatively charged.

A nucleoside

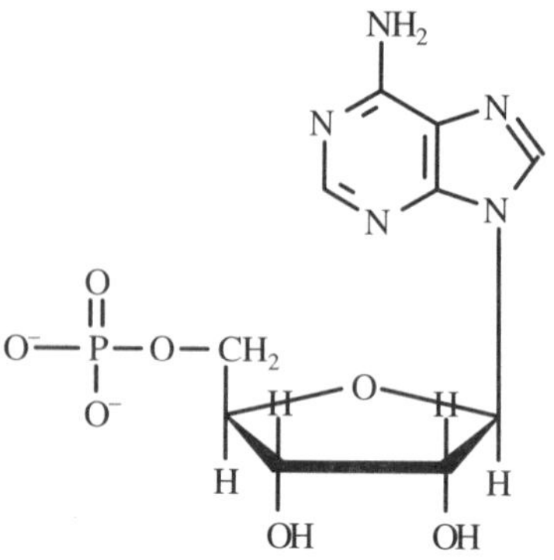

Note that a **nucleoside** is made up from a base and a sugar molecule, a **nucleotide** from a base, a sugar and an ionised phosphate group and a **nucleic acid** is a polymer of nucleotides.

A nucleic acid polymer consists of a chain of nucleotides formed by enzyme catalysed condensation reactions. The phosphate of one nucleotide combines with the hydroxyl group on the C–3 of the sugar on another nucleotide, releasing water and forming a bond. As the polymerization continues, a backbone of alternating sugar and phosphate groups is formed with the nitrogenous bases emerging from this backbone.

The sequence of these bases is important in the storage of genetic information. Thus, the DNA backbone consists of alternate phosphate and deoxyribose groups and the bases form the side chain. At the end of a nucleic acid chain is a nucleotide that does not have another nucleotide attached to its phosphate group.

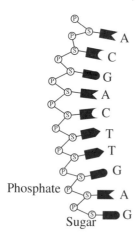

Phosphate
Sugar

Section of DNA,
deoxyribonucleic acid

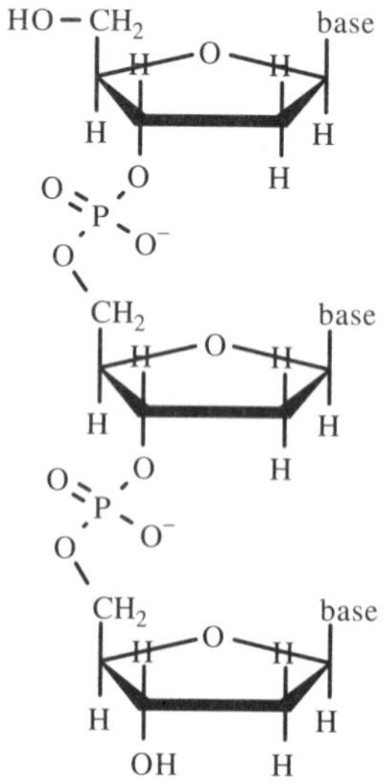

C.8.2　Describe the double helical structure of DNA.

Students should be able to describe the hydrogen bonding between specific pairs of nucleotide bases.　© IBO 2001

DNA has a secondary structure that results in the formation of a **double helix** that consists of two strands of nucleic acid that interact through intermolecular hydrogen bonding to form a double helix. The organic bases are located between the two backbones of sugar and phosphate groups, but their properties are a key to understanding the secondary structure of DNA. The structure of DNA shows that adenine (A) and thymine (T) only occur opposite each other and the same applies to cytosine (C) and guanine (G). Part of the reason for this is that only the combination of a purine and a pyrimidine give a similar distance between the two backbones of DNA, since a purine is double ringed and a pyrimidine is single ringed.

The major reason why each base combines only with one other type of base due is to the intermolecular hydrogen bonding that occurs between them and holds the double-stranded DNA molecule together. Because of their molecular geometry, adenine forms **two** strong hydrogen bonds with thymine, but adenine and cytosine do not form hydrogen bonds strong enough to hold DNA together. Cytosine and guanine form **three** strong hydrogen bonds, but any other combination of purine and pyrimidine does not have hydrogen bonds which are able to hold two strands of nucleic acid together. The double helix is further stabilised by other interactions such as dipole-dipole hydrophobic interactions and van der Waals' forces between the base pairs (previously mentioned in Section 13.2 page 464). Since uracil replaces thymine in RNA, uracil may also form strong hydrogen bonds with adenine, though these exist only in the synthesis of RNA and not in the actual DNA molecule.

Hydrogen bonds between A & T and C & G

OPTION

Option C: Human Biochemistry

The strong hydrogen bonding between the bases and the twisting of the sugar–phosphate backbone result in DNA's secondary structure taking the form of a double stranded, helical shape with a 'ladder' of bases spanning the gap between the two strands. The fact that each organic base on a strand has only one possible complement on the other (A & T and C & G; called complementary base pairs) is essential to the passing on of genetic information from one cell to the next. This pairing is based entirely on intermolecular hydrogen bonding.

The Double Helix

C.8.3 Outline the role of DNA as the repository of genetic information, including the triplet code.

The role of DNA is to reproduce itself and carry the information which encodes the proteins (including the enzymes) in any organism. DNA is the 'program' behind any organism's development. A gene is a section of a DNA molecule that codes for a protein. Note that many sections of DNA molecules are not genes - many of the genomes of higher organisms contain non-coding 'junk' DNA. A gene contains many nucleotides with a specific sequence of the four bases A, C, G and T in the required order to produce a specific protein. That is, the sequence of the organic bases in each gene represent a code that determines many of an organism's characteristics. This is possible because every protein is made based on a plan denoted by the sequence of bases in the DNA molecule. All cells in one organism have exactly the same DNA with the same sequence of base pairs; different species contain different DNA molecules. Also, genetic information must be passed on to the offspring of an organism through the transfer of DNA. Therefore, when new organisms are produced or cells divide, DNA must be accurately copied or replicated. The complementary base pairs allow this process to occur easily.

If a DNA sequence is damaged by ultraviolet (uv) light, often no protein is produced, or is produced in reduced amounts, or a different mutant protein, or damaged DNA, may be produced. The production of damaged DNA can lead to disease, for example, the uncontrolled growth of cells (cancer). In other cases, a changed base sequence may give rise to a non-harmful genetic change, for example, different hair or eye color.

Instructions for protein synthesis are encoded in DNA. DNA contains four nucleotides, but some twenty amino acids are involved in the synthesis of proteins. Clearly one nucleotide base could not be involved per amino acid as this would only specify four of the twenty amino acids. Similarly, two nucleotides would not be sufficient as the four bases would specify only $4^2 = 16$ amino acids (e.g. AA, AG, AC, AT, GC, GT, GA, GG, etc.). A three nucleotide sequence with four bases can produce a total of $4^3 = 64$ combinations of triplets to specify all the amino acids, where many of the amino acids are encoded by more than one triplet. For example, AAA and AAG both specify the amino acid lysine. The triplet code AUG signals the start of a protein chain whereas three other triplets specify the end of the protein chain. A three nucleotide sequence, called a triplet code or codon, codes for a specific amino acid in the polypeptide chain and is called the genetic code. Thus the sequence of nucleotides in DNA determines the precise arrangement of amino acids in proteins. Proteins are not made directly from the genetic information stored in the DNA in the cell nucleus. The transfer of genetic information involves transcription from DNA to messenger RNA (mRNA) and translation from mRNA to protein synthesis by transfer RNA (tRNA).

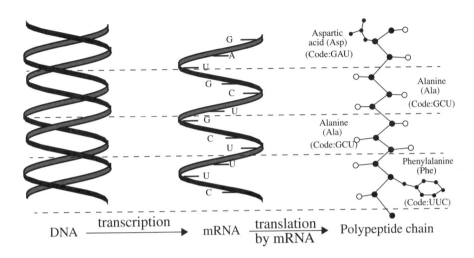

C.8.3   Describe the principles and uses of DNA profiling.

Include forensic uses and paternity cases.   © IBO 2001

One of the many useful applications of DNA technology is DNA profiling, which involves the production of a genetic 'fingerprint'. The key to DNA profiling is that all cells from an organism must create the same DNA profile. If the process is carried out extensively enough it is possible to produce a profile of sufficient detail that would make it almost impossible for any other organisms to have the same profile. A DNA profile may be obtained by two methods, both of which involve observing the number of different pieces a molecule of DNA can be split into and the size of these pieces.

The first method occurs through the use of **restriction enzymes**, which have the ability to find a certain sequence of base pairs and to cut the molecule of DNA at those sequences. Therefore, if a section of DNA is chosen that varies considerably from person to person, then each person will have this section of DNA cut into different lengths as the restriction sequences will occur at different points in each person's DNA. Another method of obtaining a unique combination of DNA sizes is through examining a section of DNA called VNTR (variable number of tandem repeats). The exact function of these parts of DNA is not known, but they consist of a short sequence of base pairs repeated many times, with the number of repeats varying from person to person. These fragments of DNA can be analysed through the use of an enzyme catalyzed reaction which copies the required section of DNA millions of times, even if the initial sample is very small. Depending on the number of repeats on the VNTR site, different sizes of DNA fragments are produced. Many people will have the same number of repeats at one VNTR site, but if numerous sites are chosen then some of these will vary in length and a

DNA profile can be created that is unique.

Once a unique combination of DNA fragments of different sizes is created, gel electrophoresis is used to make an observable DNA profile. A thin plate of electrically conducting gel is set up, a negative charge is placed at one end of the plate and a positive charge at the other. A solution of the various DNA fragments is placed on the plate. Since DNA has negatively charged phosphate groups it is attracted to the positively charged plate. The fragments of DNA move, the smaller fragments moving more quickly through the gel than the larger ones. A fluorescent dye is added which makes the DNA glow in UV light. A photograph can then be taken of the number and position of the bands of DNA that appear in the gel.

DNA profiling is mainly used to identify people. This is especially useful in helping to solve crimes, as any cells left behind at the scene of a crime in the form of blood, semen or hair roots can be used to make a DNA profile. DNA profiles can be made from all of the suspect's DNA and compared to the DNA profile collected from the scene of the crime. DNA profiling can also be used in paternity cases, especially the VNTR method, since all of the child's different VNTR lengths must come only from those that are present in the mother or the father.

13.9 METAL IONS IN BIOLOGICAL SYSTEMS

C.9.1 Explain that different metal ions fulfill different roles in the body due to their different chemical properties.

Emphasize differences in charge density, redox properties and complex ion formation. © IBO 2001

Metal ions found in the diet are essential to biological systems. Different metal ions fulfil different roles in the body due to their differences in charge density, redox properties and complex ion formation. Of these, calcium ions are the most commonly found in animals, accounting for 1.5–2% of human body mass of which 99% forms bones and teeth. An average person contains between 1 and 1.5 kg of calcium. Magnesium, potassium and sodium ions are also present in biological systems as ions in the fluids in and around the cells.

Iron was the first trace metal ion found to be essential in the human diet. Other first row transition metals such as Co, Cr, Cu and Mn are also present in trace amounts in the human body. Zinc is found in almost 100 enzymes, such as Zn^{2+} in carboxypeptidase, and is also present in insulin, a hormone. Cobalt(III) (Co^{3+}) is found in vitamin B_{12} and iron is present in the haemoglobin molecule of red blood cells so that iron deficiency produces anemia and causes fatigue as cells are deprived of oxygen. Magnesium (as ions) is a secondary element of bones and teeth as well as regulating intracellular chemical activity, helping to form proteins and transmitting electrochemical signals between cells. Manganese is essential for healthy bones and chromium plays a key role in glucose metabolism. Copper deficiency gives rise to bone disease. The need for trace amounts of some metal ions such as tin and arsenic has been established in animals such as rats but not yet in humans.

Transition metal ions have the ability to exist in multiple oxidation states and can be involved in redox reactions in biological systems. Also, transition metal ions such as Fe(II), Fe(III) and Co(III) are able to bond to several nitrogen containing bases in haemoglobin and vitamin B12 because of the presence of lone electron pairs on the nitrogen of the bases and the high charge densities (charge to size ratio) of the transition metal ions. Consequently coordinate covalent bonding takes place where the metal ion is the electron pair acceptor (Lewis base) and the nitrogen on the base, the electron pair donor (the Lewis base). This is an example of a complex ion formation in which the species containing the nitrogen donor atoms surrounding the metal ion is called a multidentate **ligand**:

structure of heme group of haemoglobin

C.9.2 Describe the importance of the difference in Na^+ and K^+ concentrations across the cell membrane.

Explain active transport using the Na^+/K^+ pump as an example. © IBO 2001

Sodium and potassium ions are two of the most important metal ions in biological systems because of their use in the transmission of nerve impulses. The potassium ion is the most prominent ion inside the cell and is responsible for the activities of many cellular enzymes. The sodium ion, which is the most abundant cation outside the cell, maintains a water balance between the fluids inside and outside the cells. Both the sodium and potassium cations are also responsible for regulating the concentration of hydrogen ions in the body and hence the acidity of the fluids. Chloride ions balance the positive charges of several cations and occur as hydrochloric acid in the stomach.

Cell surface membranes actively pump Na^+ ions out of the cell while accumulating K^+ inside the cell. This is called the Na^+/K^+ pump and is driven by ATP hydrolysis (adenosine triphosphate, an important coenzyme). The Na^+/K^+ pump is essential in osmoregulation, that is in controlling cell volume, in driving active transport of substances such as sugars and amino acids and in maintaining electrical activity in nerve cells.

OPTION

The Na⁺/K⁺ pump is driven by a protein (Na-K ATPase) molecule across the cell membrane. On the inside of the cell, it binds with 3 Na⁺ ions and an ATP molecule. The Na⁺ converts ATP to ADP (adenosine diphosphate) and the phosphate group attaches itself to the protein (a process called phosphorylation). This causes a change in the protein conformation (shape) with the release of Na⁺ ions to the outside of the cell and formation of only two binding sites for K⁺ ions. These ions cause the protein to release the phosphate group (dephosphorylation) which returns the protein to its initial shape and the K⁺ ions enter the cell. This maintains the unequal distribution of cations across the membrane which is essential for the transmission of nerve impulses.

Both Na⁺ and K⁺ have a charge of +1 but the sodium ion is smaller than the potassium ion. Thus it has a higher charge density (charge to size ratio) compared to K⁺ ions. Na⁺ ions with their higher charge density bind much more tightly to parts of the cytoplasm and are thus unable to diffuse across the cell membrane, whereas K⁺ ions with the lower charge density are able to do so quite freely.

Transmission of nerve impulses involves electro-chemical signals. A nerve impulse is the depolarization of a section of the cell membrane which moves down the nerve fiber (axon) of a nerve cell and is transmitted to other cells. Na⁺ ion channels, which participate in the propagation of the impulse down the axon, open as the membrane is depolarized and the ions rush in. A fraction of a second later, the ions are pumped out as the membrane repolarizes. Thus, without the right amounts of Na⁺ and K⁺ ions, the impulse cannot be sent effectively.

C.9.3 Outline the importance of copper ions in electron transport and iron ions in oxygen carriers. Use cytochromes and haemoglobin as examples. © IBO 2001

Cytochromes are part of the electron transfer chain which generates ATP (a form of short term stored chemical energy). Cytochromes are iron and copper containing proteins that carry energetic electrons to produce ATP (adenosine triphosphate). Living organisms use ATP to transfer useful energy ($\Delta G°$ is negative) from exothermic reactions, such as oxidation of carbohydrates and fatty acids to biosynthetic reactions and other endothermic processes that require energy. The energy produced in the oxidation of food is stored in the form of ATP (the 'energy currency').

The iron atoms of the cytochromes undergo one–electron oxidation–reduction reactions during aerobic respiration between iron(II) and iron(III) oxidation states and the copper between copper(I) and copper(II):

$$Fe^{2+} \rightleftharpoons Fe^{3+} + e^-; \quad Cu^{1+} \rightleftharpoons Cu^{2+} + e^-$$

Reduced co-enzymes such as NADH (nicotinamide adenine dinucleotide) carry hydrogen ions and electrons from the metal ions which serve as intermediates to form water and produce energy:

$$4e^- + 4\,H^+_{(aq)} + O_{2\,(g)} \rightleftharpoons 2\,H_2O_{(l)} + energy$$

This exothermic reaction is carried out in many steps involving a number of enzymes. Copper in the cytochrome oxidase is the terminal electron carrier in the electron transport chain (also called the respiratory chain) which converts oxygen to water and the energy produced is used to form ATP.

Haemoglobin is the best–known oxygen transport protein. It bonds to the oxygen in the lungs in order to transport it throughout the blood to tissues in the body. Heme is a complex of iron in a hydrophobic environment due to the non-polar side chains that surround it. This environment makes it possible for the oxygen to bind with the Fe^{2+} reversibly without oxidising the metal to Fe^{3+}.

Iron bonds to oxygen to form oxyhaemoglobin. This carries oxygen to the cells, releases the oxygen, picks up carbon dioxide and returns the CO_2 to the lungs where it is released. Most of the carbon dioxide present in the circulatory system is transported as carbonic acid, i.e. as hydrogen carbonate and hydrogen ions:

$$CO_{2\,(g)} + H_2O_{(l)} \rightleftharpoons H^+_{(aq)} + HCO_3^-_{(aq)}$$

Iron deficiency causes anemia (shortage of red blood cells) and, as a result, insufficient oxygen is carried to the cells, leading to fatigue. Species such as carbon monoxide, CO, bind tightly with Fe(II) to block its ability to pick up oxygen. This interferes with oxygen transport, depriving the body cells of vital oxygen. The heart must pump at a greater rate and if sufficient oxygen cannot be supplied, the animal can die by asphyxiation. Since the reactions of haemoglobin with both O_2 and CO are reversible, excess amounts of oxygen can eventually displaces the CO and the effect of CO metabolic poisoning can be reversed to some extent.

OPTION C – HUMAN BIOCHEMISTRY QUESTIONS

1. What is nutrition? What are nutrients? List the six groups nutrients are generally divided into.

2. Describe the requirements of the human body for a healthy diet.

3. What is calorific value? Explain how the calorific value of a food is related to its enthalpy of combustion.

4. Discuss the benefits and concerns of using genetically modified (GM) foods.

5. State the basic structure of 2–amino acids.

6. What are optical isomers? Why does the basic structure of 2–amino acids give rise to optical isomers?

7. Under what conditions will an aqueous solution of amino acids be: neutral, acidic, basic?

8. Discuss the physical properties of amino acids.

9. What is a peptide chain and how is it formed?

OPTION

10. Discuss the technique of paper chromatography. Your answer should explain the following terms: (a) stationary phase, (b) adsorption, (c) R_f value.

11. Discuss the technique of electrophoresis. Your answer should explain the following; (a) isoelectric point, (b) solubility of an amino acid at its isoelectric point, (c) the variation in the solubility of amino acid at pH values higher and lower than the isoelectric point.

12. Explain how the amino acid composition of proteins can be analyzed by chromatography and electrophoresis.

13. Describe and explain the primary, secondary, tertiary and quaternary structures of proteins.

14. List four ways in which parts of the amino acid chains interact to stabilize the tertiary protein structure. Illustrate using a diagram.

15. List the major functions of proteins in the body.

16. Describe the structural features of monosaccharides and give their empirical formula.

17. Describe the straight–chain formula of glucose and the structural difference between α–glucose and ß–glucose.

18. Draw the straight chain formula of glucose and identify two carbon atoms in the structure which are not chiral.

19. Describe the condensation of monosaccharides to form the disaccharide, lactose and the polysaccharide starch.

20. Give the names of the monosaccharides that condense to form (a) starch and (b) sucrose.

21. What is the glucoside linkage?

22. How does the structure of amylose differ from the structure of amylopectin?

23. List the major functions of polysaccharides in the body.

24. What is a triglyceride?

25. Describe the composition of fats and oils. Write a general formula for a fat or an oil.

26. Describe the difference in structure between saturated and unsaturated fats and explain the difference in their melting points.

27. Explain how one can calculate the number of C=C double bonds in a fat from addition reactions.

28. Explain the relationship between the iodine number and the degree of unsaturation in a fat or oil.

29. What is a hydrolysis reaction?

30. Describe the hydrolysis of fats to form soap.

31. Describe the action of soaps.

32. List the major functions of fats in the body.

33. Describe the term vitamin.

34. Describe the role of vitamins in metabolism.

35. What structural features make a vitamin water soluble; fat soluble?

36. By referring to the structure of vitamin A, list two functional groups present in it.

37. With reference to the structures of vitamins A and C, account for their different water solubilities.

38. Describe the structures and major functions of retinol (vitamin A), calciferol (vitamin D) and ascorbic acid (vitamin C).

39. Describe the effects of food processing on the vitamin content of food.

40. Outline the production and roles of adrenaline, thyroxine, insulin and sex hormones in the body.

41. Identify the similarities and differences between the structures of cholesterol and the sex hormones.

42. Describe the mode of action of oral contraceptives.

43. Outline the use and abuse of steroids.

44. Use a potential energy diagram to describe the basic characteristics of enzymes.

45. With respect to enzymes, explain the following terms: (a) substrate, (b) active site, (c) lock and key model.

46. Explain the relationship between enzyme activity and substrate concentration when [enzyme] << [substrate].

47. What is the significance of V_{max} and K_m in the Michaelis–Menten equation? What are the units of the two terms.

48. Given the Michaelis–Menten equation, rearrange it to give the equation of a straight line. How can the values of V_{max} and K_m be determined from the straight line equation derived?

49. Explain competitive and non–competitive inhibition.

50. State and explain the effects of heavy metal ions, extremes of temperature and pH changes on enzyme activity.

51. Describe some uses of enzymes in biotechnology.

52. Describe the structure of nucleosides, nucleotides and their condensation polymers, nucleic acids.

OPTION

53. Describe the difference in the structures of purines and pyrimidines?

54. Discuss the double helical structure of DNA.

55. What is the triplet code? Describe the role of DNA as the repository of genetic information.

56. Describe the principles and uses of DNA profiling.

57. List three metal ions that fulfil roles in the body. Why are metal ions able to play important roles in the body?

58. Describe the importance of the difference in Na^+ and K^+ ion concentrations across the cell membrane.

59. Using cytochromes and haemoglobin as examples, explain the importance of copper ions in electron transport and iron ions in oxygen carriers.

ENVIRONMENTAL CHEMISTRY (Option D)

14

Chapter contents

The effect of human activity on the environment has become increasingly global, with the effects of chemicals in air and water spanning political and natural borders. An understanding of this impact is essential within and beyond the study of chemistry.

© IBO 2001

14.1 PRIMARY AIR POLLUTION

D.1.1   Describe the sources of carbon monoxide, oxides of nitrogen and sulfur, particulates and hydrocarbons in the atmosphere.

Include both natural and man–made sources. Balanced equations should be used where possible.

D.1.2   Outline the effects of primary air pollution on health.

Students should be familiar with at least one harmful effect of each of the substances in D.1.1.

D.1.3   Discuss methods for the reduction of primary air pollution.

Limit this to the following methods:

CO–catalytic converters. NO$_x$–catalytic converters, lean burn engines, recirculation of exhaust gases. SO$_2$–alkaline scrubbing, removal of sulfur–containing compounds from coal and oil, limestone–based fluidized beds. Particulates–electrostatic precipitation. Hydrocarbons–catalytic converters.

© IBO 2001

An **air pollutant** is a substance present in sufficient concentration in the air to produce a harmful effect on humans or other animals, vegetation or materials. It can be naturally produced, such as through volcanic activity, bacterial action, etc. or produced by human activity ('man made') due to increased urbanization, industrialization (electrical power plants, industry etc.), transportation, forest fires, incineration of solid wastes etc. The effect of air pollutants depends on the amounts present, their relative toxicity and the average length of time the pollutants remain in the environment before becoming harmless by natural processes or by chemical cycles.

A **primary** air pollutant is one which is added directly to the air from a given source such as carbon dioxide from the burning of fossil fuels. A **secondary** air pollutant, on the other hand, is formed in the atmosphere through chemical reaction(s), such as the formation of ozone in photochemical smog. The five major primary air pollutants are carbon monoxide (CO), nitrogen oxides (NO$_x$), sulfur oxides (SO$_x$), particulates and hydrocarbons (HCs).

Carbon monoxide, :C≡O: (CO) is a polar molecule with covalent bonding between the atoms and is not very soluble in water. It is a colorless, odorless, tasteless, toxic compound which is formed due to the incomplete combustion of carbon and carbon–containing compounds such as fossil fuels:

$$2\,C_{(s)} + O_{2(g)} \Rightarrow 2\,CO_{(g)}$$

In the presence of excess oxygen, carbon dioxide is formed:

$$2\,CO_{(g)} + O_{2(g)} \Rightarrow 2\,CO_{2(g)} \text{ OR } C_{(s)} + O_{2(g)} \Rightarrow CO_{2(g)}$$

Carbon monoxide is a product if either there is insufficient oxygen such as in forest fires or in automobiles when poor mixing of fuel and air takes place or if there is insufficient oxygen present in an internal combustion engine. Almost 90% of all CO production comes from natural sources – most of it from the atmospheric oxidation of methane gas,

OPTION

CH_4. Methane is produced from anaerobic (lack of oxygen) conditions from the decomposition of organic matter in swamps and tropical regions (for example rice fields, rivers, lakes etc.) as well as algae and other organic matter in oceans. The other 10% CO comes from man–made sources, from the combustion of fossil fuels used in industry, forest fires and in particular gasoline (petrol) used in the internal combustion engine for transportation.

Whereas the natural sources of CO tend to be widely distributed, two major problems with CO from human activity include (1) **localization**, that is, it is produced in much smaller areas such as the down town core areas and on highways and major thoroughfares and (2) **high emission rates** at rush hours, for example. This is compounded by the fact that fungi in soil acts as 'soil sinks' converting CO to CO_2:

$$2\ CO_{(g)} + O_{2(g)} \Rightarrow 2\ CO_{2(g)}$$

The localization and high emission rates in urbanized areas occur in the places with less soil and therefore less microorganisms that can effectively reduce CO concentrations.

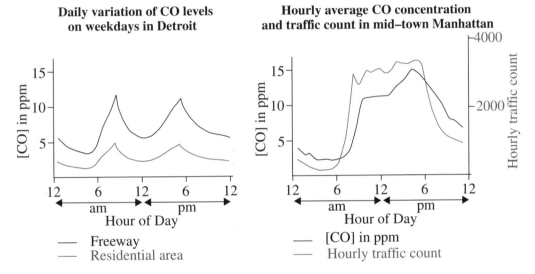

Carbon monoxide and oxygen transport: High levels of carbon monoxide have an impact on health. Hemoglobin (Hb) is the oxygen carrier in red blood cells:

$$Hb + O_2 \rightleftharpoons HbO_2;\ \text{oxyhemoglobin}$$

This is a reversible reaction which allows the hemoglobin to release its oxygen in the cell and then pick up more oxygen. However, CO not only combines with hemoglobin but also bonds much more strongly with it:

$$Hb + CO \Rightarrow HbCO;\ \text{carboxyhemoglobin}$$

Thus CO interferes with oxygen transport making it a metabolic poison. It deprives body cells of oxygen gas leading to asphyxiation. In the presence of carbon monoxide, there is oxygen depletion to the cells. The heart must therefore pump faster and this leads to shortness of breath and headaches. As more of the hemoglobin is tied up by carbon monoxide, it can lead to fatigue, drowsiness, coma, respiratory failure and finally death. Death from carbon monoxide may be prevented if a victim is immediately removed from an enclosed area such as a garage into fresh air. The reaction between hemoglobin and CO is somewhat reversible and as increasing amounts of oxygen react with the hemoglobin, the more the reverse reaction HbCO $\Rightarrow$ Hb + CO is favored (Le Chatelier's principle), thus freeing up the hemoglobin.

Solutions to carbon monoxide production: Most solutions are directed towards the automobile as it is the largest man made source of the primary pollutant. However, the problem is complicated by the presence of other pollutants, namely hydrocarbons, NO_x and particulates also produced by the automobile.

Several methods are being used including policies to encourage the use of mass transportation. Others being tested include the use of alternate fuels such as solar and battery operated cars, fuel cells, hydrogen as a fuel and changes to engine design. By far the most common method includes exhaust systems that make it possible for the oxidation of carbon monoxide to carbon dioxide (which although is a greenhouse gas is not a metabolic poison).

(a)   The **Thermal Exhaust Reactor** takes advantage of the heat of the exhaust gases and enables CO to react with more air to oxidize carbon monoxide to carbon dioxide and any unburnt hydrocarbon fuel to carbon dioxide and water.

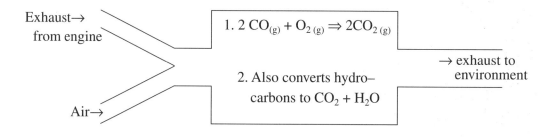

The control of pollutants from automobiles is complicated because of the presence of other primary pollutants. Thus, if a low air to fuel ratio is used (lean burning engines), there is less air present. This means more CO and hydrocarbons are produced, but at the same time it minimizes the production of nitrogen oxides (NO_x). Air can then be injected into the exhaust gases containing CO and unburnt HCs to oxidize these to carbon dioxide and water. This Thermal Exhaust Reactor method however requires expensive engine design.

(b)   **Catalytic converters** are quite remarkable in their ability not only to oxidize carbon monoxide to carbon dioxide, but also to convert NO (nitrogen monoxide) to nitrogen gas:

$$2\ CO_{(g)} + 2\ NO_{(g)} \xrightarrow{\text{catalyst \& moderate T}} 2\ CO_{2(g)} + N_{2(g)}$$

In the presence of small amounts of platinum–based catalysts, the pollutants CO and NO are converted to CO_2 and harmless nitrogen gas.

The average cost of an automobile is increased by about US \$600 – 800 and it also requires the use of high octane, non–leaded fuel since the catalyst in the converter is inactivated by the lead in leaded gasoline. Similarly, sulfur impurities in gasoline also poison the catalyst and have to be removed before gasoline can be used as fuel.

Nitrogen oxides (NO_x): There are several (8) known oxides of nitrogen of which nitrous oxide (N_2O; properly called dinitrogen monoxide) is found naturally and nitric oxide or nitrogen monoxide (NO) and nitrogen dioxide (NO_2) are found to be important components of polluted air.

	N_2O nitrous oxide (dinitrogen monoxide)	NO nitric oxide (nitrogen monoxide)	NO_2 nitrogen dioxide
Oxidation number of nitrogen:	+ 1	+ 2	+ 4
Lewis Structure	$:N=N=\ddot{O}:$	$:\dot{N}=\ddot{O}:$ odd # electrons	(Lewis structure of NO_2) odd # of electrons
Sources	All produced by natural sources from decomposition of nitrogen–containing compounds by bacterial action in soil and from lightning.	80% from natural sources (bacterial action); 20% from human sources from high temperature oxidation of N_2 in air in automobile and aircraft engines.	Nearly all made as **secondary pollutant** from NO.

There is no reaction between nitrogen gas (N_2, $:N \equiv N:$) and oxygen gas at room or moderately high temperatures due to the very high stability of the nitrogen–nitrogen triple bond and any reaction between nitrogen and oxygen gas is highly endothermic. Under conditions of high temperatures (around 1500°C found in automobile engines) a reaction between the two gases can however take place, producing nitrogen oxides, NO_x. Human activity produces about 10% of NO_x. Most human sources of NO_x are emitted as NO and a small amount as NO_2 gas during the high temperature combustion that takes place in an automobile engine, air planes and rail engines; stationary sources such as furnaces fuelled by natural gas, coal, fuel oil and wood; industrial processes such as nitric acid manufacture as well as agricultural burning and forest fires.

$$N_{2 (g)} + O_{2 (g)} \Rightarrow 2\, NO_{(g)}$$

$$N_{2 (g)} + 2\, O_{2 (g)} \Rightarrow 2\, NO_{2 (g)}$$

In the atmosphere the NO gas present (a primary pollutant) is rapidly converted to NO_2, a secondary pollutant:

$$2\ NO_{(g)} + O_{2(g)} \Rightarrow 2\ NO_{2(g)}$$

Thus, most of the man–made NO_x pollution enters the environment as NO gas. The natural decomposition of nitrogen–containing compounds by bacterial action is, however, responsible for most of the N_2O and NO found in the environment. The high energy in lightning also results in some formation of N_2O and NO. As with carbon monoxide, natural sources of NO_x are widely distributed, however, man made sources of NO_x are localized and can be present in high concentrations due to the use of automobiles.

Effect of NO_x on Health: Both nitric oxide, NO and nitrogen dioxide, NO_2, are toxic and pose health hazards to human beings and animals, with NO_2 being the more toxic. The effects of NO_2 are evident during smog episodes when polluted air from automobile exhausts is trapped near the earth's surface on windless days. The very young and the old are most susceptible to the effects of NO_2 which include irritation of the eyes and nose, breathing difficulties, respiratory distress and, if fluid accumulation takes place in the lungs (called pulmonary edema), it can lead to death.

Control and Prevention of NO_x pollution: Two methods, namely the catalytic converter and the thermal exhaust reactor, were discussed under CO reduction and are found to be effective in reducing NO_x pollution. The concentration of NO_x depends on the maximum temperature reached as well as the amount of oxygen gas available at that temperature. Another method is the exhaust gas recirculation (EGR) process in which some of the cooler exhaust gas is recirculated into the engine. This lowers the operating temperature and uses oxygen from the air for completing the oxidation of any carbon monoxide and unburnt hydrocarbons to form carbon dioxide and water. The use of lean burning engines lowers the amount of oxygen in the air to fuel mixture thus reducing the amount of NO_x produced (but producing more CO and HCs in the process).

SULFUR OXIDES, SO_x

Sulfur dioxide, SO_2, is produced by far in the largest amount and **sulfur trioxide, SO_3,** is produced in very small amounts. Once SO_2 is in the atmosphere, it is chemically converted to SO_3 in the presence of O_2. The presence of heavy metal pollutants and finely divided particulates such as ash can speed up the reaction, as can the presence of O_3 and sunlight:

$$2\ SO_{2(g)} + O_{2(g)} \Rightarrow 2\ SO_{3(g)}$$

Principal sources:
(a) Man made (anthropogenic):
It is estimated that approximately 150 million tons per year of sulfur dioxide are released annually by human activities such as:

(1)   **From sulfur containing fossil fuels such as coal:** Low grade coal can contain up to 7% sulfur impurity (although the common percentage of sulfur in coal is

between 1 and 5%). Coal contains sulfur as elemental sulfur, as iron pyrite FeS_2 and as organic sulfur, since it was present as the proteins of organisms. The combustion process converts any sulfur to sulfur dioxide:

$$S_{(s)} + O_{2\,(g)} \Rightarrow SO_{2\,(g)}$$

$$4\,FeS_{2\,(g)} + 11\,O_{2\,(g)} \Rightarrow 2\,Fe_2O_{3\,(s)} + 8\,SO_{2\,(g)}$$

Coal combustion is the major contributor to sulfur oxide pollution. Petroleum and natural gas contribute little to this as most of the sulfur is removed by bubbling hydrogen gas in the presence of a catalyst, during petroleum refining and natural gas processing. Some heavy fuels (used by ships and power stations) can have a high sulfur content, contributing to SO_2 pollution.

(2) **From smelting plants** which oxidise sulfide ores to the metal oxides:

$$Cu_2S_{(s)} + 2\,O_{2(g)} \Rightarrow 2\,CuO_{(s)} + SO_{2(g)}$$

(3) **Sulfuric acid plants** also release some sulfur dioxide. H_2SO_4 is produced by the oxidation of SO_2 gas by oxygen to form SO_3 gas which reacts with water to produce the acid.

(b) **Natural sources**: No major natural primary sources of sulfur dioxide are known although probably very small amounts are produced through volcanic and bacterial activity. However, approximately 200 million tons of sulfur dioxide are estimated to be produced as a secondary pollutant annually in the atmosphere as a result of the atmospheric oxidation of hydrogen sulfide gas, H_2S. Hydrogen sulfide gas is produced most importantly by the decay of organic matter (in swamps, oceans, etc.) and also some by volcanic activity:

$$2\,H_2S_{(g)} + 3\,O_{2(g)} \Rightarrow 2\,SO_{2(g)} + 2\,H_2O_{(l)}$$

Effects of sulfur dioxide on health: Sulfur oxides are acidic oxides. Breathing air containing fine droplets of acid irritates the whole respiratory tract from mucous membranes in the nose and throat to tissues in the lungs and has its greatest effects on the elderly, the young and those suffering from asthma. It can also cause severe eye irritation.

Methods of controlling SO_x pollution:
Several methods exist to control SO_x pollution. These include:

(1) **Converting high sulfur coal to SNG,** synthetic natural gas and remove most of the sulfur in the process of coal gasification. In this method, any sulfur is converted to hydrogen sulfide gas which is acidic and easily removed:

$$S_{(s)} + H_{2(g)} \Rightarrow H_2S_{(g)}$$

One major disadvantage is that it requires about 30% of the energy for the

OPTION

conversion of coal to SNG.

(2) **Using low–sulfur, cleaner burning coal** such as anthracite (hard coal) that has a high heat content.

(3) **Controlling before burning fossil fuel (pre–combustion method):**

(a) In the case of petroleum and natural gas, sulfur is removed by bubbling hydrogen gas, in the presence of a catalyst, during petroleum refining and natural gas processing. Any sulfur present is reduced to hydrogen sulfide gas which is an acidic gas and easily removed, thus reducing acid rain.

(b) To desulfurize (remove sulfur) from high–sulfur coal, the method of **coal washing** is used. Coal is finely ground and washed with water. Iron pyrite, FeS_2, has high density, settles rapidly and is removed. However, even in finely ground coal, a lot of sulfur is trapped below the surfaces of the particles and is therefore not removed. Organic sulfur, chemically bonded to carbon atoms in coal cannot be removed by this physical process.

(4) **Post combustion methods**, that is removal of sulfur from exhaust gases **after burning** the coal but before releasing to the atmosphere:

(a) **Limestone fluidized beds or injection systems:**

This involves adding powdered limestone, $CaCO_3$, with the coal in the combustion process. The heat from the combustion decomposes limestone to calcium oxide:

$$CaCO_{3(s)} + heat \Rightarrow CaO_{(s)} + CO_{2(g)}$$

The calcium oxide reacts with the SO_2 produced to form $CaSO_3$, calcium sulfate(IV), and in the presence of oxygen forms $CaSO_4$, calcium sulfate(VI):

$$CaO_{(s)} + SO_{2(g)} \Rightarrow CaSO_{3(s)};$$

$$2\,CaO_{(s)} + 2\,SO_{2(g)} + O_{2(g)} \Rightarrow 2\,CaSO_{4(s)}$$

The calcium sulfate, any unreacted calcium oxide and sulfur dioxide together with fly ash (particulates) are then absorbed into water in a **wet–scrubber**:

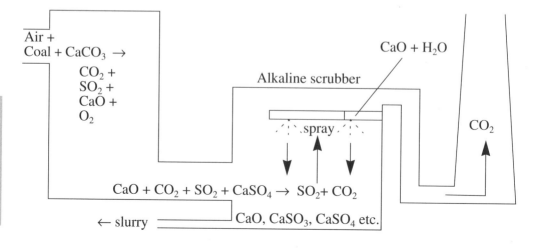

(b) **A wet–scrubber** is a cleaning device that uses a liquid, usually water based, to remove contaminants. This uses a counterflow method in which the alkaline liquid is sprayed downward while the gas stream moves upwards. The effectiveness depends on the contact between the alkaline liquid and the acidic sulfur dioxide:

$$CaO_{(aq)} + SO_{2\ (g)} \Rightarrow CaSO_{3\ (s)}$$

The waste slurry is transferred to settling ponds. Problems include the tendency of $CaSO_3$ to deposit on scrubber surfaces and the need for extremely large amounts of limestone, $CaCO_3$ which is converted to CaO by heating. Note that by this method, the sulfur dioxide is being replaced by carbon dioxide, a greenhouse gas.

Other wet–scrubbers use magnesium hydroxide as the alkaline material:

$$Mg(OH)_{2\ (aq)} + SO_{2\ (g)} \Rightarrow MgSO_{3\ (s)} + H_2O_{(l)}$$

The magnesium sulfate (IV) formed in the slurry can be heated to convert it to MgO:

$$MgSO_{3\ (s)} + heat \Rightarrow MgO_{(s)} + SO_{2\ (g)}$$

The SO_2 is used for the manufacture of sulfuric acid and the magnesium oxide is treated with water to form magnesium hydroxide and recycled:

$$MgO + H_2O \Rightarrow Mg(OH)_2$$

However, the heating requires large amounts of energy and is therefore very expensive.

PARTICULATES
These are solid particles suspended or carried in the air and are generally large enough to be seen. Natural sources of particulates include sandstorms, volcanoes and forest fires started by lightning. Typical particulates from man–made sources include:

(a) smoke and soot produced by combustion of coal, petroleum, wood etc.

(b) dust from mechanical break–up of solid matter

(c) asbestos from industrial plants. Asbestos is a fibrous material composed of silicate crystals. Having used asbestos in the past in the insulation of buildings, demolition of such buildings releases asbestos particles. Many countries now ban the use of asbestos as it causes scarring of lung tissue.

(d) metallic particles such as beryllium, mercury and arsenic from industrial plants and lead in places where leaded gasoline is still in use. Beryllium oxide is used in spark plugs and as lining in high temperature furnaces (because of its very high melting point and high electrical resistivity). Mercury is present in fly ash and is also used in the manufacture of fungicides, pulp and paper. When coal is burnt, most of the ash is carried away in the exhaust gases as finely divided powder called fly ash which consists of unburnt carbon and oxides of many metals including iron, magnesium, calcium etc., as well as sulfates. A typical coal plant produces 1000 tons of fly ash a day.

OPTION

HEALTH EFFECTS

Particulates irritate the mucous membranes and lungs.

(1)   Asbestos with very small diameter particles can be trapped in the lungs where it can remain indefinitely; in some people, the effects appear as much as 30 years after exposure has taken place. It leads to scarring of lung tissue and thickening of the lining of lungs eventually causing **asbestosis**, a disease leading to shortness of breath. Also, cancer of the lower parts of the lungs is more common among asbestos workers who smoke.

(2)   Beryllium oxide is toxic and causes **berylliosis** leading to inflammation of the respiratory system followed by pneumonia–like symptoms. It also scars lung tissues, causing shortness of breath and coughing.

(3)   Lead poisoning: Lead is found to inhibit some enzyme actions. Acute lead poisoning produces abdominal pain, nausea, numbness of hands and feet, muscle cramps and brain damage.

(4)   Mercury Poisoning: Mercury is also a metabolic poison and its toxicity is primarily due to its ability to react with and inhibit an enzyme system. Mercury poisoning (Minamata disease) produces nerve damage and can lead to death.

Note that particulates in the atmosphere play a role in catalysing the formation of secondary pollutants such as ozone:

$$O + O_2 + M \Rightarrow O_3 + M \text{ (where M is a particulate)}$$

which can cause major health hazards.

CONTROL OF PARTICULATES

Several methods exist for the removal of particulates. **Electrostatic precipitation** is the most important and effective method for the removal of very tiny particles.

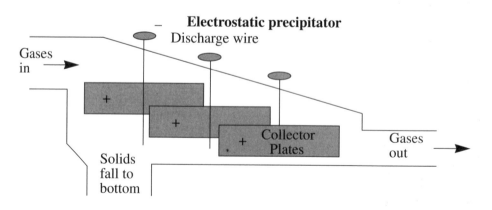

In an electrostatic precipitator, a very high voltage is applied between the discharge wires and the collector plates which ionizes the gas molecules present: $G \rightarrow G^+ + e^-$. The electrons produced collect on the particulates and the negatively charged particles are attracted to the positively charged collector plates. The collector plates have to be periodically shaken to remove the collected solid particles. This method can remove more than 98% of all particulate matter.

Hydrocarbons (HCs) are primary pollutants as these are introduced directly into the environment. These include gases or volatile organic liquids that are easily converted into gases and escape into the air. Recall that C_1 to C_4 hydrocarbons are gases and C_5 to C_{12} hydrocarbons are liquids due to the weak van der Waals' forces between these generally non–polar molecules which increase as their size increases.

Similarly to CO and NO_x, most hydrocarbons enter the environment from natural sources involving biological processes including a little from geothermal activity. Methane, the simplest alkane, and the largest natural source of hydrocarbons, is produced by the anaerobic bacterial decomposition of organic matter in bodies of water including swamps and oceans. Methane is produced as a digestive gas in many animals. Trees and plants produce most of the rest of the natural hydrocarbons, called terpenes.

Petroleum, a complex mixture of very useful organic compounds, is the key source of hydrocarbon pollution produced by human activities. These include extracting, refining, transporting and the use of petroleum products. These produce air pollution at each stage. The fraction from petroleum that is used as fuel contains volatile hydrocarbons with C_5 to C_{24} carbons. These evaporate easily in the internal combustion engine and produce vapor during storage and the filling of fuel tanks (storage tanks both at gasoline stations and in automobiles). Incomplete combustion of fuel, especially in gasoline and diesel engines, also produces unburnt hydrocarbons that are released into the atmosphere through exhausts. Photochemical smog, which is secondary pollution from automobile exhausts, contains large amounts of methyl benzene, $C_6H_5CH_3$, as well as reactive benzene derivatives. Solvents used in paints and other similar products are also human sources of volatile hydrocarbons.

Health Effects of Hydrocarbons: Whereas aliphatic hydrocarbons produce no effects until the concentrations are high, vapors of aromatic compounds cause irritation of the mucous membrane and can be fatal in large amounts. Methylbenzene, for example, causes fatigue, weakness and confusion after exposure for several hours.

Incomplete combustion of coal and wood produces fused aromatic ring compounds containing several benzene rings joined together such as benzo(α)pyrene, called polynuclear aromatic hydrocarbons; these are found to be carcinogenic. Benzo(α) pyrene is found in coal dust and produces black lungs in miners and chimney sweepers who have a high rate of skin and lung cancers.

The principal source of man–made hydrocarbon pollution are the unburnt hydrocarbons from automobile exhausts. These can be effectively removed by using a catalytic converter where the hydrocarbons are oxidized to carbon dioxide and water, as discussed earlier (see page 512). The graph shows the variation in concentration of exhaust emission gases with the composition of

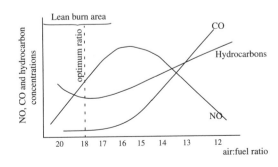

the air–fuel mixture. 'Lean burn' engines use an air:fuel ratio of approximately 18:1 by volume to minimise the production of pollutants.

AUTOMOBILE POLLUTION: SUMMARY

The sheer number of automobiles around the world makes this mode of transportation the major source of primary air pollution. These include unburnt hydrocarbon fuels that escape from the fuel tank, the engine and exhaust as well as carbon dioxide, carbon monoxide, particulates (soot) and nitrogen oxides produced after combustion as well as lead (released as lead(II) bromide) if leaded gasoline is used.

Methods of control of pollution from the automobile include:

(a)　use of non–leaded gasoline to eliminate lead pollution.

(b)　valves on gas tanks so gasoline can be pumped into the tank, but gasoline vapor cannot escape.

(c)　different air to fuel ratio produces different amounts of pollutants. Lower air to fuel ratios produce less NO_x but more CO and HCs due to incomplete combustion. Higher air to fuel ratios produce more complete burning, thus less CO and HCs but more NO_x as the more complete combustion produces higher temperatures and the presence of more oxygen favors NO_x production.

(d)　exhaust recycling (in exhaust gas recirculation) of cooler gases can reduce combustion temperature and thus less production of nitrogen oxide gases.

(e)　thermal exhaust reactor, where the exhaust gases are mixed with air to oxidize carbon monoxide to carbon dioxide and any unburnt hydrocarbons to CO_2 and H_2O.

(f)　catalytic converters seem by far the most effective way of reducing pollution from the automobile. They use platinum–based catalysts through which the exhaust gases pass and they convert unburnt HCs, CO and NO to CO_2, H_2O and N_2.

$$2\ CO_{(g)} + 2\ NO_{(g)} \xrightarrow[\text{\& moderate temp.}]{\text{catalyst}} 2\ CO_{2\ (g)} + N_{2\ (g)}$$

Because lead poisons the catalyst, the added advantage is the use of nonleaded gasoline thus eliminating lead pollution from automobiles.

SUMMARY:

	Human source	Natural Source	Effect on Health	Methods of Control
Carbon monoxide (CO)	Incomplete combustion of C–containing fossil fuels used for transportation and industry; forest fires. Localized, high emissions produced.	From atmospheric oxidation of CH_4 (from anaerobic decomposition of organic matter).	Metabolic poison. Interferes with O_2 transport; deprives body cells of O_2 leading to asphyxiation. Heart has to pump faster.	1. Thermal exhaust reactor. 2. Catalytic converter.
Nitrogen oxides (NO_x)	High temperature combustion in automobiles produces mostly NO, nitric oxide. This is oxidised to NO_2 in the atmosphere.	Decomposition of N–containing compounds by bacterial action produces N_2O, nitrous oxide, and NO. (Nearly all NO_2 is man made).	NO_2 is toxic and causes irritation of the eyes and nose, breathing problems, respiratory distress and pulmonary edema. HNO_3 (from NO_2) irritates the respiratory tract	1. Catalytic converter. 2. Lean burning engines. 3. Recirculation of exhaust gases.
Sulfur Oxides (SO_x)	Sulfur containing coal, smelting plants, sulfuric acid plants.	No major direct sources of SO_x in nature, but oxidation of H_2S gas, produced from decay of organic matter and volcanic activity.	Acid rain formed from SO_x pollution irritates respiratory tract and adversely affects the elderly, the young and asthma sufferers.	1. Removal of sulfur from fossil fuels before burning 2. Alkaline scrubbing. 3. Adding $CaCO_3$ to coal.
Particulates	Combustion of fossil fuels by industry and transportation, break–up of solid matter, industrial plants.	Blowing dust, volcanic activity, forest fires, biological sources such as pollen.	Irritation of the mucous membranes and lungs. Asbestosis and berylliosis cause scarring of lung tissue. Major effects due to the formation of secondary pollutants	1. Gravity settling chambers. 2. Cyclone separators. 3. Electrostatic precipitators.
Hydrocarbons	Petroleum extracting, refining, transporting and use; solvents. incomplete combustion of coal, wood.	CH_4 from biological processes due to anaerobic bacterial decomposition of organic matter; trees and plants produce terpenes.	Aromatic compounds cause irritation of mucous membrane. Methyl benzene causes fatigue, weakness and confusion.	1. Catalytic converters.

OPTION

14.2 OZONE DEPLETION

D.2.1. Describe the formation and depletion of ozone by natural processes.

D.2.2 List the pollutants, and their sources, that cause the lowering of ozone concentration.

Consider chlorofluorocarbons (CFCs) and nitrogen oxides.

D.2.3 State the environmental effects of ozone depletion.

Include the increased incidence of skin cancer and eye cataracts, and the suppression of plant growth.

D.2.4 Discuss alternatives to CFCs in terms of their properties.

Include hydrocarbons, fluorocarbons and hydrofluorocarbons (HFCs). Include toxicity, flammability, the relative weakness of the C–Cl bond and the ability to absorb infrared radiation.

© IBO 2001

Ozone, O_3, is a naturally occurring component of the stratosphere. It is a very pale bluish gas with an acrid (pungent–smelling) odor, very active chemical properties (a powerful oxidizing agent) and has harmful effects on living matter. It plays a different role in the upper and lower atmospheres. Inhaling a small amount of ozone can be harmful, yet it is essential to life and health by its presence in the ozone layer. The ozone layer is about 15 to 45 km above the earth's surface and holds much of the air's ozone.

Very short wavelength ultra violet (uv) light from the sun splits O_2 molecules into oxygen atoms which are extremely reactive free radicals (represented by •):

$$O_{2\,(g)} + \text{uv light} \Rightarrow 2 \bullet O$$

These oxygen atoms react with other oxygen molecules, O_2 to form O_3:

$$O_{2\,(g)} + \bullet O_{(g)} \Rightarrow O_{3\,(g)}$$

The photo–dissociation of molecular oxygen by uv light represents the principle mechanism of ozone's formation in the upper atmosphere. The reverse reaction takes place when O_3 absorbs rather longer wavelength uv light.

$$O_{3(g)} \Rightarrow O_{2(g)} + \bullet O_{(g)}$$

$$O_{3(g)} + \bullet O_{(g)} \Rightarrow 2\, O_{2(g)}$$

So, O_3 is constantly being formed and broken down. The ozone layer acts as a shield by absorbing 99% of the sun's harmful uv light of longer wavelength than that absorbed by O_2 and N_2.

Satellite data over a sixteen year period from 1979 to 1995 shows a clear decline in ozone concentration by about 6% in the latitudes 60° south to 60° north. Similarly satellite pictures show the greatest destruction of the ozone layer at the South Pole, covering an area almost equal in size to the North American continent! According to Environment Canada, the Antarctic showed a 70% decrease in the thickness of the ozone layer during the spring of 1996, while in the Arctic, the ozone values were 45% below normal. Satellite pictures over the North Pole also clearly indicate ozone holes where depletion of ozone has taken place.

Ozone in the ozone layer is being reduced by:

(1) **CFCs, chlorofluorocarbons (freons)** are used in spray cans as a propellant and in old refrigerators and air conditioners, in fire extinguishers and as solvents. When released, the CFCs, because they are chemically very inert, do not decompose and float slowly through the atmosphere into the stratosphere. When they reach the unfiltered ultraviolet rays of the sun, they are turned into extremely reactive chlorine atoms with an unpaired electron which very readily reacts with the ozone.

$$CCl_2F_2 + uv \text{ light} \Rightarrow \bullet CClF_2 + \bullet Cl$$

Note that the average bond enthalpy of C–F bond is 484 kJ mol^{-1} and only 338 kJ mol^{-1} for the C–Cl bond; the C–Cl bond is weaker and breaks. The Cl atom, also a free radical, is very reactive and readily reacts with O_3 to produce O_2:

$$\bullet Cl + O_3 \Rightarrow ClO\bullet + O_2$$

(2) Nitric oxide, formed from the high temperature reaction of N_2 and O_2 in supersonic aircraft engines, reacts with ozone reducing its concentration:

$$NO + O_3 \Rightarrow NO_2 + O_2$$

A decrease in O_3 concentration means more uv light reaches the earth, thus increasing cases of skin cancer and eye cataracts, more sunburn and damage to animals and plants including suppression of plant growth, genetic mutations and changes in the world's climate. Note that as little as 0.2 ppm O_3 near the earth's surface promotes photochemical reactions responsible for **smog.** Near the earth's surface, O_3 attacks many products such as tyres, rubber products and tobacco crops and can cause extensive crop damage.

Alternatives to CFCs:

1. **Use of propane, C_3H_8 and 2–methylpropane hydrocarbons** as refrigerant coolants. Although these do not lead to ozone depletion, they are flammable as well as being greenhouse gases (able to absorb infrared radiation) and would lead to global warming.

2. **Fluorocarbons**: These are neither toxic nor flammable and the very strong C–F bond makes them stable to uv radiation so they cannot catalyze ozone depletion. However, these are greenhouse gases and would eventually lead to an increase in the global temperature.

3 **Hydrochlorofluorocarbons, HClFCs** contain hydrogen, chlorine, fluorine and carbon atoms in their molecules. The presence of a hydrogen atom makes the compound decompose less easily since the C–H bond is stronger (412 kJ mol^{-1}) than the C–Cl bond. Nonetheless, these do reduce the ozone layer because of the presence of a C–Cl bond in the molecule and can only be considered a temporary solution.

4. **HFCs (hydrofluorocarbons)**, without any chlorine atoms, are considered good alternative to CFCs as no chlorine atoms, which are primarily responsible for ozone depletion, are involved . One such example is CF_3CH_2F, 1,1,1,2–tetrafluoroethane.

OPTION

14.3 GREENHOUSE EFFECT AND GLOBAL WARMING

D.3.1   Describe the greenhouse effect.   © IBO 2001

The temperature of the earth depends on the amount of sunlight received, the amount absorbed by the earth and then reflected back into space and the extent to which the atmosphere retains the heat. There is a natural 'greenhouse effect' which keeps the Earth's average temperature warm enough (about 16°C or 60°F) to be habitable. This effect is due to the presence of water vapor and carbon dioxide as 'greenhouse gases' found naturally in the atmosphere. Sunlight penetrates the atmosphere to warm the earth's surface. The energy radiated from the Earth as infrared radiation is absorbed by the water vapor and carbon dioxide and reradiated back to earth. Thus, greenhouse gases allow incoming solar radiation to reach the Earth, but absorb some of the heat radiated from the Earth, thus maintaining the global temperature. This is called the greenhouse effect without which the earth would be much colder than it is.

Global warming is the gradual increase in planet–wide temperatures. There is evidence to conclude that global warming is taking place. Surface land and ocean temperature records exist for more than a century and indicate that, over that time period, average global temperatures have risen by about half a degree centigrade and the rate of temperature change is significantly faster than any observed changes in the last 10,000 years.

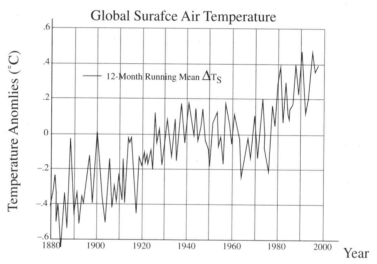

source; http//www.giss.nasa.gov/data/gistemp/12mo.rm.GLB.gif

The greenhouse effect is the trapping of heat in the atmosphere. Greenhouse gases in the atmosphere act similarly to glass or plastic on a greenhouse, that is, they act as a one way filter!

The incoming solar radiation through the earth's atmosphere is of short wavelength. Because the earth absorbs some of the energy, the outgoing radiation is of lesser energy, that is, of longer wavelength. This longer wavelength radiation is absorbed by the water vapor, carbon dioxide, ozone and other greenhouse gases and reradiated toward the earth thus causing a rise in atmospheric temperature.

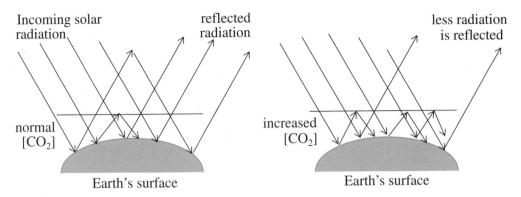

Earth's surface   Earth's surface

Increased carbon dioxide traps more of the heat radiation
escaping from the earth

In other words, the greenhouse effect allows visible and uv light of short wavelength to pass through the atmosphere to heat the air and the earth but it traps the longer wavelength infrared heat rays emitted from the warm soil and air, thus raising the temperature of the atmosphere.

D.3.2   List the main greenhouse gases and their sources, and discuss their relative effects.

The greenhouse gases to be considered are CH_4, H_2O, CO_2 and N_2O, which have natural and man-made origins. Their effects depend on their abundance and their ability to absorb heat radiation.   © IBO 2001

The major greenhouse gases are CH_4, H_2O and CO_2. Note that there are both natural and man–made sources of these gases.

The main greenhouse gases introduced into the environment by both natural and human sources are carbon dioxide, methane, water vapor and nitrous oxide (dinitrogen oxide), N_2O.

	Carbon dioxide $CO_{2\,(g)}$	Methane $CH_{4\,(g)}$	Water vapor $H_2O_{(g)}$	Dinitrogen monoxide, $N_2O_{(g)}$ (nitrous oxide)
Natural Sources	Respiration, decay of plants and animals, oxidation of soil humus, forest fires (caused by lightning).	Wetlands and termites (produce one third of total production). Bacteria in the digestive systems of cattle break down cellulose to CH_4.	Evaporation due to sunlight.	Bacterial action is the major natural source.
Human Sources	Burning of fossil fuels and wood by industry, transportation, forest fires, burning trash.	Two thirds of total production comes from cattle farming, rice fields, land fills, coal mining, petroleum and natural gas production.	Product of hydrocarbon combustion.	Use of nitrogen based fertilizers.

An estimated 25×10^8 tons of carbon dioxide are released annually into the environment by human activity. The table below shows an increase in greenhouse gases from the pre–industrial to current time period.

	Carbon dioxide	Methane	Dinitrogen oxide
Pre–industrial concentrations:	280 ppm	700 ppb	275 ppb
1994 concentrations:	350 ppm	1720 ppb	312 ppb
10 year rate of concentration change beginning 1984:	1.5 ppm per year	10 ppb per year	0.8 ppb per year
Atmospheric life (years):	200–500	7–10	120–150

The increase in concentrations of greenhouse gases from human activity provide circumstantial evidence for global warming. Atmospheric concentrations of greenhouse gases have increased significantly since the industrial revolution: CO_2 is up 25%, CH_4 is up over 145% and N_2O around 15%. The atmospheric concentration of methane is low, but it is about 30 times more effective than carbon dioxide in its ability to trap infrared radiation. However, methane has a relatively short average atmospheric lifetime compared to carbon dioxide. Compared to carbon dioxide, nitrous oxide is about 160 times more effective, whereas water is only a tenth as effective as carbon dioxide in its ability to trap infrared radiation. The concentrations of these gases in the atmosphere also vary, with water vapour being the most, and nitrous oxide the least abundant.

D.3.3   Discuss the influence of increasing amounts of greenhouse gases on global warming.

Effects include climate change, thermal expansion of the oceans and melting of the polar ice caps.   © IBO 2001

Effects of Global Warming: Over the last century there has been
- an increase in temperature by about half a degree centigrade,

- a one percent increase in precipitation and

- about 15–20 cm worldwide rise in sea levels resulting from the partial melting of glaciers and polar ice-caps and the physical expansion of ocean water caused by warmer temperatures.

The change in the climate in most regions of the world will grow as the concentration of greenhouse gases continues to increase. The climate change will impact on health, agriculture, forests, water resources, coastal areas, species diversity, species numbers and natural areas.

OPTION

Effects of Global Warming:

Health	Agriculture	Forests	Water Resources	Coastal Areas	Species and Natural Areas
Life cycles of pathogens and insects such as mosquitoes are affected by climate; greater chance of malaria, etc.	Effect on crop yields and geographic distribution of crops; some crops will thrive, others will not.	Insects and diseases may increase; increase in summer droughts would produce more forest fires. Higher temperatures and more rain should help forests grow more rapidly.	Decreased water quality due to flooding; floods more likely due to more intense rainfall; droughts more severe due to increased evaporation and drier soil.	Raise the level of seas eroding beaches, inundating low lands, increasing coastal flooding.	Loss of cold water fish habitat, shift in ecological areas, loss of habitats and species, desertification.

D.3.4   Outline the influence of particulates on the Earth's surface temperature.

Particulates can lower the temperature by reflecting the sunlight.   © IBO 2001

Between 1880 and 1940, the average temperature increased 0.4°C to 0.6°C. But between 1945 and 1957, it fell 0.2 to 0.3°C during the period of greatest expansion of fossil fuel use. Why? Cooling during the 1950s could possibly have been due to particulates emitted by gigantic volcanic eruptions in Alaska (1953) and USSR (1956) amongst others. That is, an increase in temperature due to increase in CO_2 and other greenhouse gas concentrations (the greenhouse effect) was counteracted by reflection of sunlight by particulates (however, other factors may have been important such as solar radiation not being constant as it follows an eleven year cycle). Particulates are produced by nearly all combustion and industrial processes, heavy industry and incinerators. Particulates have the effect of cooling the earth as small particles are effective scatterers of radiation; thus less radiation reaches the earth leading to decrease in temperature. Also, particulates help as nuclei in condensation of water vapor in the atmosphere. This leads to increased cloudiness and more precipitation. The increased cloudiness also causes a decrease in the average temperature near the surface of the earth.

OPTION

14.4 ACID RAIN

D.4.1 State what is meant by acid rain and outline its origins.

Rain is naturally acidic because of dissolved CO_2; acid rain has a pH of less than 5.6.

Acid rain is caused by oxides of sulfur and nitrogen. Students should know the equations for the burning of sulfur and nitrogen and for the formation of H_2SO_3 and H_2SO_4.

D.4.2 Discuss the environmental effects of acid rain and possible methods to counteract them.

© IBO 2001

Pure rain water is naturally acidic, pH $\approx$ 5.6 ([H^+] $\approx$ 2.5 × 10^{-6} mol dm^{-3}) due to dissolved carbon dioxide in water vapor reacting to form carbonic acid, a very weak acid:

$$CO_{2(g)} + H_2O_{(l)} \rightleftharpoons H_2CO_{3(aq)} \rightleftharpoons H^+_{(aq)} + HCO_3^-_{(aq)}$$

The environmental pollution called acid rain is any rain with pH less than 5.6. Recall that pH is a logarithmic scale with one pH unit corresponding to a difference in hydrogen ion concentration of a factor of 10. Thus acid rain of pH 4.2 has hydrogen ion concentration 25 times greater than pure rain water. Although extreme acid rain (pH of 1.7 recorded in Los Angles in December 1982) is rare, the average rainfall in industrialized areas of the world has [H^+] about 4 to 40 times greater than pure rain water (that is, pH 4 to 5 is common compared to pH of 5.6). A pH of 4.0 in lakes is sufficient to kill fish life and such dead lakes do exist in North America, China and Russia among other places. Note that the pH of any water sample can be measured using pH paper showing colors of various pH values, or using a universal indicator, or a calibrated pH meter.

Research shows that acid rain is associated with parts of a country where heavy industries are situated and also down–wind from such sites. Analysis of acid rain indicates that especially sulfur oxides, SO_x, and nitrogen oxides, NO_x, are mostly responsible for the rain acidity (recall that many non–metallic oxides are acidic). Snow, fog, sleet, hail and drizzle all become contaminated with acids when SO_x and NO_x are present as pollutants.

Sources of SO_x and NO_x pollutants: These were discussed in Section 14.1.

THE FORMATION OF ACID RAIN

In the presence of moisture, sulfur oxides produce acids:

$$SO_{2(g)} + H_2O_{(l)} \Rightarrow H_2SO_{3(aq)} \text{ sulfurous acid, a weak acid}$$

$$2 SO_{2(g)} + O_{2(g)} + 2 H_2O_{(l)} \Rightarrow 2 H_2SO_{4(aq)} \text{ sulfuric acid, a strong acid}$$

$$SO_{3(g)} + H_2O_{(l)} \Rightarrow H_2SO_{4(aq)} \text{ sulfuric acid, a strong acid}$$

Nitrogen dioxide is a poisonous, reddish–brown, highly reactive gas. This gas can be converted to nitric acid, HNO_3, a strong acid in a series of complicated reactions and can be summarized as:

$$4NO_{2(g)} + 2H_2O_{(l)} + O_{2(g)} \Rightarrow 4HNO_{3(aq)}$$

Nitrogen dioxide in the presence of other pollutants present in the air can also be converted to nitric acid. Thus the presence of the hydroxyl free radical, •OH, which is formed during photochemical smog can react with nitrogen dioxide, itself a free radical (with a lone electron):

$$•NO_{2(g)} + •OH_{(g)} \xrightarrow{H_2O} HNO_{3(aq)}$$

THE ENVIRONMENTAL EFFECTS OF ACID RAIN

Acid rain affects humans and aquatic life. It produces dissolution of limestone, corrosion of metals, deterioration of electrical equipment, bleaching and weakening of fabric and leather, discoloration and embrittlement of paper, acute and chronic effects on plants, significant decrease in crop yield etc.

Effects of acid rain on humans: Breathing air containing fine droplets of acid irritates the whole respiratory tract from mucous membranes in the nose and throat to the lung tissues. Also, it can cause severe eye irritation. Sulfate aerosols are also powerful irritants. The small sulfate particles penetrate the lungs where they become embedded and have adverse effects on asthmatics, the elderly and the young.

Effect on aquatic life: For example, salmon cannot survive if pH is as low as 5.5 and acidification of lakes and rivers takes place affecting aquatic life. One major effect on fish is the increased concentration of Al^{3+} resulting from the leaching of soil by acid rain. Al^{3+} affects the function of the gills.

Effect on materials: Corrosion of basic materials such as marble or limestone ($CaCO_3$) and dolomite ($CaCO_3 \cdot MgCO_3$). The insoluble carbonates are converted to more soluble sulfates:

$$CaCO_{3(s)} + H_2SO_{4(aq)} \Rightarrow CaSO_{4(aq)} + H_2O_{(l)} + CO_{2(g)}$$

The sulfates can dissolve in water leading to considerable damage to structural and artists' stone. This is called 'stone leprosy' and has caused damage to cultural monuments in places like Egypt, Greece, Mexico and Turkey. The Egyptian sphinx (pictured with restoration scaffolding) has suffered from both acid rain and being used for artillery target practice!

Corrosion of iron and steel is promoted by acid rain, a problem which is increased by high humidity, high temperatures and the presence of particulates. The overall reaction is:

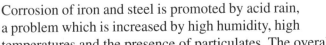

$$4Fe_{(s)} + x\,H_2O_{(l)} + 3O_{2(g)} \Rightarrow 2Fe_2O_3 \cdot x\,H_2O_{(s)}$$

OPTION

Similarly deterioration of electrical equipment takes place as a result of corrosion. Acid rain pollution causes bleaching and weakening of fabrics and leather and discoloration and embrittlement of paper. Acid rain can also leach heavy toxic metals such as lead, cadmium and mercury into the water system.

Effect on soil and vegetation: Plants can be damaged by acid concentrations and length of exposure. **Acute injury** due to short term exposure to high acid concentrations leads to attacks on cells producing dead areas of leaves which dry out and usually become bleached. **Chronic injury** due to long term exposure to even low acid concentrations disrupts chlorophyll synthesis, characterized by yellowing of leaves (as a result of acid entering the stomata of the leaves). Effects include bleached spots, yellowing of leaves, suppression of plant growth and reduction in yield. Acid rain also leaches or removes important nutrients such as Mg^{2+} from soil.

Effect on visibility: The mist of sulfuric acid and sulfate aerosols in the atmosphere can cause great loss of visibility and can curtail air flights.

CONTROLLING ACID RAIN

Most efforts at reducing acid rain are directed at the important sources of the pollutants, namely the burning of coal and the fuelling of automobile engines.

Reduction in SO_2 emissions include (refer to Section 14.1):

(1)   Use of low–sulfur, cleaner–burning coal such as anthracite (hard) coal which has high heat content. Using sub–bituminous coal and lignite of low–sulfur content does not produce as much heat because of its lower carbon (heat) content which means more of it has to be burnt.

(2)   Converting dirty high–sulfur coal to clean burning SNG, synthetic natural gas. The conversion process allows for the removal of SO_2 and thus reduces acid rain. However, a major disadvantage is that it requires about 30% of the energy for the conversion of coal to SNG.

(3)   Cleaning coal before combustion. Coal is finely ground and washed with water. Iron pyrite, FeS_2, has higher density than coal, settles more rapidly and is removed. However, only about half the sulfur is removed in this expensive way as organic sulfur is chemically bonded to carbon atoms in coal and it cannot be removed by this physical process.

(4)   Post–combustion methods.

The reduction in emissions of NO_x from automobiles can be achieved by using lower air to fuel ratio which produces less NO_x but more CO and HCs due to incomplete combustion and the use of catalytic converters which are quite remarkable in their ability to convert NO to nitrogen gas but add to the cost of a car:

$$CO_{(g)} + 2\ NO_{(g)} \Rightarrow 2\ CO_{2(g)} + N_{2(g)}$$

14.5 WATER SUITABLE FOR DRINKING

D.5.1 Discuss the demand for fresh water and reasons for the inadequacy of its supply.

Only a small fraction of the Earth's water supply is fresh water. Of this fresh water, over 80% is in the form of ice caps and glaciers. Water is mainly used for agriculture and industry. © IBO 2001

Approximately three quarters of the earth's surface is covered by water with the world's oceans containing most of it, as shown in the table below:

Distribution of Water on Earth

	oceans	glaciers, ice caps	ground water	lakes, rivers	atmosphere
%	97.3	2.1	0.6	0.015	0.001

Salty ocean water is not drinkable, leaving a minute 2.7% of the total as fresh water for drinking. Out of this, about 80% is in the form of ice in glaciers and ice caps and not readily available for human use; over 20% is found as ground water. Wells drilled into the acquifers provide a source of usable water. A tiny fraction is readily available in lakes and rivers as surface water. This is recyclable as part of the water (hydrologic) cycle, in which the sun's energy evaporates the water, from bodies of water as well as from the leaves of plants, into the atmosphere. As it rises, it cools and, if the concentration is sufficient, it returns to the earth in the form of rain or snow to repeat the cycle.

Water used by humans, whether for personal use or by industry, becomes impure and is returned to the environment into lakes, rivers, oceans, reservoirs or acquifers (natural underground reservoirs).

Fresh water is not available uniformly around the world nor necessarily where the consumption is highest. Parts of the world have enough or ample supplies, while others have almost none. It is estimated that about 40% of the world population experiences droughts. Water is a unique, highly polar substance capable of hydrogen bonding and this property allows it to dissolve many chemicals. Thus some toxic substances as well as bacteria and viruses can be carried by water. Water that is unsuitable for drinking, irrigation, industrial use or washing is considered **polluted water**. A primary hazard to people living not only in under–developed countries but also in some urban areas comes from contaminated drinking water spreading waterborne diseases such as cholera, hepatitis A, typhoid fever and dysentery (diarrhea). This is due to biological contamination of water by microorganisms from animal and human waste where adequate chemical treatment of water supplies is not carried out or where contamination takes place due to flooding.

Chemical contamination of water has increased as a result of human activities. It has been found to be cheaper to build industries on the banks of rivers so that chemical wastes can be easily removed by the flowing rivers. The extensive use of fertilizers and pesticides, the burning of coal and reactions in the automobile engines producing acid rain, oil spills, the use of detergents and cleaning substances in homes, all contribute to water pollution.

OPTION

Thus, human activities continue to pollute water. Increased population and the resulting need for agriculture and industry to meet requirements causes the demand for fresh water to rise at an alarming rate. Water for drinking purposes accounts for only a small percentage of fresh water, the rest being used for agriculture and industry. However, not all the water needs to be of drinking quality such as that used for irrigation, air conditioning and cooling, toilet flushing and a great deal of the water used by industry. The new millennium requires that water be recycled so that it can be reused and that per capita demand decreases.

The main reasons for treating drinking water are to kill any remaining disease causing microorganisms, to remove suspended particles and to remove or destroy objectionable smells and colors.

D.5.2 Compare the advantages and disadvantages of treating drinking water with chlorine and ozone.

Include cost, retention time and formation of chlorinated organic compounds.

© IBO 2001

The two bacteriocidal agents (substances that kill bacteria) in common use are chlorine, Cl_2, and ozone, O_3, gases. Both these compounds are added in very small amounts and function as strong **oxidizing agents** to kill microorganisms in water purification; these chemicals are reduced in the process:

$$Cl_{2(g)} + 2e^- \rightarrow 2Cl^-_{(aq)}$$

$$O_{3(g)} + 2e^- + H_2O \rightarrow O_{2(g)} + 2OH^-_{(aq)}$$

The microorganisms are destroyed when carbon and hydrogen are oxidized to carbon dioxide and water. Chlorination has been used for a long time and is effective in preventing the spread of water–borne diseases such as typhoid fever. One advantage of using chlorine to purify water is that it remains dissolved in water (has a higher retention time) thus providing protection against disease–causing bacteria. Disadvantages of chlorine include the fact that it is not effective against hepatitis and polio causing viruses. Chlorine also reacts with organic compounds dissolved or present in water creating chlorinated organic compounds, some of which are cancer causing (such as trichloromethane, $CHCl_3$, and tetrachloromethane, CCl_4).

Ozone is also a very effective oxidizing agent used to purify water. Its advantage is that it is also effective against viruses, unlike chlorine, and is needed in lesser quantities. Also, the oxidized organic compounds are less toxic than chlorinated organic compounds and, unlike chlorine, ozone does not give a chemical taste to the water. It is, however, more reactive than chlorine, has to be produced on site and is more expensive to produce than chlorine. Finally unlike chlorine, it does not provide long term protection against pathogens as it has a very short retention time, so the water has to be used soon after purification with ozone. An ideal solution is to use ozone for killing bacteria and viruses and then to add a much smaller amount of chlorine to provide protection until the water is consumed.

Summary: Advantages and disadvantages of treating water with chlorine and ozone:

	Chlorine	Ozone
1.	Effective against bacteria but not viruses.	Effective against both bacteria and viruses.
2.	Cheaper to produce.	More expensive to produce.
3.	Longer retention time.	Shorter retention time.
4.	Can be easily liquefied and shipped.	Must be produced on site because of high reactivity.
5.	Can form toxic chloro–organic compounds.	Oxidized products are much less toxic.
6.	Leaves a chemical taste behind.	Leaves no chemical taste behind.
7.	Functions as a strong oxidizing agent.	Stronger oxidizing agent than Cl_2.

D.5.3 Discuss ways to obtain fresh water from sea water using distillation, reverse osmosis and ion exchange.

© IBO 2001

Sea water, containing on average about 3.5% dissolved salts by mass, is not fit for human consumption. It is equally unfit for agricultural and industrial uses where the high salt content would cause dehydration of plants (water loss by the process of osmosis) and lead to corrosion of equipment. Desalination processes remove salts from sea water and brackish water to produce fresh water. Three methods in common use to **desalinate** sea water are **distillation, reverse osmosis** and **ion exchange.**

Distillation is the process that allows the separation of a volatile liquid from non–volatile materials. Heating the solution allows for the volatile water to be converted to water vapor that can be separated and collected as fresh water leaving behind the non–volatile salts in solution. Large scale desalination by distillation is made more efficient by using a multistage process to maximize the use of heat so that when condensation of vapor produces heat in one stage, it is used to heat water in the second stage and so on.

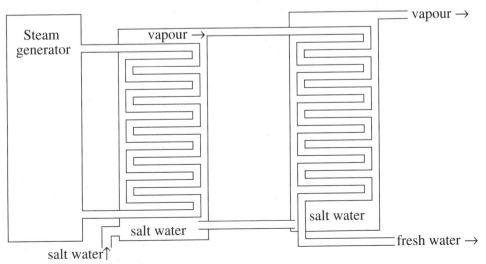

Reverse osmosis: Osmosis is the natural tendency of a solvent such as water to move from a region of high solvent concentration (purer water) to one of lower solvent concentration (less pure water) through a semipermeable membrane. A semipermeable membrane allows water, but not ions or other large molecules, to pass through it. Thus, it is a tendency to equalize concentrations across the membranes. If pure water and salt water are separated by a semipermeable membrane, then, due to osmosis, pure water (of higher solvent concentration) will move into the salt water thus diluting it. This flow of water can in fact be stopped if a pressure equal to the osmotic pressure of the solution is applied. Indeed, if the pressure applied is greater, then the flow of the solvent takes place in the opposite direction and the process is called reverse osmosis.

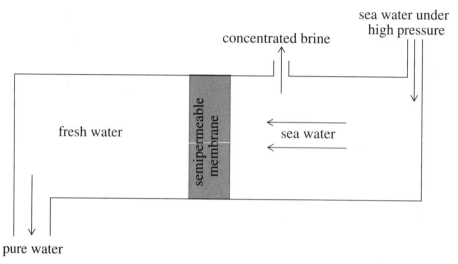

Because reverse osmosis does not require a phase change as does distillation, it thus requires less energy. Reverse osmosis plants are still too expensive for many nations to use. The world's largest desalination reverse osmosis plant is in Saudi Arabia, producing about 50% of that nation's drinking water.

Ion exchange: Ion–exchange columns containing **zeolites** (naturally occurring materials containing sodium aluminium silicates, $Na^+AlSiO_4^-$) are used to replace hard water ions such as Ca^{2+}, Mg^{2+} and Fe^{2+} with soft water ions (Na^+). The method of ion–exchange can also be used to purify brackish or sea water but requires the use of both a positive ion exchange which can replace metal ions with hydrogen ions, H^+, and a negative ion exchange which can replace anions in solution with hydroxide ions, OH^-. The H^+ ions react with the OH^- ions to form water.

Ion exchange columns contain high molar mass polymer resins represented by polymer–$SO_3^-H^+$ and polymer–$NH_3^+OH^-$ respectively. When a metal ion M^+ passes through the positive ion exchange column, it exchanges with a hydrogen ion:

$$polymer–SO_3^-H^+ + M^+ \Rightarrow polymer–SO_3^-M^+ + H^+$$

Similarly, an anion X^- passing through the negative ion column exchanges with the OH^-:

$$polymer–NH_3^+OH^- + X^- \Rightarrow polymer–NH_3^+X^- + OH^-$$

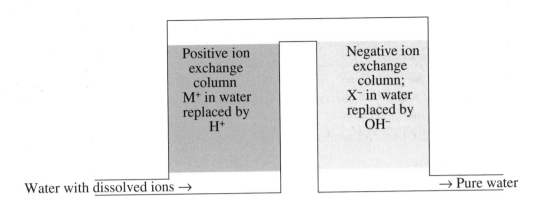

Water with <u>dissolved ions</u> →   → Pure water

Once the two columns are saturated with metal cations and anions respectively, they can be treated with sulfuric acid and sodium hydroxide respectively to reverse the processes to regenerate the original polymer resins in the columns. This is, however, a costly process.

D.5.4   Discuss ways to reduce the amount of water used and to recycle water. © IBO 2001

The presence of contaminants from human activity makes the availability and production of water for human consumption difficult. Also, agriculture and industry together use almost 90% of the water in industrial countries. For example, the production of one ton of paper or the refining of only one barrel of crude oil requires the use of about 80 000 litres of water each! The industrial use of water mainly for cooling purposes or for producing steam has particularly concentrated on recycling water as is the case with cooling towers used by industries and energy generating plants.

Instead of rain water flowing into rivers and then into oceans, dams can be built to create lakes to store water as well as to produce electricity where possible (and therefore cutting down on the use of fossil fuels). However, dams can be very expensive to build and can produce a variety of other problems including the flooding of farm land and the release of water downstream.

Not all water has to be treated to meet drinking water standards. Thus, if hazardous pollutants were removed, the waste water and sludge from sewage effluent could be used as fertilizers, as is the case in some parts of the world. Water saving shower heads, smaller sized toilets, direct reuse of water for drinking purposes from sewage (where recycling plants produce pure drinking water from sewage effluent), all save water. However, long term solutions to water usage must include conservation, reuse and less dependence on fresh water.

OPTION

14.6 DISSOLVED OXYGEN IN WATER

D.6.1 Outline the importance of dissolved oxygen in water.

D.6.2 Outline biological oxygen demand (BOD) as a measure of oxygen-demanding wastes in water.

Refer to the amount of oxygen needed to decompose waste matter over a definite period of time. No distinction between biological and biochemical oxygen demand will be made.

D.6.3 Distinguish between aerobic and anaerobic decomposition of organic material in water.

D.6.4 Describe the influence of sewage, detergents and fertilizers on the growth of aquatic plants, and the effect of their subsequent decomposition on oxygen concentration (eutrophication).

The additional nitrogen and phosphorus compounds encourage growth of aquatic plants often in the form of 'algal blooms' or, in coastal areas, 'red tides'.

D.6.5 Discuss the effect of heat on dissolved oxygen and metabolism in water.

© IBO 2001

The quality of water depends on several factors including oxygen–demanding wastes and disease–causing pathogens or microorganisms that can affect health. These can be life threatening. Other pollutants include plant nutrients that lead to growth of aquatic plants, suspended solids (undissolved particulates), substances such as benzene, chromium and mercury which are all toxic to aquatic life, dissolved minerals that give rise to salinity, excess acidity due to acid rain which can harm or destroy marine life and lead to corrosion and damage of crops and thermal pollution which can reduce the amount of dissolved oxygen in water, speeding up the rate of chemical reactions.

Human beings and land animals obtain oxygen for respiration from the air. For plants and animals to survive in aquatic systems, water must contain a minimum concentration of dissolved oxygen. The **dissolved–oxygen (DO) content** of a body of water is one of the most important indicators of its quality. Recall that whereas water is a highly polar, bent molecule, diatomic oxygen is a non–polar molecule and hence its solubility in water is very low. At 20°C, it is about 2.8×10^{-4} mol dm^{-3}. This is equivalent to 9 mg of oxygen per dm^{-3} of water (or 1000g water or in a million mg of water) and is best expressed as 9 ppm (parts per million). As the temperature rises, the solubility of any gas decreases, in contrast to that of most solids.

The quality of water, at any temperature, can be determined by the amount of oxygen present. At 20°C, DO content of 8 to 9 ppm O_2 at sea level is considered to be water of good quality. As the DO level reaches 4.5 ppm oxygen, it is considered moderately polluted and below that concentration, highly polluted.

Plant nutrients such as nitrates, from nitrogen–containing animal and human waste and fertilizers, and phosphates from detergents and fertilizers, lead to excess growth of aquatic plant life, often in the form of algal blooms. This can make water taste and smell bad and can kill shell fish as in the case of 'red tides'. Red tides are caused by several species of marine plankton (microscopic plant-like cells) that can produced chemical toxins. The process that causes pollution by such excessive growth is referred to as **eutrophication.** Dead plants fall to the bottom of bodies of water where, in the presence of oxygen, they are broken down or decay due to bacterial activity, thus depleting the concentration of oxygen. Consequently, deep water fish die of asphyxiation (lack of oxygen) and that part of the water becomes lifeless.

Organic substances such as plants from eutrophication, animal and human waste, waste from industrial processes such as meat–packing and food–processing plants and paper mills, are the main oxygen–demanding wastes. These can all be decayed by bacteria under aerobic conditions (in the presence of oxygen). Thus any carbon present is oxidized to carbon dioxide and the nitrogen and phosphorous to nitrates and phosphates respectively. **BOD,** the **Biological Oxygen Demand** (some refer to it as the Biochemical Oxygen Demand), is a measure of the amount of oxygen consumed by the biodegradable organic wastes and ammonia in a given amount of water over a time period, normally 5 days at $20°C$. The effluent sample is diluted in oxygen saturated water and enclosed without air space in a BOD sample bottle. After the 5 day incubation period, the decrease in dissolved oxygen is measured using an oxygen electrode. The greater the amount of oxygen–demanding wastes, the higher is the BOD:

BOD Values for Water

ppm BOD	Quality of Water
< 1	Almost pure water
5	Doubtful purity
20	Unacceptable purity

Untreated municipal sewage can be in the 100 to 400 ppm BOD range, whereas food–processing plants can be up to 10000 ppm, indicating very high oxygen demanding wastes present in the effluent of such plants.

If the amount of oxygen–demanding wastes is increased to a point where it consumes most of the oxygen, in a body of water, no life including aerobic bacteria is possible. The exception is anaerobic bacteria which not only survive, but thrive under such conditions. Whereas aerobic bacteria oxidize elements in organic matter so that carbon is oxidized primarily to carbon dioxide, anaerobic bacteria reduce it so that any carbon is converted to methane, CH_4. Nitrogen is reduced to ammonia and amines with a strong fishy smell and any sulfur is reduced to foul smelling hydrogen sulfide gas, H_2S. In fact the production of such foul smells is a clear indication of the anaerobic processes taking place and thus the presence of excess amounts of oxygen–demanding wastes.

Power plants and many industrial processes use huge quantities of fresh water to cool and condense steam. The cooling water subsequently becomes warm (or hot) and if this is dumped into streams, rivers or lakes, leads to **thermal pollution**. Two major effects of thermal pollution on bodies of water include that on dissolved oxygen and that on the metabolic rates of aquatic life.

The concentration of any gas such as oxygen dissolved in a liquid decreases as

OPTION

temperature is increased (that is more of the gas bubbles out). This is complicated by the fact that if the less dense warm water is not rapidly mixed with a body of deep, cooler, more dense water, it can stay on the top, is unable to absorb as much oxygen from the atmosphere and leads to overall reduced levels of dissolved oxygen.

The Effect of Temperature on the Solubility of Oxygen Gas in Water

Temperature (°C)	0	20	40
Solubility (ppm)	15	9	6.5

According to collision theory, as temperature increases, there are more frequent collisions between reacting particles and, more importantly, there are harder collisions (that is the number of particles with energy greater than the activation energy, E_a, increases). Thus, as temperature increases, the rate of a chemical reaction increases. A crude generalization (depending on the E_a value) is that the rate of a chemical reaction approximately doubles for every 10°C rise in temperature. Thus, not only is the DO (dissolved oxygen) level decreased as temperature increases, but so are the metabolic rates of aquatic animals which require more oxygen as a result. Thus, thermal pollution has adverse effects on both dissolved oxygen and the rate of consumption of oxygen in bodies of water.

14.7 WASTE WATER TREATMENT

D.7.1 Outline the primary and secondary stages of sewage treatment and state what is removed during each stage.

For primary treatment filtration, flocculation and sedimentation should be covered. For secondary treatment mention the use of oxygen and bacteria (e.g. the activated sludge process).

D.7.2 Discuss the increasing use of tertiary treatment.

Include removal of heavy metals and phosphates by chemical precipitation and nitrates by chemical or biological processes. © IBO 2001

Sewage is the water–carried wastes (that is used water) that flows away from any community. It can be more that 99.9% pure water and contain domestic, sanitary, commercial and industrial wastes. Such sewage may contain disease causing microorganisms, organic materials as well as other toxic substances such as heavy metal ions. The purpose of sewage treatment is to remove hazardous materials, reduce the BOD (Biological Oxygen Demand) of sewage and kill microorganisms prior to discharge.

Different types of sewage treatment with different levels of effectiveness are carried out in the world depending on the availability of resources since the cost increases with more advanced treatment. These are classified as **primary, secondary** and **tertiary stages** of **sewage treatment.** Each level of treatment reduces the level of the pollutants in the sewage and thus the original BOD, with the tertiary treatment being the most effective but by far the most expensive to build and operate.

In **primary sewage treatment,** the effluent is first passed through screens and traps which filter out large objects such as trash and debris and, from the surface, remove floating objects including grease (which has a high BOD). It then passes through settling tanks where smaller heavier objects such as rocks and stones settle and can be transferred to land fills. Next, the sewage passes through holding or sedimentation tanks or ponds where it is allowed to settle and sludge is removed from the bottom. The mechanical process of **sedimentation** can be speeded up by adding chemicals which allow suspended particles to join together to form large clumps. This process is called **flocculation** (the large clumps formed are called **flocs**) and can be achieved by the addition of aluminum sulfate, $Al_2(SO_4)_3$, whose aluminium ions cause particles to clump together and precipitate out. The flocs formed settle at the bottom.

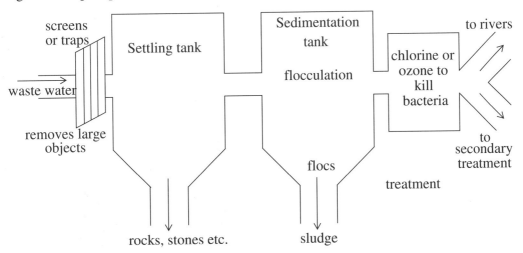

Depending on the amount of BOD wastes, primary treatment is generally not sufficient to improve the quality of water to safe levels, even if it is treated with chlorine or ozone to kill pathogens. A typical primary treatment domestic sewage plant can remove about 30 – 40% of the BOD waste and secondary treatment is essential to further reduce BOD levels.

Secondary sewage treatment involves microbial activity and requires **aeration** in which air, or air enriched with oxygen, is bubbled, using large blowers, through sewage mixed with bacteria–laden sludge. This allows aerobic bacteria to thoroughly mix with the sewage, to oxidize and break down most of the organic matter. The process is thus biological in nature and is called an **activated sludge process**.

Then the water, containing decomposed suspended particles, is passed through a sedimentation tank where large quantities of biologically active sludge collect. Part of this is recycled and the rest has to be disposed off. Secondary sewage treatment can remove most (about 90%) of organic oxygen–demanding wastes and suspended particles. Primary and secondary treatments cannot remove dissolved inorganic substances such as nitrates, phosphates and heavy metal ions, which require further treatment. The effluent is then treated with chlorine or ozone gas to kill pathogenic bacteria before release into lakes, rivers etc. or being sent to a tertiary plant for further treatment.

OPTION

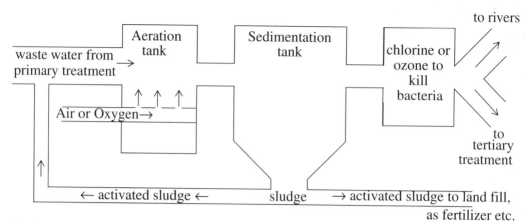

Tertiary sewage treatment involves specialized chemical, biological and or physical processes that further treat the water after it has undergone primary and secondary treatments to remove the remaining organic materials, nutrients and substances not removed by the biological processes in secondary treatment, such as toxic metal ions as well as nitrate and phosphate ions. Examples of tertiary treatment include **carbon bed, chemical precipitation** and **biological processes.**

The carbon bed method uses activated carbon black. This consists of tiny carbon granules with large surface areas which have been treated and activated by high temperatures. This then has the ability to readily adsorb organic chemicals from the waste waters. **Adsorption** is the attraction of a substance to the surface of a solid substance. Carbon beds are effective against many toxic organic materials and charcoal filters are often used to further purify tap water for drinking purposes.

Chemical Precipitation: Certain toxic heavy metal ions such as cadmium, lead and mercury can easily be precipitated as their sulfide salts whose solubilities in water are incredibly small. For the reaction:

$$MS_{(s)} \rightleftharpoons M^{2+}_{(aq)} + S^{2-}_{(aq)}$$

the K_c value (also called K_{sp}, the solubility product constant) at 25°C is of the order of 10^{-28} for CdS and PbS, and for HgS is of the order of 10^{-52}. Thus if carefully controlled amounts of hydrogen sulfide gas are bubbled through a solution containing heavy metal ions, these can be precipitated as the corresponding sulfides which can then be filtered out. Excess hydrogen sulfide (being acidic) can then be easily removed:

$$M^{2+}_{(aq)} + H_2S_{(g)} \Rightarrow MS_{(s)} + 2\,H^+_{(aq)}$$

Similarly, the presence of phosphate ions, PO_4^{3-}, can be reduced to very low levels by the addition of calcium ions, Ca^{2+}, since the solubility product constant K_{sp} of calcium phosphate is very small (1.2×10^{-26})

$$3\,Ca^{2+}_{(aq)} + 2\,PO_4^{3-}_{(aq)} \Rightarrow Ca_3(PO_4)_{2(s)}$$

The anaerobic biological process of denitrification turns the nitrogen in nitrates back to atmospheric nitrogen, N_2. This is achieved by anaerobic organisms (denitrifying bacteria). Denitrification therefore reduces nitrate contamination in ground water.

EXTENSION MATERIAL (HL ONLY)
14.8 SMOG

D.8.1   Compare reducing and photochemical smog.   © IBO 2001

Smog, a term coined from the words smoke and fog arose from the conditions of coal smoke and fog experienced by the city of London in the early part of the last century. The so-called 'London smog' or **industrial smog** or **reducing smog** is one of two types of smog caused by the combustion of sulfur containing coal (and oil) used for heating, manufacturing processes and the generation of electricity. It consists of water droplets, sulfur dioxide and trioxide, soot and ash (particulate matter) and sulfuric acid. The reducing smog is found in coal burning cities such as Chicago and Beijing which can experience cool or cold, wet winters and where thermal inversion can trap cold, still air close to the earth's surface. As a result of increased pollution controls, bans on the use of coal as a domestic fuel, and measures such as the use of alkaline scrubbers which remove SO_x and particulates pollution, severe episodes of industrial smog are on the decline. The other type of smog, called **photochemical smog** is an **oxidizing smog**. This is a chemical soup containing hundreds of different substances formed in the atmosphere as a result of free radical reactions brought about by ultra violet rays from the sun (thus called photochemical smog). It was first observed in Los Angeles in the 1940s. Automobile pollution is the main source of this type of smog and unlike industrial smog it is almost free of sulfur dioxide.

	Industrial Smog	Photochemical Smog
Main source	Pollution from burning of sulfur containing coal (& industrial oil)	Pollution from automobile exhausts
Conditions required	Cool/cold wet wintry weather; thermal inversion worsens condition	Sunlight (ultra violet radiation); warm, sunny weather; thermal inversion worsens condition
Main pollutants produced	sulfur oxides, particulates, sulfuric acid	nitrogen oxides, ozone, alkanals, peroxyacyl nitrates (PANs)
Cities with major smog	Chicago, Beijing	Los Angeles, Manila, Mexico City
Effects of smog	Breathing difficulties due to constriction of bronchial tubes by SO_2; acid rain damage to vegetation and aquatic systems, corrosion of metal, "stone leprosy" (effect on marble structures)	Effects on humans, materials and vegetation, e.g., PANs are powerful lachrymators (cause eyes to water) and cause damage to plants; O_3 is an eye irritant, causes deterioration of rubber, affects vegetation; acid rain from NO_x damages vegetation, metals, aquatic life, marble
Ways to reduce such smog	Alkaline scrubbers to reduce SO_x and particulate pollution; electrostatic precipitators to reduce particulates (see Section 14.1).	Catalytic converter to convert NO to N_2; use of lean burning engines to reduce NO_x pollution (but this produces more CO and HCs) (see Section 14.1).

OPTION

D.8.2 Describe the catalytic effect of particulates and nitrogen oxides on the oxidation of sulfur dioxide.

Particulates and SO_2: heterolytic catalysis to form SO_3; $NO_x + SO_2$ – free radical catalysis to form SO_3.

© IBO 2001

Sulfur dioxide, a primary pollutant produced from the combustion of sulfur containing coal, is oxidized to sulfur trioxide, a secondary pollutant:

$$2\ SO_{2\,(g)} + O_{2\,(g)} \rightleftharpoons 2\ SO_{3\,(g)}$$

In the presence of particulates, particularly metallic particles, which behave as heterogeneous catalysts, this reaction is speeded up. This is because the oxygen molecules are adsorbed onto the metal surface weakening the bond between the oxygen atoms and making them more susceptible to reaction with sulfur dioxide. Similarly, free radicals formed by the action of ultra violet light on nitrogen dioxide oxidize SO_2 to SO_3:

$$NO_{2\,(g)} + \text{uv light} \Rightarrow NO_{(g)} + O_{(g)}$$

$$SO_{2\,(g)} + O_{(g)} \Rightarrow SO_{3\,(g)}$$

$$NO_{2\,(g)} + SO_{2\,(g)} \Rightarrow NO_{(g)} + SO_{3\,(g)}$$

Sulfur trioxide is the anhydride of sulfuric acid. It reacts rapidly with moisture present in the air to produce sulfuric acid, a strong acid:

$$SO_{3(g)} + H_2O_{(l)} \Rightarrow H_2SO_{4(aq)}$$

D.8.3 Outline the formation of secondary pollutants in photochemical smog.

Treatment should be restricted to the formation of radicals from the reaction of nitrogen oxides with sunlight and the reaction of these radicals with hydrocarbons, leading to the formation of aldehydes and peroxyacylnitrates (PANs).

© IBO 2001

Research has clearly identified the role of sunlight in initiating photochemical smog in which particulates and unburnt hydrocarbons act as catalysts and reactants in the formation of secondary pollutants. It is found that photochemical smog follows a general, daily, cyclic pattern:

1. The release of hydrocarbons, nitrogen oxides and particularly nitric oxide, NO, as primary pollutants from the combustion of fossil fuels at high temperature in internal combustion engines and in the furnaces of power plants, cause smog. The automobile is the main source; and so nitric oxide, along with hydrocarbons and particulates, peaks during morning rush hours:

$$N_{2(g)} + O_{2(g)} \Rightarrow 2\ NO_{(g)};\ \text{primary pollutant}$$

2. The nitric oxide (systematic name: nitrogen monoxide) formed is almost immediately oxidized to brown nitrogen dioxide gas:

$$2 \, NO_{(g)} + O_{2(g)} \Rightarrow 2 \, NO_{2(g)}$$

3. As soon as solar radiation is available in the morning, photo–dissociation of the nitrogen dioxide takes place to produce oxygen atoms:

$$NO_{2(g)} + uv \; light \Rightarrow NO_{(g)} + O_{(g)}$$

The atomic oxygen formed is a highly reactive species containing unpaired electrons and is called a free radical.

4. Atomic oxygen initiates a series of important reactions to produce secondary pollutants such as ozone:

$$O_{(g)} + O_{2(g)} \Rightarrow O_{3(g)}$$

The ozone level therefore peaks later in the day. Both atomic oxygen and ozone are called photochemical oxidants. These are very reactive toxic substances produced as a result of a photo–dissociation reaction. They are capable of oxidizing other substances not easily oxidized by diatomic oxygen under atmospheric conditions. Note that diatomic oxygen and ozone are allotropes (which are different forms of the same element in the same physical state).

5. Atomic oxygen and ozone carry out the oxidation of hydrocarbons (which are the other primary pollutants produced by the automobile) to produce a wide variety of secondary pollutants including aldehydes and toxic substances such as peroxyacyl nitrates, PANs, which are powerful lachrymators (cause eyes to water). These then disperse in the atmosphere reaching a maximum concentration in the afternoon. A sequence of reactions leading to the formation of PAN can be shown as follows:

$$\underset{\text{hydrocarbon}}{R\text{–}CH_2\text{–}R} + O_3 \Rightarrow \underset{\text{aldehyde}}{RCHO} + \underset{\text{free radicals}}{RO\bullet + \bullet OH}$$

$$RCHO + O \Rightarrow \underset{\text{free radicals}}{R\text{–}C^\bullet{=}O + \bullet OH}$$

$$R\text{–}\overset{\bullet}{C}{=}O + O_2 \Rightarrow R\text{–}C\overset{\displaystyle O}{\underset{O\text{–}O\bullet}{\Vert}} \quad \text{free radical}$$

$$R\text{–}C\overset{\displaystyle O}{\underset{O\text{–}O\bullet}{\Vert}} + \overset{\bullet}{N}O_2 \Rightarrow R\text{–}C\overset{\displaystyle O}{\underset{O\text{–}O\text{–}NO_2}{\Vert}} \quad \text{PAN}$$

The sequence involved in photochemical reactions can be summarized as follows:

1. Formation of NO_x:

$$N_{2\,(g)} + O_{2\,(g)} \Rightarrow NO_{(g)};$$

$$2 \, NO_{(g)} + O_{2\,(g)} \Rightarrow 2 \, NO_{2\,(g)}$$

OPTION

2.   Photo–dissociation:

$$NO_{2\,(g)} + uv\ light \Rightarrow NO_{(g)} + O_{(g)}$$

3.   Formation of ozone and organic free radicals:

$$O_{(g)} + O_{2\,(g)} \Rightarrow O_{3\,(g)}$$

$$O_2 + O + HC \rightarrow HCO_3\ or\ O_3 + HC \Rightarrow HCO_3\ (reactive\ organic\ peroxides)$$

4.   Formation of photochemical 'soup' consisting of chemicals such as PANs:

$$HCO_3 + NO_2 \Rightarrow PAN$$

The principal sources of photochemical smog are nitrogen oxides, sunlight and hydrocarbons. It is difficult to control the formation of nitrogen oxides as well as hydrocarbons and carbon monoxide pollution from the automobile simply by adjusting the air to fuel ratio. For example, if the HC and CO concentration can be reduced by using a high air to fuel ratio, more NO_x is produced. If, on the other hand, a low air to fuel ratio is used, the NO_x amount is reduced at the expense of HC and CO pollution.

D.8.4   Discuss the formation of thermal inversions and their effects on air quality.

© IBO 2001

Under normal conditions, there is a gradual decrease in the temperature as the altitude increases. The warmer, less dense air near the earth's surface, warmed by the earth, rises. At the same time, pollutants produced near the surface of the earth move with the warm air to the upper atmosphere. Cooler air takes the place of the rising warmer air near the earth's surface, warms up and rises, in turn creating air currents which allow the pollutants produced to be dispersed. Thermal inversion (also called temperature inversion) is the abnormal temperature arrangement of air masses where a layer of warmer air is trapped between two layers of colder air.

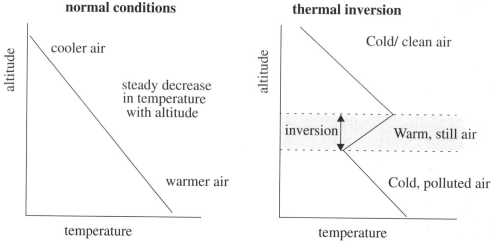

Prevailing winds give rise to the horizontal movement of air. However, surrounding hills, mountains or valleys in places such as Mexico City and Los Angeles hinder the horizontal movement of air. The flow of cold air from the surrounding hills and mountains into these cities creates the cool lower layer. Under windless conditions, pollutants can collect over a city without being dispersed. This creates a situation where warm air on top stays over a polluted air mass and the cooler, more dense, air stays near the earth, stopping vertical movement. The warm air mass effectively acts as a lid, trapping polluted air close to the ground. The warm, dry, cloudless conditions of thermal inversion are ideal for the formation of photochemical smog as any ultra violet light from the sun's rays is easily able to reach the earth.

14.9 OZONE DEPLETION

D.9.1   Explain the dependence of O_2 and O_3 dissociation on the wavelength of light.

$\lambda = 242\ nm$ $\lambda = 330\ nm$

$O_2 \Rightarrow 2O,$ $O_3 \Rightarrow O_2 + O$

The energy needed should be related to the bonding in O_2 and O_3.   © IBO 2001

Diatomic oxygen, O_2, and ozone (triatomic oxygen), O_3, are allotropes. Oxygen gas is a diatomic molecule with a double bond between the oxygen atoms (bond order of two). Ozone, on the other hand is triatomic and can be represented by two resonance structures (bond order of one and a half):

Resonance structure of ozone

The double bond in the oxygen molecule, results in a stronger bond compared to ozone. To dissociate an oxygen molecule, therefore, requires greater energy than to dissociate an ozone molecule. Since the wavelength of light is inversely proportional to its energy, the stronger double bond in the oxygen molecule requires radiation of lower wavelength (242 nm or less) compared to the dissociation of ozone which requires higher wavelength (330 nm or less). Thus, ozone absorbs harmful uv rays in the range 240 to 330 nm that oxygen does not absorb.

D.9.3   Describe the steps in the catalysis of O_3 depletion by CFCs and NO_x.

For example: $CCl_2F_2 \Rightarrow CClF_2 + Cl$
$Cl + O_3 \Rightarrow ClO + O_2$
$ClO + O \Rightarrow O_2 + Cl$
NO_x similar pathway.   © IBO 2001

Ultra violet (uv) light from the sun splits O_2 molecules into atoms:

$$O_{2\ (g)} + h\nu \Rightarrow 2\ O_{(g)}\ \text{(extremely reactive species)}$$

These oxygen atoms react with other oxygen molecules, O_2, to form O_3:

$$O_{2\ (g)} + O_{(g)} \Rightarrow O_{3\ (g)}$$

The photo–dissociation of molecular oxygen by uv light represents the principal mechanism of its formation in the upper atmosphere. The reverse reaction takes place when O_3 absorbs uv light. So, O_3 is constantly being formed and broken down. The ozone layer acts as a shield by absorbing 99% of the sun's harmful uv light.

$$O_{3(g)} + hv \Rightarrow O_{2(g)} + O_{(g)}$$

$$O_{(g)} + O_{(g)} \Rightarrow O_{2(g)}$$

Ozone can also be destroyed in a reaction with oxygen atoms:

$$O_{3(g)} + O_{(g)} \Rightarrow 2\ O_{2(g)}$$

Chlorofluorocarbons (CFCs) are stable compounds with a variety of uses such as in refrigeration and as propellants in aerosol sprays. In the upper atmosphere, uv light is able to break the weaker C–Cl bonds by homolysis to produce chlorine free radicals.

$$CCl_2F_2 + hv \Rightarrow \bullet CClF_2 + \bullet Cl$$

The chlorine free radicals can react with ozone to produce oxygen molecules and $\bullet ClO$ (this is the propagating step where one free radical is used up and another is formed in its place):

$$\bullet Cl + O_3 \Rightarrow \bullet ClO + O_2$$

The newly formed free radical $\bullet ClO$ can also react with an oxygen free radical to form a diatomic oxygen molecule and regenerate the chlorine free radical:

$$\bullet ClO + O \Rightarrow O_2 + \bullet Cl$$

These two steps combined, remove both ozone and atomic oxygen in the upper atmosphere by converting them to diatomic oxygen. In the process a chlorine free radical is reformed, that is, it effectively catalyses the conversion of ozone and atomic oxygen to oxygen gas:

$$O_{3\ (g)} + O_{(g)} \overset{\bullet Cl}{\Rightarrow} 2\ O_{2\ (g)}$$

Similarly, nitric oxide, NO, formed by the high temperature reaction between nitrogen and oxygen gases in supersonic aircraft engines reacts with ozone, reducing its concentration:

$$NO_{(g)} + O_{3\ (g)} \Rightarrow NO_{2\ (g)} + O_{2\ (g)}$$

Any NO_2 formed either by this reaction or by oxidation with O_2 also undergoes photo–dissociation in the presence of uv light to promote other photochemical reactions:

$$NO_{2\ (g)} + hv \Rightarrow NO_{(g)} + O_{(g)}$$

D.9.3 Outline the reasons for greater ozone depletion in polar regions.

Consider the seasonal variation in temperature in the upper atmosphere. Refer to surface catalysis on ice particles.

© IBO 2001

Recent data shows a decrease in ozone concentrations in Antarctica in the 1980s and 1990s compared to earlier data. This was caused by increased ozone depleting pollutants. Data also indicates that the ozone concentrations over Antarctica show a seasonal variation with a greater depletion around October during the polar spring producing the ozone hole. A return to more normal concentrations occurs in November as the spring progresses.

The ozone hole can be explained by the fact that during the South Pole winter from June to September, the temperatures are frigid, trapping very cold air at the pole and immediately converting any water vapor present into ice crystals. These ice particles behave as surface catalysts and provide the surface area over which pollutants present in the polar atmosphere combine to produce reactive chemicals such as chlorine molecules. After the long, cold winter darkness, when the sun comes out in October, the photodissociation of chlorine molecules takes place in the presence of ultra violet light from the sun's rays. This produces chlorine free radicals which catalyze the destruction of ozone over Antarctica to produce the ozone hole:

$$Cl_{2(g)} + uv\ light \rightarrow 2\ \bullet Cl_{(g)}$$
$$\bullet Cl_{(g)} + O_{3(g)} \rightarrow \bullet ClO_{(g)} + O_{2(g)}$$
$$\bullet ClO_{(g)} + O_{(g)} \rightarrow O_{2(g)} + \bullet Cl_{(g)}$$
$$O_{3(g)} + O_{(g)} \rightarrow 2\ O_{2(g)}$$

As the spring progresses in Antarctica, the ice crystals in the stratosphere melt and are no longer available as surface catalysts for the production of chlorine molecules. This, combined with the flow of air containing ozone from the lower altitude warmer regions, replaces the destroyed ozone and by November the ozone concentration increases. Similar, but not as drastic ozone depletion, has also been observed over the North Pole during the Arctic spring. The temperatures around the North Pole do not go down to the same extremes as those at the South Pole (down to $-90°C$) and the air with the ozone from lower altitudes is better able to diffuse, reducing the overall effect on the ozone layer.

D.9.4   Describe the properties required for sun-screening compounds.

Such compounds should contain conjugated double bonds, e.g. para-aminobenzoic acid (PABA), so that absorption of ultraviolet light is possible.

© IBO 2001

Melanin is a natural dark brown pigment present in the skin. People with different skin colors have different amounts of this pigment in their skin. Skin exposed to the sun's rays, tans by triggering the production of more melanin. This causes the skin to darken and so protect the lower layers from harmful solar radiation. Excess exposure to the sun's uv radiation causes skin damage and can lead to skin cancer.

The uv range is divided into three regions: near uv, A: 320 – 400 nm, mid uv, B: 280 – 320 nm and far uv, C: 200 – 280 nm. A great deal of the mid and far uv is absorbed in the ozone layer in the photo–dissociation of oxygen and ozone molecules though the filtering of mid uv by ozone is not complete. Tanning occurs as a result of exposure to light in the near uv region. Sun–screens are chemicals used to lower the dose of sunlight

OPTION

547

that the skin receives. Those which protect the skin from sun burn and from any mid uv radiation should absorb in the 280 – 320 nm range, while allowing for tanning to take place.

It is found that when electromagnetic radiation passes through a compound, such as vitamin A or PABA (para–aminobenzoic acid, $H_2N-C_6H_4-COOH$), containing conjugated (alternating) single and double bonds, a portion of the uv radiation is absorbed by the compound. The wavelength of radiation absorbed depends on the structure of the compound.

PABA

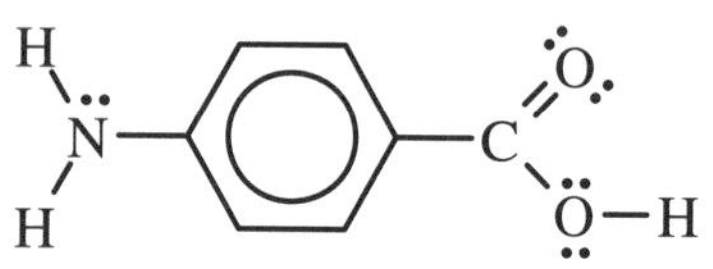

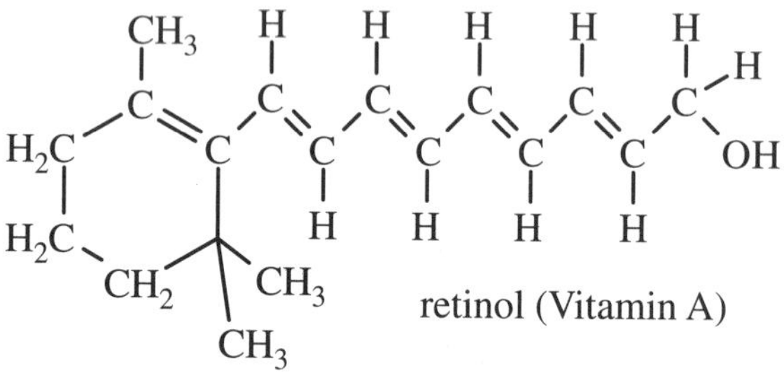

retinol (Vitamin A)

As a general rule, it is found that the wavelength at which the compound absorbs depends on the number of conjugated double bonds – the greater the number of such bonds, the longer the wavelength at which the compound absorbs light. The maximum absorption for PABA occurs at 265 nm, whereas β–carotene, a precursor of vitamin A that gives the orange color to carrots, has 11 conjugated double bonds and has a maximum absorption at about 500 nm.

PABA absorbs strongly in the ultra violet region over a range of 240 to about 290 nm, with a maximum absorption at 265 nm. It therefore protects the skin from the effects of part of the far uv region, the range 200–280 nm. It, however, does not protect the skin from the maximum intensity radiation from the sun received on the earth, which occurs at about 310 nm and which is responsible for deep burning of the skin. The absorption of radiation in the 290 to 320 nm range is of particular interest in the suppression of sunburn. A more effective sun–screen would need to contain a mixture of conjugated dienes which are able to absorb over a longer wavelength range. If one sits behind a window, the main effect is the reddening of the skin and not a sunburn because glass does not transmit much light of wavelength below 350 nm.

14.10 TOXIC SUBSTANCES IN WATER

A toxic substance (poison) is a chemical that is dangerous or causes illness or death (lethal) in small amounts. An example is the nerve gas sarin, used in the Tokyo subway incident, which was found to be extremely toxic in minute quantities. Substances such as nicotine can be moderately toxic to animals, whereas water is considered non–toxic. The lethal dose for a toxic substance varies from chemical to chemical and from one animal to another. Thus, lethal doses of poisons are expressed as milligrams of toxic substance per kilogram of body mass of the animal (mg per kg mass).

LD$_{50}$ (lethal dose in 50% of the population) is used to indicate the dose of a given toxic substance, in mg per kg body mass, that kills 50% of the laboratory animals under study such as rats, mice and guinea pigs. The smaller the value of LD$_{50}$, the more toxic the substance. Since different species react differently to various poisons, any application of data based on animal studies to human beings must be used with caution. Thus, studies are often carried out with different animals before such extrapolation is made.

On the basis of such studies, heroin has a LD$_{50}$ of between 1 and 5 mg/kg. This means that a 75 to 375 mg sample of heroin will be fatal to 50% of average people weighing 75 kg. Examples of LD$_{50}$ of other poisons include:

Toxic Substance	LD$_{50}$ (mg substance/kg body mass)
Botulism toxin	< 0.01
Potassium cyanide	between 1 and 5
Morphine	between 5 and 50
Aspirin, Sulfuric acid	between 50 and 500
Amphetamine, Nicotine	between 500 and 5000
Ethanol, Soap	between 5000 and 15000

The degree of toxicity is sometimes defined according to the mass of substance required for a lethal dose, but this tends to vary between countries. Generally, LD$_{50}$ < 1 mg/kg is considered extremely toxic, 1 – 50 mg/kg is highly toxic, 50 – 500 mg/kg is toxic, 500 – 5000 mg/kg is moderately toxic and 5000 – 15000 mg/kg is slightly toxic.

Substances can have toxicity that is short term, causing acute effects that occur shortly after intake, and long term chronic effects, due to repeated exposure, that cause damage over a longer period of time. Thus methanol's short term toxicity is not very high, however, it is metabolized to methanal, HCHO, producing chronic long term toxicity.

The maximum daily tolerance to a substance is also calculated on the basis of body mass. It is the mass of the substance that can be safely eaten on a daily basis without adverse effects and is particularly applicable to food additives. This is obtained by carrying out experiments on animals who are fed the substance in increasing quantities

OPTION

to determine the level at which acute, short term and chronic, long term toxicities occur.

It is common to carry out such studies on several species of animals and then to apply the most conservative data to humans by dividing the tolerance quantity observed by a factor of 100, to set safe standards for people. The factor of 100 is not always possible because of, for example, naturally occurring levels in the environment. Similarly, maximum daily (and yearly) tolerance levels have been established for radiation.

Safe LD_{50} and maximum daily tolerance levels are indeed difficult to establish for several reasons. Data based on animals are not necessarily applicable to humans since they can react differently to a particular chemical. Thalidomide, for example, was found so safe with animals that it was available without prescription in West Germany as a tranquilizer (often for pregnant women). Similarly, adult data cannot be used for children since adults often develop mechanisms for protection against some poisons that are not present in infants. Also, if taken in the same quantity, accumulation of a toxic substance per body mass will be higher for children than for adults because of their lower mass.

D.10.2 State the principal toxic types of chemicals that may be found in polluted water.

Include heavy metals, pesticides, dioxins and polychiorinated biphenyls (PCBs).

© IBO 2001

Toxic substances found in water are poisons which are harmful to humans, animals or aquatic life, at low concentrations. These include heavy metals and synthetic organic chemicals such as pesticides, dioxins and PCBs (polychlorobiphenyls). The heavy metal poisons found in water include cadmium, copper, lead and mercury. Mercury is converted to methyl mercury by anaerobic bacteria and accumulates in fish due to **biological magnification**. This is the process by which toxins are concentrated up the food chain as animals eat other animals. The pesticides include DDT which has been banned in many countries due to its biological magnification through the food chain. This has had disastrous effects on birds, especially eagles and ospreys, which were almost wiped out in the US by the weakening of their egg shells which were then easily damaged. Dioxin, present as an impurity in herbicides (chemicals that kill plants) exhibits extreme toxicity. PCBs are highly stable compounds used in electrical transformers.

D.10.3 Outline the sources, health and environmental effects of cadmium, mercury and lead compounds.

Cadmium-metal plating, some rechargeable batteries, pigrnents

Mercury-seed dressing to prevent mould, batteries

Lead-some kinds of paint, as tetraethyl lead in gasoline.   © IBO 2001

The three heavy metals Cd, Hg and Pb are examples of metabolic poisons which interfere with biological metabolism either by stopping or reducing the function of an important process. These interfere with enzymes which bond with the metal ions. The major sources and effects of these are given in the table below:

Heavy Metal	Sources	Health Effects	Environmental Effects
Cadmium	Byproduct of zinc–refining; rechargeable Ni–Cd batteries; metal plating and pigments	Itai–Itai disease; makes bones brittle and easily broken; kidney and lung cancer in humans	Toxic to fish; produces birth defects in mice inducing abortions
Mercury	Batteries; Hg amalgams for dental filling and Hg salts as fungicides; mercury cell in chlor–alkali industry	Minamata disease; paralysis and mental disorders	Reproductive system failure in fish; inhibits growth and kills fish; biological magnification in the food chain;
Lead	Lead paints; TEL (tetra ethyl lead) in gasoline as anti–knocking agent (banned in many countries)	Low birth mass, still birth, brain damage	Toxic to plants and domestic animals; biological magnification in the food chain

D.10.4 Describe the sources and possible health effects of nitrates in drinking water.

Include the formation of carcinogenic nitrosamines and a possible link to the formation of nitrites leading to oxygen depletion in the body.   © IBO 2001

Stable diatomic nitrogen is converted into its compounds by either being reduced to ammonia (by Haber process) or in nature it is oxidized to the nitrate ion, NO_3^-, through a series of reactions:

$$N_{2\,(g)} + O_{2\,(g)} \Rightarrow 2NO_{(g)}$$

$$2\,NO_{(g)} + O_{2\,(g)} \Rightarrow 2\,NO_{2\,(g)}$$

$$H_2O_{(l)} + 2\,NO_{2\,(g)} \Rightarrow HNO_{2\,(aq)} + HNO_{3\,(aq)}$$

HNO_2 is a weak acid and partially dissociates to produce NO_2^- ions, called nitrate(III) ions or nitrite ions; HNO_3 is a strong acid and dissociates to produce nitrate(V) ions, also called nitrate ions:

$$HNO_{2\,(aq)} \rightleftharpoons H^+_{(aq)} + NO_2^-_{(aq)} \qquad HNO_{3\,(aq)} \Rightarrow H^+_{(aq)} + NO_3^-_{(aq)}$$

About 15% of acid rain enters the environment as a result of the high temperature oxidation of nitrogen gas to nitrogen oxides, NO_x, in automobile engines (the rest comes from SO_x pollution). Ammonia reacts with the acidic conditions in soil to produce ammonium ions, NH_4^+. Oxidation due to oxygen in the soil can convert ammonium ions to nitrate ions, both of which are used by plants. Natural decay of organic matter

OPTION

converts nitrogen in proteins to NO_3^-. The nitrate ions are highly water soluble (all common nitrate salts are soluble) and NO_3^- thus ends up in the water system. Ammonium nitrate, NH_4NO_3, is used extensively as fertilizer and is a source of nitrate ions in water. Thus, in agricultural areas, nitrate concentrations, particularly in well water, can exceed the maximum safe infant level established by the World Health Organization of 10 ppm, and sometimes even the 50 ppm level set for adults.

Nitrates (and phosphates) are plant nutrients which produce growth of surface plants such as algae and eventually lead to eutrophication. This leads to bodies of water that can die following the increase of organic wastes, which then increase the BOD.

The presence of nitrate and nitrite ions in water is of health concern. Nitrites are also used as food preservatives since these are effective against the deadly microbe that causes botulism. In the late sixties, high rates of cancer of the stomach were detected in the Japanese, whose diet is rich in fish preserved using nitrites. Fish contain amines (the cause of the fishy smell) and react with nitrite ions to produce nitrosamines which have been found to be powerful carcinogens:

$$HNO_2 + R_2\text{--}HN \Rightarrow R_2\text{--}N\text{--}N{=}O + H_2O$$

$$\text{amine} \qquad \text{nitrosamine}$$

Also, nitrates present in water are converted, by the bacteria present in the human digestive system, to nitrites. Consumption from the water system of excessive nitrate ions, which are reduced to nitrite ions, can cause the 'blue baby' syndrome (a disease called methemoglobinemia). This is because nitrite ions reduce the oxygen carrying capacity of hemoglobin by oxidizing the Fe^{2+} to Fe^{3+} to form methemoglobin which is not able to transport oxygen any longer.

ENVIRONMENTAL CHEMISTRY QUESTIONS

1. What is a primary air pollutant and how is it different from a secondary pollutant?

2. List the major primary air pollutants.

3. Describe the natural and human sources of (a) carbon monoxide, (b) nitrogen oxides, (c) sulfur oxides, (d) particulates and (e) hydrocarbons in the atmosphere. Include balanced equations where possible.

4. Outline the health effects of each of the primary pollutant listed in question 3.

5. Describe and discuss methods for the control and prevention of each of the primary air pollutants listed in question 3.

6. Describe the primary and secondary pollutants produced by the automobile. Explain how these are produced, include relevant equations for the formation of the pollutants and describe current methods in use to reduce the pollution from automobile exhaust.

7. Discuss the advantages and disadvantages of lean burning engines and recirculation of exhaust gas methods to control pollution from the automobile.

8. What are allotropes? Draw the Lewis structures for the allotropes of oxygen and compare their bond strengths.

9. What are CFCs and what are their main uses?

10. Discuss the evidence for ozone depletion.

11. List the pollutants and their sources, that cause rapid ozone depletion. Include balanced equations to show how these deplete the ozone layer.

12. State the environmental effects of depletion and discuss alternatives to CFCs in terms of their properties.

13. What are some advantages and disadvantages of the alternatives to CFCs?

14. Discuss the evidence for global warming and describe the greenhouse effect.

15. List the main greenhouse gases and their sources. Discuss their relative effects.

16. Discuss the influence of increasing amounts of greenhouse gases on global warming.

17. Outline the influence of particulates on the Earth's surface temperature.

18. State what is meant by acid rain. Describe the pollutants, sources and chemical reactions leading to acid rain. Include balanced chemical equations leading to acid rain.

19. Discuss the environmental effects of acid rain.

20. Acid rain attacks and destroys marble in monuments. Explain using a balanced chemical equation.

OPTION

21. Discuss and evaluate possible methods of controlling acid rain. Include balanced equations where possible.

22. Discuss the demand for fresh water and the reasons for the inadequacy of its supply.

23. Discuss ways to reduce the amount of water used and to recycle water.

24. Using diagrams discuss ways to obtain fresh water from sea water using distillation, reverse osmosis or ion exchange. Include advantages and disadvantages of each process.

25. List some factors that influence water quality.

26. Outline the importance of dissolved oxygen in water.

27. Discuss each of the following as it relates to organic material in water: (a) aerobic decomposition, (b) anaerobic decomposition, (c) eutrophication.

28. List nutrients in water that affect the growth of aquatic plants and what is the effect of their subsequent decomposition on oxygen concentration.

29. Discuss the effects of oxygen demanding wastes on water quality.

30. Define Biological Oxygen Demand (BOD) and describe how it is a measure for oxygen demanding wastes.

31. Discuss the effect of heat on dissolved oxygen and metabolism in water.

32. Discuss the reasons for treating drinking water.

33. Compare the advantages and disadvantages of treating drinking water with chlorine and ozone. Your answer should include comparison of costs, retention time and formation of any compounds.

34. With respect to water treatment explain the following terms: (a) primary treatment, (b) filtration, (c) flocculation, (d) sedimentation, (e) secondary treatment, (f) activated sludge, (g) tertiary treatment, (h) chemical precipitation.

35. Outline the primary, secondary and tertiary stages of sewage treatment. Your answer should include the pollutants removed during each stage of water treatment and some qualitative idea of effectiveness in the removal of different pollutants for each method.

36. Discuss the effectiveness of the different water treatments and the increasing need for tertiary treatment.

37. Discuss industrial and photochemical smogs. List the similarities and differences between the two types of smog. Your answer should include the main sources of the smog, the main pollutants produced, examples of cities with each type of pollution, effect of and ways to reduce each type of smog.

38. Describe the catalytic effect of particulates and nitrogen oxides on the oxidation of sulfur dioxide.

39. Outline the steps in the formation of secondary pollutants in photochemical smog. Include balanced equations in your answer.

40. Discuss ways of controlling industrial and photochemical smog.

41. What is thermal inversion?

42. Discuss the formation of thermal inversions and their effects on air quality.

43. Explain the dependence of O_2 and O_3 dissociation on the wavelength of light.

44. Using balanced chemical equations, describe the steps in the catalysis of O_3 depletion by CFCs and NO_x.

45. Outline the reasons for greater ozone depletion in polar regions.

46. Discuss the properties required for sun–screening compounds.

47. Explain the terms LD_{50} and daily maximum tolerance with respect to toxicity.

48. Discuss the different approaches in expressing toxicity.

49. State the principal toxic types of chemicals that may be found in polluted water.

50. Discuss the sources, health and environmental effects of cadmium, mercury and lead.

51. Describe the sources and possible health effects of nitrates in drinking water.

Option D: Environmental Chemistry

CHEMICAL INDUSTRIES
(Option E)

15

Chapter contents

Chemical industries have a major place in the world economy. The industrial revolution, which commenced in the 18th century, was also a materials revolution that started with the large–scale extraction of iron. This continues to the present day with the extraction of other metals, the production of bulk chemicals such as fertilizers, the oil and plastics industries, and the speciality chemicals industry producing medicines, enzymes, catalysts and additives. When teaching this option, emphasize chemical reactions and their relevant equations.

© IBO 2001

15.1 OVERVIEW

Outline the abundance, occurrence and availability of sources of materials.

A qualitative picture only is intended. Include minerals (especially metals and their ores), petroleum and biotechnology. © IBO 2001

Chemicals produced in the largest amounts around the world include:

* sulfuric acid (used in making fertilizers, chemical processing etc.)

* ammonia (used in making fertilizers, explosives etc.)

* ethene (used in making polyehthene)

* sodium hydroxide (used to produce baking soda, in aluminium production etc.) and chlorine (used to disinfect swimming pools, drinking water, in bleach, etc.).

SOURCES OF MAJOR MATERIALS FOR THE CHEMICAL INDUSTRY

Atmosphere: Oxygen (O_2; 21%) , nitrogen (N_2; 78%) , argon (Ar; 1%)

Hydrosphere: Water (H_2O), magnesium chloride ($MgCl_2$), sodium chloride (NaCl)

Lithosphere: Limestone ($CaCO_3$), sodium chloride (NaCl), metals and their mineral ores etc.

Biosphere: Coal, petroleum, natural gas, sulfur, organic materials.

Biotechnology: In the manufacture of insulin, ethanol, biopolymers, vitamins etc.

Metals and their ores:

Metals occur mostly as compounds in the earth's crust, though some of the less active metals such as gold can be found as free ('native') elements. Metals occur as **ores**, from which they can be extracted. The preparation of metals from their ores, involves chemical **reduction**. Iron in iron(III) oxide (Fe_2O_3) is reduced to metallic iron which leads to the production of iron and steel. In nature these oxides are usually mixed with impurities and the production of iron and aluminium requires steps to remove such impurities. Aluminium, in the form of Al^{3+} ions, constitutes 7.4% by mass of the Earth's crust. Aluminium metal is soft and has a low density. Many of its alloys, however, are very strong. Hence, aluminium is an excellent choice when a lightweight, strong metal is required. In structural aluminium, the high chemical reactivity of the element is offset by the formation of a transparent, hard film of aluminium oxide, Al_2O_3, over the surface, which protects the aluminium from further oxidation.

Some Common Metals and Their Ores

Metal	Chemical Formula of Compound of the Element	Name of Mineral
Aluminium	$Al_2O_3 \bullet xH_2O$ (principal ore)	Bauxite
Calcium	$CaCO_3$	Limestone
Copper	Cu_2S	Chalcocite
Iron	Fe_2O_3 Fe_3O_4 ($FeO.Fe_2O_3$)	Haematite Magnetite

'Pure' silicon and 'The Chip':

Silicon of about 98% purity can be obtained by heating silica and coke at 3000°C in an electric arc furnace: $SiO_{2(s)} + 2C_{(s)} \Rightarrow Si_{(s)} + 2CO_{(g)}$. Silicon, at about 25%, is a major part of silicate rocks, clays and sand. The bonding between these two elements in clays and rocks literally holds together the earth's skin. SiO_2 (also called silica when pure and used in making glass) occurs naturally in large amounts in rocks and sand. Silicon for simiconductors is at least 99.999% pure.

Fossil Fuels:

Fossil fuels (natural gas, coal and petroleum) are among the major chemical raw materials produced by biological activity. Coal forms as a result of the high pressure from over burden and the decay of plant matter. Bacterial action gives peat, lignite and finally bituminous coal (these are different classifications of coal by rank depending on the percentage of carbon and moisture content). The decomposition under reducing conditions of the remains of small marine organisms is the basis of crude oil formation. Hydrocarbons of low molar mass are gases. Thus, pockets of natural gas are found in association with deposits of petroleum. Fossil fuels have a biological origin but geological conditions have transformed these into their present form.

Hydrocarbons have a lengthy list of uses. It is unfortunate that so much of their limited supply is being burned as fuel rather than conserved for future use as chemical starting materials for polymers, fibers, detergents and other goods.

Biotechnology as a source of new materials:

Human beings have been limited to the materials found on planet Earth and to relatively few chemical transformations. Technological advances in mining techniques and the control of chemical change through basic research have radically changed the materials available for human use. Discovery of new raw materials seems to have been exhausted and biotechnology is beginning to play an important role in the manufacture of new substances. Although fermentation and the large scale production of penicillin involved biotechnology, the biotechnology revolution began when the first successful gene–splicing and gene–cloning experiments produced recombinant DNA and one of the earliest benefits of this was the biosynthesis of human insulin (in the late 1970s).

E.1.2   Identify the factors that influence the establishment of a chemical industry in a particular location.

Include sources of suitable raw materials, energy supply, transport to and from the site, availability of investment, skills and labour and existence of markets for the product.
© IBO 2001

IMPORTANCE OF THE CHEMICAL INDUSTRY

The importance of the chemical industry rests on the food, clothes, medicines and the great variety of consumer articles that it produces. One of the signs of the economic development of a country is the state of its chemical industry because the chemical industry can take essentially simple and often cheap raw materials and turn them into much more valuable products. For example, the Haber process which exploits the 'free' supply of nitrogen (it still

OPTION

costs money to extract the nitrogen) from the atmosphere and converts it into ammonia and then into fertilizers and explosives upon which not only the supply of food has become dependent, but so have wars and conflicts. Thus, the commercialization of this process likely prolonged World War I by at least one year.

THE ECONOMICS OF PRODUCTION

A new manufacturing plant must consider a large number of factors affecting its economic viability. In economic terms product costs are a function of land, labour and capital. These would include raw materials, energy supply, transportation to and from the site, availability of investment, support services and the presence of markets for the product(s). The support services must include skills and labor, laboratory services (e.g. for quality control), security and fire services.

Starting Materials:

A readily obtainable supply of suitable raw materials is essential. Starting materials which are high in the electrochemical series such as aluminium and iron are abundant in the Earth' s crust, but are never found in elemental form; they are present as ores and thus have to be extracted, sometimes by expensive means. Besides the major product(s), other chemicals may be made by side reactions. Thus, any useful side products would need to be purified and sold; sometimes sheer economics may force the chemists and engineers to change the conditions required to produce the major product in order to suppress side reactions, even if the yield of the major product is reduced in the process.

Energy:

Many chemical reactions require energy to carry them out. The cost of energy is one of the most important factors in the design and running of any chemical industry. These have to be run so that the heat from an exothermic reaction in one part of the plant can be used to produce steam that drives turbines to produce electricity or to warm a building in the winter time. In some countries heat is used to warm water which is used for irrigation purposes to speed up the growth of crops for food production. Likewise an endothermic reaction may be used to cool liquid or gases from an exothermic reaction.

Note that, in order for a new product to come onto the market, it requires research in the production of the chemical using a small scale pilot study. Once the economic viability of the process is established, large scale production is started and extensive marketing is undertaken. The economic viability must address the cost of labor, maintenance of the plant and laboratory facilities, depreciation and replacement of equipment, as well as the energy and raw materials required for the manufacture of the product, transportation of it to markets, etc. It is uncommon for a new chemical industry to achieve financial profitability in its early years. The goal of any (chemical) industry is to improve the yield of the product, reduce waste and minimize costs (in order to make the maximum profit for its investors.)

Intermediates are chemicals obtained or manufactured by chemical industries that are used to make consumer products. For example, one of the chemicals produced in very large amounts is ethene. Ethene is used to make polyethene, which is also considered to be an intermediate. Polyethene is then used in the manfacture of a wide range of consumer products including packaging materials as well as rigid articles such as chairs and tables. A second example is aminobenzene (aniline) which is an intermediate used in the manufacture of brightly coloured azo compounds used in the dye industry. These synthetic dye intermediates are used to produce brightly coloured consumer products.

Sulfuric acid is the chemical produced in the largest amount. It has direct uses (for example in car batteries), but is also widely used as an intermediate in the manufacture of numerous consumer products including detergents, paints, pigments, paper and polymers.

Biotechnology: This is the synthesis of natural polypeptides in living organisms for commercial use. The protein insulin was routinely obtained from the pancreas of cattle or pigs (as a by–product of the food industry). However, this caused an allergic reaction in some people because the bovine insulin sequence is not identical to that of human insulin. Now micro–organisms have been developed using biotechnology to synthesize such polypeptides.

Knowing the role of DNA in protein synthesis, it has been possible to make important proteins and molecules such as hormones (insulin) and antibiotics. Recombinant DNA technology has made it possible to transfer genes between organisms, that is micro–organisms can receive or combine from the genes of animals and be 'genetically engineered' to carry out the synthesis of useful chemicals. Note that careful selection of yeasts in brewing to produce ethanol has been around for a long time indeed. Genetic engineering is also being used to develop new and improved varieties of plants leading to new sources of food.

15.2 PRINCIPLES OF EXTRACTION AND PRODUCTION OF METALS

E.2.1   Outline the principles used in the physical separation of materials.   © IBO 2001

There are several ways in which metals are extracted from their ores. The simplest occurs for only a few unreactive metals such as gold and some other precious metals such as platinum which are much lower in the activity series. These unreactive elements can be found in the ground such as the occurrence of gold mines in southern Africa and Alaska. Although it should be possible to dig a hole in a seam of gold rich rock and take out the lumps of metal, large pieces of gold are not generally found and the gold is present as tiny fragments mixed in with large quantities of other material. The solids removed from the mine have to be converted to powder and then the gold recovered by physical or chemical methods. The mixture of earth and rock containing gold is swirled with water. Owing to the greater density of the gold particles, they tend to lie on the bottom of the pan, while the other solid particles are washed away. This is the physical separation and purification based on the unreactivity of gold and its higher density.

After mining, many ores need to be concentrated by removing sand, rock and other impurities surrounding the mineral of interest. If the ore is heavier than the impurities, then after pulverisation the lighter impurities can be removed using a **cyclone separator**. This is a machine in which centrifugal force pushes the heavier particles to the wall and they are then collected at the bottom. The lighter particles are removed from the top. For lighter ores, or ores which do not react with water, such as sulfides and silicates, the flotation method is used, or the ore is made water repellent by treatment with oil. Air is then blown through a suspension of the ore in water and oil. Air bubbles which form on the oil reduce its density, forcing the ore to the top. In the chemical method, gold is recovered by extraction into aqueous cyanide.

E.2.2   Discuss the chemical principles involved in the extraction of metals from their ores.

> *Relate this to chemical reactions based on the reactivity series (see 10.2), but also include factors such as chemical conversion (iron), electrolytic conversion (aluminium) and energy requirements.*   © IBO 2001

The most reactive metals in groups 1, 2 and 3 (e.g., Na, Mg, Al) are high up in the reactivity series. They are present in nature as chlorides (group 1), carbonates (group 2, except for $MgCl_2$ in the sea) and oxides (group 3). These are extremely hard to break down by chemical means and their extraction is done by **electrolysis**. Two important processes that use electrolysis are:

(1)   The extraction of Na from NaCl involves the electrolysis of molten sodium chloride. The electrolysis is carried out in a Downs cell. The NaCl is mixed with $CaCl_2$ in a ratio of about 2 to 3 so as to lower the melting point of the solid in order to carry out the electrolysis at a lower temperature. A large current is passed through the cell, but at a low voltage. This both discharges the sodium effectively

and heats the mixture so that it does not crystallize. Anions go to the anode and oxidation takes place:

$$2Cl^-_{(l)} \Rightarrow Cl_{2\,(g)} + 2e^-.$$

Downs Cell schematic diagram

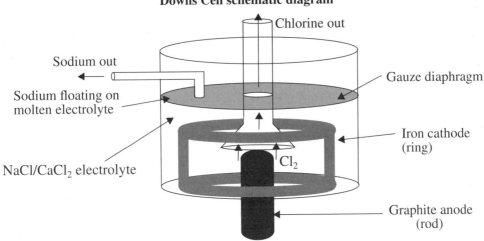

(2) Extraction of aluminium from **bauxite**: Bauxite is the major ore of Al, consisting of up to 60% by mass aluminium oxide, Al_2O_3, known as alumina. Pure alumina is needed and the impurities in the ore have to be removed. Since the melting point of alumina is very high, the electrolyte used in the smelting process contains a mixture of alumina, cryolite, Na_3AlF_6 and fluorspar, CaF_2. This lowers the operating temperature and results in the reduction of the Al^{3+} to Al. O_2 is produced at the anode from the oxidation of O^{2-}.

$$Al^{3+}_{(l)} + 3\,e^- \Rightarrow Al_{(l)};\ \text{reduction half reaction}$$

$$2\,O^{2-}_{(l)} \Rightarrow O_{2\,(g)} + 4\,e^-;\ \text{oxidation half reaction}$$

The overall reaction is: $4\,Al^{3+}_{(l)} + 6\,O^{2-}_{(l)} \Rightarrow 4\,Al_{(l)} + 3\,O_{2\,(g)}$

For sulfide ores, **roasting and reduction** are used. This method removes the metals from their sulfide ores by first roasting to turn them into oxides, followed by reduction by carbon. This is a method used for a number of the transition elements and metals such as zinc, lead and mercury: e.g.,

ROASTING: $2\,ZnS + 3\,O_2 \Rightarrow 2\,ZnO + 2\,SO_2$,

then **REDUCTION**: $ZnO + C \Rightarrow Zn + CO$.

For less reactive metals that occur chiefly as oxides, extraction is carried out by reduction with carbon, as in the important extraction of iron. The chief iron ore haematite, Fe_2O_3, is reduced in a blast furnace:

$$Fe_2O_{3\,(s)} + 3\,CO_{(g)} \rightleftharpoons 2\,Fe_{(l)} + 3\,CO_{2\,(g)}$$

OPTION

15.3 IRON AND ALUMINIUM

E.3.1   State the main sources of iron.   © IBO 2001

Iron is the most important of the industrial age metals and much of the twentieth century way of life has been based on the use of iron machinery. The main sources of iron include iron ores and scrap iron. Iron ores are mined as its oxides, Fe_2O_3, (haematite), Fe_3O_4, (magnetite) and the sulfide FeS_2, (iron pyrites). The latter is roasted in air to form the oxide and sulfur dioxide.

E.3.2   Explain the reactions that occur in the blast furnace.

Include the role of coke, limestone and the formation of slag. The relevant equations should be considered.   © IBO 2001

A mixture of limestone ($CaCO_3$), coke (C) and iron ore (e.g., Fe_2O_3) is fed from the top into the furnace. A lot of air is introduced under pressure near the bottom of the furnace where coke is oxidized exothermically to CO_2:

$$C_{(s)} + O_{2\,(g)} \rightleftharpoons CO_{2\,(g)} + heat$$

The furnace is at about 2200 K temperature in this lower region. Higher up the furnace, CO_2 reacts with coke to form carbon monoxide. This reaction is **endothermic**, with the furnace in this region cooling to 1400 K:

$$CO_{2(g)} + C_{(s)} + heat \Rightarrow 2\,CO_{(g)}$$

It is CO that plays the largest part in the reduction of the ore towards the top of the furnace. Iron oxides are reduced exothermically:

$$Fe_2O_{3(s)} + 3\,CO_{(g)} \Rightarrow 2\,Fe_{(l)} + 3\,CO_{2(g)} + heat.$$

Blast Furnace

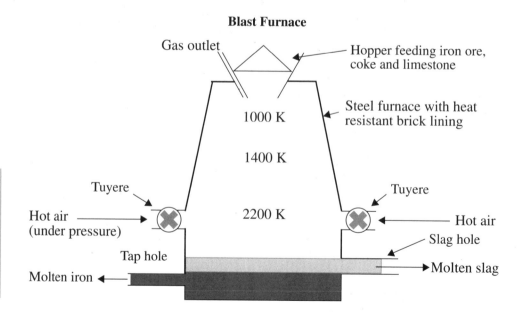

The iron produced sinks to the bottom of the furnace where the temperature is high enough to melt it. A layer of molten iron then lies on the bottom of the furnace. At the same time, because of the high temperature, the limestone in the charge decomposes to form calcium oxide and carbon dioxide:

$$\text{heat} + CaCO_{3\,(s)} \Rightarrow CaO_{(s)} + CO_{2\,(g)}$$

The highly basic calcium oxide combines with the acidic silicon(IV) oxide present as sand in the impure ore and the **amphoteric** aluminium oxide. These impurities in the ore form a molten slag of calcium silicate(IV) and calcium aluminate(III), which trickles down the stack:

$$CaO_{(s)} + SiO_{2\,(s)} \Rightarrow CaSiO_{3\,(l)}$$

$$CaO_{(s)} + Al_2O_{3\,(s)} \Rightarrow CaAl_2O_{4\,(l)}$$

At the bottom of the furnace, liquid iron and slag are tapped off every few hours. A modern furnace makes 3000 tons of iron a day using 3000 tons of coke (and 4000 tons of air) and producing a ton of slag for every ton of iron! If natural gas (CH_4, methane) is injected with the hot air only half the amount of coke is then required. Slag is used for road making and in the manufacture of cement. A furnace can operate continuously for several years before it needs relining.

E.3.3   Explain the conversion of iron into steel using the basic oxygen converter.

The Basic Oxygen Process : The most common method of making steel is to blast pure O_2 through the impure molten iron. Initially, the furnace is charged with hot, molten pig iron and lime. O_2 is blown onto the surface of the metal at great speed through water cooled pipes. The oxygen penetrates into the molten iron and oxidizes the impurities rapidly. Carbon, sulfur and phosphorous oxides are formed, which escape from the melt either as gases or by being absorbed into the slag. The oxidation of the impurities is an exothermic process and the heat evolved as the impurities are oxidized keeps the contents of the furnace in a molten state, despite a rise in the melting point as impurities are removed. (Recall: impurities lower and broaden the melting point of a substance). Alloying metals such as Mn, Co etc. as well as Al (to react with dissolved O_2), are then added to the molten metal

E.3.4   Describe the properties and uses of steel as an alloy of iron.

   Consider carbon steels and alloy steels (including stainless steel).

Some of the iron leaving the blast furnace is run into giant crucibles and made into steel as described above. Molten steel is formed after the carbon content has been reduced to a suitable level. Steels contain less than 1.5% carbon and include added metals. Many different steels are made, with different properties for different uses. The amount of carbon and the type of metal mixed with iron that largely determine the nature of the steel such as its tensile strength and other useful mechanical properties.

Steel containing a low carbon content (<0.3%) is used for making boiler plates, medium carbon content (0.3–0.7% C) is used in cars and high carbon content (0.7–1.5%) is used in cutting tools. Small amounts of other substances, such as manganese, are added to give desirable qualities such as toughness so that it can be used as tool steel. The presence of **chromium** as an additive to steel inhibits rusting and produces **stainless steel.** It also contains some Ni, but it is the formation of a coating of Cr_2O_3 that prevents the iron from rusting. Other important steel alloys, their properties and some uses are given below:

Fe + other metals	Important Properties	Some uses
Titanium steel	Withstands high temperatures	Gas turbines, spacecraft
Chromium steel	Hard	Ball bearings
Cobalt steel	High magnetic permeability	Magnets
Manganese steel	Tough tool steel	Earth–moving machinery
Stainless steel containing Cr & Ni	Non–rusting	Cutlery, sinks, car accessories, etc.

ALUMINIUM

E.3.5   Discuss the production of aluminium by electrolysis of alumina in molten cryolite.

Explain the need for cryolite as a solvent because of the very high melting point of Al_2O_3. Account for the materials used in the construction of the cell and the choice of electrodes.   © IBO 2001

Aluminium, in the form of Al^{3+} ions, constitutes 7.4% of the Earth's crust. Aluminium is obtained industrially by the electrolysis of molten aluminium oxide, Al_2O_3. This is obtained from bauxite, impure hydrated aluminium oxide, $Al_2O_3 \bullet xH_2O$. The main impurities in bauxite are iron(III) oxide, Fe_2O_3 and silicon (IV) oxide, SiO_2.

The first stage in the production of aluminium is to obtain pure aluminium oxide from the bauxite. The **amphoteric** nature of Al_2O_3 is an essential feature on which its purification is based. When the impure bauxite is treated with hot concentrated sodium hydroxide, Al_2O_3 and SiO_2 dissolve:

$$Al_2O_{3\,(s)} + 2\,OH^-_{(aq)} + 3\,H_2O_{(l)} \Rightarrow 2\,Al(OH)_4{}^-_{(aq)}\,;\ \text{aluminate ion}$$

$$SiO_{2\,(aq)} + 2\,OH^-_{(aq)} \Rightarrow SiO_3{}^{2-}_{(aq)} + H_2O_{(l)};\ \text{silicate ion}$$

but Fe_2O_3 and other basic materials remain insoluble and are removed by filtration. The solution can be treated with carbon dioxide (acidic non–metal oxide) to precipitate aluminium hydroxide:

$$CO_{2\,(g)} + Al(OH)_4^-{}_{(aq)} \rightleftharpoons Al(OH)_{3\,(s)} + HCO_3^-{}_{(aq)}$$

Sodium silicate stays in solution whereas aluminium hydroxide precipitates out. Finally, the aluminium hydroxide is heated to obtain pure Al_2O_3:

$$2Al(OH)_{3(s)} \rightleftharpoons Al_2O_{3(s)} + 3\,H_2O_{(g)}$$

Treatment of bauxite to obtain pure Al_2O_3

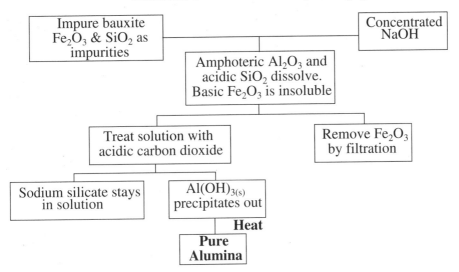

Aluminium is so reactive that it is obtained by electrolysis of molten salts, requiring high temperatures to maintain the molten state, rather than from aqueous solutions. The melting point of Al_2O_3 is > 2000°C (the cation Al^{3+} and the anion O^{2-} both have high charge densities due to their relatively small sizes and large charges, leading to very strong electrostatic interactions, high lattice energy and thus a very high melting point.). Metallic aluminium is thus obtained from the purified oxide by electrolytic processes that use molten cryolite, Na_3AlF_6, as a solvent with a much lower melting point of 1000°C. Cryolite dissolves alumina which in turn lowers the melting point of the cryolite solution to about 850°C and the electrolyte is maintained at this temperature by the current through it. The process thus requires large amounts of energy. The mixture of cryolite and alumina is electrolyzed in a cell with carbon anodes and a carbon cell lining that serves as the cathode. As the electrolysis takes place, molten Al (melting point 660°C) sinks to the bottom of the cell and is run off into molds.

Cathode half reaction (reduction): $Al^{3+}{}_{(l)} + 3\,e^- \rightleftharpoons Al_{(l)}$

Oxygen is evolved at the anode where oxidation takes place:

$$2\,O^{2-}{}_{(l)} \rightleftharpoons O_{2\,(g)} + 4\,e^-$$

The overall reaction is: $4\,Al^{3+}{}_{(l)} + 6O^{2-}{}_{(l)} \rightleftharpoons 4Al_{(l)} + 3O_{2\,(g)}$

The O_2 produced reacts with the carbon anode to form oxides of carbon. Thus the anodes gradually burn away and are replaced regularly, adding to the cost of manufacture. Every ton of Al requires half a ton of carbon. The energy released from the oxidation of the anodes is a significant factor in driving the whole process.

OPTION

Production of Aluminium

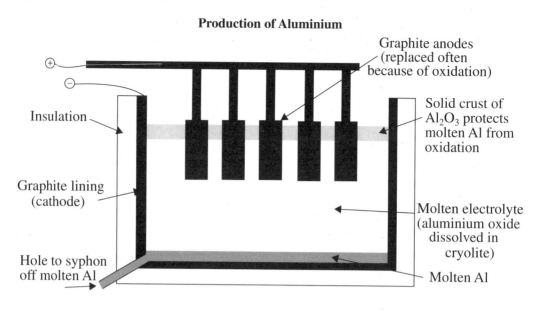

About ten times more energy is needed to produce a ton of aluminium than to produce a ton of steel. Recycled aluminium from aluminium cans requires approximately one–half the energy needed to produce the same amount of the metal from the ore.

E.3.6   Describe the main properties and uses of aluminium.

Include the properties of the aluminium oxide coating and the resulting resistance to corrosion. Compare with the properties and uses of iron and steel.

© IBO 2001

Aluminium is a soft metal with a low density. However, many of its alloys are very strong. Hence, Aluminium is an excellent choice when a strong, but lightweight, metal is required. The position of aluminium in the electrochemical series and its electrode potential suggest that it should react readily with oxygen, to form its oxide, and with water and dilute acids to produce hydrogen gas:

$$Al_{(s)} \rightleftharpoons Al^{3+}_{(aq)} + 3e^- \quad E° = +1.66 \text{ V}$$

$$3H^+_{(aq)} + 3e^- \rightleftharpoons \tfrac{3}{2} H_{2\,(g)} \quad E° = 0.00 \text{ V}$$

However, the rapid formation of a very thin layer of oxide prevents further attack by oxygen or moisture. Since the oxide layer is virtually non–porous to water, the aluminium is protected from further oxidation unlike iron, which forms a porous oxide rust layer. Oxygen and water readily penetrate the porous iron oxide layer thus allowing further rusting of the iron to continue underneath the rusted surface. As a result, aluminium is very corrosion resistant.

Aluminium is used both as a structural and decorative metal and as an electrical conductor in high–voltage transmission lines. Aluminium competes with copper as an electric conductor because of the lower density and cost of aluminium. Larger diameter

OPTION

Aluminium wire must be used to offset the lower electrical conductivity of aluminium. Chemically and physically a new kind of aluminium foil, which is very different from household aluminium foil, is an alloy containing iron, silicon and other elements. Its enhanced strength comes from the iron and its heat resistance comes from the silicon.

Most of the uses of aluminium such as saucepans, aircraft and vehicle bodywork, etc. are only possible because of the protective oxide coating which is only about 10^{-6} mm thick. The thickness of the oxide layer can be increased (to about 10^{-3} mm) by an electrolytic process known as **anodizing**. This is done by making aluminium the anode during the electrolysis of sulfuric acid. Water is oxidized to oxygen at the anode:

$$2\,H_2O_{(l)} \Rightarrow O_{2(g)} + 4\,H^+_{(aq)} + 4\,e^-$$

Oxygen released at the anode combines with the aluminium and thickens the oxide layer, thus protecting it even further. The electrolytic anodizing process can be carried out in the presence of dyes which are absorbed by the oxide layer, thus coloring the anodized material to make it suitable for different uses such as window frames and drink cans.

Iron has almost three times the density of aluminium. It has a high tensile strength and is ductile. Aluminium is relatively soft and can be easily made into a variety of shapes. Both form alloys that are harder and stronger than the pure metals.

E.3.7   Discuss the environmental impact of iron and aluminium production.

   Include the effects of mining the ore, siting the plant, energy costs and recycling the metals.   © IBO 2001

All of the processes in steel making, from the blast furnace to the final heat treatment and the production of aluminium by electrolysis, use tremendous quantities of energy, mostly in the form of heat or electricity. In the production of a ton of steel, approximately one ton of coal is consumed and produces a ton of slag! About ten times more energy is needed to produce a ton of aluminium than to produce a ton of steel. The environmental effects of mining the ore depend on the extraction method used as well as the geographic area in which the ore is found. The mined areas can be scars on the landscape unless the mining company decides to revegetate the area. The waste products of mining, 'tailings', and the metal wastes from these can be very damaging to the environment.

Recycling: When Al articles are finished with or worn out, the Al can be reclaimed and used again. Recycled aluminium stock from aluminium cans requires approximately one–half the energy needed to produce the same amount of the metal from the ore. Thus, recycling is essential because it saves money, energy and fuels; it saves the environment and the reserves of materials and it solves the problem of waste disposal. However, recycling is not always economically feasible as it can be labor intensive to collect, sort and process the material. The higher the value of the material, the more economical it is to recycle. Thus, virtually all gold is recycled, but only 40% of aluminium is recycled and a still lesser percentage of iron is currently recycled.

OPTION

15.4 THE OIL INDUSTRY

E.4.1 Outline the importance of oil as a source of chemical feedstock.

Although only about 10% of the refined products of crude oil are used as chemical feedstock, it is still the most significant source of organic chemicals. Compare the use of oil as an energy source and as a chemical feedstock.

© IBO 2001

By supplying a large part of the world's energy needs, crude oil has become the most important modern raw material. It is also a major source of organic chemicals. By itself, crude oil is not a useful resource; however, it consists of a mixture of very useful hydrocarbons ranging from petrol and other fuels for transport and oil heating systems to chemicals that can be converted to very useful polymers and detergents. Millions of tons of oil are extracted each year and processed in refineries and chemical plants, to produce useful substances ranging from fertilizers and pesticides to ointments, plastics, drugs and dyes just to mention a few.

F.4.2 Outline the removal of sulfur from crude oil.

Refer to the need for this removal and the use of sulfur in the manufacture of sulfuric acid.

© IBO 2001

Sulfur impurities in natural gas and petroleum must be removed in order to reduce the acidic sulfur oxide pollution from the burning of oil and gas (see Chapter 14). Hydrogen sulfide and other sulfide impurities are acidic and so can be extracted into solutions of basic potassium carbonate:

$$H_2S_{(g)} + CO_3^{2-}{}_{(aq)} \rightleftharpoons HS^-{}_{(aq)} + HCO_3^-{}_{(aq)}$$

After removal from this solution, some of the H_2S is burned in air at high temperature (1000°C) using aluminium oxide as a catalyst to yield sulfur dioxide:

$$H_2S_{(g)} + \tfrac{3}{2}O_{2(g)} \rightleftharpoons SO_{2(g)} + H_2O_{(g)}$$

which can be used directly to make sulfuric acid (see Chapter 8).

It is also possible to reduce the sulfur dioxide gas produced, to elemental sulfur by reaction with additional H_2S:

$$SO_{2(g)} + 2\,H_2S_{(g)} \rightleftharpoons 3\,S_{(l)} + 2\,H_2O_{(g)}$$

using Fe_2O_3 as a catalyst. This greatly reduces pollution from the burning of natural gas and petroleum. Other sulfur compounds are removed from the hydrocarbons by passing them over ZnO or activated charcoal.

E.4.3   Describe the fractional distillation of oil.

Compare simple distillation with fractional distillation. Students should understand that the vapour phase is always richer in the more volatile component. No calculations using Raoult's law or Dalton's law are required.

Simple Distillation:

The vapour pressure of a liquid increases with temperature and when it equals the surrounding (usually atmospheric) pressure, the liquid boils. For a liquid to boil it has to overcome interparticle forces and the pressure of the atmosphere. The liquid and vapour are at equilibrium at the boiling point. A liquid can be separated from non-volatile solutes by simple distillation. At its boiling point, the vapour enters the condenser which is cooled by the circulation of water through the water jacket, entering at the bottom and leaving at the top. This cools and condenses the vapour with the pure liquid collecting in the receiving flask.

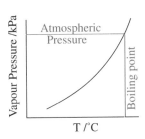

Simple distillation apparatus

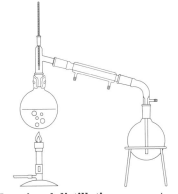

Fractional distillation:

Simple distillation cannot be used to completely separate two or more miscible liquids since all the liquids contribute to the vapour pressure and will be present in the vapour formed. Fractional distillation allows the separation of liquid mixtures based on their differing boiling points. This is because, when a mixture of liquids is boiled, the vapour phase will be richest in the most volatile liquid (with the lowest boiling point). If this vapour is condensed and collected in a container and boiled again, the vapour then formed is yet richer in the most volatile liquid. Thus, a series of evaporations and condensations should allow for the separation of the most volatile liquid. Fractional distillation achieves this usually by using a tower. The temperature in the tower decreases towards the top.

Fractional distillation apparatus

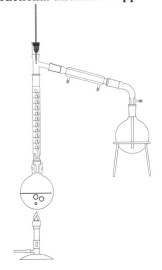

Fractional distillation of oil:

Crude oil is a complex mixture of many hydrocarbons and by itself is not of much use. In the refining process, petroleum is separated into useful fractions with each fraction containing fewer, more useful hydrocarbon mixtures. This separation is possible because the hydrocarbons are non-polar molecules with only weak van der Waals' forces between them. As the size of the molecules increases and as they have a greater number of electrons, it leads to greater distortion of the electron cloud leading to greater interparticle forces and high boiling points. The boiling points vary with molar masses with the lighter molecules being more volatile. Thus the process of fractional distillation is used to physically separate liquid hydrocarbons from crude oil based on differences in their boiling points, each fraction containing hydrocarbons of similar range boiling points.

Fractional distillation of oil requires heating crude oil to a temperature of about 400°C, which is sufficient to vaporize most of the hydrocarbons present in petroleum.

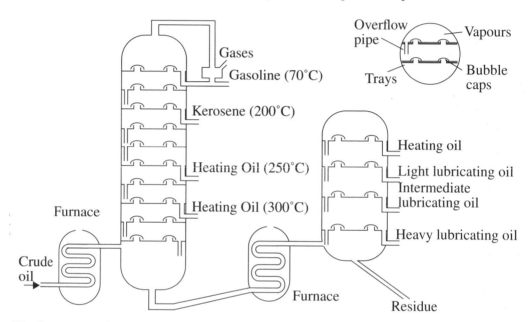

The hot vapors rise up the fractionating column, creating a temperature gradient. Bubble caps in the column allow the vapor to pass through the trays without the condensed liquid which is formed falling down the column. The liquid can then be tapped. The lighter hydrocarbons with lower boiling points condense near the top of the column, whereas heavier ones with higher boiling points condense lower down.

The residue from a fractionating column consists of hydrocarbons of very high boiling points under atmospheric conditions. The technique of **vacuum distillation** can be used to vaporize such compounds since reduced external pressure reduces the boiling point of substances in the residue. Without vacuum distillation, much higher temperatures would be required, which could decompose (break up) the hydrocarbons before separation can take place.

E.4.4   Describe cracking and its products.

Include thermal cracking (both steam and catalytic) and hydrocracking. © IBO 2001

For automobile engines to work efficiently, the fuel must burn evenly rather than exploding suddenly. If it does explode prematurely, the engine suffers from **knocking**, which leads to loss of power, fuel wastage and likely damage to the engine. The **octane number** of a fuel is a measure of how resistant it is to knocking. A fuel with a high octane number causes less knocking than a fuel with a low octane number. Aromatic and branched chain hydrocarbons are found to have high octane ratings. Other criteria the fuel must meet include the fact that it should not evaporate too easily, nor should it require more O_2 to burn than is available from the air in the pistons.

Cracking: The petroleum fractions with 1 to 12 carbon atoms in the molecule are in demand in larger quantities than the other fractions. **Pyrolysis** or **cracking** or **thermal cracking** (splitting by heat) of high molar mass alkanes gives hydrocarbons with smaller molecules. These are more easily vaporized and are, therefore, more useful fuels.

$$C_{12}H_{26(l)} \Rightarrow C_9H_{20(l)} + C_3H_{6(g)}$$

Cracking tends to produce branched–chain rather than straight–chain alkanes. So the gasoline produced this way has a higher octane rating. Thermal cracking is also used to convert alkanes into alkenes by heating the alkanes to a high temperature (800°C) and then rapidly cooling. A mixture of different products is formed, but ethene is the most favored product. C_2H_4 and other alkenes are key starting materials for the preparation of a large number of other chemicals.

$$\text{e.g. } 2\ CH_3CH_2CH_{3(g)} \Rightarrow CH_{4(g)} + CH_3CH=CH_{2(g)} + CH_2=CH_{2(g)} + H_{2(g)}$$

Catalytic cracking (cat–cracking) takes long–chain hydrocarbons and breaks them into smaller ones by passing the hydrocarbons at a lower temperature of around 500°C over a catalyst mixture of silica, SiO_2, and alumina, Al_2O_3. A variation of the cat–cracking process is called **Hydrocracking**. The catalyst is sodium aluminium silicate. In the presence of excess H_2, no alkenes are formed, only saturated hydrocarbons. The gases produced contain 2–methylpropane used to make high octane gasoline by **alkylation**.

E.4.5   Describe reforming processes and their products.

Include isomerization, cyclization and aromatization. Reforming is important in some countries as a source of hydrogen for the Haber process (see 8.2.5).

© IBO 2001

Reforming involves converting straight chain alkanes into ring molecules, arenes (aromatics) and cycloalkanes. **Isomerization**, as its name implies, involves breaking up straight chain alkanes and reassembling them as branched chain isomers. Both of these processes are important in the production of high octane gasoline.

Reforming: A huge number of important chemicals are derived from benzene such as TNT (trinitrotoluene), drugs and dyes. One source of benzene is petroleum in which unbranched chain alkanes are converted into aromatic compounds by the process of reforming. If a platinum catalyst is used, the process is called catalytic reforming or **platforming.** Naphtha, which boils between 75 and 190°C is a fraction from oil distillation that has little use by itself. However, much of it can be converted into hydrocarbons with a high octane number by the process of catalytic re–forming.

In catalytic reforming, naphtha is mixed with hydrogen and passed over a catalyst (a mixture of platinum and aluminium oxide). With high pressures (of up to 40 atm.) at temperatures of over 450°C. The reactions that take place depend on the type of hydrocarbon in the naphtha. Some of them are converted into aromatics (a process called aromatization) and some straight chain hydrocarbons rearrange into branched–chain hydrocarbons; this process is called **isomerization**. Other products are cyclic compounds (a process called cyclization). All these changes give products with increased octane numbers:

$$CH_3 - CH_2 - CH_2 - CH_2 - CH_2 - CH_3$$

$CH_3 - CH_2 - CH - CH_2 - CH_3$		
CH_3	$+H_2$	$+4H_2$
Isomerisation	cyclisation	aromatisation

H_2 is an important byproduct of catalytic reforming in cyclization and aromatization and is used for the Haber Process (see Chapter 8).

Alkylation: Smaller alkenes, obtained by thermal cracking react with alkanes in the presence of concentrated H_2SO_4 as a catalyst to form larger alkanes.

Thus, 2–methylpropene reacts with 2–methylpropane (obtained by isomerization) to give 2,2,4–trimethylpentane, a good fuel with a high octane rating as it is highly branched This is in fact the industry standard with an octane number of 100.

E.4.6   State the uses of refinery products as feedstock for the organic chemical industry.

Refinery products are used as raw materials in the manufacture of solvents, plastics, pesticides, food additives, pharmaceuticals, detergents, cosmetics and dyes.

© IBO 2001

Petrochemicals are organic compounds found in, or derived from, petroleum and used in the production of commodities other than fuels. Such compounds serve as indispensable raw materials for plastic, rubber, polymers, drugs, detergents, cosmetics, dyes etc. New developments in paints, fertilizers, pesticides and detergents have been made possible by the ready availability of petrochemicals. Fractional distillation of crude oil produces lubricating oils, wax candles, ointments, polishes and chemicals which in turn are used to produce plastics (see Section 15.5), detergents, fibers, agricultural chemicals, synthetic rubber, solvents etc. Thus, benzene from crude oil is converted to aminobenzene (phenylamine) which is used in the preparation of drugs and dyestuffs whereas methylbenzene is nitrated to produce TNT and also to produce polyurethane foams for upholstery, insulation and flotation devices.

15.5 POLYMERS

E.5.1   Describe how the properties of polymers depend on their structural features.

Include the: different amounts of branching in low- and high-density polyethene; different positions of the methyl groups in isotactic and atactic polypropene; formation of cross-links in phenol-methanal plastics (compare thermoplastics and thermosets).   © IBO 2001

Polymers: Polymers are long chain macromolecules made by joining together many smaller repeating units called **monomers**. Polyethene, a typical polymer, is a giant molecule made when hundreds of thousands of ethene molecules join together to make a long chain. Ethene molecules are the monomers, which join to make the polymer polyethene, represented by $-(C_2H_4)_n-$ where n represents a very large number of C_2H_4 molecules joined together. The empirical formula for polyethene is CH_2, just as it is for ethene.

$$nCH_2=CH_2 \Rightarrow -(C_2H_4)_n-$$

There are two main types of polymers – addition and condensation polymers. In addition polymerization, all the monomer's atoms are present in the polymer; in condensation polymerization, a small molecule (such as water) is eliminated in order for monomers to join together, i.e., the monomers have two reactive sites for the polymerization to take place (see Chapter 11).

Four factors are generally important in determining the properties of polymers:

1.   **Chain length**: The greater the average chain length, the greater are the intermolecular forces and hence the higher the strength and melting point.

2.   **Intermolecular forces (IMFs)**: The stronger the IMFs, the higher the strength and the melting point of the polymer.

3.   **Branching**: A straight chain polymer can pack closer together. The presence of branches limits how close polymer chains can come to each other, thus lowering IMFs, leading to lower density and melting point.

4.   **Cross–linking**: The greater the cross–linking between the chains, the more rigid the polymer.

Thermoplastic and thermosetting polymers: Thermoplastic polymers can be molded when they are hot; they keep their new shape on cooling. On reheating, the polymer can be molded into another shape. Thermosetting polymers can also be molded when they are heated, however, on cooling they set permanently into their new shape as the heating causes substantial cross linking to occur. Reheating has no effect on the polymer, but too high a temperature can decompose a thermosetting plastic. Cross linking is achieved either by making the polymer with side chains that will react to make the crosslinks, or, by adding a second substance that will produce the crosslinks with the original polymer chains.

Different properties arise from the stereochemistry of the polymers. First, consider linear polymers in which the polymer chains are not literally all in straight lines, but rather

OPTION

where the carbon backbone of the polymer takes up a zig–zag pattern (recall the tetrahedral structure for C bonded to four other atoms). In **branched** polymers the side chains grow off the main chain. In **crosslinked** polymers, two different chains are connected by short lengths of another chain which in some cases may be only two or three atoms long. A crosslinked polymer is found to be more rigid than a linear or branched polymer. The amount of cross–linking determines how rigid the final structure becomes. A good example of this is the vulcanization of rubber. Natural rubber is a soft, sticky substance which hardens to a useless material unless it is treated with sulfur, or some other chemical. Rubber is built from isoprene (2–methyl–1,3–butadiene) monomers.

When rubber is heated with sulfur it maintains its spring for longer periods of time than natural rubber. The sulfur atoms create strong covalent links between the chains so that treated rubber retains the shape into which it was molded. This led to the discovery of rubber tires and the use of rubber in hoses, shoes and balls.

The phenol-methanal plastics (shown at right) are examples of polymers with extensive cross-links that produce rigid plastics. They are excellent electrical insulators, non-flammable and chemically inert. These plastics are used in electrical plugs, sockets, switches, casings for electronic equipment, etc.

Polyethene, made either as a **low–density** or **high–density** polymer, depending on reaction conditions, has many different uses. Both contain saturated, strong, covalent bonds within the polymer chains, making the polymers resistant to chemical reactions and good electrical insulators. Because the intermolecular forces between both types of polymers are weak van der Waals' forces, both become soft and melt on heating and can be molded to form thin films and sheets and be made into rods and tubes. Low density polymers (melting point about 100°C) are used in making plastic bags, wrappers, squeeze bottles, plastic bowls, etc. High density polyethene has a higher tensile strength and melting point (about 135°C) and is used for making rigid articles such as buckets, milk bottle crates, disposable syringes, etc. Polyethene is light, impermeable to water and can be pigmented, giving rise to articles with a wide variety of attractive colors.

Tacticity is the way groups are arranged along a polymer backbone chain. For example polypropene is made by the polymerisation of propene:

$$n \; CH_2=CH-CH_3 \implies \left(CH_2 - \underset{\underset{CH_3}{|}}{\overset{\overset{H}{|}}{C}} \right)_n$$

The carbon atoms in the polymer backbone are not arranged in a linear pattern, but rather in a zig-zag manner (with tetrahedral angles):

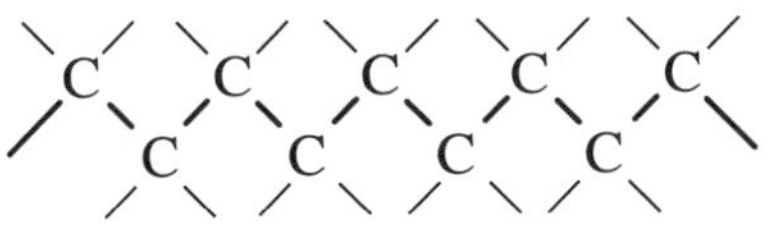

The hydrogen and the methyl side chain (–CH$_3$) can appear on either side of the backbone. If the methyl groups are all on the same side (and the H atoms on the opposite side), the polymer is is said to be isotactic. If the arrangement is random, the polymer is called atactic and is the more likely. Polymers with regular isotactic arrangements can pack more easily into crystals and fibres and have generally more useful properties than atactic ploymers. Thus, atactic polypropylene is soft and not very strong whereas isotactic polypropylene is strong and is used to make fibres, ropes, carpets, etc.

Isotactic polypropylene

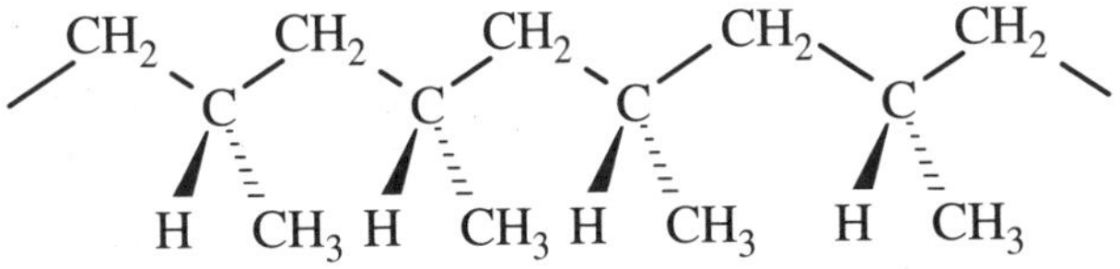

Atactic polypropylene

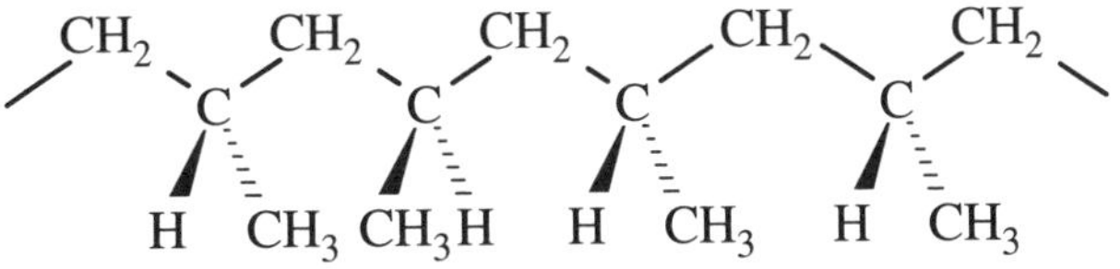

E.5.2   Describe ways of modifying the properties of polymers.

Include the use of: plasticizers in polyvinyl chloride; volatile hydrocarbons in the formation of expanded polystyrene; air in the manufacture of polyurethane foams.   © IBO 2001

Plasticizers in polyvinyl chloride:

The stronger dipole-dipole intermolecular forces between chains in the polymer polyvinyl chloride (PVC) lead to a rigid plastic. A plasticizer is a substance added to a polymer to allow the chains to slide over each other, producing a softer plastic. Medical products such as blood bags and intravenous drip tubes tend to be made of polyvinyl chloride containing a diethylhexyl phthlate plasticizer. A 10% concentration of the phthalate produces a semi-rigid PVC and higher concentrations produce the more flexible polymer.

Volatile hydrocarbons in the formation of expanded polystyrene:

This involves the polymerisation of styrene in the presence of a volatile hydrocarbon of low boiling point such as pentane, C$_5$H$_{12}$. This produces polystyrene containing the volatile hydrocarbon which causes it to expand to several times its original size. These expanded polystyrenes have reduced densities and are very good thermal insulators and are used, for example, in making disposable coffee cups.

OPTION

Air in the manufacture of polyurethane foams:

A 'blowing agent' such as air produces a polyurethane foam that is soft and which has a low density. Such foams are used as cushioning materials for furniture. More often, in the case of polyurethane, water is used to produce the foaming agent carbon dioxide since the isocyanate group reacts with water to produce CO_2.

$$-NCO + H_2O \Rightarrow -NH_2 + CO_2$$

F.5.3   Discuss the advantages and disadvantages of polymer use.

Consider strength, density, insulation, lack of reactivity, use of natural resources, disposal and biodegradability. Use polyethene, polyurethane foams, polyvinyl chloride and phenol-methanal plastics as examples.   © IBO 2001

The source of most synthetic polymers is petroleum, a non–renewable resource. Crude oil is the most convenient and economical resource currently available for the manufacture of plastics so the advisability of using 90% of this non-renewable resource as a fuel must be questioned. In theory, it should be possible to convert renewable agricultural resources such as wood, cotton, straw and starch into new synthetic polymers. This will require research to develop new techniques, which would have implications for land use, crop production, the environment and costs.

The disposal of polymers is, of course, of key importance since currently a great deal of plastics end up in landfills (which are estimated to contain about 20% plastics). Disposal of plastics include four approaches:

1.   **Combustion**: Complete combustion or incineration of plastics, primarily consisting of C and H, can be a very good method of disposal. The products are primarily CO_2 and H_2O and the process produces a great amount of energy which can be used constructively. Thus, buried plastics represent a high energy content in landfills. Incineration can lead to a large reduction in plastic waste while producing useful energy. However, incineration does present problems namely: (i) CO_2 produced is a greenhouse gas, (ii) chlorinated polymers such as PVCs produce $HCl_{(g)}$ on combustion, leading to acid rain and (iii) some printed plastic contains heavy metals such as Pb and Cd, which are toxic.

2.   **Biodegradability**: i.e., the use of bacteria and fungi to break down the plastics. Microorganisms are able to break down natural polymers such as cellulose or proteins from plants into simpler molecules using enzymes. For example, starch, a naturally degradable polymer, can be incorporated into a plastic to make it biodegradable. However, the rate of decomposition, the products of such processes and the environmental impact of the product for each plastic would have to be studied (and understood) before such products become commercially available. The whole question of biodegradability in landfills is complicated by the fact that such landfills are often lined to stop leaching into the water table. Unfortunately, such covering produces **anaerobic**, oxygen–free, environments where biodegradation by aerobic microorganisms cannot take place.

3. **Recycling:** Recycling can reduce the amount of new plastic manufactured. However, this requires energy and depending on the quality of the plastic, can be quite energy demanding. The amount of plastic recycled ranges from about 2% of the packing plastics in the US to as much as 50% in Germany and is therefore very dependent on government policies. There is a clear increase in the recycling of plastic bottles which are easy to melt and reuse. This is true of any polymer that is not extensively cross–linked. The molten polymer can either be used in the manufacture of new products if the waste is made of similar monomers or it can be used to make plastic of lower quality with appropriate uses such as cheap plastic lumber. However, the sorting of plastic waste is labour intensive.

4. **Conservation**: As a society we have become voluminous users of plastics which are made from a non–renewable resource. Conservation, recycling and minimal use of plastics should be a key strategy in extending the life of non–renewable resources (Reduce, Reuse, Recycle).

Properties and uses of some plastics

Polymer	Type of plastic	Properties	Uses
Polyethene $(-CH_2-CH_2-)_n$	Thermoplastic; becomes soft and melts on heating; can be moulded, excellent insulators; unreactive.	(a) Low density polymer, low melting point (~100°C). (b) High density polymer, high tensile strength, higher melting point (~140°C).	(a) Packaging material, plastic bags etc. (b) Plastic Chairs, tables, rigid bottles etc.
Polyurethane foams	Thermosetting can be made flexible by adding a blowing agent. Produce toxic vapours in fires.	(a) Flexible polyurethane foams have low strength and low density. (b) Rigid polyurethanes have higher tensile strength and density.	(a) Materials for furniture etc. (b) Insulators in building panels etc.
Polyvinyl chloride (PVC)	Thermoplastic polymer with wide range of physical properties; plasticizers added which make it more flexible	(a) Flexible PVC has low tensile strength and density. (b) Rigid PVC has higher density and strength.	(a) Raincoats, handbags, shower curtains, etc. (b) Pipes, tiles, rigid bottles, etc.
Phenol-methanal plastics	Cross-linked by covalent bonding.	Chemically inert; electrical and thermal insulators; non-flammable; high density, high strength.	Electric switches, electronic casings, utensil handles, etc.

OPTION

EXTENSION MATERIAL (HL ONLY)

15.6 SILICON

E.6.1   Describe the extraction and purification of silicon.

Include zone refining.   © IBO 2001

Silicon is the most important element used in the semiconductor industry without which it would be impossible for the industry to exist. Silicon occurs naturally as silicon (IV) oxide, SiO_2, in sand, quartz and as a number of silicates, SiO_3^{2-}. Impure silicon (of about 98% purity) is obtained by reducing silica with coke using heat:

$$SiO_{2(s)} + 2\ C_{(s)} + heat \Rightarrow Si_{(s)} + 2\ CO_{(g)}$$

Higher purity Si is produced by reducing silicon tetrachloride, $SiCl_4$, with hydrogen gas or Mg:

$$SiCl_4 + 2\ Mg \Rightarrow Si + 2\ MgCl_2 \text{ or } SiCl_4 + 2\ H_2 \Rightarrow Si + 4\ HCl$$

In order to use this silicon in the semiconductor industry, it must be further refined by a melting process called **zone refining**. In this method, a silicon bar containing impurities is pushed very slowly through a heater or furnace which is at the melting point of Si. As the Si melts and the rod moves through, the rod that emerges, cools and pure silicon crystallizes from the molten state more readily than the impurities, which interfere with the regular repeating packing present in a pure crystal. The impurities remain in the molten zone and are concentrated at one end of the rod.

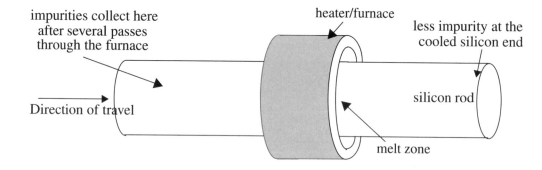

It is possible to produce silicon containing less than 1 ppb (part per billion) of impurities (such as B, Al and As) after zone refining the bar several times.

E.6.2   Compare the electrical conductivity of a semiconductor with that of metals and non-metals.

Relate this to the ionization energies of semiconductors compared to metals and non-metals.   © IBO 2001

E.6.3   Explain the doping of silicon to produce n-type and p-type semiconductors.

In p-type semiconductors, electron holes in the crystal are created by introducing a small percentage of a group 3 element (eg In, Ga). In n-type semiconductors inclusion of a group 5 element (eg As) provides extra electrons.   © IBO 2001

Silicon as a semiconductor: Semiconductors are a special class of materials which have an electrical resistance between those of electrical conductors and electrical insulators and are better conductors under certain circumstances. Thus, they conduct electricity better as the temperature rises, that is the electrical resistance falls as the temperature rises.

Note that the electrons in the shell of an isolated atom have discrete energy levels. The valence electrons, present in the highest energy levels, are used in bond formation. In metals, electrons in the valence shell can move easily to an unfilled higher energy level making electric conduction possible. Electrons in metals are delocalised; they are in effect free from individual atoms and are able to move through the metal when a potential difference is applied across it. Si contains 4 valence electrons. As each atom forms four tetrahedrally directed covalent bonds to other silicon atoms, a macromolecular crystal structure in three dimensions is built up.

Doping of semiconductors is carried out by adding certain substances to molten silicon. This can be done by exposing the semiconductor to the vapor of the substance which is added in the furnace. The chosen substance is added in carefully controlled amounts to bring its content up to only a few parts per million. The atoms of the added substance are therefore well spaced out in the semiconductor so that its crystal structure is not weakened. The process is called **doping** and the added substances are called **dopants**.

There are two types of semiconductors: **n–type** and **p–type**. In n–type semiconductors, the dopants are Group V (or 15) elements, such as arsenic and antimony, which have 5 electrons in the outer shell. When an arsenic dopant atom replaces an atom of silicon in the structure, it uses four of its five valence electrons to form covalent bonds with silicon atoms. The fifth electron is supplied to the material, creating a negative charge. These are called n–type semiconductors. The added atoms are called **donor atoms** because they donate electrons to the material. The addition of donor atoms leaves the crystal uncharged overall because the additional electrons are associated with additional positive charges on the donor nuclei.

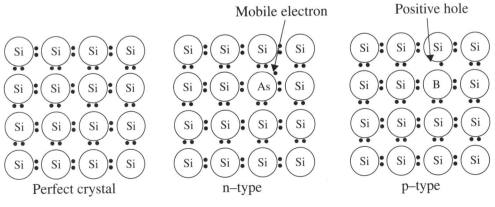

Mobile electron   Positive hole

Perfect crystal   n–type   p–type

In p–type semiconductors, the dopants are Group III (or 13) elements, such as boron and gallium (Ga) or indium (In), which have three electrons in the outer shell. When a boron atom replaces a silicon atom, it forms three electron pair bonds with three silicon atoms, but the fourth bond is incomplete as it has only one electron. The vacancy is called an **electron hole** and is positively charged, producing a p–type semiconductor. The added atoms are called **acceptor atoms** because they can accept electrons to fill the holes in the bonds.

A typical solar (photo–voltaic) cell consists of two layers of almost pure silicon; one has a trace of arsenic (n–type) and the other a trace of boron (p–type). The n–type has atoms with an extra electron which is relatively free to move where as the p–type layer has atoms short of an electron. When the two layers are placed together, the extra electron from the n–type moves to the p–type layer and pairs up. When sunlight strikes such a surface, the sun's energy is able to unpair the electrons which move back to the n–type layer. If an external circuit is present, the electron can flow back to the p–type layer. The advantages of solar cells are many. These include no moving parts, no liquids and no corrosive chemicals. They generate electricity as long as the sun is shining. The disadvantages include the need for large surfaces, the fact that pure silicon is very expensive and that the solar cells only work when the sun is shining and produce low power outputs (see Chapter 16, Section F.9).

A SOLAR POWERED GARDEN LIGHT

15.7 ELLINGHAM DIAGRAMS

E.7.1   Analyse Ellingham diagrams to predict the feasibility of reducing metal oxides.

© IBO 2001

Changes in free energy are related to enthalpy and entropy changes and the temperature by the Gibb's Free Energy Equation: $\Delta G° = \Delta H° - T\Delta S°$; it is the difference between the heat produced in a reaction and the energy demand due to the entropy factor. A negative free energy change implies a spontaneous reaction, that is one capable of doing useful work (the reverse is then true for non–spontaneous reactions; $\Delta G = 0$ for a reaction at equilibrium). $\Delta G°_f$, the change in free energy of formation of an element, in its stable state under standard conditions (of 298K and 1 atm pressure), is by definition, equal to zero. Also, ΔG values are not an indication of the speed of a reaction but rather of reaction spontaneity (see Chapter 6):

ΔH	$T\Delta S$	$\Delta G = \Delta H - T\Delta S$
– (minimum energy)	+ (maximum entropy)	$\Delta G = -$ (reaction spontaneous at all temperatures)
–	–	$\Delta G = -$ at low T
+	+	$\Delta G = -$ at high T
+	–	$\Delta G = +$ at all T

If one were to plot a graph of ΔG_f against temperature (K), the slope of the line would be equal to $-\Delta S$, provided ΔH and ΔS are independent of temperature, which is usually the case. Such graphs showing the energy changes in the conversion of an element to its oxides are known as Ellingham diagrams (see graphs below).

For the reaction of a metal M with oxygen to produce the metal oxide MO, e.g.:

$$2M_{(s)} + O_{2(g)} \Rightarrow 2MO_{(s)}$$

ΔH is negative (exothermic reaction) and ΔS is also negative since 1 mole of gas in the reactant is converted to solid product. Thus $-\Delta S$ is positive as shown by the upward slope in the graph below. Any sudden change in the slope is due to a change in ΔS as a result of a phase change such as at the melting point of the metal. Above the boiling point of the metal, for example at ~600 K in the case of Hg, ΔS is even more negative since 3 moles of gaseous reactants are being converted to solid product, giving rise to a steeper slope.

Consider the reduction by aluminium of chromium oxide, Cr_2O_3. The two equations to consider are:

$$2Cr_{(s)} + \tfrac{3}{2}O_{2(g)} \Rightarrow Cr_2O_{3(s)}$$

and

$$2Al_{(s)} + \tfrac{3}{2}O_{(g)} \Rightarrow Al_2O_{3(s)}$$

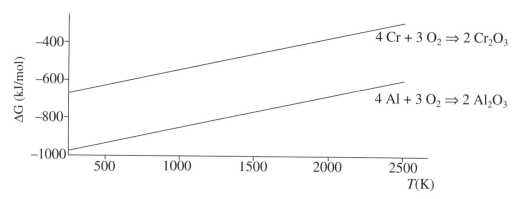

The line for oxidation of Cr is above that of Al. This means Cr_2O_3 is less stable compared to Al_2O_3 at all temperatures (since the lines do not cross) and Al will be able to reduce Cr_2O_3 to Cr. Thus, the lower the ΔG line on the Ellingham diagram, the more stable the compound. Hence the reduction of chromium(III) oxide by aluminium: $2\,Al + Cr_2O_3 \Rightarrow 2\,Cr + Al_2O_3$ is energetically feasible.

Ellingham diagram

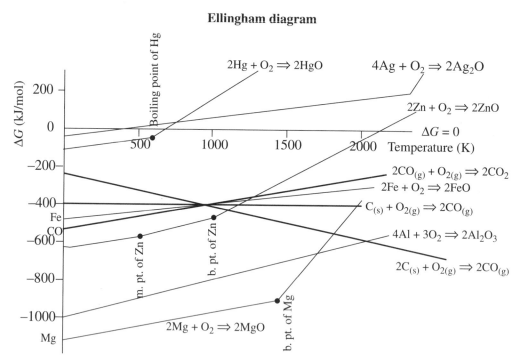

Three additional lines in the above graph include:

(1): $$2\,CO_{(g)} + O_{2(g)} \Rightarrow 2\,CO_{2(g)}$$

(2): $$C_{(s)} + O_{2(g)} \Rightarrow CO_{2(g)}$$

(3): $$2\,C_{(s)} + O_{2(g)} \Rightarrow 2\,CO_{(g)}$$

because these are often used to reduce metal oxides to metals.

In the oxidation of $C_{(s)}$ to $CO_{2(g)}$ (equation 2 above), the C/CO_2 line is more or less horizontal (because one mole of gaseous reactant is being converted to one mole gaseous product), whereas the line for the formation of CO from carbon (equation 3) has a positive change in entropy (because one mole of reactant gas is being converted to two moles of product gases) giving rise to the downward slope since $- \Delta S$ (given by the slope) is negative. On the other hand, the formation of CO_2 from CO line (equation 1) involves a decrease in entropy (since 3 moles reactant gases are converted to 2 moles of products; $\Delta S = -$) giving rise to a positive, upward slope. Note that all three lines meet at approximately 1000 K.

For a metal oxide to decompose to the metal, that is, $2MO_{(s)} \Rightarrow 2M_{(s)} + O_{2(g)}$, ΔG must be negative (for the reaction to be spontaneous). Thus, if the Ag/Ag_2O line is considered, ΔG is positive above ~400 K and thus silver is found as the metal rather than the oxide in nature. Similarly, mercury can be obtained by heating HgO to above 750 K, since above this temperature ΔG is positive for the Hg/HgO line.

The lower the line, the more stable the oxide. Hence if magnesium is heated with zinc oxide it will reduce to zinc, but the reverse reaction (reducing magnesium oxide with zinc) does not occur.

Ellingham diagrams are graphs of ΔG_f, the change in free energy of formation (kJ mol^{-1}) with temperature. These are useful in explaining and predicting the reduction of metal ores by carbon and carbon monoxide to the metal, that is, in the extraction of metals from their ores.

Note that the height of the line in an Ellingham diagram indicates the instability of the oxide (or the sulfide ore) since the higher the line, the more positive the ΔG (relatively speaking), the less spontaneous the formation of the oxide (or the sulfide).

Often, less reactive metals exist in nature as oxides or sulfides, e.g. Al_2O_3, Fe_2O_3, Fe_3O_4, ZnS, PbS, CuS, etc. Consider the blast furnace reactions. The coke undergoes combustion at the bottom of the furnace producing about 1900K temperature. According to the graph, CO is more stable compared to CO_2 at T > 1000K, that is, carbon reduces carbon dioxide to carbon monoxide only above 1000K. Thus, at 1900K, CO is formed. It cools as it rises up the furnace and at a temperature of about 1000K the CO/CO_2 line falls below that of the Fe/FeO line so that CO is able to reduce the iron oxide to iron.

The Al/Al_2O_3 line would not reach $\Delta G = 0$ until well above 5000K (meaning to decompose it by just heating would require well over 5000 K!). Also, this line is below all the carbon lines until over 2000 K. These temperatures are considered uneconomical by industry. Hence aluminium is obtained commercially by electrolysis.

The decomposition of ZnO to Zn and O_2 does not occur until over 2000 K. However, ZnO can be reduced to Zn using carbon monoxide at around 1200 K, because above 1200K, ΔG for the reaction $2 C_{(s)} + O_{2(g)} \Rightarrow 2 CO_{(g)}$ is more negative than for the reaction $2 Zn_{(s)} + O_{2(g)} \Rightarrow 2 ZnO_{(s)}$.

Similarly, for the reaction $2 Mg + O_2 \Rightarrow 2 MgO$, ΔG is negative well up to 2000 K and MgO does not break down even when heated to this high temperature. However, coke can reduce MgO to Mg (with the formation of CO) above 1900K since CO is more stable than MgO above that temperature. Note that whenever a phase change is involved, (e.g., boiling point or melting point), ΔS is more negative and ΔG therefore less negative, e.g., compare: $2 Mg_{(s)} + O_{2(g)} \Rightarrow 2 MgO_{(s)}$; $2 Mg_{(g)} + O_{2(g)} \Rightarrow 2 MgO_{(s)}$; the second reaction has a more negative ΔS.

The test for the extraction of a metal from its ore is whether or not the free energy change for the reaction is negative at a particular temperature. An Ellingham diagram allows us to find this out by looking at graphs rather than performing calculations.

15.8 MECHANISMS IN THE ORGANIC CHEMICALS INDUSTRY

E.8.1 Compare and discuss the mechanisms of thermal and catalytic cracking.

Thermal cracking involves a free-radical mechanism whereas catalytic cracking has an ionic mechanism.
© IBO 2001

Recall that most cracking is used to produce shorter chain products (for the production of fuels). **Catalytic cracking** involves breaking long–chain hydrocarbons into smaller ones using a catalyst mixture of silica, SiO_2, and alumina, Al_2O_3, at ~500 °C:

$$C_{12}H_{26} \Rightarrow C_9H_{20} + C_3H_6$$

Thermal cracking is used to convert alkanes into alkenes at high temperatures. Together with ethene, a mixture of products is usually formed. C_2H_4 and other alkenes are key starting materials for the preparation of a large number of other chemicals.

$$\text{e.g. } 2 CH_3CH_2CH_{3(g)} \Rightarrow CH_{4(g)} + CH_3CH=CH_{2(g)} + CH_2=CH_{2(g)} + H_{2(g)}$$

The thermal cracking takes place via a **free radical mechanism**. Recall that this mechanism involves three steps: initiation, propagation and termination. The thermal cracking of ethane can be used to show the free radical mechanism of the process:

1. **Initiation step:** Formation of free radicals – these are very reactive species containing unpaired electrons:

    $$C_2H_6 + heat \Rightarrow 2 \bullet CH_3$$

    The bond cleavage is more likely to occur between C–C bond (B.E.= 348 kJ/ mol) rather than C–H bond (B.E.=412 kJ/mol)

2. **Propagation step:** This is where one free radical is used up, but another produced in its place:

    $$C_2H_6 + \bullet CH_3 \Rightarrow CH_4 + \bullet C_2H_5$$

    $$\bullet C_2H_5 \Rightarrow C_2H_4 \text{ (alkene)} + \bullet H$$

    $$C_2H_6 + \bullet H \Rightarrow \bullet C_2H_5 + H_2$$

Ethene and hydrogen would be the main products.

3.   **Termination step:** This is where free radicals combine, e.g.:

$$\cdot H + \cdot CH_3 \rightarrow CH_4$$

A large hydrocarbon such as octane, C_8H_{18} decomposes in several ways:

$$C_8H_{18} \overset{heat}{\Rightarrow} C_8H_{16} + H_2$$

$$\Rightarrow C_4H_{10} + C_4H_8$$

$$\Rightarrow C_4H_8 + C_3H_6 + CH_4$$

Catalytic cracking breaks large molecules into small ones, but more importantly produces branched chain hydrocarbons with higher octane numbers which are more suitable as fuels. Catalytic cracking involves an **ionic mechanism** through the formation of carbocations (electron deficient carbons with a positive charge on them; also called carbonium ions). Because carbocations rearrange more easily than free radicals as a result of which catalytic cracking produces rearrangements much more readily than the free radical thermal cracking process does. Rearrangement takes place (since a tertiary carbocation is more stable than a secondary one which is more stable than a primary one) to form molecules with more branched chains so that if a carbocation is formed reactions such as those shown below take place:

$$CH_3-CH_2-CH_2-C^+H-CH_3 \Rightarrow CH_3-C^+H_2 + CH_2=CH-CH_3 \text{ (fragmentation)}$$

$$CH_3-C^+H_2 + R-H \Rightarrow CH_3-CH_3 + R^+ \text{ (hydride ion transfer)}$$

$$H_3C-CH_2-CH_2-\underset{\underset{H}{|}}{C^+}-CH_3 \Rightarrow H_3C-\underset{\underset{CH_2-CH_3}{|}}{C^+}-CH_3 \quad \text{(rearrangement)}$$

The first equation represents the cracking of the larger hydrocarbon into a smaller (alkene) molecules. The second one is in effect the using up of a carbocation and the production of another. The third equation is where rearrangement takes place to produce a branched chain molecule with a higher octane rating.

E.8.2   Describe the mechanism involved in the manufacture of low-density polyethene.

This is a free-radical mechanism.   © IBO 2001

Recall the addition polymerization for the formation of polyethene from ethene:

$$nCH_2 = CH_2 \Rightarrow -(CH_2-CH_2)_n-$$

It may be easy to assume that the π–bond in each ethene breaks to give the two bonds at the end of the molecule to form the macromolecular polymer. Evidence from kinetic studies of polymerization reactions is, however, necessary to elucidate the mechanisms for such reactions. Low density polyethene is made at high pressure (1500 atm), a temperature of 200°C and in the presence of organic peroxides which are a source of free radicals.

OPTION

$$nCH_2 = CH_2 \xrightarrow[\text{peroxides}]{200°C; \ 1500 \ atm} -(CH_2-CH_2)_n-$$

low density polyethene

Recall that a free radical mechanism involves initiation, propagation and termination steps; also, peroxides contain a very weak O–O bond in the R–O–O–R functional group.

Mechanism

1. **Initiation step:** Peroxides decompose to produce alkyl free radicals ($\cdot$R):

$$R-\underset{O}{\overset{\parallel}{C}}-O-O-\underset{O}{\overset{\parallel}{C}}-R \xrightarrow{\text{heat}} 2 \ R-\underset{O}{\overset{\parallel}{C}}-O\cdot \Longrightarrow 2\,CO_2 + 2R\cdot$$

2. **Propagation step:**

    The alkyl free radicals react with the alkene to produce a longer alkyl free radical:

    $$R\bullet + CH_2 = CH_2 \Rightarrow R-CH_2-CH_2\bullet$$

    The chains add successive ethene units to produce longer alkyl free radicals:

    $$R-CH_2-CH_2\bullet + CH_2{=}CH_2 \Rightarrow R-CH_2-CH_2-CH_2-CH_2\bullet$$

    Also: $R-CH_2-CH_2-CH_2-CH_2-R + \bullet R \Rightarrow R-CH_2-C\bullet H-CH_2-CH_2-R + RH$, which leads to chain branching.

3. **Termination step:** The alkyl free radicals either combine to form a longer chain molecule or the transfer of a hydrogen atom occurs to form a combination of an alkane and alkene:

    $$2R-CH_2-CH_2-CH_2-CH_2\bullet \Rightarrow (R-CH_2-CH_2-CH_2-CH_2)_2- \ \ \text{or}$$

    $$2R-CH_2-CH_2-CH_2-CH_2\bullet \Rightarrow R-CH_2-CH = CH-CH_3 + R-CH_2-CH_2-CH_2-CH_3$$

E.8.3 Outline the use of Ziegler-Natta catalysts in the manufacture of high-density polyethene.

The mechanism is ionic but details are not required.   © IBO 2001

High–density polyethene is formed at much lower pressures (5–7 atm) and lower temperatures in the presence of special catalysts. The polymerization produces linear, regular arrangements of groups along the chains which fit together much better in a crystal structure. These high density polymers thus have stronger van der Waal's forces. They have much higher melting points and are stiffer, harder, have a greater tensile strength and are chemically inert compared to low density, branched polymers with lower melting point, lower strength and chemical resistance which are thus less useful.

The **Ziegler–Natta catalysts** used in the production of high–density polymers are not soluble in alkane solvents. The reaction mixture is thus a heterogeneous one and polymerization takes place at the surface of the transition metal ion catalyst. As a result the process is also called **coordination polymerization** (because of the coordination/bonding between the unsaturated reactive center of the monomer and the transition metal). This polymerization uses an ionic mechanism but its details are not fully understood.

The typical compounds used as catalysts are: titanium (IV) chloride, $TiCl_4$, and triethylaluminium, $(C_2H_5)_3Al$. They react together to give an organotitanium compound $Ti–CH_2–CH_3$ which is believed to play a key role. The titanium is the site for the coordination with the alkene. Bonding between the partially positive metal and the alkene's π bond develops. This is followed by insertion of the alkene into the hydrocarbon chain bonded to the titanium atom.

$$Ti\overset{\delta+}{-}CH_2-CH_3 \qquad\qquad Ti\overset{\delta+}{-}CH_2-CH_2-CH_2-CH_3$$
$$CH_2{=}CH_2 \qquad\qquad\qquad CH_2{=}CH_2$$

15.9 THE CHLOR–ALKALI INDUSTRY

E.9.1   Discuss the production of chlorine by the electrolysis of sodium chloride.

Explain why an electrolytic process is required and why the diaphragm cell is preferable to the mercury cathode cell.   © IBO 2001

The **chlor–alkali** industry is the name given to a group of related industries that produce chlorine, sodium hydroxide and sodium carbonate. These chemicals are used in huge quantities in many different chemical processes. Cl_2 and $NaOH$ are made from the electrolysis of $NaCl_{(aq)}$ and it produces H_2 as a by product.

The production of chlorine and sodium hydroxide: Chlorine and sodium hydroxide are both made by the electrolysis of brine (salt water) by various commercial methods. First sodium chloride is obtained from deposits of rock salt which can be mined directly, but more often water is pumped into the deposits and the salt removed as brine. The resulting solution can be purified. If solid sodium chloride is required, it can be produced by crystallizing it out from the solution. Evaporated sea water can also be used for salt production.

The mercury cell process: Brine is continuously passed into a cell that has graphite anodes and a moving layer of mercury as the cathode. Chloride ions are discharged in preference to the hydroxide ions in water. However, in this cell sodium ions are discharged in preference to water or hydrogen ions owing to the use of mercury as the cathode rather than another material. Sodium reacts with the mercury, making an alloy known as an amalgam. The amalgam travels out of the cell into a chamber containing water. It is at this stage that sodium hydroxide is produced:

OPTION

Anode half reaction: $\qquad\qquad\qquad\quad 2\,Cl^- \Rightarrow Cl_{2\,(aq)} + 2e^-$

Cathode half reaction: $\quad 2\,Na^+_{(aq)} + 2e^- \Rightarrow 2\,Na_{(l)};\; 2\,Na_{(l)} + 2\,Hg_{(l)} \Rightarrow 2\,NaHg_{(l)}$

$$2\,NaHg_{(l)} + 2\,H_2O_{(l)} \Rightarrow 2\,Na^+_{(aq)} + 2\,OH^-_{(aq)} + 2\,Hg_{(l)} + H_{2(g)}$$

The overall equation for the reactions taking place is:

$$2\,NaCl_{(aq)} + 2\,H_2O_{(l)} \Rightarrow 2\,NaOH_{(aq)} + H_{2(g)} + Cl_{2\,(g)}$$

The chlorine gas produced by the oxidation of Cl^- at the anode is slightly impure owing to it being mixed with water vapor. The latter is removed by drying the gas with concentrated sulfuric acid.

The mercury cell

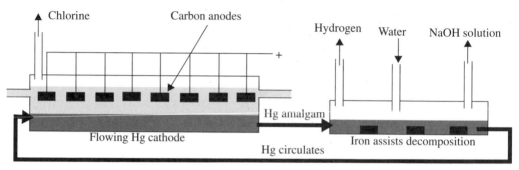

The diaphragm cell process: In a diaphragm cell, the anode and cathode are in two compartments separated by a diaphragm. Diaphragms were made of asbestos. Asbestos fibres, however, scar lung tissue and cause asbestosis. Thus, diaphragm cells tend to use ion-selective membrane technology. The anode is made from titanium, sometimes with a coating of platinum, and the cathode is made from steel. In the anode compartment, chlorine is given off by the oxidation of Cl^-:

$$2\,Cl^-_{(aq)} \Rightarrow Cl_{2(g)} + 2\,e^-$$

At the cathode, water is reduced to hydrogen gas:

$$2\,H_2O_{(l)} + 2\,e^- \Rightarrow 2OH^-_{(aq)} + H_{2(g)}$$

Hydroxide ions are formed, therefore the solution becomes increasingly alkaline. The overall result is that the brine loses its chloride ions and becomes richer in hydroxide ions as a result of electrolysis:

$$2\,NaCl_{(aq)} + 2\,H_2O_{(l)} \Rightarrow Cl_{2(g)} + H_{2(g)} + 2\,NaOH_{(aq)}$$

Several things, however, can occur unless the process is carefully monitored. In the cold, chlorine reacts with hydroxide ions; ClO^-, chlorate (I) ions are produced:

$$Cl_{2\,(aq)} + 2\,OH^-_{(aq)} \Rightarrow 2\,Cl^-_{(aq)} + ClO^-_{(aq)} + H_2O_{(l)}$$

If hydroxide ions reach the anode, they can be discharged. If this happens, oxygen is given off due to oxidation of water and the OH^- at the anode:

$$2\,H_2O_{(l)} \Rightarrow O_{2(g)} + 4\,H^+_{(aq)} + 4\,e^-$$

$$4\,OH^-_{(aq)} \Rightarrow 2\,H_2O_{(l)} + O_{2(g)} + 4\,e^-$$

This contaminates the chlorine and makes the isolation of pure chlorine more difficult. To avoid these problems, the brine in the anode compartment is kept at a slightly higher pressure than in the cathode compartment. This makes it less likely that the solution around the cathode will reach the anode. The membrane keeps the two solutions apart while allowing ions to move between them, thus keeping the current flowing.

The diaphragm cell

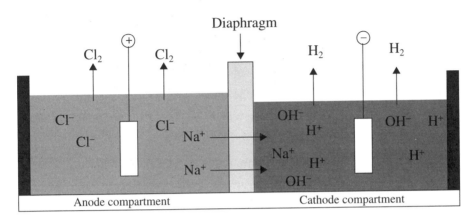

SUMMARY

The production of chlorine and sodium hydroxide is carried out by the electrolysis of a saturated salt solution called brine in two types of cells:

(i)   The mercury cell which uses a layer of mercury as the cathode; Na^+ ions are discharged at the cathode to produce Na which reacts with Hg to form an amalgam of sodium and mercury,

cathode half-reaction (reduction): $Na^+ + e^- \Rightarrow Na$; $Na + Hg \Rightarrow NaHg$ (amalgam)

$2\ NaHg_{(s)} + 2\ H_2O_{(l)} \Rightarrow 2\ Na^+_{(aq)} + 2\ OH^-_{(aq)} + 2\ Hg_{(l)} + H_{2(g)}$

anode half-reaction (oxidation): $2\ Cl^-_{(aq)} \Rightarrow Cl_{2(g)} + 2\ e^-$

(ii)   The diaphragm cell which separates the anode and the cathode by an ion-selective membrane,

anode half-reaction (oxidation): $2\ Cl^-_{(aq)} - 2\ e^- \Rightarrow Cl_{2(g)}$

cathode half-reaction (reduction): $2\ H_2O_{(l)} + 2\ e^- \Rightarrow H_{2(g)} + 2\ OH^-_{(aq)}$

In both cells, a solution of sodium hydroxide remains and is separated for commercial use.

E.9.2   Outline the importance of the products of this process.

The process produces sodium hydroxide with chlorine and hydrogen as by-products.

© IBO 2001

OPTION

Sodium chloride is readily available as a raw material. With the use of electrical energy, electrolysis of an aqueous solution of sodium chloride produces three very important chemicals, namely $Cl_{2(g)}$ produced at the anode due to the oxidation of the chloride ions, $H_{2(g)}$ produced at the cathode due to the reduction of H_2O (or H^+ ions from water) and sodium hydroxide left in solution :

$$2\ NaCl_{(aq)} + 2\ H_2O_{(l)} \Rightarrow Cl_{2(g)} + H_{2(g)} + 2\ NaOH_{(aq)}$$

Some uses of chlorine	Some uses of sodium hydroxide	Some uses of hydrogen
Manufacture of solvents	Inorganic chemicals	Foodstuffs - margarine
PVC manufacture	Organic chemicals	HCl manufacture
Bleaching paper products	Paper products - converting wood to pulp	Future potential use in fuel cells
Disinfecting drinking and swimming pool water	Aluminium industry	
Production of inorganic chemicals	Soap manufacture	

E.9.3   Discuss the environmental impact of this process.

Include reasons why the diaphragm cell has replaced the mercury-cathode cell in many parts of the world, and that knowledge of the effect on the ozone layer has led to reservations about the use of chlorine-containing solvents.   © IBO 2001

The amount of mercury escaping around a mercury cell plant is always controlled and minimised but almost inevitably some mercury enters the sodium hydroxide solution. Mercury reacts with many organic molecules and it is now established that organo–mercury compounds find their way into the food chain of animals.

Intake of mercury compounds results in a sickness called Minamata disease (first identified in this Japanese town). Mercury is converted to methyl–mercury ions by bacterial action, enters the food chain and ends up in fish, leading to biological magnification when fish is the main diet for people. Methyl–mercury compounds, can form strong covalent bonds to sulfur atoms in the –SH groups present in the cysteine units in some proteins, thus seriously altering their properties. Mercury poisoning can cause inflammation of gums, nausea, diarrhoea, kidney failure, blindness, damage to the brain and damage to the central nervous system!

Minamata disease has been largely responsible for the replacement of the mercury cell by the diaphragm cell. However, the use of an asbestos diaphragm presents problems of its own as it has been identified as causing respiratory tract cancer and asbestosis. Asbestos is considered to be responsible for cancer deaths, second only to cigarette related cancer deaths. Thus asbestos is no longer the only diaphragm material; a fluoropolymer akin to PTFE which incorporates sulphonated or carboxylated sites is used instead.

Amongst its many uses, chlorine is used in the manufacture of chlorine–containing solvents and CFCs. Besides their use as solvents, they are used as aerosol propellants, refrigerants in automobiles, home and commercial air conditioners, in refrigerators and freezers and in fire extinguishers. It is the high strength of the C–Cl and the C–F bonds that makes these molecules stable. This and their low densities make it possible for these substances to reach the upper atmosphere without decomposing. This is where a major concern arises because of the interference of CFCs with the ozone layer (see Chapter 14, Section D.2). Energy from ultra violet rays in the upper atmosphere is able to dissociate CFCs into free radicals, for example:

$$CCl_2F_2 + h\nu \Rightarrow \cdot CClF_2 + \bullet Cl$$

The formation of the extremely reactive chlorine free radical leads to reaction with ozone in the ozone layer:

$$\bullet Cl + O_3 \Rightarrow O_2 + \bullet ClO$$

The $\bullet$ClO radical can react with an oxygen atom to produce oxygen gas and the chlorine free radical:

$$\bullet ClO + O \Rightarrow O_2 + \bullet Cl$$

The overall effect is the conversion of ozone to diatomic oxygen leading to depletion of the ozone layer! The ozone layer is essential to the survival of species on Earth as it 'filters' out the harmful ultra violet rays, preventing them from reaching the Earth's surface. In nature, the formation and decomposition of O_3 happens in a dynamic, steady state which keeps the concentration of ozone in the ozone layer more or less constant via the action of the four following reactions:

$$O_2 + uv \Rightarrow 2\,O$$

$$O_2 + O \Rightarrow O_3$$

$$O_3 + uv \Rightarrow O_2 + O$$

$$O_3 + O \Rightarrow 2\,O_2$$

The presence of CFCs and other gases (such as NO_x from supersonic transports, etc.) has been found to be responsible for the destruction of O_3 in the ozone layer. As a result of the Montreal Protocol, the use of chlorinated solvents has been greatly curtailed.

QUESTIONS ON THE CORE MATERIAL

INITIAL OVERVIEW

1. Outline the abundance, occurrence and availability of sources of raw materials for the chemical industry.

2. Identify the factors that influence the establishment of a chemical industry in a particular location.

3. Outline the division of the chemical industry into intermediates and consumer products.

4. Discuss the increasing importance of biotechnology in chemical manufacture.

PRINCIPLES OF EXTRACTION AND PRODUCTION

5. Explain using the reactivity series why elements are rarely found free in nature and have to be extracted and processed before they can be used.

6. Outline the key steps involved in the extraction of a metal from its ore.

7. Outline the principles used in the physical separation of materials.

8. Discuss the chemical principles involved including energy requirements and use of catalysts in the extraction of the following substances from their ores:

    (a)   iron   (b)   chlorine   (c)   aluminium

METALS – IRON AND ALUMINIUM

9. State the main sources of iron.

10. Explain in detail the extraction of iron from its ore. Include the reactions that occur in the blast furnace. Write balanced equations for the various reactions, give the oxidation numbers of the elements involved and identify the oxidizing and reducing agents for each redox reaction.

11. Why is limestone added in the process of iron extraction and what happens to the products formed as a result?

12. Describe the conversion of iron into steel in the basic oxygen converter. Why is this process utilized once the iron is produced?

13. How and why is iron different from steel?

14. Describe the main properties and uses of steel.

15. Describe the principal uses of iron and steel.

16. Describe the production of pure alumina from bauxite. Explain the chemical processes involved in the reactions.

17. Discuss the production of aluminium by electrolysis of alumina (Al_2O_3) in molten cryolite (Na_3AlF_6). Explain the role of cryolite. Identify the electrode at which the metal is formed and explain why. Include the oxidation and reduction half reactions, the overall chemical reaction and identify the oxidizing and reducing agents. Account for the materials used in the construction of the cell and the choice of electrodes.

18. Describe the main properties of aluminium. What properties of aluminium make it useful in a wide range of consumer products?

19. Explain the principal uses of aluminium and compare these with the uses of iron and steel.

20. Why does aluminium not corrode as does iron? What advantages are there in using iron instead of aluminium?

21. Discuss the environmental impact of iron and aluminium production. Include the effects of mining of the ore, siting of the plant and recycling of the metals.

THE OIL INDUSTRY

22. Describe the importance of oil as a source of chemical feedstock.

23. Outline the removal of sulfur from crude oil.

23. Describe cracking and its products. Include catalytic cracking, thermal cracking and hydrocracking.

25. Describe the process of simple distillation.

26. Compare simple distillation with fractional distillation.

27. Describe the fractional distillation of oil.

28. Describe reforming processes and their products. Your answer should include isomerism (thermal and catalytic reforming), cyclization and aromatization.

29. Why is the process of reforming important from an industrial point of view?

30. State the uses of refinery products as feedstock for the organic chemical industry.

31. Describe how low and high density polyethene properties differ, based on their structures.

32. Define the terms isotactic and atactic with respect to polypropene.

33. Describe how the properties of polypropene depend on its structural features.

34. Compare thermoplastics and thermosets.

35. Describe how the properties of phenol-methanal plastics depend on the formation of cross-links in the polymer.

OPTION

SILICON

36. Describe the extraction and purification of silicon. Include balanced equations and explain the zone refining process with a simple schematic diagram.

37. Compare the electrical conductivity of a semiconductor with that of metals and non-metals.

38. Explain the doping of silicon to produce n–type and p–type semiconductors.

EXTENSION MATERIAL (HL ONLY)
ELLINGHAM DIAGRAMS

39. Explain how Ellingham diagrams can be used to predict the feasibility of reducing metal ores.

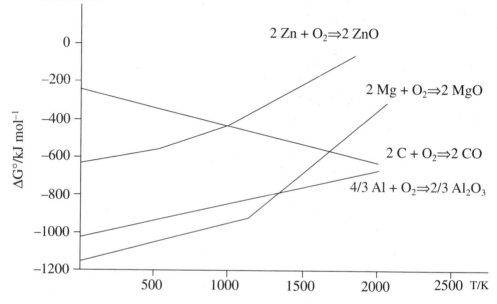

40. Why is there no change in gradient for Al_2O_3, one change in gradient in the MgO line and two changes in the gradients for the ZnO graph?

41. Explain which metal oxide will be reduced by aluminium at 1000 K and which will not and why.

42. Deduce the temperature above or below which magnesium oxide can be reduced by solid carbon and explain your reasoning.

EXTENSION MATERIAL (HL ONLY)
MECHANISMS IN THE ORGANIC CHEMICALS INDUSTRY

43. Discuss and compare the mechanisms of thermal and catalytic cracking.

44. Describe the mechanism involved in the manufacture of low density polythene.

45. Outline the use of Ziegler-Natta catalysts in the manufacture of high density polyethene.

EXTENSION MATERIAL (HL ONLY)
THE CHLOR–ALKALI INDUSTRY

46. Explain why an electrolysis process is required for the production of chlorine from sodium chloride.

47. What are the products of the electrolysis of molten sodium chloride and why are these different from the electrolysis of aqueous sodium chloride? Give the respective anode and cathode reactions to explain your answer.

48. Describe the production of chlorine by the electrolysis of sodium chloride by two methods. Explain which one is preferred and why.

49. Outline the importance of the products of the electrolysis of aqueous sodium chloride.

50. Discuss the environmental impact of the processes used for the production of chlorine, sodium hydroxide and hydrogen from sodium chloride.

OPTION

Option E: Chemical Industries

FUELS AND ENERGY (Option F)

16

Chapter contents

The development of human society has been directly related to the ability to use and manipulate fuels for energy production. This option considers the chemical principles and environmental issues associated with the use of fossil fuels, and nuclear and solar energy. © IBO 2001

16.1 ENERGY SOURCES

F.1.1   State desirable characteristics of energy sources.

These include energy released at reasonable rates (neither too fast nor too slow) and minimal pollution.

F.1.2   Outline current and potential energy sources.

Consider fossil tuels, nuclear (fission and fusion), electrochemical cells, solar energy and alternative sources (eg wind, tidal, geothermal).   © IBO 2001

Energy is the capacity to do work. The sun is the source of most of the energy on the Earth. Photosynthesis in green plants and certain bacteria converts the radiant energy into chemical energy which is stored in sugars and other compounds of carbon. The plants then become the source of energy for living things. Solar energy also provides heat energy which causes evaporation of water which then gains **potential energy** due to its position. The potential energy is converted into **kinetic energy** (energy of motion) of a flowing stream or river which can be harnessed to run turbines to produce electricity. Potential and kinetic energy are considered types of energy. Rain water by itself releases energy at too slow a rate and dams are built to store the potential energy, which is then released at a reasonable rate. Thus, the quality of energy is an important factor in determining the usefulness of energy. Since, according to the second law of thermodynamics, whenever energy is used, some is always lost into the environment as a less useful form of energy.

In order for energy sources to be useful, these must involve processes which move towards lower energy states and release energy at reasonable rates. A primary source of energy is where only one transformation is carried out to obtain heat, for example, in the burning of natural gas or coal on site. The burning converts coal or gas via chemical combustion to heat. A secondary source of energy requires more than one transformation. Also, often long distance transportation is involved, as in the production of electricity by burning coal or oil, producing steam and turning turbines to produce electricity. Thus, heating a house with oil is far more efficient than using electricity as there is much less wastage of energy (second law of thermodynamics).

A **renewable energy** source is considered a permanent energy source, that can be replenished as it is used (such as solar, wind, tidal). A non–renewable energy source, on the other hand, is considered to be a temporary source; one which is depleted as it is used such as coal, oil and natural gas.

Compounds of high potential energy in nature are particularly valuable as fuel because of their very high quality. Fossil fuels, such as natural gas, coal, gasoline and oil, are mostly carbon (as in coal) or hydrocarbons (as in methane, propane, octane, etc.) result from the anaerobic decay of prehistoric plants and animals. On combustion, these produce carbon dioxide and water and a great amount of energy. Thus, hydrocarbons such as octane in petroleum deposits produce much useful heat on combustion :

$$C_8H_{18(l)} + 12.5\ O_{2(g)} \Rightarrow 9\ H_2O_{(l)} + 8\ CO_{2(g)};\ \Delta G^\theta = -5272\ kJ\ mol^{-1}$$

These are all, however, non–renewable sources of energy. Other high quality energy forms include solar energy, wind energy, tidal/wave power and fissile materials such as U–235 and Pu–239. Besides dispersed rainwater, the energy stored in oceans is low quality heat which cannot be harnessed easily, although research is ongoing in this area.

Solar energy has many advantages including being fairly non–polluting and it is available freely during sunlight. However, a variation in sunlight is caused by seasons, geography, cloud cover and of course day and night. As a result, solar energy needs to be collected and requires efficient storage for use at nights and under cloudy conditions. Solar energy is harnessed in several ways. These include passive solar heating which involves designing buildings with windows positioned to capture the maximum amount of heat, using materials which facilitate the process of heat collection and storing the energy collected for use at night. Active solar heating involves using solar collectors placed on the roofs and sides of buildings to capture the maximum amount of solar radiation. The heat is stored and used when necessary. Solar energy can also be used directly by solar or photovoltaic cells. Solar energy can also be used to electrolyse water to produce hydrogen gas (for use in fuel cells), for charging batteries, pumping water to reservoirs with higher potential energy etc. Also, lenses or mirrors can be used to concentrate solar radiation.

In addition to the radiation (light) energy and thermal (heat) energy from the sun which must be stored for continuous use, other forms of energy on the Earth include:

(1)   **Chemical energy** is released during a chemical reaction. Chemical energy can also be converted to electrical energy in electrochemical cells (batteries) and fuel cells.

(2)   **Nuclear energy,** results from fission or fusion. Fission, the bombardment of U–235 or P–239 by neutrons to split it into atoms of lighter elements produce the uncontrolled energy in nuclear fission bombs. Subsequently this has been harnessed to produce electrical energy, however, this requires controlling the rate of fission and the amount of heat generated. Control rods (made of cadmium or graphite which are neutron absorbers), between the fuel rods containing the fissile material, are designed to control the rate of fission. The coolant (water or heavy water) functions as a moderator (some nuclear power plant use graphite as a moderator). It slows the neutrons produced by the nuclear reaction, making it possible for more fission to take place. It cools the fuel rods and prevents the core of a nuclear reactor from melting as well as removing the heat.

Fusion, the source of the sun's energy, has yet to be harnessed efficiently enough on Earth to produce energy. Technical problems include producing the incredibly high temperatures (around $10^8 °C$) and holding the plasma together for a long enough time for fusion to take place. So far the energy required to heat the plasma and maintain the confinement has been greater than the energy released. The hydrogen bomb is an example of unconfined nuclear fusion.

(3)   **Wind, hydropower** and **biomass** are all indirect forms of renewable solar energy. The most common wind generator consists of two or three blades on a horizontal axis resembling airplane propellers. Although complicated to manufacture and

OPTION

needing high wind speeds to start, the blades can rotate at up to six times the speed of the prevailing wind. Commercial development of wind generators requires windy sites which are not always readily available. The advantages of wind power include its cost (it is relatively cheap), its non–polluting nature and that it is an infinite resource. Disadvantages include its variable power, possible changes in weather if used on a large scale and the need to store energy for use when no wind is blowing.

(4)   **Tidal** ('moon') power is a potential source of energy. One disadvantage is that it is not a continuous source of energy since electricity can only be generated when the tides are coming in or going out, thus requiring energy storage.

(5)   **Geothermal** energy from the interior of the earth which is heated by gravitational forces and natural radioactivity is used commercially in places such as California, Iceland and New Zealand.

An experimental wind power station in Western Australia

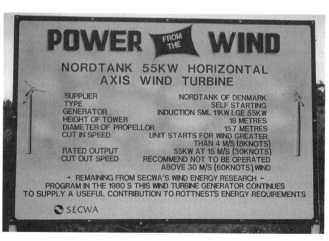

16.2 FOSSIL FUELS

F.2.1   Describe the formation and characteristics of coal, oil and natural gas. © IBO 2001

Fossil fuels have been produced from the slow decomposition of plant and animal matter over millions of years. These are naturally occurring carbon or hydrocarbon deposits, formed from the remains of once living organisms that are used as fuels. Petroleum, natural gas and coal are fossil fuels.

COAL is a highly complex substance occurring in large underground deposits and consisting of carbon and various carbon compounds. Coal was formed from plants in vast forests and swamps that covered large areas of the world in the geological past. Coal is solidified plant material which has been deposited in rock layers, has undergone partial decay and has been subjected to geological heat and pressure from the over–laying rocks over periods of millions of years. Energy stored in coal is originally from the sun via photosynthesis.

Coal is a readily combustible rock containing between 40 and 98% carbon with varying amounts of volatile materials and some moisture. Volatile matter includes oxides of carbon, hydrogen gas, methane and other hydrocarbons, ammonia and hydrogen sulfide. Mineral matter includes clay, iron sulfide, carbonates ($CaCO_3$, $FeCO_3$) and sand (SiO_2, which can be present in very large quantities – up to a third). Thus besides carbon, coal is made up of the elements H, O, N, S plus smaller amounts of other elements. Coal can contain up to 5% sulfur present as FeS_2 and organically bonded. Coal with higher percentage of sulfur is considered 'dirty' fuel because of the SO_2 pollution it generates, leading to acid rain.

Coal is analyzed on the basis of four items: its water content, mineral impurity (ash), volatile materials and fixed carbon content. The last two are the principal contributors of energy. Coal quality increases in rank as the percentage of carbon in the coal increases. The ratio of hydrogen to carbon atoms in coal is of the order of 0.7 and the compounds present are mainly unsaturated closed ring aromatic compounds.

The main types of coal are:

1.   **Peat** is the first step in changing organic matter into coal, where wood fragments can still be seen; it has low carbon content and heat value and high moisture content.

2.   **Lignite** is also low grade coal; it contains up to 40% moisture and is of low heat value.

3.   **Sub–bituminous** coal is black coal; it contains up to 30% moisture and is used primarily for thermal generation.

4.   **Bituminous** or ordinary coal is found to be the most abundant; it contains up to 86% carbon and is used for domestic and industrial purposes.

5.   **Anthracite** or hard coal contains up to 98% carbon by mass; it has a brilliant lustre and burns slowly with a blue flame.

OPTION

Sources of Coal: Most of the world's coal is found in the northern hemisphere, with China, Russia, Western Europe and the US accounting for 70% of the world's known recoverable reserves (meaning 80% of the total; the last 20% is assumed to be too difficult and expensive to recover).

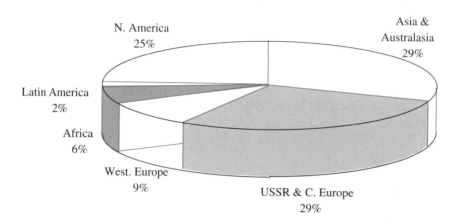

World Coal Reserves (1990)

It is estimated that the world has about 300 to 350 years supply of recoverable coal reserves. Small, labor intensive mines should stretch this further, as is the case in China and parts of the former Soviet Republics which have numerous local coal pits.

Petroleum or crude oil is a dark, thick useless mixture of over 200 useful hydrocarbons (with smaller quantities of other materials). Petroleum contains gases and solids as well as liquids.

Whereas coal is derived from plants, the origin of petroleum seems to be marine organisms, called plankton, as it is almost always found in rocks of oceanic origin formed 50 to 500 million years ago. As a result of weathered rock materials being carried to the sea, the animal remains were embedded inside the earth. Under anaerobic conditions (low concentrations of oxygen) and high pressures from rocks these animal remains changed into hydrocarbon residues producing crude oil. Earth movements must have caused migration of crude oil through porous rock since it is sometimes found away from its places of formation. This is the case for the oil fields of the Middle East, North Sea and North America where the petroleum was trapped between porous and impermeable rock.

Crude oil from wells is a dark, foul–smelling liquid. It contains straight and branched–chain saturated hydrocarbons (alkanes), cycloalkanes, aromatic compounds and compounds of N, O and S in smaller quantities. It can contain between 1 and 5% sulfur, which can be a source of SO_2 pollution and so is normally removed before use. Crude oil is easy to transport as it is a liquid. However, it contains more impurities than natural gas but is more abundant and is a dirtier fuel than natural gas. Not much energy is required to either pump oil or transport it in pipelines or tankers (although the gigantic problems of tanker crashes and pipeline leakages can lead to environmental catastrophes).

Petroleum resources are difficult to assess for several reasons: (1) major oil companies have the technology to provide estimates but may wish to keep these secret and (2) exploration costs vary so that investment in searching for new resources is possible only when the price is high. Rough estimates range from 30 to 50 years supply of recoverable petroleum resources world wide. The Middle East has over 50% of proven oil reserves and over 30% of global production. The thirteen Organization of Petroleum Exporting Countries (OPEC) have about three quarters of the world reserves and produce just over 50% of global needs.

Natural gas is formed from the decomposition that produced crude oil and coal deposits. It is a mixture of gaseous hydrocarbons, mostly methane, with smaller amounts of other gases such as nitrogen and carbon dioxide, hydrogen sulfide and low boiling point hydrocarbon liquids such as pentanes. It is found trapped under pressure in underground reservoirs capped with impermeable rock. With the availability of tankers which can carry liquefied natural gas (LNG), the use of natural gas has increased, but reserves are considered to be less than for crude oil. Of the fossil fuels, natural gas is in the shortest supply; reserves are expected to decline over the next 30 years or so.

Natural gas is considered an excellent fuel because it is clean–burning with no solid residue, which is easy and cheap to transport and has a higher heat output than most other fuels. Impurities in natural gas are easily removed. These include water vapor (removed using solid dry agents), CO_2 and H_2S (both acidic and removed by a reaction with a base such as hydroxylamines). If natural gas contains more than 95% methane, such as that in the North Sea fields, it is called **dry natural gas.**

F.2.2   Determine and compare the enthalpies of combustion of coal, oil and natural gas.

Calculations could be made using enthalpies of formation or from experimental data. Cross reference with 15.1.   © IBO 2001

The **standard enthalpy change of combustion,** ΔH^θ_{comb} is the heat evolved when one mole of a substance is completely burnt in oxygen under standard conditions; ΔH^θ_{comb} is always negative:

$$C_{(graphite)} + O_{2\,(g)} \Rightarrow CO_{2\,(g)}; \qquad \Delta H^\theta_{comb} = -393.5 \text{ kJ mol}^{-1}$$

$$CH_{4\,(g)} + 2\,O_{2\,(g)} \Rightarrow CO_{2\,(g)} + 2\,H_2O_{(l)}; \quad \Delta H^\theta_{comb} = -890.4 \text{ kJ mol}^{-1}$$

The enthalpy of combustion of a fuel can be determined in the laboratory using calorimetry. For example, a known mass of octane, C_8H_{18}, liquid (found in gasoline) can be burnt and the heat produced used to raise temperature of a known mass of water. Knowing also the specific heats of water and the container, the enthalpy of combustion can be calculated. The diagram shows a simplified version of this device, which is known as a 'bomb calorimeter'.

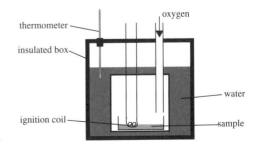

EXAMPLE

Experimentally it is found that when 1.00 g of octane is burnt, it raises the temperature of 200 g of water by 27.2 °C. The mass of the calorimeter is 135 g. The specific heat of water is 4.184 J g^{-1} °C^{-1} and the specific heat of the calorimeter is 0.840 J g^{-1} °C^{-1}. Calculate the enthalpy of combustion of octane.

SOLUTION

Heat produced by the combustion of 1.00 g of octane

= heat absorbed by the water + heat absorbed by the calorimeter

= (mass × specific heat × ΔT)$_\text{water}$ + (mass × specific heat × ΔT)$_\text{calorimeter}$

= (200. g × 4.184 $\frac{\text{J}}{\text{g °C}}$ × 27.2°C) + (135 g × 0.840 $\frac{\text{J}}{\text{g °C}}$ × 27.2°C)

= 22.76 + 3.08 kJ

= 25.8(4) kJ

Thus 1.00 g of octane (M_r = 114.3) produces 25.8(4) kJ
Therefore 1 mol produces 2950 kJ and ΔH_comb = −2950 kJ (3 significant figures).

This is much less than the literature value of −5512 kJ due to heat loss to the surroundings.

$$C_8H_{18\,(l)} + \frac{25}{2}\,O_{2\,(g)} \Rightarrow 8\,CO_{2\,(g)} + 9\,H_2O_{(l)}; \Delta H^\theta{}_\text{comb} = -5512 \text{ kJ mol}^{-1}$$

Note that much less energy per mol is produced by methane compared with octane since fewer bonds are broken and made during its combustion process.

The enthalpy of combustion depends on two factors:

- the number of bonds being broken and made (i.e. the size of the molecule) and
- the type of bonds being broken.

Comparing the enthalpies of combustion of methane and methanol:

$$CH_{4\,(g)} + O_{2\,(g)} \Rightarrow CO_{2\,(g)} + 2\,H_2O_{(l)}; \Delta H^\circ{}_\text{comb} = -890.4 \text{ kJ mol}^{-1}$$

$$CH_3OH_{\,(l)} + \frac{3}{2}\,O_{2\,(g)} \Rightarrow CO_{2\,(g)} + 2\,H_2O_{(l)}; \Delta H^\circ{}_\text{comb} = -715.0 \text{ kJ mol}^{-1}$$

Both produce the same amount of products, but in methanol there is one oxygen bonded to the other atoms. Thus when methanol burns, fewer bonds are made in the products in this case producing less energy than when methane burns.

F.2.3   Outline the composition and characteristics of the crude oil fractions used for fuel.

Students should have general, rather than specific, knowledge about the types of compounds found in each fraction, the boiling point range and the uses of the fractions.   © IBO 2001

Fractions	Carbon chain Composition	Boiling Point Range, °C	Major Uses
Gaseous Hydrocarbons	$C_1 - C_4$ (CH_4 is main component)	0 – 20 (gases)	Gaseous fuels for automobiles, cooking, domestic and industrial heating; CH_4 used for producing H_2 for Haber process.
Petroleum ether or naptha	$C_5 - C_7$	20 –100 (liquids)	Solvents for varnishes, dry cleaning; as a cracking stock for methane.
Gasoline	$C_5 - C_{12}$	40 – 175 (readily vaporize in car engines)	Fuels for internal combustion engines.
Kerosene oil	$C_{12} - C_{18}$	175 – 300 (liquids)	Jet engine and diesel fuel.
Gas oil or diesel oil	$C_{18} - C_{24}$	300 – 400 (liquids)	Diesel fuel, cracking stock to produce gasoline.
Lubricating oil, wax oil, greases	$C_{20} - C_{30}$	non–volatile fraction	Lubricants, cracking stock.
Paraffin wax	$C_{25} - C_{40}$	high boiling point solids	Candles, packaging, polishing wax, petroleum jelly, water proofing.
Residue, bitumen	$> C_{30}$	high boiling point solids	Asphalt (road surfaces), roofing, water proofing.

F.2.4   Describe how the components of a hydrocarbon fuel relate to its octane rating.

Octane rating is a measure of the ability of a fuel to resist 'knocking' when burnt in a standard test engine. A fuel is rated relative to heptane (rating of 0) and 2,2,4-trimethylpentane (rating of 100). The role of lead additives in fuels and the role of aromatic compounds in unleaded fuels should be mentioned.   © IBO 2001

The ability of a gasoline to perform in an internal combustion engine is rated according to its **octane number** or **rating**. The octane rating is a measure of the ability of a fuel to resist 'knocking' when burnt in a standard test engine. The more knocking a fuel causes, the poorer the fuel, the lower its octane rating. Thus, octane rating is a measure of the

OPTION

burning efficiency of a fuel. It is found, for example, that straight chain hydrocarbons such as heptane are poor fuels (and assigned an octane rating of zero). 2,2,4 – trimethylpentane is a very efficient fuel and is assigned a value of 100. It is found that aromatic compounds have high octane ratings.

Straight chain hydrocarbons with low octane ratings are converted into branch–chain and aromatic compounds with higher octane ratings by one of two methods:

1. **Isomerization**: This converts straight–chain to better burning branch–chain hydrocarbon molecules by heating with $AlCl_3$ as a catalyst.

$$CH_3-CH_2-CH_2-CH_2-CH_2-CH_2-CH_3 \longrightarrow CH_3-CH_2-\underset{\underset{CH_3}{|}}{\overset{\overset{CH_3}{|}}{C}}-CH_2-CH_3$$

2. **Reforming** (or **plat–forming** if Pt is used as a catalyst):

    This converts straight chain alkanes and cycloalkanes into higher octane aromatic compounds:

C_7H_{16}	$\Rightarrow$	$C_6H_5CH_3$	$+$ 4 H_2
heptane		methyl benzene	
C_6H_{12}	$\Rightarrow$	C_6H_6 + 3 H_2	
cyclohexane		benzene	

The addition of organo lead compounds such as tetraethyl lead (TEL) to gasoline (at around 0.1% by volume) improves octane rating. Also, by forming a fine lead coat on the valves, engine performance is improved. The combustion products of such organo lead compounds are almost all toxic, particularly to children and their use has been largely discontinued. They have been replaced by aromatic compounds and other additives.

F.2.5   Explain the processes of coal gasification and liquification.

Gasification produces synthesis gas and liquification produces liquid hydrocarbons. Relevant equations should be used. Advantages include the elimination of SO_2 pollution and the ease of transportation. The main disadvantage is the energy cost of the processes. © IBO 2001

Coal gasification is the most economical way of converting dirty coal into clean burning gaseous fuel.

It involves four steps:

1. **Hydrogasification**; coal is reacted with superheated steam between 500–1000 °C to produce carbon monoxide and hydrogen gas;

$$C_{(s)} + H_2O_{(g)} \overset{heat}{\Rightarrow} CO_{(g)} + H_{2(g)} \text{ (+ impurities)}$$

The impurities are collected and removed. The mixture of CO and H_2, is called **synthesis gas**, and is often directly used in industry as a fuel.

2. **Catalytic increase of hydrogen gas:** The coal gas is reacted with more steam to increase the amount of hydrogen:

$$CO_{(g)} + H_2O_{(g)} \Rightarrow CO_{2(g)} + H_{2(g)}$$

3. The **removal of impurities** such as acidic carbon dioxide gas and water and desulfurization, that is removal of the hydrogen sulfide gas. The H_2S gas can be oxidized to sulfur and sold as a by–product.

4. **Catalytic Methanation**: The water gas with the increased hydrogen (produced in step 2) is passed over a heated catalyst:

$$3 H_{2(g)} + CO_{(g)} \Rightarrow CH_{4(g)} + H_2O_{(g)}$$

Note that this reaction is the exact reverse of forming H_2 gas for the Haber process.

The water vapor is removed, leaving behind clean burning, high energy value methane fuel, called **Synthetic Natural Gas (SNG).**

Advantages of coal gasification include the elimination of pollution by sulfur dioxide (and thus acid rain) and particulates, and, the ease with which gaseous or liquid fuels can be transported. However, a major disadvantage is that the process requires about 30% of the energy content of the coal for the conversion!

Coal Gasification Process Summary

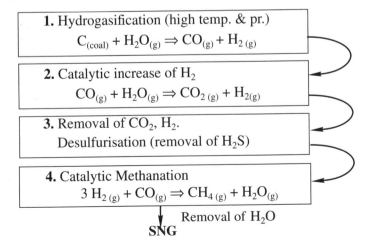

Coal liquification turns coal into synthetic liquid fuels such as methanol or gasoline. The starting point in the **Fischer–Tropsch** process are the gasification products created when coal is heated with superheated steam between 500 – 1000°C to produce CO and hydrogen gas:

$$C_{(s)} + H_2O_{(g)} \Rightarrow CO_{(g)} + H_{2\,(g)}$$

This mixture is passed over an iron or cobalt catalyst to form a variety of liquid fuels:

$$CO_{(g)} + H_{2\,(g)} \Rightarrow HCHO_{(g)};\ \text{methanal}$$

$$HCHO_{(g)} + H_{2(g)} \Rightarrow CH_3OH_{(l)};\ \text{methanol}$$

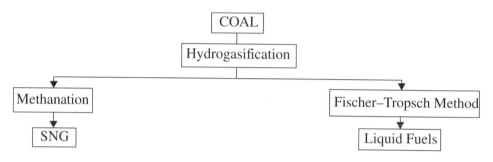

It is the amount of hydrogen introduced that determines whether the product is alkanal or alkanol. By varying the conditions of the reaction, higher molar mass alkanols and hydrocarbons can be formed. Thus the complex coal molecules are broken down by the coal gasification process and converted into useful fuels by the Fischer–Tropsch process. This expensive process, developed in Germany, is extensively used in places such as South Africa where coal is plentiful and oil resources scarce.

In the **Bergius process**, coal is ground to a powder, mixed in hot solvent and treated with hydrogen gas at high temperature and pressure in the presence of a platinum catalyst. The unsaturated hydrocarbons in coal become saturated and under heat these break into smaller molecules. Thus coal changes to a mixture of hydrocarbons (synthetic crude oil) that can be refined into fractions. The Bergius process yields hydrocarbons (**Synthetic Natural Liquid, SNL**) that fall into the gasoline, diesel and jet fuel range. A general equation for the Bergius process can be written as:

$$n\ C_{(coal)} + (n+1)\ H_{2(g)} \xrightarrow{\text{catalyst, Pt}} C_nH_{2n+2}$$

The process can also proceed via methanol produced by the Fischer-Tropsch process, which is then dehydrated to give $C_5 – C_{12}$ hydrocarbons, for example:

$$6\ CH_3OH_{(l)} \Rightarrow C_6H_{12\,(l)} + 6\ H_2O_{(l)}$$

Note that the usual route to methanol synthesis involves the reaction:

$$CO_{(g)} + 2\ H_{2\,(g)} \xrightarrow[\text{catalyst}]{400°C,\ \text{high T}} CH_3OH_{(l)}$$

F.2.6   Describe how the burning of fossil fuels produces pollutants.

The primary pollutants are CO, CO₂, SO₂, NOₓ particulates (fly ash) and
hydrocarbons.   © IBO 2001

Although coal is the most plentiful fossil fuel, it is also the most polluting and produces CO_2, SO_2 (leading to acid rain) and particulates (fly ash), and is therefore considered a dirty fuel. Because coal contains carbon, (complete) combustion produces carbon dioxide. Although CO_2 is part of the cycle involving animal and plant life through respiration and photosynthesis, the industrial revolution has seen the percentage of CO_2 in the atmosphere increase by 7.4% by volume from 1900 to 1970 because of fossil fuel combustion (see Chapter 14).

Excess carbon dioxide in the atmosphere has a couple of detrimental effects:

1. CO_2 is an acidic (non–metal) oxide; it can thus increase acidity of soils and cause stone leprosy (eating away of basic rock such as marble) due to acid rain:

$$CO_{2(g)} + H_2O_{(l)} \rightleftharpoons H_2CO_{3(aq)} \rightleftharpoons H^+_{(aq)} + HCO^-_{3(aq)}$$

2.   It can increase the temperature of the atmosphere through the Greenhouse Effect which is the trapping of heat in the atmosphere. $CO_{2(g)}$ in the atmosphere behaves like glass or plastic on a greenhouse by acting as a one way filter allowing high energy, shorter wave length radiation to penetrate the atmosphere, but absorbing and re-radiating the longer wavelength radiation toward the earth, thus raising atmospheric temperature.

Coal contains between 0.5 and 5% sulfur and the combustion of coal produces SO_2 pollution:

$$S_{(coal)} + O_{2(g)} \Rightarrow SO_{2(g)}$$

Approximately 80% of SO_2 pollution comes from coal burning power plants. Because it is possible to remove sulfur from coal either by **pre–combustion** or, more commonly, by **post–combustion**, concentrations of SO_2 are decreasing. The pre-combustion method involves washing coal – finely ground coal is washed with water. This removes FeS_2, but not organically bonded sulfur. The post–combustion method removes the SO_2 after burning the coal but before releasing it to the atmosphere and involves adding limestone to the furnace. The heat produced decomposes the limestone to calcium oxide:

$$CaCO_{3(s)} + heat \Rightarrow CaO_{(s)} + CO_{2(g)}$$

The highly basic CaO reacts with the acidic SO_2 gas to produce solid calcium sulfite, $CaSO_3$, which is removed as waste slurry, in a **scrubber**.

Particulates are the solid particles suspended or carried in the air and produced as smoke and dust by the combustion of coal, petroleum etc. **Fly ash** is the particulate product of coal combustion. Coal is pulverized (crushed to powder) and used as fuel while most of the ash is carried away in the exhaust gases as a finely divided gray

OPTION

powder called fly ash. It consists of carbon and oxides of Fe, Mg, Ca, Al, S, Ti, P, Na, Ni and sulfates. 5 to 15% of the initial mass of coal appears as fly ash in gaseous emissions or as other solid waste from a coal plant. It represents those elements which are converted into solid oxides on combustion. Because these are metal oxides, they tend to be basic and on dissolving in water produce basic water pollutants.

Sulfur containing compounds in petroleum are removed because, amongst other problems, the combustion of fuels from petroleum produces sulfur dioxide if the sulfur is not removed. This is done by reacting petroleum with hydrogen gas under pressure, to produce acidic H_2S gas which is easily removed.

Incomplete combustion of gasoline in automobiles is the major source of carbon monoxide (CO), nitrogen oxides (NO_x), hydrocarbon and particulate pollution. This happens when insufficient oxygen in air is present for complete combustion or if the air and fuel are not properly mixed as is often the case when a car engine is not adequately tuned. Two major problems with CO production from human activity is localization (produced in small high traffic areas) and high emission peaks (at rush hours and in traffic jams).

CO interferes with oxygen transport by binding strongly with the hemoglobin:

$$hemoglobin + O_2 \rightleftharpoons oxyhemoglobin$$

$$hemoglobin + CO \Rightarrow carboxyhemoglobin\ (COHb)$$

COHb loses its ability to carry oxygen gas, leading to metabolic poisoning. It deprives body cells of essential oxygen leading to asphyxiation. In the presence of CO, there is oxygen depletion; the heart must pump faster leading to shortness of breath, headaches and in some cases death through respiratory failure.

Most human sources of NO_x pollution are emissions of $NO_{(g)}$ caused by high temperatures in automobile engines (there is no reaction between nitrogen and oxygen gas in the air).

$$N_{2\,(g)} + O_{2\,(g)} \xrightarrow{\text{high temperature}} 2\,NO_{(g)}$$

This is a colorless, odorless, nonflammable, toxic, reactive gas which, in the air, is rapidly converted to NO_2:

$$2\,NO_{(g)} + O_{2(g)} \Rightarrow 2\,NO_{2(g)}$$

NO_2 is a toxic, brown, choking gas which is a necessary component of photochemical smog, the type sometimes experienced in Los Angeles and Mexico City. The presence of solar radiation photodissociates $NO_{2(g)}$:

$$NO_{2(g)} \xrightarrow{\text{u.v.}} \bullet NO_{(g)} + O\bullet_{(g)}$$

The formation of the **oxygen free radical** is the key to the series of reactions which produce smog, (and including chemicals such as ozone and PAN, peroxyacylnitrate, a powerful lachrymator which causes eyes to produce tears in high traffic areas).

Automobiles in many countries use a catalytic converter to reduce both NO and CO emissions. Using rhodium, an expensive transition metal, as a catalyst, unburned hydrocarbons, CO and NO are converted to CO_2, H_2O and N_2 gas:

$$2\ CO_{(g)} + 2\ NO_{(g)} \Rightarrow 2\ CO_{2\ (g)} + N_{2\ (g)}$$

A large part of hydrocarbon pollution comes from the combustion of volatile petroleum fuels. Hydrocarbons are released when these fuels from the production stage are transferred to an automobile gasoline tank and through exhaust gases which always contain some unburned hydrocarbon fuels.

The production of pollutants by the automobile is complicated by the presence of other pollutants, namely, CO, hydrocarbons (HCs), nitrogen oxides (NO_x) and particulates. Thus at low air–fuel ratio (when there is less air), NO_x is minimized, but produces high levels of $CO_{(g)}$ and hydrocarbons. At high air–fuel ratios (rich in air), CO and HCs are reduced, but, more NO_x is produced. Natural gas, on the other hand, is a clean–burning fuel because pollution–causing impurities are removed beforehand, but, the combustion of natural gas does produce CO_2, a greenhouse gas.

Thermal pollution: The ultimate form which energy takes when used is **heat**. Heat is given off by electricity generating plants (coal burning etc.), machines, appliances, lights, industrial activity, heating buildings etc. The production of **waste heat** is an unavoidable consequence of using energy!

According to the second law of thermodynamics (namely 'you cannot break even'), when a heat engine (e.g. a steam turbine) is used to perform work (e.g. turn a generator), only some energy is converted to work and the rest is given off as waste energy (an example of inefficiency). For example, in a typical fossil fuel plant, only about 40% of energy is converted to electricity. Most of the wasted heat energy is absorbed by the cooling tower used by the generating plant. Typically the temperature of the cooling water increases by about 11°C and is normally released into the environment from which it was obtained. When this warm water disrupts animal and plant life, it is called thermal pollution. Electricity generating stations transfer waste heat to the atmosphere through cooling ponds and/or cooling towers (where warm water is sprayed down through cool air or flows through pipes with large surface areas).

Effects of thermal pollution: If warm water is discharged into lakes or rivers, the increased temperature of the water: (a) decreases the amount of dissolved O_2 in the water which can affect aquatic organisms; (b) tends to stimulate the animals to be more active and greater activity increases the animals' need for O_2 which has already been reduced by the higher temperature and (c) leads to increased growth and development of aquatic life e.g. green algae, which in turn leads to the aquatic system being choked with plant life.

However, thermal pollution can be used to our advantage! For example, in France, warm water (35°C) is used in agriculture to speed up crop production; this could help with world food production!

F.2.7   Discuss the advantages and disadvantages of the different fossil fuels.

Consider the cost of production and availability (reserves) as well as pollution.

© IBO 2001

	COAL	PETROLEUM	NATURAL GAS
Availability	About 300 – 350 years supply	About 30 – 50 years supply	About 30 years supply
Pollution	CO_2 – greenhouse gas SO_2 – acid rain Particulates (fly ash) Thermal pollution	CO_2 – greenhouse gas CO (metabolic poison) NO_x (leading to photochemical smog) Thermal pollution	CO_2 – greenhouse gas; NO_x (otherwise very clean burning fuel) Thermal pollution
Cost of production	Open–pit mining: low Coal mines have higher cost of production; Cheaper than petroleum	Depends on location. e.g., more expensive in off–shore arctic waters	Usually associated with coal and oil production; cost mainly that of transportation
Advantages	Cheap and plentiful; ash produced can be used in making roads, etc.	Sulfur easily removed and few particulates	Cleanest burning fuel
Disadvantages	'Dirty fuel'; produces SO_2 and particulates (use of electrostatic precipitators can remove 99% of dust); greenhouse gases are produced	Limited supplies; photochemical smog, greenhouse gases produced	Limited supplies; greenhouse gases are produced

16.3 NUCLEAR ENERGY

F.3.1 Distinguish between nuclear reactions and chemical reactions.

Emphasize that in nuclear reactions nuclei are converted to other nuclei, while in chemical reactions only valence electrons are involved and atoms do not change into other atoms.

F.3.2 Write balanced nuclear equations.

Both the atomic number and mass number must be balanced. © IBO 2001

Ordinary chemical reactions involve only valence electrons and atoms do not change in identity, for example, the combustion of heptane:

$$C_7H_{16\,(l)} + 11\ O_{2(g)} \Rightarrow 7\ CO_{2\,(g)} + 8\ H_2O_{(l)} + heat$$

In nuclear reactions, however, nuclear transformations take place, that is nuclei are involved and may be converted into other nuclei. Thus a new element or different isotope of the original element can be formed. Nuclear reactions occur naturally in radioactive elements whose nuclei are unstable (radiation is emitted to increase nuclear stability) and occur artificially as a result of bombardment of atoms with protons, neutrons or other high energy particles.

Recall isotopic symbols as $^A_Z X$ (or $^A X_Z$ or $^A X$), where X is the chemical symbol of the element, **Z, the atomic number,** (the number of protons in the nucleus) and A is the **mass number,** (the sum of the number of protons and neutrons; i.e. the total number of nucleons in the nucleus).

Balanced nuclear equations require that both the atomic number and mass number must be balanced. Consider the following examples:

1. When Be–9 is bombarded with alpha particles (helium nuclei, ^4_2He), a neutron
   (^1_0n) is given out. Write a balanced nuclear reaction and identify the other product.

$$^9_4Be + ^4_2He \rightarrow ^1_0n + ^{12}_6X$$

   Product X must have atomic number $= (4 + 2) = 6$, that is carbon. Its mass number must be $(9 + 4 - 1) = 12$. Thus X is C–12 isotope.

2. When N–14 is bombarded with neutrons, a proton is emitted. Identify the other product.

$$^{14}_7N + ^1_0n \rightarrow ^1_1p + ^A_ZX$$

   $A = 14 + 1 - 1 = 14$, $Z = 7 + 0 - 1 = 6$, thus X is C–14 isotope.

Note the notations for the common particles encountered in nuclear reactions:

proton: ^1_1p; electron: $^{-1}_0e$ or $^{-1}_0\beta$ (for beta particles); neutron: ^1_0n, alpha particles: $^4_2\alpha$ or ^4_2He (helium nuclei), gamma rays: γ or $^0_0\gamma$ (high energy electromagnetic radiation or photons). Note that a positron has the same mass as an electron, but has a positive charge; that is $_{1}^{0}e$. This is not observed in natural radioactivity, but is produced artificially; e.g. P–30 is a positron emitter: $_{15}^{30}P \rightarrow _{1}^{0}e + _{14}^{30}Si$.

Here, a proton is converted to a neutron, with the emission of a positron, as happens with light nuclei which have too few neutrons to be stable. As the atomic number Z increases, radioisotopes are more likely to be neutron rich, hence α or β decay will occur.

F.3.3   Describe the nature of α, β and γ radiation.

Compare the charge, mass, penetrating power and behaviour in an electric field.

© IBO 2001

Radioactivity: The French physicist Henri Becquerel (1896) accidentally discovered radioactivity which is the ability of some isotopes to undergo reactions involving nuclear change or transformations. In natural radioactivity, it is the conversion of unstable nuclei to more stable nuclei.

Experiment to show the **three** types of radioactive decay.

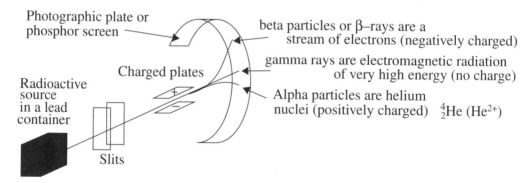

Types of radioactivity

Name	Symbol	Mass (a.m.u.)	Charge	Description	Penetrating Power
alpha	α	1	+2	Helium ions $_{2}^{4}He$; 'alpha'	Low; stopped by paper or skin
beta	β	0.0005	−1	high speed electrons, $_{-1}^{0}e$	Moderate; stopped by 1 mm thick Al foil
gamma	γ	0	0	High energy electromagnetic radiation	High; stopped by ~10 mm Pb sheet

Because of their relatively low penetrating power, alpha and beta particles are relatively harmless unless a radioactive source is taken into the body by swallowing or breathing in. However, high–energy beta particles can burn the skin and penetrate to the tissues beneath it. Gamma rays, on the other hand, because of their high penetration power are very dangerous. Exposure to gamma rays can cause damage to tissues resulting in various forms of cancer, cataracts and genetic damage to reproductive cells can lead to mutations, a result of which can be deformities in new born babies.

Examples of specific radioactive decay (remember that atomic and mass numbers must balance):

1.   U–238 is an alpha emitter:

$$^{238}_{92}U \rightarrow \, ^{4}_{2}He + \, ^{234}_{90}Th$$

2.   Np–239 is a beta emitter:

$$^{239}_{93}Np \rightarrow \, ^{0}_{-1}e + \, ^{239}_{94}Pu$$

This is possible if a neutron in Np–239 splits into an electron and a proton (in a complex series of steps), thus forming Pu–239. The result of beta–particle emission is an increase in the atomic number (number of protons) by 1 and a decrease in the number of neutrons by 1, as a result of which the mass number remains unchanged.

3.   In natural radioactivity, decay of gamma rays always takes place with alpha– or beta–emission, never by itself. Thus Ra–226 emits both alpha and gamma rays:

$$^{226}_{88}Ra \rightarrow \, ^{222}_{86}Rn + \, ^{4}_{2}\alpha + \, ^{0}_{0}\gamma$$

Of course, there would be no difference to the balanced nuclear reaction if gamma rays are not included. (However, among artificially produced radio–isotopes, some gamma-only emitters exist; $^{A}_{Z}X^{*} \rightarrow \, ^{A}_{Z}X + \, ^{0}_{0}\gamma$.)

F.3.4   State the concept of half-life.

Half-life is independent of the amount of a radioactive sample.   © IBO 2001

Half-Life, $t_{1/2}$, for a radioactive substance is the time required for one–half of the initial amount of radioactive material to decay. It is independent of the amount of a radioactive sample, that is these are all first order reactions. Each radioactive isotope has its own characteristic half life which can range from 10^{-6} seconds to a few billion years! e.g. C–14 has $t_{1/2} = 5730$ years; Pu–239 (a product of nuclear reactions and a highly toxic substance) has $t_{1/2} = 24{,}000$ years! It is an exponential decay, so if one starts with say

100 g of a radioactive sample at time zero, then after one–half life, 50 g of the original isotope will be left as half will have been converted to the products.

Half lives	Mass (g)
Initially	100
after $t_{1/2}$	$\left(\dfrac{100}{2^1}\right) = 50$
after $2t_{1/2}$	$\left(\dfrac{100}{2^2}\right) = 25$
after $3t_{1/2}$	$\left(\dfrac{100}{2^3}\right) = 12\frac{1}{2}$
after $4t_{1/2}$	$\left(\dfrac{100}{2^4}\right) = 6\frac{1}{4}$
after $5t_{1/2}$	$\left(\dfrac{100}{2^5}\right) = 3\frac{1}{8}$

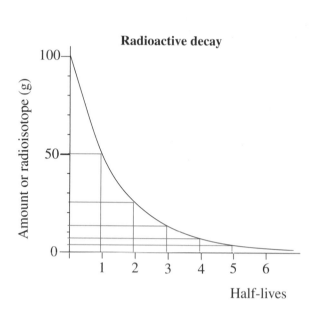

Thus, the Pu–239 produced in nuclear plants now as a waste product will be with us for thousands of years to come because it will take approximately 170,000 years for it to decay to less than 1% of the present amount and more like 250,000 years to reach relatively safe levels!

One of the best–known uses of the half–lives of radioisotopes is the carbon–14 dating method. The age of ancient materials made of plant or animal matter can be established on the basis of their $^{14}_{6}C$ content. Carbon dioxide in the atmosphere consists mainly of carbon–12 with trace amounts of carbon–14, which is radioactive and decays. However, the concentration of carbon–14 in living things does not decrease because it is constantly being formed in the atmosphere from the action of cosmic rays (assumed to have constant intensity) on nitrogen, $^{14}_{7}N$. All plants absorb carbon dioxide from the atmosphere and as long as the plant is living, the amount of carbon–14 incorporated into the molecules it produces remains a constant fraction of the amount of carbon present. When the plant dies, exchange with the atmosphere ceases and the amount of carbon–14 diminishes with time as it continues to decay. Since it is known that the half–life of carbon–14 is about 6000 years, it is possible to obtain a good measure of the age of an object by determining the amount of radioactive carbon remaining in it. A wooden dish that contains only 25% of the carbon–14 that trees have today is therefore approximately 11,000 to 12,000 years old. The carbon–14 dating technique is limited for the dating of objects of organic origin that are not that old – about 8 to 9 half–lives (50,000 years). At this age, it is difficult to measure accurately the very small amount of carbon–14 remaining. Other isotopes with much longer half lives are used for older objects.

F.3.5 Apply the concept of half-life in calculations.

Restrict this to whole numbers of half-lives.

EXAMPLE

Predict the amount of $_{83}^{212}Bi$ remaining if you observe 10.0 g decay over a period of 121 minutes. $t_{1/2} = 60.5$ min.

SOLUTION

Start with 10g, after $t_{1/2} = 60.5$ min., 5g left, after two $t_{1/2} = 2 \times 60.5$ min., 2.5 g left.

EXAMPLE

Consider an ancient scroll which gives 1.25 d.p.m. (disintegrations per minute) of radioactivity due to C–14 compared to a freshly made scroll which gives 10 d.p.m. If $t_{1/2}$ C–14 = 5730 years. Calculate the age of the ancient scroll.

SOLUTION

Initially	$1 \times t_{1/2}$	$2 \times t_{1/2}$	$3 \times t_{1/2}$
10 d.p.m. $\rightarrow$	5 d.p.m. $\rightarrow$	2.5 d.p.m. $\rightarrow$	1.25 d.p.m.

$\therefore 3 \times 5730 = 17190$ years old

F.3.6 Compare nuclear fission and nuclear fusion.

Fusion and fission are similar in that they both convert matter into energy. The energy, ΔE, is produced from the mass defect, Δm, which is the difference in mass between the reactants and the products. This energy is given by Einstein's equation: $\Delta E = \Delta mc^2$ where c is the velocity of light.

Nuclear fission is the splitting of a heavy nucleus into two or more lighter nuclei (called fission fragments) with the simultaneous release of neutrons and large amounts of energy. The additional neutrons released can induce further fission:

$$_{92}^{235}U + _{0}^{1}n \rightarrow [_{92}^{236}U] \rightarrow _{56}^{141}Ba + _{36}^{92}Kr + 3_{0}^{1}n + energy$$
$$\text{unstable}$$

The **critical mass** is the mass of the fissionable material in a certain volume needed to sustain a chain reaction. A chain reaction occurs when the uranium sample is large enough for most of the neutrons emitted to be captured by another nucleus before passing out of the sample. Also, for a chain reaction to occur, there must be a balance between the net production of neutrons and the loss of neutrons caused by:

(i)   the capture of neutrons by uranium atoms without fission happening

(ii)   the capture of neutrons by other materials in the sample and

(iii) the escape of neutrons without being captured. Thus critical mass is very important.

OPTION

Nuclear fusion brings together nuclei of two lighter elements to form a heavier nucleus with the release of energy. The heavier nucleus is more stable than the two lighter nuclei (that is there is a net loss of mass) and energy is released:

$$_1^2H + _1^2H \rightarrow _2^3He + _0^1n + energy$$

The energy of the sun is produced from the fusion of protons; H and He comprise approximately 99% of the sun's mass. Nuclei must overcome the extremely high electric repulsion between the positive nuclei in order to fuse. As a result, extremely high temperatures (approximately 10^8 K) and pressures are required. Fusion is also called a **thermonuclear reaction**. The hydrogen bomb is an example of uncontrolled nuclear fusion. Controlled fusion is not yet possible, but scientists predict that the appropriate technology will be available around the year 2050. Technical problems with fusion are related to the fact that pushing the positively charged nuclei together and holding them together requires enormous amounts of energy.

Thus, the problems with fusion are:

(i)   the production of **plasma**. At very high temperatures the atoms are stripped of their electrons and the intensely hot mixture of positive nuclei and free electrons is called plasma. This process needs upwards of 40 million K! (between 40 and 100×10^6 K),

(ii)   that the plasma must be held together long enough (about 1 second) for the fusion reaction to become self sustaining.

(iii) that enough energy must be produced to make the process commercially profitable.

There are several advantages of nuclear fusion:

1.   The fuel deuterium ($_1^2H$ or $_1^2D$) is abundant (there are about 10^{22} deuterium atoms in 1 dm^3 of sea water!). In fact, the fuel is limitless and cheap.

2.   Fusion is considered much less dangerous than fission with regard to producing radioactive waste products.

3.   Massive shipments of radioactive fuel would not be required as they are in fission. Also, far less waste has to be stored.

4.   Theft of fuel material (plutonium) from fission reactors and waste facilities, for the production of nuclear weapons, is eliminated.

Besides the technical problems at the moment, tritium, $_1^3H$ (an isotope of hydrogen) is produced and is very radioactive. If $_1^3H$ can be isolated it can then be used as a fusion fuel as well. Also, $_1^3H$ has a much shorter half life than many fission products.

$$_1^2H + _1^3H \rightarrow _2^4He + _0^1n + energy$$

F.3.7 Explain the functions of the main components of a nuclear power plant.

Include the fuel, moderator, control rods, coolant and shielding. The materials used for the different components should be considered. © IBO 2001

A nuclear power plant has many similarities to the fossil fuel power plant. Both require turbines and generators and the heat produced by the reactions converts water to steam which turns the turbines. It is the source of the heat that is different and requires substantially different arrangement in and around the reaction vessel, which contains the core, in order to safely generate electricity.

An atomic reactor (pile) is used to produce controlled nuclear fission and consists of:

1. **Carefully diluted fissionable (fissile) material**: enriched U–235 (about 3%) or Pu–239 is used in fuel rods that can be inserted or removed from the reactor core. In nature, U exists as the fissile U–235 (0.7%) and the non–fissile U–238 (99.3%). The ore is treated in a series of complicated physical and chemical processes to enrich the U–235 to the required level. The non–fissile U–238 absorbs neutrons to produce Pu–239, which is in fact fissile and becomes part of the fuel. Pu–239, when separated from spent fuel rods, can also be used as a fuel for another type of reactor, called the Breeder reactor. In typical pressurised water reactors, the non–fissile fragments formed also absorb some of the neutrons (but do not split). As the reaction progresses and fragments collect, the chain reaction eventually stops – in about 3 years. Thus the fuel rods have to be replaced even though about 30% of the U–235 is still present. The unspent fuel contains high levels of radioactive waste which have to be isolated and stored.

2. **Moderators** are essential for the fission reaction: A moderator is used to slow down the neutrons so that they are more easily absorbed by nuclei. The water or graphite surrounding the fuel rods helps to maintain the reaction by acting as a moderator.

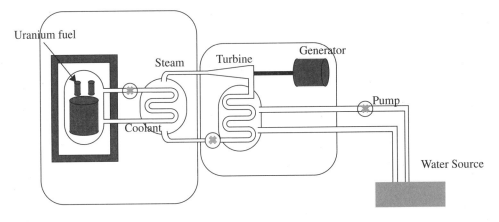

3. **Control Rods**: As the nuclear reaction progresses and more neutrons are produced, the reaction can become **self perpetuating** or a **chain reaction** in which the neutrons from one fission result in the fission of just one other nucleus. The chain reaction is thus controlled by restricting the number of free neutrons

OPTION

available for subsequent fission. Control rods made up of substances that can easily absorb neutrons can be lowered into the reactor core to control the chain reaction. Substances such as boron and cadmium are examples of materials used as control rods.

4. **Coolant** to extract the heat produced: The heat produced in the core heats the water in the primary loop. In the more common reactors the water is kept at high pressure (**PWR – Pressurised Water Reactors**) to allow it to absorb more heat without boiling. The heated water is surrounded by the secondary loop where the steam generator absorbs the heat and, because the water is at lower pressure, turns it into steam which is used to turn the turbine. Breeder reactors use liquid sodium as a coolant.

5. **Shielding of the reactor core**: This is achieved by three successive barriers as shown in the diagram: the casing for the pellets, the steel reactor vessel and the containment building. Shielding is essential to prevent the escape of highly radioactive and toxic materials into the environment.

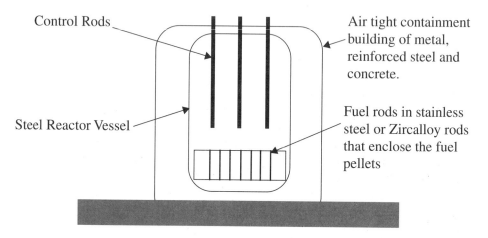

Breeder reactors:

A breeder reactor is a nuclear fission reactor that transforms non–fissionable U–238 into fissionable Pu–239 by placing it around the core where it produces more fissionable fuel than it consumes. Non–fissionable U–238, on neutron bombardment, undergoes the following nuclear transformation (amongst others):

$$^{238}_{92}U + ^{1}_{0}n \Rightarrow ^{239}_{92}U$$

$$^{239}_{92}U \Rightarrow ^{0}_{-1}e + ^{239}_{93}Np$$

$$^{239}_{93}Np \Rightarrow ^{0}_{-1}e + ^{239}_{94}Pu$$

The Pu–239 formed is fissionable. If all the non–fissionable U–238 were used in breeder reactors, then the supply of energy would be increased enormously. Pu–239 from spent fuel rods containing U–235 and U–238 can also be recovered and used as a fuel. A typical fission reaction involves the formation of Sr–90 and Ba–147, although many other products are possible:

$$^{239}_{94}\text{Pu} + ^{1}_{0}\text{n} \rightarrow ^{90}_{38}\text{Sr} + ^{147}_{56}\text{Ba} + 3\,^{1}_{0}\text{n} + \text{energy}$$

The non–fissionable U–238 is placed outside the fissioning Pu–239 which also consists of U–235. U–235 is used as a source of neutrons. Suppose 100 fissions are required to sustain a chain reaction. Since each fission, on the average produces 2.5 neutrons, then 100 fissions will produce 250 neutrons. Of the 250 neutrons, 100 are required to maintain the chain reaction at the same power level. Thus 150 neutrons are left. Some are lost. If 110 neutrons are captured by non–fissionable U–238, then 110 Pu–239, which is fissile, will be produced. Thus 100 fissions produce 110 Pu–239 leading to a 10% increase in the amount of fuel, and is thus called a breeder reactor.

F.3.8 Discuss the differences between conventional power generation and nuclear reactors.

© IBO 2001

Fossil fuel power plants have three main components:

1. **Boilers** in which fuel is burnt to provide high pressure steam.

2. The steam then drives **turbines**.

3. The turbines drive **generators** that produce electricity. Generators have large coils of wire rotating quickly in a magnetic field, producing an electric current.

A fossil fuel plant for generating electricity

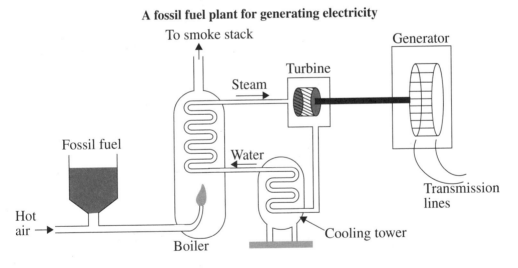

The percentage of the available energy converted to electricity from the burning of fossil fuels is not very high; it is about 30% for coal and 40% for oil or natural gas-fired power plants. Thus about 60-70% of the total energy available is lost to the environment (about half via the cooling towers). However, electricity is a very convenient form of high-grade energy which can be easily distributed by electrical cables with little loss of energy.

In a fossil-fuel power plant, the coal, oil or gas is burnt in a huge furnace producing heat and hot gases. In a boiler, water is converted into high-pressure steam at a temperature

OPTION

of about 560°C. The steam passes through pipes to the high-pressure cylinders of the steam turbines. A turbine consists of a ring of blades, which turn under the force of the steam. The potential energy of the high pressure steam is thus converted into kinetic (or mechanical) energy of the turning turbines. As the temperature and pressure of the steam drops, much larger turbine blades are required. The low temperature and pressure steam returns to the boiler for reheating before it enters the pressure cylinders. The condenser below the turbine condenses steam back to water which can be reused. The condensation process produces a partial vacuum which allows more energy to be extracted from the steam, thus increasing its efficiency. Condensers require large amounts of cooling water which subsequently has to cool in large cooling towers before re-use.

The similarities and differences between conventional power reactors and nuclear reactors.

Similarities	Differences	
	Conventional Power	Nuclear Reactors
1. Generators to produce electricity	1. Ordinary chemical combustion reaction to produce heat	1. Nuclear fission to produce heat from mass defect, $\Delta E = \Delta mc^2$
2. Turbines	2. Fuel does not have to be enriched	2. U–235 fuel has to be enriched by complex methods
3. Thermal power		
4. Cooling tower	3. Fuel burnt in a furnace; requires air	3. Fuel rods in an airtight building; neutrons cause fission
5. Thermal pollution		
	4. Requires no containment building	4. Requires containment building to isolate radioactive fuel
	5. Requires only one (primary) heat transfer loop or cycle	5. Uses two heat transfer loops – a primary to carry heat from reactor and a secondary where steam is produced
	6. Products are CO_2 (green house gas) + SO_2 (very little from natural gas) + particulates	6. Products can be highly radioactive but no CO_2 produced
	7. All fuel can be used up	7. About 30% unspent fuel unusable. Spent fuel highly radioactive
	8. SO_2 can be removed using scrubbers and particulates using electrostatic precipitators	8. Used fuel rods require expensive reprocessing; accidents can release radioactive materials
	9. No melt down possible	9. Failure of control or cooling system can lead to melt down
	10. Fly ash can be used in road making	10. Nuclear waste has to be stored and eventually disposed of

F.3.9   Discuss the concerns about safety in nuclear power plants.

Consider the effects of: escape of radioactive materials at various stages; radioactive contamination of ordinary materials; escape of sodium from a breeder reactor; loss of control of a nuclear reaction; nuclear waste.   © IBO 2001

Even if the control rods and the cooling system of a nuclear power plant fails, a nuclear plant cannot detonate (or explode) like a nuclear bomb. This is because the U–235 fissionable material present is not concentrated enough for an uncontrolled chain reaction to occur. However, concerns and potential problems of controlled nuclear fission include:

1.   **Problems with nuclear fuel cycle**: Mining produces a low level of radioactivity, leading to possible water contamination by radioactive substances. There is a threat to miners from radioactive dust and radioactivity in spent uranium ore as well as a wider public danger of accidents during transportation and the possibility of hijacking and sabotage of the fuel.

2.   **Problems in operation:** Failure of control rods and cooling systems can lead to a meltdown (similar to the Three Mile Island accident) probably leading to a release of radioactive materials. Note that several safety systems exist such as control rods, containment buildings, etc., their purpose being to reduce the possibility of meltdowns. Also, thermal pollution, that is heat loss to the environment, which is unavoidable.

3.   **A fast breeder reactor uses liquid sodium** (m. pt. 98 °C, b. pt. 890°C with a very high capacity to absorb heat) in its primary and secondary loops to remove the heat produced by the nuclear reaction. The tertiary loop contains water which is converted to steam. Escape of liquid sodium from the breeder reactor and its subsequent contact with water would be disastrous. Also, the mishandling of Pu–239, the fissile material used in breeder reactors, would be disastrous since Pu–239 is extremely toxic (carcinogenic) and can be made into a nuclear fission bomb. The Canadian nuclear reactor (**CANDU**) uses heavy water, D_2O as the moderator which could lead to the release of heavy water into the surrounding environment.

4.   **Spent fuel** consists of highly radioactive and dangerous fission products. Although most have short half lives and decay rapidly, others like Sr–90 and Cs–137 have longer half lives (about 30 years). However, some have much longer half lives. Pu–239 for example, has a half life of 24,000 years. This means it will be present for about 10 half lives before most of it will have decayed to a level considered relatively safe, i.e. for around 250,000 years.

5.   **Reprocessing:** This is the separation of U–235 and Pu–239 (both of which are fissionable) from spent fuel, for recycling. Also, certain byproducts may be useful in medicine or for research. What is left after reprocessing is considered nuclear waste. Note: long term storage of nuclear waste is most problematic, as is concern about possible theft of Pu–239 from nuclear facilities.

6.   **Nuclear waste** is presently stored in pools of water. Long term storage of nuclear waste seems most problematic for fission products with long half lives. Currently, no method of permanent storage is accepted. Possibilities include permanent burial in dry, earthquake free places e.g. salt mines (considered most likely), in underground holes under the Antarctic ice sheet or in deep ocean trenches. Other options include storage in surface warehouses or shooting nuclear waste into space! Transmutation into harmless isotopes would be the ideal solution but this is not presently feasible. For liquid wastes, solidification in glass or ceramic form followed by burial in metal containers may be a solution.

STORAGE OF NUCLEAR WASTES - SUMMARY:

High level waste:

Source: Nuclear industry and military complexes.

Characteristics: Radioactivity is high, the isotopes have long half lives. They are generally produced in small amounts.

Storage: Contained securely by making into glass followed by burial deep underground in non-leachable environment.

Low level waste:

Source: Coolant from nuclear power plants, radioisotopes used in hospitals and for monitoring the thickness of paper, plastic etc.

Characteristics: Radioactivity is low, the isotopes have short half lives. They are generally produced in large amounts.

Storage: These isotopes are stored until radioactivity is reduced to relatively low levels or they are diluted.

Spent fuel is often stored in pools of water to absorb heat and to allow high activity isotopes with short half lives to decay.

"Fission energy is safe only if a number of critical devices work as they should, if a number of people in key positions follow all their instructions, if there is no sabotage, no hijacking of the transports, if no reactor fuel processing plant or reprocessing plant or repository anywhere in the world is situated in a region of riots or guerrilla activity and no revolution or war – even a "conventional one" – takes place in these regions . . . No acts of God can be permitted."

Hannes Alfvén

OPTION

16.4 SOLAR ENERGY

Solar energy is transmitted **nuclear fusion energy.** Characteristics of solar energy include:

1. It is infinite and is readily available. It is free and requires no purification.

2. It is a clean form of energy and one of the safest. Many applications appear to be essentially pollution free.

3. Although large areas of land are needed, the environmental impact is small compared to strip mining, oil spills, etc.

4. No major breakthroughs are needed to harness solar energy as it is already being used for solar hot water heaters for homes (they, however, do need large scale use to make them cheaper.) Solar collectors are used for the purpose.

5. The use of photovoltaic cells convert solar energy into electrical energy directly as used in space vehicles. These are not feasible economically now but the technology is well known.

6. Often solar energy is available where it can be used, that is it does not require transportation costs like coal and oil.

7. Political problems should be minimum because no one owns the sun; thus it cannot be turned off or the price raised (like oil).

8. The direct use of solar energy does not deplete (reduce) the resources of the earth.

9. Some economists think widespread use of solar energy could stabilize economies and reduce inflation!

It not been taken advantage of for several reasons including:

1. Other sources of energy have been cheaper (e.g. gasoline in North America).

2. Solar energy is widely dispersed, so it must be concentrated to be used.

3. It is not available at night when the need is highest.

4. Because supply varies with cloud cover. An effective method of storing solar energy is needed so it can be used when needed.

5. Regions that need the most energy for heating are those that get the least amount of sunshine.

6. Large scale conversion to electricity is not, at present, economically competitive.

OPTION

F.4.1   State how solar energy can be converted to other forms of energy.

Include chemical energy (biomass), thermal energy (passive and active methods) and electricity generation (direct and indirect methods).   © IBO 2001

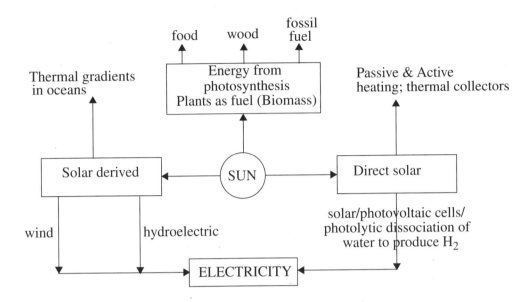

F.4.2   Describe the role of photosynthesis in converting solar energy to other forms of energy.

Products of photosynthesis are used for food, primary fuels and conversion to other fuels, e.g. ethanol. The equation for photosynthesis is required.   © IBO 2001

Only about 0.1% of the total solar energy falling on the Earth is used to form plant energy via photosynthesis. Photosynthesis is a complex process but can be represented by the overall reaction in which carbon dioxide and water are converted to energy rich carbohydrates such as glucose in the presence of solar energy and chlorophyll. The carbon dioxide is reduced to form glucose, $C_6H_{12}O_6$. In this process, water is oxidized to oxygen gas:

$$6\ CO_{2(g)} + 6\ H_2O_{(l)} \Rightarrow C_6H_{12}O_6 + 6\ O_{2\ (g)}$$

Photosynthesis is initiated by light energy. Green plants contain two kinds of chlorophyll α and β. Both are complex organic ring structures that contain a magnesium atom. They absorb red light in the visible spectrum and are thus green in colour. Excited forms of chlorophyll use the solar energy they have absorbed to carry out the endothermic conversion of water and carbon dioxide to produce glucose and oxygen. Plants then convert the glucose to starch and cellulose.

OPTION

F.4.3 Discuss how biomass can be converted to energy.

Include: direct combustion; combustion of waste materials from other processes; production of biogas; production and use of ethanol. Mention the advantages and disadvantages of each method. The equation for the formation of ethanol from glucose is required.

© IBO 2001

Biofuels and Biomass: 0.1% of solar radiation arriving on earth is used for photosynthesis. Biofuels are renewable energy sources derived mainly from living things, which store solar radiation via photosynthesis. Biomass is dry plant materials and organic waste and includes vegetable matter such as trees, crops and natural vegetation, animal dung and domestic and industrial organic waste. It has been used by man for thousands of years in the form of wood. Note that all fossil fuels originally were biomass. Biomass contributes 15% to world energy supplies. Biofuels are obtained by processing the different types of biomass.

Advantages of biofuels include the fact that they are renewable, available and are relatively non–polluting. Disadvantages include the fact that they replace food crops, deplete soil nutrients and their fermentation waste is polluting.

The direct production of energy comes from the combustion of wood and other plant substances and waste to produce heat. Use is also made of liquid plant and animal products such as seed oil for fuel.

The indirect conversions include:

(i) **Thermal**:

 Gasification – heat in limited air to produce biogas, SNG, methanol.

 Pyrolysis – heat in absence of oxygen to produce oil (SNL) and SNG.

 Hydrogenation – biomass reacted with CO and steam to produce heavy oil.

(ii) **Biological**:

 Anaerobic – bacterial decay of organic matter produces biogas – mixture of CH_4 (70%) and CO_2.

Fermentation of carbohydrates produces ethanol:

$$C_6H_{12}O_{6\,(s)} \Rightarrow 2\, C_2H_5OH_{(l)} + 2\, CO_{2\,(g)}$$

Ethanol can be obtained from sugar, root crops (especially cassava) and cereals. It can be used for heating and automobiles when combined with gasoline containing 10% by volume maximum ethanol (called **gasohol**). The use of gasohol requires no modification to automobiles.

Currently ethanol is more expensive per litre than gasoline because it requires as much energy to process as is obtained from it. Other disadvantages include the fact that it can absorb water because of hydrogen bonding and can separate from gasoline as well as cause corrosion. It also has lower energy content and provides fewer kilometers per litre than gasoline. Large amounts of water are needed to produce it and much waste is generated. It uses cropland and ecological problems arise with the cultivation of a single crop.

Advantages of using ethanol include renewability, higher octane rating and lower emissions of CO and NO_x; also, it can be made from surplus or waste agricultural products, trees can be grown on land not supporting food crops and the technology is available.

F.4.4   Outline the principles of using solar energy for space heating.
Examples should include storage of heat by water and rocks.   © IBO 2001

The warmth of the sun can be used to heat homes by heating the air and house structure using solar collectors. The simplest application of solar energy is passive heating. A well insulated building with the majority of its windows facing towards the sun is the main requirement for space heating from direction sunlight, that is, maximum amount of heat is collected and stored by the structure. It is most effective if it is used to heat structures with a high thermal capacity such as tanks of water or thick stone walls.

Passive solar heating

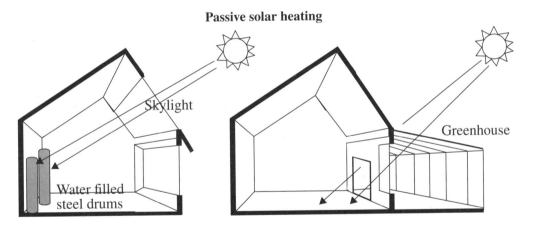

Passive heating can also be used for water heating using solar collectors. These are painted black to allow absorption of all frequencies and are inclined so sunlight falls perpendicularly as much as possible. These are used where relatively low temperatures are required, for example in greenhouses and domestic hot water heating. The solar collectors are placed below storage tanks so that hot water rises to the tank.

Advantages of passive heating include its relative low cost, no moving parts are involved and thus low maintenance costs, reliability and long life. However, it must be designed into the building, is relatively difficult to control, is useless for concentrating large amounts of energy and requires back–up heating systems.

In an active space heating system, the heat is stored and distributed by pumps and fans. The energy is collected using flat or inclined bed black collectors against the side of the

OPTION

building and facing the sun. Liquid water or air is heated in the collectors. The heated liquid is then pumped into tanks and stored, or, heated air is blown through a storage pit filled with rocks. At night this is recirculated as heat into the house.

On sunny or lightly overcast days, temperatures of 90 °C in the heat transfer fluid can be reached even in winter using flat–bed collectors. The current cost in North America is approximately U.S.$15,000. It is possible to get almost completely self–heated homes using this method.

Active solar heating

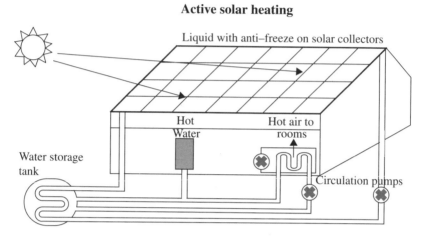

The advantages of active heating are that it need have relatively little influence on architectural design and it is easy to control. However, it is more expensive, requires maintenance and is less efficient as multiple transfers of energy are involved (second law of thermodynamics). There are advantages and disadvantages in using air versus liquid in the active space heating system. If air is used, it does not freeze (or boil) at the temperatures involved, is not corrosive and can circulate directly to various places. However, the ductwork and storage required are bulky, leaks are hard to detect and the system is costly to fit into an existing building. Water on the other hand transfers heat more efficiently, requires a smaller area for storage and the piping and plumbing is relatively easy to retrofit. However, problems include freezing and boiling (protection using anti–freezes is required), corrosion can occur and leaks can cause damage.

F.4.5   Discuss the methods for converting solar energy into electricity.

Include parabolic mirrors and photovoltaic cells. Consider the advantages and disadvantages of each method.   © IBO 2001

Several methods are used to convert solar energy into electricity:

1.   **Indirect** use of sun's thermal energy to heat water for conventional generation:

   (i)   Using specially coated surfaces made of aluminium oxide; these have high absorbency for solar radiation and can withstand continuous heating to 540°C for extended periods of time – up to 40 years. The solar energy is used to convert water into steam which turns turbines to generate electricity.

(ii) Parabolic mirrors can be used to focus the sun's heat onto a pipe containing heat exchanging fluid that is then used to make stem to generate electricity.

(iii) Energy is concentrated by converging lenses or mirrors; needs computers to control mirrors to track the sun and focus its rays on large electricity – generating steam boilers. By this method, the boiler can be heated to 1500°C.

These methods require huge numbers of coated surfaces or mirrors which have to be moved to track the sun across the sky and which must be placed far apart to avoid shadows. However, sunlight is a resource that will not run out until the distant future. It does not deplete the Earth's resources.

2. **Direct** conversion of solar energy to electricity using photovoltaic (or solar) cells: Most of the satellites orbiting the earth are powered by solar cells. Solar cells, are maintenance free and easy to use. These convert energy from the sun directly into electricity and are found to be about 13–14% efficient. The advantages of solar cells are many. They have no moving parts, no liquids, no corrosive chemicals and will generate electricity for a very long time, provided they are exposed to solar radiation. The disadvantages include the need for large collecting areas, the large cost of pure silicon and that they only work when the sun is shining and provide low power.

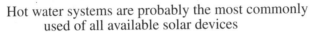

Hot water systems are probably the most commonly used of all available solar devices

OPTION

16.5 ELECTROCHEMICAL ENERGY

F.5.1   Explain the workings of lead-acid storage batteries and dry cell (zinc-carbon and alkaline) batteries.

Include the relevant half-equations.   © IBO 2001

Electrochemical cells are devices that produce electricity, that is, they convert chemical energy to electrical energy using spontaneous redox reactions. Primary cells are not rechargeable; once chemicals have been used up, no further reaction is possible. Secondary cells are voltaic cells which, by using reversible electrochemical reactions, are rechargeable (use electricity to reverse the chemical reaction). These are sometimes called storage cells or accumulators.

Primary Cells:

1.   **A Common Dry Cell** contains a carbon cathode, a zinc anode and a moist paste of graphite, NH_4Cl and MnO_2 as the electrolyte. The electrolyte, which is moist enough to allow ionization, is present as a paste rather than as a liquid.

Anode (oxidation) reaction: $Zn_{(s)} \Rightarrow Zn^{2+}_{(aq)} + 2\ e^-$ at the negative terminal

Cathode (reduction) reaction: $2\ NH_4^+_{(aq)} + 2\ e^- \Rightarrow 2\ NH_{3(g)} + H_{2(g)}$ at the positive terminal. Note that a sealed cell would explode if gases are not used up.

MnO_2 provides oxygen that reacts with H_2 to give H_2O and is itself reduced to $Mn_2O_{3(s)}$:

$$2MnO_2 + H_{2(g)} \Rightarrow Mn_2O_{3(s)} + H_2O_{(l)}$$

Similarly Zn^{2+} combines with NH_3 to form a complex ion:

$$Zn^{2+}_{(aq)} + 4\ NH_{3\ (aq)} \Rightarrow Zn(NH_3)_4^{2+}_{(aq)}$$

Such a cell provides 1.5V when new and cells are made in a variety of sizes and shapes. Disadvantages include: (1) If current is drawn too rapidly, the hydrogen gas produced cannot be consumed rapidly enough; the cathode is polarized (i.e. covered in gas bubbles) and the voltage drops. (2) Spontaneous but slow direct reaction gives poor shelf–life and (3) They are not rechargeable.

2.   **An Alkaline Battery** is somewhat more expensive but has a longer shelf–life, provides 1.54V and avoids some of the problems of a common dry cell.

Oxidation of Zn takes place under alkaline or basic conditions at the negative terminal:

$$Zn_{(s)} + 2\ OH^-_{(aq)} \Rightarrow ZnO_{(s)} + H_2O_{(l)} + 2e^-$$

Reduction half reaction at the positive terminal:

$$2\ MnO_{2\ (s)} + H_2O_{(l)} + 2e^- \Rightarrow Mn_2O_{3\ (s)} + 2OH^-_{(aq)}\ ;\ \text{no gases formed}$$

OPTION

Advantages include: (1) No decline in performance under high current loads and (2) able to produce more electric current for longer periods of time. However, the cells are not rechargeable.

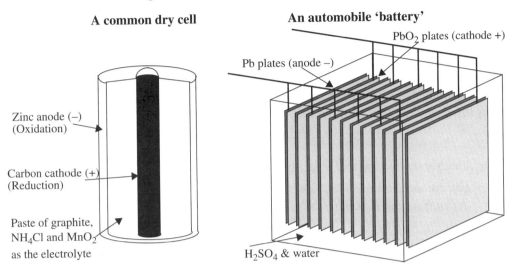

A common dry cell

An automobile 'battery'

PbO_2 plates (cathode +)

Pb plates (anode −)

Zinc anode (−)
(Oxidation)

Carbon cathode (+)
(Reduction)

Paste of graphite, NH_4Cl and MnO_2 as the electrolyte

H_2SO_4 & water

Secondary Cells:

These electrochemical cells are reversible, and can be recharged; the original reactant concentration can be restored by applying an external source of electricity in the opposite direction.

1.   **Automobile Batteries**: called lead storage or lead–acid batteries; the acid is H_2SO_4:

Anode: oxidation half reaction (at the negative terminal): $Pb_{(s)} \Rightarrow Pb^{2+}_{(aq)} + 2\ e^-$

Cathode: reduction half reaction (at the positive terminal):

$$PbO_{2\ (s)} + 4\ H^+_{(aq)} + SO_4^{2-}_{(aq)} + 2\ e^- \rightleftharpoons PbSO_{4\ (s)} + 2\ H_2O_{(l)}$$

Net Result: $Pb_{(s)} + PbO_{2(s)} + 2\ H_2SO_{4\ (aq)} \rightleftharpoons 2\ PbSO_{4(s)} + 2\ H_2O_{(l)}$

The cathode plates of a lead-acid battery are made of lead (in practice an alloy) which become covered with porous lead(IV) oxide during the discharging process with the consumption of H_2SO_4. With the production of water the electrolyte becomes dilute (1 mol water produced for each mol acid used up). Thus, the state of a battery can be determined from the density of the electrolyte solution.

The voltage produced is 2V. Thus, for a 12 V car battery, six 2V cells are arranged in series. This produces 12 volts but internal resistance also increases, thus producing less current than a single cell. The reverse reaction takes place when the battery is being charged.

Advantages: It can deliver large amounts of energy for short time periods and is rechargeable (by generator driven by car's engine). Disadvantages: Owing to the high density of lead, there is a high mass to charge ratio (bulky) and acid spillage is a possibility.

OPTION

2. **Nickel–Cadmium Batteries** are rechargeable, light–weight and produce a constant potential of 1.4V. The oxidizing and reducing agents can be regenerated by recharging;

Anode: $Cd_{(s)} + 2OH^-_{(aq)} \Rightarrow Cd(OH)_{2 (s)} + 2e^-$ oxidation half reaction

Cathode: $e^- + NiO(OH)_{(s)} + H_2O_{(l)} \Rightarrow Ni(OH)_{2 (s)} + OH^-_{(aq)}$ reduction half reaction

Insoluble hydroxides of Cd and Ni deposit on electrodes and half reactions are easily reversed during charging. These are more expensive, produce a lower voltage, but have longer life than lead-acid accumulators.

F.5.2   Identify the factors that affect the voltage and power available from a battery.

Voltage depends primarily on the nature of the materials used while power depends on their quantity.   © IBO 2001

Electrical Characteristics of Batteries:
A battery is a group of cells connected together to provide different voltages, current, etc.

Voltage (volts): The simplest requirement of a cell, is to deliver voltage at or near that required for the purpose. This depends on the reaction the cell is based on and on the concentrations of the chemicals. The voltage, but also its internal resistance can be increased by joining a number of cells in series.

Internal Resistance (ohms): Every cell experiences internal resistance owing to the finite rate at which ions can diffuse. This must be low enough to deliver desired current – the higher the internal resistance, the lower the current the cell can deliver.

Current (amps): This is important because of how it affects voltage. The current a cell can deliver depends on the size of the electrodes and the way they are arranged. If too much current is obtained from too small a cell, voltage drops so far that voltage requirement cannot be met. The current may be increased and internal resistance lowered by joining a number of cells in parallel.

Capacity: A cell must have sufficient capacity to maintain minimum voltage for a period of time. The total energy that can be obtained from a cell under normal conditions is called its capacity or power.

Note that, according to Ohm's Law: voltage = current × resistance

SUMMARY

1. Voltage depends only on the chemical properties of materials used in its construction.

2. The size of a cell and the quantities of active materials in it do not affect generated voltage – but they do determine the total electrical energy (power) and maximum current it can provide.

OPTION

3.   The limitations can be measured in terms of the internal resistance of the cell.

4.   The size of this internal resistance determines the maximum current the cell will provide in any given external circuit.

5.   The ability to maintain constant voltage is related to physical size – the larger a cell, the larger the active electrode surfaces and the more electrolyte in contact with them and therefore the lower the internal resistance. In general then, a good voltage under heavy load can be maintained only with a large cell.

6.   Thus batteries are groups of cells connected together in series, parallel or series–parallel to provide different voltages, current capacities, etc. This depends on use e.g. some batteries have to stand idle between periods of use, others may have rapid on and off use, still others may be used steadily until discharged.

F.5.3   Explain how a hydrogen-oxygen fuel cell works.

Include the relevant half-equations.   © IBO 2001

A **fuel cell** is a device that converts the chemical energy of fuels directly to electrical energy. Normally fuels are burned converting chemical energy to heat which makes steam that turns turbines to produce electricity. This is a highly inefficient method. Fuel cells differ from electrochemical cells ('batteries') in two ways:

1.   In fuel cells, the fuel is fed in continuously. Thus fuel cells are energy conversion devices whereas batteries are energy storage devices.

2.   The electrodes in fuel cells are made of inert materials (such as porous carbon impregnated with platinum as a catalyst).

The cathode and anode are separated by the electrolyte ($KOH_{(aq)}$). In a hydrogen-oxygen fuel cell, the oxidation of hydrogen gas by oxygen takes place in a controlled manner.

A hydrogen-oxygen fuel cell

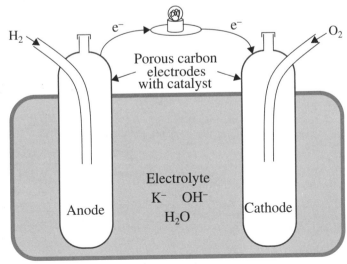

The oxidation process leads to the loss of e^- by the H_2 at the anode. The e^- flow out of the fuel cell and back to the cathode via an external circuit to reduce the O_2. Most commonly, the reactions take place in basic solution:

Oxidation half reaction: $2\ H_{2\ (g)} + 4\ OH^-_{(aq)} \Rightarrow 4\ H_2O_{(l)} + 4\ e^-$; at the anode

Reduction half reaction: $O_{2\ (g)} + 2\ H_2O_{(l)} + 4\ e^- \Rightarrow 4\ OH^-_{(aq)}$; at the cathode

Overall reaction: $2\ H_{2\ (g)} + O_{2\ (g)} \Rightarrow 2\ H_2O_{(l)}$

The net result is the oxidation of H_2 and the reduction of O_2.

Half reactions in acidic conditions are also possible:

Oxidation half reaction: $2\ H_{2\ (g)} \Rightarrow 4\ H^+_{(aq)} + 4\ e^-$; at the anode

Reduction half reaction: $O_{2\ (g)} + 4\ H^+_{(aq)} + 4\ e^- \Rightarrow 2\ H_2O_{(l)}$; at the cathode

Advantages and disadvantages of fuel cells:

Advantages:
Fuel cells are highly efficient (70-80%) since they convert the chemical energy of the fuels directly to electrical energy. Thus these greatly reduce thermal pollution, as well as being less polluting in general. Fuel cells also tend to be light in weight.

Disadvantages:
These include technical problems ranging from leaks to corrosion and catalytic failures.

Fuel cells are used in the space program. These usually operate at about 70-140°C, generate about 0.9 V and the water produced can be purified and used for drinking. Some fuel cells are used for commercial production of electricity in Japan.

EXTENSION MATERIAL (HL ONLY)
16.6 STORAGE OF ENERGY AND LIMITS OF EFFICIENCY

F.6   Storage of Energy and Limits of Efficiency

F.6.1   *Discuss the advantages and disadvantages of energy storage schemes. Include both pumped storage and conversion to hydrogen.*   © IBO 2001

In dealing with alternate sources of energy such as solar and wind power, it becomes clear that periods of energy demand do not always coincide with the availability of power as on a cold, windless, winter's night. It thus becomes essential to store surplus energy for use when demand increases. The idea then is to store unused energy and deliver it when and where necessary tailoring supply to meet demand. This is easily done with fossil fuels, but not with some of the renewable energy sources, which require both short and long–term storage. Storing energy in a form that can be easily converted to electrical energy seems very appropriate as electricity can be produced readily from primary and secondary energy sources.

1.   **Hydrogen economy**: Hydrogen gas is a very good secondary source of energy. Hydrogen can be readily made from water. Thus alternate energy sources or extra energy at off peak times, can be stored either through electrolysis or a series of chemical reactions which decompose water to produce hydrogen gas. Unlike fossil fuels, the only product of combustion of hydrogen is water. However, several disadvantages exist in this method including the expense the energy required in producing hydrogen gas, storage, difficulties (hydrogen has a very low density and a boiling point of 20 K) and high flammability.

The hydrogen energy cycle for energy storage can be represented as follows:

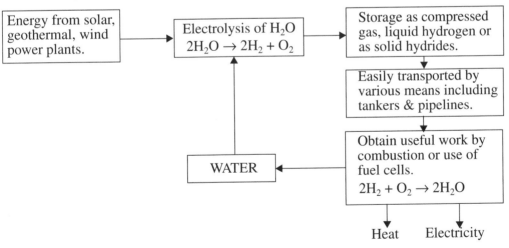

Hydrogen is a non–polluting form of energy. Its only product of combustion is water. It is therefore an ideal fuel for converting and storing other forms of energy. Hydrogen is so light that it goes straight up and disperses rapidly. Hydrogen could be shipped through pipelines to markets. Hydrogen pipelines would also make it feasible to locate nuclear plants in remote areas. Solar and wind generators could fit into such a system. The existing natural gas pipelines could easily be adapted to hydrogen delivery.

2. For large scale consumption, pumped water storage schemes can use excess electrical power to drive water uphill (raising its potential energy) using pump–turbines which pump water to a high reservoir. When the demand increases, the water is allowed to run back down. The pump now acts as a turbine and the stored potential energy of the water is turned into mechanical energy which generates hydroelectric power.

The largest such storage system in the world is in Michigan, USA where Lake Michigan is used as the lower reservoir and the upper reservoir is a man–made lake. Problems with such sites include huge costs, identifying locations with suitable height differences, environmental impacts and efficiency (since only about two thirds of the energy used for pumping the water to higher elevations is recovered).

3. For small scale consumption, energy can be stored by charging batteries.

16.7 NUCLEAR STABILITY

F.7.1 Predict nuclear stability and mode of decay from neutron to proton ratios.

Students should be familiar with the belt of stability in the graph of number of neutrons against number of protons for various stable nuclei. © IBO 2001

Spontaneous radioactivity involves unstable nuclei which decay with the eventual formation of a stable nuclei. Thus some nuclei are stable and others are not, for example, C–12 and C–14, H–1 and H–3. The isotopes in these examples have the same number of protons but differ in the number of neutrons. Two important factors determine nuclear stability:

　　1. **the mass number** (which is the total number of nucleons in the nucleus) and

　　2. **the neutron to proton ratio**.

This is because in a nucleus, the positively charged protons repel each other and as the number of protons increases in a nucleus, the forces of repulsion between the protons increases drastically. Thus, a greater proportion of neutrons is required for a nucleus to remain stable as the atomic number increases. This is evident from the graph of the number of neutrons against the number of protons present in stable nuclei.

A 1:1 n to p ratio holds true for the stable nuclei of the first twenty elements or so in the periodic table. This ratio increases to 1.5 to 1 around atomic number 80. Elements above atomic number 83 with 209 nucleons do not exist as stable isotopes. Thus for polonium, with 84 protons, the repulsive forces due to

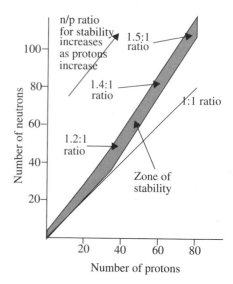

the 84 protons are so large that regardless of the number of neutrons, its nuclides are unstable.

When the n to p ratio is too large or too small, the nucleus is unstable, the atom is called a radionuclide and undergoes radioactive decay. If a **radionuclide** has a higher n to p ratio than for a stable nucleus, that is if it has an excess of neutrons and therefore a neutron disintegrates to form a proton with the emission of a beta particle:

$$\ _0^1n \Rightarrow \ _1^1p + \ _{-1}^0e$$

This decreases the n to p ratio and may be repeated until it reaches the stable value and no further radioactive decay takes place. An example of β decay is:

$$\ _{93}^{239}Np \Rightarrow \ _{-1}^0e + \ _{94}^{239}Pu$$

If, on the other hand, a radionuclide has a lower n to p ratio, it has an excess of protons and therefore a proton is transformed to a neutron either by positron emission or by electron capture. An inner-orbital electron is captured, the rate at which this happens is slow and gamma rays are always produced:

$$\ _1^1p \Rightarrow \ _0^1n + \ _1^0e \quad \text{or} \quad \ _1^1p + \ _{-1}^0e \Rightarrow \ _0^1n$$

$$\ _{15}^{30}P \Rightarrow \ _{14}^{30}Si + \ _1^0e \ ; \text{positron emission}$$

$$\ _{18}^{37}Ar + \ _{-1}^0e \Rightarrow \ _{17}^{37}Cl \ ; \text{electron capture}$$

In both positron emission and electron capture by a nucleus, the nucleus produced has one less proton. Note that positron emissions are short lived and when they collide with electrons, high energy photons are formed:

$$\ _{-1}^0e + \ _1^0e \Rightarrow 2 \ _0^0\gamma$$

If however, the number of nucleons exceeds 209, the limit for stable nuclei and therefore lies beyond the stable value, several decays are required in order to attain stability. For example the radioisotope U–238 undergoes a series of 14 decays (including eight α decays) before the final product Pb–206 is formed; this is called the U–238 decay series. Note that during α decay, the emission of a helium nucleus decreases the number of nucleons. This is supplemented by β decays to maintain a favourable n:p ratio. Part of the uranium decay series is shown below:

$$\ _{92}^{238}U \Rightarrow \ _2^4\alpha + \ _{90}^{234}Th$$

$$\ _{90}^{234}Th \Rightarrow \ _{-1}^0\beta + \ _{91}^{234}Pa$$

$$\ _{91}^{234}Pa \Rightarrow \ _{-1}^0\beta + \ _{92}^{234}U$$

$$\ _{92}^{234}U \Rightarrow \ _2^4\alpha + \ _{90}^{230}Th$$

F.7.2 Calculate the energy released in a nuclear reaction. © IBO 2001

What is the source of the tremendous energy of fission and fusion? It comes from mass being converted to energy as indicated by Einstein's equation: $E = mc^2$, where E is the energy, m the mass and c the velocity of light equal to 2.998×10^8 m s^{-1}. Thus a very small amount of matter should produce a tremendous amount of energy. If the mass is in kg and the velocity of light in meters per second, the units of energy turn out to be **Joules**. A unit of energy can therefore be considered a unit of mass. Since 1 atomic mass unit is equal to 1.661×10^{-27} kg, then

$$E = mc^2 = 1.661 \times 10^{-27} \text{ kg} \times (2.998 \times 10^8 \text{ m/s})^2 = 1.493 \times 10^{-10} \text{ J}$$

Thus, destroying one hydrogen atom gives approximately 1.5×10^{-10} J of energy. 5.0 g of

hydrogen atoms would give $1.5 \times 10^{-10} \text{ J} \times 5.0 \text{ mol} \times 6.02 \times 10^{23} \, \dfrac{\text{atom}}{\text{mol}} \approx 4.5 \times 10^{14}$ J of

energy. This is enough to heat approximately 10^9 kg (i.e. one million tons) of water from 0°C to 100°C!

Consider thorium–228, an alpha–emitter that produces radium–224:

$$^{228}_{90}\text{Th} \Rightarrow {}^{224}_{88}\text{Ra} + {}^{4}_{2}\text{He}$$

The mass of the products equals 228.022800 atomic mass units whereas the reactant is 288.028726. The difference equals 0.005926 atomic mass units.
This loss corresponds to a mass of $0.005926 \times 1.661 \times 10^{-27}$ kg.
Thus: $E = 0.005926 \times 1.661 \times 10^{-27}$ kg$\times (2.998 \times 10^{-8}$ m s$^{-1})^2 = 8.847 \times 10^{-13}$ J per atom. 1 mol Th–228, mass $\approx$ 228 g, containing 6.023×10^{23} atoms would produce 5.329×10^{11} J $\approx$ 533 billion Joules of energy! This value is about a million times greater than typical enthalpy changes for chemical reactions, which are measured in kilojoules.

F.7.3 Define and determine mass defect and nuclear binding energy.

Nuclear binding energy is a quantitative measure of nuclear stability. The graph of nuclear binding energy per nucleon against mass number should be used to explain why the products are more stable than the reactants in both nuclear fission and nuclear fusion, and consequently why both processes are exothermic.

© IBO 2001

Mass Defect and **Nuclear Binding Energy**: Consider a helium atom. It is made up of 2 protons, 2 electrons and 2 neutrons. The relative mass of the helium atom (4.002604) is very slightly less than the sum of the relative masses of 2 protons, 2 electrons and 2 neutrons (the sum of masses of 2p, 2e and 2n is equal to 4.032982). Thus if any separate protons, neutrons and electrons are combined to form an atom, there is a loss of mass. This is called **mass defect** and the energy equivalent to the mass defect, which can be calculated using Einstein's equation $E = mc^2$, is called its **nuclear binding energy**. If one wanted to break up a helium nucleus into protons and neutrons, one would have to supply enough energy, equivalent to its mass defect, to be able to do so.

OPTION

To obtain an idea of the relative stabilities of different nuclei it is better to divide the binding energy by the total number of nucleons. The binding energy per nucleon for various elements are shown below:

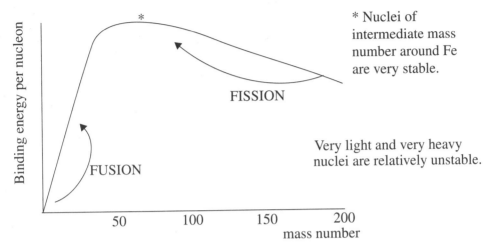

Note that the greater the binding energy per nuclear particle, the more stable the nucleus. The diagram above explains why both fission and fusion produce energy. In fission there is the splitting of a large unstable nuclei into smaller more stable nuclei e.g.

$$^{235}_{92}U + {}^{1}_{0}n \rightarrow {}^{141}_{56}Ba + {}^{92}_{36}Ba + 3\, {}^{1}_{0}n$$

The more stable nuclei contain less mass per nuclear particle. In the process, mass must be changed into large amounts of energy according to Einstein's equation. Similarly for fusion:

(a)   Deuterium – Deuterium fusion: ${}^{2}_{1}H + {}^{2}_{1}H \rightarrow {}^{3}_{2}He + {}^{1}_{0}n$ + energy

A tremendous amount of energy is released because He–3 has a greater binding energy per nucleon than H–2. D–D fusion occurs in a hydrogen bomb and inside stars. Similarly for:

(b)   Deuterium – Tritium fusion: ${}^{2}_{1}H + {}^{3}_{1}H \rightarrow {}^{4}_{2}He + {}^{1}_{0}n$ + energy.

The products of fusion consist of much more stable nuclei (because of the steep rise in binding energy per nucleon with much higher binding energy for He nuclei compared to the H nuclei) and thus fusion produces much more energy compared to fission.

Note that the binding energy is between protons and neutrons and NOT between atoms which is due to interaction of valence electrons only.

16.8 RADIOACTIVE DECAY

F.8.1 Calculate the change in activity over a period of time.

See the data booklet for the integrated form of the rate equation. © IBO 2001

Radioactive decays are first order reactions with constant half lives and equations used in kinetics, namely $\ln\left(\dfrac{x_0}{x}\right) = kt$ or $x = x_0 e^{-kt}$ can be used for such problems.

Thus a graph of $\ln\left(\dfrac{x_0}{x}\right)$ against t should be a straight line through the intercept with slope $= k$.

At one half–life, time $t = t_{1/2}$ and $x = 0.5x_0$ by definition.

Thus $\ln\left(\dfrac{x_0}{0.5x_0}\right) = kt_{1/2}$ or $t_{1/2} = \ln\left(\dfrac{2}{k}\right) = \dfrac{0.693}{k}$. Since k is a constant, then $t_{1/2}$ is also a constant, independent of the initial amount, and can be used to calculate k.

EXAMPLE

After 2 hours, a solution containing 1.30×10^{-6} mol per dm^3 of $^{240}AmCl_3$ contained only 1.27×10^{-6} mol per dm^3 of radioactive substance. What is the half life for Am–240?

SOLUTION

$$\log\left(\frac{x_0}{x}\right) = \frac{kt}{2.303}$$

$$\therefore k = \log\left(\frac{x_0}{x}\right) \times \frac{2.303}{t}$$

$$= \log\left(\frac{1.30}{1.27}\right) \times \frac{2.303}{2}$$

$$= 1.17 \times 10^{-2} \text{ hours}^{-1}$$

$$t_{1/2} = \frac{0.693}{k}$$

$$= \frac{0.693}{1.17 \times 10^{-2}}$$

$$= 59 \text{ hours}$$

Alternatively, the problem can be solved using the equation $x = x_0 e^{-kt}$.

EXAMPLE

Radium–226 has a half–life of 1620 years. Calculate the first order rate constant k, and the fraction remaining after 100 years.

SOLUTION

$$k = \frac{0.693}{t_{1/2}}$$

$$= \frac{0.693}{1620}$$

$$= 0.000428$$

$$= 4.28 \times 10^{-4} \text{ year}^{-1}$$

$$\log\left(\frac{x_0}{x}\right) = \frac{kt}{2.303}$$

$$= \frac{4.28 \times 10^{-4} \times 100}{2.303}$$

$$= 0.0186$$

$$\therefore \frac{x_0}{x} = 1.044 \text{ ; thus fraction remaining} = \frac{x}{x_0} = \frac{1}{1.044} = 0.965 \Rightarrow 96.5\% \text{ remains.}$$

F.8.2   Describe the different types of nuclear waste, their characteristics and their sources.

F.8.3   Compare the storage and disposal methods for different types of nuclear waste.

Nuclear power generator stations discharge low level radioactive materials – in the form of gases into the atmosphere, and, in the form of liquids into lakes and seas. These discharges are supposed to be limited to relatively safe levels as determined by the atomic energy commissions in various countries.

Waste from spent fuel: When the percentage of enriched U–235 drops from 3% to less than 1%, chain reaction cannot continue and the fuel rods, now consisting of spent fuel, have to be removed and stored. Besides the U–235 present, neutron bombardment of the U–238, in the fuel leads to the formation of Np–239 and Pu–239.

$$^{238}_{92}U + ^{1}_{0}n \Rightarrow ^{239}_{92}U \Rightarrow ^{0}_{-1}e + ^{239}_{93}Np \Rightarrow ^{0}_{-1}e + ^{239}_{94}Pu$$

The Pu–239 formed is fissile. It is also an α-emitter and as it has a half–life of 24000 years it will take about a quarter of a million years to decay to safe levels. Similarly other radioisotopes formed as a result of α and β emissions produce radionuclides of the actinide series including thorium, americium and curium, all of which are highly poisonous with long half lives causing very long term waste disposal problems.

The products of fission of U–235 produce lighter isotopes such as Sr–90 and Cs–137 which are highly radioactive (gamma emitters) with half–lives in the order of about 30 years and will therefore be around for several hundred years to come.

OPTION

Currently, spent fuel is most often stored in pools of water, usually on site; the water absorbs the heat as the wastes decay. Because of the long half–lives of radioisotopes involved, long–term safe storage is of concern because of the possibility of these radioisotopes leaching into water tables. The most common approach being investigated is the burial of nuclear waste in deep, remote places which are geologically stable such as salt beds and granite. Existence of salt beds suggest lack of water, thus eliminating the problem of leaching. Granite sites are considered extremely stable geologically; whether these can stand volcanic activity, high temperatures due to depth in the earth or the heating due to radioactive decay is another matter.

High–level radioactive waste products of long–half lives are considered to pose the greatest hazard. Research into vitrification, that is converting these products into borosilicate glass, has been underway for some time, as has the possibility of synthetic ceramics containing titanium compounds resembling natural rock, which is excellent at containing radioactive materials in nature.

Radioactive isotopes of half–life in the range of 10 to 40 years (and therefore active up to 400 years) have been buried underground or at sea, in steel drums, in concrete. Corrosion of steel drums at sea has been, however, a serious problem.

Low–level radioactive waste is produced in large volumes and is stored safely in steel drums until all the radioactivity has stopped. It is then discarded as waste. This low–level waste includes clothes and protective gear and materials that may have come in contact with other radioisotopes.

16.9 PHOTOVOLTAICS

F.9.1   State that silicon and germanium are semiconductors.

F.9.2   Compare the electrical conductivity of a semiconductor with the conductivity of metals and non-metals.

Relate this to the ionization energies of semiconductors compared to metals and non-metals.

F.9.3   Explain the doping of silicon to produce n-type and p-type semiconductors.

In p-type semiconductors, electron holes in the crystal are created by introducing a small percentage of a group 3 element (eg In, Ga). In n-type semiconductors inclusion of a group 5 element (eg As) provides extra electrons.

F.9.4   Describe how sunlight interacts with semiconductors.

Photons interact with crystals to release electrons.   © IBO 2001

Silicon and germanium are semiconductors: semiconductors are a special class of materials which have an electrical resistance between those of electrical conductors and electrical insulators and are better conductors under certain circumstances. Thus they conduct electricity better (that is, the resistance falls) as the temperature rises.

Note that the electrons in the shell of an isolated atom have discrete energy levels. The valence electrons, present in the highest energy levels are used in bond formation. Metals have few valence electrons, vacant orbitals and low ionization energies, the latter two conditions being necessary for metallic bonding. Low ionization energies of metals means valence electrons are rather weakly held by the nuclei. The valence electrons are very mobile and the interaction of the positive cations with the valence electrons accounts for metallic bonding. In metals, electrons in the valence shell can move easily to an unfilled higher energy level making electric conduction possible. The valence electrons in metals are delocalized; they are in effect free from individual atoms and are able to move through the metal when a potential difference is applied across it (see Chapter 4).

Si and Ge both contain 4 valence electrons. As each atom forms four tetrahedrally directed covalent bonds to other silicon atoms, a macromolecular crystal structure in three dimensions is built up in the pure element. At absolute zero temperature, Si and Ge would, like most non-metals, be insulators (non–conductors of electricity). At room temperatures, because they have rather low ionisation energies compared with other non-metals, some valence electrons gain enough energy from the vibration of atoms in the crystal lattice to move between atoms and hence behave as a semiconductor. Such substances are called **intrinsic semiconductors** since the origin of their electrical conductivity is from within the crystals.

Across a period, such as $n = 3$ (the third period), recall that valence electrons are being added to the same principal energy level, whereas the nuclear charge increases. Thus the atomic radius decreases, the valence electrons are closer to the nucleus and ionization energy increases. Whereas metals with low ionization energies are very good conductors of electricity, Si and Ge are semiconductors. Non–metals with high ionization energies are poor conductors of electricity and are considered to be insulators.

Semiconductors are made by adding certain substances to silicon and germanium to increase their conductivity. This can be done by exposing the semiconductor to the vapor of the substance to be added in the furnace. The chosen substance is added in carefully controlled amounts to bring the content up to only a few parts per million. The atoms of the added substance are therefore well spaced out in the semiconductor so that its crystal structure is not weakened. The process is called **doping** and the added substances are called **dopants**.

There are two types of semiconductors: **n–type and p–type**. In n–type semiconductors, the dopants are Group V (or 15) elements, such as arsenic (As) or antimony (Sb), which have 5 electrons in their outer shells. When an arsenic dopant atom replaces an atom of silicon in the structure, it uses four of its five valence electrons to form covalent bonds with silicon atoms. The fifth electron is supplied to the material, creating a potentially negative charge. It is not negative overall as it has one more proton. These are called n–type semiconductors. The added atoms are called **donor atoms** because they donate electrons to the material.

In p–type semiconductors, the dopants are Group III (or 13) elements, such as boron, gallium (Ga) or indium (In) which have three electrons in the outer shell. For example,

OPTION

when a boron atom replaces a silicon atom, it forms three electron pair bonds with three silicon atoms, but the fourth bond is incomplete as it has only one electron. The vacancy is called an **electron hole** and creates a potentially mobile positive charge and is called a p–type semiconductor. Again, the crystal has no overall charge. The added atoms are called **acceptor atoms** because they can accept electrons to fill the holes in the bonds.

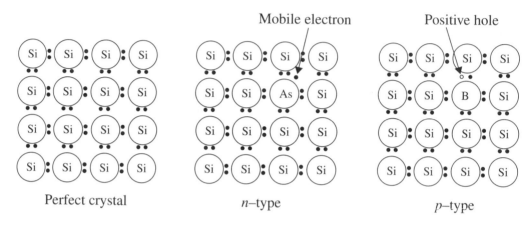

Perfect crystal   *n*–type   *p*–type

When n–type and p–type conductors are placed together, electrons flowing through the p–type electrode stop at the pn–junction. Electrons flowing through the n–type electrode pass through the junction because they can pass from a structure with surplus electrons into a structure with electron holes. A junction of this kind acts as a **rectifier** and can transform alternating current into direct current. A **transistor** is a device which uses semiconductor electrodes to control the flow of electric current by altering the electrical potential at the junction rather than driving the current. A silicon chip 0.5–1.0 cm across may contain up to 200,000 transistors in one integrated circuit.

A typical photo–voltaic solar cell consists of two layers of almost pure silicon; one has a trace of arsenic (n–type) and the other a trace of boron (p–type). The n–type has an extra electron which is relatively free to move whereas the p–type is short of an electron. When the two layers are placed together, the extra electron from the n–type moves to the p–type layer and it pairs up. When sunlight strikes such a surface, the sun's energy is able to unpair the electrons (that is, photons from sun's energy interact with the crystal to release electrons) which move back to the n–type layer creating a potential difference. If an external circuit is present, the electrons can flow through it back to the p–type layer.

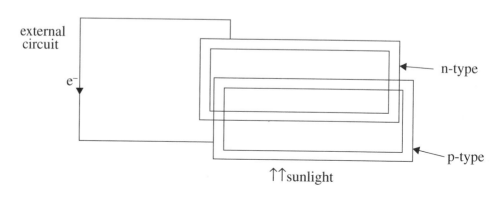

QUESTIONS ON THE CORE MATERIAL (SL & HL)
ENERGY SOURCES

1. State the desirable characteristics of energy sources.

2. Outline current and potential energy sources.

FOSSIL FUELS

3. Describe the formation of coal, oil and natural gas.

4. In what sorts of geological formations are petroleum and natural gas likely to be found?

5. How does the formation of coal differ from that of petroleum?

6. Describe the characteristics of coal, oil and natural gas as fuels.

7. What are the main ways of classifying coal? What is this classification based on?

8. What elements and compounds are present in coal?

9. How does the composition of coal differ from that of petroleum?

10. Define the term standard molar enthalpy change of combustion, $\Delta H°_{comb}$.

11. 1.00 g benzene burns in excess oxygen to produce 42.0 kJ of energy as determined by the use of a calorimeter. Write a balanced equation for the reaction and calculate the standard molar enthalpy change of combustion for benzene. If the experimental data was not given, what data from a data booklet would you use to calculate $\Delta H°_{comb}$ for benzene?

12. Given $\Delta H°_f (H_2O) = -242$ kJ mol^{-1}, $\Delta H°_f (CO_2) = -393$ kJ mol^{-1}, $\Delta H°_f (CH_4) = 74.9$ kJ mol^{-1} and $\Delta H°_f (C_4H_{10}) = -125$ kJ mol^{-1}, calculate the standard molar enthalpy changes of combustion of methane and butane.

13. Given the standard change in enthalpy of formation for propane is -104 kJ mol^{-1}, calculate the standard change in enthalpy of combustion for propane from data given in the above question.

14. Outline the composition and characteristics of the crude oil fractions used for fuel.

15. What is it meant by octane number? What is its significance?

16. Describe how the components of a hydrocarbon fuel relate to its octane rating.

17. Explain the processes of coal gasification and liquefaction. Include the equations for the main chemical reactions involved.

18. What are the advantages and disadvantages of coal gasification and liquefication?

19. Write an essay on coal. Your answer should identify the different grades of coal and the basis used for the classification. Compare coal with other fossil fuels as a source of air pollution and explain any differences. Describe how air pollution from the combustion of coal may be reduced.

20. Discuss coal as an energy source. Your answer should explain its origins, world coal reserves, pollution associated with its use and ways of converting coal to other fuels.

21. Coal is a most abundant fossil fuel as a primary energy source and its consumption is expected to increase in the next 50 years. Explain the meaning of the terms fossil fuels and primary energy source. Outline the advantages and disadvantages of coal as a primary energy source. Why is the consumption of coal expected to increase in the next 50 years?

22. Describe the key components of natural gas and petroleum.

23. Explain the nature of petroleum and how it is formed.

24. List the major fossil fuels in order of their abundance. Describe the origin of fossil fuels. Compare the pollution produced by these fossil fuels and explain which one causes the most environmental damage and why.

25. Discuss the advantages and disadvantages of the different fossil fuels.

26. State the main types of pollutants produced by the burning each of the various fossil fuels and describe how the burning of fossil fuels produces each type of pollutant.

NUCLEAR ENERGY

27. Distinguish between nuclear reactions and chemical reactions.

28. Explain nuclear fission using a typical balanced equation for the nuclear reaction.

29. Describe how a fission process is started.

30. Write balanced nuclear equations for a fission and fusion reaction of your choice.

31. Would you expect a radioactive decay to have an activation energy? Explain your answer.

32. Describe the nature of α, β and γ radiation and state how to differentiate between them. In your answer compare the charge, mass and penetrating power of each.

33. State the concept of half–life. Draw and describe the graph for the decay of a radio–isotope.

34. Explain how long it would take for a radioactive substance to decay to less than 1% of its original amount? 0.1% of its original amount? On the basis of your answer how long would it take for Pu–239, an extremely carcinogenic substance produced in nuclear reactors, to decay to relatively safe levels given its half–life is about 24 000 years?

35. Fission products such as Sr–90 and Cs–137 have half–lives in the order of 30 years. How long will it take these substances to decay to relatively safe levels? Explain your answer.

36. Why is the carbon–14 dating method suitable for objects that are not older than about 50 000 years?

37. Describe a chain reaction.

38. Compare nuclear fission and nuclear fusion. Include balanced equations.

39. Identify the forms in which energy is released in a nuclear power plant and explain how they are converted into the form in which it is used.

40. Explain the functions of the main components of a nuclear power plant.

41. Discuss why certain fuels such as uranium and plutonium are used in nuclear reactors.

42. Describe the advantages and disadvantages of nuclear fission as a source of energy. Your answer should include the effect of each of the concerns raised.

43. Discuss the differences between conventional power generation and nuclear reactors.

44. Discuss the concerns about safety in nuclear power plants.

45. What fuel is used in controlled nuclear fusion? What is plasma? List some advantages of controlled nuclear fusion.

46. Write an essay on nuclear fission as a commercial source of energy. Your answer should include the fuel used, the source of energy and how it is utilized and the advantages and disadvantages of nuclear fission as a source of energy.

47. Explain the difference between a typical nuclear fission reactor and a breeder reactor.

48. Explain briefly each of the following: critical mass, natural radioactivity, artificial radioactivity, half–life, the law of conservation of mass–energy and Einstein's equation.

49. Explain how a breeder reactor can produce more fuel than it consumes.

SOLAR ENERGY

50. Describe the characteristics of solar energy.

51. State how solar energy can be converted to other forms of energy.

52. Describe the role of photosynthesis in converting solar energy to other forms of energy. Include a balanced chemical equation.

53. Discuss how biomass can be converted to energy. Your answer should include direct combustion, combustion of waste materials from other processes, production of biogas and production and use of ethanol. For each method, state the advantages and disadvantages. Give the equation for the formation of ethanol from glucose.

54. Outline the principles of using solar energy for space heating. Your answer should include storage of heat using water and rocks.

OPTION

55. What are the differences between passive and active solar heating? What are their advantages and disadvantages?

56. Discuss the methods by which solar energy can be converted to electricity. Your answer should include parabolic mirrors and photovoltaic cells. Discuss the advantages and disadvantages of each method.

57. What is biomass?

58. Name and write a chemical equation for the process which converts solar energy into chemical energy. What are the advantages and disadvantages of using biomass as a large scale source of energy. How is ethanol produced for fuel? What is gasohol? What are the advantages and disadvantages of ethanol as an automobile fuel?

59. Describe a photovoltaic cell and how it operates.

60. What are the advantages and disadvantages of utilising solar energy?

ELECTROCHEMICAL ENERGY

61. What is an electrochemical cell? How is it different from an electrolytic cell?

62. State the materials used as electrodes and electrolytes in the lead–acid storage batteries and dry cells. Write balanced half reactions and overall equations for the reactions in each case. Explain the workings of each.

63. For the ordinary dry battery (Leclanché cell), show the make up of the cell and label the anode and cathode. Write balanced equations for the reactions taking place at each electrode and the overall reaction. Explain the workings of the zinc-carbon battery.

64. What is a fuel cell? Explain how a hydrogen-oxygen fuel cell works. What are the advantages of using fuel cells over obtaining energy from the combustion of fossil fuels? What are the problems with current fuel cells?

65. Explain the factors that affect the voltage and power available from a battery.

66. Comment on the advantages and disadvantages of batteries as sources of energy.

EXTENSION MATERIAL (HL ONLY)
STORAGE OF ENERGY AND LIMITS OF EFFICIENCY

67. Discuss the advantages and disadvantages of pumped storage schemes.

68. Write an essay on hydrogen gas as a way of storing energy. In your answer explain what features make hydrogen attractive as a fuel. What is the source of hydrogen and what primary energy sources can be used to produce it? What are the potential uses of hydrogen gas as a fuel and what are the disadvantages of using it?

69. Discuss the limits of energy conversion.

NUCLEAR STABILITY

70. Explain why the neutron/proton ration increases as the atomic number increases in a nucleus. If a nucleus has (a) a larger n/p ratio and (b) a smaller n/p ratio than in the belt of stability, explain the nuclear process that must take place in each case for the nucleus to become stable. What happens to the nucleus if the number of nucleons exceed 209?

71. Calculate the energy equivalent of the mass defect of He.

72. Define 'mass defect', 'nuclear binding energy' and 'nuclear binding energy per nucleon'.

73. Why do some nuclei undergo fission whereas others undergo fusion? Explain your answer in terms of binding energy.

RADIOACTIVE DECAY

74. Describe the different types of nuclear waste, their characteristics and their sources.

75. Compare storage and disposal methods for different types of nuclear waste.

PHOTOVOLTAICS

76. What are semiconductors? Name two semiconductors. Based on ionization energies, compare the properties of semiconductors with those of metals and insulators.

77. Explain the difference between n-type and p-type semiconductors. Describe how the properties of an intrinsic semiconductor can be altered by doping.

78. Describe how sunlight interacts with semiconductors.

MODERN ANALYTICAL CHEMISTRY (Option G)

17

Chapter contents

Emphasize problem solving and using the information gained from one or more techniques throughout this option. Students should understand the chemical principles behind each analytical technique but are not expected to have a detailed knowledge of the instruments themselves.

© IBO 2001

17.1 ANALYTICAL TECHNIQUES

G.1.1 State the reasons for using analytical techniques

Analytical techniques are used in structure determination, in analysis of composition of substances and to determine purity.

G.1.2 Outline the information that can be obtained from analytical techniques, singly or in combination.

Students should be able to draw upon a range of contexts to illustrate the information obtained by using a technique or range of techniques.

***Visible and ultraviolet (uv) spectroscopy**–assaying of metal ions, organic structure determination and detection of drug metabolites.*

***Infrared (ir) spectroscopy**–organic structure determination, information on strengths of bonds, secondary structure of proteins and measuring degree of unsaturation of oils and fats.*

***Mass spectrometry**–organic structure determination and isotopic dating (e.g. ^{14}C dating).*

***Gas chromatography**–mass spectrometry (GC–MS–drug and food testing and forensic science.*

Chemical analysis may be divided into structural analysis, qualitative analysis and quantitative analysis. In structural analysis the object is to determine the chemical structure of a pure substance, i.e. the way in which the atoms present are joined together and, in the case of large molecules, the way in which the molecule is arranged in three–dimensions. An example of this kind of analysis would be determining the structure of a protein molecule. Qualitative analysis is designed to find out what components are present in a complex mixture of substances. Often the emphasis is on the detection of one particular component, for example the use of a forbidden colouring material in a processed food. In quantitative analysis the amount of a particular substance in a mixture is determined, for example the percentage of copper in brass.

In the past almost all analyses were carried out by 'wet' chemical techniques, such as testing to see if certain characteristic chemical reactions occurred (structural and qualitative analysis), or the use of volumetric and gravimetric techniques (quantitative analysis). Although these techniques still have important applications, nowadays most analysis is carried out by 'physical methods', some of which are described below. These are usually faster, more precise and easier to automate than 'wet' methods.

17.2 PRINCIPLES OF SPECTROSCOPY

G.2.1   Describe the electromagnetic spectrum.

X–ray, uv, visible, ir and radio (including microwave) should be identified. Highlight the variation in wavelength, frequency and energy across the spectrum.

G.2.2   Distinguish between absorption and emission spectra and how each is produced. *Cross reference with 2.2.1.*

G.2.3   Describe the atomic and molecular processes in which absorption of energy takes place.

Cross reference with 2.2. The description should cover vibrations, rotation and electronic transitions only.

G.2.4   Describe the operating principles of a double–beam infrared spectrometer.

A schematic diagram of a simple double–beam spectrometer is sufficient. This example is chosen to illustrate the general principles of how spectrometers operate. Mention could be made of modern methods of processing signals by Fourier transformation.   © IBO 2001

Many physical techniques involve spectroscopy, i.e. the way in which the absorption or emission of electromagnetic radiation by substances varies with frequency. There are many kinds of electromagnetic radiation ranging from γ–rays through to radio waves and beyond. These are all very similar and can be considered to be a kind of wave. A wave has certain characteristics such as amplitude, wavelength and frequency. As shown on the Figure 17.1, the **wavelength** (λ, in units of distance, e.g. m) is the distance between successive peaks on the wave. The **frequency** (f, in units of Hertz, Hz = s^{-1}) is the number of peaks that pass a fixed point every second. Therefore if this is multiplied by the distance between the peaks (wavelength), then it gives the **velocity** of the wave. All electromagnetic waves travel at the same speed in a vacuum ($c = 3 \times 10^8$ m s^{-1}), so the relationship between frequency and wavelength shown below holds for all electromagnetic waves.

Figure 17.1 – An electromagnetic wave

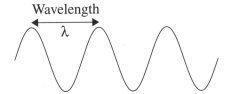

Wavelength

λ

velocity = frequency × wavelength

$$c = f . \lambda$$

It is found that electromagnetic radiation also has a particle nature and that the energy carried by a quantum of radiation is related to the frequency of the radiation by the equation $E = h . f$ (where h = Planck's constant, 6.626×10^{-34} J s). This means that particles of high frequency (and hence short wavelength) radiation carry a great deal of energy and those of low frequency radiation much less. A particle (atom, molecule or ion) can absorb a quantum of light and this will affect its state. The way in which its state is affected will depend on the amount of energy that the quantum carries. γ–rays, the highest frequency radiation, can bring about changes in the nucleus. X–rays cannot do this but they do have enough energy to remove electrons in inner filled shells of atoms.

OPTION

Ultraviolet and visible light have enough energy to affect the valence electrons. All of these types of radiation can break chemical bonds and initiate reactions hence, except for visible light (which can only break very weak bonds), they are potentially harmful. Infrared radiation can stimulate the vibrations of molecules, whilst microwaves affect their rotational state. Radio waves do not directly affect molecules under normal circumstances, but they can alter the spin state of some nuclei when they are exposed to magnetic fields (see NMR spectroscopy, Section17.5, page 666).

Figure 17.2 – The electromagnetic spectrum

Wavelength
(nanometres)

Changes to

Visible

Wavelength (nm)	Colour
400	Violet
	Blue
500	Green
600	Yellow
	Orange
700	Red

10^{-4} — γ–rays — Nucleus

10^{-1} — X–rays — Inner electrons

UV

10^{4} — IR — Outer electrons / Molecular: Vibrations

Microwaves — Rotations

10^{9}

10^{14} — Radio waves — Nuclear spin

Decreasing frequency

Decreasing energy

Increasing wavelength

In **emission spectroscopy** the frequency of the radiation emitted by excited particles dropping to a lower energy state, is studied. For example the coloured light from a neon lamp is an emission process. In **absorption spectroscopy** radiation of a wide range of frequencies is passed through the sample and the way in which the absorption of radiation varies with its frequency is studied. Energy of particular frequencies is absorbed and used to enable a particle to move from a lower to a higher energy state. The red colour of red paint is the result of an absorption process because of the wide range of frequencies in the white light shining on it. The paint absorbs the blue, green and yellow colours because their energy corresponds to the energy difference between filled and vacant orbitals. It reflects the red light because its energy is not sufficient to allow electrons to move to a higher orbital.

Figure 17.3 Emission and Absorption Spectroscopy

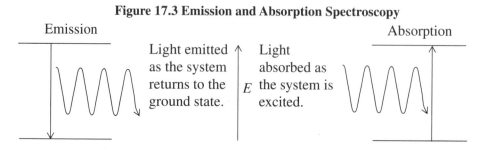

Emission

Light emitted as the system returns to the ground state.

E

Light absorbed as the system is excited.

Absorption

Many measurements in spectroscopy employ '**double–beam**' instruments that allow the radiation passing through the sample to be continually compared with identical radiation that has not passed through the sample. In these instruments the radiation from the source is split into two equal beams that pass along parallel paths. The sample is placed in one beam, whilst the second, known as the reference beam, is identical (i.e. a similar container and a similar solvent, if one is used) except for the fact that the substance being studied is missing. The light from the source passes through a monochromator which only allows radiation of a particular wavelength to pass through it. This monochromatic (single colour) light then strikes a beam splitter which directs half of the radiation through the sample and the other half through the reference cell. The two beams are then recombined at the detector. The signal from the sample and reference beams are then compared electronically to see if the sample absorbs radiation of the frequency that the monochromator is set to and the output sent to the recorder. As the spectrum of the sample is scanned, the frequency of the radiation that the monochromator transmits is varied and a graph of absorption against frequency/wavelength drawn. The principle of the double–beam instrument (either uv–visible or ir – they differ only in the source and detector) is illustrated in Figure 17.4 below.

Figure 17.4 – A double–beam spectrometer

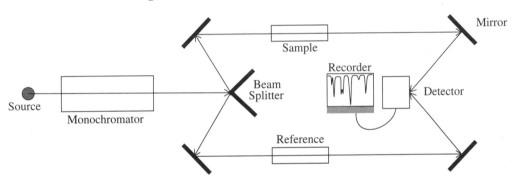

A recent development has been **Fourier transform spectroscopy**. This works in a totally different manner. A single beam of radiation containing all the frequencies of interest is passed through the sample and then split so that it travels along two separate paths. The length of one of these is varied and the way in which the intensity alters (owing to the interference pattern produced) as the difference in path length changes is measured. Using sophisticated computer technology, the whole absorption spectrum can be calculated from this. One of the main advantages of this technique is that it is far more sensitive, as the full power of the radiation source is used, rather than just the narrow range of frequencies from the monochromator. The spectrum can also be found much more rapidly than with a conventional spectrometer.

OPTION

17.3 VISIBLE AND ULTRAVIOLET SPECTROSCOPY

G.3.1   Describe the factors that affect the colour of transition metal complexes.

Cross reference with 13.2.6. The factors are the identity of the metal (e.g. Mn^{2+}, Fe^{2+}), oxidation number (eg Fe^{2+}, Fe^{3+}) and the identity of the ligand. Limit this to octahedral complexes in aqueous solution.

G.3.2   Describe the effect of different ligands on the splitting of the d orbitals in transition metal complexes.

The ligands should be limited to NH_3, H_2O and Cl^-.

G.3.3   State that organic molecules containing a double bond absorb ultraviolet radiation.

Refer to conjugated and delocalized systems: arenes, alkenes and natural products, eg chlorophyll.

G.3.4   Describe the effect of the conjugation of double bonds in organic molecules on the wavelength of the absorbed light.

Retinol and phenolphthalein are suitable examples.

G.3.5   Predict whether or not a particular molecule will absorb ultraviolet or visible radiation.

G.3.6   State the Beer–Lambert law.

$$\log_e\left(\frac{I_0}{I}\right) = \varepsilon l c$$

G.3.7   Construct a calibration curve and use the Beer–Lambert law to determine the concentration of an unknown solution.

© IBO 2001

The energy carried by a quantum of light in the UV and visible regions of the spectrum corresponds to the difference in energy between filled and unfilled electron orbitals in many ions and molecules. In some simple ions (e.g. the sodium ion) the difference in energy between the highest filled orbital and the lowest unfilled orbital (i.e. the 2p and the 3s for Na^+) is quite large and so they only absorb very short wavelength UV light. In the transition metals, the difference in energy between filled and unfilled d–orbitals is much smaller so that these ions absorb energy in the far UV and visible regions, the latter being responsible for the fact that many of these ions are coloured. For example aqueous copper(II) ions appear blue in colour because they absorb light in the red and green regions of the visible spectrum.

In transition metals light can be absorbed because, even though in an isolated atom the d-orbitals are all of the same energy, when the atom is surrounded by charged or polar ligands the interaction of the different orbitals with the electric fields of these ligands varies and hence they have different energies (see Section 3.5, page 103). This usually causes the d-orbitals to split into two groups with three orbitals at a lower energy and two at a slightly higher energy.

The difference in energy between these two groups of orbitals is smaller than that between most electron orbitals and corresponds ($\Delta E = h.f$) to light in the visible region of

OPTION

the spectrum (see Figure 3.9, page 108). The exact difference in energy between the two groups of d-orbitals, and hence the colour of the light absorbed (remember the colour it appears is the complementary colour of the absorbed light) depends on a number of factors:

- the element being considered (especially the nuclear charge)
- the charge on the ion
- the ligands surrounding the ion
- the number and geometrical arrangement of the ligands

The first point is easily illustrated by considering manganese(II), which has an almost colourless hexaaquo ion $[Mn(H_2O)_6]^{2+}$ and iron(III), which has a yellow-brown hexaaquo ion $(Fe(H_2O)_6)^{3+}$, even though they both have the same electronic structure [Ar] $3d^5$. This is a result of the differing charges on the two nuclei. An example of the second factor is the two oxidation states of iron, where $[Fe(H_2O)_6]^{2+}$ is pale green and $[Fe(H_2O)_6]^{3+}$ is yellow-brown. Here the nuclear charge is constant, but there is a difference in the electronic structures - [Ar] $3d^6$ and [Ar] $3d^5$ respectively. The nature of the ligand is well illustrated by copper(II). With water there is the familiar pale blue colour of the hexaaqua ion, $[Cu(H_2O)_6]^{2+}$. If the ligands are gradually replaced by ammonia, to give for example $[Cu(NH_3)_4(H_2O)_2]^{2+}$, the colour deepens to a dark royal blue. If the water ligands are gradually replaced by chloride ions the colour changes through green to the yellow of $[CuCl_4]^{2-}$. Obviously this last case also results from a change in the number and geometry of the ligands, which can lead to quite marked changes of colour. The hexaaqua ion of cobalt, $[Co(H_2O)_6]^{2+}$, is for example pale pink (i.e. blue, green and yellow light are weakly absorbed), but the tetrachloro ion, $[CoCl_4]^{2-}$ is dark blue (i.e green, yellow and red light are strongly absorbed).

In the same way that atoms and ions have atomic orbitals, molecules have molecular orbitals, some of which are filled, others of which are unfilled. In simple molecules, such as water, as in simple ions, the difference in energy between the highest filled orbital and the lowest unfilled orbital is again quite large and so that they too only absorb very short wavelength UV light. The difference in energy in molecules that have double bonds (i.e. C=C and C=O, structural elements known as '**chromophores**') is much less, especially if these are '**conjugated**' (i.e. alternate double and single bonds), and/or involve extensive delocalised bonds (e.g. in a benzene ring). Molecules of this kind absorb light in the far UV and visible regions. For example 1,10–diphenyl– 1,3,5,7,9– decapentene which, as shown below, has two benzene rings and an extensive chain of conjugated double bonds, and is an orange colour because it absorbs blue and green light.

If we examine the structures of a number of compounds to identify these structural elements it is possible to predict to what extent these will absorb UV and visible light. Consider the compounds below.

2.3–dichloropentane contains only σ – bonds and so will only absorb short wavelength UV light.

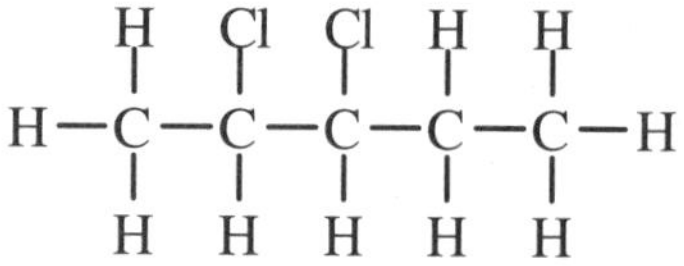

Pent–3–enoic acid contains isolated double bonds, so that it will absorb in the mid UV region.

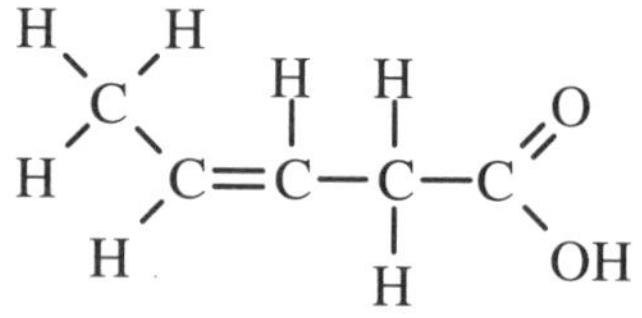

In pent–2–enoic acid the double bonds are conjugated and so the UV absorption will be at a longer wavelength.

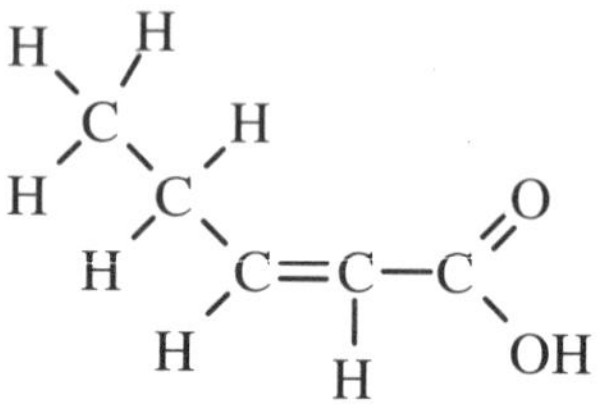

It is only when there is an extended system of delocalised bonds and conjugated double bonds, as in the diazonium compound formed between 2–naphthol and phenylamine that the absorption moves into the visible region to produce a coloured compound (in this case, red).

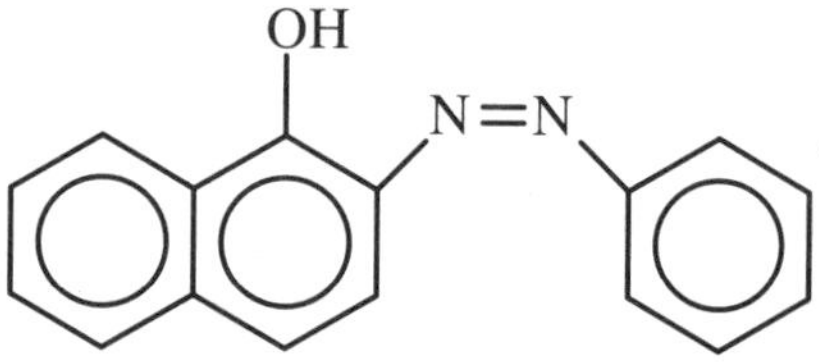

Other substances that absorb visible light as a result of extended conjugated systems are chlorophyll (vital for photosynthesis), retinol (vital for vision, see Table 21 of the IB Data Booklet) and the indicator phenolphthalein. Also, many drugs and their matabolites absorb light in the UV region.

The amount of light of a particular frequency which a solution absorbs will depend on the nature of the compound (which determines the molar extinction coefficient, ε), its concentration (c in mol dm^{-3}) and the distance the light passes through the solution (l, in cm). The intensity of the light (I) is found to decay exponentially as it passes through the solution, giving rise to a logarithmic relationship:

$$I = I_0 10^{-\varepsilon l c}$$

therefore, taking logarithms

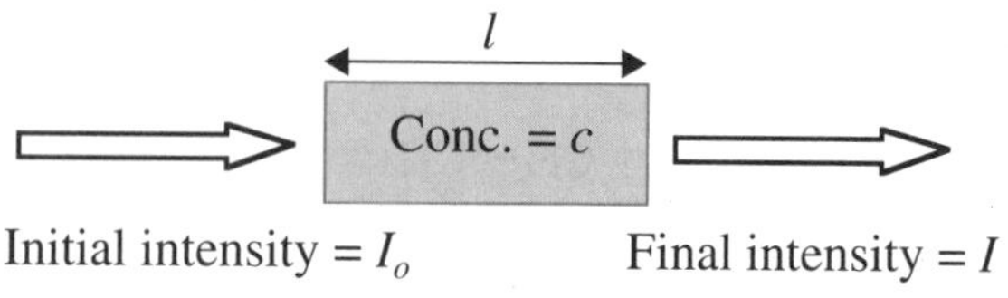

Initial intensity = I_o Final intensity = I

$$A = \log_{10}\left(\frac{I_0}{I}\right) = \varepsilon l c$$

OPTION

This is known as the **Beer–Lambert law**, and A is known as the absorbance of the solution, the reading given directly by most UV/visible spectrophotometers (though some also give the percentage transmittance, T, where $T = \dfrac{I}{I_o} \times 100$. The molar extinction coefficient (ε) is a measure of how strongly the compound absorbs light. The larger the value of ε, the stronger the absorption – the permanganate ion (MnO_4^-) for example has a very large extinction coefficient. Even though the Beer-Lambert law only holds precisely for dilute solutions, this relationship means that a graph of absorbance (A) against concentration (c) is linear, making it easy to use this technique to determine the concentration of a given species in a solution. The molar extinction coefficient (ε) may be found from the gradient, knowing the path length (l). It is equal to the logarithm of the fractional decrease in intensity of the monochromatic light as it passes through 1 cm of 1 mol dm^{-3} solution and therefore has units of dm^3 mol^{-1} cm^{-1}.

An example is the absorption of iodine in aqueous 0.1 mol dm^{-3} potassium iodide at 306 nm. The graph of absorbance against concentration as light passes through a 1 cm cell is shown in Figure 17.5. As expected it is linear and from the gradient, the molar extinction coefficient may be determined as $\dfrac{2.3}{1 \times 0.015} = 153.3$ dm^3 mol^{-1} cm^{-1}.

Figure 17.5 - The dependence of the absorption of iodine at 306 nm on concentration.

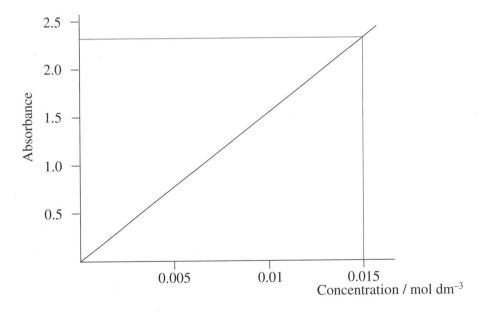

17.4 INFRARED SPECTROSCOPY

G.4.1 Describe what occurs at a molecular level during the absorption of infrared radiation by molecules.

H_2O, $-CH_2-$, SO_2 and CO_2 are suitable examples. Stress the change in bond polarity as the vibrations (stretching and bending) occur.

G.4.2 State the relationship between wavelength and wavenumber.

An inverse relationship exists (ie the wavenumber is the number of wavelengths that make up one cm). High wavenumber implies high energy.

G.4.3 Deduce the functional groups in an organic molecule from its infrared spectrum.

Examples should contain up to three functional groups. Students are not required to learn the characteristic absorption frequencies of functional groups, but must be familiar with the relevant information in the data booklet. The precise wavenumber of the absorption depends upon neighbouring atoms. © IBO 2001

A quantum of infrared radiation does not have sufficient energy to excite an electron to a higher energy level, but it does have sufficient energy to excite a molecule to a **higher vibrational level**. There are two types of vibrational motion that most molecules are capable of – stretching motions, where the bonds become longer then shorter, and bending motions, where the length of the bonds stays constant, but the angle between them increases and decreases. This latter kind of motion is, of course, not possible in diatomic molecules. These types of motion are shown for water in Figure 17.6 below:

Figure 17.6 – The bending and stretching motions of water

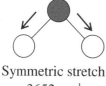 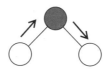 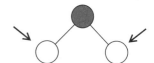

Symmetric stretch	Asymmetric stretch	Symmetric bend
3652cm^{-1}	3756 cm^{-1}	1595 cm^{-1}

The 'wavenumbers' at which these motions absorb infrared radiation are shown under each mode. In infrared spectroscopy, the **wavenumber** (= 1/wavelength in cm) is traditionally used rather than frequency. It is equal to the number of wavepeaks in 1 cm of the wave. For example if infrared radiation has a wavelength of 2000 μm (0.002 cm) then it will have a wavenumber of $1/0.002 = 500 \text{ cm}^{-1}$. The higher the wavenumber, the higher the frequency and the more energy each quantum of radiation carries ($E = hf$). Note that the stretching motions generally require more energy and therefore occur at a higher frequency (and hence greater wavenumber) than bending motions.

In order to absorb infrared light a vibrational motion must result in a change in the dipole moment of the molecule. Consider the hydrogen chloride molecule, $^{\delta+}H - Cl^{\delta-}$. It is, as shown, a polar molecule and as the bond stretches, the distance between the atoms increases and so the dipole moment, which depends on both the partial charges and their separations, also increases. Hence the vibration of this bond absorbs infrared radiation of a particular frequency (2990 cm^{-1}). A careful study of the infrared absorption spectrum also yields data about the strength of the bond between the atoms. All of the vibrations of water lead to a change in dipole moment and hence to infrared absorption. In a symmetrical linear molecule, such as carbon dioxide, the symmetrical stretching mode does not change the dipole of the molecule (or, more precisely, it maintains the symmetry that leads to the molecule being non-polar) and hence it does not give rise to an infrared absorption, though other vibrations which affect the dipole absorb I.R. radiation, as shown in Figure 17.7:

Figure 17.7 – The bending and stretching motions of carbon dioxide

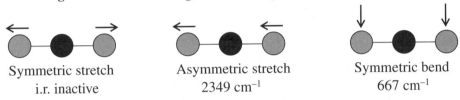

Symmetric stretch
i.r. inactive

Asymmetric stretch
2349 cm^{-1}

Symmetric bend
667 cm^{-1}

Likewise the symmetrical stretching mode of a symmetrical tetrahedral molecule is not infrared active, because it does not result in any change of the dipole of the molecule. Although not infrared active, the frequency of many of these vibrations may be found by the closely related technique of Raman spectroscopy. Sulfur dioxide is non-linear (effect of non-bonding e-pair) and so similar in shape to water. Hence, in contrast to carbon dioxide, even the symmetric stretch causes a change in dipole and is i.r. active.

Many bonds in molecules tend to absorb infrared radiation of a particular frequency, largely irrespective of the rest of the molecule, hence absorption of radiation of this frequency indicates the presence of this bond in a molecule. This is of particular use in deducing the structure of organic molecules. This is fully described in Section 11.2, page 356 and an example given in the diagram below. Note that the precise wavenumber depends to some extent on the other groups present, so a range of frequencies is associated with that bond.

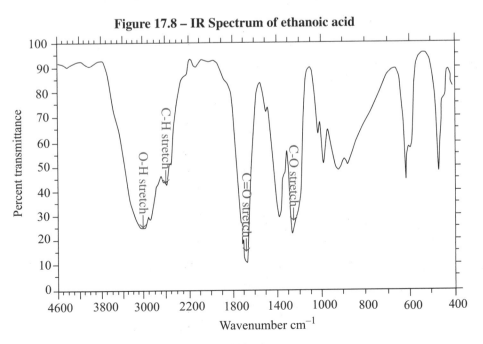

Figure 17.8 – IR Spectrum of ethanoic acid

17.5 NUCLEAR MAGNETIC RESONANCE (NMR) SPECTROSCOPY

G.5.1 State that atoms with an odd mass number can be detected by NMR spectroscopy.

G.5.2 Analyse simple NMR spectra.

The emphasis is on ^1H spectra. Interpretation should include the: number of peaks, chemical shift (with tetramethylsilane (TMS) as the reference standard), area under each peak, splitting patterns (treatment of spin-spin coupling constants is not required, but students should be familiar with splitting patterns for simple molecules ie doublet, triplet and quartet).

G.5.3 Outline how NMR is used in body scanners.

Protons in water in human cells can be detected by magnetic resonance imaging (MRI), giving a three-dimensional view of organs in the human body. © IBO 2001

Fundamental particles, such as protons, neutrons and electrons have a property called spin and there is a magnetic moment associated with this. As a result in a magnetic field the particle can either align itself with or against the magnetic field. In many nuclei the spins of the nucleons (i.e. protons and neutrons) cancel each other out, so that the nucleus does not have an overall magnetic moment, but where there is an odd number of nucleons then this cannot occur. As a result the nucleus has a residual spin and hence in a magnetic field it can align itself with or against the field.

Useful nuclei with a non–zero magnetic moment are ^1H, ^{13}C, ^{19}F and ^{31}P. The two states that they have in a magnetic field are at different energies and for strong magnetic fields, often produced using superconducting electromagnets, the difference in energy between the two states is equal to a quantum of energy in the radio frequency region of the electromagnetic spectrum. Nuclei can therefore absorb radio frequency energy of the appropriate frequency and move ('flip') from the lower energy state to the higher energy state. In this way it is similar to UV, visible and IR spectroscopy.

When electrons are in a magnetic field they orbit in such a way as to set up a magnetic field that opposes the applied field (Lenz's law). This means that the magnetic field experienced by the nucleus, and hence the precise frequency at which it absorbs radiation, depends on the electron density near to the nucleus and therefore on the chemical environment of the nucleus. Because chlorine is more electronegative than iodine, the hydrogen atom in H–Cl has less electrons near to it, so that it experiences a stronger magnetic field and will therefore absorb radiation of a higher frequency than the hydrogen atom in H–I. In molecules that have a number of hydrogens in different chemical environments, then each hydrogen will produce an absorption at a different frequency and the strength of the absorption will be proportional to the number of hydrogen atoms in that environment. In ethanol (CH_3–CH_2–OH) for example, there are three absorption peaks with an intensity ratio of 3 : 2 : 1 (see Figure 17.6 or, better, Figure 11.4, page 360). The absorptions of neighbouring atoms interfere with each other and in a high resolution spectrum this leads to splitting of the absorption into a number of closely grouped peaks.

This 'chemical shift' (often given the symbol δ) is however very small – in the parts per million (ppm) range and the frequency of radiation is very dependent on the strength of the applied magnetic field and it is difficult to ensure that this remains constant to a comparable accuracy. The problem is overcome by mixing another substance with the sample and recording the frequency at which absorption occurs relative to this 'internal standard'. The substance chosen as the internal standard is tetramethylsilane (TMS) which has the formula $(CH_3)_4Si$. This has the advantage of being chemically inert, producing a single strong signal, as it has 12 hydrogens in identical chemical environments and, because of the low electronegativity of silicon, it absorbs radiation of a frequency rather different from that of most other compounds, so that it does not interfere with their absorption signals. The chemical shift (in ppm) is then measured relative to this arbitrary standard.

In organic chemistry ^1H NMR spectroscopy is particularly useful as the chemical shift of the absorption signals, their relative intensity and the splitting pattern caused by hydrogens on neighbouring carbon atoms are often sufficient to allow the structure of the molecule to be determined, as described in Section 11.2 (page 356). An example of such a 'low resolution' NMR spectrum, for ethanol, is given in Figure 11.4 (page 360). Under higher resolution some of the peaks are seen to split, as shown in Figure 17.9 below, also for ethanol. The precise frequency at which the absorption occurs is influenced by the direction of the magnetic field of any hydrogens attached to the neighbouring carbon atom. The signal of the CH_3– group (δ = 1.1) is therefore affected by the alignment of the hydrogens of the $–CH_2$– group. There are three combinations for this (↑↑, ↑↓, or ↓↓) so the signal is split into three (a triplet). Similarly the signal of the $–CH_2$– group (δ = 3.8) is split into a quartet by the possible alignments of the hydrogens in the CH_3– group. The general rule is that the number of peaks is equal to the number of hydrogens on the neighbouring carbon plus one. The O–H signal is not split because the rapid exchange of this atom between ethanol molecules averages out the different possible spins. NMR spectra also often include an 'integration trace', which gives the areas under the peaks. The distance this rises at each peak is proportional to the number of hydrogen atoms responsible for that peak, so in the ethanol NMR spectrum below the relative ratio can be seen to be 1 : 2 : 3, something that is often not easy to determine by direct observation when the peak is split.

Figure 17.9 – High resolution NMR spectrum of ethanol with TMS reference

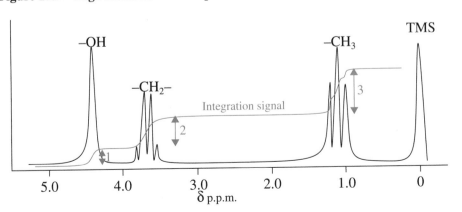

Although ^1H NMR spectra are the most common, other NMR spectra also produce useful information. The most commonly encountered are ^{13}C NMR spectra. ^{13}C only accounts for about 1% of naturally occurring carbon, so it is unlikely that two ^{13}C atoms will occur next to each other, hence splitting of the signal is usually a result of interaction with hydrogen atoms (proton coupling). This interaction is easily removed by a certain experimental technique (proton decoupling) and so two different types of NMR spectra may be encountered, both of which are illustrated in Figure 17.10, which shows the ^{13}C NMR spectrum of a compound $C_2H_2Cl_4$. The spectrum clearly shows that the two carbon atoms are different, hence it must be $ClCH_2-CCl_3$ rather than $Cl_2CH-CHCl_2$ and this is confirmed by the splitting pattern:

Figure 17.10 – ^{13}C NMR spectrum of a compound $C_2H_2Cl_4$

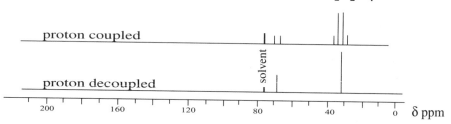

The **body scanner** also operates on the principle of NMR spectroscopy. The main constituents of the body that contains hydrogen atoms, and hence produce signals, are water and lipids. Different parts of the body have different water-lipid ratios in the tissue and therefore absorb radio frequency radiation in different ways. The patient is placed in a strong magnetic field and as the scanner is moved around the body data about the absorption at various angles can be accumulated to allow a three–dimensional image of the various organs to be built up.

17.6 MASS SPECTROMETRY

G.6.1 Discuss how the molecular mass and molecular formula of a compound may be obtained from the molecular ion peak.

Spectrometers have sufficient accuracy to allow identification of the molecular formula from the molecular mass using the masses of the commonest isotopes of C, H, N and O.

G.6.2 Analyse molecular mass spectra.

Stress the importance of isotopes and relate these to the $(M + 1)^+$ peak for ^{13}C and the $(M + 2)^+$ and $(M + 4)^+$ peaks for chlorine and bromine. Include recognition of molecular fragments (see 20.1.3). © IBO 2001

The simple mass spectrometer was outlined in Section 2.2, page 65. In it atoms or molecules are ionised and the relative abundances of the ions of different masses are found by accelerating the ions and then bending them in a magnetic field. In the case of molecules, the bonds frequently break as a result of the ionisation process resulting in fragments, of a lower mass than the ion from the original molecule (the '**molecular ion**'), which produce a '**fragmentation pattern**'. The precise mass of the molecular ion, because the atomic masses are not precise integers, can be used to determine the molecular formula of a substance. Similarly the fragmentation patterns that they produce are very useful in the identification of molecules, particularly organic molecules, as described in Section 11.2, page 356.

Compounds of elements that contain significant amounts of isotopes of different masses will give rise to separate peaks for the different isotopes. Chlorine for example contains both ^{35}Cl and ^{37}Cl in a ratio of approximately 3:1. This is clearly shown in the spectrum of chloroethene in Figure 17.11 below. The two molecular ion peaks at 62 and 64 correspond to the molecular ions $C_2H_3{}^{35}Cl^+$ and $C_2H_3{}^{37}Cl^+$ respectively and have heights in the ratio 3:1. The minor peaks at 35 and 37 obviously correspond to $^{35}Cl^+$ and $^{37}Cl^+$ produced by fragmentation. The very prominent peaks around 26 are produced by ions comprising a pair of carbon atoms with varying numbers of hydrogen atoms attached.

Figure 17.11 – The mass spectrum of chloroethene

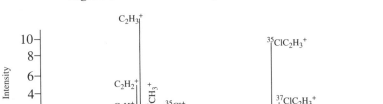

In the mass spectrum of the Cl_2 molecule there are peaks at 70 ($^{35}Cl-^{35}Cl)^+$, 72 ($^{35}Cl-$ $^{37}Cl)^+$ and 74 ($^{37}Cl-^{37}Cl)^+$ with an intensity ratio of 9 $\left(\frac{3}{4} \times \frac{3}{4}\right)$: 6 $\left(2 \times \frac{3}{4} \times \frac{1}{4}\right)$: 1 $\left(\frac{1}{4} \times \frac{1}{4}\right)$.

Molecules containing bromine shows similar pairs of peaks for its isotopes ^{79}Br and ^{81}Br, though these two isotopes are present in approximately equal amounts.

Even though ^{13}C only accounts for approximately 1% of natural carbon, intense peaks in the mass spectra of organic species frequently have a smaller peak at one mass number greater, especially if they contain a large number of carbon atoms, owing to the presence of ^{13}C. Peaks one or two mass numbers less are usually due to the loss of one or more hydrogen atoms. Mass spectrometry can be used to detect the percentage of ^{14}C present in a sample in the process known as radiocarbon dating.

17.7 CHROMATOGRAPHY

G.7.1 State the reasons for using chromatography.

Chromatography can be used to separate substances for analysis and to determine purity. Highlight the coupling of chromatography with other techniques.

G.7.2 State that all chromatographic techniques require a stationary phase and a mobile phase.

Components in a mixture have different tendencies to adsorb onto a surface or dissolve in a solvent. This provides a means of separating the components of a mixture.

G.7.3 Explain how the phenomena of adsorption and partition can be used in chromatographic techniques.

Each of these phenomena gives rise to different chromatographic techniques. Molecular exclusion is not required.

G.7.4 Outline the use of paper chromatography, thin-layer chromatography (TLC), column chromatography, gas-liquid chromatography (GLC) and high performance liquid chromatography (HPLC).

An outline of the operation for each technique is all that is required. This should include an understanding of R_f values where relevant.

G.7.5 Deduce which chromatographic technique is most appropriate for separating the components in a particular mixture.

© IBO 2001

In chemistry the concept of a pure substance (i.e. one that contains only one compound) is vital and so techniques that can identify whether a sample is a pure substance or a mixture are important. The term chromatography is used to describe a range of closely related techniques used to separate mixtures. Most of them are used for **analytical** purposes, i.e. to see what is present in the mixture, rather than for **preparative** purposes, i.e. to obtain a pure sample of one of the components of the mixture.

All chromatographic techniques involve two phases, a **stationary phase** and a **mobile phase**. The mobile phase moves past (or through) the stationary phase and the components are separated according to how much time each component spends in the different phases, because of the extent to which they bond to the phases.

Imagine a moving conveyor belt and a group of people standing together alongside it. The people all jump on to the conveyor belt, but one group (A) counts to five and then

OPTION

jumps off. When off, they count to ten and jump on again, then after five, off again and so on. The second group (B) count to ten when they jump on the conveyor and five when they jump off, ten when they are on again etc. After a minute or so, it is quite obvious that the people in group B will have travelled rather further than those in group A, so that the 'mixture' of people has been separated.

Hence, all chromatography operates on the principle of partition. This is either the way in which a substance distributes itself between two immiscible phases or the way it bonds to the surface of a solid. The differences lie only in the nature of the two phases and hence the type of bonding that operates between the components of the mixture and these phases. The most commonly encountered techniques are paper chromatography; thin–layer chromatography; column chromatography; ion–exchange chromatography; gas–liquid chromatography and high performance liquid chromatography. The way in which these are carried out and the underlying theory of each is described below. Sometimes chromatography, as its name suggests, is used to separate coloured substances and the components can then be detected by their colour. More often it is used with colourless substances and in these cases a variety of special techniques must be used to detect the presence of the components of the mixture.

In **paper chromatography** a spot of the mixture is applied to absorbent paper, rather like filter paper. The end of this is then dipped in the solvent used to 'develop' the chromatogram. The solvent soaks through the paper by capillary action, moving past the spot where the mixture was applied and onwards. The components that bond strongly to the solvent will be carried along in the direction that the solvent is moving, whereas those that do not bond to it will remain almost stationary. Figure 17.12 below shows one common arrangement for carrying out paper chromatography, though many others are possible.

Figure 17.12 – Paper chromatography

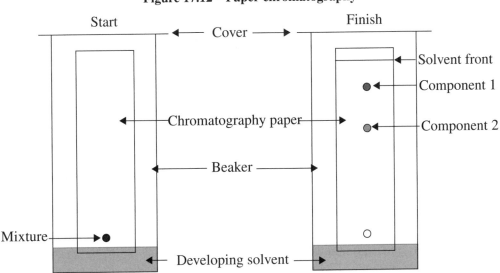

In the above diagram as the organic solvent soaks through the paper, Component 1 is very soluble in the solvent, which is the mobile phase, and only poorly in water held in the absorbent pores of the paper, which acts as the stationary phase. Component 1 has therefore moved almost as far as the solvent. Component 2, because of its different structure, bonds more strongly to the stationary aqueous phase and so does not move as far. This technique relies on the partition of the components of the mixture between a mobile non–aqueous phase and a stationary aqueous phase. Paper chromatography can be used to separate the coloured components of an ink, or the different amino acids from a mixture of amino acids (see Chapter 13).

Thin layer chromatography (TLC) is very similar in practice to paper chromatography, the physical arrangement being almost identical to that shown in the previous diagram. The difference is that the stationary phase is a thin layer, usually of silicon dioxide (silica), on a glass or plastic support. This means that the separation is not the result of the partition of the components between two liquids, but it depends on the extent to which they bond to the surface (i.e. are <u>ads</u>orbed by) of the stationary layer of silica, which in turn mainly depends on the polarity of the substance. Because the particles in TLC are much finer than the pores in paper it usually gives better separation.

In both paper and thin layer chromatography, components can be identified by their R_f **value**, where:

$$R_f = \frac{\text{Distance moved by component}}{\text{Distance moved by solvent}}$$

In the example in Figure 17.12, the R_f value of component 1 is greater than that of component 2.

EXAMPLE
Find the R_f value of component shown on the paper chromatograph below:

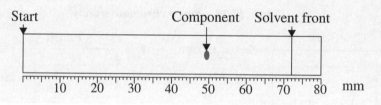

SOLUTION

$$R_f = \frac{\text{Distance moved by component}}{\text{Distance moved by solvent}} = \frac{49}{72} \approx 0.68$$

The principle of **column chromatography** is very similar to thin layer chromatography, as the stationary phase is usually silicon dioxide or aluminium oxide (alumina) and separation depends on whether a component is strongly adsorbed onto the surface of this or remains dissolved in the mobile phase of solvent used to elute the column. The oxide powder is packed into a column with the solvent and the mixture applied at the top of the packing, as shown in Figure 17.13. The solvent (also known as the eluant) is allowed to slowly drip out of the bottom of the column, controlled by a tap, and fresh solvent added at the top so that the packing never becomes dry. As the mixture moves down it will separate out into its components, as shown. This technique can be used to obtain a pure sample of the various components as they can be collected separately when they elute from the bottom of the column and the solvent evaporated. If the components are colourless, then separate fractions of the eluate must be collected and tested for the presence of the components of the mixture.

Figure 17.13 – An illustration of column chromatography

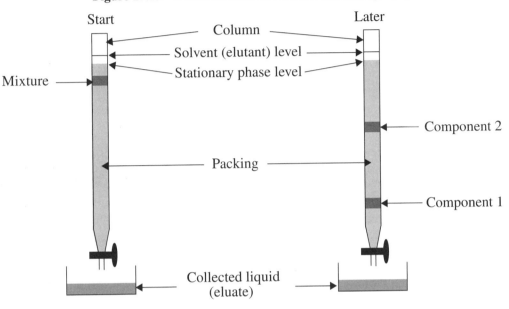

The physical arrangement for **ion–exchange chromatography** is very similar to that for column chromatography, though instead of the column being packed with powdered oxide, it is packed with beads of ion–exchange resin as the stationary phase. An ion–exchange resin (see Chapter 14) is a polymer that has ionic groups bonded to it. Most commonly these are negatively charged ionic groups (cation exchange resin), but resins with positive groups (anion exchange resin) also exist. Each negatively charged group has a free cation closely associated with it, held in place by electrostatic attraction. These cations may be displaced by other cations from the solution that bond more strongly to the charged group. If, for example, a mixture of metal cations is passed through a column packed with cation exchange resin, then those that bond strongly to the resin will not move very fast, those that bond less strongly will move faster, so that the mixture will separate.

In **gas liquid chromatography** (GLC), the mobile phase is a gas and the stationary phase is packed into a very long (often a number of metres) thin column, that is coiled into a helix. There are various types of stationary phases that may be used. Sometimes the column is packed with an oxide (usually SiO_2 or Al_2O_3), or more frequently these days (HRGC - high resolution gas chromatography) a very thin column is coated on the inside with an oxide layer, and in these cases separation occurs because molecules of the mixture are adsorbed onto the surface of the oxide. Sometimes, the oxide will be just acting as a support for a high boiling point oil or wax. In this case separation depends on the partition of the components between the gas phase and solution in the oil.

OPTION

Figure 17.14 - Schematic diagram of gas chromatography

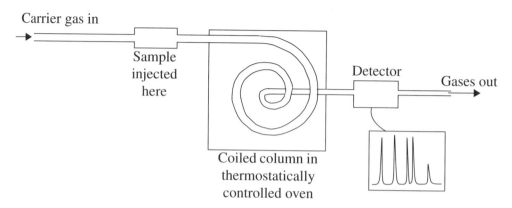

The mixture, which must vaporise at the temperature used, is usually injected, by means of a hypodermic syringe, into a steady gas flow at the start of the column. One great advantage of the technique is the very small samples required, of the order of a microlitre ($1 \ \mu l = 10^{-6} \ dm^3$). The rate at which the sample passes through the column can be controlled by the temperature and for this reason the column is housed in an oven.

The components of the mixture are detected as they reach the end of the column, either by the effect they have on the thermal conductivity of the gas, or by the current that results from the ions formed when they are burnt in a flame. The results are shown as a graph of the detector signal against the time since the mixture was injected into the gas flow. The components can often be identified from the time taken for them to emerge from the column (called the retention time) and the area under the peak is proportional to the amount of the component in the mixture. A typical GLC chromatogram is shown in Figure 17.15(a).

Figure 17.15 – Typical glc and hplc chromatograms

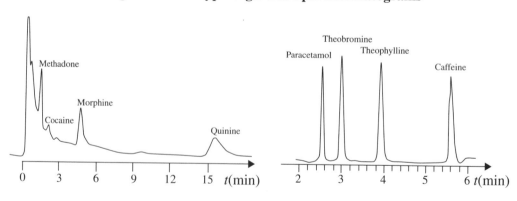

(a) typical glc to show the detection of drugs in a urine sample

(b) typical hplc to show the components of a propriety cold treatment

It can be seen that gas chromatography allows the number of components in a mixture to be identified and the relative amounts of these can be determined from the area under the peak. For more precise work, the system can be calibrated using samples of known concentration under identical conditions. A very powerful technique (**Gas Chromatography – Mass Spectrometry**, GC–MS) involves coupling the output of the gas chromatography column to the input of the mass spectrometer. This means that each component is definitely identified as it elutes by means of its mass spectrum. This is particularly useful in food and drug testing as well as in forensic science.

The principle of **High Performance Liquid Chromatography** (HPLC) is basically very similar to gas chromatography except that the mobile phase is a liquid, forced under high pressure (up to 10^7 Pa) through a rather shorter column (usually 10–30 centimetres long), rather than a gas. Its advantage over gas chromatography lies in the fact that it can be used for non-volatile and ionic substances. One of the major weaknesses of this technique is that the detector systems are less sensitive than those usually used in gas chromatography. The most commonly used detection system is the absorption of UV light, though there are a wide variety of other detector systems (e.g. fluorescence and conductivity) that find specialist use.

Usually ('normal phase') the packing is either a polar oxide (silicon dioxide or aluminium oxide), or an inert support coated with a thin layer of a polar liquid, as the stationary phase and a non–polar liquid is used as the mobile phase. In such as system the less polar components elute before the more polar. The polarity of the phases can however be reversed ('reverse phase', i.e. a non-polar packing and a polar mobile phase) so that the more polar components elute first. A typical HPLC chromatogram is shown in Figure 17.15 (b).

When facing an analytical problem it is important to select the correct technique. This will depend on what is required (Is it qualitative or quantitative? Are the components known or must they be identified?), how much of the material is available (kilograms or micrograms?), how low are the concentrations of the substances to be detected (~ 0.01 mol dm^{-3} or 10^{-6} mol dm^{-3}), and on the nature of the sample (Is it volatile? How polar is it?). For a volatile sample, generally gas chromatography on a suitable column will offer the best solution. For a non–volatile sample HPLC will often provide the solution. Column chromatography is most suitable for preparative purposes, whilst paper and thin layer techniques involve the minimum amount of apparatus, if all that is required is a simple qualitative check. Some common applications of the different techniques are given in Table 17.1 below:

OPTION

Table 17.1 – Summary of some chromatographic techniques

Technique	Stationary Phase	Mobile Phase	Typical application
Paper chromatography	Trapped water in the paper	Organic solvent	Detection of amino acids in a mixture Testing food colours to see if they are single dyes or mixtures
Thin layer chromatography	Oxide coating	Organic solvent	Detection of amino acids in a mixture Testing food colours to see if they are single dyes or mixtures
Column chromatography	Oxide packing or ion exchange resin	Organic solvent	Preparative, e.g. separation of the chlorophylls and carotene in plant extract
Gas-liquid chromatography	Oxide or non-volatile liquid on the solid support	Gas	Analysis of vegetable oil mixtures Analysis of gas mixtures, especially from petrochemicals Analysis of components of fruit odours Detection of drugs in urine Detection of steroids
High Performance Liquid Chromatography	Oxide packing Ion exchange resin Molecular sieve	Liquid	Analysis of sugars in fruit juices Analysis of additives in margarine Analysis of pesticide residues Detection of ions in body fluids Detection of levels of alcohol in blood

OPTION

QUESTIONS FOR OPTION G

1. Which of the following types of radiation has quanta of the highest energy?

A X-rays
B UV light
C IR light
D Microwaves

2. Green light has a wavelength of 500 nm. What is the frequency of this light?

A 0.002 Hz
B 3.31×10^{-31} Hz
C 7.55×10^{35} Hz
D 6.00×10^{14} Hz

3. A 1×10^{-4} mol dm^{-3} solution of an organic compound in a 1 cm cell has an absorbance of 0.5 at a wavelength of 300 nm. What is the numerical value of its molar extinction coefficient at this wavelength.

A 5×10^{-5}
B 5×10^3
C 2×10^5
D 6.00×10^{-2}

4. At a particular wavelength the molar extinction coefficient of aqueous copper sulfate is 300 dm^3 mol^{-1} cm^{-1}. Approximately what percentage of the incident light of this wavelength will pass through a 0.01 mol dm^{-3} in a 1 cm cell?

A 10%
B 1%
C 0.1%
D 0.01%

5. A species has an infrared absorption at 2000 cm^{-1}. What is the wavelength of the light?

A 2×10^5 m
B 20 m
C 5×10^{-2} m
D 5×10^{-6} m

6. Transition metal ions tend to absorb light in the visible region of the spectrum. Explain why this occurs and why the precise colour may vary with the other species present.

OPTION

In terms of the colours of light absorbed in this way, explain why aqueous nickel sulfate appears a green colour. The intensity of green light passing through a particular sample of aqueous nickel sulfate is I_1. If the concentration of the salt is doubled, but all other factors are kept constant, how will the intensity of the light that now passes, I_2, be related to I_1? What changes must be made to the distance that the light passes through the solution in order to restore the intensity of the transmitted light to I_1?

7. Aqueous nickel(II) ions form a brightly coloured complex with an organic ligand. Various volumes of equimolar solutions of the two species are mixed and the absorbance recorded. Use the results below to derive the probable formula of the complex ion formed, explaining your method.

Volume of Ni^{2+} solution cm^3	Volume of ligand solution cm^3	Absorbance
0	10	0
2	8	1.27
4	6	1.71
6	4	1.26
8	2	0.63
10	0	0

7. Consider the IR absorption spectrum below. Use a table of infrared absorption frequencies to assign **two** of the peaks. Also identify **two** groups that are **not** present in the compound.

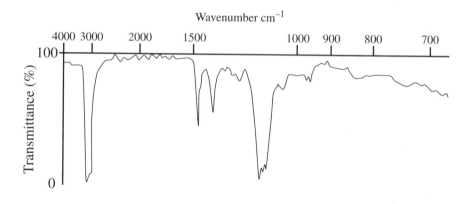

Which region of the spectrum is known as the 'fingerprint' region? Explain how this region can be of use and why, in terms of the absorptions that occur in this region, it has this characteristic.

9. Boron trifluoride, BF_3, is a trigonal planar molecule that absorbs radiation in the infrared region of the spectrum. What changes in the molecule lead to it absorbing in this spectral region? Not all changes of this type are infrared active. Explain why this is so and use sketches to illustrate one that would be IR active and one that would not.

10. The position of absorption bands in IR spectra are usually quoted in wavenumbers, with units of cm^{-1}. How is this related to the frequency of the radiation? Water absorbs radiation at $3652\ cm^{-1}$. What is the wavelength and frequency of this radiation?

11. Explain why some atomic nuclei, such as ^{19}F, give rise to NMR spectra whilst others, such as ^{16}O do not. The nuclei of a particular isotope do not always absorb energy of exactly the same frequency, why is this?

12. Use a table of chemical shifts to predict the absorptions that would occur (both the chemical shift in ppm and the relative intensity) in the NMR spectrum of 3–methylbutanal:

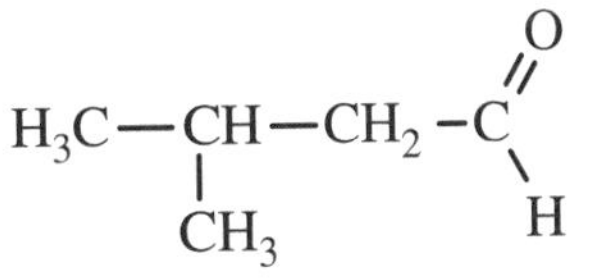

$$H_3C-CH-CH_2-C\overset{O}{\underset{H}{\diagdown}}$$
$$|$$
$$CH_3$$

There are a number of possible isomers of this compound. Name the isomer that would have the simplest NMR spectrum and describe the NMR spectrum that it would produce.

13. Identify the organic molecule responsible for the NMR spectrum shown below, explaining how you reach your conclusion, including reference to the splitting pattern.

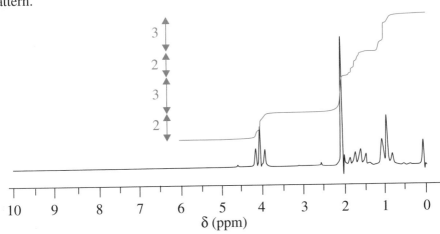

14. When introduced into a mass spectrometer, dichloroethene gives a distinctive spectrum:

a) What peaks would you expect to result from the molecular ion? Give the masses you would expect them to occur at and the relative intensities of these peaks.

b) In what way might you expect the spectrum to reveal whether the dichloroethene is the 1.1 or a 1.2 isomer?

c) There are two possible 1.2 isomers. Given pure samples of each how could you use a mass spectrometer to differentiate between them. Would there be simpler ways of achieving this? Describe one.

15. a) What is the empirical formula of a hydrocarbon that contains 83.3% carbon by mass?

b) How could you use the mass spectrum to find the molecular formula of the compound. Outline how the mass spectrum could be used to confirm that it was indeed a hydrocarbon and not an oxygen/nitrogen containing molecule.

c) Assume the molecular formula is C_5H_{12}. Consider the possible isomers and the way in which these might split up in a mass spectrometer to produce fragments around 55-57, 40-43 and 25-29. How might you attempt to deduce which isomer you had from the mass spectrum?

16. The mass spectrum below is that of a carboxylic acid.

a) Identify the carboxylic acid in question.

b) Give the formulae of the species that give rise to the peaks labelled A to F.

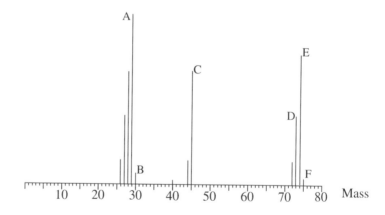

17. a) All chromatography depends upon a separation between two phases. What are these phases in the case of paper chromatography? The paper chromatogram of an orange dye is illustrated. Explain the separation of the two components in terms of their relative affinities for the stationary and mobile phases.

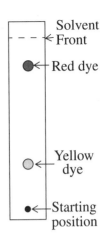

b) Calculate the R_f values of the components.

c) Gas–liquid chromatography (GLC) and high performance liquid chromatography (HPLC) are both far more widely used than paper chromatography. Give at least two reasons why these techniques are preferred.

d) Give an example of a mixture for which GLC would give better results than HPLC and one for which the reverse is true. In each case state why that technique is to be preferred.

18. Many chromatographic techniques are used to detect the presence of a particular substance. Column chromatography can however also be used as a preparative technique, i.e. to produce a sample of a substance. Explain how you would attempt to use this technique to produce pure samples of the different dyes comprising universal indicator.

One particular type of column chromatography is ion–exchange chromatography. Explain how this technique works and give an example of a mixture that it could be used to separate.

19. When a mixture of the four isomeric alkanols with the molecular formula C_4H_9OH is passed through a gas chromatography column they are separated with 2,2-dimethylpropanol eluting first and butanol eluting last.

a) What does this show about the relative attraction of butan-1-ol and 2,2-dimethylpropanol for the packing of the column? Explain how this leads to the separation of the two compounds.

b) How could the relative amounts of the four isomers in the mixture be found?

c) By what methods might the alkanols be detected as they elute from the column?

d) How would the time taken for the substances to elute be affected if the temperature of the column was increased?

OPTION

20. Consider the following techniques:

gas–liquid chromatography   NMR spectroscopy   mass spectrometry

column chromatography   IR spectroscopy   UV–visible spectroscopy

For each of the following problems, say which of the above techniques would be the most appropriate and justify your choice.

a) Determining the concentration of an aqueous solution of copper(II) sulfate.
b) The presence of 2–methylheptane in petrol.
c) Whether a sample is propan–1–ol or propan–2–ol.
(Assume no pure samples or data on these is available)
d) Obtaining a pure sample of pure 4–nitrobenzene from a mixture with 2–nitrobenzene.
e) Assessing the ^{16}O to ^{18}O ratio in a sample of ice from Antarctica.

21. Modern analytical techniques have had a great impact in many other fields, but probably the greatest has been upon the medical sciences. Discuss **three** examples where three **different** techniques have contributed to the medical sciences and describe how their introduction has led to improvements.

THEORY OF KNOWLEDGE

18

THEORY OF KNOWLEDGE AND CHEMISTRY

For those not involved in teaching the program, TOK has always seemed something of an enigma. What is this strange subject that lies at the heart of the IB Diploma, but appears to have no syllabus? Indeed there are teachers who fear it because they see it as undermining the foundations of their subject!

In TOK there are no absolutes. Each TOK teacher has a slightly different perception of the program, so what is written here must be prefaced with the remark that this is the personal perspective of one of the authors, though one who has taught TOK for over a decade and been an external assessor in the subject for about half of that time.

TOK is about liberating students from thinking that there are always right answers and that "they" can always provide these. Its ultimate aim is to prompt students to always ask
> **"What is the evidence for the knowledge that I have just encountered?"**
and possibly the subsidiary question of
> **"What are the advantages of accepting this knowledge as true?"**
They must come to terms with the fact that they cannot always go to the original sources, either because of limitations of time, intellect and/or opportunity. And that some things must be taken on trust, but it should be the informed trust of
> **"This is what the best informed people in the community currently accept."**
rather than the more absolute faith of
> **"This is the way the world is."**

As a result TOK is not so much about content, but more about the approach to teaching. It is about having this approach in one's own personal background and seizing every opportunity that arises to share this conviction with the students, through whatever subject is being studied at the time. This integration of TOK thought into subject areas is a far more effective way of achieving the aims than dedicated specialist lessons - the very best of TOK teaching usually occurs outside TOK lessons and perhaps, given the perfect school program and perfect teachers, TOK would become redundant.

Chemistry, like the other sciences and mathematics (though of course proof in the latter is of a very different nature philosophically speaking) are often seen by students in terms of these absolutes. Science proves the way the world is. Science provides the answers. The major contribution the science teacher can make to TOK is perhaps dispelling this myth that some students still espouse as they enter the final two years of secondary education. Exposing students to some of the "failed" theories of science, plus conveying the fact that people "really did believe this" is I think important. The Phlogiston Theory is of course one that springs readily to mind in a chemical context, but there are perhaps many more recent minor examples than we sometimes realise. I confess to occasionally straying across the borderline into Physics - giving the students a photocopy from a page of an old Encyclopaedia Britannica in which heat is described in terms of the Caloric Theory. After enquiring what they think of the theory, I reveal the source before asking them where they would go to start finding out about something. This can be a salutary experience. I also justify an excursion into Physics on the grounds that, as far as I am aware, no Chemist has come up with a statement that has proved so wonderfully incorrect as that made by Michelson (of the Michelson-Morley experiment fame) about a decade before relativity and quantum mechanics started to turn Physics on its head:

"The more important fundamental laws and facts of physical science have all been discovered, and these are now so firmly established that the possibility of their ever being supplanted in consequence of new discoveries is exceedingly remote. Our future discoveries must be looked for in the sixth place of decimals."

Perhaps Michelson could have benefited from a couple of TOK classes? Seriously though, realising what we are currently teaching may, a century from now, be viewed in the same way that we view the "plum pudding" atom is something we all need to be aware of.

On the subject of atoms, when students first encounter s,p and d orbitals, they often become agitated and ask why, if this is the "truth", did we make them learn 2,8,8 etc. just a year ago. Is this now the real truth or are we going to teach them some new truth in another six months time. This is a splendid platform from which to launch forth into the fact that when God gave Moses the 10 Commandments on the top of Mt. Sinai, he omitted to add the true description of atomic structure to the bottom of the tablet, so we really don't know what is "true", we can only produce explanations that seem to fit with the observed facts. Do we know atoms exist in the same way as we know this book exists? Furthermore, is it not sensible for people to acquire knowledge of an appropriate degree of sophistication to their needs, with the option of revising this as it becomes necessary? To some people knowing that Mr. Smith lives in North America may be valuable. For others knowing that his house is in Detroit may be required. Some may need to know that he is currently in his bathroom getting shaved.

Reflecting on scientific method is I think also a very important contribution that science teachers can make to TOK. There is the classical Aristotelian - Baconian model of:

Observation $\Rightarrow$ Hypothesis $\Rightarrow$ Experiment $\Rightarrow$ Confirmation

It is worth asking whether people do observe the universe with an open mind to discover the initial hypothesis - did people really look at combining mass data and postulating the basics of atomic theory, or did they have the concept of combining atoms in mind and then look through pre-existing data for support? How many times must a hypothesis be proved before it becomes a theory, or even the ultimate "Law"? Does my dropping a stone really add to our certainty about the Law of Gravity?

As a Popper fan, I feel much more in tune with the concept of falsifiability. If a theory does not lead to falsifiable predictions it is not scientific (Mendeleev's Periodic Table predictions?) and a hypothesis can never be proved, only disproved. With reference to this latter, I really enjoy discussing possible mechanisms in the light of available kinetic data. You can never prove a mechanism, just disprove possible mechanisms. In fact it can be said that science really only progresses when an established theory proves to be inadequate (like ozone having a permanent dipole!). What we currently believe to be true is only a temporary resident waiting only for the day when its limitations are discovered. Ultimate "truth", if one feels the necessity for such a hypothesis, is well beyond what man can aspire to, at least in the field of science.

This of course is a very different concept to "Science divining the ultimate reality of the universe", which is the paradigm from which many students start. "Paradigm" of course is another concept worthy of exploration along with the other ideas of Thomas Kuhn regarding scientific revolutions. Modern chemistry, in contrast to many other disciplines, is a bit short of good examples in this regard, though with an interested group the transition from valence-bond to molecular-orbital theory could be pursued. More generally I resort to Relativity, which most are vaguely familiar with at a popular level, or plate-tectonics, which I tell them had not been invented when I was at school!

It is the ability of the physical sciences to make accurate predictions that many feel differentiates them from the social sciences. We know that when we mix equal volumes of 1 M strong acid and 1M strong base, the temperature will rise by a certain amount. It is of course interesting to reflect that this is may be in part because of the large populations chemists deal with. When we dehydrate butan-2-ol can we predict in advance whether a particular molecule will form but-1-ene or but-2-ene? Many will feel that it is the scope for creativity that differentiates the fine arts from the sciences, but there was no shortage of imagination in coming up with the concept of the double helix for example. Serendipity obviously has its place in scientific discovery, but how many potential Marsdens would have dismissed as "instrumental error" the 1 in 2000 alpha particles that bounced back?

Anybody inspired to go slightly further with TOK type thought might like to do a little reading around. They could do worse than start with the appropriate section of the TOK teacher's "bible" ("Man is the Measure" by Reuben Abel). A few other titles that are worth delving into are:

What is this thing called science A.F. Chalmers
The common sense of science J. Bronowski
The act of creation A. Koestler
Popper B. Magee

Perhaps it is not totally inappropriate to leave this section with a quotation from Zen and the Art of Motorcycle Maintenance. It refers to the law of gravity, but you can substitute any theory you like:

"It seems completely natural to presume that the law of gravity existed before Newton...........
So when did it start? Has it always existed?............
Before the sun and the stars were formed the law of gravity existed.................
Sitting there with no mass, no energy, not in anybody's mind, because there wasn't anybody the law of gravity still existed?................
If the law of gravity existed I don't know what a thing has to do to be non-existent!"

ANSWERS

EXERCISE 1.1

1. D 2. C 3. B

4(a) element; (b) mixture; (c) mixture; (d) element; (e) compound
5. (a) mixture; (b) compound; (c) mixture; (d) element; (e) compound.

EXERCISE 1.2

1. D 2. C 3. C 4. D 5. C 6. D

7. a) 0.20 b) 1.2×10^{23} c) 3.6×10^{23} 8. a) 3.61×10^{24} b) 5.4×10^{23}

EXERCISE 1.3

1. A 2. C 3. D

4. a) H_2SO_4, b) NaOH, c) HNO_3, d) NH_3, e) HCl, f) CH_3COOH, g) $CuSO_4$, h) CO,
i) SO_2, j) $NaHCO_3$
5. a) NaCl b) CuS c) $ZnSO_4$ d) Al_2O_3 e) $Mg(NO_3)_2$ f) $Ca_3(PO_4)_2$ g) HI h) $(NH_4)_2CO_3$
i) CH_4 j) PCl_5

EXERCISE 1.4

1. D 2. A 3 a) 127.9 b) 106.4 c) 132.1 d) 126.1 e) 152.0 f) 233.3

EXERCISE 1.5

1. B 2. D 3. A 4. B 5. A

6. a) 51.1 g, b) 7.47 g, c) 10.7 g, d) 68.7 g, e) 1.90 g
7. a) 1.00, b) 3.00, c) 25.8, d) 5.44 8. a) 150 g mol^{-1}, b) 128 g mol^{-1}
9. 1.245×10^{23} molecules
10. a) 3.41×10^{-4}, b) 5.68×10^{-3}, c) 2.05×10^{22}

EXERCISE 1.6

1. D 2. C 3. B 4. D 5. B 6. C 7. A 8. B 9. D 10. B

11. 36.29% 12. a) Fe_2O_3 b) SiF_4 c) $C_2H_2O_4$ 13. SnO_2 14. $CuSO_4.5H_2O$
15. 66700 g mol^{-1} 16. $K_2Cr_2O_7$ 17. 354.5; 47.4% carbon, 2.56% hydrogen,
50.0% chlorine
18. a) 0.409 g carbon and 0.0453 g hydrogen b) 0.545 g oxygen c) $C_3H_4O_3$
19. $C_2H_5N_3O_2$; $C_4H_{10}N_6O_4$ 20. 56.67%

EXERCISE 1.7

1. C 2. B 3. A

4. a) CaO + 2 HNO_3 $\Rightarrow$ $Ca(NO_3)_2$ + H_2O b) 2 NH_3 + H_2SO_4 $\Rightarrow$ $(NH_4)_2SO_4$
c) 2 HCl + $ZnCO_3$ $\Rightarrow$ $ZnCl_2$ + H_2O + CO_2 d) SO_2 + 2 Mg $\Rightarrow$ S + 2MgO
e) Fe_3O_4 + 4 H_2 $\Rightarrow$ 3 Fe + $4H_2O$ f) 2 K + 2 C_2H_5OH $\Rightarrow$ 2 KC_2H_5O + H_2
g) 2 $Fe(OH)_3$ $\Rightarrow$ Fe_2O_3 + 3 H_2O h) CH_3CO_2H + 2 O_2 $\Rightarrow$ 2 CO_2 + 2 H_2O
i) 2 $Pb(NO_3)_2$ $\Rightarrow$ 2 PbO+4 NO_2+O_2
j) 2 $NaMnO_4$ +16 HCl $\Rightarrow$ 2 NaCl + 2 $MnCl_2$ + 5 Cl_2 + 8 H_2O
5. a) $CuCO_3$ $\Rightarrow$ CuO + CO_2 b) NiO + H_2SO_4 $\Rightarrow$ $NiSO_4$ + H_2O
c) 2 Fe + 3 Br_2 $\Rightarrow$ 2 $FeBr_3$ d) PbO_2 + 2 CO $\Rightarrow$ Pb + 2 CO_2 e) 2 $FeCl_2$ + Cl_2 $\Rightarrow$ 2 $FeCl_3$
f) C_2H_5OH + 3 O_2 $\Rightarrow$ 2 CO_2 + 3 H_2O g) Ag + 2 HNO_3 $\Rightarrow$ $AgNO_3$ + NO_2 + H_2O
h) MnO_2 + 4HCl $\Rightarrow$ $MnCl_2$ + Cl_2 + $2H_2O$ i) SO_2 + $2H_2S$ $\Rightarrow$ 3S + $2H_2O$
j) $4NH_3$ + $5O_2$ $\Rightarrow$ 4NO + $6H_2O$

EXERCISE 1.8

1. C 2. B 3. a) 2 $KClO_{3(s)}$ $\Rightarrow$ 2 $KCl_{(s)}$ + 3 $O_{2(g)}$ b) 0.4 moles c) 2.45 g   4. 37.7 g

5. a) MnO_2 ; Mn_3O_4, b) $3\ MnO_2 \Rightarrow Mn_3O_4 + O_2$, c) 0.353 g

EXERCISE 1.9

1. a) Limiting reagent is Al, yield is 1.2 moles b) Limiting reagent is I_2, yield is 2.57 g
c) 1.03 g excess aluminium
2. a) Limiting reagent is SbF_3, CCl_4 is in excess b) 101.5 g c) 20.9 g
3. a) Limiting reagent is salicylic acid b) 1.30 kg c) 90.6%

EXERCISE 1.10

1. C 2. D 3. A 4. B 5. D
6. 30 cm^3 of oxygen remains unreacted 7. 1.20×10^{23} 8. 46.8 g mol^{-1}
9. 0.761 g dm^{-3} 10. 2.40×10^5 dm^3 (240 m^3)

EXERCISE 1.11

1. A 2. D 3. B
4. a) 0.75 mol dm^{-3} b) 0.0250 mol dm^{-3} c) 0.0811 mol dm^{-3}
5. a) 2.1 moles, b) 0.0020 moles, c) 2.55×10^{-4} moles
6. a) 0.4 dm^{-3} b) 2.94 dm^{-3} c) 0.720 dm^{-3} (=720 cm^{-3})
7. Weigh out precisely 2.922 g of solid sodium chloride (0.0500 moles) and make it up to
500 cm^3 of solution in a 500 cm^3 volumetric flask.
8. Measure out 240 cm^3 of 2.0 mol dm^{-3} hydrochloric acid (0.48 moles) and make this
up to 1.2 dm^3 of solution. 9. 1.25 mol dm^{-3}
10. $[NO_3^-] = 0.8$ mol dm^{-3}, $[Cl^-] = 0$ mol dm^{-3}, $[H^+] = 0.4$ mol dm^{-3},
$[Pb^{2+}] = 0.2$ mol dm^{-3}

EXERCISE 1.12

1. C 2. A 3. D
4. a) 0.0125 moles b) 0.0125 moles c) 0.625 mol dm^{-3}
5. a) 3.75×10^{-4} moles b) 1.875×10^{-4} moles c) 0.556 g dm^{-3}
6. a) $Ag^+_{(aq)} + Cl^-_{(aq)} \Rightarrow AgCl_{(s)}$, b) 4.00×10^{-3} moles, c) 2.00×10^{-3} moles, d) 90.66%
7 a) 5.01×10^{-4} moles, b) 2.51×10^{-3} moles, c) 0.711 g, d) 0.268 g, $x = 6$
8 a) 9.46 mol dm^{-3}, b) 105.7 cm^3
9 a) $6\ Fe^{2+}_{(aq)} + Cr_2O_7^{2-}_{(aq)} + 14\ H^+_{(aq)} \Rightarrow 6\ Fe^{3+}_{(aq)} + 2\ Cr^{3+}_{(aq)} + 7\ H_2O_{(l)}$,
b) 3.74×10^{-4} moles, c) 2.24×10^{-3} moles, d) 96.4%
10. 122 g mol^{-1}, possibly benzoic acid (C_6H_5–COOH)

EXERCISE 1.13

1. a) 0.0050, b) 0.010, c) 0.005, d) 0.9 g, e) 90%
2. 82.6%; It was assumed that the impurities in the marble reacted with neither acid nor
alkali. It was assumed that none of the evolved carbon dioxide remained in solution to
react with the alkali.
3. a) 12.0 g mol^{-1} b) 24.0 g mol^{-1} c) 36.0 g mol^{-1}. Answer b) is most likely as this molar
mass corresponds to magnesium, which is a divalent metal, rather than to carbon or
chlorine.

Answers

EXERCISE 1.14
1. C 2. C 3. A

4. a) 4.376×10^5, b) 2.3×10^{-7}, c) 4.15×10^8, d) 3.72×10^{-2}, e) 4.768×10^2, f) 3.26×10^0
5. a) 820000 b) 0.00629 c) 271 380 000 000 d) 0.0000002 e) 42 f) 0.589

EXERCISE 1.15
1. B 2. D 3. B 4. B

5 a) 0.028, b) 28, c) 3.76×10^5, d) 0.00175, e) 2×10^9

EXERCISE 2.1
1. D 2. B 3. C
4. a) electron; b) neutron; c) electron; d) proton; e) electron
5.

Element	Protons	Neutrons	Electrons
Helium	2	2	2
Nitrogen	7	7	7
Aluminium	13	14	13
Manganese	25	30	25
Iodine	53	74	53

6. a) Atoms that have the same atomic number (number of protons), but a different number of neutrons (mass number). b) mass numbers 10 and 11 $^{10}_{5}B$ and $^{11}_{5}B$ c) 10.8
7.

	No. Protons	No. Neutrons	No. Electrons	Atomic No.	Mass No.
Isotope 1	29	34	29	29	63
Isotope 2	29	36	29	29	65

therefore 72.5% ^{63}Cu and 27.5% ^{65}Cu
8.

Isotope	No. protons	No. neutrons	No. electrons
$^{3}_{1}H$	1	2	1
$^{15}_{7}N$	7	8	7
$^{57}_{26}Fe$	26	31	26
$^{90}_{38}Sr$	38	52	38
$^{235}_{92}U$	92	143	92

9.

Isotope	No. protons	No. neutrons	No. electrons
$^{3}_{1}H^{-}$	1	2	2
$^{24}_{12}Mg^{2+}$	12	12	10

$^{27}_{13}Al^{3+}$	13	14	10
$^{34}_{16}S^{2-}$	16	18	18
$^{48}_{22}Ti^{4+}$	22	26	18

10. $(70 \times 0.20) + (71 \times 0.27) + (72 \times 0.080) + (73 \times 0.37) + (74 \times 0.080) = 72$

EXERCISE 2.2

1. a) They are bombarded with fast moving electrons.
b) The paths of the moving ions are deflected by a magnetic field.
c) They are collected on a metal plate and the current flowing to neutralise the charge on the plate is recorded. (A number of other possible correct answers)
2. A doubly charged germanium-70 would produce a peak at a mass of 35.

3. a) $^{188}_{76}Os$ – 14%; $^{189}_{76}Os$ – 17%; $^{190}_{76}Os$ – 27%; $^{192}_{76}Os$ – 42%   b) 190

2.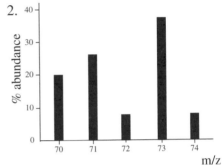

EXERCISE 2.3

1. C 2. A 3. D 4. C
5. a) 2,2 b) 2,8,3 c) 2,7 d) 2,8,8 e) 2,8,6
6. a) They are isotopes of the same element. b) Chemical properties depend primarily on the number of electrons that an atom has and the nuclear charge affecting these. Both isotopes have the same number of electrons and the same nuclear charge.

EXERCISE 2.4

1. C 2. C 3. B 4. C 5. B 6. B 7. C 8. D
9. a) $1s^2 \, 2s^2 \, 2p^6 \, 3s^2 \, 3p^6 \, 3d^5 \, 4s^2$ b)$1s^2 \, 2s^2 \, 2p^6 \, 3s^2 \, 3p^4$ c)$1s^2 \, 2s^2 \, 2p^6$
d)$1s^2 \, 2s^2 \, 2p^6 \, 3s^2 \, 3p^6 \, 3d^5$ e)$1s^2 \, 2s^2 \, 2p^6 \, 3s^2 \, 3p^6 \, 3d^9 \, 4s^2$ (exception $3d^{10} \, 4s^1$ not required)
10. Na Li O N Ne
11.

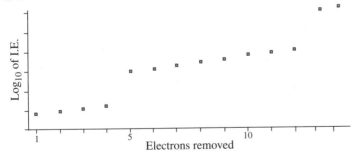

b)
Four electrons are lost relatively easily and they can be thought of as being in the highest energy level. The next eight are rather more difficult to remove and they may be thought of as being in the intermediate level. The remaining two electrons are very difficult to remove and can be thought of as forming the lowest energy level.
c) As successive electrons are removed, the electron–electron repulsion acting on the remaining electrons, which to some extent counteracts the attractive force of the nucleus, decreases. This means that as more electrons are removed from an energy level, (or as

more electrons are removed, the remaining electrons are more attracted to the nucleus) so that the energy required to remove the remaining electrons increases.

12. a) In both cases the effective nuclear charge acting on the outermost electron is +1. The electron being lost in sodium however is further from the nucleus and so less strongly held by electrostatic forces than the electron in lithium.

b) In oxygen one of the 2p–orbitals is doubly filled. This means that there is increased repulsion between the two electrons sharing the orbital. This increased repulsion more than offsets the effect of the increase in nuclear charge on going from nitrogen to oxygen.

c) In beryllium the electron lost comes from a 2s energy level, whereas in boron the electron lost comes from a 2p orbital, which is at a higher energy than the 2s. This difference in energy of the 2s and 2p orbitals more than offsets the greater nuclear charge in boron.

13. a) V^{3+} b) $1s^2\, 2s^2\, 2p^6\, 3s^2\, 3p^6\, 3d^3\, 4s^2$

c) The electronic structure of the ion could not be that of an atom because the 3d level contains electrons, but there are no electrons in the 4s level. In neutral atoms electrons always at least partially fill the 4s before starting to fill the 3d.

14. a) The element is aluminium. (It must be in group 3 because 3 electrons are easily lost before a sudden increase in IE, but it cannot be boron because it contains at least 6 electrons.)

b) About 4.4 (just slightly greater than that for the last electron shown.)

c) They would be greater because even though the two elements have the same effective nuclear charge, the electrons being lost would be closer to the nucleus and hence more strongly attracted.

15. a) B and D b) A – the first three electrons have much lower ionisation energies than the fourth.

c) A and D or E and D. d) C – it has a high first ionisation energy and it must have more than four electrons in the outer shell as there is no sudden increase in ionisation energy.

EXERCISE 3.1

1. A 2. C

3. a) 7 b) 2 c) One of Na, Mg, Al, Si, P, S, Ar d) One of F, Br, I, At e) Halogens

EXERCISE 3.2

1. C 2. D 3. D 4. C

5. Al, Mg, Ca, Ba, Cs

6. a) Decrease–the valence shell electrons are further away from the charge on the nucleus.

b) Decrease – the nuclear charge increases and valence electrons are in the same main energy level thus pulling the valence electrons closer in.

c) Increase – the increased electron–electron repulsion pushes the electrons further from the nucleus or, due to the greater number of electrons compared to protons, each electron is less attracted.

d) Decrease – the valence electrons are further from the nucleus so are more easily lost.

e) Decrease – the increasing nuclear charge attracts the valence electrons more strongly.

EXERCISE 3.3

1. C 2. A 3. B 4. A 5. A

6. a) $2\,Na + 2\,H_2O \Rightarrow 2\,NaOH + H_2$

b) The sodium would fizz around on the surface as a molten blob, slowly dissolving.
c) Redox d) With lithium the reaction takes place gently and with potassium the reaction is so violent that the hydrogen ignites with a lilac flame.

7. a) Purple b) White c) Black d) Yellow-brown e) Yellow

8. a) $Ag^+_{(aq)}+Br^-_{(aq)} \Rightarrow AgBr_{(s)}$ b) Add aqueous lead nitrate. If I^- is present a yellow precipitate forms. If Br^- is present the precipitate will be white $Pb^{2+}_{(aq)}+2I^-_{(aq)} \Rightarrow PbI_{2(s)}$. Alternatively add chlorine water followed by an immiscible organic solvent (e.g. hexane) and if the organic solvent turns purple as a result of iodine dissolving in it, I^- is present $Cl_{2(aq)} + 2I^-_{(aq)} \Rightarrow I_{2(aq)} + 2Cl^-_{(aq)}$. If Br^- was present the bromine formed will turn the organic layer brown $Br_{2(aq)} + 2I^-_{(aq)} \Rightarrow I_{2(aq)} + 2Br^-_{(aq)}$.

9. a) Yes √ the colourless (pale green solution) will turn yellow–brown

$Cl_2 + 2Br^- \Rightarrow Br_2 + 2Cl^-$ b) No reaction

c) Yes √ the yellow–brown solution will turn to another yellow–brown solution and with excess bromine a black solid will form $Br_2 + 2I^- \Rightarrow I_2 + 2Br^-$ d) No.

10. a) Going from left to right the oxides change from basic to amphoteric to acidic in character.

Acidic, SO_2 (or SO_3 or oxides of P): $SO_2 + H_2O \rightleftharpoons HSO_3^- + H^+$

Amphoteric, Al_2O_3

Basic, Na_2O (or MgO): $Na_2O + H_2O \Rightarrow 2Na^+ + 2OH^-$

b) The oxidising strength decreases going down the group. Going down the group the electron being gained is successively further away from the nucleus and hence are less strongly attracted.

c) The reducing strength increases going down the group. Going down the group the electrons are successively further away from the nucleus and hence are more easily lost.

EXERCISE 3.4

1. C 2. B

3. a) With sodium chloride there is no chemical reaction, the ions that exist in the solid just become free to move. In the case of phosphorus trichloride, there is a hydrolysis reaction to produce a solution containing ions: $PCl_3 + 3H_2O \Rightarrow H_3PO_3 + 3H^+ + 3Cl^-$

b) i Add aqueous silver nitrate to both solutions and a white precipitate would be formed in both cases. ii Test both solutions with blue litmus paper. The solution formed from the phosphorus trichloride is acidic and will turn it red, but that from the sodium chloride is neutral and so will not affect it.

4. Basic - Na_2O or MgO. These react with acids, but not with bases, e.g.
$Na_2O + 2HCl \Rightarrow 2NaCl + H_2O$; $MgO + H_2SO_4 \Rightarrow MgSO_4 + H_2O$ Amphoteric-Al_2O_3. This reacts with both acids and bases, e.g. $Al_2O_3 + 6HCl \Rightarrow 2AlCl_3 + 3H_2O$
$Al_2O_3 + 2NaOH + 3H_2O \Rightarrow 2NaAl(OH)_4$ Acidic - P_4O_{10}, P_4O_6, SO_2, or SO_3. These dissolve in water to form acidic solutions, e.g.
$P_4O_{10} + 6H_2O \Rightarrow 4H^+ + 4H_2PO_4^-$; $SO_2 + H_2O \rightleftharpoons H^+ + HSO_3^-$

5. The elements change from metallic (e.g. Na) to non–metallic (e.g. P) because as the charge on the nucleus increases going from left to right across the period, so do the ionisation energies and electronegativities of the elements. At the left hand side the elements bond by metallic bonding, with the valence electrons being delocalised. The chlorides are ionic because the elements readily lose electrons to form cations as a result

of their low ionisation energies. The elements in the middle and right of the period are joined by covalent bonds, though in the centre this occurs as giant structures, whereas on the right hand side the structure is molecular. The chlorides of the elements in the middle and right of the period are all molecular covalent, because the ionisation energies are too high for cation formation.

EXERCISE 3.5

1. B 2. C 3. C 4. D 5. B

6. a) Elements in the s–block of the periodic table have a small number of electrons in their valence shell, that are relatively easily lost. The energy required to remove electrons from the filled inner shells is however so great that it is never energetically feasible. In the case of transition metals such as manganese the first few ionisation energies are somewhat higher, but even so manganese will always lose its two 4s electrons (the 3d electrons are buried under the 4s cloud). The ionisation energies for the 3d electrons are quite high, but there is no sudden rise in ionisation energy until all the 4s and 3d electrons have been lost, corresponding to the +7 state. Hence the precise oxidation state achieved depends on the oxidising agents present and the complex ions that can form.

b) The hexaaquanickel(II) ion reacts with chloride ions from the acid to form the tetrachloronickel(II) complex ion.

$[Ni(H_2O)_6]^{2+} + 4Cl^- \Rightarrow NiCl_4^{2-} + 6H_2O.$

The energies of the d–orbitals in the two ions are slightly different and hence they absorb light of a different wavelengths, giving slightly different colours.

c) In order to form a bond to the metal ion, a species must have a lone pair of electrons that it can share with the ion to form a dative covalent bond (Lewis acid-base reaction). Ammonia has a lone pair of electrons on the nitrogen, but methane does not.

7. a) The blue and colourless solutions initially react to form a pale blue precipitate, but in the presence of excess ammonia this dissolves to form a dark blue solution.

b) The colourless gas reacts to change the colour of the solution from orange to green due to Cr^{3+} ions.

c) The pale green colour of the aqueous iron(II) sulfate darkens to a yellow–brown colour when it is heated with the colourless hydrogen peroxide. When aqueous sodium hydroxide is added a red–brown precipitate forms.

d) When the black powder is added to the colourless hydrogen peroxide, there is an evolution of bubbles of a colourless gas. Finally the test tube contains a colourless liquid and the black powder remains unchanged.

8. Haber process and Contact process. (Other answers possible)

a) Iron metal, vanadium(V) oxide.

b) $N_2 + 3H_2 \rightleftharpoons 2NH_3$; $2SO_2 + O_2 \rightleftharpoons 2SO_3$

Both of these processes involve heterogeneous catalysts. These are in a different phase to the reactants (iron, for example provides an active surface on which the reaction occurs). A homogeneous catalyst is in the same phase as the reactants and is consumed in one step of the mechanism, but regenerated during a subsequent step.

9. a) $[Cu(H_2O)_6]^{2+}$ changing to $[CuCl_4]^{2-}$. b) $[Cu(NH_3)_4]^{2+}$.

c) $[CoCl_4]^{2-}$ changing to $[Co(H_2O)_6]^{2+}$. d) $Cr_2O_7^{2-}$ changing to CrO_4^{2-}.

e) MnO_4^- changing to MnO_4^{2-}.

10. a) Octahedral b) +2 in $[Fe(CN)_6]^{4-}$ and +3 in $[Fe(CN)_6]^{3-}$

c) ⁻:CN. The presence of a lone pair allows complex formation.

11. a) The third ionisation energy of Ti is not much higher than the second ionisation energy, because it comes from a 3d orbital, which is of similar energy to the 4s orbital, hence Ti can quite easily lose a third electron. In the case of Ca the third electron would have to come from a 3p orbital, which is at a much higher energy, hence Ca does not readily lose a third electron.

b) V^{3+} has electrons in the 3d sub–level. These electrons can move from one 3d orbital to another of higher energy and this process involves the absorption of light in the visible region of the spectrum, making the compound coloured. In the case of Sc^{3+} there are no electrons in the d–orbital, hence this cannot occur so the compounds are colourless.

c) V^{3+} has electrons in the 3d sub–level which it can readily lose and hence act as a reducing agent, likewise it can accept another electron into this orbital and act as an oxidising agent. Sc^{3+} has a noble gas structure with filled electron shells. Losing an additional electron would require a great deal of energy and hence does not occur. Similarly because the nuclear charge is less than vanadium, gaining a single electron into an outer shell is not energetically feasible.

d) Cu^+ has a completely filled d–orbital hence electron transitions cannot occur between these and absorb light in the visible region. In Cu^{2+} there is a vacancy in the d–orbitals allowing such transitions and the absorption of light.

e) The complex has an octahedral geometry. Three identical ligands can either occupy sites all at 90° to each other, or a pair of identical ligands can be directly opposite each other.

12.

a)

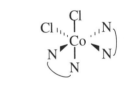

a) The left hand diagram and the right hand diagrams are geometrical isomers of each other, the left had being the 'trans–' form and the right hand ones both 'cis–' forms.

b) The pair of right hand diagrams are non–superimposable mirage image forms (i.e. enantiomers. It can be seen that the mirror image of the more symmetrical trans form is superimposable on the original and so enantiomeric forms do not exist.

EXERCISE 4.1

1. D 2. D 3. B 4. a) potassium bromide b) lithium nitride c) barium sulfide
d) aluminium iodide e) beryllium oxide 5. a) AB b) BA c) A_2B d) AB_3 e) B_3A_2

EXERCISE 4.2

1. C 2. B 3. C 4. C 5. C
6. a) No compound (He is a noble gas) b) HCl c) NCl_3 d) SiF_4 e) P_2O_3
7. a) covalent b) covalent c) ionic d) covalent e) no compound
8.

a) H :Cl:

b) O :: O

c) H : P : H
         H

d) : F : O : F :

e) H : C :: O
         H

EXERCISE 4.3

1. A 2. A

3. a) tetrahedral b) trigonal pyramid c) non–linear or bent or angular or 'V'- shaped d) trigonal pyramid e) tetrahedral

4.

a) 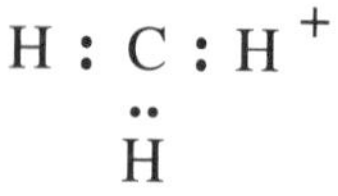 $H : C : H \overset{+}{}$
    $\overset{..}{H}$

trigonal planar
120°

b) 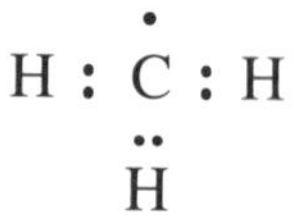 $H : \overset{\bullet}{C} : H$
       $\overset{..}{H}$

trigonal pyramid
~115°

c) 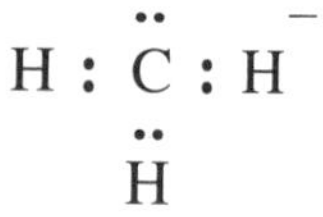 $H : \overset{..}{C} : H \overset{-}{}$
       $\overset{..}{H}$

trigonal pyramid
~107°

5.

a) 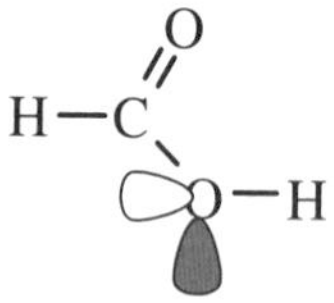
H—C with =O and O—H

120° round C,
C–O–H ~104°

b) 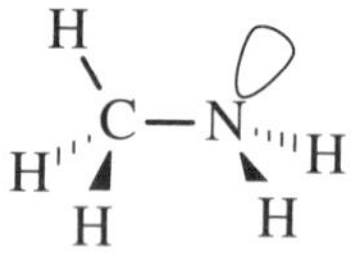
H C—N H with H H

~109° round C,
~107° round N

c)
H—C≡N

180°

d) 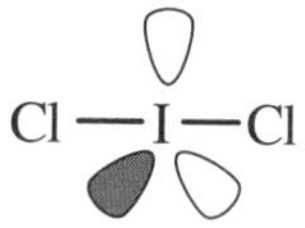
Cl—I—Cl

180°

EXERCISE 4.4

1. C 2. C 3. a) non-polar b) polar c) slightly polar d) polar e) non-polar
4. a) N b) O c) F d) neither e) O
5. a) C-Cl will be the most polar, C=C the least polar b) A will be polar and B non-polar. In A the bond dipoles do not cancel whereas B has symmetrical electron distribution since the bond dipoles cancel c) Put some of each liquid into a burette and allow it to run through the jet. Bring an electrically charged plastic rod close to, but not touching the stream of liquid. If the liquid is A, the stream will deflect and if it is B it will not deflect.
6.

Lewis structure	Diagram	Shape/ bond angle	Polarity
 $: \overset{..}{Cl} : Be : \overset{..}{Cl} :$	$Cl - Be - Cl$	180° Linear	Non-polar
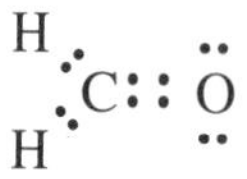 $\overset{H}{\underset{H}{}} C :: O$	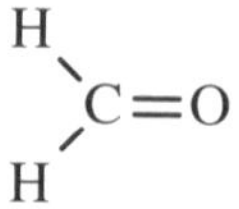 $\overset{H}{\underset{H}{}} C=O$	120° Trigonal planar	Polar
 $: \overset{..}{F} : N :: N : \overset{..}{F} :$	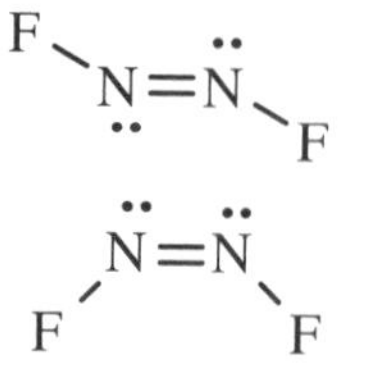 $\overset{F}{} N=N \overset{}{F}$ and $N=N$ with F F	117° Planar	Non-polar polar

Lewis structure	Diagram	Shape/ bond angle	Polarity
$\left[\begin{array}{c}:\!\ddot{C}l\cdots\ddot{C}l:\\ \cdots I \cdots\\ :\!\ddot{C}l\cdots\ddot{C}l:\end{array}\right]^{-}$	Cl⟍ ⋰Cl I Cl⟋ ⋱Cl	90° Square planar	Non-polar
$\left[\begin{array}{c}:\!\ddot{F}\cdots\ddot{F}:\\ \cdots P \cdots\\ :\!\ddot{F}\cdots\ddot{F}:\end{array}\right]^{-}$	F |⸝F :P ⟍ | F F	~90° & 120° 'Saw-horse'	Polar

EXERCISE 4.5

1. C

2. a) Hybridisation is the combining of a number of atomic valence orbitals to form an equal number of identical orbitals of equal energy to be used in the formation of covalent bonds. In this case one s–orbital and two p–orbitals have combined to form three sp^2 hybrid orbitals.

b) The shape of BF_3 is trigonal planar. This is also the shape of sp^2 hybrid orbitals.

c) As the shape of the BF_4^- ion is tetrahedral, the hybridisation must be sp^3.

EXERCISE 4.6

1. D

2. a) The single bond is a σ-bond. The double bond is a σ-bond and a π-bond. The triple bond is a σ-bond and two π-bonds.

b) The shortest bond would be in C≡O, the bond in O=C=O would be intermediate in length and that in CH_3-OH would be the longest.

EXERCISE 4.7

1. B

2. a) $\left[\begin{array}{c} O\\ O\;N\;O \end{array}\right]^{-}$

b) This would predict that one of the nitrogen oxygen bonds would be shorter than the other two. Also with the charge all on one oxygen it is unlikely that it would have the precise trigonal planar symmetry found.

c) The bonding is better described by considering the nitrogen and oxygen atoms to be joined by three σ-bonds and for there also to be a delocalised π-bond that connects all four atoms.

d) The σ-bonds would be formed between sp^2 hybrid orbitals on the oxygen and nitrogen atoms. The delocalised π-bond would be the result of the interaction of the p-orbitals, on all of the atoms, that are at right angles to the sp^2 hybrid orbitals.

e) The bond between the nitrogen and the oxygens would be equivalent to $1\frac{1}{3}$ bonds and each oxygen atom would carry a charge of $-\frac{1}{3}$.

f) It would be expected that the N–O bond length in the nitrate ion (bond order $1\frac{1}{3}$)
would be longer than the N=O bond in nitric acid, but shorter than the N–O bond.

EXERCISE 4.8

1. D 2. A 3. B 4. D 5. B

6. a) These molecules have only van der Waals' forces between them. The strength of
these forces increases with molar mass, so that the intermolecular forces are strongest in
iodine, making it a solid, intermediate in bromine, hence it is a liquid, and least in
chlorine, which is therefore a gas.

b) Water molecules are held together by relatively strong hydrogen bonds. Sulfur is not
sufficiently small and electronegative enough to give rise to hydrogen bonding in
hydrogen sulfide, which therefore has a much lower boiling point as a result of the
weaker intermolecular forces.

c) Hydrogen bonding can occur between the -OH groups on the ethanol molecules,
hence there are quite strong intermolecular forces between the molecules. Although
methoxymethane contains an oxygen, there are no suitable hydrogen atoms for hydrogen
bonding to take place, hence the intermolecular forces are only the much weaker dipole-
dipole forces, resulting in a lower boiling point.

d) The strength of the van der Waals' forces between these molecules will increase with
the surface area of the molecule, hence they are weakest in the more spherical molecule,
the weaker the forces and the lower the boiling point. The shape of pentan-3-ol is more
spherical than pentan-1-ol, hence its lower boiling point.

e) sulfur dioxide is a polar molecule and hence it will have dipole-dipole forces between
its molecules. These are stronger than the van der Waals' forces between chlorine
molecules, hence its higher boiling point, in spite of its lower molar mass..

7. The hydrides of fluorine, oxygen and nitrogen (HF, H_2O, H_3N) can all form hydrogen
bonds between their molecules, whereas the hydrides of the elements lower down in the
same group (e.g. HCl, H_2S and H_3P) only have van der Waals' forces and dipole-dipole
interaction between their molecules. Hydrogen bonds are much stronger than van der
Waals' forces and the dipole-dipole interaction, so the hydride of the first element in
each group has the higher boiling point. Other differences would include the first
element in each group having a higher melting point, a greater latent heat of fusion, a
greater latent heat of vaporisation and high surface tension in the liquid state. Some
more specific differences would include:

  NH_3 is much more soluble in water than PH_3, this is partly because it can hydrogen
  bond to the solvent.

  HF is a weak acid whereas HCl is a strong one. In part this is due to the fact that HF
  molecules are stabilised by being able to hydrogen bond to the water. Also, H–F is a
  relatively strong bond compared to H–Cl.

  Ice (solid H_2O) is relatively hard and brittle. This is because it is held together by
  hydrogen bonding between the water molecules, which are stronger than other
  intermolecular forces, making it quite hard, and if the crystal is distorted these
  directional bonds break causing the crystal to cleave.

EXERCISE 4.9

1. a) The strength of metallic bonding and hence the boiling point, will increase with the
number of electrons per atom that participate in the delocalised bonding. Also, the
decreasing ionic size of the metal cations is another factor. Sodium has only one valence

electron to contribute, hence its low boiling point, magnesium two, resulting in a greater boiling point, and aluminium three accounting for it having the highest boiling point.
b) The bonding in metals is not between one atom and another, but between the cations and the mobile flux of electrons that surrounds them. This means that they can move relative to each other without the need to break bonds.
c) The delocalised electrons are capable of moving freely throughout the solid, hence they are capable of conducting an electric current from one part of the solid to another.

EXERCISE 4.10

1. A 2. D 3. D 4. D 5. A 6. B 7. B
8. a) Silicon carbide b) Naphthalene c) Rubidium chloride d) Scandium e) Naphthalene f) Rubidium chloride g) Scandium h) Scandium i) Silicon carbide j) Rubidium chloride
9. a) Magnesium would be malleable, conduct electricity and have a higher melting point.
Iodine would be brittle, would not conduct electricity and would have a lower melting point (any two of these differences). b) The mixture would have small grey and black particles visible. The compund would be a uniform white solid.
c) MgI_2. It will be ionically bonded. d) When the compound is added to water it will dissolve, but neither component of the mixture would dissolve.
e) When the mixture is shaken with the non-polar solvent, the iodine would dissolve in the solvent, but the magnesium would not. The magnesium could then be filtered off and the iodine recovered by evaporating the solvent.
10. Covalent bonds are not weak. Diamond one of the hardest known substances is held together only by covalent bonds. Many substances have molecular covalent bonding and in these, even though the covalent bonds are strong, there are relatively weak forces between the molecules. It is these that are overcome when a substance melts. It would be more accurate to state that "Sugar has a molecular covalent structure and the forces between the molecules are much weaker than the ionic bonds that exist in salt."
11. Ethanoic acid dissolves in water because its -OH group can form hydrogen bonds to the water. Sodium ethanoate dissolves in water because it is an ionic solid and the strong hydration interaction between the ions and the polar water molecules enables the strong forces between the ions in the solid to be overcome. Ethyl ethanoate has two hydrocarbon regions which cannot bond to the water and these would disrupt the hydrogen bonding between water molecules if it were to dissolve, hence it is not soluble.
12. Going from left to right, sodium oxide has an ionic structure. There are quite strong electrostatic forces between the ions hence the melting point is quite high. In magnesium oxide, the bonding is also ionic, but the fact that there are equal numbers of the two ions and that these have double charges results in a very high melting point. Aluminium oxide and silicon dioxide have a giant covalent structures so that to melt them involves overcoming strong covalent bonds, resulting in a high melting point. The remaining oxides, those of phosphorus, sulfur and chlorine, have a molecular covalent structure, so that melting them only depends on overcoming relatively weaker intermolecular forces. The lower the molar mass of the compound, the lower the melting point and this accounts for the decrease in melting point of these from phosphorus, through sulfur to chlorine.

EXERCISE 5.1

1. D 2. B 3. B

Answers

4. Helium has a lower molar mass than air (i.e. nitrogen and oxygen) and so, at a given temperature, its particles are moving faster. This means that they collide with the walls of the balloon more frequently than molecules of N_2 and O_2 in air. For this reason the number of molecules per second striking a microscopic hole in the balloon and hence escaping will be greater for helium than it would be if it were inflated with air.

5. The alcohol molecules need a certain minimum amount of kinetic energy in order to escape from the surface of the liquid. This means that only the more energetic molecules escape, hence the average kinetic energy of the remaining molecules falls. Temperature is a measure of the average kinetic energy of the molecules and hence a decrease in this is experienced as a drop in temperature of the alcohol.

6. a) A is at a low temperature, B at a higher temperature and C at the highest temperature.
b) A is the gas with the greatest molar mass, B has a lower molar mass and C is the one with the lowest molar mass.

7. a) $NH_{3\,(g)} + HCl_{(g)} \Rightarrow NH_4Cl_{(s)}$ b) Molecules of NH_3 and HCl escape from the solution. These particles in the gas phase are in constant random motion, hence they will move from a region of high concentration to one of low concentration. c) Diffusion.
d) A e) The particles of HCl, having a greater molar mass than those of NH_3, move at a lower speed, therefore in a given time they will have moved a shorter distance.
f) The time taken for the reaction to occur would be less.
g) As the temperature increases the average kinetic energy of the molecules, and hence their speed, increases. This means the time taken for them to meet is less.

8. a) A = solid C = liquid E = gas b) B = melting, D = boiling.
c) When there is a change of state the energy supplied is used to overcome the attractive forces between the molecules, rather than to increase their kinetic energy.
d) During B the particles become free to move at random and so no longer have fixed positions. During D the distance between the particles of the substance become a lot greater. e) Impurities always reduce the melting point of a substance, therefore change B will occur at a lower temperature. f) If the time for D was much shorter, less energy is needed to overcome the forces between the particles, hence the intermolecular forces are weaker.

EXERCISE 5.2
1. A 2. A 3. D 4. B 5. C 6. B 7. D 8. C
9. $N_2 = 76$ kPa, $O_2 = 20$ kPa, Ar = 1 kPa
10. 0.67 atmospheres
11. a) 96.8 kPa, b) 0.0139 moles, c) 83.2%
12. a) If the temperature increases the particles of the gas will move faster, therefore they will collide more frequently and forcefully with the walls of the container and each collision will have a greater impact. Hence pressure will increase with increasing temperature and vice versa. If the volume increases then particles will, on average, have to travel further before colliding with the walls so the number of collisions per second will decrease. Hence an increase in volume will decrease pressure and vice versa. If more gas is introduced into the container, then there will be more particles colliding with the wall each second. Hence an increase in amount of gas increases pressure and vice versa.
b) Gases at the same temperature and pressure all have the same average kinetic energy.

As this is equal to $\frac{1}{2}mv^2$, if m is greater v must be smaller. Hence gases of a high molar mass move more slowly all other factors being equal. If a particle is moving more slowly, it will take it longer to move a certain distance, hence its rate of diffusion will be less.

c) Consider the same number of moles of H_2 and SF_6 in identical containers at the same temperature. The H_2 molecules move faster (see part b) and so collide with the walls more frequently. Even though the SF_6 molecules collide with the walls less frequently, each time they do so the collision has a greater impact. These two factors cancel each other out so that the resultant pressure is the same for both gases.

d) High pressure and low temperature. If the distance between the particles is decreased, by increasing the pressure, and the energy they possess is reduced, by decreasing the temperature, then intermolecular forces become significant. These are greater for SF_6 than for H_2, so their properties will no longer be virtually identical. Also at high pressures the total volume decreases, so volume of the particles becomes significant and as SF_6 is larger than H_2 their properties will no longer be virtually identical.

13. a) 1100 dm^3 b) 100 g (n.b. H_2)

14. Mass of gas in flask $= 4.685$ g; Volume of flask (assuming density of water $= 1$ kg dm^{-3}) $= 0.8043$ dm^3; The flask contains 0.03193 moles at this T & P, hence the molar mass $= 146.7$ g mol^{-1}.

15. a) i 50% ii 43.1% b) Both are 75 kPa. c) The propane. It has the lower molar mass, therefore its particles will have the greater velocity and hence collide with the walls more frequently. There is therefore a greater chance that in a given time it will strike the hole and hence escape.

16. The pressure in both flasks must be equal, therefore

$$P = \frac{nRT}{V} = \frac{x \times R \times 600}{V} = \frac{(2-x) \times R \times 300}{V} \Rightarrow 600x = 600 - 300x \Rightarrow x = \frac{6}{7}$$

Therefore there is 8/7 mole in the flask at 27 K and 6/7 mole in the flask at 127 K.

$$P = \frac{nRT}{V} = \frac{\frac{6}{7} \times 8.31 \times 400}{5} = 570 \text{kPa}$$

EXERCISE 6.1

1. B 2. C 3. A 4. a) $Mg + H_2SO_4 \Rightarrow MgSO_4 + H_2$
b) Exothermic c) The chemical potential energy of the reactants is higher than that of the products.
5. a) Cl-Cl and O=O; absorbs energy. b) Cl-O releases energy.
c) It is the energy change when molar quantities of the reactants, as in the balanced equation, are completely converted to the products. d) Positive e) Endothermic

4 d)

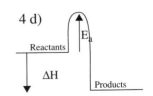

EXERCISE 6.2

1. B 2. C 3. B 4. C 5. D 6. A 7. D
8. Heat energy absorbed $= m.s.\Delta T = 100 \times 4.18 \times 4.5 = 1881$J
Amount of ammonium nitrate $= m/M = 8.00/80.06 = 0.100$ mol

Answers

Enthalpy of solution = 1881/0.100 = 18810 J mol^{-1} = 18.8 kJ mol^{-1}

9. a) 3 cm^3 b) 2.3 g c) 0.050 moles d) $C_2H_5OH + 3 O_2 \Rightarrow 2 CO_2 + 3 H_2O$

e) 1350×0.050 = 67.4 kJ

10. a) Heat energy absorbed by the aluminium = $m.s.\Delta T$ = 0.1×875×80 = 7000J

b) Heat energy absorbed by the water = $m.s.\Delta T$ = 500×4.18×80 = 167200J

Total energy absorbed = 167200 +7000 = 174200J = 174.2 kJ

c) Amount of butane = m/M = 14.5/58 = 0.25 moles

d) Enthalpy of reaction = 174.2 / 0.25 = 697 kJ mol^{-1}

e) Much of the heat generated by the combustion of the gas would be lost to the surroundings.

EXERCISE 6.3

1. D 2. A

3. Let required enthalpy change = ΔH Applying Hess' law, 2.ΔH + (–120) = (–800)

ΔH = (120-800)/2 = –340 kJ mol^{-1}

4. –126 kJ mol^{-1}

5. a) Weigh out a sample of the solid (i.e. CaO or CaCO$_3$). Take a known volume of dilute hydrochloric acid, so that the acid will be in excess. Measure the temperature of the acid and then add the solid. Stir the mixture, monitoring the temperature and record the maximum temperature reached.

b) The calcium oxide, because the carbonate forms a gas and heat will be lost through the evolution of hot gas. OR The calcium carbonate, because the oxide is likely to have absorbed water vapour from the air converting it to the hydroxide.

c) The specific heat capacity of dilute hydrochloric acid is required.

d) Calculate the heat evolved in the two reactions ($m.s.\Delta T$) and knowing the number of moles of calcium compound taken in each case, calculate ΔH for the two reactions. The required enthalpy change is ΔH for the carbonate reaction minus ΔH for the reaction with the oxide.

EXERCISE 6.4

1. A 2. A 3. Equation: $2 CO_{(g)} + O_{2(g)} \Rightarrow 2 CO_{2(g)}$

Bonds broken 2×(C≡O) + O=O = (2×1073) + 496 = 2642 kJ mol^{-1}.

Bonds made 4×743 = 2972 kJ mol^{-1}.

Overall enthalpy change = 2642 – 2972 = –330 kJ mol^{-1} for 2 moles of CO, so for 1 mole = –165 kJ mol^{-1}

4. Enthalpy change in breaking bonds = (944) + (3×242) = 1670 kJ mol^{-1}

Overall enthalpy change = 1670 – (6×N-Cl) = +688 kJ mol^{-1}

Enthalpy of N-Cl bond = 1/6 (1670 - 688) = 164 kJ mol^{-1}

5. Equation:$C_3H_{6(g)} + H_{2(g)} \Rightarrow C_3H_{8(g)}$. Bonds broken C-C + H-H = 348 + 436 = 784kJmol^{-1}

Bonds made 2×(C-H) = 2×412 = 824 kJ mol^{-1}.

Enthalpy change = 784 – 824 = –40 kJ mol^{-1}

The actually value is much more exothermic than this value. The reason for this is that the bond angle in cyclopropane is 60°, much less than the normal tetrahedral angle of 109°. The resulting strain in the molecule increases the chemical potential energy of cyclopropane. This is released when it is converted to propane and the additional potential energy is converted to heat energy.

Also, bond enthalpy values for C–C and C–H are only average values obtained from a series of compounds and are not exact values for the reaction.

EXERCISE 6.5

1. C 2. B 3. A 4. a) Equation: $Zn_{(s)} + Cl_{2(g)} \Rightarrow ZnCl_{2(s)}$

$\Delta H = \Delta H_f(ZnCl_2) - [\Delta H_f(Zn) + \Delta H_f(Cl_2)] = -416 - [0 + 0] = -416 \text{ kJ mol}^{-1}$

b) Equation: $2 H_2S_{(g)} + SO_{2(g)} \Rightarrow 2 H_2O_{(l)} + 3 S_{(s)}$

$\Delta H = [2\Delta H_f(H_2O) + 3\Delta H_f(S)] - [2\Delta H_f(H_2S) + \Delta H_f(SO_2)] = -233 \text{ kJ mol}^{-1}$

c) Equation: $2 Pb(NO_3)_{2(s)} \Rightarrow 2 PbO_{(s)} + 4 NO_{2(g)} + O_{2(g)}$

$\Delta H = [2\Delta H_f(PbO) + 4\Delta H_f(NO_2) + \Delta H_f(O_2)] - [2\Delta H_f(Pb(NO_3)_2)] = +598 \text{ kJ mol}^{-1}$

5. For the equation $CH_2Cl_{2(l)} + O_{2(g)} \Rightarrow CO_{2(g)} + 2 HCl_{(g)}$ $\Delta H = -458 \text{ kJ mol}^{-1}$. For the equation $CH_2Cl_{2(l)} + 2 O_{2(g)} \Rightarrow CO_{2(g)} + H_2O_{(l)} + Cl_{2(g)}$ $\Delta H = -560 \text{ kJ mol}^{-1}$. The latter is much closer to the experimental value, so this is presumably the reaction occurring.

6. a) $4 CH_3NHNH_{2(l)} + 5 N_2O_{4(g)} \Rightarrow 4 CO_{2(g)} + 12 H_2O_{(l)} + 9 N_{2(g)}$

b) $[4\times(-395) + 12\times(-244)] - [4\times(+13) + 5\times(+9)] = -4605 \text{ kJ mol}^{-1}$

c) The products of the reaction are common, rather inert substances and so are unlikely to lead to pollution problems.

7. a) Burn both of the compounds in a calorimeter to measure their enthalpies of combustion and then combine these using a Hess' Law cycle to determine the enthalpy change for the hypothetical reaction.

b) Bonds broken = C–C + O–H = 346 + 464 = 810 kJ mol^{-1}

Bonds made = C–O + C–H = 358 + 413 = 771 kJ mol^{-1}. Enthalpy change = +39 kJ mol^{-1}

c) $\Delta H = -280 - (-327) = +47 \text{ kJ mol}^{-1}$ d) The enthalpy of formation data will give the best agreement, because bond enthalpy data applies to general values for the bonds, the actual values of which vary slightly from molecule to molecule.

EXERCISE 6.6

1. C 2. C 3. B 4. $-363.5 \text{ kJ mol}^{-1}$ 5. -377 kJ mol^{-1}. If two moles of calcium were reacted with one mole of fluorine, then the formation of two moles of CaF would release 754 kJ mol^{-1}, but 1214 kJ mol^{-1} would be released if only one mole of CaF$_2$ was formed and the excess calcium remained unreacted so this is the reaction that occurs.

EXERCISE 6.7

1. A 2. B 3. B

4. -161 kJ mol^{-1}

5. Using the theoretical value (+833) the enthalpy of solution is +5 kJ mol^{-1}. Using the experimental value (+905) the enthalpy of solution is +77 kJ mol^{-1}. The theoretical latter value is only slightly endothermic (small enough for entropy factors to compensate for see next section) and so the solid would be expected to be slightly soluble. In the case of sodium chloride the theoretical and experimental values are similar, hence sodium chloride is soluble. The actual value for silver chloride is very different from the theoretical owing to the presence of significant covalent character in the bonding. This results in an enthalpy of solution that is too endothermic to be compensated for by entropy factors, hence silver chloride is insoluble.

EXERCISE 6.8

1. D 2. B 3. a) An increase in entropy. Increase in the number of moles of gas.

b) A decrease in entropy. Formation of a solid from aqueous solution.

c) A decrease in entropy. Decrease in the number of moles of gas.

d) A decrease in entropy. Decrease in the number of moles of gas.

e) Little change in entropy. Number of moles of gas constant.

EXERCISE 6.9

1. C 2. B 3. a) -334 J mol^{-1}K^{-1} b) -598 kJ mol^{-1} c) 2007 J mol^{-1}K^{-1}

d) The total entropy change for the universe must be positive if a reaction is spontaneous. The total entropy change is the sum of the changes for the system and the surroundings. = 2007 - 334 = 1673 J mol^{-1}K^{-1} therefore the reaction is spontaneous at 298K. As the temperature increases, the entropy change for the surroundings, which is positive becomes less. The optimum condition is therefore a low temperature.

4. Consider the conversion of the cis- to the trans- isomer. ΔG = 64.1 - 67.1 = -3.0 kJ mol^{-1}

This is negative, therefore the product, the trans- isomer is the more stable. For "perfect equilibrium" ΔG is zero. $\Delta G = \Delta H - T.\Delta S$ = -4400 - (-5).T = 0. T = 4400/5 = 880K. The temperature at which the equilibrium is balanced would be 607°C.

5. a) The gradient represents the entropy change in the reaction. At the first gradient change the entropy reverses so that it becomes positive rather than negative. This means that the entropy of the products has increased, so probably the discontinuity is due to lead oxide becoming a gas. The second discontinuity is in the opposite direction, so corresponds to lead itself becoming a gas, making the entropy change less favourable.

b) At temperatures below ~1000K carbon is a more powerful reductant than carbon monoxide, but above this temperature the reverse is true.

c) Hydrogen will not reduce Al$_2$O$_3$ at any temperature. It will reduce PbO at almost all temperatures shown on the graph. It will only reduce ZnO at temperatures below ~1500K.

6. a) +214 J mol^{-1}; b) Ice is the stable form as ΔG for melting is positive; c) –266 J mol^{-1};

d) 273 K (actual value using the data given is 272.7) – this is the melting point of ice, when it is in equilibrium with water.

e) ΔS for melting will be larger, therefore the temperature required for ΔG to be equal to zero (assuming ΔH unchanged) will be smaller. This corresponds to the lowering of the freezing point of ice caused by a solute.

EXERCISE 7.1

1. B 2. C 3. A

4. a)

b) The reaction rate is greatest at the start of the reaction. This can be seen by the fact that the gradient of the curve is greatest at the start of the reaction.

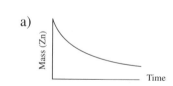

c) Possibilities include:

• Collecting the gas and recording its volume against time.

• Recording the change in total mass of the beaker and contents against time.

• Titrating samples from the reaction mixture with an aqueous alkali of known concentration.

EXERCISE 7.2

1. C 2. D 3. A

4. The determination of the reaction rate would be best determined using a spectrophotometer. Probably setting the wavelength to red (complimentary colour of green) or blue (complimentary colour of orange would yield acceptable results. (The best way would be to scan the complete spectrum of both dichromate(VI) and chromium(III) and then select the wavelength where they have the greatest difference in absorption.). Mix together aqueous dichromate(VI) and aqueous sulfur dioxide (suitable concentrations to give a reasonable rate of reaction would have to be determined by trial and error), then transfer the mixture rapidly to a cuvette in the spectrophotometer. Record the absorption of the solution at different times, or preferably continually using a link to a computer. Draw a graph of absorption against time. The relative rate can be determined from the gradient of the graph. If a concentration–absorption calibration has been carried out at the wavelength used, this can be converted to a concentration–time graph and the absolute rate calculated. The major precaution would be to measure the temperature and try to keep it constant.

5. Many possible answers, this is just a possible example.

a) The reaction of marble (calcium carbonate) chips with hydrochloric acid.

b) The variation of the total mass of the reaction system with time. As a gas with quite a high molar mass is evolved there is a significant change in total mass during the reaction. This technique is relatively easy to carry out and yet provides quite a high degree of precision.

c) The concentration of hydrochloric acid. The acid was diluted before adding to the marble chips, but the total volume was kept constant.

d) The technique could be used to investigate the effect of temperature. This would be done by heating the acid to different temperatures before adding it to the marble chips. The precaution would be to monitor the temperature of the mixture during the course of the reaction and to use these values rather than the starting temperature of the acid as the cold marble chips will cause a drop in temperature.

EXERCISE 7.3

1. A 2. B 3. A 4. D 5. C

6. a) The rate of a chemical reaction depends on the collision rate between the reactants. Increasing the concentration of the reactants increases the collision rate and hence the reaction rate. b) In order for reaction to occur on collision, the energy of the collision must be greater than the activation energy for the reaction and the reactive parts of the molecule must come into contact during the collision. c) As the temperature is increased the kinetic energy of the particles increases and so the proportion of the collisions, with the required activation energy, and hence the rate, also increases. A small increase in the collision rate will also occur.

7.

c) The lead dioxide is acting as a catalyst.

d) By increasing the temperature.

7. a)&b)

EXERCISE 7.4

1. D 2. D 3. C 4. D 5. B

6. a) Comparing 1 and 2, doubling [CH$_3$COCH$_3$] doubles the rate of reaction. Comparing 2 and 4, halving [I$_2$] has no effect on the rate of reaction. Comparing 1 and

Answers

6, doubling $[H^+]$ doubles the rate of reaction. The rate expression is: Rate $= k.[CH_3\text{-CO-}CH_3].[H^+]$

b) The reaction is first order in $CH_3\text{-CO-}CH_3$. The reaction is zero order in I_2. The reaction is first order in H^+. The reaction is second order overall.

c) Rate $= k.[CH_3\text{-CO-}CH_3].[H^+] = 4\times10^{-6}$
$k = 2\times10^{-5}mol^{-1}dm^3s^{-1}$.

7. a) The reaction is first order in the ester. The fact that the first and second half–life are equal when the other reagent is in large excess demonstrates this.

b) The half-life is 140 s. $k_1 = 4.95\times10^{-3}s^{-1}$ c) Because this is present in excess and so its concentration does not change significantly during the course of the reaction.

d) The experiment could be repeated with a high concentration of ester and a low concentration of hydroxide ions.

e) Rate $= k_2.[ester].[OH^-]$. $k = 2.475\times10^{-2}$ mol^{-1} dm^3 s^{-1} If $[OH^-]$ is virtually constant because it is present in excess, then Rate $= (k_2.[OH^-]).[ester]$. This gives first order kinetics with an apparent rate constant $(k_2.[OH^-]) = 0.2.k_2 = 4.95\times10^{-3}$ s^{-1}.

EXERCISE 7.5

1. C 2. D 3. B 4. D

5. a) a) The reaction is second order in A and zero order in B, therefore Rate $= k.[A]^2$
b) Substituting: $3.2\times10^{-4} = k \times(0.2)^2$, $k = 3.2\times10^{-4} / 0.04 = 8\times10^{-3}mol^{-1}dm^3s^{-1}$
c) Rate $= k.[A]^2 = 8\times10^{-3}\times(0.1)^2 = 8\times10^{-5}mol$ dm^{-3} s^{-1} d) i A+A $\Rightarrow$X (slow RDS) then X+B$\Rightarrow$C+D+A (fast) iiA+B $\Rightarrow$ C+D (slow RDS) or other possibilities.

EXERCISE 7.6

1. A 2. A 3. C 4. B 5. D

6. a) & b)

With heterogeneous catalyst

c) The reaction is endothermic, so the container will become cooler.
d) This would increase the rate of reaction. The reason for this is that the shape of the distribution of kinetic energies amongst the molecules will change so that a greater proportion of the molecules, and hence of the collisions, will have the required activation energy. There will also be a slight increase in the collision rate.

e) Increasing the pressure (and hence the concentration) of the gas.

f) The reaction could be monitored by shining a light, preferably a blue light, through the gas and recording the variation of the intensity of the light with time.

7. a) The reaction is first order because the first and second half lives are equal. In order to calculate the rate constant the concentration of the benzenediazonium chloride would need to be known.

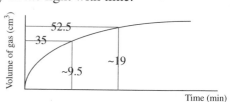

b) The precautions necessary would be to maintain the temperature, not only of the water bath, but of the whole apparatus (because of the effect of temperature on gas volume), constant.

c) In order to determine the activation energy the rate would have to be measured at different temperatures with all other conditions constant. The activation energy can be found from the gradient of a graph of ln(rate) against $1/T$ with all other conditions constant.

EXERCISE 8.1

1. C 2. a) $PCl_{5\ (s)} \rightleftharpoons PCl_{3\ (s)} + Cl_{2\ (g)}$ b)i It will start to dissociate. ii The rate will decrease as its concentration decreases iii Zero, because neither of the reactants are present to react. iv The rate of the reverse reaction will increase as the concentrations of phosphorus(III) chloride and chlorine increase. v Eventually they will become equal. vi A state of equilibrium is achieved. vii The flask will contain phosphorus(V) chloride, phosphorus(III) chloride and chlorine. The last two will have the same concentration, but this will be different to the concentration of phosphorus(V) chloride.
No. A state of equilibrium will never be reached, because the products will escape and the reverse reaction will never reach a rate equal to the forward reaction.

EXERCISE 8.2

1. C 2. D 3. C 4. A 5. D 6. B 7. C 8. A
9. a) $N_{2\ (g)} + 3\,H_{2\ (g)} \rightleftharpoons 2\,NH_{3\ (g)}$ b) and c)

$$N_2 + 3H_2 \qquad 2\,NH_3$$

335kJmol^{-1} With catalyst

-92kJmol^{-1}

d) Finely divided, because the reaction occurs on the surface of the catalyst, so increasing the surface area increases the rate of reaction.
e) It will increase the rate of both the forward and reverse reactions, by increasing the collision rates.
10. a) Initially the nitrogen monoxide and oxygen react to form nitrogen dioxide. The rate of this reaction will fall as the gases are consumed. Initially there is no nirogen dioxide, so the reverse reaction does not occur, but as nitrogen dioxide is formed by the forward reaction, the rate of the reverse reaction increases. Eventually the rates of forward and reverse reactions become equal. b) $2NO_{(g)} + O_{2\ (g)} \rightleftharpoons 2NO_{2\ (g)}$
c) Using air instead of oxygen decreases the concentration of oxygen and hence reduces the rate of the forward reaction, without affecting the reverse reaction. The equilibrium therefore shifts to the left, decreasing the concentration of NO_2, producing a lighter colour.
11.

Equilibrium	Effect of change	Balance by
a	Shifts to the left	Increasing the temperature
b	Shifts to the left	Increasing the pH (reducing $[H^+]$)
c	Shifts to the left	Decreasing the pressure
d	Shifts to the right	Increasing the temperature
e	Shifts to the right	Increasing $[NH_3]$

Answers

12. a) The equilibrium will shift to the left. According to Le Chatelier's principle, a decrease in temperature shifts the position of equilibrium in the direction of the exothermic change. In this case this is towards the left hand side or decreasing temperature shifts the equilibrium in the reverse direction to compensate for some of the heat taken away by reducing the temperature.

b) This will shift the position of equilibrium to the right, increasing the amount of hydrogen iodide. According to Le Chatelier's principle, adding more of a reagent shifts the position of equilibrium in the opposite direction.

c) Increasing the pressure will have no effect on the position of equilibrium. According to Le Chatelier's principle, increasing the presure shifts the equilibrium to the side with least moles of gas, but in this case there are two moles of gas on each side of the equilibrium.

13. a) The amount of yellow solid would increase and the amount of brown liquid would decrease. According to Le Chatelier's principle, increasing the presure shifts the equilibrium to the side with least moles of gas. In this case this is the right hand side, so more of the yellow ICl_3 is formed.

b) According to Le Chatelier's principle, a decrease in temperature shifts the position of equilibrium in the direction of the exothermic change. If the amount of yellow solid increases, one can conclude that the forward reaction is exothermic.

14. a) $2 SO_{2 (g)} + O_{2 (g)} \rightleftharpoons 2 SO_{3 (g)}$ b) i Increase the rate of the forward reaction. ii Increases the rate of the reverse reaction. iii The proportions of the components will be unaffected. c) Increasing the pressure shifts the position of equilibrium to the side with the least number of moles of gas. In this case this is the right hand side, so increasing the pressure would increase the amount of sulfur trioxide.

d) Because the forward reaction is exothermic, an increase in temperature would shift the equilibrium to the left, hence decreasing the proportion of sulfur trioxide.

EXERCISE 8.3

1. D 2. A 3. B

4. a) NH_4HS is a solid so that its concentration cannot vary, therefore it is omitted from the equilibrium constant expression, so that the units are just $[NH_3]\times[H_2S]$, i.e. $mol^2 dm^{-6}$. b) $K_c = [NH_3].[H_2S] = 0.00001$, $[NH_3] = 3.16\times10^{-3} mol dm^{-3}$.

c) i Increases the mass of solid. ii Decreases $[H_2S]$. iii Does not affect the value of K_c.

5. a) They show that the forward reaction of the equilibrium is exothermic as an increase in temperature causes a decrease in the amount of product. b) $0.596 mol^{-2}dm^6$.

6. a) $\dfrac{[COCl_2]}{[CO].[Cl_2]}$ b) $0.417 mol^{-1} dm^3$

c) $[CO] = 1.60$; $[Cl_2] = 1.20$; $[COCl_2] = 0.400 mol dm^{-3}$ d) $0.208 mol^{-1} dm^3$

e) As the temperature is constant, the value of K_c must remain constant, so the system is now no longer at equilibrium. The equilibrium must shift to the right so as to increase the value of the equilibrium constant expression

f) Yes. Le Chatelier's principle states that an increase in total pressure (this will be required to reduce the volume) will shift the equilibrium in the direction of the least moles of gas. For this equilibrium this is a shift to the right, increasing the amount of product.

EXERCISE 8.4

1. C 2. A 3. B

4. a) The temperature at which the vapour pressure equals the extenal pressure.
b) The lower the boiling point, the weaker the intermolecular forces. c) Between 69 °C and 81°C. The vapour pressure of the mixture will be greater than that of hexane, but lower than that of cyclohexane. This means that the temperature required for it to equal the external pressure will be intermediate between the boiling points of the pure components.
d) The vapour will be richer in the more volatile component, hexane. At the boiling point of the mixture, the vapour pressure of the hexane in the mixture would be greater than that of the cyclohexane. e) The proportion of the hexane in the distillate will continually increase and that of the cyclohexane decrease. f) Fractional distillation.
g) The separation of the components of petroleum (crude oil) or the components of air.

EXERCISE 8.5

1. A 2. D

3. $\quad \Delta T = K \times \dfrac{n \times m_{st}}{M_{st}} \times \dfrac{1000}{m_{sv}}$

$\quad M_{st} = K \times \dfrac{n \times m_{st}}{\Delta T} \times \dfrac{1000}{m_{sv}} = 20.1 \times \dfrac{1 \times 1.50}{4.7} \times \dfrac{1000}{50} = 128.3$

4. $K = \Delta T \times \dfrac{1}{n_{st}} \times \dfrac{m_{sv}}{1000} = 1.2 \times \dfrac{1}{0.0135} \times \dfrac{20}{1000} = 1.78$ K mol^{-1} kg.

5. $\qquad\qquad \Pi V = nRT$

$\quad n = \dfrac{\Pi V}{RT} = \dfrac{330 \times 0.5}{8.31 \times 298} = 0.0666$ moles

From mass and molar mass, $5/150 = 0.0333$ moles, therefore the solute must dissociate into two particles.

EXERCISE 8.6

1. D 2. D

3. Initially: $p(O_2) = 20$ kPa; $p(N_2) = 80$ kPa; $p(NO) = 0$
   At equilibrium $p(O_2) = 19.4$ kPa; $p(N_2) = 79.4$ kPa; $p(NO) = 1.2$ kPa

4. a) Molar mass = 136, therefore $[Ca^{2+}] = [SO_4^{2-}] = 6.34/136 = 0.0466$ mol dm^{-3}

$K_{sp} = [Ca^{2+}].[SO_4^{2-}] = (0.0466)^2 = 2.17 \times 10^{-3}$ mol^{2}dm^{-6}

b) $[Ca^{2+}] = [SO_4^{2-}] = 0.1/2$ (as V doubles when the solutions are mixed)
$[Ca^{2+}].[SO_4^{2-}] = (0.05)^2 = 2.5 \times 10^{-3}$

This is greater than 2.17×10^{-3}, so a precipitate will form

5. a) $K_{sp} = [Mg^{2+}].[OH^-]^2 = x.(2x)^2 = 4x^3 = 2 \times 10^{-11}$; $x = 1.71 \times 10^{-4}$ mol dm^{-3}

In g dm^{-3} = $M_r \times n = 58 \times 1.71 \times 10^{-4} = 0.00992$ g dm^{-3}

b) $[OH^-] = 2 \times 1.71 \times 10^{-4} = 3.42 \times 10^{-4}$ mol dm^{-3}

c) $0.00992 \times 50/1000 = 4.96 \times 10^{-4}$ g

d) $[Mg^{2+}] = \dfrac{2 \times 10^{-11}}{(10^{-2})^{-2}} = 2 \times 10^{-7}$ mol dm^{-3}

Answers

e) $2\times10^{-7} \times 50/1000 \times 58 = 5.81 \times 10^{-7}$ g

The hydroxide ions displace the position of the equilibrium:

$Mg(OH)_2 \rightleftharpoons Mg^{2+} + 2\ OH^-$

to the left, hence decreasing the solubility (common ion effect).

6 a) $ZnCO_{3\ (s)} \rightleftharpoons Zn^{2+}_{\ (aq)} + CO_3^{2-}_{\ (aq)}$

$Zn(OH)_{2\ (s)} \rightleftharpoons Zn^{2+}_{\ (aq)} + 2\ OH^-_{\ (aq)}$

b) $K_{sp}(ZnCO_3) = [Zn^{2+}].[CO_3^{2-}]$

$K_{sp}(Zn(OH)_2) = [Zn^{2+}].[OH^-]^2$

c) $ZnCO_3$: $x^2 = 1.4\times10^{-11}$, therefore $x = 3.74\times10^{-6}$ mol dm^{-3}

$Zn(OH)_2$: $4x^3 = 2.0\times10^{-17}$, therefore $x = 1.71\times10^{-6}$ mol dm^{-3}

Hence zinc carbonate is the more soluble

d) For $ZnCO_3$ to precipitate, $[Zn^{2+}] = 1.4\times10^{-11}/0.1 = 1.4\times10^{-10}$ mol dm^{-3}

For $Zn(OH)_2$ to precipitate, $[Zn^{2+}] = 2.0\times10^{-17}/(0.1)^2 = 2.0\times10^{-15}$ mol dm^{-3}

Therefore the hydroxide precipitates first.

EXERCISE 9.1

1. D 2. C 3. B

4. a) $Fe_{(s)} + H_2SO_{4\ (aq)} \Rightarrow FeSO_4 + H_{2\ (g)}$

b) $PbCO_{3\ (s)} + 2\ HNO_{3\ (aq)} \Rightarrow Pb(NO_3)_{2\ (aq)} + H_2O_{(l)} + CO_{2\ (g)}$

c) $ZnO_{(s)} + 2\ HCl_{(aq)} \Rightarrow ZnCl_{2\ (aq)} + H_2O_{(l)}$

d) $Ca(OH)_{2\ (s)} + 2\ HNO_{3\ (aq)} \Rightarrow Ca(NO_3)_{2\ (aq)} + 2\ H_2O_{(l)}$

e) $2\ NaHCO_{3\ (s)} + H_2SO_{4\ (aq)} \Rightarrow Na_2SO_{4\ (aq)} + 2\ H_2O_{(l)} + 2\ CO_{2\ (g)}$

f) $H^+_{\ (aq)} + OH^-_{\ (aq)} \Rightarrow H_2O_{(l)}$

5.a) Diprotic acids are acids in which each molecule of acid can donate two hydrogen ions.

b) An amphiprotic species is one that can both accept and donate hydrogen ions, i.e. can act as both an acid and a base. For example the hydrogencarbonate ion can act as an acid to form the carbonate ion (CO_3^{2-}), or it can act as a base and form carbonic acid (H_2CO_3).

c) e.g. Water $H_2O_{(l)} \rightleftharpoons OH^-_{\ (aq)} + H^+_{\ (aq)}$; $H_2O_{(l)} + H^+_{\ (aq)} \rightleftharpoons H_3O^+_{\ (aq)}$

or hydrogenphosphate $HPO_4^{2-}_{\ (aq)} \rightleftharpoons H^+_{\ (aq)} + PO_4^{3-}_{\ (aq)}$; $HPO_4^{2-}_{\ (aq)} + H^+_{\ (aq)} \rightleftharpoons H_2PO_4^-_{\ (aq)}$

EXERCISE 9.2

1. C 2. A 3. A

4. a) $NH_{3\ (aq)} + H_2O_{(l)} \rightleftharpoons NH_4^+_{\ (aq)} + OH^-_{\ (aq)}$. The hydroxide ions make the solution alkaline or NH_4^+ is a weak acid and OH$^-$ is a strong base, thus the solution is basic. b) A **base** is a species that accepts a hydrogen ion, for example NH_3 accepts a hydrogen ion to form NH_4^+. **Weak** means that the base is not completely converted to hydroxide ions in aqueous solution, so aqueous ammonia molecules are in equilibrium with ammonium and hydroxide ions.

c) A lower pH. The sodium hydroxide is totally converted to sodium and hydroxide ions, so [OH$^-$] = 0.1 mol dm^{-3} whereas in ammonia the ammonia is in equilibrium with the ammonium and hydroxide ions, so [OH$^-$] is much less than 0.1 mol dm^{-3}. This means that the pH is lower in the ammonia solution.

5. a) $HCl_{(aq)} + H_2O_{(l)} \Rightarrow H_3O^+_{(aq)} + Cl^-_{(aq)}$. The acid is fully dissociated.
$CH_3COOH_{(aq)} + H_2O_{(l)} \rightleftharpoons H_3O^+_{(aq)} + CH_3COO^-_{(aq)}$. The acid is only partially dissociated.
b) The concentration of ions in the hydrochloric acid (strong acid) is much greater than that in the ethanoic acid (weak acid) so it has a much greater conductivity.
c) If the acids were added to magnesium ribbon (or any other reactive metal or metal carbonate) the rate of reaction, and hence of evolution of gas, would be much greater for the strong acid. Or if titrated with a strong base, NaOH, the equivalence point with the strong acid will be 7, whereas with the weak acid, it will be greater than 7 (approximately 9)

EXERCISE 9.3

1. B 2. B 3. D

4. a) 10^{-3} mol dm^{-3} b) 10^{-11} mol dm^{-3} c) 1 mol dm^{-3} 5. a) 4 b) 2 c) 7

6. The hydrochloric acid is full dissociated and so $[H^+] = 5 \times 10^{-4}$ mol dm^{-3}, hence the pH is between 3 and 4. The ethanoic acid is only partially dissociated and so, even though its concentration is much greater than that of the hydrochloric acid, the concentration of hydrogen ions and hence the effect on universal indicator, is similar.

7. a) $n = \dfrac{m}{M} = \dfrac{0.63}{63} = 0.01, c = \dfrac{n}{v} = \dfrac{0.01}{0.1} = 0.1 \text{moldm}^{-3}$ b) 1 c) 10^{-13} mol dm^{-3}

d) $HNO_2 \rightleftharpoons H^+ + NO_2^-$ e) The pH would be greater than that of nitric acid, as nitrous acid is only partially dissociated, so the hydrogen ion concentration will be much lower than in nitric acid, giving a greater pH.

8. Hydrochloric acid is a strong monobasic acid ($HCl \Rightarrow H^+ + Cl^-$), hence the $[H^+] = 0.01$ mol dm^{-3} and the pH is 2. sulfuric acid is a strong dibasic acid ($H_2SO_4 \Rightarrow 2H^+ + SO_4^{2-}$), hence the $[H^+] = 0.02$ mol dm^{-3} and the pH is less than 2. Ethanoic acid is a weak monobasic acid, and hence there is an equilibrium between the undissociated acid and the ions ($CH_3COOH + H_2O \rightleftharpoons H_3O^+ + CH_3COO^-$). This means that $[H^+]$ is much less than 0.01 mol dm^{-3} and hence the pH is much greater than 2.

EXERCISE 9.4

1. B 2. D

3. a) A buffer solution is one that maintains an approximately constant pH when small amounts of acid or base are added to it. b) $NH_3 + H_2O \rightleftharpoons NH_4^+ + OH^-$. When a small amount of acid is added, the hydrogen ions from the acid will react with the hydroxide ions in the equilibrium above. This will cause the equilibrium to shift to the right, forming more hydroxide ions until their pH is restored to almost the original value. If a small amount of alkali is added, then the hydroxide ions will react with ammonium ions, displacing the above equilibrium to the left until the hydroxide ion concentration falls to almost its initial value.

EXERCISE 9.5

1. A 2. B 3. C

4. a) Amount of HCl $= c.V = 0.2 \times 0.015 = 3 \times 10^{-3}$ moles
HCl + $NH_3 \Rightarrow NH_4Cl$, therefore amount of ammonia $= 3 \times 10^{-3}$ moles

$c = \dfrac{n}{V} = \dfrac{3 \times 10^{-3}}{0.020} = 0.15$ mol dm^{-3} b)i $[OH^-] = \sqrt{(K_b.[B])} = \sqrt{(10^{-4.7} \times 0.15)} = 1.73 \times 10^{-3}$;

Answers

pOH = 2.76, so pH = 14-2.76 = 11.24

ii At the mid point [B] = [BH⁺], so pOH = pK_b = 4.7. pH = 14-4.7 = 9.3

iii [H⁺] = $\sqrt{(K_a.[HA])}$ = $\sqrt{(10^{-9.3} \times 0.15)}$ = 8.67×10⁻⁶, therefore pH = 5.06

d) The section of the curve around pH 9 is the buffering region, this is because the addition of a small amount of acid or alkali has little effect on the pH.

e) Firstly the pH would remain at about pH 13 until almost the equivalence point. Secondly twice the volume of acid would be required to reach the equivalence point.

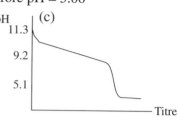

EXERCISE 9.6

1. C 2. B 3. C 4. D

5. a)HCl; HPO_4^{2-}; $C_5H_5NH^+$; $H_3N-NH_3^{2+}$; ⁻OOC–COOH. b)NO_3^-; I^-;SO_4^{2-}; NH_3; $HONH_2$. c)HSO_4^- and $N_2H_5^+$. d) e.g.H_2O Conjugate base OH^- Conjugate acid H_3O^+ or HCO_3^- Conjugate base CO_3^{2-} Conjugate acid H_2CO_3

6. a)i) An acid is a species that can donate hydrogen ions to another species.

ii) A base is a substance that can accept a hydrogen ion from another species.

b) $HNO_3 + H_2SO_4 \rightleftharpoons H_2NO_3^+ + HSO_4^-$. Sulfuric acid donates a proton to nitric acid, and thus behaves as an acid. On donating the proton it produces HSO_4^-.

c) $HNO_3 + H_2SO_4 \rightleftharpoons H_2NO_3^+ + HSO_4^-$

d) Conjugate acid‾base pair means that the two species are related by the gain/loss of only a single hydrogen ion (H⁺).

EXERCISE 9.7

1. C 2. a) A Lewis acid is a species that can accept a non-bonding electron pair to form a dative covalent bond.

c) A dative bond. Both of the electrons in the bond came from the chloride ion.

d)i Trigonal planar ii Tetrahedral

b)

:Cl:
:Cl:Al   +   :Cl: ⟶   :Cl:Al:Cl:
:Cl: :Cl:

3. a) Lewis base – the P in the PH_3 has a lone pair of electrons that it can donate.

b) Lewis acid – the B in the BCl_3 has an incomplete valence shell, so can accept a pair of electrons.

c) Lewis base – the S in the H_2S has a lone pair of electrons that it can donate.

d) Lewis base – the S in the SF_4 has a lone pair of electrons that it can donate.

e) Lewis acid – the Cu^{2+} has incomplete p and d orbitals, so it can accept a pair of electrons.

EXERCISE 9.8

1. D 2. C 3. C 4. D 5. C 6. B 7. C

8. a) 1.14 b) 8.34 c) 1.48×10⁻⁶ mol dm⁻³ d) 0.00437 mol dm⁻³ e) 13.13

9. a) $K_b = \dfrac{[BH^+][OH^-]}{[B]} = \dfrac{0.1 \times 10^{-4.7}}{0.1} = 10^{-4.7} = 2.00 \times 10^{-5}$ mol dm⁻³

b) The solution must be more acidic, so the equilibrium given above must be displaced to the left. This requires the addition of more ammonium chloride.

c) $[BH^+] = \dfrac{K_b[B]}{[OH^-]} = \dfrac{2.00 \times 10^{-5} \times 0.1}{1 \times 10^{-5}} = 0.2$ mol dm^{-3}

d) Ethanoic acid and sodium ethanoate (or any similar strength weak acid and conjugate base).

10. a) 0.00100 mol dm^{-3} b) 1.0×10^{-11} mol dm^{-3} c) Greater as each Ba(OH)$_2$ forms two OH$^-$ ions.

11. a) 7.21 b) [H$^+$] = $\sqrt{(0.02 \times 6.17 \times 10^{-8})}$ = 3.51×10^{-5}, therefore pH = 4.45 c) 1.62×10^{-7} mol dm^{-3}

12.a) $K_a = \dfrac{[H^+].[A^-]}{[HA]} = \dfrac{(10^{-4.67})^2}{0.28} = 1.63 \times 10^{-9}$ mol dm^{-3} b) Weaker (pK$_a$ =

8.79), the greater pK$_a$, the weaker the acid.

c) $K_a = \dfrac{[H^+].[A^-]}{K_a} = \dfrac{(10^{-5})^2}{1.63 \times 10^{-9}} = 0.0613$ mol dm^{-3}

13. a) HCN$_{(aq)}$ $\rightleftharpoons$ H$^+_{(aq)}$ + CN$^-_{(aq)}$

b) [H$^+$] = $\sqrt{(K_a.[HA])}$ = $\sqrt{(10^{-9}.3 \times 0.01)}$ = 2.24×10^{-6}, therefore pH = 5.65. This is considerably greater than the pH of a strong acid of this concentration (pH = 2).

c) Percentage = $\dfrac{100 \times [H^+]}{[HA]} = \dfrac{100 \times 2.24 \times 10^{-6}}{0.01} = 0.0224\%$. If diluted, the

percentage increases. d) pK$_b$ of conjugate base = 14 - pK$_a$ = 14 - 9.3 = 4.7

[OH$^-$] = $\sqrt{(K_b.[A^-])}$ = $\sqrt{(10^{-4.7} \times 0.1)}$ = 1.41×10^{-3}, therefore [H$^+$] = 7.08×10^{-12} & pH = 11.15

EXERCISE 9.9

1. C 2. B 3. C
4. a) Slightly acidic – salt of a weak base and strong acid. b) Neutral – salt of a strong base and a strong acid. c) Slightly acidic – salt of a small, highly charged cation.
d) Slightly alkaline – salt of a strong base and a weak acid.

EXERCISE 9.10

1. B 2. a) Methyl orange b) Because the titration involves a weak base and a strong acid, the rapid change of pH at the end point will be from about 2 to 6. Methyl orange changes colour within this pH range. c) From red to yellow. d) The indicator is itself a weak acid, so enough alkali must be added to react with this as well as with the other acid present - this amount is assumed to be negligible. e) Bromophenol blue. Because its pK$_a$ is 4.0, the mid point of its color change will be at about pH 4, which is within the expected pH change at the equivalence point.
3. a) Ethanoic acid is a weak acid, so only partially dissociated in aqueous solution.
b) Phenolphthalein; c) The rapid change in pH at the equivalence point is only about 1 unit, too small for most indicators to completely change colour. d) For Curve b, when the volume of alkali added is twice that required for neutralisation, [NH$_3$] = [NH$_4^+$] and hence the pH at this point is equal to the pK$_a$.

4. a) i. The sudden drop in pH would occur at ~12.5 cm^3 as H$_2$SO$_4$ is dibasic.

ii. The sudden drop in pH at ~25 cm^3 would only go to ~pH=6 and this would gradually fall as excess ethanoic acid is added.

b) Phenolphthalein would be an appropriate indicator for all three as the rapid changes in pH at the equivalence point all pass through the range for phenolphthalein (10 to 8). Methyl orange, which changes between pH 4.5 and 3.0 would only change colour with the two strong acids, it would not change colour with ethanoic acid.

5. a) HS^- b) $H_2S_{(aq)} \rightleftharpoons HS^-_{(aq)} + H^+_{(aq)}$ c) $c = \dfrac{m}{MV} = \dfrac{3.4}{34} = 0.10 \, mol \, dm^{-3}$

d) $[H^+] = \sqrt{(K_a.[HA])} = \sqrt{(9.55\times10^{-8}\times0.1)} = 9.77\times10^{-5}$, therefore pH = 4.01

e) A buffer solution is one that maintains an approximately constant pH when small amounts of acid or base are added to it.   f) The hydroxide ions would react with the hydrogen ions. As a result the equilibrium in b) will shift to the right, producing more hydrogen ions, until the pH is restored to almost its original level. g) 0.196 mol dm^{-3}

h) pH = 7.31 i) 9.77×10^{-3} mol dm^{-3} . The concentration is so low that it would soon be consumed if an acid were added. j) The solution has a pH of 4.01 (see d), so with bromothymol blue it will be yellow (the "acid" colour), and with methyl yellow it will also be yellow (the 'alkali' colour).

k) Indicators are weak acids/bases in which the colours of the acidic and basic forms (HIn and In$^-$ in the equilibrium $HIn_{(aq)} \rightleftharpoons H^+_{(aq)} + In^-_{(aq)}$) have different colours. If an acid is added, the hydrogen ions drive the equilibrium to the left producing one colour. If an alkali is added, then this reacts with the hydrogen ions driving the equilibrium to the right, giving another colour. The pH at which this occurs will depend on the pK_a value of the acid. Bromothymol blue would be the more suitable, because it would change colour when the pH reached about 7, near to the expected equivalence point. Methyl yellow is already in the alkaline form and so would never change colour if titrated with an alkali. m) $S^{2-}_{(aq)} + H_2O_{(l)} \rightleftharpoons HS^-_{(aq)} + OH^-_{(aq)}$ n) The hydrogensulfide ion is amphiprotic, i.e. it can both gain and lose hydrogen ions. o) 0.0891 mol dm^{-3} p) 1.26×10^{-13} mol dm^{-3} q) Add either hydrogensulfide ions, or a dilute acid to convert sulfide ions to hydrogensulfide ions.

EXERCISE 10.1

1. B 2. D 3. B 4. C 5. C
6. a) +2 b) 0 c) +4 d) +4 e) +1 f) -2 g) +4 h) +1 i) +5 j) +6
7. a) Any compound of Fe^{2+} e.g. $FeSO_4$, $FeCl_2$ etc. b) NH_3, NH_4^+ c) MnO_4^- d) CH_2Cl_2, CH_2O e) PCl_5, $POCl_3$, P_4O_{10} (P_2O_5)
8. a) +2 to +1, reduced b) +4 to +4, neither c) –3 to +1, oxidised d) –2 to +2, oxidised
e) +2 to +2$\frac{1}{2}$, oxidised   9. a) The nitrogen in the hydrazine has an oxidation state of -2 and in dinitrogen tetroxide it is +4. In the element the oxidation state is zero, so in the case of hydrazine the nitrogen is oxidised and in the case of dinitrogen tetroxide it is reduced.
b) $2N_2H_4 + N_2O_4 \rightleftharpoons 3N_2 + 4H_2O$ c) The products are both common, stable, inert, non–toxic species and hence cannot be considered pollutants.
10. a) $(NH_4)_2Cr_2O_7$ b) This gives the oxidation number of the chromium in the dichromate ion. c) There are two chromium atoms, each of which change their oxidation state from +6 to +3, so the total change in oxidation state is -6. d) -3 e) There are two nitrogens and a total increase in oxidation number of +6, therefore each increases by +3.
f) 0 g) N_2 h) Orange to green. i) The reaction is exothermic.

EXERCISE 10.2

1. D 2. A 3. B 4. a) $Zn \Rightarrow Zn^{2+} + 2e^-$ b) $Br_2 + 2e^- \Rightarrow 2 Br^-$ c) $H_2S \Rightarrow S + 2 H^+ + 2 e^-$

d) $HNO_3 + H^+ + e^- \Rightarrow NO_2 + H_2O$ e) $VO_3^- + 6 H^+ + 2 e^- \Rightarrow V^{3+} + 3 H_2O$

5. a) $PbO_2 + 4 H^+ + Sn^{2+} \Rightarrow Sn^{4+} + Pb^{2+} + 2 H_2O$ b) $2 Co^{3+} + Sn^{2+} \Rightarrow Sn^{4+} + 2 Co^{2+}$

c) $PbO_2 + 2 H^+ + NO_2^- \Rightarrow NO_3^- + Pb^{2+} + H_2O$

d) $ClO_3^- + 6 H^+ + 3 Sn^{2+} \Rightarrow 3 Sn^{4+} + Cl^- + 3 H_2O$ e) $ClO_3^- + 3 NO_2^- \Rightarrow 3 NO_3^- + Cl^-$

6. a) $Mg + Pb^{2+} \Rightarrow Mg^{2+} + Pb$ b) $SO_2 + I_2 + 2 H_2O \Rightarrow SO_4^{2-} + 2 I^- + 4 H^+$

c) $H_2O_2 + 2 H^+ + 2 Fe^{2+} \Rightarrow 2 Fe^{3+} + 2 H_2O$

d) $3 Zn + Cr_2O_7^{2-} + 14 H^+ \Rightarrow 3 Zn^{2+} + 2 Cr^{3+} + 7 H_2O$

e) $6 MnO_4^- + 5 CH_3OH + 18 H^+ \Rightarrow 6 Mn^{2+} + 5 CO_2 + 19 H_2O$

7. a) +5 in ClO_3^- -1 in Cl^- +7 in ClO_4^- b) $ClO_3^- + H_2O \Rightarrow ClO_4^- + 2 H^+ + 2 e^-$

c) $ClO_3^- + 6 H^+ + 6 e^- \Rightarrow Cl^- + 3 H_2O$ d) $4 KClO_3 \Rightarrow 3 KClO_4 + KCl$

e) When combining the half equations the water and hydrogen ion terms cancel out, so no other reagent is needed.

8. a) $C_2H_5OH + H_2O \Rightarrow CH_3COOH + 4 H^+ + 4 e^-$ b) -2 to 0 c) $O_2 + 4 H^+ + 4 e^- \Rightarrow 2 H_2O$

d) $C_2H_5OH + O_2 \Rightarrow CH_3COOH + H_2O$

e) The activation energy for reactions involving molecular oxygen is quite high owing to the strength of the O=O bond. The bacteria produce enzymes that catalyse the change by reducing this activation energy.

EXERCISE 10.3

1. A 2. B 3. C

4. a) +2 to +1;

b) A blue solution and a colourless solution react to give a brown solution and a white precipitate.

c) $I_2 + 2 S_2O_3^{2-} \Rightarrow 2 I^- + S_4O_6^{2-}$; d) +2 to $+2\frac{1}{2}$

e) Starch solution. The solution will change from blue to colourless.

f) Moles of $S_2O_3^{2-} = c \times V = 0.2 \times 0.015 = 3 \times 10^{-3}$

Moles of $Cu^{2+} = 2 \times$ moles of $I_2 =$ moles of $S_2O_3^{2-} = 3 \times 10^{-3}$

$[Cu^{2+}] = n/V = 3 \times 10^{-3}/0.02 = 0.15$ mol dm^{-3}

5. a) From colourless to purple (from excess MnO_4^-).

b) Moles $Fe^{2+} = m/M_r = 2.00/55.85 = 0.0358$

$MnO_4^- + 8 H^+ + 5 Fe^{2+} \Rightarrow Mn^{2+} + 4 H_2O + 5 Fe^{3+}$

Moles $MnO_4^- = 1/5$ moles Fe $= 0.0358/5 = 7.16 \times 10^{-3}$

Volume required $= n/V = 7.16 \times 10^{-3}/0.2 = 0.0358$ dm$^3 = 35.8$ cm^3

EXERCISE 10.4

1. B 2. B 3. B

4. a) A pale green gas and a colourless solution reacting to form a red–brown solution.

b) There would be no reaction, the bromine would remain a red–brown colour.

c) Chlorine is a more powerful oxidising agent than bromine. Hence in the first case the chlorine is able to oxidise the bromide ions to bromine, but in the second case the bromine is not a powerful enough oxidising agent to oxidise chloride ions to chlorine.

5. You could put strips of the metal M into aqueous solutions of salts of metals such as copper sulfate, zinc chloride and magnesium nitrate. If a layer of the metal in solution forms on the surface of metal M, then metal M is more reactive than the metal in solution.

Alternatively strips of the other metals, such as copper, zinc etc. could be placed in an aqueous solution of MSO_4. If a layer of the metal M forms on the surface of the metal strip, then the metal that the strip is made from is more reactive than metal M.

EXERCISE 10.5

1. D 2. C 3. A

4. a) A temperature of 298K, all concentrations 1 mol dm^{-3}, (pressure of 101.3 kPa less vital here). b) A standard hydrogen electrode. c) A **high resistance** voltmeter.
d) A piece of filter paper dipped in aqueous potassium nitrate (many other possibilities).
e) i From the manganese to the silver. ii A new layer of silver metal will form on the surface. iii The manganese electrode will slowly dissolve. iv The cations will move towards the silver electrode and the anions will move towards the manganese electrode.

f) $Ag_{(s)}| Ag^+_{(aq)}||Mn^{2+}_{(aq)}| Mn_{(s)}$, $2 Ag_{(s)} + Mn^{2+}_{(aq)} \rightleftharpoons 2 Ag^+_{(aq)} + Mn_{(s)}$

g) -1.98 V; h) $\Delta G = -z.F.E^\theta = -2 \times 96500 \times (-1.98) = +382$ kJ mol^{-1}. Therefore as ΔG is large and positive, the reaction is not spontaneous.

i) Decrease. The silver equilibrium $(Ag^+ + e^- \rightleftharpoons Ag)$ will shift to the left, making its potential more negative, hence the difference in electrode potentials will be smaller.

EXERCISE 10.6

1. B 2. C 3. B

4. a) ionic b) i No; ii Yes; iii Yes c) i Electrolysis; ii Electrolyte; iii Electrodes d) Anode – positive; cathode – negative e) The anode.
5. a) The ions in the solid are firmly held in fixed places and so are not able to move and carry the current.

b) It could be melted, or it could be dissolved in water. c) $2 Cl^- \Rightarrow Cl_2 + 2 e^-$

d) Bubbles of yellow–green gas. e) $Cu^{2+} + 2 e^- \Rightarrow Cu$ f) A layer of a red–brown solid
g) Reduction, because the copper ions are gaining electrons.

EXERCISE 10.7

1. D 2. A 3. D
4. a) The chloride ion. b) Oxidation. c) The ion from the calcium chloride.
d) $2 Cl^- \Rightarrow Cl_2 + 2 e^-$; e) Bubbles of yellow–green gas would be evolved.
f) If the chloride ion concentration was quite low, then the water might be oxidised to oxygen, rather than the chloride ions to chlorine.
g) The calcium ion. h) The water will be changed most easily.
i) $2 H_2O + 2 e^- \Rightarrow H_2 + 2 OH^-$
j) Bubbles of colourless gas would be evolved.
k) The solution would eventually become calcium hydroxide.
l) ΔG is probably positive as energy is required for the change to occur.
5. a) The Faraday constant represents the electrical charge carried by one mole of electrons. b) $Q = I.t = 0.2 \times (5 \times 60 \times 60) = 3600$ C
c) Amount of electrons passed = 0.0373 mol. Reaction is $Cu^{2+} + 2e^- \Rightarrow Cu$, Amount of

$Cu = \frac{1}{2}$ amount of electrons $= 0.01865$ mol. Mass of $Cu = n.M = 0.01865 \times 63.55$

$= 1.185$ g

EXERCISE 11.1

1. B 2. A 3. A 4. D 5. D

6. a) Homologous series b) $C_nH_{2n+1}NO_2$ c) The boiling points would increase with increasing numbers of carbon atoms, owing to an increase in the strength of the van der Waals' forces between the molecules. d)i More soluble in water because the oxygens on the nitro groups can hydrogen bond to the water molecules. ii Less volatile because the nitro group would make the molecules polar and so dipole-dipole bonds will exist between them, increasing the boiling point. e) Compounds in the same homologous series tend to have similar chemical reactions, so the product would be $C_5H_{11}NH_2$.

EXERCISE 11.2

1. C 2. A

3. Spectrum A is that of methanol, spectrum B that of methanoic acid. The key difference in the two spectra is the $>C=O$ peak at ~ 1750 cm^{-1} in spectrum B, also the O–H peak in this spectrum is at a slightly lower wavenumber (~ 3000 cm^{-1}). In the methanol spectrum (A) the O–H is characteristically at a slightly greater wavenumber (~ 3300 cm^{-1}), so it can be seen as separated from the C–H absorptions at ~ 2900. Both spectra show clear C–O peaks, at ~ 1000 cm^{-1} in the methanol and at ~ 1100 cm^{-1} in the methanoic acid.

4. a) 750 cm^{-1} is C–Cl; 3000 cm^{-1} is C–H.

b) If there is only one NMR signal and the molecule contains a C–C bond (assume only one), then the possibilities are Cl–CH$_2$–CH$_2$–Cl, Cl$_2$CH–CHCl$_2$, or CH$_3$–CCl$_3$. The last of these is the one with an M_r nearest to 130.

5. a) 121 is caused by the loss of a hydrogen atom from the molecular ion.

b) $(122-104) = 18$; 104 is caused by the loss of a water molecule from the molecular ion.

c) $(122-93) = 29$; 93 is caused by the loss of CHO or C_2H_5 from the molecular ion.

6. a) The molecular ion is at 72.

b) $(72-57) = 15$, thus peak at 57 is caused by the loss of CH$_3$; $(72-43) = 29$, thus peak at 43 due to loss of C_2H_5 or CHO; $(72-29) = 43$, thus peak at 29 due to loss of CH$_3$-CO.

c) The probable structure is CH$_3$–CH$_2$–CO–CH$_3$.

7. a) 0.9 is R–CH$_3$; 1.3 is R–CH$_2$–R; 2.0 is either R$_3$CH or CH$_3$–CO–O–R, 4.1 is R–CO–O–CH$_2$–R.

b) The ratio in the peak order

0.9	:	1.3	:	2.0	:	4.1 is
2	:	3	:	3	:	2

c) The probable structural formula is CH$_3$–CH$_2$–CH$_2$–O–CO–CH$_3$, with the assignment being in the order that the hydrogens appear in this formula, 0.9, 1.3, 4.1, 2.0. (n.b. close inspection will show that the peaks labelled as '1.3' in fact occur at a slightly higher chemical shift owing to the fact that the oxygen further down the chain is having an effect.)

8. a) 0.9; 2.3; 7.3.

b) 0.9 is a methyl group (R–CH$_3$); 2.3 is a on a carbon next to a benzene ring

(CH₃–⬡) 7.3 is a hydrogen attached to a benzene ring H–⬡

c) The ratio in the peak order 0.9:2.3:7.3 is 3:2:5.

d) The molecule is most likely ethylbenzene CH₃–CH₂–⬡

9. From the IR spectrum, notable features are the presence of a C⁻O peak (at 1243 cm⁻¹), a >C=O peak (at 1741 cm⁻¹) and a C–C peak (at 2964 cm⁻¹).
From the mass spectrum, the molar mass would appear to be 88. There is a very strong peak at 43 (often caused by $CH_3^-CO^+$) and a peak at 29 (probably $CH_3–CH_2^+$).
From the NMR spectrum there would appear to be 3 types of hydrogen, possible assignments being:

δ	Hydrogen	Intensity
1.3	R–CH₂–R	3
2.1	CH₃–CO	3
4.2	CH₃–O	2

Taking all of this into account, the compound is probably ethyl ethanoate (CH₃–CO–O–CH₂–CH₃), the chemical shift for the CH₃ on the ethyl group being affected by the oxygen further down the chain.

10. a) Molecular ion peaks at 124 (large), 126 (smaller) and 128 (very small) isotopes of Cl. Peaks at 35 and 37 below the molecular ion peaks corresponding to loss of Cl twin peaks, 2 apart for fragments as they contain only one Cl.

b) Absorption between 700 and 800 cm⁻¹ from C–Cl vibration. Absorption between 1610 and 1680 cm⁻¹ from C=C vibration.

c) Two separate signals corresponding to =CH–C and C–CH₂–Cl. The relative intensities of the signals would be 1:2. One signal at 3.2–3.7 ppm corresponding to C–CH₂–Cl. One signal at 4.9 to 5.9 ppm corresponding to =CH–C.

EXERCISE 11.3

1. A 2. B

3. a) CH₃–CH₂–CH₂–CH₂–CH₃ b) CH₃CH₂CH(C₂H₅)CH₂CH₂CH₃ c) CH₃–CH₂–Br

d) H₃C—CH₂-C=CH₂
          |
          CH₃

e) H₃C—CCl₂—CH—COOH
                |
                CH₃

4. a) Methylpropene;

b) 3–chloropentane; c) 3–iodobutan–1–ol; d) 4–hydroxy–4–methylpentanoic acid

EXERCISE 11.4

1. D 2. A 3. a)

H₃C—CH—CH₂-CH₃
     |
H₃C—O

or CH₃CH₂-O-CH₂-CH₂-CH₃

b) H₃C—O—CH₂-CH—CH₃
                |
                CH₃

c) CH₃–CH₂–CH₂–CH₂–CH₂–O–H

4. CH₃–CH₂–CH₂–CH₂–CH₂–CH₃ Hexane; CH₃–CH₂–CH₂–CH(CH₃)–CH₃
2–methylpentane;

CH$_3$–CH$_2$–CH(CH$_3$)–CH$_2$–CH$_3$ 3–methylpentane;

CH$_3$–CH(CH$_3$)–CH(CH$_3$)–CH$_3$ 2,3–dimethylbutane;

CH$_3$–C(CH$_3$)$_2$–CH$_2$–CH$_3$ 2,2–dimethylbutane

5. a)   Butan–1–ol   CH$_3$–CH$_2$–CH$_2$–CH$_2$OH

         Butan–2–ol   CH$_3$–CH$_2$–CH(OH)–CH$_3$

         Methylpropan–1–ol   CH$_3$– CH(CH$_3$)–CH$_2$OH

         Methylpropan–2–ol   (CH$_3$)$_3$C–OH

b) Butan–2–ol can exist as a pair of enantiomers. This is the only isomer in which there are four different groups attached to one carbon atom and thus has an asymmetric/chiral centre.

c) Pass polarised light through the pure liquid and see, using a polarimeter, whether the two samples both rotated the plane of polarisation in the same direction or in different directions.

d) It is probable that the product would comprise almost entirely of one enantiomer.

e) Normal chemical synthesis would yield a mixture containing equal amounts of the two enantiomers, a racemic mixture. This is because there is an equal probability of the two enantiomers forming when the asymmetric carbon atom is created.

f) CH$_3$–O– CH$_2$–CH$_2$–CH$_3$

g) Less soluble because the hydroxy group can hydrogen bond better to the water molecules than the 'bridging' oxygen.

EXERCISE 11.5

1. C 2. C

3.

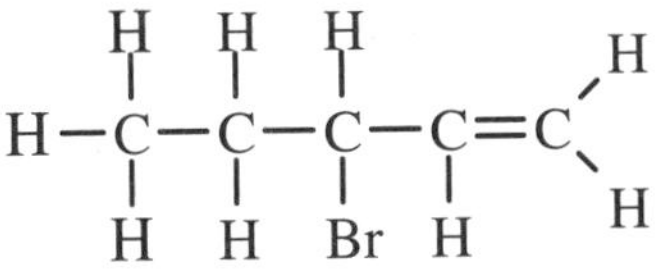

a)

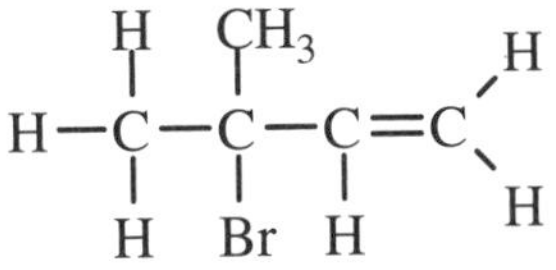

b) 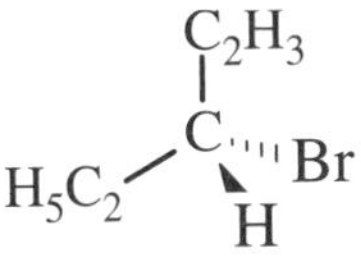 and

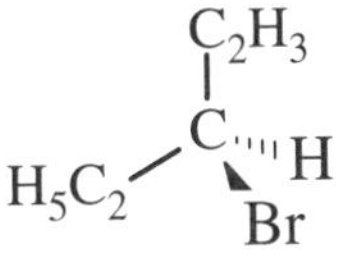

c)

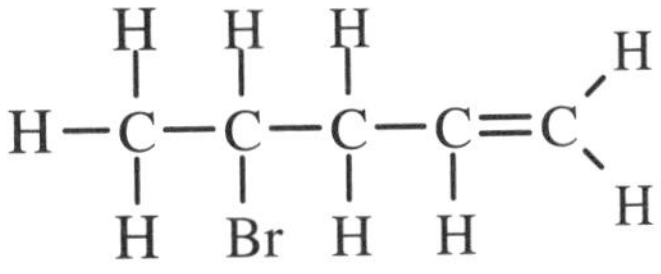

d)

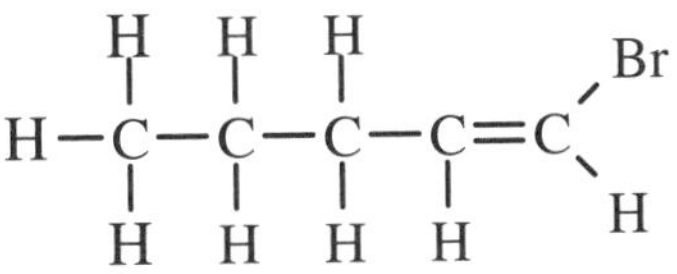

e)

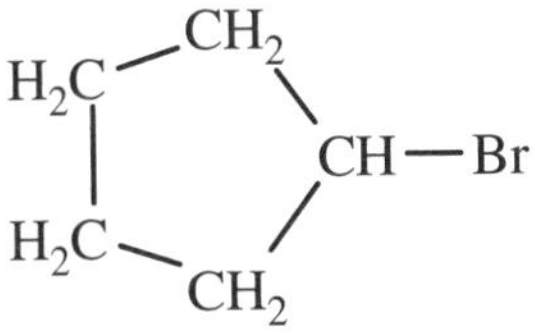

4. a) *Optically active* means that the substance will rotate the plane of polarisation of polarised light. A *racemic mixture* is one that contains equal amounts of two enantiomers. b) The natural lactic acid would comprise just one enantiomer, whereas the synthetic product would be a racemic mixture. c) If polarised light were passed through a solution of the sample in a polarimeter, the synthetic product would have no effect, but the natural product would rotate the plane of polarisation of the light.

5.a) Because it contains an asymmetric/chiral carbon atom (labelled *) C$_2$H$_5$–*CHBr–CH$_3$ the molecule can exist in two enantiomeric forms.

b) If the starting alkene was orientated:

$$H_3C \diagdown \quad \diagup CH_3$$
$$C = C$$
$$H \diagup \quad \diagdown H$$

Then the attack from the H–Br could occur from either above or below the molecule and these produce the two different enantiomers. These are equally probable and hence there are equal amounts of the two enantiomers and the mixture would therefore be optically inactive.

EXERCISE 11.6

1. A 2. C 3. A 4. D 5. B 6. A, 7. D

8. a) $CH_3\text{-}CH_2\text{-}CH=CH\text{-}CH_3$ b) $C_5H_{10\,(l)} + 7\frac{1}{2}O_{2\,(g)} \Rightarrow 5CO_{2\,(g)} + 5H_2O_{(l)}$ c) Heat energy.

d) Carbon monoxide , or carbon e) Carbon monoxide is a toxic gas, carbon particles contribute to smog formation. f) $CH_3\text{-}CH(CH_3)\text{-}CH=CH_2$ 3-methylbut-1-ene.

9. a)Bromoethane, $CH_3\text{-}CH_2\text{-}Br$ b) Addition reactions c) Hydrogen gas and a nickel catalyst d) The starting material would turn bromine water from orange to colourless, whereas the product would not do this. e) A high pressure (~70 atm), a temperature of about 300°C and a phosphoric acid catalyst. f) But-2-ene g) $CH_3\text{-}CH_2\text{-}CH(OH)\text{-}CH_3$

10. The answer should refer to the symmetry of the benzene ring, its lack of reaction with bromine water and thermochemical anomalies.

EXERCISE 11.7

1. D 2. C 3. B

4. a) By passing the vapour over a heated alumina catalyst, or by heating the butan–1–ol with excess concentrated sulfuric acid. b) But–1–ene, $CH_3\text{–}CH_2\text{–}CH=CH_2$

c) It would turn bromine water from orange to colourless.

5. a) Acidified potassium dichromate(VI) b) From orange to green. c) Bubbles of carbon dioxide gas would be evolved.

6. a) Ethyl ethanoate, $CH_3\text{–}CH_2\text{–}O\text{–}CO\text{–}CH_3$ b) Esters c) Concentrated sulfuric acid
d) $CH_3\text{–}CH_2\text{–}CH_2\text{–}CO\text{–}O\text{–}H$

EXERCISE 11.8

1. B 2. B

3.

The reaction is described as S_N1 because the reaction is a first order (i.e. independent of the nucleophile concentration) nucleophilic substitution reaction.

EXERCISE 11.9

1. A 2. B

3. a) A *monomer* is a small molecule that can form two or more covalent bonds to other similar molecules in order to form a large molecule. A *polymer* is a large molecule formed by the joining together of a large number of small molecules.

b) [-CH$_2$CHCl-]$_n$ formed from CH$_2$=CHCl.

c)

EXERCISE 11.10

1. D 2. A 3. C

4. When shaken with bromine water hexane and hexene would both form immiscible layers, whereas ethanol and ethanoic acid would dissolve into the solution. The hexene would decolourise the bromine water (brown to colourless) when shaken, whereas the hexane would not. When tested with litmus paper, the ethanoic acid would change the litmus paper from blue to red, whereas the ethanol would not affect it.

5.

6. a) Propanoic acid; Methylpropane; Butane; Propene b) C and G, butan-1-ol
c) B and D, C$_4$H$_{10}$ d) E, Br-CH$_2$-CHBr-CH$_3$ e) A, in aqueous solution the -COOH group dissociates to form H$^+$ ions. f) A, methanol (CH$_3$OH); conc. H$_2$SO$_4$, methyl propanoate; sweet smelling. g) CH$_3$-CH$_2$-CH(OH)-CH$_3$, butan-2-ol. Other answers possible.

7. a) C$_2$H$_5$OH + CH$_3$COOH $\rightleftharpoons$ CH$_3$COOC$_2$H$_5$ +H$_2$O
b) C$_2$H$_5$OH + 2[O] $\Rightarrow$ CH$_3$COOH + H$_2$O reflux with acidified potassium dichromate(VI) solution
or 2 Cr$_2$O$_7^{2-}$ + 16 H$^+$ + 3 C$_2$H$_5$OH $\Rightarrow$ 4 Cr^{3+} + 3 CH$_3$COOH + 11 H$_2$O warm with ethanoic acid and conc. sulfuric acid. c) C$_2$H$_5$OH $\Rightarrow$ C$_2$H$_4$ + H$_2$O heat with excess concentrated sulfuric acid, or pass ethanol vapour over strongly heated alumina.

8. a) Add bromine water. With hexene the colour of the lower aqueous layer will change from orange to colourless. With hexane the lower aqueous layer will remain orange.
b) Add universal indicator. The ethylamine will change the indicator colour from green to blue. With the ethanamide the indicator will remain green.
c) Warm with a little acidified potassium dichromate(VI). With the 2–methylpropan–1–ol the colour will change from orange to green. With the 2–methylpropan–2–ol the colour will remain orange.

9. a) CH$_3$–CH$_2$–CO–OH + CH$_3$–OH $\Rightarrow$ CH$_3$–CH$_2$–CO–O–CH$_3$ + H$_2$O
b) CH$_3$–CH$_2$–CH=CH$_2$ + HCl $\Rightarrow$ CH$_3$–CH$_2$–CHCl–CH$_3$

10. D

Answers

11 a)

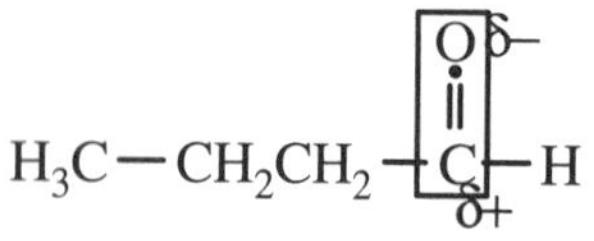

H₃C—CH₂CH₂—$\overset{\overset{O^{\delta-}}{\underset{\displaystyle\parallel}{}}}{\underset{\delta+}{C}}$—H

nucleophilic attack

b)

$\overset{\displaystyle H}{\underset{\displaystyle CH_3}{\overset{|}{H_3C-C-}}}\overset{\displaystyle O}{\overset{\parallel}{C}}-H$

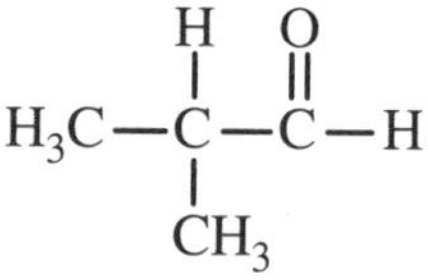

2-methylpropanal,
easily oxidised isomer.

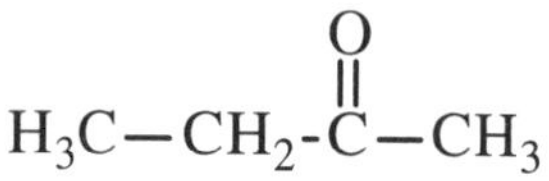

$\overset{\displaystyle O}{\overset{\parallel}{H_3C-CH_2-C-CH_3}}$ Butanone, not easily oxidised isomer.

c) i Add both X and Y to a little powdered calcium carbonate. X would give no reaction, but with Y there would be bubbles of gas evolved. ii Acidified potassium dichromate(VI).

12. a) When a mixture of ethanol and acidified potassium dichromate(VI) is distilled, the product is ethanal (CH_3–CHO). If the mixture is refluxed the product of further oxidation is ethanoic acid (CH_3COOH).

b) When 1-bromobutane (C_4H_9–Br) is warmed with dilute aqueous potassium hydroxide 1-butanol (C_4H_9OH) is the product. When it is added to a boiling, concentrated ethanolic solution of potassium hydroxide an elimination reaction gives but–1–ene (C_2H_5–CH=CH₂).

13. a)

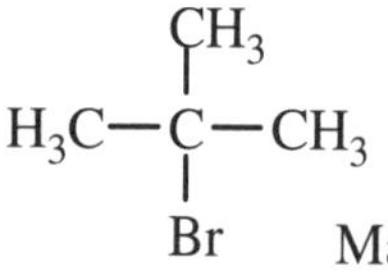

$\overset{\displaystyle CH_3}{\underset{\displaystyle Br}{\overset{|}{\underset{|}{H_3C-C-CH_3}}}}$ Major product

$\overset{\displaystyle CH_3}{\overset{|}{H_3C-CH-CH_2-Br}}$ Minor product

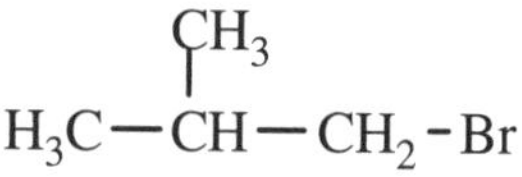

b)i Aqueous sodium hydroxide ii From A, methylpropan-2-ol, a tertiary alkanol will be formed. From B, methylpropan-1-ol, a primary alkanol will be formed.

14. Electrophilic addition $C_2H_4 + Br_2 \Rightarrow C_2H_4Br_2$
The mechanism of the first stage of the addition is:

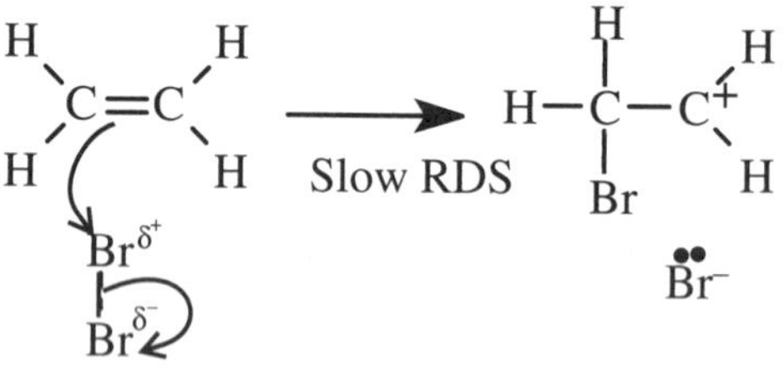

Then in the second stage, this carbocation will react with the bromide ion to complete the addition process:

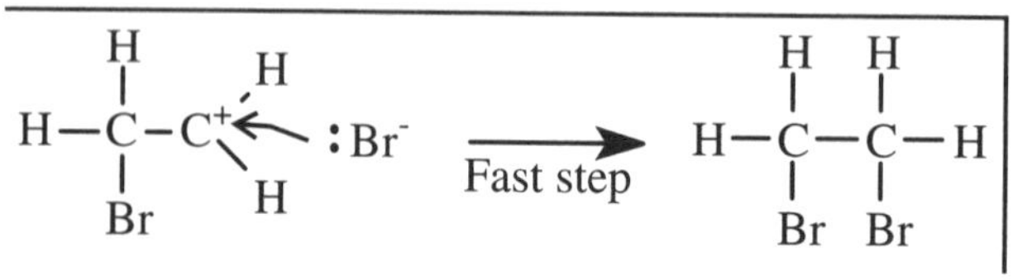

Nucleophilic addition H_3C—CHO + HCN ⟶ $\overset{\displaystyle H_3C-CH-OH}{\underset{\displaystyle CN}{\overset{}{\underset{|}{}}}}$

This reaction requires a base to convert the hydrogen cyanide into the more nucleophilic cyanide ion: $HCN + OH^- \Rightarrow CN^- + H_2O$

The cyanide ion then acts as a nucleophile and attacks the carbonyl carbon to produce an intermediate anion. This reacts with the water present to form the product, known as a cyanohydrin (hydroxyl nitrile), and regenerate the base catalyst.

Nucleophilic substitution $CH_3I + OH^- \Rightarrow CH_3OH + I^-$
There are two possible mechanisms for nucleophilic substitution. The example above will occur by an S_N2 mechanism:

$$H-\overset{\frown}{\underset{\cdot\cdot}{O}^-} : CH_3I \longrightarrow \overset{\text{Activated complex}}{[H-O\cdot\cdot CH_3^{\cdot\cdot}I]^-} \longrightarrow H-O-CH_3 + :I^-$$

Nucleophilic addition-elimination
$CH_3\text{-}CO\text{-}CH_3 + (NO_2)_2C_6H_3\text{-}NH\text{-}NH_2 \Rightarrow (CH_3)_2C=N\text{-}NH\text{-}C_6H_3(NO_2)_2 + H_2O$
In this a lone pair on the terminal nitrogen acts as the nucleophile and an addition reaction occurs by nucleophilic attack on the carbonyl carbon followed by the oxygen gaining a hydrogen from the water. A hydrogen ion is then lost by the nitrogen that acted as the nucleophile.

In the second elimination stage, the other hydrogen on the nitrogen attached to the former carbonyl group is lost as is the -OH group, probably after initial protonation, to form a carbon-nitrogen double bond.

15.
a)

$$H_3C-CH_2-\overset{\overset{\textstyle O}{\|}}{C}-CH_3$$

b)

$$H_5C_2-\overset{\overset{\textstyle H}{|}}{\underset{\underset{\textstyle N-NH-C_6H_3(NO_2)_2}{\|}}{C}}-H$$

c)

$$H_3C-\overset{\overset{\textstyle H}{|}}{\underset{\underset{\textstyle O-CO-CH_3}{|}}{C}}-CH_3$$

d) $O=C=O$ (the earlier products of $H\text{-}CO\text{-}H$ and $H\text{-}CO\text{-}OH$ oxidise easily)
16. a) The white solid would dissolve to give a colourless solution. b)The orange solution and the colourless liquid would react to give an orange-yellow precipitate.
c) The colourless liquid and the purple solution would react to give a colourless solution.
17. a) Add both to a little powdered calcium carbonate. In the case of the ethanol there would be no reaction, in the case of the ethanoic acid bubbles of colourless gas would be produced. b) Warm both with a little acidified potassium dichromate(VI) solution. With

the propanal the solution would turn from orange to green. With the propanone it would remain orange c) Add 2,4–dinitrophenylhydrazine solution. With the butanal an orange–yellow precipitate would form. With the butan–1–ol the solution would remain clear orange. d) Either repeat test a), in which case the butanoic acid would react the same as the ethanoic acid and the butanone the same as the ethanol. Or repeat test c), in which case the butanoic acid would react the same as the butanol and the butanone would react the same as the butanal. e) Add bromine water. With the hexan–1–ol it would remain an orange brown colour, but with the cyclohexene it would change colour from orange–brown to colourless. Or add a small piece of sodium. With the hexan–1–ol it would react to give off bubbles of colourless gas, but with the cyclohexene there would be no reaction.

18. The strength of the acid largely depends on the extent to which the anion becomes stable by reducing the charge on the oxygen atom. In ethanol the loss of a hydrogen ion would result in the negative charge being totally localised on the oxygen atom. The resulting ethoxide ion is not as stable, hence ethanol is not acidic. In phenol, a little of the charge can be distributed on to the benzene ring through the delocalised π–bond system, making phenol very weakly acidic. In ethanoic acid there is complete delocalisation of the charge between the two equivalent oxygen atoms of the ethanoate ion, hence it is a weak acid. In trichloroethanoic acid, the electron attracting inductive effect of the chlorine atoms further reduces the electrical charge on the oxygens with the result that it is quite a strong acid.

19. The reaction is: $CH_3\text{-}CH{=}CH_{2(g)} + H_2O_{(g)} \rightleftharpoons CH_3\text{-}CH(OH)\text{-}CH_{3(g)}$ ΔH negative
In the equilibrium two moles of gas are converted into one mole of gas, therefore a high pressure would favour a high yield of product, as Le Chatelier's principle predicts that an increase in pressure will shift the equilibrium to the side with the least moles of gas. Le Chatelier's principle also predicts that a decrease in temperature will shift the equilibrium in the exothermic direction, therefore a low temperature will produce a higher yield of product (but at a slower rate!). In the initial step of the reaction a hydrogen ion adds on to the double bond. This can produce two possible carbocations: $CH_3\text{-}C^+H\text{-}CH_3$
and $CH_3\text{-}CH_2\text{-}CH_2^+$. The former is a secondary carbocation and is therefore more stable than the latter which is a primary carbocation since the electron releasing inductive effect of the two methyl groups stabilises the positive charge more in the secondary carbocation. Propan-2-ol, the product from the reaction of the secondary carbocation with water, will therefore predominate.

20. A: $CH_3\text{-}CH_2\text{-}CH_2\text{-}CH_2\text{-}Cl + OH^- \Rightarrow CH_3\text{-}CH_2\text{-}CH_2\text{-}CH_2\text{-}OH$ (butan-1-ol) + Cl^-
B $CH_3\text{-}CH_2\text{-}CH_2\text{-}CH_2\text{-}Cl + OH^- \Rightarrow CH_3\text{-}CH_2\text{-}CH{=}CH_2$ (but-1-ene) + H_2O + Cl^-
A would be favoured by a lower temperature, B by a higher temperature. A would be favoured by a lower concentration of alkali, B by a higher concentration. A would be favoured by having the alkali dissolved in water, B by having it dissolved in alcohol.

21.a) Methylamine acts as a weak base, therefore an aqueous solution will contain hydroxide ions produced according to the equilibrium:
$CH_3\text{-}NH_{2(aq)} + H_2O_{(l)} \rightleftharpoons CH_3\text{-}NH_3^+{}_{(aq)} + OH^-{}_{(aq)}$
The presence of hydroxide ions will increase the pH of the solution.

b) The intermolecular forces in chloropropane are van der Waals' forces and dipole-dipole forces. Water contains very strong hydrogen bonds between the molecules. If a substance is to dissolve in water it must break these bonds and this is only energetically favourable if the substance can itself hydrogen bond to the water, or dissociate into ions. Chlorobutane cannot form hydrogen bonds, hence it is insoluble. c) A molecular covalent substance (CH_3-CO-NH_2) of quite low molar mass (~60) existing as a solid at room temperature and pressure indicates that the presence of quite strong intermolecular forces. In the case of ethanamide, these are hydrogen bonds. The oxygen of the carbonyl group can form hydrogen bonds to the hydrogen atoms attached to the nitrogen of a neighbouring molecule.

22. a)

$$H_3C \diagdown C=O \diagup H$$

Ethanal

$$H_3C - \overset{\displaystyle \overset{OH}{|}}{\underset{\displaystyle \underset{H}{|}}{C}} - C \diagup {\overset{O}{}} \diagdown {O-H}$$

2-hydroxypropanoic acid

b) X is

$$H_3C - \overset{\displaystyle \overset{OH}{|}}{\underset{\displaystyle \underset{H}{|}}{C}} - C \equiv N$$

c) Reflux ethanal with hydrocyanic acid (HCN) and a strong base catayst.

d)

$$N \equiv C : ^- \quad \overset{H_3C}{\underset{H}{\diagup}} \overset{\delta+}{C} = O^{\delta-} \quad \overset{H^+}{\Rightarrow} \quad C \equiv N - \overset{\displaystyle \overset{CH_3}{|}}{\underset{\displaystyle \underset{H}{|}}{C}} - OH$$

Nucleophilic attack

e) Warm with an aqueous solution of a strong acid

f) Hydroxypropanoic acid contains an asymmetric carbon atom, i.e. one that is bonded to four different groups:

$$H_3C \diagup \overset{\displaystyle \overset{COOH}{|}}{C} \diagdown {}^{\text{''}H} \atop OH \qquad\qquad H^{\text{''}} \diagup \overset{\displaystyle \overset{COOH}{|}}{C} \diagdown CH_3 \atop HO$$

g) Optical activity is the ability of a substance to rotate the plane of polarisation of polarised light. One of the two enantiomers above will rotate the light clockwise, the other anticlockwise.

h)Which enantiomer is produced depends on whether the nucleophilic attack occurs from above or below the plane of the carbonyl group. As there are equal probabilities of the two attacks, equal amounts of the two products are produced (a racemic mixture). This has no effect on polarised light as the rotations of the two enantiomers cancel each other out.

INDEX

INTERNATIONAL BACCALAUREATE

CHEMISTRY

SECOND EDITION

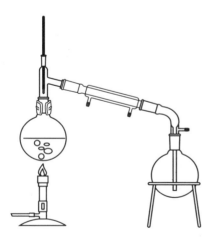

John Green:
Li Po Chun United World
College of Hong Kong

Sadru Damji:
Upper Canada College,
Toronto